Data Mining:
Next Generation Challenges and Future Directions

Data Mining:
Next Generation Challenges
and Future Directions

Edited by

Hillol Kargupta, Anupam Joshi,
Krishnamoorthy Sivakumar, and Yelena Yesha

AAAI Press / The MIT Press

Menlo Park, California • Cambridge, Massachusetts • London, England

Copublished and distributed by The MIT Press,
Massachusetts Institute of Technology,
Cambridge, Massachusetts, and London, England.

ISBN 0-262-61203-8

To Mom, Dad, Kakali, Rinku, Badal, and Priyanka.

–Hillol Kargupta

Dedicated to my wife, daughter, parents and brothers — for family is the foundation of all intellectual activity.

–Anupam Joshi

To my parents, husband Yaacov and daugther Rose.

–Yelena Yesha

Manufactured in the United States of America

10 9 8 7 6 5 4 3 2 1

Contents

Counterterrorism, Privacy, and Data Mining

Scientific Data Mining

Web, Semantics, and Data Mining

Foreword

Ramasamy Uthurusamy

As an application-driven multidisciplinary endeavor, the knowledge discovery and data mining (KDD) field has made significant progress in the past decade and a half. KDD had created a sharp discontinuity in economic affairs and opened up opportunities for businesses to do things with data that had not been done before, and allowed things to be done in new ways. The field is vibrant with significant impact on a wide variety of science, business, and technology areas where it has become necessary to deal with exponentially increasing volume of data. Stored data, due to innovative technologies and rapidly decreasing cost, is doubling every nine months, growing twice as fast as Moore's Law. This glut of data and advances in computational resources are fueling the ever-increasing demand for KDD tools that allows one to make sense of all that data and gain insight.

Three fundamental ideas distinguish KDD from other fields. First, it did bring awareness to the scientific community, the need to deal with and make sense of ever growing data that the industry and business communities are facing. It is not just the very large size of the database, but also the very high dimensionality of the data that demanded new research efforts. Second, it also emphasized the need for a discovery component, the fundamental part of any KDD application and solution. Third, it attempted to steer practitioners towards a process and system-centric view of KDD for it to be effective in solving real world problems.

These ideas were actually catalysts in getting the tools and techniques of KDD used not by people and businesses that had, and now have, to deal with massive data but by small and medium industries and retailers who have relatively small and medium databases, but who saw an opportunity to make better sense of and effective use of this data. This evolution also indicates two possible trends. The "Microsoft-way" will move the field towards "data mining for the masses." The "GM-way" will move it towards "KDD for business and industry," where massive data is easy to collect but difficult to exploit and use. The two have parallels in mainframe computing and desktop computing.

KDD had been a catalyst in educating the professionals on the need for data cleaning through the discovery that only ten percent of collected data is ever used and forty percent of all collected data have errors in them. The original process centric view of KDD espoused the three "I"s (Integrated, Iterative, and Interactive) as basic for KDD. These are central to the ideas of computer assisted human discovery and human assisted computer discovery.

Going forward, the issues of "interestingness," "privacy," "standards," "data cleaning," "visualization," "incorporating domain knowledge," and more importantly the "process and system centric approaches" will require much needed attention. In addition, a concerted effort is needed to facilitate the database, machine learning, and statistics communities to interact closely and cooperate in order to focus on solving KDD challenges.

I envision the convergence of semantic web, P2P, Internet2, grid computing, web services, and ontological engineering that will lead to interesting new avenues of KDD research. More importantly, I believe "KDD for strategic intent" to be a very promising high impact business application area. An example is how Harrahs achieved significant growth and gains over competing casinos by formulating strategies based on the results of mining customer data. The concept of utilizing KDD tools and techniques to formulate corporate strategies that provide competitive edge is at the core of the original intent of KDD.

While KDD has made impressive progress, it faces greater than ever challenges and opportunities. My congratulations go to Hillol Kargupta, Joshi, Sivakumar, and Yesha for knitting together this collection of contributions from leading researchers and practitioners that summarizes their initiatives to address some of the next generation challenges and to identify the future directions of the field.

This book is rich in theory and practice and a conduit for translating good theory into good practice. The challenges and potential research directions are described in four sections. The chapters have interleaved themes of distributed KDD, intrusion detection, privacy and security issues, terrorism, counter-terrorism, and intelligence, ontologies, simulation, and foundational issues, system architecture, and framework. The types of data that posed challenges to the various research efforts reported include: stream, temporal, mobile, wireless, pervasive, scientific, distributed, text, unstructured, multimedia, multi-relational, medical, biological, simulation, spatial, protein contact maps, environmental, nonstationary time-series, heterogeneous sequences, police incident-reports, industrial and commercial, and patents. The KDD tools and techniques researched include: multi-query optimization, query answering, network protocol for high performance transport, data sampling, data reduction, association rule, temporal mining, supervised and unsupervised learning, summarization, inductive logic programming, graph modeling, latent semantic indexing, and grid computing. This extensive firsthand description of academic and industrial research allows one to understand the issues and the progress made in addressing them.

The nature and diversity of the research presented in a consistent and organized collection that provides a current synopsis of challenges, the complexity and interconnectedness of the problems, the credibility of the researchers and practitioners and their presentations and insights, make this book a compelling read.

Preface

Hillol Kargupta, Anupam Joshi,
Krishnamoorthy Sivakumar, and Yelena Yesha

The field of data mining deals with the problem of scalable data analysis by paying close attention to computing, storage, communication, and human-factor-related issues. Over the last decade, data mining technology has made serious impact in many different domains, from credit-card fraud detection and customer relations management to drought modeling and intrusion detection. New algorithmic challeneges and application areas are emerging at a rate that is often difficult to manage. This book freezes time for a moment, gleans the field of data mining, and offers a perspective on some emerging directions. The book's concept emerged from the 2002 National Science Foundation workshop on Next Generation Data Mining. Many data mining researchers and practitioners gathered in Baltimore, Maryland to share perspectives of the past and ideas for the future. The workshop crystalized the need for a book that identifies some of the emerging issues in the field of data mining. A lot of effort by the authors, publisher, and the editors over the last year and half has finally brought this book to where it is today. Before inviting the reader to enjoy its content, we would like to take an opportunity, in this preface, to present the reader with the book's overall roadmap.

Over the last few years, data mining researchers have begun to examine the new issues that arise when, for a variety of reasons, all the data to be analyzed cannot be aggregated at a single site. This situation has led to the development of "distributed" data mining approaches. The advent of pervasive computing, sensor networks, and privacy-sensitive multiparty data present clear examples where centralization of data is either not possible, or at least not always desirable. Chapter 1 by Kargupta and Sivakumar provides a nice tutorial-like overview of the distributed data mining area. It surveys key techniques for distributed data mining and presents some challenges for the future.

Chapter 2, by Alan Demers, Johannes Gehrke, and Mirek Riedewald, focuses on a particular application area for distributed data mining, namely intelligence data. They describe the problems involved in this domain and identify the research challenges involved, such as online data mining, mining streaming data and model management. They also present a possible architecture of such a system, as well as preliminary results from their own research.

In Chapter 3, Joydeep Ghosh, Alexander Strehl, and Srujana Merugu present an interesting problem, given multiple partitions (clusters) of the same underlying data done by different entities using potentially different algorithms and criteria. The problem is compounded by the fact that the underlying algorithms and features are not shared because of concerns related to privacy, intellectual property, or other legal issues. The authors outline the problem and some example applications, and show preliminary results that appear promising on both real and synthetic data sets.

An important player in the world of modern distributed systems is grid computing. Much like the computational grid created by the high-performance computing community, researchers now envisage a data or knowledge grid as well. We can expect that this grid will provide plenty of data that can be mined, but only in a distributed manner. Chapter 4, by Mario Cannataro, Domenico Talia, and Paolo Trufino, shows how the grid interacts with distributed data mining technology. They describe both the challenges involved as well as a prototype system.

A related effort looks at integrating data mining with the underlying networking layer and explore cross layer issues. In chapter 5, Robert Grossman and his colleagues suggest that when data mining does involve significant data transfer, and where high bandwidth optical pipes are available, relying on off-the-shelf TCP/IP stacks built into most operating systems is not appropriate. They present an approach which combines a novel transport protocol with dynamic lightpath setups to support remote analysis of extremely large data sets.

Mining data streams is clearly a hard problem, since the data is seen only once. Chapter 6, by Chris Gianella, Jiawei Han, Jian Pei, Xifeng Yan, and Philip Yu, examines the problem of finding frequent patterns in such streams. They argue that since the underlying data distribution can change, different patterns may be "frequent" at different times. They present an approach that computes all frequent patterns, and updates them as needed. Their approach provides approximate support guarantees for patterns that are time sensitive, and they show that it can be implemented with limited memory resources.

Sampling as a method of data deflation before analysis is well known in the data mining community. Chapter 7, by Hervé Brönnimann, Bin Chen, Manoranjan Dash, Peter Haas, and Peter Scheuermann describes two approaches to data reduction based on sampling that are geared towards mining association rules. While both approaches use greedy heuristics, they show that one approach provides a guaranteed level of accuracy and is more accurate for a given sample size, but takes longer to run. They also show how these algorithms can be adapted to work in streaming data environments.

In chapter 8, Milind R. Naphade, Chung-Sheng Li, and Thomas S. Huang focus on detecting recurrent events in digital media streams. In particular, they present a novel approach to capture the "structure" in video streams such as news or sports productions. Their approach is probabilistic in nature, and embeds short term models based on statistics in a longer term model that describes the transitions between the short-term models. They show that the approach can be extended to work in other situations where multimodal sensor data streams are involved.

In chapter 9, Bhavani Thuraisingham discusses some of the technical challenges for applying data mining for counter-terrorism applications. She provides an overview of different types of terrorism-related threats and describes how data mining techniques could provide solutions to counter-terrorism. She also raises concerns for privacy and some potential solutions.

In chapter 10, Paola Sebastiani and Kenneth D. Mandl deal with the issue of biosurveillance and early outbreak detection in the context of our public health infrastructure. They note that early detection of covert biological attacks requires real-time mining of data streams and identify some of the possible solutions.

In chapter 11, Levent Ertöz and his colleagues introduce the Minnesota Intrusion Detection System (MINDS), which uses a collection of different data mining techniques to detect attacks against computer networks and systems. Their chapter discusses some of the techniques used in MINDS and offers results on on live network traffic at the University of Minnesota. The performance of the MINDS system in anomaly detection look very promising compared to the existing signature-based systems for intrusion detection.

Chapter 12 deals with related applications of data mining technology in counter-terrorism. In this chapter, Daniel Barbará, James Nolan, David Schum, and Arun Sood present an architecture to manage a large, distributed volume of evidence for counter-terrorism applications. Their chapter offers an interesting application of the data mining technology in intelligence gathering and evidence linking with human in the loop.

Most data-mining methods assume data is in the form of a feature-vector (a single relational table) and cannot handle multi-relational data. Inductive logic programming is a form of relational data mining that discovers rules in first-order logic from multi-relational data. In chapter 13, Raymond Mooney and his colleagues discuss the application of inductive logic programming to relational data mining and link discovery. Link discovery concerns the identification of complex relational patterns that indicate potentially threatening activities in large amounts of relational data and is an important task in data mining for counter-terrorism.

Privacy preserving data mining deals with obtaining valid data mining results without learning the underlying data values. This field has recently received increased attention from the research community as well as other communities dealing with law enforcement and counter-terrorism. Despite the attention, however, there is no universally accepted notion of what privacy preserving means. In chapter 14, Chris Clifton, Murat Kantarcoglu, and Jaideep Vaidya provide a framework and metrics for discussing the meaning of privacy preserving data mining, as a foundation for further research in this field.

Recent advances in computer hardware and numerical methods have made it possible to simulate physical phenomena at very fine temporal and spatial resolutions, which generate enormous datasets. In chapter 15, Raghu Machiraju and his colleagues describe a unified framework that promises to provide a novel method to explore large simulation data sets. They discuss applications to two scientific phenomenon: temporally varying solid and fluid systems. Both applications have hidden hierarchies of features as well as many abstract multidimensional feature characterizations (e.g. shapes).

In chapter 16, Mohammed Zaki, Jingjing Hu, and Chris Bystroffz describe how data mining can be used to extract valuable information from protein contact maps. The contact map provides a host of useful information about the protein structure. For example, clusters of contacts represent certain secondary structures, and also capture nonlocal interactions, giving clues to the tertiary structure. Using contact maps and a hybrid mining approach, they construct contact rules to predict the structure of an unknown protein. They also mine nonlocal frequent dense contact patterns that discriminate physical from nonphysical maps.

As data mining techniques are being increasingly applied to scientific and other nontraditional domains, it is becoming apparent that existing approaches for modeling characteristics of underlying physical phenomena and processes are limiting because they cannot model the domain's requirements. An alternate way is to use graphs to capture, in a single and unified framework, many of the spatial, topological, geometric, and other relational characteristics present in such datasets. The added power provided by graph-modeling can only be realized if computationally efficient and scalable algorithms for many of the classical data-mining tasks, such as frequent pattern discovery, clustering, and classification, become available. In chapter 17, Michihiro Kuramochi, Mukund Deshpande, and George Karypis present algorithms for finding frequently occurring patterns and building predictive models for graph datasets.

Environmental and Earth sciences concerns with the collection, assimilation, cataloging, and dissemination or retrieval of a vast array of environmental data (e.g., satellite imagery of different resolutions; aerial photos, radar and other monitoring networks; models of the topography; spatial attributes of the landscape such as roads, rivers, parcels, schools, zip code areas, city streets and administrative boundaries; census information; and digital terrain models). In chapter 18, Nabil Adam, Vijayalakshmi Atluri, Dihua Guo, and Songmei Yu describe the complex nature of the queries posed to such databases and argue that data warehousing and data mining techniques must be employed to efficiently process these queries. Research challenges in environmental data warehousing and mining related to data model and on-line analytical processing operations, as well as the challenges in extending traditional data mining techniques to mine environmental data are also discussed.

In chapter 19, Shashi Shekhar, Pusheng Zhang, Yan Huang, and Ranga Vatsavai provide a survey of data mining techniques for spatial datasets and discuss future research needs. Extracting interesting and useful patterns from spatial datasets is more difficult than extracting the corresponding patterns from traditional numeric and categorical data due to the complexity of spatial data types, spatial relationships, and spatial autocorrelation.

With recent innovations in data collection technologies in many emerging scientific applications, there is a need for a paradigm shift from a traditional hypothesize-and-test process to a partial automation of hypothesis generation, model construction, and experimentation. To develop appropriate knowledge discovery tools in support of the paradigm shift in sciences, numerous data mining challenges should be solved. Towards that end, Zoran Obradovic and Slobodan Vucetic, in chapter 20, consider data mining challenges of (1) mining of heterogeneous data; (2) learning from biased labeled samples; (3) enhancing predictive modeling by exploiting large unlabeled databases; and (4) reducing large datasets with a controllable information loss for a more efficient mining in a distributed environment. Effective methods for addressing these problems are described. Applications on six scientific and engineering problems in precision agriculture, electric power systems and biochemistry are also illustrated.

The potential of extracting valuable knowledge from the Web has been quite evident from its very beginning. Web mining (i.e. the application of data mining techniques to extract knowledge from Web content, structure, and usage) is a collection of technologies that fulfill this potential. In chapter 21, Jaideep Srivastava, Prasanna Desikan, and Vipin Kumar provide a brief overview of the field, both in terms of technologies and applications, and outline future research directions.

In chapter 22, Svetlana Mironova and her colleagues present two advancements in the development of algorithms and software for the mining of textual information. The General Text Parser software environment, with network storage capability, is object-oriented software (C++, Java) designed to provide information retrieval and data mining specialists the ability to parse and index large text collections. The General Text Parser utilizes latent semantic indexing for the construction of a vector space information retrieval model. Users can choose to store the files generated by the General Text Parser on a remote network in order to overcome local storage restrictions and facilitate file sharing. For feature extraction from textual information, a supervised learning algorithm for the discovery of finite state automata, in the form of regular expressions, is presented. The automata generate languages that consist of various representations of features useful in information extraction.

In chapter 23, Anupam Joshi and Jeffrey Undercoffer, examine the intersection of data mining with the semantic web (in particular with ontologies and reasoning) and show how the two can operate in synergy to better distributed data mining, in particular through distributed intrusion detection. Based upon an analysis of over 4,000 classes of computer attacks and their corresponding attack strategies, they have developed a target-centric ontological framework that models computer attacks and uses data mining techniques to identify and specify instances of the ontology. An example of the Mitnick Attack (an attack that combine a denial of service and TCP hijacking in a distributed manner), is used to illustrate the utility of an ontology. They define an intrusion detection system model that employs data mining techniques for initial hypothesis testing and then use semantic reasoning to further test events that are initially identified as falling outside the bounds of normal system activity.

Web mining aims to discover insights about the meaning of Web resources and their usage. Because of the primarily syntactical nature of data that Web mining uses, the discovery of meaning is impossible, based on these data alone. Therefore, formalizations of the semantics of Web resources and navigation behavior are increasingly being used. In chapter 24, Bettina Berendt, Gerd Stumme, and Andreas Hotho discuss the interplay of the semantic web with Web mining, with a specific focus on usage mining. Semantic web mining aims to combine the two fast-developing research areas of the semantic web and Web mining. One of the aims of the semantic web is to enrich the World Wide Web by machine-processable information, which supports the user in his or her tasks.

Data mining is a fast growing field that has many emerging areas in different application domains. No single book can cover all those topics. However, this book makes an effort to put together a collection of some of those topics in order to facilitate the development of a new generation of data mining algorithms, systems, and applications. We hope that the reader enjoys the book.

Pervasive, Distributed,
and Stream Data Mining

Chapter 1

Existential Pleasures of Distributed Data Mining

Hillol Kargupta and Krishamoorthy Sivakumar

Advances in computing and communication over wired and wireless networks have resulted in many pervasive distributed computing environments. The Internet, intranets, local area networks, ad hoc wireless networks, and sensor networks are some examples. These environments often come with different distributed sources of data and computation. Mining in such environments naturally calls for proper utilization of these distributed resources. Moreover, in many privacy sensitive applications different, possibly multiparty, data sets collected at different sites must be processed in a distributed fashion without collecting everything to a single central site. However, most off-the-shelf data mining systems are designed to work as a monolithic centralized application. They normally download the relevant data to a centralized location and then perform the data mining operations. This centralized approach does not work well in many of the emerging distributed, ubiquitous, possibly privacy-sensitive data mining applications.

This chapter offers a perspective of the emerging field of distributed data mining (DDM) (Kargupta et al. 2000b, Park and Kargupta 2002) that deals with the problem of mining data using distributed resources. DDM pays careful attention to the distributed resources of data, computing, communication,

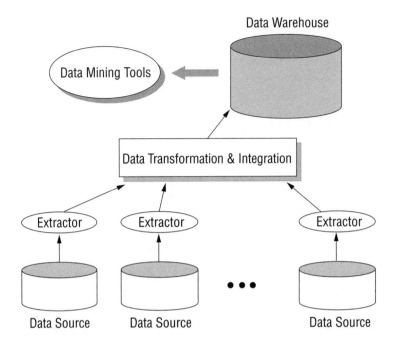

Figure 1.1: Mining in a data warehouse-based architecture.

and human factors in order to use them in a near optimal fashion. Figure 1.1 shows the structure of a typical DDM application that runs over a network of multiple data sources and compute nodes. This chapter presents an overview of the capabilities of the state-of-the-art DDM algorithms reported in existing literature.

The organization of this chapter is as follows: Section 1.1 discusses some of important applications of DDM technology that emerged over the last several years. Section 1.2 presents a brief overview of research related to DDM. Section 1.3 discusses the common data models considered in the DDM literature. Section 1.4 considers the techniques for computing statistical aggregates from distributed data. Section 1.6 reviews distributed clustering techniques. Section 1.7 discusses distributed association rule learning algorithms. Section 1.8 considers Bayesian network learning from distributed data. Section 1.9 explores the techniques for distributed classifier learning. Finally, section 1.11 concludes this chapter by identifying some future research directions.

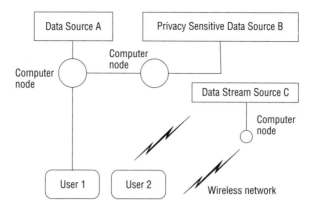

Figure 1.2: A typical distributed data mining environment.

1.1 Emerging Applications of Distributed Data Mining

DDM applications come in different flavors. When the data can be freely and efficiently transported from one node to another without significant overhead, DDM algorithms may offer better scalability and response time by (1) properly redistributing the data in different partitions or (2) distributing the computation, or (3) a combination of both. These algorithms often rely on fast communication between participating nodes. However, when the data sources are distributed and cannot be transmitted freely over the network due to privacy-constraints or bandwidth limitation or scalability problems, DDM algorithms work by avoiding or minimizing communication of the raw data. Both of these scenarios have interesting real-life applications. The following discussion offers some of the emerging ones where the DDM technology is finding increasing attention.

1.1.1 Mobile and Wireless Applications

There are many domains where distributed processing of data is a natural and scalable solution. Distributed wireless applications define one such domain. Consider an ad hoc wireless sensor network where the different sensor nodes are monitoring some time-critical events. Central collection of data from every sensor node may create heavy traffic over the limited bandwidth wireless channels and this may also drain a lot of power from the devices. Figure 1.3 illustrates this point. It shows that the battery power needed to transmit data over a standard cellular digital packet data (CDPD) network from one node

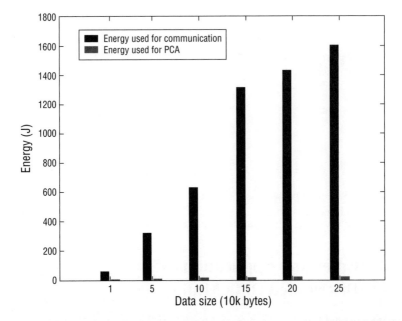

Figure 1.3: Comparison of the battery power needed to transmit data over CDPD wireless networks with that for performing PCA in a HP Jornada 690 (Hitachi SuperH SH-3 133MHz processor with 32MB RAM running Windows CE). The results clearly show that the power consumed by the on-board computation is a lot less compared to that needed to transmit to a remote desktop machine over CDPD wireless networks.

to another is an order or two more than than that needed to perform principal component analysis (PCA) on the same data set using a HP Jornada 690 (Hitachi SuperH SH-3 133MHz processor with 32MB RAM running Windows CE) system. Further discussion on the power consumption characteristics of popular data mining techniques can be found elsewhere (Bhargava, Kargupta, and Powers 2003). This result points out that it may be worthwhile to perform some of the data analysis on-board the sensor node (possibly equipped with a relatively low-end processor) instead of sending all the data to a remote node (at least from a power efficiency perspective).

Transmitting data to a central site over a low-bandwidth wireless network may drain out power dramatically and local processing of the data may be a better choice from the power consumption perspective. A distributed architecture for data mining is likely to reduce the communication load and also reduce the battery power more evenly across the different nodes in the sensor network.

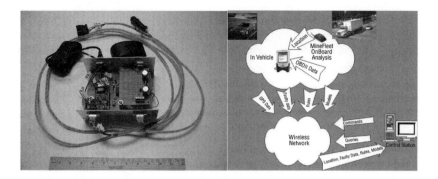

Figure 1.4: Left: On-board hardware for tapping onto the vehicle data bus. Right: Architecture of the vehicle data mining system.

Power consumption is not the only issue. DDM over wireless networks also allows the application to run efficiently even in the presence of severe bandwidth constraints. Therefore, it is not surprising to see a growing number of DDM systems for mobile applications (Kargupta et al. 2002b, Bhargava, Kargupta, and Powers 2003). For example, the distributed vehicle data stream mining system connects to the vehicle data bus in real time and monitors the data using a PDA-based platform and communicates with the remote control station over wireless networks. Figure 1.4 shows the on-board hardware developed at the DIADIC laboratory of the University of Maryland, Baltimore County and a screen-shot of the desktop-based interface that interacts with the remote on-board devices over wireless networks. This system continuously monitors and mines the on-board data stream generated by the different vehicle systems. The control station allows the user to monitor and mine a large number of vehicles in a fleet. This particular application deals with distributed mobile data sources and static user of the control station. There are also many mobile applications that deal with static data sources and mobile users. The MobiMiner system for mining and monitoring stock market data, reported elsewhere (Kargupta et al. 2002a), is an example of that.

We believe that in the near future we will see more mobile applications of the DDM technology for personalization, process monitoring, intrusion detection in ad hoc wireless networks, and other related domains.

1.1.2 Large Scale Scientific, Business, and Grid Mining Applications

The wireless domain is not the only example. In fact, most of the applications that deal with time-critical or large-quantity of distributed data may benefit by paying careful attention to the distributed resources for computation, storage, and the cost of communication. The world wide web is a very good example. It contains distributed data and computing resources. An increasing number of databases (e.g. weather databases, astrophysical data from virtual observatories, oceanographic data at www.noaa.gov), and data streams (e.g. financial data at www.nasdaq.com, emerging disease information at www.cdc.gov) are coming online. It is easy to think of many applications that require regular monitoring of these diverse and distributed sources of data. A distributed approach to analyze this data is likely to be more scalable and practical, particularly when the application involves a large number of data sites. The distributed approach is also finding applications in mining remote sensing and astronomy data. For example, the NASA earth observing system (EOS), a data collector for a number of satellites, holds many data sets that are stored, managed, and distributed by the different EOS data and information system (EOS-DIS) sites that are geographically distributed all over the USA. A pair of Terra spacecraft and Landsat 7 alone produces about 350 GB of EOSDIS data per day. An online mining system for EOS data streams may not scale if we use a centralized data mining architecture. Mining the distributed EOS repositories and associating the information with other existing environmental databases may benefit from DDM (Chen et al. 2002). In astronomy, the size of telescope image archives continue to increase very fast as information is collected for new all-sky surveyors such as the GSC-II (McLean et al. 1998) and the Sloan Digital Survey (Szalay 1998). DDM may offer a practical scalable solution for mining these large distributed astronomy data repositories.

As we mentioned earlier, DDM may also be useful in grid environments (Cannataro, Talia, and Trunfio 2001; Chervenak, Foster, Kesselman, Salisbury, and Tuecke 2000; Chervenak et al. 1999; Ćurčin et al. 2002) with multiple compute nodes connected over high speed networks. Even if the data can be centralized using the relatively fast network, proper balancing of computational load among a cluster of nodes may require a distributed approach. Moreover, a distributed environment requires proper management of other distributed resources like data, privacy, and collaborative user-interaction. Several new distributed data mining applications belong to this category. The Kensington enterprise data mining system[1] and some of the counterterrorism applications reported elsewhere (Grossman 2002) belong to this category.

1.1.3 DDM from Multiparty, Privacy-Sensitive Data

The data privacy issue is playing an increasingly important role in many data mining applications. If a consortium of different banks wants to collaborate for detecting frauds and intrusions (Stolfo et al. 1997) then a centralized data

---

[1] http://www.inforsense.com

mining system would require collection of the potentially privacy-sensitive proprietary data from every bank to a single site. In many situations that is not acceptable. However, this may not be necessary if DDM is our choice of technology. DDM systems may be able to learn models from distributed data without exchanging raw data. This may allow both detection of fraud and preserving the privacy of the data.

The growing number of applications of data mining techniques for counterterrorism and security also beg for such privacy-preserving distributed data mining algorithms that can analyze multiparty distributed data without downloading the data to a single location. A growing number of DDM algorithms are now explicitly designed for privacy sensitive applications (Kantarcioglu and Clifton 2002; Kargupta et al. 2002a; Vaidya and Clifton 2002). We shall revisit this issue in section 1.10. Next, let us briefly discuss some of the fields that are related to DDM and their relevant contributions.

1.2   Historical Background

Although large scale exploratory analysis of data in a distributed environment is a relatively new development, the field has a strong connection with many fields. This section discusses this connection between DDM and a few other related fields.

Many DDM systems adopt the multiagent system (MAS) architecture. MAS has its root in distributed artificial intelligence (DAI), which investigates AI-based search, learning, planning, and other problem-solving techniques for distributed environments. Early research is in this area includes blackboard systems (Nii 1986), classifier systems (Holland 1975), production systems (Newell and Simon 1963), connectionism (Rumelhart and McClelland 1986), Minsky's "society of mind" concept (Minsky 1985), cooperative problem solving (Durfee, Lesser, and Corkill 1989), Actor framework (Agha 1986), and the contract net protocol (Smith 1980; Davies and Smith 1983). The emergence of distributed environments, such as the Internet and e-commerce have catalyzed many applications of DAI/MAS technology and extensive literature on multiagent communication (Finin, Labrou, and Mayfield 1997), negotiation (Rosenschein 1994) search (Lander and Lesser 1992), architectural issues (Woolridge and Jennings 1995), and learning (Sen 1997) is now available. While most of these topics are relevant to the DDM, DAI/MAS learning and architectural issues are probably the most relevant topics to DDM. However, existing literature on multiagent learning does not typically address the issues involved with large scale distributed data analysis. In DAI/MAS the focus is more on learning control knowledge (Byrne and Edwards 1995; Carmel and Markovitch 1995; Joshi 1995; Sen and Sekaran 1995), adaptive behavior (Mor, Goldman, and

Rosenschein 1995; Sandholm and Crites 1995; Weiß 1995), and other related issues. However, several efforts reported in the DAI/MAS literature do consider data intensive applications such as information discovery in the world wide web (Lesser et al. 1998; Menczer and Belew 1998; Moukas 1996).

The field of high performance parallel and distributed computing is also closely related to DDM in many ways. High performance parallel computing environments are often used for fast mining of large data sets. There exists a large volume of parallel data mining (PDM) literature (Alsabti, Ranka, and Singh 1997; Freitas and Lavington 1998; Kamath and Musick 2000; Zaki, Ogihara, Parthasarathy, and Lei 1996; Zaki, Parthasarathy, and Li 1997; Parthasarathy et al. 2001; Han, Karypis, and Kumar 1997; Joshi et al. 2000) Most of the PDM techniques assume existence of high speed network connections between the computing nodes. That is usually not available in many of the distributed and mobile data mining applications. Nevertheless, the development of DDM has been strongly influenced by the PDM literature.

Data fusion refers to seamless integration of data from disparate sources. Among the extensive literature on data fusion, the distributed approach of multisensor data fusion is very relevant to DDM. Typically, the multisensor data fusion algorithms work based on the following general mechanism: each sensor makes a local decision; all local decisions are then combined at a fusion center to produce a global decision. The objective of this approach is to determine the optimum local and global decision rules that maximize the probability of signal detection. This process shares striking procedural similarities with DDM. The Bayesian (Hoballah and Varshney 1989), the Neyman-Pearson (Viswanathan and Varshney 1997) criteria, and statistical hypothesis testing techniques are also frequently used for multisensor data fusion applications.

1.3 Data Models in DDM

In contrast to the different related fields discussed in the previous section, the field of distributed data mining deals with data analysis from distributed data. DDM algorithms depend on the nature of the data models distributed across the different participating sites. Most DDM algorithms are designed to work with either the *homogeneous* or *heterogeneous* data distribution, that can be defined using the relational (tabular) model.

In a relational database the schema provides the information regarding the relations stored. Homogeneous schemas contain the same set of attributes across different data sites. Distributed data mining from similar databases (e.g. customer transaction databases, maintenance reports) usually deal with the homogeneous situation. It is commonly referred to as the horizontal data partitioning. Most early DDM algorithms were designed to deal with the homogeneous data model (Kargupta, Hamzaoglu, and Stafford 1997; Stolfo et al. 1997).

A growing number of DDM algorithms (Kargupta et al. 2001; Strehl and Ghosh 2002) consider distributed data with heterogenous schemas defined by different sets of attributes across data sites (vertical partitioning). The data records at each site are usually somehow connected or linked through either an identifier or a common attribute. Most heterogenous DDM algorithms deal with the scenario where every participating table shares a common key column that links corresponding rows across the tables. For example, in a spatial database the location coordinates can serve as a key, whereas in a temporal database, the time stamp of the observation can serve the same purpose.

Most of the first generation DDM algorithms were applied on static databases located at different sites. However, the field has witnessed a growing number of applications (Oats, Schmill, and Cohen 1997) that deal with data streams where the different sites generate a continuous flow of time critical data. Mining communication data streams, vehicle health data streams, and financial data streams are some examples.

There is also a growing trend toward developing DDM algorithms for mining semi-structured data and unstructured data . We have seen several such applications (Kargupta, Hamzaoglu, and Stafford 1997; Sayal and Scheuermann 2000), particularly in the context of web and text data mining.

Bioinformatics data mining is another emerging application area of DDM. Applications in this domain normally deal with different types of data such as sequence, text, and images. Although the bioinformatics data is heterogeneous, the DDM applications share the flavor of semistructured data mining.

The following section considers different classes of DDM algorithms and reviews the relevant literature.

1.4 DDM Algorithms: An Overview

This section presents an overview of the state-of-the-art DDM algorithms. It considers some of the main data analysis algorithms in a typical data mining suite and discusses the state of the technology of their corresponding distributed counterparts. Most data mining sessions start with a data-preprocessing stage. This includes normalization, cleaning, feature selection, and if necessary representation construction. The preprocessing stage is followed by a different data modeling and analysis stages that sometimes involve clustering, predictive modeling, classification, association analysis, and other related techniques. This section follows the same structure in order to give the reader a flavor of what the field of DDM can offer today. Our discussion makes sincere effort to point the reader to appropriate existing DDM literature. However, space constraints often limit the depth of the discussion necessary to expose all the techniques to full details. Therefore, we focus on only a handful of different techniques. The following section starts with the data preprocessing and statistical aggregate computation.

1.5 Data Preprocessing and Computing Statistical Aggregates from Distributed Data

Data preprocessing is an important step in data mining and DDM is no exception. This step often requires computing statistical aggregates like the mean, variance, and covariance. They are additive by definition; this property can be exploited for implementing a distributed version of the algorithms to compute these statistics from homogeneous distributed data. The univariate statistical aggregates can also be computed from distributed heterogeneous sites by directly using their standard implementation scheme. However, more advanced techniques for data filtering and representation construction offer difficult challenges. The following sections describe some of them and their current algorithmic solutions reported in the DDM literature.

1.5.1 Principal Component Analysis from Distributed Data

Principal component analysis (PCA) is frequently used for constructing the representation of the data. It often reduces the dimension of the data by a large factor and constructs features that capture the maximally varying directions in the data. PCA is frequently used for clustering, classification, and predictive model building.

PCA from distributed homogeneous data is a relatively straight forward task in most cases. Since the covariance matrix is additively decomposable, one can simply compute the covariance matrix at each of the local participating sites and send those matrices to the central site. The central site can construct the global covariance matrix by adding the local covariance matrices with appropriate weights. This can be followed by a regular PCA of the global covariance matrix. The global eigenvectors can be broadcasted to the local sites and they can be subsequently used for projecting the local data for clustering and other related applications.

PCA from distributed heterogeneous data is a relatively more challenging problem. The collective principal component analysis (CPCA) algorithm (Kargupta et al. 2000a; Kargupta et al. 2001) offers one way to perform distributed PCA from heterogeneous sites. The main steps of the CPCA algorithm are given below:

1. Perform local PCA at each site; select dominant eigenvectors and project the data along them.

2. Send a sample of the projected data along with the (dominant) eigenvectors.

3. Combine the projected data from all the sites.

4. Perform PCA on the global data set, identify the dominant eigenvectors, and transform them back to the original space.

To compute exact principal components (PCs), in principle, we need to reconstruct the original data from all projected local samples. However, since the PCA is invariant under a linear transformation, the global PCs are computed directly from projected samples. The size of samples is a lot smaller than that of the original data. In other words, we can exploit the dimensionality reduction already achieved at each of the local sites.

Random projection techniques have recently gained popularity for constructing a similarity-preserving low-dimensional representation of the data. Distributed random projection may have a similar impact in DDM applications (Kargupta 2004a, b).[2] The following section reviews some of the existing techniques for computing statistical aggregates.

1.5.2 Computing Statistical Aggregates from Distributed Data Streams

A number of online monitoring applications involve processing queries on continuous streams of data that originate from different locations. Typical examples include monitoring computer networks to detect distributed denial-of-service (DDoS) attack[3] (Householder et al. 2001), monitoring web usage logs to identify the most popular web documents (Arlitt and Jin 1999), and monitoring telephone call record statistics. In these applications, the specific characteristic (of the data stream) to be monitored involve numeric values of item frequencies that are atypical (exceptionally large or small). Streaming data rates often exceed the capacity of the monitoring system in terms of storage, communication, and processing resources. Moreover, continuous transmission of a large number of rapid data streams to a central location can be impractical.

A useful class of queries involve monitoring and reporting the k largest values from a distributed data stream. For example, in an application involving monitoring HTTP requests across a distributed set of mirrored websites,

---

[2]Chris Gianella, Kun Liu, Todd Olsen, and Hillol Kargupta are preparing a paper tentatively entitled "Communication Efficient Construction of Decision Trees Over Heterogeneously Distributed Data."

[3]See "Denial of Service Attacks using Nameservers," www.cert. org.

one might like to know the web documents that are currently the most popular across all servers. Bobcock and Olston (2003) provide a distributed top-k monitoring algorithm that uses arithmetic constraints at remote stream sources and significantly reduces communication. The main steps of the algorithm are as follows: (1) Initially, maintain at a central coordinator site, a valid top-k set $\mathcal{T}$. Install a set of arithmetic constraints at each remote site over the partial data values there, to ensure continuing validity of $\mathcal{T}$. (2) As updates occur, the remote sites track changes to partial (local) data values, ensuring that the arithmetic constraint remains satisfied. As long as all the arithmetic constraints across all sites hold, no communication is necessary and the current top-k set $\mathcal{T}$ remains valid. (3) When one or more arithmetic constraints is violated, a distributed process called *resolution* takes place. This checks (and alters, if necessary) whether the current top-k set remains valid. If the top-k set has changed, new arithmetic constraints are installed (by the central site) at the remote sites.

This approach is flexible and can be easily adapted to applications where the exact top-k set is not required and a prespecified degree of error $\epsilon > 0$ is acceptable. This can further reduce the cost of monitoring and communication.

1.6   Distributed Clustering

The main objective of distributed clustering algorithms is to cluster the distributed data sets without necessarily downloading all the data to the single site. Some of them work by exchanging statistics computed at the local sites. Others work by exchanging local cluster information among the sites and then performing a metalevel clustering for merging the local clusters. Most clustering algorithms can be divided in two general categories based on the type of data distribution that they can handle. First we discuss the homogeneous case.

1.6.1   Homogeneous Case

Forman and Zhang (2000) proposed a center-based distributed clustering algorithm that only requires the exchange of sufficient statistics, which is essentially an extension of their earlier parallel clustering work (Zhang, Hsu, and Forman 2000). The recursive agglomeration of clustering hierarchies by encircling tactic (RACHET) (Samatova et al. 2002) is also based on the exchange of sufficient statistics. It collects local dendograms that are merged into a global dendogram. Each local dendogram contains descriptive statistics about the local cluster centroid that is sufficient for the global aggregation. However, both approaches need to iterate until the sufficient statistics converge or the desired quality is achieved.

Parthasarathy and Ogihara (2000) note that finding a suitable distance metric is an important problem in clustering, including distributed clustering. They define one such metric based on association rules. However, this approach is still restricted to homogeneous tables. In contrast, McClean and her colleagues (McClean, Scotney, and Greer 2000) consider the clustering of heterogeneous distributed databases. They particularly focus on clustering heterogeneous datacubes comprised of attributes from different domains. They utilize Euclidean distance and Kullback-Leibler information divergence to measure differences between aggregates.

The PADMA system (Kargupta, Hamzaoglu, and Stafford 1997) is yet another distributed clustering-based system for document analysis from homogeneous data sites. Distributed clustering in PADMA is aided by relevance feedback-based supervised learning techniques. Additional work on parallel and distributed clustering is reported elsewhere (Dhillon and Modha 1999; Zhang, Hsu, and Forman 2000).

1.6.2   Heterogeneous Case

Clustering heterogeneous, distributed data sets constitute an important class of problems. Kargupta, et. al. (2001) proposed a distributed clustering algorithm based on CPCA. This technique first applies a given off-the-shelf clustering algorithm to the local principal components. Then the global principal components are obtained from an appropriate data subset (projected) that is the union of all representative points from local clusters. to obtain new clusters, which are subsequently combined at the central site. A collective approach toward hierarchical clustering is proposed elsewhere (Johnson and Kargupta 1999).

Recently an ensemble approach to combining multiple clustering has been proposed by Strehl and Ghosh (2002). Given r different clusterings (possibly with different number of clusters in each clustering), they propose a framework to construct an ensemble of clusters in a way to maximize the shared information between original clusters. In order to quantify the shared information, they use a mutual information-based approach. Mutual information essentially denotes how two clusters are similar in terms of distributions of shared objects.

A distributed clustering algorithm for mining click-stream data is reported elsewhere (Sayal and Scheuermann 2000). This algorithm works by generating local clusterings and then combining them by analyzing the local cluster descriptions. A cluster is represented using a set of transaction ids. The combining phase uses duplicate cluster removal and a technique for generating maximal large itemsets (where items correspond to the transaction ids) to define the new global clusters.

1.7 Distributed Association Rule Mining

Two main approaches to distributed association rule mining are Count Distribution (CD) and Data Distribution (DD). CD especially considers the homogeneous DDM case. Each data site computes support counts for the same candidate itemsets independently, which are then gathered at a central site to determine the large itemsets for the next round. In contrast, DD focuses on maximizing parallelism through data redistribution; it distributes candidate itemsets so that each site computes a disjoint subset. It requires the exchange of data partitions, and is therefore only viable for machines with high-speed communications.

Agrawal and Shafer (1996) introduced a parallel version of Apriori. It requires $O(|C| \cdot n)$ communication overhead for each phase, where $|C|$ and n are the size of candidate itemset C and the number of data sites, respectively. The fast distributed mining (FDM) algorithm (Cheung et al. 1996) reduces the communication cost to $O(|C_p| \cdot n)$, where C_p is the potential candidate itemset (or, the union of all locally large itemsets). FDM notes that any globally large itemset should be identified locally large at one or more sites. However, this approach does not scale well in n, especially when the distributed data is skewed in distribution. Schuster and Wolff (2001) proposed the distributed decision miner algorithm that reduces communication overhead to $O(Pr_{above} \cdot |C| \cdot n)$, where Pr_{above} is the probability that a candidate itemset has support greater than a given threshold.

Jensen and Soparkar (2000) proposed an association rule-mining algorithm from heterogeneous relational tables. It particularly considers mining from star schema of n primary tables $T_1, \cdots, T_n$ (with one primary key) and one relationship table T_r. They assume that T_r contains all foreign keys to each T_i, and exploit the foreign key relationships to develop a decentralized algorithm. Since each foreign key is a unique primary key in the corresponding table, explicit join operation can be avoided during the computation of the support of an itemset. Another association rule mining technique from heterogeneous data is also reported (Vaidya and Clifton 2002).

1.8 Bayesian Network Learning from Distributed Data

In this section we first provide a brief introduction to Bayesian networks (BN) and discuss related literature. We then present an overview of our collective framework for learning a BN from distributed data.

A BN is a probabilistic graphical model that represents uncertain knowledge (Pearl 1988, Jensen 1996). It can be defined as a pair $(\mathcal{G}, p)$, where

$\mathcal{G} = (\mathcal{V}, \mathcal{E})$ is a directed acyclic graph (DAG). Here, $\mathcal{V}$ is the node set which represents variables in the problem domain and $\mathcal{E}$ is the edge set which denotes probabilistic relationships among the variables. For a variable $X \in \mathcal{V}$, a parent of X is a node from which there exists a directed link to X. Let $pa(X)$ denote the set of parents of X. The set of conditional distributions $\{P(X \mid pa(X)), X \in \mathcal{V}\}$ are called the parameters of a Bayesian network.

We now review important literature on learning BNs. Learning parameters of a BN from complete data is discussed in Buntine (1991). Learning parameters from incomplete data using gradient methods is discussed in Binder et al. (1997). Lauritzen (1995) has proposed an EM algorithm to learn BN parameters, whereas Bauer, Koller, and Singer (1997) describe methods for accelerating convergence of the EM algorithm. Learning using Gibbs sampling is proposed by Gilks, Richardson, and Spiegelhalter (1996). The Bayesian score to learn the structure of a BN is discussed by Cooper and Herskovits (1992). Learning the structure of a BN based on the minimal description length (MDL) principle is presented by Lam and Bacchus (1994). Learning BN structure using greedy hill-climbing and other variants is introduced by Heckerman and Gieger (1995), whereas Chickering (1996) introduced a method based on search over equivalence network classes. Learning the structure of BN from incomplete data, is considered in Chickering and Heckerman (1997), Cheeseman and Stutz (1996), and Friedman (1998). See Buntine (1991), Friedman and Goldszmidt (1997), and Lam and Bacchus (1994) for discussions on how to sequentially update the structure of a network as more data is available. Lam and Segre (1997) report a technique to automatically produce a BN from discovered knowledge using a distributed approach. An important problem is how to learn the BN from data in distributed sites. The centralized solution to this problem is to download all datasets from distributed sites. Kenji (1997) worked on the homogeneous distributed learning scenario.

In the following, we provide a brief overview of our collective approach to learning a BN that is specifically designed for a distributed data scenario. The primary steps in this approach are: (a) learn local BNs (local model) involving the variables observed at each site based on local data set, (b) at each site, based on the local BN, identify the observations that are most likely to be evidence of coupling between local and nonlocal variables. Transmit a subset of these observations to a central site, (c) at the central site, a limited number of observations of all the variables are now available. Using this, learn a nonlocal BN consisting of links between variables across two or more sites, (d) Combine the local models with the links discovered at the central site to obtain a collective BN.

The nonlocal BN constructed at the central site would be effective in identifying associations between variables across sites, whereas the local BNs would detect associations among local variables at each site. The conditional probabilities can also be estimated in a similar manner. Those probabilities that involve only variables from a single site can be estimated locally, whereas the ones that involve variables from different sites can be estimated at the central site. Finally, a collective BN can be obtained by taking the union of nodes and edges of the local BNs and the nonlocal BN and using the conditional probabilities from the appropriate BNs.

Selection of observations (for transmission to a central site — step b) that are most likely to be evidence of strong coupling between variables at two different sites is done as follows. For simplicity, we will assume that the data is distributed between two sites. At each local site, a local BN is first learned using only samples in this site. This would give a BN structure involving only the local variables at each site and the associated conditional probabilities. Let $p_A(.)$ and $p_B(.)$ denote the estimated probability function involving the local variables. The observations at each site are ranked based on how well it fits the local model, using the local (marginal) probability functions. The observations at site A with large likelihood under $l_A(.)$ are evidence of "local relationships" between site A variables, whereas those with low likelihoods under $l_A(.)$ are possible evidence of "cross relationships" between variables across sites. Let $S(A)$ denote the set of keys associated with the latter observations (those with low likelihood under $l_A(.)$). The sites A and B transmit the set of keys S_A, S_B, respectively, to a central site, where the intersection $S = S_A \cap S_B$ is computed. The observations corresponding to the set of keys in S are then obtained from each of the local sites by the central site.

Chen, Sivakumar, and Kargupta (2001 and 2001b) have shown that the above collective approach to learning a BN is well suited for a scenario with multiple data streams. Further improvements to the above collective BN learning algorithm, for both structure and parameter learning, has been reported by Chen and Sivakumar (2002) and Chen, Sivakumar, and Kargupta (2003).

1.9 Distributed Classifier Learning

Learning classifiers from distributed data sites poses an important class of problems. First we discuss the problem for homogeneous case. The heterogeneous scenario will follow that discussion.

1.9.1 Learning Classifiers from Homogeneous Sites

Most algorithms for distributed classifier learning from homogeneous data sites are related to ensemble learning techniques (Dietterich 2000; Opitz and Maclin 1999; Bauer and Kohavi 1999; Merz and Pazzani 1999). The ensemble approach has been applied in various domains to increase the classification accuracy of predictive models. It produces multiple models (base classifiers) and combines the outputs of the base modules in order to enhance accuracy.

The ensemble approach is directly applicable to the distributed scenario. Different models can be generated at different sites and ultimately aggregated using ensemble strategies. Several ensemble-based techniques have been reported in the literature. Fan, Stolfo, and Zhang (1999) discussed an AdaBoost-based ensemble approach from this perspective. Breiman (1999) considered arcing as a way to aggregate multiple blocks of data, especially in online setting. An experimental investigation of stacking (Wolpert 1992) for combining multiple models was reported elsewhere (Ting and Low 1997).

The meta-learning framework (Chan and Stolfo 1993a, 1993b, 1998) offers another possible approach to learn classifiers from homogeneous, distributed data. In this approach, supervised learning techniques are first used to learn classifiers at local data sites; then metalevel classifiers are constructed by either learning from a data set generated using the locally learned concepts or combining local classifiers using ensemble techniques. The metalevel learning may be applied recursively, producing a hierarchy of metaclassifiers. Metalearning follows three main steps: (1) Generate base classifiers at each site using a classifier learning algorithm. (2) Collect the base classifiers at a central site. Produce metalevel data from a separate validation set and predictions generated by the base classifier on it. (3) Generate the final classifier (metaclassifier) from metalevel data.

Learning at the metalevel can work in many different ways. For example, we may generate a new dataset using the locally learned classifiers. We may also move some of the original training data from the local sites, blend it with the data artificially generated by the local classifiers, and then run a learning algorithm to learn the metalevel classifiers. We may also decide the output of the metaclassifier by counting votes cast by different base classifiers. A metalearning-type technique known as *knowledge probing* is reported in Guo and Sutiwaraphun (2000). A Java-based distributed system for metalearning is reported elsewhere (Stolfo et al. 1997; Lee, Stolfo, and Mok 2000).

Metalearning illustrates two characteristics of DDM algorithms — parallelism and reduced communication. All base classifiers are generated in parallel and collected at the central location along with the validation set; the communication overhead is usually negligible compared to the transfer of entire raw data from every site.

Cho and Wüthrich (2002) proposed a distributed rule-based classifier system that selects k appropriate rules out of n $(>> k)$ rules learned from different sites. They empirically argued that a properly chosen set of k rules is sufficient for constructing a good ensemble classifier. In their approach, each rule is supposedly learned from an equal sized data called *fragment*. In order to select the optimal set of k rules, they ordered the original n rules and picked the top k. For the ordering criteria, they considered *confidence, support and deviation*, where confidence refers to the accuracy of a rule, support denotes the significance of a rule with respect to the entire data, and deviation is the degree of misclassification.

Gorodetski and his colleagues (2000) addressed distributed learning in data fusion systems. For *base classifiers*, they developed a technique that learns a wide class of rules from an arbitrary formula in first order logic. This is particularly applied as a visual technique to learn rules from databases. In order to overcome deficiencies of local learning (base classifiers), they adopted a randomized approach to select subsets of attributes and cases that are required to learn rules from distributed data, which results in a metalevel classifier.

The following section explores different distributed classification algorithms from heterogeneous sites.

1.9.2   Learning Classifiers from Heterogeneous Sites

Homogeneous DDM algorithms usually do not work well for mining heterogeneous sites. In the heterogeneous case, each local site observes only partial information. Therefore, a DDM algorithm must be able to learn a model using different features observed at different sites without downloading all the data to a single location. Ensemble-based approaches described in the previous subsection usually generate high variance local models (Tumer and Ghosh 2000) and fail to detect the interaction between features observed at different sites. This makes the problem fundamentally challenging.

In some applications, heterogeneous DDM may not require detecting interactions between features from different sites. In other words, the underlying problem may be site-wise decomposable. This scenario is relatively easy to handle. An ensemble-based approach to learn distributed classifiers is likely to work well for this case. Even if the application does not involve distributed data, vertical partitioning of data for decomposing the learning problem into smaller subproblems can speed up the process (Provost and Buchanan 1995). However, assumption of site-wise decomposability is not necessarily correct in every application. In the general case, heterogeneous DDM may require building classifiers using nonlinearly interacting features from different sites.

The WoRLD system (Aronis et al. 1997) also works by making some assumptions about the class of DDM problems. It works by collecting first order statistics from the data. It considers the problem of concept learning from heterogeneous sites by developing an "activation spreading" approach. This approach first computes the cardinal distribution of the feature values in the individual data sets. Next, this distribution information is propagated across different sites. Features with strong correlations with the concept space are identified based on the first order statistics of the cardinal distribution. Since the technique is based on the first order statistical approximation of the underlying distribution, it may not be appropriate for data mining problems where concept learning requires higher order statistics.

There exist a few DDM algorithms that use an ensemble of classifiers for mining heterogeneous data sites. However, these techniques use special-purpose aggregation algorithms in order to handle some of the issues discussed earlier in this section. The aggregation technique proposed by Tumer and Ghosh (2000) uses an order statistics-based approach for combining high variance local models generated from heterogeneous sites. The technique works by ordering the predictions of different classifiers and using them in an appropriate manner. Their work developed several methods, including selection of an appropriate order statistic as the classifier and taking a linear combination of some of the order statistics ("spread" and "trimmed mean" classifiers). It also analyzes the error of such a classifier in various situations. Although these techniques are more robust than other ensemble based models, they do not explicitly consider interactions across multiple sites.

Park and his colleagues (2002) developed a technique to learn decision trees from heterogeneous, distributed sites. The approach can be classified as an ensemble-based approach. However, they also proposed a Fourier spectrum-based technique to aggregate the ensemble of decision trees. They note that any pattern involving features from different sites cannot be captured by simple aggregation of local classifiers generated using only the local features. In order to detect such patterns, they first identify a subset of data that none of the local classifiers can classify with high confidence. This subset of the data is merged at the central site and another classifier (central classifier) is constructed from it. When a combination of local classifiers cannot classify a new observation with a high confidence, the central classifier is used instead. This approach exhibits a better performance than a simple aggregation of local models. However, its performance is sensitive to the confidence threshold.

Kargupta and his colleagues considered a *collective* framework to address data analysis in heterogeneous DDM environments and proposed the *collective data mining* (CDM) (Kargupta et al. 2000b) framework. CDM can be deployed for learning classifiers and predictive models from distributed data. Instead of combining incomplete local models, it seeks to find globally meaningful pieces of information from each local site. In other words, it obtains local building blocks that directly constitute the global model. Given a set of labeled training data, CDM learns a function that approximates it. The foundation of CDM is based on the observation that any function can be represented in a distributed fashion using an appropriate set of basis functions. When the basis functions are orthonormal, the local analysis produces correct and useful results that can be directly used as a component of the global model without any loss of accuracy. Since data modeling using canonical, nonorthogonal basis functions do not offer problem decomposability needed in a DDM application, CDM does not directly learn data models in popular representations like polynomial, logistic functions, decision trees, and feed-forward neural nets. Instead, it first learns these models in some appropriately chosen orthonormal basis space, guarantees the correctness of the generated model, and then converts the model in orthonormal representation to the desired forms.

The main steps of CDM can be summarized as follows: (1) Generate approximate orthonormal basis coefficients at each local site. (2) Move an appropriately chosen sample of the data sets from each site to a single site and generate the approximate basis coefficients corresponding to nonlinear cross terms. (3) Combine the local models, transform the model into the user described canonical representation, and output the model. Here nonlinear terms represent a set of coefficients (or patterns) that cannot be determined at a local site. In essence, the performance of a CDM model depends on the quality of estimated crossterms. Typically, CDM requires an exchange of a small sample that is often negligible compared to the entire data.

The CDM approach was originally explored using two important classes of function induction problems — learning decision trees and multivariate regressors. Fourier and Wavelet-based representations of functions have been proposed elsewhere (Kargupta et al. 2000b; Hershberger and Kargupta 2001) for constructing decision trees and multivariate regressors respectively. The Fourier spectrum-based approach works by estimating the Fourier coefficients (FCs) from the data. It estimates the local FCs from the local data and FCs involving features from different data sites using a selected small subset of data collected at the central site.

It has been shown elsewhere (Kargupta et al. 2000b; Park, Ayyagari, and Kargupta 2001; Kargupta et al. 2002a) that one can easily compute the Fourier spectrum of a decision tree and the vice versa. This observation can be exploited to construct decision trees from the estimated FCs. However, fast estimation of FCs from data is a nontrivial job. Estimation techniques usually work well when the data is uniformly distributed. This problem is addressed by the development of a resampling-based technique (Ayyagari and Kargupta 2002) for the estimation of the Fourier spectrum.

The collective multivariate regression (Hershberger and Kargupta 2001) chooses wavelet basis to represent local data. For each feature in the set wavelet transformation is applied and significant coefficients are collected at the central site. Then regression is performed directly on the wavelet coefficients. This approach has a significant advantage in terms of communication reduction since a set of wavelet coefficients usually represents raw data in a highly compressed format.

The CDM framework has recently been extended to the unsupervised DDM domain. A discussion on collective principal component analysis, collective clustering, and collective Bayesian learning from heterogeneous, distributed data was presented earlier in this chapter.

1.10 Privacy Preserving Distributed Data Mining

Privacy is an important issue in many applications. A growing body of literature on privacy-sensitive data mining is emerging. Most of these algorithms can be divided into two groups. One approach adopts a distributed framework; the other approach adds random noise to the data in such a way that the individual data values are distorted while still preserving the underlying distribution properties at a macroscopic level. We now briefly discuss these two approaches.

The distributed approach supports computation of data mining models and extraction of "patterns" at a given node by exchanging only the minimal necessary information among the participating nodes without transmitting the raw data. The field of DDM (Kargupta et al. 2000b; Park and Kargupta 2002) produced several distributed algorithms that are sensitive to privacy. For example the metalearning based JAM system (Stolfo et al. 1997) was designed for mining multiparty distributed sensitive data such as financial fraud detection. The Fourier spectrum-based approach to represent and construct decision trees (Kargupta and Park 2003, Ayyagari and Kargupta 2001), the collective hierarchical clustering (Johnson and Kargupta 1999) are examples of additional distributed data mining algorithms that may be used with minor modifications for privacy-preserving mining from distributed data. In the recent past, several distributed techniques to mine multiparty data have been reported. A privacy preserving technique to construct decision trees (Quinlan 1986) proposed elsewhere (Lindell and Pinkas 2000), multiparty secured computation framework (Du and Atallah 2001), association rule mining from homogeneous (Kantarcioglu and Clifton 2002) and heterogeneous (Vaidya and Clifton 2002) distributed data sets are some examples. There also exists a collection of useful privacy-sensitive data mining primitives such as secure sum computation (Schneier 1995), and secure scalar product computation (Vaidya and Clifton 2002).

There is also a somewhat different approach and the algorithms that belong to this group work by first perturbing the data using randomized techniques. The perturbed data is then used to extract the patterns and models. The randomized value distortion technique for learning decision trees (Agrawal, Evfimievski, and Srikant 2003) and association rule learning (Evfimievsi 2002) are examples of this approach. Additional work on randomized masking of data can be found elsewhere (Traub, Yemini, and Woz'niakowski 1984). However, the idea of using white noise for preserving privacy has been questioned elsewhere (Kargupta, Liu, and Ryan 2003). They reported a spectral filter for filtering the perturbed data and showed that the random perturbation technique may not preserve a whole lot of privacy in many cases. Random multiplicative noise using projection matrices have been explored elsewhere (Liu, Kargupta, and Ryan 2003) for privacy-preserving distributed data mining. This paper exploited the inner-product preserving property of random matrices and developed a "double-sided" (both row and columnwise) projection of data matrix that allows computing the correlation matrix from the projected data.

1.11   Conclusions and Future Direction

In this chapter we have offered a perspective on the existing pleasures in the field of distributed data mining. We have discussed some of the DDM algorithms reported in the literature, their strengths, and weaknesses. We also discussed some of the key emerging application areas. However, we did not make any effort to review the DDM systems research because of limited space. A review of the systems issues in DDM research can be found elsewhere (Park and Kargupta 2002). As a research area DDM still has many open challenges. Some of the future directions are discussed in the following paragraphs.

One of the most important challenges facing the DDM technology is the transition of DDM algorithms from the design board to world of real applications. Many of the DDM algorithms are developed based on the relational data models. While they remain valid in many applications, there are other situations where the existing data models do not fit very well. Many real-life DDM applications deal with data distribution scenarios that are neither homogeneous nor heterogeneous in their traditional sense described in this chapter. We may have heterogeneous data sites that share more than one attribute. We may not have any well-defined key that links multiple rows across the sites. We need to address these issues. We certainly need more algorithms for the heterogeneous scenarios. Also distributed data mining from semistructured, unstructured, and stream data needs further exploration.

DDM frequently requires exchange of data mining models among the participating sites. Therefore, seamless and transparent realization of DDM technology will require standardized schemes to represent and exchange models. The predictive model markup language (PMML (Grossman et al. 1999), cross-industry standard process model for data mining (CRISP-DM), and other related efforts are likely to be very useful for the development of DDM.

Distributed data mining for wireless applications needs a lot of work on both algorithmic and systems issues. Bandwidth limitation is one of the major constraints in this domain. However, it also has other constraints, such as power consumption. Most DDM algorithms that are designed for desktop-based applications hardly pay any attention to their power consumption characteristics. The next generation DDM algorithms will have to pay attention to this aspect and we need research for developing power efficient DDM algorithms and systems.

Finally, data privacy is likely to remain an important issue in data mining research and application. The field of privacy-preserving data mining algorithms is still in its early stage and the privacy-preserving properties of at least some of them need more investigation. Overall, the field needs lot of work for defining privacy in a rigorous manner, developing formalism to prove privacy-preserving properties of data mining algorithms, and designing a new class of algorithms that can mine privacy-sensitive data in an asynchronous distributed manner.

Acknowledgments

We acknowledge supports from the NASA (NRA) NAS2-37143 and the United States National Science Foundation CAREER award IIS-0093353. We would also like to thank B. H. Park for help with some of the figures.

Hillol Kargupta is an associate professor in the Department of Computer Science and Electrical Engineering at the University of Maryland Baltimore County. He is also affiliated with AGNIK LLC in Columbia, Maryland. His research interests include mobile and distributed data mining and computation in gene expression. He can be reached at hillol@cs.umbc.edu

Krishamoorthy Sivakumar is an assistant professor at the School of Electrical Engineering and Computer Science, Washington State University. His research interests include data mining from distributed databases, privacy-sensitive data mining, and statistical signal and image processing. He can be reached at siva@eecs.wsu.edu.

Chapter 2

Research Issues in Mining and Monitoring of Intelligence Data

Alan Demers, Johannes Gehrke,
and Mirek Riedewald

There has recently emerged a heightened awareness of the importance of effective intelligence gathering and associated intelligence data processing by the U.S. Government. A new effort called the "Knowledge Discovery and Dissemination Working Group" has started research on an information infrastructure that will meet the needs of U.S. intelligence and law enforcement agencies for the next decades. From the discussions and projects some basic architectural requirements are emerging. In particular, operational and legal requirements for intelligence agencies lead to two separate architectural areas, which we call *information spheres.*

A *local* information sphere exists within each government agency. Its goal is to perform online analysis and data mining of multiple high-speed data streams, with essentially unrestricted local access to all data managed by the system. The *global* information sphere spans all participating government agencies, and mediates inter-agency collaboration. It addresses the sometimes conflicting requirements of allowing analysts from different government agencies to efficiently share information, hypotheses and evidence without violating applicable laws regarding privacy and civil rights.

Each local information sphere must continuously process high-speed data streams from a variety of sources, performing on-line data mining and trigger evaluation as well as supporting interactive data analysis for analysts. We believe that a distributed mining and monitoring system is best suited to implement this vital functionality of a local information sphere. Note that the architecture of such a system needs to follow the plug-and-play paradigm in order to support easy integration of new data mining and analysis operators and to be easily extended with new functionality. The requirements of the global information sphere present additional research challenges, particularly in the areas of privacy preserving data mining and information integration (Agrawal and Srikant 2000; Evfimievski, Srikant, Agrawal, and Gehrke 2002; Gehrke 2002; Lindell and Pinkas 2002; Vaidya and Clifton 2002). In this chapter we focus on issues related to the local information sphere.

The remainder of the chapter is organized as follows. In section 2.1 we introduce the general architecture for a distributed data mining and monitoring application. Section 2.2 discusses selected challenging research problems that need to be addressed for an efficient and effective implementation of this architecture. Some recent results that we extend in our ongoing research towards this goal are presented in section 2.3. Section 2.4 concludes this chapter.

2.1   Overview of the Architecture

An effective data mining and monitoring system supports fast and efficient information exchange and at the same time has to protect the privacy of individuals. Balancing these two conflicting goals is a nontrivial challenge, which we address with the information sphere architecture.

Typically a person's private information is not "private" in the sense that no one else knows that information. For instance, our primary care physician has access to our medical records, the human resource department knows our income, and the bank has all data about our finances. Privacy is ensured by not allowing each of these entities to freely exchange their data. Similarly, there are laws that govern the information exchange between different units in the government. Notice that in this chapter we will not address authentication and security challenges within the system. Instead we keep the design general enough to accommodate relevant technology.

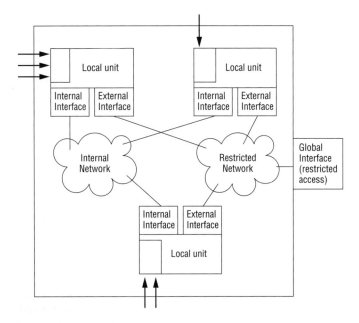

Figure 2.1: Local information sphere.

2.1.1 Local Information Sphere

Whenever information is allowed to flow freely, the information infrastructure should support unrestricted access to all data in the most efficient way. This is the goal of the local information sphere. Figure 2.1 shows a schematic drawing of the architecture. Its basic components are local processing units (cf. figure 2.2). These units consist of one or more processors with large main memory and essentially unrestricted archival capabilities, e.g., large hard disk drives or RAID arrays. We do not advocate any specific technology; for example, a local processing unit could be a massively parallel machine or a cluster of PCs. An internal network connects different local units through their internal interfaces. The design goal for internal interfaces and the internal network is to optimize for fast unrestricted information sharing. There is no requirement that all processing units be centrally located. In practice, these units are more likely to be geographically distributed, and the internal network will be a secure wide-area network (WAN).

The units in a local information sphere process potentially massive streams of incoming information. Examples of such streams are newsfeed data and continuously arriving measurements from sensors, as well as reports from analysts, and other intelligence feeds. Current database technology is inadequate

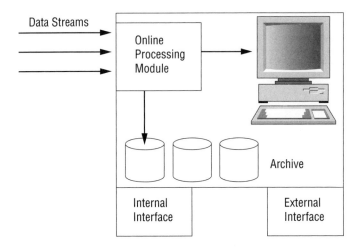

Figure 2.2: Local information sphere.

for processing and extracting information from these streams in real-time. A variety of different data stream query processors is under development that focus on processing high-speed data streams and associated research problems. Examples are Stanford's STREAM Project (Babcock, Babu, Datar, Motwani, and Widom 2002; Babu and Widom 2001), the Aurora system (Çetintemel, Cherniack, Convey, Lee, Seidman, Stonebraker, Tatbul, and Zdonik 2002), Berkeley's Telegraph (Hellerstein et al. 2000), the NiagaraCQ query engine (Chen, DeWitt, Tian, and Wang 2000), and sensor database systems (Bonnet, Gehrke, and Seshadri 2001). However processing data streams is just one of the challenges when implementing a local information sphere. We will discuss a plethora of concrete problems in section 2.2.

2.1.2 Global Information Sphere

As we mentioned previously, protecting privacy requires limiting the flow of data about individuals between different agencies or even between departments within an agency. On the other hand the combined information in all local information spheres might reveal important facts that could not be derived from any local sphere individually. This dilemma can be addressed by allowing the extraction and exchange of aggregate information that hides individual records until there is enough evidence to justify a further investigation. Consequently the different local information spheres are connected to each other within a global information sphere (figure 2.3).

While the efficiency of data sharing operations between local information

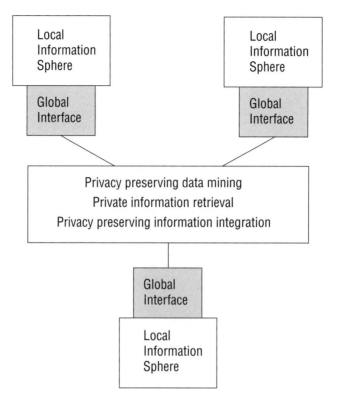

Figure 2.3: Local information sphere.

spheres is important, a primary goal of the global information sphere is to preserve the privacy of data at the local information sphere. This includes protecting not only the privacy of each individual's data in different local spheres, but also the privacy of information retrieval by analysts. The latter refers to the fact that knowing which queries an analyst poses to a database will also reveal information about this analyst's knowledge. There are similar problems regarding the integration of different data sources within the global information sphere, which also have to be addressed in a privacy preserving manner. Consequently, local information spheres are connected using interfaces that support privacy preserving data mining and private information retrieval rather than free access to all data. Notice that this requires a separate external interface and a restricted network for the processing units within each local information sphere (cf. figure 2.1). A detailed discussion of all research issues in the global information sphere is beyond the scope of this chapter.

2.2   Research Problems in the Local Information Sphere

In the following subsections we discuss challenging research problems in distributed mining and monitoring. The selection of topics is by no means complete; it contains our personal bias and focuses on issues related to processing data streams. More information on the current status of data stream processing in the database community can be found in a special issue of the *IEEE Computer Society Bulletin of the Technical Committee on Data Engineering* (Gehrke 2003).

2.2.1   Multiquery Optimization

An important activity of automatic mining tools as well as human analysts is the generation of hypotheses from available evidence. These hypotheses are continuously re-evaluated based on newly arriving information. New data could also initiate the (automatic) evolution of an existing hypothesis, or even the creation of a new hypothesis. From an analyst's point of view the system should be able to support the concurrent evaluation of as many hypotheses as possible. Apart from the obvious challenge of how to automatically evolve or create a hypothesis, there are nontrivial issues in multiquery optimization of such hypotheses (Sellis 1988). Several of the hypotheses might be partly based on the same evidence or be affected by the same incoming data item. Detecting such commonalities automatically and evaluating or updating multiple hypotheses together allows the system to scale with increasing load in terms of the number of concurrently evaluated hypotheses as well as the speed of the incoming data records. To be able to guarantee real-time (or near real-time) processing, the time permissible for finding affected hypotheses and evaluating and updating them is governed by the rate of the incoming data stream. Note that the workload is not static, but rather evolves as analysts and automatic tools add, remove, and change hypotheses. Instead of recomputing the "optimal" system configuration each time the workload changes, *incremental* query addition and deletion techniques are required (Chandrasekaran, Cooper, Deshpande, Franklin, Hellerstein, Hong, Krishnamurthy, Madden, Raman, Reiss, and Shah 2003; Raman and Hellerstein 2002).

2.2.2   Online Processing of Resource-Intensive Queries

When processing queries over massive data streams, the amount of available main memory is typically the bottleneck. For example, joining two streams of relational tuples requires the system to store the complete streams, which ultimately will result in a memory overflow. Similarly, detecting if newly arriving information affects a hypothesis might require large amounts of memory, as shown in the following example. (Note that also other approaches are possible [Cortes and Pregibon 2001].)

Fraud Detection Example. Consider a large telecommunications company with the problem of detecting fraudulent telephone numbers, where a phone number is fraudulent if the owner of the phone number never pays his or her telephone bill. For ease of terminology, let us call such a fraudulent phone number a *bad phone number*. One simple space of hypotheses is "phone number x is bad," for all possible x within the network of the telecom company. Assume that, for a phone number x, we believe x is bad if x was called from a bad number, or if x ever called a bad number — once we believe that x is bad an analyst will more closely examine the calling pattern of x for deeper analysis. If x was called by y at a time t at which y was not known to be bad, the call seems irrelevant for our long-running hypothesis query about x. However, if it turns out later that y is bad, the call at time t suddenly becomes very relevant, and thus we require quick access to it.

In this simple example, the main memory of a modern PC might be large enough to store a day's calling records. However, for more complex scenarios and multiple hypotheses in-memory storage will no longer be an option, and we need to resort to disk-based storage of older data. (See section 2.2.3 on research problems in a high-speed queryable archive.) In the example, the main challenge is to identify the information that is most relevant in establishing a hypothesis, and to keep that information in main memory. The relevance will typically depend on information that arrives in the future.

In general, the goal is to make a system in the local information sphere degrade gracefully with increasing load. Graceful degradation can be achieved along two dimensions — accuracy and response time. When only a fraction of the relevant data can be kept in memory, either an approximate answer will be obtained, or accessing the archive for computing the exact result will slow down the computation (Haas and Hellerstein 2001). New techniques are needed that can adapt to resource bottlenecks by choosing an "optimal" trade-off depending on application requirements (e.g., if it is more desirable to get a fast approximate result rather than a slow exact result, and what tolerable approximations are) (Hellerstein et al. 2000). Possible solutions are discussed next.

Load Shedding. One concept for addressing resource (especially memory) bottlenecks is *load shedding* (Çetintemel, Cherniack, Convey, Lee, Seidman, Stonebraker, Tatbul, and Zdonik 2002). When a process detects that it is approaching its memory limit, it starts preemptively discarding the "least relevant" data from memory to make room for newly arriving "important" information. A fundamental question is whether, or with what probability, a load shedding technique can guarantee that it will not miss the needle in the haystack, i.e., a piece of evidence that might be needed later on for proving or discarding a hypothesis.

In intelligence scenarios, load shedding needs to be combined with techniques that keep track of those data items that were directly written to secondary storage without appropriately being processed by queries — the knowledge of *what* was missed facilitates incremental postprocessing of queries using the archive. Other provisioning techniques that require further investigation are mechanisms for prioritizing resources among the different queries (this could be referred to as "query shedding") and tools for capacity planning that make recommendations for system upgrades if bottlenecks persist and the system is permanently "falling behind."

2.2.3 High-Speed Archiving and Indexing

Within the local information sphere a high-performance *archive* will play an important role. This archive permanently records all relevant information and hence is essential for offline "deep mining" and other post-arrival analysis as well as simple storage of all evidence. We believe that a traditional database system is insufficient for this purpose, as current systems are unable to keep up with the rate of data arrival and the temporal and spatiotemporal nature of the data.

The archive, however, is not accessed exclusively by mining tools. Due to the limited amount of fast memory, even some online queries might have to access the archive from time to time, for example to retrieve older records in order to increase the accuracy of a query answer. As in data warehousing, we expect benefits from multiquery optimization of accesses to the archive and from generating indexes for supporting expensive queries.

There are important differences between an archive for intelligence data at a local information sphere and a data warehouse. For intelligence applications we cannot afford to apply data in batches overnight, as responses to critical situations must be immediate. Hence we need new update and indexing techniques that take the temporal nature of the data into account, can handle extremely high update rates, and can adapt to varying input rates and resource availability. Here we can build on research in the areas of log-structured file systems (Rosenblum and Ousterhout 1992), temporal access methods (Muth, O'Neil, Pick, and Weikum 2000), and bulk-updated indexes (Arge, Hinrichs, Vahrenhold, and Vitter 2002).

There are other interesting and little researched issues for stream archives. For instance, if the system maintains statistics about a data stream, this information can be used to optimize the creation of indexes (similar to the recent work on index tuning wizards or index advisors) (Chaudhuri and Narasayya

1997; Valentin, Zuliani, Zilio, Lohman, and Skelley 2000) or to optimize the physical layout of the archive.

In addition to the problems mentioned so far, there are also generic requirements on such an archive, which are little different from requirements on other archives (e.g., fault-tolerance, recoverability, concurrency control, availability, etc.).

2.2.4 Foundations of Data Stream Queries

There is a lot of previous work on active databases and publish-and-subscribe systems (Widom and Ceri 1996; Fabret, Jacobsen, Llirbat, Pereira, Ross, and Shasha 2001). It is important to evaluate the extent to which some of these techniques can be employed within the local information sphere. For instance, could a hypothesis be expressed as a trigger or as a subscription? Is the event-condition-action model adequate? What are the tradeoffs in terms of query performance and expressiveness?

A fundamental problem is to determine the memory consumption of a query. For instance, it is important to understand what classes of queries can be computed in $O(1)$, $O(\log^{O(1)} n)$, or $o(n)$ space, where n is the number of data items in the stream seen so far (Babcock, Babu, Datar, Motwani, and Widom 2002). Related to this problem is the question of how additional knowledge about the stream, e.g., *stream punctuations* (Tucker and Maier 2002), might be used to reduce the space consumption of a query. For instance, when performing a simple SQL group-by computation over a data stream, all groups for which it is known that no more elements will arrive can be removed from the operator state and sent to the output. Punctuations bring up a fascinating set of research problems, such as what types of punctuations are feasible and useful, and also the problem of who annotates the stream with the relevant punctuations.

2.2.5 Parallel and Distributed Stream Processing

Scalability, both in terms of the number of queries and the data arrival rate, is clearly a basic requirement of a data mining system at a local information sphere. An obvious solution for dealing with massive data streams in a scalable manner is to make use of local parallelism by distributing the processing across multiple nodes, for example in a "blade-farm" or in a cluster of PCs with network-attached storage. The research challenges here lie in the "parallelization" of hypothesis maintenance and online data stream query processing.

A second challenge comes from the potentially physical distribution of the data stream sources — even within a local information sphere. This requires techniques for distributed processing and mining of high-speed data streams. While processing different streams locally at individual sites can be scaled through local parallelism, queries that have to access multiple physically distributed streams are punished by network latency and transfer times and restricted bandwidth. As in a conventional distributed database system, we believe that the distribution of data and queries should be transparent to the analyst.

Triggered by advances in communication technology the interest in distributed data mining has increased rapidly over the past few years. Traditional data mining approaches are based on a centralized application that downloads all relevant data from the sources, potentially shipping large amounts of data over the network. The goal of distributed data mining techniques is to not only reduce the amount of network traffic, but also to distribute load among the different local units, taking the availability of the distributed resources into account. The underlying idea typically is to let the same algorithm operate on several units concurrently, producing a local model at each site. Then the local models are aggregated to produce the final model (Park and Kargupta 2003). Currently various approaches exist for distributed classifier learning, association rule mining, and clustering (Kargupta, Huang, Sivakumar, and Johnson 2001; Schuster and Wolff 2001). (See the excellent book *Advances in Distributed and Parallel Knowledge Discovery* by Hilol Kargupta and Philip Chan (2000) for an overview.) Despite current advances, there has been little work on distributed mining of data streams in real-time.

2.2.6   New Data Mining Models

In many intelligence applications the values of the events on which hypotheses are based on are probabilistic in nature. For example, automated text processing tools that work over the output of automated natural language processing tools might only produce facts that are correct with high probability. We need to develop data mining algorithms and potentially new data mining models that take this inherent uncertainty in the records from which the models are constructed into account. Similarly, we need to develop data mining models that are temporal in nature, maybe drawing from work on time series analysis from the statistics literature. There has been early work that exploits the temporal nature of events, such as the work on sequential patterns or periodic association rules (Agrawal and Srikant 1995; Mannila, Toivonen, and Verkamo 1997; Özden, Ramaswamy, and Silberschatz 1998); one possible first step would be to extend these approaches to other data mining models. In addition, we need models for more complex data records, such as graph-structured data (Zaki 2002).

2.2.7 Data Mining Model Management

As noted previously, intelligence applications use large amounts of data of various types, which may be derived from sources of questionable reliability, and thus must be considered probabilistic in nature. Under these conditions, hypothesis generation (either automatically or manually) is a difficult problem. Even determining the best way to find supporting evidence for a hypothesis can be a difficult task, requiring considerable skill and experience. We do not understand yet how a successful analyst goes about his/her work, but in general the best techniques are likely to be complex and domain-specific.

Analysts could benefit from a data mining model management system that would enable them to mine hypotheses and queries for techniques that have proven successful in similar situations in the past. For example, given a hypothesis that "organization X is dangerous," an analyst might wish to understand how one of his colleagues acquired evidence about a similar organization six months earlier.

A related issue, which we term *meta-mining*, is mining on-line queries themselves for trends or similarities. When development of hypotheses by several independent analysts (who in general have access to different data) results in related or identical online queries, this could indicate a trend that should cause the system to generate an alert. In this way, the system might recognize significant events that would escape the notice of any individual analyst.

2.3 Recent Results

In this section, we survey some of our own recent results that are particularly applicable to some of the research problems that we outlined in the previous section.

2.3.1 Sketches for Data Streams

The computation of sketches is one technique for real-time processing of data streams. Sketches support the maintenance of summary statistics in the online processing module of a local unit (figure 2.2). We discuss recent results on using sketches to compute join statistics and show how sketches can be used for the distributed computation of summary statistics.

Computing Summaries Using Sketches

In the following we summarize some of the techniques presented in Dobra, Garofalakis, Gehrke, and Rastogi (2002). More specifically, in the following we discuss sketch-based techniques for answering queries of the form

"$Q_{\text{COUNT}} = \text{SELECT COUNT(*) FROM } R_1, R_2, \ldots, R_r \text{ WHERE } \mathcal{E}$" over data streams $R_1, \ldots, R_r$. Here $\mathcal{E}$ represents the conjunction of n equi-join constraints of the form $R_i.A_j = R_k.A_l$ ($R_i.A_j$ denotes the jth attribute of relation R_i). Intuitively the query computes the number of tuples in the cross-product of $R_1, \ldots, R_r$ that satisfy the equality constraints in $\mathcal{E}$ over the join attributes. The technique can be easily extended to handle other aggregate operators like SUM or AVERAGE. For simplicity from now on we will assume a renaming of the $2n$ join attributes in $\mathcal{E}$ to $A_1, A_2, \ldots, A_{2n}$ such that each equi-join constraint in $\mathcal{E}$ is of the form $A_j = A_{n+j}$, for $1 \leq j \leq n$. Also, let $\text{dom}(A_i) = \{1, \ldots, |\text{dom}(A_i)|\}$ be the domain of attribute A_i.

In order to be able to process massive data streams with limited resources, algorithms are needed that can summarize the streams in a concise, but reasonably accurate synopsis. A major challenge is to construct synopses that can be set up for any available amount of memory and provide approximate answers to user queries along with guarantees on the quality of the approximation. Within a local processing unit these synopses enable real-time decision making, e.g., for generating early alerts that trigger further investigation or filtering and ranking of incoming information.

The sketch-based randomized algorithm for producing a probabilistic estimate of the result of the above mentioned COUNT query is an extension of the technique proposed by Alon, Matias, and Szegedy (1996). Essentially, we construct a random variable X that is an unbiased estimator for the query result (i.e., $E[X] = Q_{\text{COUNT}}$), and whose variance can be appropriately bounded from above. Then, by employing the standard averaging and median-selection trick of Alon, Matias, and Szegedy (1996), the accuracy and confidence of X to compute an estimate of Q_{COUNT} is boosted to guarantee a small relative error with high probability.

Such a random variable X can be constructed as follows. For each pair of join attributes A_j, A_{n+j} in $\mathcal{E}$, we build a family of four-wise independent random variables $\{\xi_{j,l} : l = 1, \ldots, |\text{dom}(A_j)|\}$, where each $\xi_{j,l} \in \{-1, +1\}$. The key here is that every equi-join attribute pair A_j and A_{n+j} shares the same ξ family, and so for all $l \in \text{dom}(A_j)$, $\xi_{j,l} = \xi_{n+j,l}$. However, a distinct ξ family is generated for each of the n distinct equi-join pairs by using mutually-independent random seeds. Thus, random variables belonging to families defined for different attribute pairs are completely independent of each other. The family for attribute pair A_j, A_{n+j} can be efficiently constructed on-line using only $O(\log |\text{dom}(A_j)|)$ space. Hence the space requirement for all n families of random variables is $\sum_{j=1}^{n} O(\log |\text{dom}(A_j)|)$.

For each stream R_k, we define the atomic sketch X_k to be equal to $\sum_{\mathcal{I} \in \mathcal{D}_k} (f_k(\mathcal{I}) \prod_{j \in S_k} \xi_{j,\mathcal{I}[j]})$. Here S_k denotes the join attributes in R_k; $\mathcal{D}_k$ denotes the projection of the crossproduct of the domains of the join attributes in $\mathcal{E}$ on S_k. Function $f_k(\mathcal{I})$ computes the number of tuples in R_k that match $\mathcal{I}$, and

$\mathcal{I}[j]$ is the value of attribute A_j of $\mathcal{I}$. The COUNT estimator random variable is defined as $X = \prod_{k=1}^{r} X_k$ (i.e., the product of the atomic sketches X_k).

Note that each atomic sketch X_k can be efficiently computed as tuples of R_k are streaming in. More specifically, X_k is initialized to 0 and, for each tuple t in the R_k stream, the quantity $\prod_{j \in S_k} \xi_{j,t[j]}$ is added to X_k, where $t[j]$ denotes the value of attribute A_j in tuple t.

Dobra, Garofalakis, Gehrke, and Rastogi (2002) show that X indeed is an unbiased estimator for the query result, and they derive tight bounds for the variance of X for acyclic join graphs (the join graph for Q_{COUNT} is an undirected graph consisting of a node for each R_i and an edge for each join-attribute pair A_j, A_{n+j} between the nodes containing these join attributes). Although the estimator is unbiased, it has a significant variance, which can be reduced by standard averaging and median selection of several sketches. Hence a user can easily select the appropriate tradeoff between resource consumption and result accuracy depending on the application requirements.

Dobra, Garofalakis, Gehrke, and Rastogi (2002) also demonstrate that (approximate) statistics (e.g., histograms) on the distributions of join-attribute values can be used to reduce the variance in the randomized answer estimate. These novel sketch-partitioning techniques significantly boost the accuracy of approximate answers by (1) intelligently partitioning the attribute domains so that the self-join sizes of the resulting partitions are minimized, and (2) judiciously allocating space to independent sketches for each partition.

Maintaining Distributed Sketches

In the discussion so far we have assumed that atomic sketch X_k is computed by a single local processing unit, which has seen all tuples of stream R_k. However in practice stream R_k might be a logical data stream defined over several physical streams, which arrive at different processing units of the local information sphere. Also, in order to process massive data streams, the local processing unit might be a parallel machine or a cluster of workstations.

We formalize this problem as follows. Let R_k be a data stream that consists of I_k substreams $R_k^{(i)}$ such that $R_k = \bigcup_{i=1}^{I_k} R_k^{(i)}$ (note that the operator preserves duplicates). Each of these substreams captures the tuples that arrive at a certain location i (i.e., local processing unit or machine/processor within a certain processing unit). As before we wish to compute Q_{COUNT}, however, this time over the distributed substreams $R_k^{(i)}$.

Recall that in the centralized view X_k is computed as:
$$\sum_{\mathcal{I} \in \mathcal{D}_k} (f_k(\mathcal{I}) \prod_{j \in S_k} \xi_{j,\mathcal{I}[j]}).$$
Since R_k is the (duplicate preserving) union of all substreams $R_k^{(i)}$, we can compute $f_k(\mathcal{I})$ as $f_k(\mathcal{I}) = \sum_{i=1}^{I_k} f_k^{(i)}(\mathcal{I})$ where $f_k^{(i)}(\mathcal{I})$ is defined as f_k,

but restricted to the corresponding substream $R_k^{(i)}$. Let $X_k^{(i)}$ be computed as $\sum_{\mathcal{I} \in \mathcal{D}_k} (f_k^{(i)}(\mathcal{I}) \prod_{j \in S_k} \xi_{j,\mathcal{I}[j]})$. Then we can obtain X_k simply as $\sum_{i=1}^{I_k} X_k^{(i)}$. Notice that for this to work all we need to do is ensure that each $X_k^{(i)}$ is computed using the same family $\xi_{j,\mathcal{I}[j]}$.

The distributed computation of X_k is performed as follows. First we select n mutually-independent random seeds (one for each distinct equi-join pair of Q_{COUNT}) as before in the centralized algorithm. These seeds are then replicated at each processor that is involved in the computation of any of the $X_k^{(i)}$. Since the $\xi_{j,\mathcal{I}[j]}$ are generated deterministically from the random seeds, it is ensured that the different $X_k^{(i)}$ use the same families of random variables, and hence their sum is equal to X_k.

The above algorithm greatly reduces computation overhead for distributed computation of stream summaries. Instead of collocating the substreams, only the compact partial sketches need to be forwarded to a node that wishes to compute Q_{COUNT}. The same technique can be used to parallelize the computation of Q_{COUNT}. Each incoming tuple of stream R_k can be routed to *any* of the participating I_k processors, taking load and access costs into account. As long as each of these processors uses the same random seeds, each sketch X_k can be obtained by adding the corresponding partial results, essentially resulting in a perfectly parallelizable algorithm for the computation of Q_{COUNT}.

2.3.2 Joining Data Streams

This subsection gives an overview of our ongoing research on matching events in massive data streams with limited resources. We discuss the actual online problem and a related static optimization problem, which is fundamental for understanding the problem complexity (Das, Gehrke, and Riedewald 2003).

Matching Event Streams in Real Time

To date most data stream related research has focused on computing aggregates and summaries, e.g., work by Datar, Gionis, Indyk, and Motwani (2002); Gehrke, Korn, and Srivastava (2001); Gilbert, Kotidis, Muthukrishnan, and Strauss (2001); and Thaper, Guha, Indyk, and Koudas (2002). On the other hand it is equally important to be able to detect and react to correlated occurrences of individual events. Such events might arrive in different streams, potentially at different local processing units. Event matches are detected by computing the (distributed) join of two or more data streams. To make the computation feasible, the matching is typically restricted to the most recent events, for example, those that arrived within the last day. Intuitively the interval of valid events "slides" along the time axis (its endpoint is the current time "now"), hence this matching process is referred to as a *sliding window join*.

A major challenge is to join massive data streams with fluctuating arrival rates using only limited resources. We have developed novel lightweight semantic stream join heuristics that perform the computation in a best effort manner. With sufficient memory and computing resources the exact result is obtained, while during periods of resource shortage the result quality degrades gracefully. More precisely, our goal is to achieve the best possible approximate result subject to given memory constraints. To evaluate the quality of our online techniques we also developed an optimal offline benchmark algorithm. This enabled us to show that our online algorithms can not only handle very high data rates, but at the same time maintain a close to optimal approximation quality. This work is part of our ongoing effort to develop efficient stream join techniques for all relevant approximation quality measures.

The Static Join Optimization Problem

As mentioned before, events in two different data streams are matched by computing the sliding window join of the streams. Whenever a new tuple (without loss of generality we assume that events are represented by relational tuples) arrives in one stream any of the most recent tuples from the other stream could match it. Hence, to guarantee that no match is missed, the algorithm requires enough buffer memory to store the valid events (i.e., the tuples in the sliding windows) of both streams. If the buffer is too small, some valid event tuples have to be dropped *before* they expire. These prematurely dropped tuples are lost for the computation. If a matching tuple arrives in the other stream, the corresponding match therefore can not be detected any more. Our goal is to minimize the number of lost matches for a given amount of available buffer memory. Note that other approximation quality measures are possible, but not discussed here.

More precisely, we consider the following static load shedding problem. Given two relations A and B (which correspond to the window contents) we wish to compute their equality join. As motivated before, due to reasons such as memory or processing time restrictions, a total of k tuples need to be dropped from the input buffers for A and B such that the number of lost result tuples is minimized. We will refer to this join as a *k-truncated join* of A and B. Thus our aim is to find a set of k tuples to be dropped from the input relations such that the size of the k-truncated join result is as large as possible.

We can model the above as a graph problem, as follows: Consider a bipartite graph $G(V_A, V_B, E)$, with its two partitions V_A and V_B representing the relations A and B respectively. Each partition has one node for every tuple in the relation it represents. We have an edge between a node $n_A \in V_A$ and a node $n_B \in V_B$ if the tuples corresponding to n_A and n_B satisfy the join condition.

Thus the bipartite graph G has an edge for every result tuple of the join of A and B. Since our join condition is an equality on one or more of the attributes of A and B, it is easy to see that G will consist of a union of mutually disjoint fully connected bipartite components (called *Kurotowski* components). Each Kurotowski component can be represented by a pair of integers m, n where m and n are the number of nodes from V_A and V_B respectively in the component. We denote such a Kurotowski component by $K(m, n)$. Thus our k-truncated join approximation problem is equivalent to finding a set of k nodes in the bipartite join-graph whose deletion results in the deletion of the lowest number of edges (which represent join tuples). Note that dropping a tuple from one of the input relations means that all output tuples produced by this tuple are lost. Hence our definition of a node deletion requires that deleting a node results in the deletion of all edges incident on that node. For arbitrary bipartite graphs, i.e., bipartite graphs not necessarily representing a join, the above problem can be shown to be NP-hard (Das, Gehrke, and Riedewald 2003).

We are now ready to state a couple of versions of the k-truncated join approximation problem, modeled as a graph optimization problem as described below.

Primal Version

Input: A bipartite graph consisting of c mutually disjoint Kurotowski subgraphs specified by the c integer pairs $K(m_1, n_1), K(m_2, n_2) \ldots K(m_c, n_c)$, and an integer k.

Output: A set of k nodes from the bipartite graph whose *deletion* from the graph results in the deletion of the lowest number of edges. Note that when we delete a node, all edges incident on the node are deleted.

A potentially useful variant of the above problem is the k_1, k_2-truncated join approximation problem in which we are required to delete k_1, k_2 tuples from the two joining relations respectively as opposed to k tuples overall.

Dual Version

Input: A bipartite graph consisting of c mutually disjoint Kurotowski subgraphs specified by the c integer pairs $K(m_1, n_1), K(m_2, n_2) \ldots K(m_c, n_c)$, and an integer k.

Output: A set of k nodes to be *retained* in the bipartite graph such that the subgraph induced by them has the highest number of edges amongst all subgraphs with k nodes.

Since an optimal solution to the primal version where k nodes are selected for deletion is an optimal solution to the dual problem where $n - k$ nodes are retained (n is the total number of nodes in the bipartite graph), an optimal algorithm for either one of them trivially implies an optimal algorithm for the other.

An Optimal Solution

We consider the dual formulation, where a total of k nodes need to be retained. Given c Kurotowski components, we order the components from $1 \ldots c$ as per some arbitrary ordering, and let $K(m_i, n_i)$ denote the ith component ($0 \le i \le c$) as per this ordering.

Given a single Kurotowski component $K(m, n)$, the optimal way to retain $0 \le p \le m + n$ nodes (or equivalently, to delete $m + n - p$ nodes), from it is to retain $m' \le m$ nodes from the first partition and $n' \le n$ nodes from the second partition such that $m' \cdot n'$ (i.e., the number of retained edges) is as large as possible. It can easily be shown that this corresponds to choosing $m' \le m$ and $n' \le n$ such that $|m' - n'|$ is minimized for $m' + n' = k$. Thus, the p nodes to be retained can be chosen one by one by selecting alternately a node from the m partition followed by a node from the n partition till a count of p is reached, and if all the nodes of one of the partitions are exhausted before a count of p is reached, we simply select the remaining nodes to be retained from the larger partition. Let $C_{m,n}(p)$ denote the maximum number of edges that can be retained when p ($\le m + n$) nodes are retained from a Kurotowski $K(m, n)$ component. It can be shown that $C_{m,n}(p)$ can be computed as follows (w.l.o.g., assume $m \ge n$):

$$C_{m,n}(p) = \begin{cases} (p/2)^2 & \text{if p} \le \text{2n, p even} \\ (p^2 - 1)/4 & \text{if p} \le \text{2n, p odd} \\ n(p - n) & \text{else.} \end{cases}$$

Let $T(i, j)$ denote the optimal cost (i.e., the maximal number of edges) of retaining j nodes from the first i Kurotowski components, as per our ordering. Then,

$$\begin{aligned} T(1, j) &= C_{m_1, n_1}(j) \\ T(i, j) &= max\{T(i - 1, j), T(i - 1, j - 1) + C_{m_i, n_i}(1), \\ &\quad T(i - 1, j - 2) + C_{m_i, n_i}(2), \ldots, \\ &\quad T(i - 1, j - m_i - n_i) + C_{m_i, n_i}(m_i + n_i)\} \text{ for i} > 1 \ . \end{aligned}$$

Intuitively the second formula states that the optimal way to retain j nodes from i components is to choose the best from the following options: Either retain j nodes optimally from the first $i - 1$ components, or retain $j - 1$ nodes optimally from the first $i - 1$ components and retain 1 node optimally from the

i^{th} component, or retain $j - 2$ nodes optimally from the first $i - 1$ components and retain 2 nodes optimally from the ith component, and so on. The actual value we are interested in is $T(c, k)$. By keeping track of the terms that provide the maximum in the second formula above, we can also maintain the exact set of nodes retained from each component in the optimal solution.

To compute $T(c, k)$, we need to compute $c \cdot k$ entries in the dynamic programming matrix T, and each entry takes $O(k)$ time to compute. Thus, the overall running time of this algorithm is $O(c \cdot k^2)$. By considering a three-dimensional matrix T with entries of the form $T(c, k_1, k_2)$ representing the optimal way to retain k_1 nodes from the "left" partition and k_2 nodes from the "right" partition of the first c Kurotowski components, it is possible to extend the above algorithm to handle the variant where one needs to delete k_1, k_2 nodes from the two bipartite partitions respectively, instead of k nodes overall.

Strictly speaking, the above algorithm is pseudo-polynomial for the problem formulation as stated above because its input is of size $(O(c \cdot \log(max_i \{m_i, n_i\}) + \log k))$, i.e., logarithmic in k. However, in the actual join computation all tuples have to be examined in order to obtain the problem parameters, which is a cost of $\Omega(k)$. Thus the dynamic programming scheme finds the optimal solution in time polynomial in the size of the input relations.

2.4   Conclusions

We have outlined a set of challenging research problems in distributed mining and monitoring. As part of the Himalaya Data Mining Project at Cornell University, our group is addressing a subset of these problems.[1]

Acknowledgements

The high-level architecture that we reviewed in the introduction to this chapter was defined in collaboration with the Knowledge Discovery and Dissemination working group, and we would like to thank the members of its steering committee for helpful discussions. Our earlier work on data stream processing and mining was coauthored jointly with Alin Dobra, Venkatesh Ganti, Minos Garofalakis, Flip Korn, Wei-Yin Loh, Raghu Ramakrishnan, Rajeev Rastogi, and Divesh Srivastava (Dobra, Garofalakis, Gehrke, and Rastogi 2002; Dobra, Garofalakis, Gehrke and Rastogi 2002; Ganti, Gehrke, and Ramakrishnan 2001; Ganti, Gehrke, and Ramakrishnan 2002; Ganti, Gehrke, Ramakrishnan, and Loh 2002; Garofalakis, Gehrke, and Rastogi 2002; Gehrke, Korn, and Srivastava 2001).

---

[1]More information about our ongoing research can be found at www.cs.cornell.edu/database.

This work was funded by National Science Foundation grants 0084762 and 0121175, the KD-D Initiative, the Cornell Information Assurance Institute, the Cornell Intelligent Information Systems Institute, and by gifts from Microsoft and Intel. Any opinions, findings, conclusions or recommendations expressed in this material are those of the author(s) and do not necessarily reflect the views of the sponsors.

Alan Demers is a professor in the Department of Computer Science at Cornell University. His current research interests include distributed databases and peer-to-peer networking protocols.

Johannes Gehrke is an assistant professor in the Department of Computer Science at Cornell University. His research interests are in data mining and distributed query processing. His home page is located at www.cs.cornell.edu/johannes.

Mirek Riedewald is a research associate in the Department of Computer Science at Cornell University. His research interests include database and information systems, especially data stream processing, online analytical processing (OLAP), and distributed systems. For more information, see www.cs.cornell.edu/~mirek.

Chapter 3

A Consensus Framework for Integrating Distributed Clusterings Under Limited Knowledge Sharing

*Joydeep Ghosh, Alexander Strehl,
and Srujana Merugu*

The notion of integrating multiple data sources and/or learned models is found in several disciplines, for example, the combining of estimators in econometrics (Granger 1989), evidences in rule-based systems (Barnett 1981) and multi-sensor data fusion (Dasarathy 1994). Multi-learner systems that integrate the information contained in a number of noninteracting component learners have proved very useful in various distributed data mining scenarios. A simple, but effective type of such multi-learner systems is an *ensemble* of models (learners), in which each component learner tries to solve the same task and the results of the different components are integrated using a suitable combining scheme. Until now, ensembles have mainly been used for classification and regression tasks, and spectacular improvements in accuracy and robustness have been obtained for a wide variety of data scts (Sharkey 1999, Ghosh 2002, Kittler and Roli 2001). They have achieved main-stream status in difficult data mining tasks, and ensemble techniques such as bagging and boosting are now part of commercial data mining packages such as SAS Enterprise Miner. However, very little work has been done on applying the notion of ensembles to address clustering tasks. It turns out that combining multiple clusterings is a much more difficult problem, but at the same time is relevant to an increasing number of real-life applications. Thus, it is an area that needs to be addressed by next generation data mining technology.

This chapter discusses a certain scenario for combining multiple clusterings, explains why this scenario is important, formulates a solution in terms of an optimization problem and suggests some approaches to solve this problem. Specifically, we address the problem of *combining* multiple partitionings of a set of objects *without* accessing the original features or internals of individual clustering algorithms. Thus, our work focuses on distributed computing scenarios where the combiner can only examine the outputs (cluster labels) of multiple clustering algorithms, and even the number of clusters obtained may differ from site to site. We call this scenario the *cluster ensembles* problem (Strehl and Ghosh 2002a, 2002b). The reasons for restricting access to original data and individual clustering algorithms will be evident shortly. The cluster ensemble design problem is much more difficult than designing classifier ensembles because cluster labels are symbolic and so one must also solve a correspondence problem. In addition, the number and shape of clusters provided by the individual solutions may vary significantly from site to site due to differences in the clustering method used, the clustering objective, as well as the particular view of the data available at those sites. Moreover, the desired number of clusters is often not known in advance, unlike in the typical classification setting.

3.0.1 Motivation

There are two primary motivations for developing cluster ensembles as defined above: to exploit and reuse existing knowledge implicit in legacy clusterings, and to enable clustering over distributed datasets. We will consider these two application domains in greater detail in the following paragraphs.

Knowledge Reuse

In several applications, a variety of clusterings for the objects under consideration may already exist, and one desires to either integrate these clusterings into a single solution, or use this information to influence a new clustering (perhaps based on a different set of features) of these objects. Our first encounter with this application scenario was when clustering visitors to an retailing website based on market basket analysis, in order to facilitate a direct marketing campaign (Strehl and Ghosh 2000). The company already had a variety of legacy customer segmentations based on demographics, credit rating, geographical region, purchasing patterns in their retail stores, and so on. They were obviously reluctant to throw out all this domain knowledge, and instead wanted to reuse such pre-existing knowledge to create a single consolidated clustering. Note that since the legacy clusterings were largely provided by human experts or by other companies using proprietary methods, the information in the legacy segmentations had to be used *without* going back to the original features or the algorithms that were used to obtain these clusterings. This experience was instrumental in our formulation of the cluster ensemble problem. Another notable aspect of this engagement was that the two sets of customers, purchasing from retail outlets and from the website respectively, had significant overlap, but were not identical. Thus in the cluster ensemble problem, we provision for missing labels in the individual clusterings.

Another application involving legacy solutions is segmenting of mortgage loan applicants based on the information in the application forms, supplemented by pre-existing groupings of the applicants indicated by proprietary external sources such as the FICO scores provided by Fairs Isaac.

Distributed Data Mining

The desire to perform distributed data mining is being increasingly felt in both government and industry (Park and Kargupta 2003). Often, related information is acquired and stored in geographically distributed locations due to organizational or operational constraints (Kargupta and Chan 2000), and one needs to process data in situ as far as possible. In contrast, machine learning algorithms invariably assume that data is available in a single centralized location. But this may not be desirable because of the computational, bandwidth and storage costs. In certain cases, it may not even be possible due to a variety of real-life constraints including security, privacy, proprietary nature of data and the accompanying ownership issues, need for fault tolerant distribution of data and services, real-time processing requirements, statutory constraints imposed by law, etc. (Prodromidis, Chan, and Stolfo 2000). Interestingly, the severity of such constraints is becoming very evident of late as several government agencies are attempting to integrate their databases and analytical techniques.

A cluster ensemble can perform feature-distributed clustering (FDC) in situations where each processor/clusterer has access to only a limited number of features or attributes of each object, i.e., it observes a particular *aspect* or *view* of the data. Aspects can be completely disjoint features or have partial overlaps. In gene function prediction, separate gene clusterings can be obtained from diverse sources such as gene sequence comparisons, combination of DNA microarray data from many independent experiments, and mining of the biological literature (e.g., MEDLINE).

An orthogonal scenario is object-distributed clustering (ODC), wherein each processor or clusterer has access to only a subset of all objects, and can thus only cluster the observed objects. For example, corporations tend to split their customers regionally for more efficient management. Analysis such as clustering is often performed locally, and a cluster ensemble provides a way of obtaining a holistic analysis without complete integration of the local data warehouses.

One can also consider the use of cluster ensembles for the same reasons as classification ensembles, namely to *improve the quality and robustness* of results. It turns out that clustering algorithms provide a variety of ways of producing diverse results that can be ably exploited by the ensemble techniques described in this chapter. As this class of applications is not the focus of this work, the reader is referred to Strehl and Ghosh (2002a) instead.

3.0.2 Related Work

There are several techniques where multiple clusterings are created and evaluated as intermediate steps in the process of attaining a single, higher quality clustering. For example, Fisher examined methods for iteratively improving an initial set of hierarchical clustering solutions (Fisher 1996). A way of obtaining multiple approximate k-means solutions in main memory after making a single pass through a database, and then combining these means to get a final set of cluster centers is presented in Fayyad, Reina, and Bradley (1998). In all these works, a summary representation of each cluster in terms of the base features is available to the integration mechanism, as opposed to our knowledge reuse framework wherein only cluster labels are available. More recently, an evidence accumulation framework was proposed wherein multiple k-means, using a much higher value of k than the final anticipated answer, were run on a common data set (Fred and Jain 2002). The results were used to form a co-occurrence or similarity matrix that is is analogous to the one used for the CSPA algorithm of subsection 3.1.2, except that the clusterings generated by Fred and Jain (2002) are not legacy, but are generated from a common data set and feature space. Also, they are at a much finer level of resolution than that desired by the final clustering, since the purpose of running multiple clusterings is to get a more robust similarity matrix that has the flavor of the shared nearest neighbor technique.

One use of cluster ensembles is to exploit multiple existing groupings of the data. Several analogous approaches exist in supervised learning scenarios (class labels are known), under categories such as life-long learning (Thrun

1996), learning to learn (Thrun and Pratt 1997) and knowledge reuse (Bollacker and Ghosh 1999), but we have not seen these applied to totally unsupervised settings. Another application of cluster ensembles is to combine multiple clusterings that were obtained based on only partial sets of features. This problem has been approached recently as a case of collective data mining (Kargupta and Chan. Johnson and Kargupta (1999) introduced a feasible approach to combining distributed agglomerative clusterings is introduced. First, each local site generates a dendrogram (Jain and Dubes 1988, Ghosh 2003). The dendrograms are collected and pairwise similarities for all objects are created from them. The combined clustering is then derived from the similarities. Kargupta, Huang, Krishnamoorthy, and Johnson (2001) introduced a distributed method of principal components analysis for clustering. The information sharing in these approaches is less restrictive than what is allowable in cluster ensembles.

Notation

Let $\mathcal{X} = \{x_1, x_2, \ldots, x_n\}$ denote a set of objects/samples/points. A partitioning of these n objects into k clusters can be represented as a set of k sets of objects $\{\mathcal{C}_\ell | \ell = 1, \ldots, k\}$ or as a label vector $\lambda \in \mathbb{N}^n$. A clusterer Φ is a function that delivers a label vector (with possibly missing values) given a tuple of objects. Note that a given clusterer may access only a limited number of object features (as in FDC) or may be clustering only some of the elements of $\mathcal{X}$ (as in ODC). Some clusterers may provide additional information such as description of cluster means, but we shall not use such information in our approach. Figure 3.1 shows the basic setup of the cluster ensemble: A set of r labelings $\lambda^{(1,\ldots,r)}$ is combined into a single labeling λ (the *consensus labeling*) using a consensus function $\Gamma : \{\lambda^{(q)} \mid q \in \{1, \ldots, r\}\} \to \lambda$.

A superscript in brackets denotes an index and not an exponent.

Organization

In the next section, we recapitulate our recent formulation of a cluster ensemble as an optimization problem (Strehl and Ghosh 2002a). A different normalization function is proposed that is more general in that it caters to both balanced and nonbalanced clustering situations. Three effective and efficient combining functions Γ, as well as a direct optimization approach are then described and compared. In section 3.2, we describe applications of cluster ensembles for the distributed data mining scenarios described above, and show results on both real and artificial data. Section 3.3 concentrates on knowledge reuse when legacy clusters are of variable resolution.

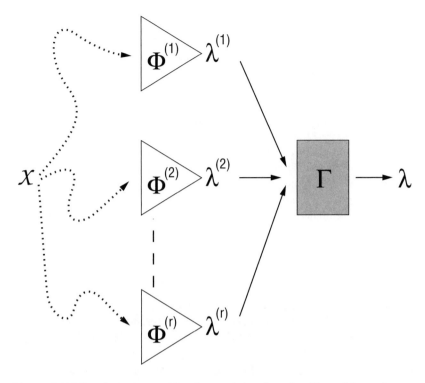

Figure 3.1: The cluster ensemble. A consensus function Γ combines cluster-ings $\lambda^{(q)}$ from a variety of sources, without resorting to the original object features $\mathcal{X}$ or algorithms Φ.

3.1 Cluster Ensembles

Let the set of clusterings $\{\lambda^{(q)} \mid q \in \{1, \ldots, r\}\}$ be denoted by Λ, and let the q-th clustering have $k^{(q)}$ clusters. If there is no a priori information about the relative importance of the individual clusterings, then a reasonable goal for the consensus answer is to seek a clustering that shares the most information with the original clusterings.

Mutual information, which is a symmetric measure to quantify the statistical information shared between two distributions, provides a sound indication of the shared information between a pair of clusterings. Let $I(X, Y)$ denote the mutual information between two random variables X and Y, and $H(X)$ denote the entropy of X. It can be shown that $I(X, Y)$ is a metric. There is no upper bound for $I(X, Y)$, so for easier interpretation and comparisons a normalized version of $I(X, Y)$ that ranges from 0 to 1 is desirable.

Several normalizations are possible based on the observation that $I(X,Y) \leq \min(H(X), H(Y))$. These include normalizing using the arithmetic or geometric mean of $H(X)$ and $H(Y)$. Since $H(X) = I(X,X)$, we prefer the geometric mean because of the analogy with a normalized inner product in Hilbert space. Thus, the normalized mutual information (NMI)[1] used is:

$$NMI(X,Y) = \frac{I(X,Y)}{\sqrt{H(X)H(Y)}}. \tag{3.1}$$

One can see that $NMI(X,X) = 1$, as desired. For consensus clustering, the random variables are represented by the cluster labelings $\lambda^{(a)}$ and $\lambda^{(b)}$, with $k^{(a)}$ and $k^{(b)}$ groups respectively, and equation 3.1 needs to be estimated by the sampled quantities provided by the clusterings. We denote the resulting normalized mutual information measure by $\phi^{(\mathrm{NMI})}(\lambda^{(a)}, \lambda^{(b)})$.

Based on this pairwise measure of mutual information, we can now define a measure between a *set* of r labelings, Λ, and a *single* labeling $\hat{\lambda}$ as the average normalized mutual information (ANMI):

$$\phi^{(\mathrm{ANMI})}(\Lambda, \hat{\lambda}) = \frac{1}{r} \sum_{q=1}^{r} \phi^{(\mathrm{NMI})}(\hat{\lambda}, \lambda^{(q)}). \tag{3.2}$$

We propose the optimal combined clustering $\lambda^{(k-\mathrm{opt})}$ to be the one that has maximal average mutual information with all individual labelings $\lambda^{(q)}$ in Λ given that the number of consensus clusters desired is k, i.e.,

$$\lambda^{(k-\mathrm{opt})} = \arg\max_{\hat{\lambda}} \phi^{(\mathrm{ANMI})}(\Lambda, \hat{\lambda}), \tag{3.3}$$

where $\hat{\lambda}$ goes through all possible k-partitions. Note that this formulation treats each individual clustering equally. One can easily generalize this definition to a weighted average, which may be preferable if certain individual solutions are more important than others.

There may be situations where not all labels are known for all objects, i.e., there are missing data in the label vectors. For such cases, the consensus clustering objective from equation 3.3 can be generalized by computing a weighted average of the mutual information with the known labels, with the weights proportional to the comprehensiveness of the labelings as measured by the fraction of known labels.

---

[1] Our earlier work (Strehl and Ghosh 2002b) used a slightly different normalization suitable for obtaining balanced clusters.

3.1.1 Direct Optimization Approaches

Since we now have an objective function (equation 3.3), an initial temptation is to directly optimize it. It turns out that an exhaustive search through all possible clusterings with k labels for the one with the maximum ANMI is formidable since for n objects and k partitions there are

$$\frac{1}{k!} \sum_{\ell=1}^{k} \binom{k}{\ell} (-1)^{k-\ell} \ell^n$$

possible clusterings, or approximately $k^n/k!$ for $n \gg k$ (Jain and Dubes 1988). For example, there are 171,798,901 ways to form 4 groups of 16 objects. However, a variety of well known greedy search techniques, including simulated annealing and genetic algorithms, can be tried to find a reasonable solution. Typically such approaches are computationally too expensive to be relevant in a data mining context. However, to get a feel for the quality-time tradeoffs involved, we devised and studied the following greedy optimization scheme that operates through single label changes:

The most representative single labeling (indicated by highest ANMI with all r labelings) is used as the initial labeling for the greedy algorithm. Then, for each object, the current label is changed to each of the other $k-1$ possible labels and the ANMI objective is re-evaluated. If the ANMI increases, the object's label is changed to the best new value and the algorithm proceeds to the next object. When all objects have been checked for possible improvements, a sweep is completed. If at least one label was changed in a sweep, we initiate a new sweep. The algorithm terminates when a full sweep does not change any labels, thereby indicating that a local optimum is reached. The algorithm can be readily modified to probabilistically accept decreases in ANMI as well, as in a Boltzmann machine.

As with all local optimization procedures, there is a strong dependency on the initialization. Running this greedy search starting with a random labeling is often computationally intractable, and tends to result in poor local optima. Even with an initialization that is close to an optimum, computation can be extremely slow due to exponential time complexity. Experiments with $n = 400$, $k = 10$, $r = 8$ typically averaged one hour per run on a 1 GHz PC using our implementation.

3.1.2 Consensus Function Heuristics

Earlier (Strehl and Ghosh 2002a, b), we introduced three efficient heuristics to solve the cluster ensemble problem. All three algorithms approach the problem by first transforming the set of clusterings into a hypergraph representation. Essentially each object is a vertex, and all the members of a given cluster in any solution are connected by an hyperedge. So, the total number of hyperedges is simply the sum of the number of clusters over all r clusterings. Based on this representation, the three heuristics were proposed (details can be found in Strehl and Ghosh 2002a). We discuss them briefly in the following paragraphs.

Cluster-based Similarity Partitioning Algorithm (CSPA)

Based on a coarse resolution viewpoint that two objects have a similarity of 1 if they are in the same cluster and a similarity of 0 otherwise, a $n \times n$ binary similarity matrix can be readily created for each clustering. The entry-wise average of r such matrices representing the r sets of groupings yields an overall similarity matrix $\mathbf{S}$ with a finer resolution. The entries of $\mathbf{S}$ denote the fraction of clusterings in which two objects are in the same cluster. Now, we can use the similarity matrix to recluster the objects using any reasonable similarity-based clustering algorithm. We chose to partition the induced similarity graph (vertex = object, edge weight = similarity) using METIS (Karypis and Kumar 1998) because of its robust and scalable properties.

CSPA is the simplest and most obvious heuristic, but its computational and storage complexity are both quadratic in n, as opposed to the next two approaches that are near linear in n.

HyperGraph Partitioning Algorithm (HGPA)

The second algorithm is a direct approach to cluster ensembles that repartitions the data using the given clusters as indications of strong bonds. The cluster ensemble problem is formulated as partitioning the hypergraph by cutting a minimal number of hyperedges. We call this approach the hypergraph-partitioning algorithm (HGPA). All hyperedges are considered to have the same weight. Also, all vertices are equally weighted. Note that this includes n_ℓ-way relationship information, while CSPA only considers pairwise relationships. Now, we look for a hyperedge separator that partitions the hypergraph into k unconnected components of approximately the same size. Note that obtaining comparable sized partitions is a standard constraint in graph-partitioning based clustering approaches as it avoids trivial partitions (Karypis, Han, and Kumar 1999). On the other hand this means that if the natural data clusters are highly imbalanced, a graph-partitioning based approach is not appropriate. For the results of this chapter, we maintain a vertex imbalance of at most 5% following constraint: $k \cdot \max_{\ell \in \{1,\dots,k\}} \frac{n_\ell}{n} \le 1.05$.

Hypergraph partitioning is a well-studied area (Kernighan and Lin 1970, Alpert and Kahng 1995) and algorithm details are omitted here for brevity. We used the hypergraph partitioning package HMETIS (Karypis, Aggarwal, Kumar, and Shekhar 1997). HMETIS gives high-quality partitions and is very scalable.

Meta-Clustering Algorithm (MCLA)

The meta-clustering algorithm (MCLA) is based on clustering clusters. It also yields object-wise confidence estimates of cluster membership. First, we represent each cluster by a hyperedge. The idea in MCLA is to group and collapse related hyperedges and assign each object to the collapsed hyperedge in which it participates most strongly. The hyperedges that are considered related for the purpose of collapsing are determined by a graph-based clustering of hyperedges. We refer to each cluster of hyperedges as a meta-cluster. Collapsing reduces the number of hyperedges from $\sum_{q=1}^{r} k^{(q)}$ to k. For details, see Strehl and Ghosh (2002a).

3.1.3 Discussion and Comparison

In this section, we compare the heuristics with the direct approach, and also do a sanity check to see if the NMI criteria is indeed meaningful. Let us first take a look at the worst case time complexity of the proposed algorithms. Assuming quasi-linear (hyper-)graph partitioners such as (H)METIS, CSPA is $O(n^2 kr)$, HGPA is $O(nkr)$, and MCLA is $O(nk^2 r^2)$. The fastest is HGPA, closely followed by MCLA since k tends to be small. CSPA is slower and can be impractical for large n. The greedy approach is the slowest and often is intractable for large n. It should also be noted that none of the three heuristics are based on pure hill-climbing. While they of course cannot guarantee the global optimum solution, they all operate more globally and are less susceptible to settling at the local minima closest to the initial condition.

We performed a controlled experiment that allows us to compare the properties of the three proposed consensus functions. First, we partition $n = 400$ objects into $k = 10$ groups at random to obtain the original clustering κ.[2] We duplicate this clustering $r = 8$ times. Now in each of the 8 labelings, "noise" is introduced by replacing some of of the labels with random labels from a uniform distribution from 1 to k. The fraction of the total labels that are replaced is called the "noise fraction," and forms the X axis of figure 3.2. Then, we feed the noisy labelings to the proposed consensus functions. The resulting combined labeling is evaluated in two ways. First, we measure the normalized objective function $\phi^{(\mathrm{ANMI})}(\Lambda, \lambda)$ of the ensemble output λ with all the individual labels in Λ. Second, we measure the normalized mutual information of each consensus labeling with the original undistorted labeling using $\phi^{(\mathrm{NMI})}(\kappa, \lambda)$. For better comparison, we added a random label generator as a baseline method. Also, performance measures of a hypothetical consensus

---

[2]Labels are obtained by a random permutation. Groups are balanced.

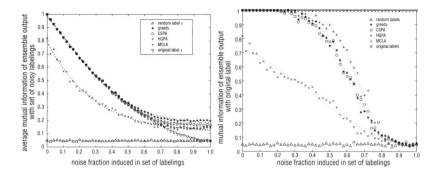

Figure 3.2: Comparison of consensus functions in terms of $\phi^{(\mathrm{ANMI})}(\boldsymbol{\Lambda}, \lambda)$ (left) and in terms of $\phi^{(\mathrm{NMI})}(\kappa, \lambda)$ (right) for various noise levels. A fitted sigmoid (least squared error) is shown for all algorithms to show the trend.

function that returns the original labels are included to illustrate maximum performance for low noise settings.[3]

Figure 3.2 shows the results. As noise increases, labelings share less information and thus, maximum obtainable $\phi^{(\mathrm{ANMI})}(\boldsymbol{\Lambda}, \lambda)$ decreases, and so does $\phi^{(\mathrm{ANMI})}(\boldsymbol{\Lambda}, \lambda)$ for all techniques (figure 3.2(top)). HGPA performs the worst in this experiment, which we believe is due to the lacking provision of partially cut edges. In low noise, both, MCLA and CSPA recover the original labelings. MCLA retains more $\phi^{(\mathrm{ANMI})}(\boldsymbol{\Lambda}, \lambda)$ than CSPA in presence of medium to high noise. Interestingly, in very high noise settings CSPA exceeds MCLA's performance. Note also that for such high noise settings, the original labels have a lower average normalized mutual information $\phi^{(\mathrm{ANMI})}(\boldsymbol{\Lambda}, \lambda)$. This is because the set of labels are almost completely random and the consensus algorithms recover whatever little common information is present whereas the original labeling is now almost fully unrelated. However, realistically noise should not exceed 50% and MCLA seems to perform best in this simple controlled experiment.

For less than 50% noise, the algorithms essentially have the same ranking regardless of whether $\phi^{(\mathrm{ANMI})}(\boldsymbol{\Lambda}, \lambda)$ or $\phi^{(\mathrm{NMI})}(\kappa, \lambda)$ is used. Since in a real setting noise is expected to be much less than 50%, this indicates that our proposed objective function $\phi^{(\mathrm{ANMI})}(\boldsymbol{\Lambda}, \lambda)$ is a suitable choice in real applications where κ and hence, $\phi^{(\mathrm{NMI})}(\kappa, \lambda)$ is not available.

The direct greedy optimization approach performs similar to CSPA in terms of $\phi^{(\mathrm{NMI})}(\kappa, \lambda)$, but scores less than MCLA in most cases. In terms of $\phi^{(\mathrm{ANMI})}(\boldsymbol{\Lambda}, \lambda)$, the greedy approach returns a higher score than CSPA,

---

[3]In low noise settings, the original labels are the global maximum, since they share the most mutual information with the distorted labelings.

HGPA, and MCLA only for unrealistically high (>75%) noise levels. More importantly, the greedy approach is tractable only when there are very few datapoints, dimensions, and clusters, due to its high computational complexity.

A Supra-Consensus Function

Our objective function has an added advantage that it allows one to add a stage that selects the best consensus function without any supervision information, by simply selecting the one with the highest ANMI. So, for the experiments in this article, we first report the results of this supra-consensus function Γ, obtained by running *all three* algorithms, and selecting the one with the greatest ANMI. Then, if there are significant differences or notable trends observed among the three algorithms, this further level of detail is described. Note that the supra-consensus function is completely unsupervised and avoids the problem of selecting the best combiner for a dataset beforehand.

3.2   Empirical Studies

We illustrate the cluster ensemble applications on two real and two artificial data-sets. In table 3.1, some basic properties of the datasets (left) and parameter choices (right) are summarized. (2D2K) is the simplest, containing 500 points each of two 2-dimensional (2D) Gaussian clusters with means $(-0.227, 0.077)^\dagger$ and $(0.095, 0.323)^\dagger$ and diagonal covariance matrices with 0.1 for all diagonal elements. The second artificial data-set, 8D5K, contains 1000 points from 5 multivariate Gaussian distributions (200 points each) in 8D space. Again, clusters all have the same variance (0.1), but different means.[4]

The third data-set (PENDIG) for pen-based recognition of handwritten digits is taken from the University of California, Irvine's Machine Learning Repository. It contains 16 spatial features for each of the 7,494 training and 3,498 test cases (objects). There are ten classes of roughly equal size (balanced clusters) in the data corresponding to the digits 0 to 9. The fourth data-set, YA-HOO, is for text clustering and contains 20 original Yahoo! news categories.[5]. The raw 21839×2340 word-document matrix consists of the nonnormalized occurrence frequencies of stemmed words, using Porter's suffix stripping algorithm. Pruning all words that occur less than 0.01 or more than 0.10 times on average because they are insignificant (e.g., haruspex) or too generic (e.g., new), respectively, results in $d = 2903$. The default k used for YAHOO is

---

[4]Both artificial data-sets are available for download at http://strehl.com/.

[5]The data is publicly available from ftp://ftp.cs.umn.edu/dept/users/boley/ (K1 series) and was used by Boley, Gini, Gross, Han, Hastings, Karypis, Kumar, Mobasher, and Moor (1999) and Strehl, Ghosh, and Mooney (2000)

Name	Features	# Features	# Categories	Balance	Similarity	Default # Clusters
2D2K	real	2	2	1.00	Euclidean	2
8D5K	real	8	5	1.00	Euclidean	5
PENDIG	real	16	10	0.87	Euclidean	10
YAHOO	ordinal	2903	20	0.24	Cosine	40

Table 3.1: Overview of datasets for cluster ensemble experiments. Balance is defined as the ratio of the average category size to the largest category size.

taken as 40 (two times the number of categories), since some categories seem to be multi-modal.

Evaluation of the quality of a clustering is a nontrivial and often ill-posed task. In fact, many definitions of objective functions for clusterings exist (Jain and Dubes 1988). Since for our data sets either the generative models or the class labels are known, we can use an extrinsic measure based on comparing category labels to class labels, as opposed to intrinsic measures such as compactness and separation. Normalized mutual information is chosen as it is impartial with respect to k as compared to other extrinsic criteria such as purity and entropy. It reaches its maximum value of 1 only when the two sets of labels have an exact one-to-one correspondence.

3.2.1   Feature-Distributed Clustering (FDC)

In feature-distributed clustering (FDC), we show how cluster ensembles can be used to combine a set of clusterings obtained in a distributed environment from partial views of the data. We run several clusterers, each having access to only a restricted, small subset of features. Note that because of the current lack of public domain datasets for distributed clustering, in our experiments these partial views had to be created from a common feature space. In a real-life scenario, the different views would be determined a priori in an application-specific way. Each clusterer has access to all objects. The clusterers find groups in their views or subspaces using the same clustering technique. In the combining stage, individual cluster labels are integrated using our supra-consensus function.

Table 3.2 summarizes the results. Each dataset was projected onto much lower dimensional, randomly chosen subspaces, for r times; a graph-partition based clustering was done on each projection, and the results integrated using the supra-consensus function. For example, in the YAHOO case, 20 clusterings were performed in 128-dimensions (occurrence frequencies of 128 random words) each. The average quality amongst the results was 0.16 and the best quality was 0.20. Using the supra-consensus function to combine all 20 labelings yields a quality of 0.31, or 156% higher mutual information than

Input and Parameters					Quality		
data	sub space #dims	# models r	all features $\phi^{(\mathrm{NMI})}(\kappa, \lambda^{(\mathrm{all})})$	consensus $\phi^{(\mathrm{NMI})}(\kappa, \lambda)$	max subspace $\max_q \phi^{(\mathrm{NMI})}(\kappa, \lambda^{(q)})$	average subspace $\mathrm{avg}_q \phi^{(\mathrm{NMI})}(\kappa, \lambda^{(q)})$	min subspace $\min_q \phi^{(\mathrm{NMI})}(\kappa, \lambda^{(q)})$
2D2K	1	3	0.84747	**0.68864**	0.68864	0.64145	0.54706
8D5K	2	5	1.00000	**0.98913**	0.76615	0.69823	0.62134
PENDIG	4	10	0.67805	**0.63918**	0.47865	0.41951	0.32641
YAHOO	128	20	0.48877	**0.41008**	0.20183	0.16033	0.11143

Table 3.2: FDC results. The consensus clustering is as good as or better than the best individual subspace clustering.

the average individual clustering. In all scenarios, the consensus clustering is as good or better than the best individual input clustering and always better than the average quality of individual clusterings. Also, the supra-consensus function chooses either MCLA and CSPA results, but the difference is not statistically significant.

3.2.2 Object-Distributed Clustering (ODC)

A dual to the application described in the previous section, is object-distributed clustering (ODC). In this scenario, individual clusterers have a limited selection of the object population but have access to all the features of the objects they are provided with. This is somewhat more difficult than FDC, since the labelings are partial. Because there is no access to the original features, the combiner Γ needs some overlap between labelings to establish a meaningful consensus.[6]

In many application scenarios, object-distribution can result naturally from operational constraints. For example, datamarts of individual stores of a retail company may only have records of visitors to that store, but there are enough people who visit more than one store of that company to result in the desired overlap.

In this subsection, we will discuss how one can use consensus functions on overlapping subsamples. We propose a wrapper to any clustering algorithm that simulates a scenario with distributed objects, and a combiner that does not have access to the original features. For experimental purposes, we divide the data into p overlapping partitions such that on an average, each object resides in v partitions. For simplicity, each partition is of the same size, i.e. nv/p. Each partition is processed by independent, identical clusterers (chosen appropriately for the application domain). For simplicity, we use the same number of clusters k in the subpartitions. Since every partition only looks at a fraction of the data, there are missing labels in the individual clusterings.

---

[6]If features are available, one can merge partitions based on their locations in feature space to reach consensus.

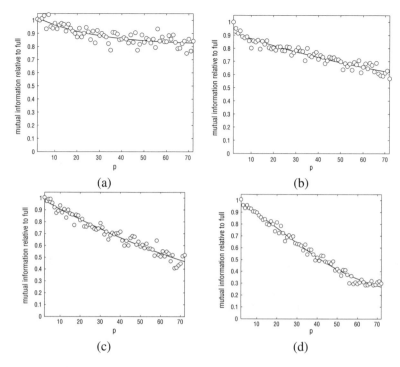

Figure 3.3: ODC results. Clustering quality (measured by relative mutual information) as a function of the number of partitions, p, on various data sets. (a) 2D2K. (b) 8D5K. (c) PENDIG; (d) YAHOO. The sum of the number of samples over all partitions is fixed at $2n$. Each plot contains experimental results using graph partitioning in the inner loop for $p = [2, \dots, 72]$.

Given sufficient overlap, the supra-consensus function Γ ties the individual clusters together and delivers a consensus clustering.

Figure 3.3 shows our results for the four data-sets when graph partitioning was used as the clusterer in each processor. Each plot in figure 3.3 shows the relative mutual information (fraction of mutual information retained as compared to the reference clustering on all objects and features) as a function of the number of partitions. We fix the sum of the number of objects in all partitions to be double the number of objects (repetition factor $v = 2$). Within each plot, p ranges from 2 to 72 and each ODC result is marked with a o. Clearly, there is a tradeoff in the number of partitions versus quality. As p approaches vn, each clusterer only receives a single point and can make no reasonable grouping. For example, in the YAHOO case, for $v = 2$ processing on 16 partitions still retains around 80% of the full quality.

Distributed clustering using a cluster ensemble also provides a speedup when the inner loop clustering algorithm has superlinear complexity ($> O(n)$) and a fast consensus function (such as MCLA and HGPA) is used. For example, let us assume that the inner loop clusterer has a complexity of $O(n^2)$ (e.g., similarity-based approaches or efficient agglomerative clustering) and one uses only MCLA and HGPA in the supra-consensus function.[7] The overhead for the MCLA and HGPA consensus functions grows linearly in n and is negligible compared to the $O(n^2)$ clustering. Hence the asymptotic sequential speedup is approximately $s^{(\text{ODC-SEQ})} \approx \frac{p}{v^2}$. Each partition can be clustered without any communication on a separate processor. At integration time only the n-dimensional label vector (instead of, e.g., the entire $n \times n$ similarity matrix) has to be transmitted to the combiner. Hence, ODC does not only save computation time, but also enables trivial p-fold parallelization. Consequently, if a p-processor computer is utilized, an asymptotic speedup of $s^{(\text{ODC-PAR})} \approx \frac{p^2}{v^2}$ is obtained. For example, 2D2K (YAHOO) can be sped up 64-fold using 16 processors at 90% (80%) of the full length quality.

3.3 Integrating Clusterings of Varying Resolutions

When clusterings are done in a distributed fashion, perhaps by different organizations with different data-views or goals, it is quite likely that k will vary from site to site. Is our consensus clustering fairly robust to such variations? To address this question, we ran experiments where clusterings over a range of k were integrated. While one would expect that different sites are looking at different features if they select different values of k, to remove this additional source of variability, we just used the same set of features for all clusterings. Also, since 2D2K is very simple, we replaced it with NEWS20, which consists of newsgroup data with 20 categories.[8] We sampled the original dataset to get a reduced data set of 2000 documents (100/category), each represented by a 1151 dimensional feature vector.

Table 3.3 summarizes the experiments performed. Spherical K-means is used for the last two datasets because they are so high-dimensional and non-Gaussian that regular K-means performs miserably on them (Strehl, Ghosh, and Mooney 2000). Ensemble-A indicates the original ranges of k chosen. We found that, given a wide range of k, ANMI would typically peak around the most appropriate value of k, hence it could be used to narrow down the range of k for re-consideration by the consensus function. This observation results

---

[7]CSPA is $O(n^2)$ and would reduce speedups obtained by distribution.
[8]Available from http://www.ai.mit.edu/people/jrennie/20Newsgroups/.

in Ensemble-B, where we zoom into a narrower range of k. For example, for 8D5K, for the first set of k values, the average mutual information varies quite smoothly and peaks around $k = 6$, as shown in the figure 3.4. So we chose the new range of k to be 4 to 8 and we find that $k = 5$ gives the highest ANMI value. Incidentally, this highlights an added benefit of using a cluster ensemble, since it gives a good indication of the natural number of clusters in the data.

First, as a sanity check, we plotted for each clustering, the average mutual information shared with the set of all clusterings and the mutual information shared with the original clustering (figure 3.5). The correlation coefficient, averaged over all the eight sets of clusterings in the experiments is 0.9023, which is quite high. This justifies our approach of picking solutions based on their average mutual information with respect to the entire set of clusterings.

Table 3.4 shows the mutual information values between the different clusterings and the original categorization of the corresponding data set. For each data set, the "A" and "B" versions indicate which ensemble was chosen, and only the supra-consensus results are shown for brevity. The average clustering quality is obtained by computing the average of the pairwise mutual information of each clustering with the original categorization. The natural-k clustering is the solution obtained by directly applying the clustering algorithm to get natural-k clusters. The max-ANMI clustering, on the other hand refers to the clustering in the given set that has the highest average mutual information with respect to the entire set of clusterings.

From the table, we notice that the quality of the consensus clustering is better than that of the natural-k clustering, the max-ANMI clustering and also the average quality of the ensemble itself, except in the case of the YAHOO dataset. This indicates that the consensus method is a good way to obtain a high quality clustering when the number of clusters is not known. It is indeed remarkable that the consensus method performs better than the natural-k clustering though it does not have access to the raw data. This can be probably be explained by the fact that the consensus method is based on multiple clusterings and is less likely to be stuck in a local minimum than the natural-k clustering. Furthermore, the quality of a max-ANMI clustering is also higher than the average of the corresponding ensemble. So the max-ANMI clustering can be used to obtain a moderately good solution when it is not possible or expensive to perform the consensus.

The deviation in the case of the YAHOO dataset is most likely because the original manually assigned categories are somewhat different from the natural clustering of the data, and the categories are highly imbalanced as well. The low NMI values of the YAHOO clusterings as well as the lower correlation value (0.6086) between the average NMI and the NMI values in the YAHOO clusterings seem to substantiate this. Hence, it is not very surprising that the

Dataset	Clust. Algo.	Similarity	Natural-k	Ensemble-A	Ensemble-B
8D5K	k-means	Euclidean	5	$k \in \{2:2:10\}$	$k \in \{4:1:8\}$
PENDIG	k-means	Euclidean	10	$k \in \{2:4:30\}$	$k \in \{8:1:12\}$
NEWS20	Spherical k-means	Cosine	20	$k \in \{5\} \bigcup \{10:10:60\}$	$k \in \{14:2:26\}$
YAHOO	Spherical k-means	Cosine	20	$k \in \{5\} \bigcup \{10:10:60\}$	$k \in \{14:2:26\}$

Table 3.3: Details of the datasets and cluster ensembles with varying k. The notation $k \in \{a:b:c\}$ indicates that k ranges from a to c in steps of b.

Ensemble	Consensus	Average	Natural-k	Max-ANMI
A-8D5K	1.0000	0.8242	1.0000	0.9603
B-8D5K	1.0000	0.8921	1.0000	1.0000
A-PENDIG	0.7023	0.6514	0.6624	0.7035
B-PENDIG	0.6800	0.6641	0.6624	0.6624
A-NEWS20	0.6723	0.6282	0.6438	0.6689
B-NEWS20	0.7029	0.6559	0.6438	0.6881
A-YAHOO	0.4998	0.5267	0.5097	0.5437
B-YAHOO	0.5017	0.5224	0.5097	0.5442

Table 3.4: Normalized mutual information of the clusterings with respect to the corresponding original categorization.

clustering obtained using the consensus methods does not perform very well for this dataset.

3.4   Future Directions

Consensus clustering provides a very general framework to help enable federated data mining systems working on top of distributed and heterogeneous databases, even under severe data and knowledge sharing constraints. The purpose of this chapter was to present the basic problem formulation and demonstrate that good results can be obtained even under fairly severe data sharing restrictions. It provides another advance towards the goal of building robust, distributed data mining systems that can accommodate various privacy restrictions.

To make further progress in this direction, several issues, both theoretical and practical, need further investigation. First, the average normalized mutual information (ANMI) objective may not be suitable in certain scenarios. A straightforward extension is to consider a weighted average if one has some information about the relative importance of individual clustering solutions. In other situations, one may want to select the most suitable among the original r solutions, rather than a hybrid consensus. An analogy can be made with applications such as facility location where a k-mediods solution is preferred

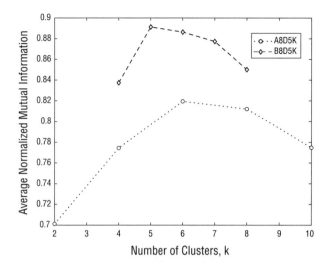

Figure 3.4: Plot showing the variation of ANMI with respect to the number of clusters k.

to a k-means even though the latter will typically give a better result in terms of lower distortion. One reason for this can be that a specific solution is more interpretable than a consensus one, and further inspection of this solution — both the objects/features used and the algorithm selected — may provide additional insights into the problem. Perhaps the solution will be to simply pick the clustering that has maximum average mutual information with all the other solutions, but this needs more careful investigation. Another theoretical extension will to develop a consensus framework for soft clusterings such as those obtained through fuzzy C-means or by applying the expectation-maximization technique to a suitable mixture model. Extensions to incrementally acquired or streaming data are also desired.

From the application viewpoint, it will be worthwhile to continue experimentation with large, distributed data sets from a variety of sources. This will shed further light on the capabilities and biases of the proposed heuristics. We are actively looking for more real-life data sets for this purpose, but currently there seems to be virtually no substantial public-domain benchmarks in this area. Finally, in some applications, a variety of hybrids of the investigated FDC and ODC scenarios may be encountered. For example individual data repositories can have records on overlapping sets of objects and, at the same time, have limited overlap in the available features for these objects. One can abstract FDC, ODC as well as this hybrid situation as special cases of each clusterer viewing a portion of the complete object-feature matrix, and it may be possi-

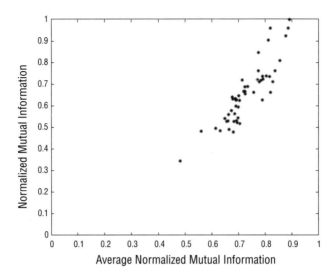

Figure 3.5: Plot of the cluster quality values with respect to the average mutual information shared with the members of the ensemble.

ble to obtain a general solution based on this viewpoint. Next-generation data miners to urged to further build on privacy preserving distributed clustering models and demonstrate their impact on a wide range of real-life application scenarios.

Acknowledgements

We would like to thank Intel Corporation (Grant 8032) and IBM ACAS for their generous support of this work.

Joydeep Ghosh (ghosh@ece.utexas.edu) is a full professor of electrical and computer engineering at The University of Texas at Austin.

Srujana Merugu (merugu@ece.utexas.edu) is a graduate student in the department of electrical and computer engineering, University of Texas at Austin.

Alexander Strehl, Ph.D., (alexander@strehl.com) is with McKinsey, Germany.

Chapter 4

Design of Distributed Data Mining Applications on the Knowledge Grid

Mario Cannataro, Domenico Talia,
and Paolo Trunfio

In many scientific and business areas, massive data collections of terabyte and petabyte scale need to be analyzed. Moreover, in several cases data sets must be shared by large communities of users that pool their resources from different sites of a single organization or from a large number of institutions. Grid computing has been proposed as a novel computational model, distinguished from conventional distributed computing by its focus on large-scale resource sharing, innovative applications, and, in some cases, high-performance orientation. Today grids can be used as effective infrastructures for distributed high-performance computing and data processing (Foster, Kesselman, and Tuecke 2001).

Together with the grid shift towards industry and business applications, a parallel shift toward the implementation of data grids has been registered. Data grids are designed to manage large data sets in remote repositories and also for moving them about with the same ease that small files can be moved. They represent an extension and enhancement of computational grids driven by the need to handle large data sets without constant, repeated authentication. Their main goal is to support the implementation of distributed data-intensive applications. Significant efforts are the EU DataGrid, the particle physics data grid, the Japanese grid DataFarm, and the Globus data grid (Chervenak, Foster, Kesselman, Salisbury, and Tuecke 2001).

Data grid middleware is crucial for the management of data on grids, however in several scientific and business applications is also vital to have tools and environments that support the process of analysis, inference, and discovery over the available data. The evolution of data grids is represented by knowledge grids that offer high-level tools and techniques for the distributed mining and extraction of knowledge from data repositories available on the grid. The development of such an infrastructure is the main goal of our work focused on the design and implementation of an environment for geographically distributed high-performance knowledge discovery applications called *knowledge grid*. The KNOWLEDGE GRID can be used to perform data mining on very large data sets available over grids to make scientific discoveries, improve industrial processes and organization models, and uncover business valuable information.

This chapter is organized as follows. Section 4.2 describes the KNOWLEDGE GRID general architecture and the features of the main components. Sections 4.3 and 4.4 discuss the basic steps to design, build, and execute a distributed data mining application using the tools offered by the KNOWLEDGE GRID. Section 4.5 outlines the system prototype and section 4.6 discusses what is needed to support the entire KDD process on grids. Section 4.7 describes related work and section 4.8 concludes the chapter and suggests future research activities in the area.

4.1   The KNOWLEDGE GRID Architecture

The KNOWLEDGE GRID architecture (Cannataro and Talia 2003) is defined on top of grid toolkits and services, i.e. it uses basic grid services to build specific knowledge extraction services. Following the integrated grid architecture approach, these services can be developed in different ways using the available grid toolkits and services. The current implementation is based on the Globus toolkit (Foster and Kesselman 1997). Like Globus, the KNOWLEDGE GRID offers global services based on the cooperation and combination of local services. We designed the KNOWLEDGE GRID architecture so that more specialized data mining tools are compatible with lower-level grid mechanisms and also with the data grid services. This approach benefits from "standard" grid services which are more and more utilized and offers an open parallel and

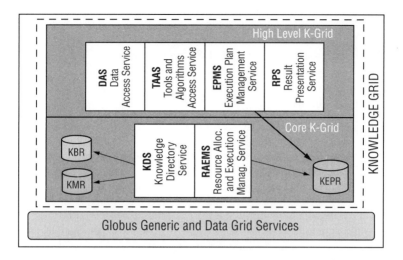

Figure 4.1: The KNOWLEDGE GRID architecture.

distributed knowledge discovery architecture that can be configured on top of grid middleware in a simple way.

4.1.1 KNOWLEDGE GRID Services

KNOWLEDGE GRID services are organized in two hierarchical levels: (1) the core K-grid layer and (2) the high level K-grid layer. The former refers to services directly implemented on the top of generic grid services, the latter is used to describe, develop, and execute distributed knowledge discovery computations over the KNOWLEDGE GRID. KNOWLEDGE GRID layers are depicted in figure 4.1. The figure shows layers as implemented on the top of Globus services. The KNOWLEDGE GRID data and metadata repositories are also shown. In the following paragraphs, the term *K-grid node* will denote a Globus node implementing KNOWLEDGE GRID services.

Core K-Grid Layer

The core K-Grid layer layer offers basic services for the definition, composition, and execution of a distributed knowledge discovery computation over the grid. Its main goal is the management of all metadata describing features of data sources, third party data mining tools, data management, and data visualization tools and algorithms. Moreover, this layer coordinates the application execution by attempting to fulfill the application requirements and the available grid resources. This layer comprises two main services: (1) knowledge directory service and (2) resource allocations and execution management service.

Knowledge directory service (KDS) extends the basic Globus monitoring and discovery service (MDS) and it is responsible for maintaining the metadata describing all the data and tools used in the KNOWLEDGE GRID. They comprise the following:

- Repositories of data to be mined (data sources).

- Tools and algorithms used to (1) extract, filter and manipulate data (data management tools), (2) analyze (mine) data, and (3) visualize, store and manipulate mining results.

- Distributed knowledge discovery execution plans. An execution plan is an abstract description of a KNOWLEDGE GRID application, that is a graph describing the interaction and data flow between data sources, data mining (DM) tools, visualization tools, and result storing.

- Knowledge obtained as result of the mining process, i.e. learned models and discovered patterns.

The metadata information is represented by XML (extensible markup language) documents and is stored in a knowledge metadata repository (KMR). Whereas it could be infeasible to maintain the data to be mined in an ad hoc repository, it could be useful to maintain a repository of the discovered knowledge. This information (see below) is stored in a knowledge base repository (KBR); metadata describing them are managed by the KDS. Recently, we are moving towards RDF schema and we developed a DAML+OIL-based ontology for the Data Mining domain that is used to classify data mining software (Cannataro and Comito 2003). We will have a two-layers metadata organization: ontological data (represented by RDF schema files) and specific metadata regarding the instance of each data mining resource (e.g. availability, location, and configuration).

KDS is then used not only to search and access raw data, but also to find previously discovered knowledge that can be used to compare the output of a given mining computation when data change, or to apply data mining tools in an incremental way. Data management, analysis, and visualization tools are usually pre-existent to the KNOWLEDGE GRID (i.e. they resides over file systems or code libraries). Another important repository is the knowledge execution plan repository (KEPR) that holds the execution plans of data mining processes.

The resource allocation and execution management service (RAEMS) is used to find the best mapping between an execution plan and available resources, with the goal of satisfying the application requirements (computing power, storage, memory, database, network bandwidth and latency) and grid constraints. The mapping has to be effectively obtained (co-)allocating resources. After the execution plan activation, this layer manages and coordinates the application execution. Other than using KDS and Globus MDS services, this layer is directly based on the Globus resource allocation manager (GRAM). Resource requests of each single data mining program are expressed using the resource specification language (RSL). The analysis and processing of the execution plan will generate global resource requests that in turn are translated into local RSL requests for local GRAMs.

High Level K-Grid Layer

The high level K-grid layer includes services used to compose, validate, and execute a parallel and distributed knowledge discovery computation. Moreover, the layer offers services to store and analyze the discovered knowledge. There are four main services: data access service (DAS), tools and algorithms access service (TAAS), execution plan management service (EPSM), and results presentation service (RPS).

The data access service (DAS) is responsible for the search, selection data search services), extraction, transformation, and delivery (data extraction services) of data to be mined. The search and selection services are based on the core KDS service. On the basis of the user requirements and constraints, DAS automates (or assists the user in) the searching and finding of data sources to be analyzed by the DM tools. The extraction, transformation, and delivery of data to be mined are based on the Global access to secondary storage (GASS) services of Globus and make use of KDS.

The tools and algorithms access service (TAAS) is responsible for the search, selection, downloading of data mining tools and algorithms. The metadata regarding their availability, location, and configuration are stored into the KMR and managed by the KDS, whereas the tools and algorithms are stored into the local storage facility of each K-grid node. A node wishing to "export" data mining tools to other users has to "publish" them using the KDS services, which store the metadata in the local KMR.

An execution plan is represented by a graph describing the interaction and data flows between data sources, extraction tools, DM tools, visualization tools, and storing of knowledge results in the KBR. The execution plan management service (EPMS) allows a user to describe the execution plan, using a visual composition tool where the programs are connected to the data sources. However, due to the variety of results produced by DAS and TAAS, different execution plans can be produced, in terms of data and tools locations, strategies to move or stage intermediate results and so on. Thus, EPMS tools generate a set of different, possible execution plans that meet user, data,

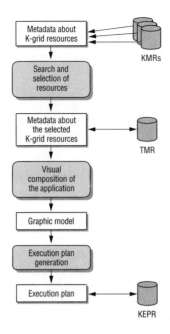

Figure 4.2: The application design process.

and algorithms requirements and constraints. Execution plans are stored in the knowledge execution plan repository (KEPR).

Result visualization is a significant step in the data mining process that can help users in the model interpretation. The results presentation service (RPS) specifies how to generate, present and visualize the knowledge models extracted (e.g., association rules, clustering models, classifications), and offers the API to store them in different formats in the Knowledge Base Repository. The result metadata are stored into the KMR to be managed by the KDS.

4.2   Design of a Knowledge Discovery Application

The design of a knowledge discovery application on the KNOWLEDGE GRID is composed of the following 3 steps (shown in figure 4.2): (1) search and selection of the resources to be used in the knowledge discovery application; (2) visual composition of the application through a graphic model that represents the involved resources and their relationships; (3) generation of the execution plan corresponding to the graphic model of the application.

4.2.1   Resources Search and Selection

The design process starts by searching and selecting the resources needed in a distributed data mining application. This step is accomplishes through the DAS and TAAS tools that search the XML metadata documents stored into the KMRs of the participant K-grid nodes. Such analysis aims to find specific information about useful resources (e.g., software implementing a desired data mining algorithm, data sources about a specific argument, etc.), and it is performed on the basis of the search parameters and selection filters chosen by the user. Metadata describing selected resources (i.e., those satisfying the searching and filtering criteria) are then stored into the task metadata repository (TMR), a local storage space that contains information about resources (computational nodes, data sources and software) selected to perform an application. The TMR is organized as a set of directories: each one is named with the fully qualified hostname of a grid node, and contains metadata documents about resources of those nodes.

4.2.2   Visual Composition of a Data Mining Application

High-level design of data mining applications is a key issue for a large use of knowledge discovery processes. According to a visual composition approach, a user designs an application through a graphical interface that allows her/him building a graph whose nodes represent the resources and whose edges represent the relationships among the resources. In the graphic model a graph node is implemented as an *object*, and a graph edge as a *link*.

An object can represent three types of resources: (1) *software* (e.g., data mining software, extraction and filtering software, visualization tools, etc.); (2) *data* (e.g., input data sets, intermediate results, inferred models, etc.); and (3) *grid nodes* (workstations, cluster of workstations, parallel computers, etc.).

A link can represent different actions, such as data transfer, programs execution and input/output relations: a *data transfer* link is used to specify resource transfer among different locations of the grid; the *execute* link is used to specify an application run on a grid node; and the *input/output* links are used to declare the input and output of a program.

Each *element* (object and link) in the graphic model has an associated set of features. For example, a grid node object will be characterized by a hostname, cpu speed, memory size, etc.; a data transfer link will be characterized by source and destination, protocol name and parameters, etc. Such features can be completely or partially specified by a user. In particular, an element in the graphic model can be *completely specified,* if the user indicates all the parameters that allow for univocally identifying and using the resource or perform the operation or *generic*, if the user does not indicate all the resource/operation parameters, but she/he specifies only a set of desired features or constraints.

For example, in a graphic model a user could specify the following objects: (1) a grid node object representing a specific host k1.deis.unical.it; (2) a grid node object representing a generic host having cpu speed greater than 2 GHz and memory size equals to or greater than 1 gigabyte; (3) a software object representing the completely specified algorithm AutoClass on the host g1.isi.cs.cnr.it; and (4) a software object representing a generic classification algorithm capable to classify the dataset Unidb stored on the host k3.deis.unical.it.

Likewise, in a graphic model a user could insert the following links: (1) a data transfer link representing the completely specified file transfer of the dataset Unidb from the host k3.deis.unical.it to the host g1.isi.cs.cnr.it using the grid-ftp protocol with 16 sockets and TCP buffer size of 64 kB; and (2) a data transfer link representing a generic file transfer operation capable to minimize the transfer time of the dataset Unidb from the host k3.deis.unical.it to the host g1.isi.cs.cnr.it.

The design of the graphic model for a data mining application is supported by a visual environment of the EPMS service. The visual environment will provide a set of graphic objects representing completely specified resources (i.e., well known software, data, grid nodes whose metadata are yet stored in the TMR at the start of the design session) and a set of graphic objects representing generic resources (i.e., generic software, data, grid nodes of which the user must specify required characteristics or constraints during the design process).

A user composes those objects to design the application graph, linking them by means of the graphic links (data transfer, execute, input and output) provided by the visual environment. During the graphic model design, a validation process verifies the consistency of the resulting graph, allowing, with a context-sensitive control, to create links only if they represent actions that can be effectively executed. For instance, it allows for inserting only an input or output link between a software object and a data object, but it does not allow a user to insert an execution link between a grid host object and a data object.

4.2.3 Execution Plan Generation

This phase translates the graphic model of an application into an *execution plan* represented by an XML document. Basically, this step is performed by a parser that analyzes the graphic model and generates its equivalent XML representation. The parser performs its goal taking into account the properties of the involved resources and the parameters of the operations.

The XML execution plan describes a data mining application at high level, neither containing physical information about resources (which are identified by metadata references), nor about status and current availability of such re-sources. Moreover, in this phase the generic objects and links in the graphic model are not resolved to completely specified resources and operations: this process is performed in the next phase, when an instantiated execution plan is produced.

To show the structure of an execution plan we consider the following ex-ample: a user needs to perform a clustering operation on a dataset Unidb stored on the host k3.deis.unical.it. The user specifies that the clustering will be per-formed on a generic remote host (with some desired performance features), by means of the clustering algorithm AutoClass available on that host.

A user can design this simple application as follows:

- The dataset Unidb is copied from the host k3.deis.unical.it to a generic host gnode1 that offers the AutoClass software

- A clustering operation on the dataset Unidb is performed by means of the AutoClass software on the host gnode1

- The inferred clustering model is copied from gnode1 to k3.deis.unical.it.

Figure 4.3 shows the main elements of the execution plan for this example. The execution plan gives a list of tasks and task links, which are specified using the XML tags Task and TaskLink, respectively. The label attribute for a Task element identifies each basic task in the execution plan, and it is used in linking various basic tasks to form the global task flow.

Each Task element contains a task-specific subelement, that indicates the parameters of the particular represented task. For instance, the task identi-fied by the dt1 label contains a DataTransfer element, indicating that it is a data transfer task. The DataTransfer element specifies the protocol, source, and destination of the data transfer. The href attributes of such elements spec-ify respectively the location of metadata about protocol, source and destina-tion objects. In this example, metadata about source of data transfer in the dt1 task are provided by the Unidb.xml file stored in the directory named k3.deis.unical.it of the TMR, whereas metadata about destination are provided by the Unidb.xml file stored in the directory named gnode1 of the same TMR. The first of such XML documents provides metadata about the Unidb dataset when stored on k3.deis.unical.it, whereas the second one provides metadata about Unidb when, after the data transfer, is stored on gnode1. The TaskLink elements represent the relations among tasks of the execution plan. For in-stance, the showed TaskLink elements indicate that the task ex1 follows the task dt1, and the task dt2 follows the ex1 one, as specified by their from and to attributes.

```
<ExecutionPlan>
    ...
    <Task ep:label="dt1">
        <DataTransfer>
            <Protocol ep:href="k3.deis.unical.it/GridFTP.xml"
                      ep:title= "GridFTP on k3.deis.unical.it"/>
            <Source ep:href="k3.deis.unical.it/Unidb.xml"
                      ep:title="Unidb on k3.deis.unical.it"/>
            <Destination  ep:href="gnode1/Unidb.xml"
                      ep:title="Unidb on gnode1"/>
        </DataTransfer>
    </Task>
    <Task ep:label="ex1">
        <Execution>
            <Program ep:href="gnode1/AutoClass.xml"
                      ep:title= "AutoClass on gnode1"/>"
            <Input ep:href="gnode1/Unidb.xml"
                      ep:title="Unidb on gnode1"/>
            ...
            <Output ep:href="gnode1/Unidb-model.xml"
                      ep:title="Unidb-model on gnode1"/>
        </Execution>
    </Task>
    <Task ep:label="dt2">
        <DataTransfer>
            <Protocol    ep:href="k3.deis.unical.it/GridFTP.xml"
                      ep:title= "GridFTP on k3.deis.unical.it"/>
            <Source ep:href="gnode1/Unidb-model.xml"
                      ep:title="Unidb-model on gnode1"/>
            <Destination ep:href="k3.deis.unical.it/Unidb-model.xml"
                      ep:title="Unidb-model on gnode1"/>
        </DataTransfer>
    </Task>
    <TaskLink ep:from="dt1" ep:to="ex1"/>
    <TaskLink ep:from="ex1" ep:to="dt2"/>
</ExecutionPlan>
```

Figure 4.3: Extract of an execution plan.

4.3   Execution of a Knowledge Discovery Application

The execution of a knowledge discovery application on the KNOWLEDGE GRID is composed of the following steps (shown in figure 4.4): (1) Instantiation of the execution plan; (2) translation of the instantiated execution plan into a specific grid *broker script*; and (3) application execution, i.e., submission of the broker script to the allocation manager of the underlying grid middleware, and results presentation.

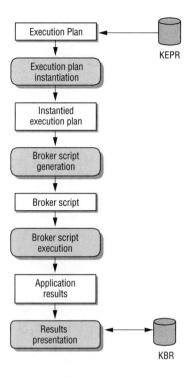

Figure 4.4: The application execution process.

4.3.1 Execution Plan Instantiation

As mentioned before, the resources and operations involved in an execution plan are identified by references to the relative metadata. Since a resource or operation can be completely specified or generic, also the relative metadata document can be completely specified (i.e., it contains all the parameters that allow to identify and use the resource or perform the operation) or generic (i.e., it does not contains all the parameters of the resource or operation, but specifies it a set of desired characteristics or constraints).

The goal of this step is to map all the generic resources and operations in the execution plan into completely specified resources and operations, on the basis of the desired characteristics or constraints indicated in the relative metadata document. The output of this steps is an instantiated execution plan that specifies all the details of resources and operations, and allows for effectively executing the application in an optimized way.

To show the task performed in this step, we consider the following example. A user needs to perform a clustering algorithm on the completely specified

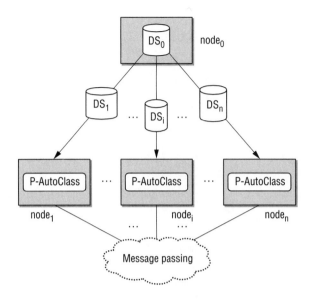

Figure 4.5: Parallel data clustering application over the KNOWLEDGE GRID.

data set DS_0 stored on the grid node $node_0$. To do this, the user wishes to use the parallel clustering algorithm P-AutoClass (Foti, Lipari, Pizzuti, and Talia 2000) on a set of n grid nodes.

The user designs such application specifying that (see figure 4.5): (1) the data set DS_0 is divided in a set of disjoint partitions $DS_1...DS_n$ (the size of each partition is not specified by the user); (2) the partitions $DS_1...DS_n$ are moved to the nodes $node_1...node_n$ (that are generic nodes offering the P-AutoClass software); and (3) the data mining operation is executed in parallel on the nodes $node_1...node_n$ (inter-process communication among the P-AutoClass processes is performed using the *MPI* primitives).

The resulting execution plan includes (1) a set of completely specified resources (e.g., the node $node_0$, the data set DS_0); and (2) a set of generic resources and operations (e.g., nodes $node_1...node_n$, partitions $DS_1...DS_n$, the specification for transferring the partitions to the nodes).

This step aims to map all the generic resources and operations into completely specified ones. Therefore, the resulting instantiated execution plan indicates n real nodes matching the generic nodes $node_1...node_n$ requirements (that is, n machines executing P-AutoClass that can cooperate via message passing); and how to divide the data set DS_0 (i.e., it specifies the size of each partition DS_i).

The size of the ith partition can be obtained on the basis of the expected performance of the destination node, and on the basis of the communication performance between the origin and the destination nodes, according to the following formula:

$$size(DS_i) = size(DS_0)\frac{F_i}{\sum_{j=1}^{n} F_j} \tag{4.1}$$

where

$$F_i = \frac{f_1(cpuspeed(node_i), bandwidth(link_{0,i}), ...)}{f_2(cpuload(node_i), latency(link_{0,i}), ...)} \tag{4.2}$$

4.3.2   Broker Script Generation

The instantiated execution plan generated at the previous step defines completely the application, by using a language that is independent from the grid middleware on which the application will be executed. The goal of this step is to translate such instantiated execution plan into a specific broker script that can be submitted to the allocation manager of the underlying grid middleware for its execution.

The RAEMS provides a set of software components to translate the execution plan in different broker scripts. For instance, the RAEMS provides a Globus broker adapter that translates the instantiated execution plan into the equivalent resource specification language (RSL) script. RSL is a structured language offered by the Globus Toolkit[1] by which resource requirements and parameters can be specified. In opposition with the XML execution plan, the RSL script describes entirely an instance of the designed computation, i.e., it specifies all the physical information needed for the execution (e.g., name and location of resources, software parameter, etc.). Figure 4.6 shows an extract of a sample RSL script.

4.3.3   Application Execution and Results Presentation

In KNOWLEDGE GRID, the execution of an application is performed by directly submitting the broker script to the resource allocation manager of the underlying grid. For example, an RSL script generated by the Globus broker adapter can be submitted to the Globus resource allocation manager (GRAM)[2] of a grid node running Globus. The GRAM interprets the RSL script and executes the data mining application that it represents. Finally, the output of the data mining application (the inferred model) is collected and moved to the user KBR and visualized by means of the RPS tools.

---

[1] http://www.globus.org/gram/rsl_spec1.html
[2] http://www.globus.org/gram

```
+
...
(&(resourceManagerContact= k3.deis.unical.it)
  (subjobStartType= strict-barrier)
  (label= dt1)
  (executable= $(GLOBUS_LOCATION)/bin/globus-url-copy)
  (arguments= -vb Œnotpt gsiftp://k3.deis.unical.it/.../Unidb
                 gsiftp://g1.isi.cs.cnr.it/.../Unidb
  )
)
...
(&(resourceManagerContact= g1.isi.cs.cnr.it)
  (subjobStartType= strict-barrier)
  (label= ex1)
  (executable= .../autoclass)
  ...
  )
)
...
```

Figure 4.6: The extract of a sample RSL script.

4.4   A Prototype

The main design and development functionalities of the KNOWLEDGE GRID discussed in the previous two sections have been implemented in a toolset named *VEGA* (a visual environment for grid applications) (Cannataro, Congiusta, Talia, Trunfio 2002). It provides a set of facilities supporting the design and execution of knowledge discovery applications over computational grids running the Globus Toolkit environment. VEGA allows to design and execute a knowledge discovery application through the following steps: (1) visual composition of the application, (2) validation of the graphic model, (3) execution plan generation, and (4) execution of the application.

The visual composition phase is performed by means of a graphical interface (see figure 4.7), which provides the user with a set of graphical objects representing the resources. Those objects can be composed using visual facilities that allow for inserting links among them, thus composing a graphical representation of the application.

A complex application is composed of several jobs. The design environment is organized in *workspaces*. Jobs in a given workspace are intended to be executed concurrently, whereas workspaces are executed sequentially. To this end a priority relationship is maintained between the workspaces according to the order of their creation. For an application composed of a set of workspaces,

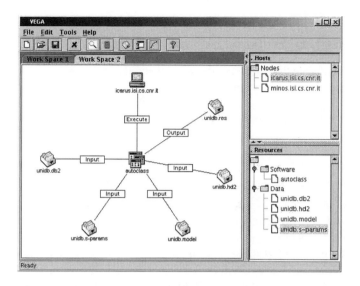

Figure 4.7: The VEGA user interface.

the environment must handle with the case of a task in a given workspace that needs to operate on resources generated by tasks in previous workspaces. Such resources are not yet physically generated in a workspace when a user is composing the next workspace of the application; this will occur only at run time. Thus, the environment is able to recognize such a situation during the composition of a workspace and it generates the needed virtual resources making them available to all the following workspaces. For instance, if in *workspace 1* a software component *S* is transferred to a node *N*, a new metadata document is created for *S* and stored in the directory *N* of the TMR. That document specifying the new location of *S* is marked as temporary until the data transfer is performed. However, if *workspace 2* is opened in the same session (i.e. it is scheduled after workspace 1), the software *S* is displayed as already available under the resources of *N*. The environment allows also for storing a graphical composition in a binary file, which can be next retrieved for modifications by the user.

The environment permits to browse the TMR in order to search and choose the resources to be used in the application. Selected hosts are displayed into the hosts panel, and the user can explore resources of each one by clicking on its label. Those resources are displayed by categories into the resources panel. Each graphical object is associated with information about the related resources; such information is used for the creation of the internal model and for the execution plan generation.

The environment handles three kinds of objects: *software*, *data* and *nodes*. It allows the user to drag the objects presented in the hosts and resources panels into the active workspace. After this, the user can link those objects in order to indicate the interaction between them. During the visual composition phase the objects can be involved in several operations, such as insertion and movement in a workspace, selection, linking with other objects, etc. Links can represent different actions, such as data transfer, programs execution and input and output relations. The environment performs the labeling of the links and the attribution of the others properties characterizing them. For each link type it is possible to set related parameters (e.g., protocol and destination path of the data transfer, job-manager of the execution, etc.).

The validation of the graphic model is performed during the visual composition and at its completion. During the composition the environment verifies the consistency of the graphic model, allowing, by a context-sensitive control, to create links only if they represent actions that can be effectively executed (as we discussed in section 4.2). At the completion of the graphic model the environment tries to catch error occurrences that cannot be recognized during the pre-processing phase. For example, it indicates if the graphic model in a workspace does not contain at least one host.

The execution plan generation step is performed by analyzing the graphic model produced during the visual composition, and is able to generate the equivalent XML execution plan and RSL script.

The execution of the application is performed by authenticating the user on the grid through the Globus grid security infrastructure (GSI) services[3] and submitting the RSL script to the Globus GRAM for its execution.

Even if scalability is an issue in distributed computing, distributed data mining go beyond the scalability issue by meeting real necessity of analyzing distributed data sets spread on a computer network. Currently we are using VEGA to compose distributed data mining applications on grids. Recently we implemented a distributed classification application based on voting to get the best classification model. The source data set was that used in the 1999 KDD Cup competition; it is composed of about 5 millions of tuples. We partitioned it on three grid nodes and run the C4.5 algorithm on each partition. Three different classification trees were obtained ad the most accurate of them was selected (99% of accuracy). Whereas the application on a single machine took about one hour (3480 secs.), by using three nodes we obtained a very accurate classification model in 23 minutes (1380 secs.) including data transfer and voting times. The resulting speed up is 2.5.

---

[3] See http://www.globus.org/security

4.5   Knowledge Discovery on the KNOWLEDGE GRID

In the previous sections it has been shown as the basic components of a distributed knowledge discovery application, that is data sources, tools, and results (knowledge extracted in the KDD process and considered useful to be stored in the KBR), are searched, combined, and executed through knowledge execution plans. In this section we will detail how the main steps of the KDD process are supported by the KNOWLEDGE GRID.

The main steps of the KDD process are (1) data cleaning; (2) data integration; (3) data transformation; (4) data selection; (5) data mining; (6) pattern evaluation; and (7) knowledge presentation.

Steps 1 to 3 can be viewed as a pre-processing phase and usually in a traditional environment they are performed once, prior to start mining phase, and need not to be repeated. In a grid environment this property does not hold because data sources are owned by independent organizations, and grid nodes offering data mining algorithms may dynamically appear and disappear. Therefore, in general those steps could be re-executed with the data mining step. Data cleaning and integration are mainly bound to the kind of data sources, so information about how to perform such steps and what tools to use will be stored as metadata about data sources (into the KMR). Moreover, the KMR will contain metadata about those data cleaning and integration tools.

Although from a computational point of view, the pre-processing phase is treated as a normal computation over the grid (i.e. the jobs executing the pre-processing phase are dispersed into the overall execution plan), we want emphasizes the different steps of the KDD process as phases of a KNOWLEDGE GRID computation. In particular, to support all those phases, the complete knowledge execution plan need to comprise a *pre-processing* (data preparation) phase, an *execution phase* (mining and evaluation), and a *visualization phase*.

Following a (1) pre-processing phase, the (2) mining and (3) pattern evaluation phases are executed in an interactive and iterative way: after a pattern (result) is evaluated, it can be accepted, (4) stored in the KBR and visualized, or the user can decide to change some parameters and repeat phases 2 and 3. From a computational point of view the interaction with the user requires to synchronize the computation (a sort of synchronization barrier) over all the grid jobs. In the KNOWLEDGE GRID this can be obtained by assigning to each phase a specific workspace and synchronizing the flow among them.

Usually during a session the data sources and the K-grid nodes remain available, so phase 1 should not be repeated. If a pre-existing knowledge execution plan is loaded, the system has to check the availability of data sources and algorithms, and in general has to repeat the data preparation phase. As an example, the system has to check that both the K-grid nodes are available and the user continues to have authorization over their resources.

Extraction, transformation, and loading (ETL) tools designed in the database and data warehouse fields are currently used in commercial KDD systems. Key issues to adapt such tools in a grid environment are support of heterogeneity (data sources format, ownership, access policies, etc); support of distribution and large data size (the pre-processing phase, if not scheduled accordingly to the previous constraints can result in large overhead); support of an interactive and iterative interaction model through workspaces synchronization; scalability, by using parallelism and data grid services (e.g. GridFTP, replica management, and so on).

4.6 Related Work

Recently proposed systems and models that share with the KNOWLEDGE GRID the goal of supporting the data mining process in the context of grids are Discovery net (D-NET), algorithm development and mining (ADaM), and Data-Centric grid. D-NET is a distributed data mining system designed at the Imperial College whose main goal is to design, develop and implement an infrastructure to effectively support scientific knowledge discovery processes from high-throughput informatics. In this context, a series of testbeds and demonstrations are being carried out, for using the technology in the areas of life sciences, environmental modeling and geo-hazard prediction. ADaM is an agent-based data mining framework developed at the University of Alabama. Initially, this framework was adopted for processing large datasets for geophysical phenomena. More recently, it has been ported to the NASA information power grid (IPG) environment, for the mining of satellite data. Differently from the two environments discussed above, the Datacentric grid is a system directed at knowledge discovery on grids designed for mainly dealing with immovable data.

Those software environments aim at offering high-level services and techniques for exploiting the basic grid services in designing and implementing distributed knowledge discovery. The importance of both those technologies make research area very critical and, at the same time, very promising for providing tools, environments, and applications for solving data-intensive complex problems and implementing distributed knowledge management systems.

The KNOWLEDGE GRID was designed to support the development of distributed knowledge discovery applications, as an integration of services and resources available on the grid, such as data mining tools, data sources, storage, and computing nodes. Moreover, even though the KNOWLEDGE GRID was mainly intended to support knowledge discovery, its services offer functionalities that can be useful to develop a more general class of distributed applications, built as a composition of services and resources from different application domains. In this respect, the KNOWLEDGE GRID approach presents similarities with works in the area of problem solving environments (PSEs), and in the field of PSE toolkits in particular.

A *PSE* is an environment that provides all the computational facilities needed to solve a given class of problems (Gallopoulos, Houstis, Rice, 1994). The features of a PSE include advanced solution methods, automatic selection of solution methods, and ways to incorporate novel solution methods. Besides the successfully development of PSEs for diverse application fields, such as signal processing and linear algebra, in recent years significant research efforts have been devoted to build PSE toolkits, i.e., systems that allow to create PSEs tailored to diverse application domains.

A popular PSE toolkit that was usefully integrated into grid computing systems to build a number of domain specific environments is NetSolve from the University of Tennessee and the Oak Ridge National Laboratory (Arnold, Agrawal, Blackford, Dongarra, Miller, Seymour, Sagi, Shi, and Vadhiyar 2002). NetSolve adopts a client/agent/server design. The client issues requests to agents; the agents allocate servers to service those requests; the servers receive inputs for the problem, do the computation, and return the output to the client. Through NetSolve a client can access remote computers with complete opacity, and can use software resources without the tedium of installation and maintenance.

Another significant system is SciAgents from Purdue University (Drashansky, Houstis, Ramakrishnan, Rice 1999), an agent-based approach to build a multidisciplinary problem solving environment (MPSE), i.e., a framework for combining PSEs for tailored, flexible multidisciplinary applications. SciAgents is specially suited for a distributed high performance computing environment; it allows extensive reuse of legacy software and provides a natural approach to parallel and distributed problem solving. Comparing our system with NetSolve and SciAgents, we see that the KNOWLEDGE GRID itself, providing a flexible integration of services for resource discovery, job management and security, could be effectively devised as a data mining oriented PSE toolkit to build environments for different classes of data intensive distributed applications.

Dynamic service composition is another research area whose experiences could suggest how to enhance the design of current KNOWLEDGE GRID functionalities. The term "service composition" refers to the techniques of composing arbitrarily complex services from relatively simpler services available over the internet (Chakraborty and Joshi 2001). As in the KNOWLEDGE GRID, key issues in service composition are service discovery, service coordination and management, fault tolerance, and scalability. A significant contribution in this area is represented by Web services, a set of technologies that allow designers to reuse software components and to integrate distributed applications over the Internet. A key topic in the KNOWLEDGE GRID is represented by mechanisms needed to compose reusable complex knowledge discovery applications starting from basic mining services. Although most of the existing service composition platforms relates to services residing over the internet, the KNOWLEDGE GRID could benefit from work in this area for developing such functionalities, in particular under the OGSA architecture (see next section), that adopts the model of web Services as core technology.

4.7 Conclusions and Future Work

Distributed data mining is the core element of network-based knowledge discovery tools and knowledge management environments. These systems may become feasible through the exploitation of geographically distributed grid services that are becoming available.

The grid infrastructure is growing up very quickly and is going to be more and more complete and complex both in the number of tools and in the variety of supported applications. Along this direction the grid services are shifting from generic computation-oriented services to high-level information management and knowledge discovery services.

The KNOWLEDGE GRID system we discussed here is a significant component of this trend. It integrates and completes the data grid services by supporting distributed data analysis and knowledge discovery and management services that will enlarge the application scenario and the community of grid computing users.

In this area, future research directions and challenges that could be investigated are described in the following paragraphs:

Use of the open grid services architecture (OGSA) model for implementing knowledge discovery services on grids. Recently, the grid research community initiated a development effort to align grid technologies with web services technologies, using the OGSA architecture. OGSA enables the integration of services and resources across distributed, heterogeneous, dynamic environments and communities (Talia 2002). To achieve this integration, the OGSA model adopts the web services description language (WSDL) and defines the grid service concept as a web service that provides a set of well-defined interfaces and follows specific conventions. A grid service implements one or more interfaces that correspond to WSDL *portTypes*. We are going to design a prototype of the KNOWLEDGE GRID in terms of the OGSA model. In this implementation, each of the KNOWLEDGE GRID services is exposed as a persistent service, using the OGSA conventions and mechanisms. According to this approach, the various services provided by the KNOWLEDGE GRID will implement several *portTypes* through which the services can be exported towards knowledge discovery applications.

An interesting direction for future work is the modeling through ontology of basic software and data components in a KNOWLEDGE GRID application. In particular, we are developing DAMON, an ontology for the data mining domain that offers application designers a reference model for the different kind of data mining tasks, methodologies and software available to solve a given problem, helping them find the most appropriate solution (Cannataro and Comito 2003). With the DAMON ontology we aim to realize a semantic modeling of user tasks/needs and of the resources characterizing data mining software, to offer high level services for dynamic software searching and applications composition. DAMON will be used as an ontology-based assistant that suggests, to the KNOWLEDGE GRID application designer, what to do and what to use on the basis of her or his needs as well as a tool that makes possible semantic search (concept-based) of data mining software. In more general terms, we think the use of ontologies to describe grid resources will simplify and structure the systematic building of grid applications through the composition and reuse of software components and the development of knowledge-based services allowing more effective resource management and scheduling.

Another research challenge that may offer some positive results in a near future is based on the exploitation of peer-to-peer (P2P) computing in designing knowledge discovery services on grids. P2P is, at the same time, a set of protocols, a computing model, and a design philosophy for distributed, decentralized, self-organizing systems. P2P is emerging as a computing model in highly dynamic environments, and so it could be a natural candidate model for next generation grids. It will play a central role as the basic technology on which fundamental tasks of future grids, such as presence management, dynamic resource discovery and sharing, collaboration, and self-configuration will be developed (Cannataro and Talia 2003b).

Finally, the development of knowledge discovery-based problem solving environments (PSEs) on grids can be another research direction to be pursued. Large and complex data sets are used in many scientific and engineering applications. Novel PSEs should be devised to include data mining facilities as components integrated in multistep solving processes.

Acknowledgements

This work has been partially funded by the project "MIUR and CNR Programme Legge 449/97-99, Fondo Speciale SP3: GRID COMPUTING: Tecnologie abilitanti e applicazioni per eScience."

Mario Cannataro is an associate professor of computer engineering at the University "Magna Graecia" in Catanzaro, Italy. His interests include grid computing, bioinformatics, and adaptive web systems. He can be reached at cannataro@unicz.it.

Domenico Talia is a professor of computer science at the University of Calabria, Italy. His interests include grid computing, peer-to-peer computing, and knowledge discovery. He can be reached at talia@deis.unical.it.

Paolo Trunfio is a Ph.D. student in computer engineering at the University of Calabria, Italy. His interests include grid computing and peer-to-peer systems. He can be reached at trunfio@deis.unical.it.

Chapter 5

Photonic Data Services: Integrating Data, Network and Path Services to Support Next Generation Data Mining Applications

Robert L. Grossman, Yunhong Gu, Dave Hanley, Xinwei Hong, Jorge Levera, Marco Mazzucco, David Lillethun, Joe Mambretti, and Jeremy Weinberger

A fundamental challenge for next generation data mining is to develop systems for remote data analysis and distributed data mining, which scale to large and very large data sets. The data may be at rest, in the sense that it resides on remote disks and tapes or it may be in motion, in the sense that it is collected and streamed from a remote instrument.

The analysis and mining of this type of data is difficult for several reasons. First, the majority of prior work has focused on agent-based systems in which local models are built on data in place and at rest, the models moved, and then combined at a central location.

Second, transmission control protocol-based (TCP) data transport itself becomes a bottleneck when working with remote and distributed data, even in high bandwidth networks, due to TCP's current congestion control mechanism (Bannister, Chien, Faber, Falk, Grossman, and Leigh 2004). This is because the congestion control mechanism for TCP behaves poorly for flows over links with a high bandwidth delay product. The bandwidth delay product can be approximated by multiplying the round trip time for a packet by the maximum bandwidth of the least capable link that a packet transverses. As an example, a standard TCP flow over a 155 megabit-per-second optical character-3 (OC) link connecting Chicago, Illinois and Amsterdam, The Netherlands is in practice limited to about 5 megabits-per-second unless extensive network tuning is undertaken.

Finally, in the last few years, we have gained a better understanding of the primitives required to integrate data mining with databases. On the other hand, we do not yet have a good understanding of the primitives required for distributed, high performance data mining.

In this chapter, we introduce an architecture for remote data analysis and distributed data mining that integrates services to set up optical paths, network protocols designed for high performance networks, and data services supporting the remote analysis and distributed mining of large data sets. We also show experimentally the speedup that is gained with this approach for some typical data mining algorithms such as computing simple correlations for streaming data.

We believe that the work described here is novel for two reasons. First, this is the first chapter that we know of describing an architecture for integrating (a) data services supporting primitives to facilitate remote data analysis and distributed data mining, (b) network protocols designed to move packets efficiently over high performance networks, and (c) services designed to set up paths on demand for photonic networks when required by applications. Integrated services like these can provide the foundation for scaling distributed data mining to large data sets. We call this architecture "photonic data services" (PDS).

Second, this is the first experimental study that we are aware of demonstrating the feasibility of the *distributed* mining of gigabyte-size data sets that are separated by thousands of miles and over a hundred milliseconds in packet round trip time.

In section 5.1, we describe related work. In section 5.2, we describe the basic idea. In section 5.3, we describe the architecture we introduce called *PDS*. In sections 5.6, we describe the three main layers of PDS. In section 5.7, we describe the testbed we use for our experiments. In section 5.8, we describe our experimental studies involving distributed mining of geoscience data. We end the chapter in section 5.9 with a summary and conclusion.

5.1   Background and Related Work

In this chapter, we are concerned with supporting remote data analysis and distributed data-mining applications with high performance data transport services. In addition, many applications will also require high performance compute services, which we do not address. Today, these would be typically provided by local compute clusters or by virtual compute clusters accessed via a computational grid (Foster and Kesselman 1999) or computational middleware architecture.[1]

There have been three main architectural approaches to date for distributed data mining: agent based systems, data grid based systems, and data web based systems. We consider each in turn.

The first approach is to use agents over commodity networks to move data, remotely control the data mining algorithms at the different sites, and to collect the intermediate results and models. Systems with this architecture include the JAM system developed by Stolfo, Prodromidis, and Chan (1997), the BODHI system developed by Kargupta, Hamzaoglu, and Stafford (1997), the Kensington system developed by Darlington, Guo, Sutiwaraphun, and To (1997), and the Papyrus system developed by Grossman, Bailey, Ramu, Malhi, Sivakumar, and Turinsky (1999).

The second approach is to use cluster middleware. Systems with this architecture include those developed by Parthasarathy and Subramonian (2000), Moore, Baru, Marciano, Rajasekar, and Wan (1999), and Grossman, Bailey, Ramu, Malhi, Sivakumar, and Turinsky (1999). More recently, Globus has emerged as the dominant middleware for working with distributed clusters (Foster and Kesselman 1999). The Globus infrastructure for data intensive computing is called the data grid, and includes services for parallel TCP striping (GridFTP), and data replication services (Globus Replica Catalog and Globus Replica Management).[2]

Other grid middleware services that have been used for data mining include DataCutter developed by Beynon, Kurc, Catalyurek, Chang, Sussman, and Saltz (2001) and Discovery Net developed by Patrick and Guo (2002). For example, Du and Agrawal (2002) recently used DataCutter for some distributed data mining experiments.

The third approach, and the one described in this chapter, is to use data webs, which are web based infrastructures for data (Grossman, Hornick, and Meyer 2002). Unlike grid middleware, which is built over authentication, authorization and access (AAA) control mechanisms for rationing and scheduling presumably scarce high performance computing resources (Foster and Kesselman 1999), data webs are built using World Wide Web Consortium

---

[1] See the NSF middleware initiative, www.nsf-middleware.org.
[2] Globus data grid, http://www.globus.org/datagrid/.

W3C standards and emerging standards for web services and packaging (SOAP and XML). Data webs in contrast to data grids are designed to encourage the open sharing of data resources without AAA controls, in the same way that the web today encourages the sharing of document resources without authentication, authorization and access controls.[3]

For small data sets, data webs use W3C standards and emerging standards to manage both the data and metadata. These include HTTP, the data web transport protocol (DWTP) and other emerging standards for transport (Grossman and Mazzucco 2002), and SOAP and XML for packaging.[4] For large data sets, this infrastructure is used just for the metadata, while specialized network protocols and data services (the photonic data services described below) are used to manage the data itself. Providing separate mechanisms for control paths and data paths is an old idea in high performance computing going back to at least the IBM High Performance Storage System (HPSS). Developing the appropriate data web services and protocols to work with large remote and distributed data is a fundamental research challenge.

As mentioned previously, the performance of data flows with large bandwidth delay products (BDP) is usually quite poor in practice (Bannister, Chien, Faber, Falk, Grossman, and Leigh 2004).

There have been several approaches for dealing with this problem. One approach to improving TCP performance for data intensive applications is to adjust the TCP window size to be the product of the bandwidth and the RTT delay of the network (Jacobson, Braden, and Borman 1992). This approach requires modifying and tuning the kernel of each of the operating systems transporting the packets and ensuring that the networking hardware can support these large or jumbo packets.

Another approach to overcoming the limitations of TCP is to stripe TCP over several standard TCP network connections. In contrast to the first approach, this can be done at the data middleware or application level. This approach has been implemented several times, including PSockets (Grossman, Sivakumar, and Bailey 2000) and GridFTP (Chervenak, Foster, Kesselman, and Tuecke 2000). It has been observed that effectively utilizing high performance links can require dozens to hundreds of sockets. This can create an overhead, limiting the usefulness of this approach. In addition, the window size must be carefully tuned, as with the first approach.

Another approach is to use a protocol that combines a user datagram protocol-based (UDP) data channel with a TCP-based control channel. UDP can effectively transport data at high rates even over high BDP paths. The TCP control channel can be used to create a reliable algorithm, while the appropriate rate and congestion control algorithms can be used in the control channel

---

[3]See the W3c semantic web, www.w3.org/2001/sw/.
[4]See the W3c semantic web, www.w3.org/2001/sw/.

so that the algorithm is friendly to other flows. PDS uses a protocol called SABUL (Grossman, Mazzucco, Sivakumar, and Pan 2004), which takes this approach and is described in more detail below. Since SABUL is based upon TCP and UDP, it can be deployed as an application library without making any changes to the existing network infrastructure.

Another approach is to improve TCP in various ways. High speed TCP (Floyd 2002), scalable TCP (Kelly 2002), and FAST are examples of this approach. Although these approaches all appear to be promising, work is still required to understand their friendliness, performance, and scalability. In addition, new TCP variants require significant changes to the current network infrastructure.

Another approach is to create entirely new protocols, such as explicit control protocol (XCP) (Katabi, D.; Handley, M.; and Rohrs 2002) and the datagram congestion control protocol (DCCP).[5] Again, deploying these new protocols will take some time due to the significant changes required to the current network infrastructure.

5.2 The Basic Idea

Today, data-intensive applications working with remote and distributed data are generally based upon standard networking (IP) and transport (TCP) protocols. For data mining applications running on commodity networks analyzing small data sets these protocols work extremely well. Data mining applications involving large, distributed data sets have generally used specialized networks such as NSF's vBNS network or the internet 2's Abilene network. In practice, very large bandwidth applications have to be scheduled on these networks and require the use of specialized transport protocols (Grossman, Sivakumar, and Bailey 2000).

As optical networking architectures become more common, a new possibility is emerging. A bandwidth-demanding application can request an optical connection between the data sources and the data sinks for a specific application. More specifically, the application can request the set up, status and tear down of the required optical paths. Clearly there is a crossover point: for short transfers of small data, TCP is clearly preferable, while for long transfers of very large data, a dedicated optical path might be preferable.

For the purposes here, the layered network model we use is a standard extension of the standard 5-layer model in which we split the top layer into a layer providing specialized data services for remote data analysis and distributed data mining and a top application layer. More generally, two additional layers would be added between layers 5 and 6 below: one for the description of

---

[5]http://www.icir.org/kohler/dcp/.

Layer	Description	Implementation
6	Application	DWTP applications
5	Data Services	SOAP, DWTP
4	Network Protocol	TCP, UDP, SABUL
3	Internet Protocol	IP
2	Path Services	ODIN
1	Physical Links	WDM, Ethernet, ...

Table 5.1: Layered network model.

data services (for example, WSDL) and one for the discovery of data services (for example, UDDI).[6]

1. *Physical Links.* We assume that the physical links are provided by multichannel wavelength-division multiplexed (WDM) communications, as well as by ethernet, and other technologies.

2. *Path Services Layer.* We assume that there are services allowing us to set up paths between devices, tear-down paths, check the status of paths, set up routing, etc.

3. *Internet Layer.* This layer provides a common network addressing and routing across multiple networks. For our applications, we use the internet protocol (IP) in this layer.

4. *Network Protocol Services Layer.* We assume that there are transport services including TCP, UDP, and other more specialized protocols providing high performance over the paths. Our applications use specialized high-performance protocols in this layer.

5. *Data Services Layer.* We assume that there are standard services for moving data such as SOAP-based web services, as well as more specialized data services designed for performance networks.

6. *Application Layer.* We assume that the remote data analysis and distributed data mining applications can request standard and specialized network services depending upon application requirements.

In this chapter, we describe specialized integrated services for layers 2, 3, and 5 and illustrate their use on the analysis of distributed geoscience data.

---

[6]See the W3c semantic web, www.w3.org/2001/sw/.

5.3 Photonic Data Services

In this chapter, we introduce the idea of integrating (1) specialized photonic path services; (2) high performance network protocols and (3) high performance data services providing data mining primitives for remote data analysis and distributed data mining. We call these integrated services "photonic data services," or PDS.

As an example, consider a distributed data mining application in which 1.8 gigabytes of vegetation data over a region specified by latitude and longitude coordinates will be correlated with 1.8 gigabytes of climate data over the same region. Assume both data sets are in the US in different locations, but that the client doing the correlation is in Amsterdam.

Assume that both data sources are connected to the client by an OC-12 network operating at 622 megabits per second. Today, the data would be moved to a common location using a standard network protocol such as TCP, merged, and then correlated. Without the correlation, this process takes over 3000 seconds, as we will see in section 5.8.

In general an experimental OC-12 is not available. Using the photonic data services described below, a photonic path can be set up in less than a minute and the two 1.8 gigabyte streams transported and merged in less than 70 seconds, as we will see in section 5.8. As the path services software matures, we expect the minute set up time to be reduced substantially, so that a data mining computation that today requires about an hour could be done in about a minute.

In the next three sections, we describe the three service layers we have implemented and integrated to create photonic data services to support data mining. Our implementation of the path services is called ODIN (Lillethun, Mambretti, and Weinberger 2002); our implementation of the network protocol services is called SABUL (Grossman, Mazzucco, Sivakumar, and Pan 2004); our implementation of the streaming merge—which is the data service or data mining primitive for the example above—is called the continuously generated merge or CGM (Mazzucco, Ananthanarayan, Grossman, Levera, and Rao 2002). The work described in this chapter is the first time we have integrated these three service layers and performed experimental studies using them.

5.4 Path Services

The path services used in PDS are called the "optical dynamic intelligent network service layer," or ODIN (Lillethun, Mambretti, and Weinberger 2002). We now describe these systems following Lillethun, Mambretti, and Weinberger (2002). ODIN receives requests for circuits by applications, which for PDS are usually from the data service layer, and contacts the required network switches, including both optical-domain DWDM switches and traditional ethernet switches and IP routers, to set up the circuits. ODIN also provides services to tear down paths and to check their status.

ODIN consists of two subsystems: one, called the "terascale high performance optical resource regulator," or THOR, interfaces to the optical fabric; while the other, called the "dynamic ethernet intelligent transit interface" or DEITI, interfaces to the traditional ethernet/IP fabric.

ODIN is designed to dynamically provision and control global light paths. The ODIN subsystem THOR is based on new signaling methods for dynamically provisioning light paths. These light paths can be used to create optical VPNs (OVPNs), as well as to extend these light paths to edge resources through other types of dynamically provisioned paths, such as vLANs.

Currently, ODIN sets up paths only within a single administrative domain. In future work, similar path services are planned for multiple administrative domains.

5.5 Network Protocol Services

In this section, we describe a network protocol designed for high performance data transfer called the "simple available bandwidth utilization library," or SABUL following Grossman, Mazzucco, Sivakumar, and Pan (2004). We emphasize that several of the other network protocols mentioned above could also be used. We chose to use SABUL since as an application-level library no change to the existing network infrastructure was required. In addition, SABUL does not require the sometimes delicate tuning required by IETF RFC 1323.

The idea behind SABUL is simple. SABUL combines the UDP protocol in order to send data at a high rate with the TCP protocol in order to do this in a reliable fashion. UDP has no flow control, rate control, or reliable transmission mechanisms. SABUL implements these control functions in a separate TCP control channel. This approach is in contrast to the approach of other high performance protocols such as NETBLT (Clark, Lambert, and Zhang 1987), which combine the data and control channels.

In SABUL, the packets on the UDP channel consist of the usual UDP header plus a 32 bit field for a sequence number. On the TCP channel, each packet consists of: a list of lost data packets, a field stating the requested data rate, and a field reserved to report the state of the receiver's available buffer size. We define the *communication state* information to be the information contained in these TCP packets.

The flow is assumed to be unidirectional. Data is sent to the receiver over the UDP channel, while current communication state information is sent over the TCP channel, from the receiver to the sender. Since the communication state information is passed over TCP, its arrival is ensured; since the amount of this information is relatively small, it has a negligible effect on the overall performance of SABUL.

One of the advantages of SABUL is its continuous updating of state information. In contrast, NETBLT uses a mechanism that sends buffers of data at a fixed rate. At the end of transmission of each buffer, the receiving side of NETBLT sends the sender a list of packets that were lost in the transmission of this buffer. The sender then resends these packets; the process continues until all packets in the buffer are accounted for. Then the next buffer can be transmitted by NETBLT. NETBLT needs to block until all packets are accounted for on the sending side before sending another buffer. This process can be further delayed since packet loss information is transmitted unreliably by the receiver to the sender (since this information is sent over UDP). Another deficit of NETBLT is that it needs to wait for at least one round trip time to get each update of packets lost.

In SABUL, however, each time the receiver notices at least one missing packet, it uses the TCP channel to transmit to the sender a list of packets that were lost. It does not have to block the sending of packets over the UDP channel to wait for an incoming packet containing the communication state information. This allows for changing the rate and flow of data, and retransmission of any missing packets during the transmission of the data. The list of missing packets is updated every time a missing packet is received. If during a predefined amount of time no packet was lost, and thus no transmission sent to the sender on the TCP channel, the receiver sends a notification of this fact to the sender with communication state information. This allows the sender to empty its buffer of packets, which have successfully been received and adjust the rate and flow if necessary.

5.6 Data Services

In this section, we describe data services designed to be component services or primitives for distributed data mining applications. This section is adapted from Grossman and Mazzucco (2002).

The data model, access model, and query model for PDS are based on data webs. Data webs are web-based infrastructures designed to facilitate the analysis and mining of remote and distributed data (Grossman and Mazzucco 2002). Data webs use a protocol for working with remote data called the "data web transfer protocol," or DWTP (formerly known as the dataspace transfer protocol or DSTP) in the same way that the standard web uses http to access remote documents. Data webs also support access to remote data using SOAP as the packaging protocol.

The PDS experiments described below use a data web implementation called *DataSpace,* which we sketch briefly below (Grossman and Mazzucco 2002).

Distributed Columns of Numerical Data. The data model for PDS is simple. Data is divided into rows (data records) and columns (data fields or data attributes). Both may be distributed over the web. Access to the data itself is through a DWTP server. The current DataSpace DWTP servers can also access data using SOAP. Physically, the data itself may be stored as files, in databases, or using other specialized storage mechanisms. Logically, data is just a distributed collection of columns.

Universal Correlation Keys. A universal correlation key (UCK) is a globally unique id (GUID) and is used for relating columns of data on two different DWTP servers. Each column of data is associated with at least one column of UCKs.

Multidimensional UCKs. UCKs may be combined to provide multidimensional keys. This is essential for working with scientific and engineering data, such as the geoscience data used in the experiments below. For example, this data uses latitude and longitude as the UCKs.

Column Based Metadata. Associated with each column of data is attribute metadata and with each data set (a collection of columns) data set metadata. DWTP applications may or may not use this metadata. On the other hand, this metadata is essential for building and deploying statistical models. DWTP servers provide a simple mechanism for associating metadata to columns and collections of columns.

Universal correlation keys enable distributed columns to be correlated in the following fashion: Pairs (k_i, x_i), where k_i is a UCK value and x_i is an attribute value, on DWTP server 1 can be combined with pairs (k_j, y_j) on DWTP server 2 to produce a table (x_k, y_k) in a DWTP client. The DWTP client can then, for example, find a function $y = f(x)$ relating x and y. This simple mechanism of distributed columns identified by UKCs (perhaps vector valued) is sufficient information for many data mining algorithms.

Depending upon the request, DWTP servers return one or more columns, one or more rows, or entire tables. DWTP uses XML to describe the metadata. On the other hand, for efficiency and scalability, by default data *itself* is transmitted as records delimited by carriage returns, with fields delimited by commas. As an alternative, data may also be transmitted using SOAP. The DWTP client may also indicate that a specialized high performance protocol such as SABUL should be used for the data channel. To summarize, the DWTP protocol uses XML for metadata and small data, while data is typically streamed, with large amounts of data streamed using SABUL or other high performance network protocols.

The DWTP protocol includes commands for retrieving metadata, retrieving UCKs, retrieving data and subsets of data, and mechanisms for sampling, working with missing data, and merging by UCKs.

5.7 Physical Testbed

We assume that our network consists of dense wavelength-division multiplexed optical devices together with standard ethernet/IP devices. For our experiments we used the Chicago area OMNInet (Mambretti 2002) and the global terra wide data mining testbed (TWDM).[7]

OMNInet is an optical networking testbed deployed in the Chicago metropolitan area. OMNInet currently provides 1 GE and 10 GE services between Northwestern, the University of Illinois at Chicago, and the StarLight facility in Chicago. OMNInet is operated by a research consortium consisting of iCAIR at Northwestern, the Electronic Visualization Laboratory at the University of Illinois at Chicago, Argonne National Laboratory, SBC, and Nortel.

TWDM is a testbed built on top of DataSpace for the remote analysis, distributed mining, and real time exploration of scientific, engineering, business, and other complex data. Currently, the TWDM testbed consists of five geographically distributed workstation clusters linked by optical networks through StarLight in Chicago. These sites include StarLight itself, the Laboratory for Advanced Computing at UIC, iCAIR at Northwestern University, SARA in Amsterdam, and Dalhousie University in Halifax. SARA is connected to StarLight via the Netherlands' Surfnet network and Dalhousie is connected to StarLight via Canada's CANARIE network.

The experimental setup was as follows. Data servers were located at the SARA research facility in Amsterdam and at the University of Illinois at Chicago and connected via an OC-12 network. The merge was done at the StarLight facility in Chicago. StarLight and the University of Illinois at Chicago are located several miles apart. The machine performing the distributed merge was connected by OC-12 paths to both remote data sources.

The machine in Amsterdam was a dual P4, 1700 Mhz, with 512 megabytes of random-access memory. The machines in Chicago were dual PIIIs, 1000 Mhz, with 512 megabytes of random-access memory. The machines were all running Linux, with the 2.4.x kernels. The network traffic was over SurfNet and OMNInet with routing providing 622 megabits per second of maximum bandwidth.

---

[7] www.ncdm.uic.edu/testbeds.htm.

5.8 PDS Application: Lambda Joins

In this section, we describe a sample distributed data mining application developed using photonic data services. The core application is the merging of distributed geoscience data from the National Center for Atmospheric Research, (NCAR) Community Climate Model.[8] We have described previously the remote analysis of small NCAR data sets with DWTP clients and servers (Grossman and Mazzucco 2002) over the commodity internet.

For the work described in this section, we integrated the data services provided by DWTP servers, the network protocol services provided by SABUL, and the path services provided by ODIN. To support the correlation of distributed data in the NCAR format, we separately developed a continuous merge algorithm for streaming data over high performance networks called the "continuously generated merge," or CGM (Mazzucco, Ananthanarayan, Grossman, Levera, and Rao 2002). Once the streaming data has been merged, simple counts using a finite buffer can be done in a variety of ways (Grossman, Levera, and Mazzucco 2002).

This approach is quite general and, for example, could be used to merge and do simple analyses of other distributed data using multidimensional keys.

5.8.1 Continuously Generated Merge (CGM) Algorithm

We now briefly review the CGM algorithm following Mazzucco, Ananthanarayan, Grossman, Levera, and Rao (2002). In the CGM algorithm we assume the data is partially presorted. Without loss of generality, assume there are two data streams, A and B, being drawn into a client in approximately ascending order and we are trying to merge on one UCK. The CGM algorithm depends upon two parameters: a parameter N determining the number of records in a window, which is used to buffer the streaming data, and N_h, the number of entries in two auxiliary hash tables. The algorithm has an even step and an odd step. The even steps of the algorithm are as follows:

1. The client grabs some fixed number of records N, from both stream A and stream B and places them in window A and window B respectively (each has room for exactly N records).

2. A hash is done on the value of each UCK in window A and the record is placed in the appropriate location in hash table A, overwriting any previous record.

3. A hash is done on the value of each UCK in window B and if the value hashes to an occupied location in hash table A, both the records are

---

[8]www.cgd.ucar.edu/cms/ccm3/.

Rand %	Match %	Time *sec*	Data Rate *Mb/s*
2	96.6	513	4.68
10	89.9	540	4.44
20	81.5	531	4.52
33	73.1	563	4.26

Table 5.2: Results from the CGM algorithm using TCP and DWTP.

merged. If the value does not hash to an occupied location in hash table A, then the record is placed in the appropriate location in hash table B, overwriting any previous record.

In the odd steps of the algorithm, the above algorithm is executed, but reversing the roles of A and B.

5.8.2 Experimental Results

The results in table 5.2 are from the CGM algorithm running using TCP as the network protocol and DWTP as the data service protocol. Each data stream was 300 megabytes in size. The CGM algorithm used a hash table size of 50,000 and a window size of 10,000. The data was atmospheric data from NCAR. The randomization was done by replacing every n'th row (for example, for 10 percent every 10th row) with a random row that was within 50,000 lines of the current row.

As can be seen from the table, the average speed varied between 4–5 megabits per second, despite the fact that each link had a maximum available bandwidth of 622 megabits per second. We note that this type of result is typical.

Tables 5.3 and 5.4 show results from the CGM algorithm running SABUL as the network protocol, DWTP as the data service protocol, and ODIN to provide path service. In this experiment, ODIN was called statically, not dynamically by the application. The data size this time was 1.8 gigabytes so that in total 3.6 gigabytes of data were merged by the algorithm. The average speed varies between 400–500 megabits per second. This means that CGM over SABUL was about 600 times faster on average, since the amount of data was 6 times greater and the elapsed time was about 100 times greater.

When testing the algorithm we realized the largest single affect on the performance of the merge was the length of the record. The longer the record size the memory copying required, the greater the merge time. To illustrate this we ran two tests. In the first, both data files contain 1 UCK and 1 attribute; in the second, both data files contain 1 UCK and 7 attributes.

Rand %	Match %	Time *sec*	Data Rate *Mb/s*
2	99	53.3	550
10	91	52.4	550
20	83	56.2	512
33	78	54.6	527

Table 5.3: Results from the CGM algorithm using SABUL.

Rand %	Match %	Time *sec*	Data Rate *Mb/s*
2	99	66.3	434
10	92	65.7	438
20	82	64.2	449
33	79	65.1	442

Table 5.4: Results from the CGM algorithm using DWTP and ODIN.

5.9   Summary and Conclusion

In this chapter, we have introduced an architecture called "photonic data services," or PDS, which integrates data services, network protocol services, and path servers. With intelligent path services, distributed data mining applications can intelligently signal for a special photonic path, use this for distributed data mining, and then release it for use by other applications. With high performance network protocols, data mining applications can work effectively with remote gigabyte size data sets over high performance networks. These types of protocols are sometimes several hundred times faster than traditional protocols over the same high performance networks. With specialized data services such as streaming merges, distributed data mining services can effectively correlate distributed gigabyte size data sets.

In this chapter, we have provided experimental evidence that our implementations scale to remote gigabyte-size data sets that can be distributed over thousands of miles and accessed via long haul networks with packet round trip times (RTT) of a hundred milliseconds or more. Compared to current implementations of data mining primitives for merging two data streams and computing counts, our photonic data services are significantly faster. For example, to stream two 1.8 gigabyte data streams of geoscience data using latitude and longitude as keys across the Atlantic, merge the results by key, and compute simple counts required over an hour with conventional services and less than a minute using the photonic data services described in this chapter. We emphasize that both experiments used the same high performance network.

Data webs built with this architecture complement data grids that require authentication, authorization and access controls supplied by Globus and other grid middleware, and the various custom agent based distributed data mining systems that have developed over the past several years. Data webs, and indeed data grids, built over photonic data services are one means of meeting the challenges posed by the large distributed and streaming data sets that will become more common with next generation data mining applications.

Robert Grossman is a professor of mathematics, statistics, and computer science at the University of Illinois at Chicago and Managing Partner of Open Data Partners, LLC. His research interests include high performance and distributed data mining. His web site is: www.lac.uic.edu/ grossman.

Yunhong Gu is a Ph.D candidate in computer science at the University of Illinois at Chicago and a research assistant at the Laboratory for Advanced Computing. His research interests are data mining and high-speed networks.

David Hanley has a bachelor's degree from the University of Illinois at Chicago and is pursuing his master's degree in computer science. He is the coauthor of two computer books and numerous papers and has won a series of computer programming contests.

Xinwei Hong is a postdoctoral research associate at the National Center for Data Mining, University of Illinois at Chicago. He received his Ph.D. in electronics and information engineering from Huazhong University of Science and Technology in 1998. His current research interests include developing high-speed data delivery over high-performance wide-area networks.

Jorge Levera is a Ph.D candidate in computer science at the University of Illinois at Chicago and a research assistant at the Laboratory for Advanced Computing. His research interests are data mining and high-speed networks.

David Lillethun is a research associate at the International Center for Advanced Internet Research. His research interests include control planes for advanced optical networks and intelligent systems for large scale infrastructure based on dynamic wavelength switching.

Joe Mambretti is Director, International Center for Advanced Internet Research, at Northwestern University (www.icair.org), Director, Metropolitan Research and Education Network (www.mren.org), and a partner in the StarLight international advanced networking facility (www.startap.net/starlight)

Marco Mazzucco just completed a postdoctoral fellowship at the Univeristy of Wales, Swansea. He worked on an ESPRERC funded project in theoretic computer science under the direction of Dr. Martin Otto. He currently does research and consulting for the National Center for Data Mining. He received his Ph.D. in mathematics at UIC in 2000.

Jeremy Weinberger is a former research associate at the International Center for Advanced Internet Research, Northwestern University. He is currently enrolled in a Ph.D. program in computer science at New York University. His research interests include systems, distributed systems, large scale infrastructure, advanced networks, and specialized interactive environments.

Chapter 6

Mining Frequent Patterns in Data Streams at Multiple Time Granularities

Chris Giannella, Jiawei Han, Jian Pei,
Xifeng Yan, and Philip S. Yu

Frequent-pattern mining has been studied extensively in data mining, with many algorithms proposed and implemented, for example, Apriori (Agrawal and Srikant 1994), FPgrowth (Han, Pei, and Yin 2000), CLOSET (Pei, Han, and Mao 2000), and CHARM (Zaki and Hsiao 2002). Frequent pattern mining and its associated methods have been popularly used in association rule mining (Agrawal and Srikant 1994), sequential pattern mining (Agrawal and Srikant 1995), structured pattern mining (Kuramochi and Karypis 2001), iceberg cube computation (Beyer and Ramakrishnan 1999), cube gradient analysis (Imielinski, Khachiyan, and Abdulghani 2002), associative classification (Liu, Hsu, and Ma 1998), frequent pattern-based clustering (Wang, Yang, Wang, and Yu 2002), and so on.

Recent emerging applications, such as network traffic analysis, web click stream mining, power consumption measurement, sensor network data analysis, and dynamic tracing of stock fluctuation, call for study of a new kind of data called "stream data." Stream data takes the form of continuous, potentially infinite data streams, as opposed to finite, statically stored data sets. Stream data management systems and continuous stream query processors are under intense investigation and development. Besides querying data streams, another important task is to mine data streams for interesting patterns.

There are some recent studies on mining data streams, including classification of stream data (Domingos and Hulten 2000, Hulten, Spencer, and Domingos 2001) and clustering data streams (Guha, Mishra, Motwani, and O'Callaghan 2000, O'Callaghan, Mishra, Meyerson Guha, and Motwani 2002). However, it is challenging to mine frequent patterns in data streams because mining frequent itemsets is essentially a set of join operations, as illustrated in Apriori, whereas join is a typical *blocking operator,* i.e., computation for any itemset cannot complete before seeing past and future data. Since one can only maintain a limited size window due to the nature of stream data, it is difficult to mine and update frequent patterns in a dynamic, data stream environment.

In this chapter, we study this problem and propose a new methodology: *mining time-sensitive data streams.* Previous work (Manku and Motwani 2002) studied the *landmark model,* which mines frequent patterns in data streams by assuming that patterns are measured from the start of the stream up to the current moment. The landmark model may not be desirable since the set of frequent patterns usually are time-sensitive and in many cases, *changes* of patterns and their trends are more interesting than patterns themselves. For example, a shopping transaction stream could start long time ago (e.g., a few years ago), and the model constructed by treating all the transactions, old or new, equally cannot be very useful at guiding the current business since some old items may have lost their attraction; fashion and seasonal products may change from time to time. Moreover, one may not only want to fade (e.g., reduce the weight of) old transactions but also find changes or evolution of frequent patterns with time. In network monitoring, the changes of the frequent patterns in the past several minutes are valuable and can be used for detection of network intrusions (Dokas, Ertoz, Kumar, Lazarevic, Srivastava, and Tan 2002).

In our design, we actively maintain pattern frequency histories under a tilted-time window framework in order to answer time-sensitive queries. A collection of patterns along with their frequency histories are compressed and stored using a tree structure similar to FP-tree (Han, Pei, and Yin 2000) and updated incrementally with incoming transactions. In Han, Pei, and Yin (2000), the FP-tree provides a base structure to facilitate mining in a static batch environment. In this chapter, an FP-tree is used for storing transactions for the current time window; in addition, a similar tree structure, called *pattern-tree,* is used to store collections of itemsets and their frequency histories. Our time-sensitive stream mining data structure, *FP-stream,* includes two major components: (1) an pattern-tree, and (2) tilted-time windows.

We have organized this chapter in the following way. First, we develop a data structure, FP-stream, supporting time-sensitive mining of frequent patterns in a data stream. Next, we develop an efficient algorithm to incrementally maintain an FP-stream. Then, we describe how time-sensitive queries can be answered over data streams with an error bound guarantee.

The remainder of the chapter is organized as follows. Section 6.1 presents the problem definition and provides a basic analysis of the problem. Section 6.2 presents the FP-stream data structure. Section 6.3 introduces the maintenance of tilted-time windows, while section 6.4 discusses the issues of minimum support. The algorithm is outlined in section 6.5. Section 6.6 reports the results of our experiments and performance study. Section 6.7 discusses how the FP-stream can be extended to included fading time windows. Section 6.8 discusses some of the broader issues in stream data mining and how our approach applies.

6.1 Problem Definition and Analysis

Our task is to mine frequent patterns over arbitrary time intervals in a data stream, assuming that one can only see the set of transactions in a limited size window at any moment.

To study frequent pattern mining in data streams, we first examine the same problem in a transaction database. To justify whether a single item i_a is frequent in a transaction database *DB,* simply scan *DB,* and count the number of transactions in which i_a appears (the frequency). The frequency of every single item can be computed in one scan of *DB.* However, it is too costly to compute, in one scan, the frequency of every possible combination of single items because of the huge number of such combinations. An efficient alternative proposed in the Apriori algorithm (Agrawal and Srikant 1994) is to count only those itemsets whose every proper subset is frequent. That is, at the k-th scan of *DB,* derive the frequent itemsets of length k (where $k \geqslant 1$), and then derive the set of length $(k + 1)$ *candidate itemsets* (i.e. those whose every length k subset is frequent) for the next scan.

There are two difficulties in using an Apriorilike algorithm in a data stream environment. Frequent itemset mining by Apriori is essentially a set of join operations as shown in (Agrawal and Srikant 1994). However, join is a typical *blocking operator* (Babcock, Babu, Datar, Motwani, and Widom 2002), which cannot be performed over stream data since one can only observe at any moment a very limited size window of a data stream.

To ensure the completeness of frequent patterns for stream data, it is necessary to store not only the information related to frequent items, but also that related to infrequent ones. If the information about the currently infrequent items was not stored, such information would be lost. If these items become frequent later, it would be impossible to figure out their correct overall support and their connections with other items. However, it is also unrealistic to hold all streaming data in the limited main memory. Thus, we divide patterns into three categories: *frequent patterns, subfrequent patterns,* and *infrequent patterns.*

Definition 1 The *frequency* of an itemset I over a time period T is the number of transactions in T in which I occurs. The *support* of I is the frequency divided by the total number of transactions observed in T. Let the $min\_support$ be σ and the *relaxation ratio* be $\rho = \epsilon/\sigma$, where ϵ is the maximum support error. I is *frequent* if its support is no less than σ; it is *subfrequent* if its support is less than σ but no less than ϵ; otherwise, it is *infrequent.* ∎

We are only interested in frequent patterns. But we have to maintain subfrequent patterns since they may become frequent later. We want to discard infrequent patterns since the number of infrequent patterns are really large and the loss of support from infrequent patterns will not affect the calculated support too much. The definition of frequent, subfrequent, and infrequent patterns is actually relative to period T. For example, a pattern I may be subfrequent over a period T_1, but it is possible that it becomes infrequent over a longer period T_2 ($T_1 \subset T_2$). In this case, we can conclude that I will not be frequent over period T_2. In our design, the complete structure, FP-stream, consists of two parts: (1) a global frequent pattern-tree held in main memory, and (2) tilted-time windows embedded in this pattern-tree. Incremental updates can be performed on both parts of the FP-stream. Incremental updates occur when some infrequent patterns become (sub)frequent, or vice versa. At any moment, the set of frequent patterns over a period can be obtained from FP-stream residing in the main memory (with a support error bounded above by ϵ).

6.2 Mining Time-Sensitive Frequent Patterns in Data Streams

The design of the *tilted-time window* (Chen, Dong, Han, Wah, and Wang 2002) is based on the fact that people are often interested in recent changes at a fine granularity, but long term changes at a coarse granularity. Figure 6.1 shows such a tilted-time window: the most recent 4 quarters of an hour, then the last 24 hours, and 31 days. Based on this model, one can compute frequent itemsets in the last hour with the precision of a quarter of an hour, the last day with the precision of an hour, etc. This model registers only $4 + 24 + 31 = 59$ units of time, with an acceptable trade-off of lower granularity at distant times.

As shown in figure 6.2, for each tilted-time window, a collection of patterns and their frequencies can be maintained. Assuming these collections

Figure 6.1: Natural tilted-time window frames.

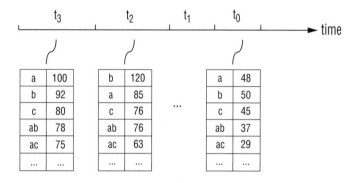

Figure 6.2: Pattern frequencies for tilted-time windows.

contain the frequent patterns (and possibly more), the following queries can be answered: (1) what is the frequent pattern set over the period t_2 and t_3? (2) what are the periods when (a, b) is frequent? (3) does the support of (a) change dramatically in the period from t_3 to t_0? and so on. That is, one can (1) mine frequent patterns in the current window, (2) mine frequent patterns over time ranges with granularity confined by the specification of window size and boundary, (3) put different weights on different windows to mine various kinds of weighted frequent patterns, and (4) mine evolution of frequent patterns based on the changes of their occurrences in a sequence of windows. Thus we have the flexibility to mine a variety of frequent patterns associated with time.

A compact tree representation of the pattern collections, called pattern-tree, can be used. Figure 6.3 shows an example. Each node in the pattern tree represents a pattern (from root to this node) and its frequency is recorded in the node. This tree shares a similar structure with an FP-tree. The difference is that it stores patterns instead of transactions. In fact, we can use the same FP-tree construction method demonstrated by Han, Pei, and Yin (2000) to build this tree by taking the set of patterns as input.

The patterns in adjacent time windows will likely be very similar. Therefore, the tree structure for different tilted-time windows will likely have considerable overlap. Embedding the tilted-time window structure into each node, will likely save considerable space. Thus we propose to use only one pattern

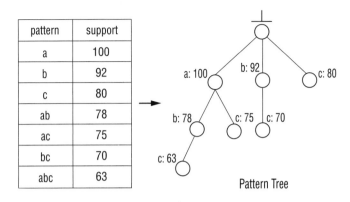

Figure 6.3: Pattern tree.

tree, where at each node, the frequency for each tilted-time window is maintained. Figure 6.4 shows an example of a pattern tree with tilted-time windows embedded. We call this structure an *FP-stream*.

6.3 Maintaining Tilted-Time Windows

With the arrival of new data, the tilted-time window table will grow. In order to make the table compact, tilted-time window maintenance mechanisms are developed based on a tilted-time window construction strategy.

6.3.1 Natural Tilted-Time Window

For the natural tilted-time window discussed before (shown in figure 6.1), the maintenance of windows is straightforward. When four quarters are accumulated, they merge together to constitute one hour. After 24 hours are accumulated, one day is built. In the natural tilted-time window, at most 59 tilted windows need to be maintained for a period of one month. In the following section, we introduce a logarithmic tilted-time window schema, which will reduce the number of tilted-time windows used.

6.3.2 Logarithmic Tilted-Time Window

As an alternative, the tilted-time window frame can also be constructed based on a logarithmic time scale as shown in figure 6.5. Suppose the current window holds the transactions in the current quarter. Then the remaining slots are for the last quarter, the next two quarters, 4 quarters, 8 quarters, 16 quarters, etc.,

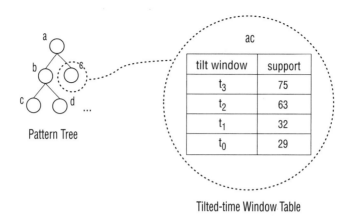

Figure 6.4: Pattern-tree with tilted-time windows embedded.

Figure 6.5: Tilted-time window frame with logarithmic partition.

growing at an exponential rate of 2. According to this model, one year of data will require $log_2(365 \times 24 \times 4) + 1 \approx 17$ units of time instead of $366 \times 24 \times 4 = 35,136$ units. As we can see, the logarithmic tilted-time window schema is very space-efficient.

Formally, we assume that the stream of transactions is broken up into fixed sized batches $B_1, B_2, \ldots, B_n, \ldots$, where B_n is the most current batch and B_1 the oldest. For $i \geqslant j$, let $B(i,j)$ denote $\bigcup_{k=j}^{i} B_k$. For a given itemset, I, let $f_I(i,j)$ denote the frequency of I in $B(i,j)$ (I is omitted if clear from context). A logarithmic tilted-time window is used to record frequencies for itemset I. The following frequencies are kept

$f(n,n); f(n-1, n-1); f(n-2, n-3); f(n-4, n-7), \ldots.$

The ratio r between the size of two neighbor tilted-time windows reflects the growth rate of window size, which usually should be larger than 1. The above example illustrates a logarithmic tilted-time window with ratio of 2. Note that there are $\lceil log_2(n) \rceil + 1$ frequencies. So even for a very large number of batches, the maximum number of frequencies is reasonable (e.g., 10^9 batches requires 31 frequencies).

However, in a logarithmic tilted-time window, intermediate buffer windows need to be maintained. These intermediate windows will replace or be merged with tilted-time windows when they are full.

6.3.3 Logarithmic Tilted-Time Window Updating

Given a new batch of transactions B, we describe how the logarithmic tilted-time window for I is updated. First, replace $f(n, n)$, the frequency at the finest level of time granularity (level 0), with $f(B)$ and shift $f(n, n)$ back to the next finest level of time granularity (level 1). $f(n, n)$ replaces $f(n - 1, n - 1)$ at level 1. Before shifting $f(n-1, n-1)$ back to level 2, check if the intermediate window for level 1 is full. If not, $f(n-1, n-1)$ is not shifted back; instead it is placed in the intermediate window and the algorithm stops (in the example in the previous subsection, the intermediate window for all levels is empty). If the intermediate window is full (say with a frequency f), then $f(n-1, n-1)+f$ is shifted back to level 2. This process continues until shifting stops. Consider the following example over batches $B_1, \ldots, B_8$. The tilted-time window initially looks like

$\quad f(8, 8); f(7, 7); f(6, 5); f(4, 1)$.

$f(8, 8)$ resides in the window for granularity level 0, $f(7, 7)$ for level 1, $f(6, 5)$ for level 2, $f(4, 1)$ for level 3. The intermediate windows at each level are empty and thus not shown. Upon arrival of B_9 we update the tilted-time window

$\quad f(9, 9); f(8, 8)[f(7, 7)]; f(6, 5); f(4, 1)$.

$f(9, 9)$ replaces $f(8, 8)$ at level 0 which is shifted back to level 1 replacing $f(7, 7)$. Since the intermediate window for level 1 is empty, $f(7, 7)$ is put into the window and the shifting stops ([$\ldots$] denotes an intermediate window). Upon arrival of B_{10}, updating requires several steps. First, we replace $f(9, 9)$ by $f(10, 10)$ and shift $f(9, 9)$ back. The intermediate window at level 1 is full, so the frequencies at level 1 are merged (producing $f(8, 7) = f(8, 8) + f(7, 7)$). $f(8, 7)$ is shifted back to level 2 replacing $f(6, 5)$. Since the intermediate window at that level is empty, $f(6, 5)$ is put into the intermediate window and the shifting stops. The result is

$\quad f(10, 10); f(9, 9); f(8, 7)[f(6, 5)]; f(4, 1)$.

Upon arrival of B_{11} we update and get

$\quad f(11, 11); f(10, 10)[f(9, 9)]; f(8, 7)[f(6, 5)]; f(4, 1)$.

Finally, upon arrival of B_{12} we get

$\quad f(12, 12); f(11, 11); f(10, 9); f(8, 5)[f(4, 1)]$.

Notice that *only one* entry is needed in intermediate storage at any granularity level. Hence, the size of the tilted-time window can grow no larger than $2\lceil log_2(N) \rceil + 2$ where N is the number of batches seen thus far in the stream. There are two basic operations in maintaining logarithmic tilted-time windows: One is frequency merging; and the other is entry shifting. For N batches, we would like to know how many such operations need to be done for each pattern. The following claim shows the amortized number of shifting and merging operations need to be done, which shows the efficiency of logarithmic scale partition. For any pattern, the amortized number of shifting and merging operations is the total number of such operations performed over N batches divided by N.

Claim 6.3.1 *In the logarithmic tilted-time window updating, the amortized number of shifting and merging operations for each pattern is* $O(1)$.

6.4 Minimum Support

Let $t_0, \ldots, t_n$ be the tilted-time windows which group the batches seen thus far in the stream, where t_n is the oldest (be careful, this notation differs from that of the B's in the previous section). We denote the window size of t_i (the number of transactions in t_i) by w_i. Our goal is to mine all frequent itemsets whose supports are larger than σ over period $T = t_k \cup t_{k+1} \cup \ldots \cup t_{k'}$ ($0 \leqslant k \leqslant k' \leqslant n$). The size of T is $W = w_k + w_{k+1} + \ldots + w_{k'}$. If we maintained all possible itemsets in all periods no matter whether they were frequent or not, this goal could be met.[1] However, this will require too much space, so we only maintain $f_I(t_0), \ldots, f_I(t_{m-1})$ for some m ($0 \leqslant m \leqslant n$) and drop the remaining tail sequences of tilted-time windows. Specifically, we drop tail sequences $f_I(t_m), \ldots, f_I(t_n)$ when the following condition holds,

$$\forall i, m \leqslant i \leqslant n, f_I(t_i) < \sigma w_i \text{ and } \sum_{j=0}^{i} f_I(t_j) < \epsilon \sum_{j=0}^{i} w_j. \tag{6.1}$$

As a result, we no longer have an exact frequency over T, rather an *approximate frequency* $\hat{f}_I(T) = \sum_{i=k}^{min\{m-1,k'\}} f_I(t_i)$ if $m > k$ and $\hat{f}_I(T) = 0$ if $m \leqslant k$. The approximation is less than the actual frequency

$$f_I(T) - \epsilon W \leqslant \hat{f}_I(T) \leqslant f_I(T). \tag{6.2}$$

Thus if we deliver all itemsets whose approximate frequency is larger than $(\sigma - \epsilon)W$, we will not miss any frequent itemsets in period T Manku and Motwani (2002) discussed the landmark case. However, we may return some itemsets whose frequency is between $(\sigma - \epsilon)W$ and σW. This is reasonable when ϵ is small.

Based on inequality (6.2), we draw the following claim that the pruning of the tail of a tilted-time window table does not compromise our goal.

---

[1] Maintaining only frequent tilted-time window entries will not work. As the stream progresses, infrequent entries may be needed to account for itemsets going from infrequent to frequent.

Claim 6.4.1 *Consider itemset I. Let m be the minimum number satisfying the condition (6.1). We drop the tail frequencies from $f_I(t_m)$ to $f_I(t_n)$. For any period $T = t_k \cup \ldots \cup t_{k'}$ ($0 \leqslant k \leqslant k' \leqslant n$), if $f_I(T) \geqslant \sigma W$, then $\hat{f}_I(T) \geqslant (\sigma - \epsilon)W$.*

The basic idea of claim 6.4.1 is that if we prune I's tilted-time window table to $t_0, \ldots, t_{m-1}$, then we can still find all frequent itemsets (with support error ϵ) over any user-defined time period T. We call this pruning *tail pruning*.

Itemsets and their tilted-time window tables are maintained in the FP-stream data structure. When a new batch B arrives, mine the itemsets from B and update the FP-stream structure. For each I mined in B, if I does not appear in the structure, add I if $f_I(B) \geqslant \epsilon|B|$. If I does appear, add $f_I(B)$ to I's table and then do tail pruning. If all of the windows are dropped, then drop I from FP-stream.

This algorithm will correctly maintain the FP-stream structure, but not very efficiently. We have the following antimonotone property for the frequencies recorded in tilted-time window tables.

Claim 6.4.2 *Consider itemsets $I \subseteq I'$ which are both in the FP-stream structure at the end of a batch. Let $f_I(t_0), f_I(t_1), \ldots, f_I(t_k)$ and $f_{I'}(t_0), f_{I'}(t_1), \ldots, f_{I'}(t_l)$ be the entries maintained in the tilted-time window tables for I and I', respectively. The following statements hold.*

1. $k \geqslant l$.
2. $\forall i, 0 \leqslant i \leqslant l, f_I(t_i) \geqslant f_{I'}(t_i)$.

Claim 6.4.2 shows the property that the frequency of an itemset should be equal to or larger than the support of its supersets still holds under the framework of approximate frequency counting and tilted-time window scenario. Furthermore, the size of the tilted-time window table of I should be equal to or larger than that of its supersets. This claim allows for some pruning in the following way. If I is found in B but is not in the FP-stream structure, then by claim 6.4.2 part 1, no superset is in the structure. Hence, if $f_I(B) < \epsilon|B|$, then none of the supersets need be examined. So the mining of B can prune its search and not visit supersets of I. We call this type of pruning *type I pruning*.

By claim 6.4.1 and 6.4.2, we conclude the following antimonotone property, which can help in efficiently cutting off infrequent patterns.

Claim 6.4.3 *Consider a pattern $I \subseteq I'$, the following statements hold.*

1. *If the tail frequencies $f_I(t_m) \ldots f_I(t_n)$ can be safely dropped based on claim 6.4.1, then I' can safely drop any frequency among $f_{I'}(t_m) \ldots f_{I'}(t_n)$ if it has.*

2. *If all the frequencies $f_I(t_0) \ldots f_I(t_n)$ can be safely dropped based on claim 6.4.1, then I' together with all its frequencies can be safely dropped.*

Claim 6.4.3 part 2 essentially says that if all of I's tilted-time window table entries are pruned (hence I is dropped), then any superset will also be dropped. We call this type of pruning *type II pruning*.

6.5 Algorithm

In this section, we describe in more detail the algorithm for constructing and maintaining the FP-stream structure. In particular we incorporate the pruning techniques into the high-level description of the algorithm given in the previous section.

The update to the FP-stream structure is bulky, done only when enough incoming transactions have arrived to form a new batch B_i. The algorithm treats the first batch differently from the rest as an initialization step. As the transactions for B_1 arrive, the frequencies for all items are computed, and the transactions are stored in main memory. An ordering, *f_list*, is created in which items are ordered by decreasing frequencies (just as was done by Han, Pei, and Yin [2000]). This ordering remains fixed for all remaining batches. Once all the transactions for B_1 have arrived (and stored in memory), the batch in memory is scanned creating an FP-tree pruning all items with frequency less than $\epsilon|B_1|$. Finally, an FP-stream structure is created by mining all ϵ-frequent itemsets from the FP-tree (the batch in memory and transaction FP-tree are discarded). All the remaining batches B_i, for $i \geqslant 2$, are processed according to the algorithm below.

Algorithm 1 (FP-streaming) (Incremental update of the FP-stream structure with incoming stream data)

Input: (1) An FP-stream structure, (2) a $min\_support$ threshold, σ, (3) an error rate, ϵ, and (4) an incoming batch, B_i, of transactions (these actually are arriving one at a time from a stream), (5) an item ordering *f_list*.

Output: The updated FP-stream structure.

Method:

1. Initialize the FP-tree to empty.

2. Sort each incoming transaction t, according to *f_list,* and then insert it into the FP-tree *without* pruning any items.

3. When all the transactions in B_i are accumulated, update the FP-stream as follows.

(a) Mine itemsets out of the FP-tree using FPgrowth algorithm in Han, Pei, and Yin 2000 modified as below. For each mined itemset, I, check if I is in the FP-stream structure. If I is in the structure, do the following.

    i. Add $f_I(B)$ to the tilted-time window table for I as described in section 6.3.3.

    ii. Conduct tail pruning.

    iii. If the table is empty, then FPgrowth stops mining supersets of I (Type II Pruning). Note that the removal of I from the FP-stream structure is deferred until the scanning of the structure (next step).

    iv. If the table is not empty, then FPgrowth continues mining supersets of I.

If I is not in the structure and if $f_I(B) \geqslant \epsilon|B|$, then insert I into the structure (its tilted-time window table will have only one entry, $f_I(B_i)$). Otherwise, FPgrowth stops mining supersets of I (Type I Pruning).

(b) Scan the FP-stream structure (depth-first search). For each itemset I encountered, check if I was updated when B was mined. If not, then insert 0 into I's tilted-time window table (I did not occur in $B)^2$. Prune I's table by tail pruning.

Once the search reaches a leaf, if the leaf has an empty tilted-time window table, then drop the leaf. If there are any siblings of the leaf, continue the search with them. If there were no siblings, then return to the parent and continue the search with its siblings. Note that if all of the children of the parent were dropped, then the parent becomes a leaf node and might be dropped. ∎

6.6 Performance Study and Experiments

In this section, we report our performance study. We describe first our experimental set-up and then our results.

6.6.1 Experimental Set-Up

Our algorithm was written in C and compiled using gcc with the -lm switch. All of our experiments are performed on a SUN Ultra-5 workstation using a

---

[2] By recording some additional time-stamp information, these zero tilted-time window entries could be dropped. However, in the interests of simplicity, we did not do so and leave it for future work.

333 MHz Sun UltraSPARC-IIi processor, 512 MB of RAM, and 1350 MB of virtual memory. The operating system in use was SunOS 5.8. All experiments were run without any other users on the machine.

The stream data was generated by the IBM synthetic market-basket data generator, (managed by the Quest data mining group).[3] In all the experiments 3M transactions were generated using 1K distinct items. The average number of items per transaction was varied as described below. The default values for all other parameters of the synthetic data generator were used (i.e., number of patterns 10000, average length of the maximal pattern 4, correlation coefficient between patterns 0.25, and average confidence in a rule 0.75).

The stream was broken into batches of size 50K transactions and fed into our program through standard input. The support threshold σ was varied (as described below) and ϵ was set to 0.1σ.[4] Note that the underlying statistical model used to generate the transactions does not change as the stream progresses. We feel that this does not reflect reality well. In reality, seasonal variations may cause the underlying model (or parameters of it) to shift in time. A simple-minded way to capture some of this shifting effect is to periodically, randomly permute some item names. To do this, we use an item mapping table, M. The table initially maps all item names to themselves (i.e. $M(i) = i$). However, for every five batches 200 random permutations are applied to the table[5].

6.6.2   Experimental Results

We performed two sets of experiments. In the first set of experiments, σ was fixed at 0.005 (0.5 percent) and ϵ at 0.0005. In the second set of experiments σ was fixed at 0.0075 and ϵ at 0.00075. In both sets of experiments three separate data sets were fed into the program. The first had an average transaction length 3, the second 5, and the third 7. At each batch the following statistics were collected: the total number of seconds required per batch (TIME),[6] the size of the FP-stream structure at the end of each batch in bytes (SIZE),[7] the total number of itemsets held in the FP-stream structure at the end of the batch (NUM ITEMSETS), and the average length of an itemset in the FP-stream at the end of each batch (AVE LEN). In all graphs presented the x axis represents the batch number. Moreover "support" is used to denote σ.

---

[3] Available at http://www.almaden.ibm.com/cs/quest/syndata.html/#assocSynData

[4] Not all 3M transactions are processed. In some cases only 41 batches are processed (2.05M transactions), in other cases 55 batches (2.75M transactions).

[5] A random permutation of table entries i and j means that $M(i)$ is swapped with $M(j)$. When each transaction $\{i_1, \ldots, i_k\}$ is read from input, before it is processed, it is transformed to $\{M(i_1), \ldots, M(i_k)\}$.

[6] Includes the time to read transactions from standard input.

[7] Does not include the temporary FP-tree structure used for mining the batch.

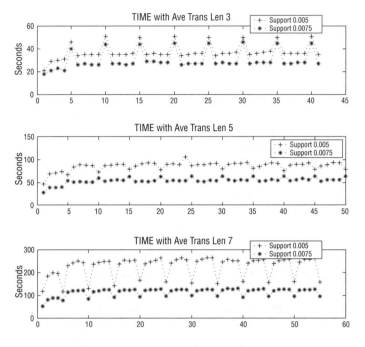

Figure 6.6: FP-stream time requirements.

Figures 6.6 and 6.7 show TIME and SIZE results, respectively. In each figure the top graph shows the results for average transaction length 3, the middle one shows average transaction length 5, and the bottom one shows average transaction length 7.

As expected, the item permutation causes the behavior of the algorithm to jump at every five batches. But, stability is regained quickly. In general, the time and space requirements of the algorithm tend to stabilize or grow very slowly as the stream progresses (despite the random permutations). For example, the time required with average transaction length 5 and support 0.0075 (middle graph figure 6.6) seems to stabilize at 50 seconds with very small bumps at every 5 batches. The space required (middle graph figure 6.7) seems to stabilize at roughly 350K with small bumps. The stability results are quite nice as they provide evidence that the algorithm can handle long data streams.

The overall space requirements are very modest in all cases (less than 3M). This can easily fit into main memory. To analyze the time requirements, first recall that the algorithm is to be used in a batch environment. So, we assume that while the transactions are accumulating for a batch, updates to the FP-stream structure from the previous batch can be commencing. The primary

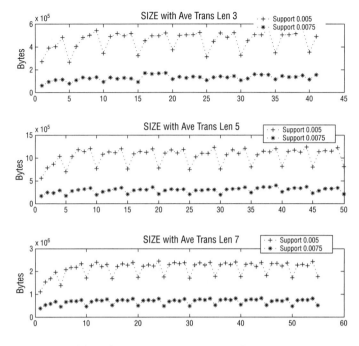

Figure 6.7: FP-stream space requirements.

requirement, in our opinion, is that the algorithm not fall behind the stream. In other words, as long as the FP-stream structure can be updated before the next batch of transactions is processed, the primary requirement is met. Consider the case of average transaction length three and $\sigma = 0.0075$ (top graph in figure 6.6). The time stabilizes to roughly 25 seconds per batch. Hence, the algorithm can handle a stream with arrival rate 2000 transaction per second (batch size divided by time). This represents the best case of our experiments. In the worst case (average transaction length 7 and $\sigma = 0.0075$) the rate is roughly 180 transactions per second. While this rate is not as large as we would like, we feel that considerable improvement can be obtained since the implementation is currently simple and straight-forward with no optimizations.

In some circumstances it is acceptable to only mine small itemsets. If the assumption is made that only small itemsets are needed, then the algorithm can prune away a great deal of work. Figure 6.8 shows the time performance of the algorithm when the length of the itemsets mined in bounded by two. We see that the times for average transaction length 3 (figure 6.8 top graph) are not much smaller than those where all itemsets were mined (figure 6.6 top graph). But the difference is significant for average transaction length 7. Here

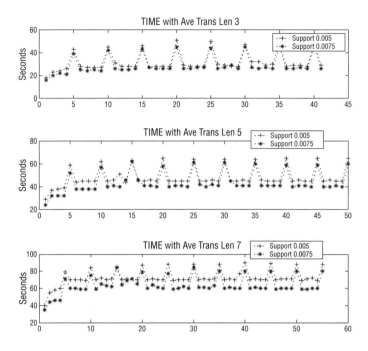

Figure 6.8: FP-stream time requirements—itemset lengths mined are bounded by two.

the algorithm with itemsets of length bounded by two at support 0.005 can handle a stream with arrival rate 556 transactions pre second (the unbounded itemset lengths algorithm could handle a rate of 180).

An interesting observation can be made concerning the spikes and troughs in figures 6.6 and 6.7. Considering SIZE we see that the random permutations cause a narrow trough (drop) in space usage. We conjecture that the permutations cause some itemsets in the tree to be dropped due to a sharp decrease in their frequency. Considering TIME we see that the permutations cause a narrow spike (increase) in the top graph at both support thresholds. In the middle graph the spiking behavior persists for threshold 0.0075 but switches to troughs for threshold 0.005. Finally, in the bottom graph, troughs can be seen for both thresholds.

The switching from spikes to troughs is an interesting phenomena. As of yet we do not know its cause but do put forth a conjecture. When an item permutation occurs, many itemsets that appear in the FP-stream structure no longer appear in the new batch and many itemsets that do not appear in the structure appear in the new batch. This results in two competing factors: (1)

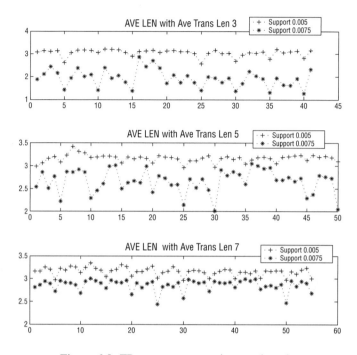

Figure 6.9: FP-stream average itemset length.

mining the batch requires less work because itemsets in the structure that do not appear in the batch need not be updated; and (2) mining the batch requires more work because itemsets not in the structure that were subfrequent in the current batch need be added. When the average transaction length is small (say 3), condition (2) dominates—resulting in a spike. When it is large (say 7), condition (1) dominates—resulting in a trough.

Finally, we describe some results concerning the nature of the itemsets in the FP-stream structure. Figures 6.9 and 6.10 show the average itemset length and the total number of itemsets, respectively.[8]

Note that while the average itemset length does not seem to increase with average transaction length, the number of itemsets does. This is consistent with our running the Apriori program of C. Borgelt[9] on two datasets consisting of 50K transactions, 1K items, and average transaction lengths 5 and 7, respectively. The support threshold in each case was 0.0005 (corresponding to ϵ in our $\sigma = 0.005$ experiments). The itemsets produced by Apriori should be exactly the same as those in the FP-stream after the first batch (the leftmost point

---

[8]The maximum itemset length was between 8 and 11 in all experiments.
[9]fuzzy.cs.uni-magdeburg.de/ borgelt/software. html/#assoc

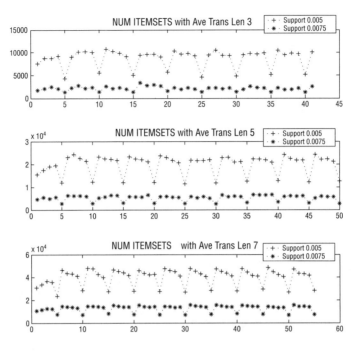

Figure 6.10: FP-stream total number of itemsets.

in middle and bottom graphs in figure 6.10). We observed that the make-up of the itemset lengths from Apriori was nearly the same for both datasets: $\approx 3\%$ size one, $\approx 33\%$ size two, $\approx 23\%$ size three, $\approx 18\%$ size four, $\approx 12\%$ size five, $\approx 7\%$ size six, $\approx 3\%$ size seven, and $\approx 1\%$ sizes eight, nine, and ten combined.

6.7   Time Fading Framework

In the previous discussion, we introduced natural and logarithmic tilted-time window partitions. Both of them give finer granularity to the recent and coarser granularity to the past. However, they do not discount the support of past transactions. In order to discount the past transactions, we introduce a fading factor ϕ. Suppose we have fixed sized batches $B_1, B_2, \ldots, B_n$, where B_n is the most current batch and B_1 the oldest. For $i \geq j$, let $B(i, j)$ denote $\bigcup_{k=j}^{i} B_k$. For $B(i, j)$, the actual window size is $\sum_{k=j}^{i} |B_k|$. In a fading framework, the faded window size for $B(i, j)$ is $\sum_{k=j}^{i} \phi^{i-k} |B_k|$ and its faded support is $\sum_{k=j}^{i} \phi^{i-k} f_I(B_k)$. We do not change Algorithm 1, that means, we still drop infrequent patterns whose support is less than ϵ. Assume the real faded support of I for $B(i,j)$ is $f_I = \sum_{k=j}^{i} \phi^{i-k} f_I(B_k)$, the approximate support we get for I is $\hat{f}_I$, then we have

$$f_I - \epsilon \sum_{k=j}^{i} \phi^{i-k} |B_k| \leqslant \hat{f}_I \leqslant f_I \qquad (6.3)$$

Inequality (6.3) is consistent with inequality (6.2) if actual support is replaced with faded support and the actual window size is replaced with the faded window size. When we merge two tilted-time windows, t_i and t_{i+1}, the merged frequency is $\hat{f}_I(t_i) + \hat{f}_I(t_{i+1}) \times \phi^{l_i}$, where l_i is the number of batches contained in tiled-time window t_i. As we can see, our tilted-time window framework also works for time fading model by changing the definition of merging operation. The claims discussed before also hold for the time fading model.

6.8   Broader Stream Mining Issues

In the last few years a great deal of work has been conducted on the managing and mining of stream data (see Babcock, Babu, Datar, Motwani, and Widom [2002] for a good survey). One of the broader issues addressed is the development of systems for processing queries on data streams. For example, the data stream management system (DSMS) at Stanford University aims to serve the analogous role of a relational DBMS on data streams. Also, the issue of stream data mining has been addressed by extending static data mining models to a stream environment — classification (Domingos and Hulten 2000; Hulten, Spencer, and Domingos 2001), clustering (Guha, Mishra, Motwani, and O'Callaghan 2000; O'Callaghan, Mishra, Meyerson Guha, and Motwani 2002), and frequent itemset discovery (Manku and Motwani 2002).

Dong, Han, Lakshmanan, Pei, Wang, and Yu (2003) argue that "online mining of the changes in data streams is one of the core issues" in stream data mining and that the previously mentioned studies have not addressed this issue substantially. Dong and colleagues describe three categories of research problems: modeling and representation of changes, mining methods, and interactive exploration of changes.

Modeling and representation of changes refers to the development of query languages for specifying mining queries on changes in data streams and the development of methods of summarizing and representing discovered changes. Mining methods refers to the development of efficient algorithms for evaluating specific change mining queries as well as general queries specified by a change mining query language. Finally, interactive exploration of changes refers to the development of methods to support a user's evaluation of changes. For example, a user may initially want to monitor changes at a high level, then more closely inspect the details of interesting high-level changes.

We envision the FP-stream model as a foundation upon which frequent itemset change mining queries can be answered. For example, the change in frequency of itemsets across multiple time granularities can be computed.

Acknowledgments

We express our thanks to An-Hai Doan for his constructive comments on a draft of the paper. Our work was supported in part by U.S. National Science Foundation (NSF) IIS-02-09199 and (NSF) IIS-08-08215, the University of Illinois, and an IBM faculty award. C. Giannella thanks the National Science Foundation for their support through grant IIS-0082407.

Chris Giannella is a Ph.D. candidate in computer science at Indiana Univeristy, Bloomington. He can be reached at cgiannel@acm.org.

Jiawei Han is a professor of computer science at the University of Illinois at Urbana-Champaign. He can be reached at hanj@cs.uiuc.edu.

Jian Pei is an assistant professor of computer science and engineering at State University of New York at Buffalo. He can be reached at www.cse.buffalo.edu/faculty/jianpei or jianpei@cse.buffalo.edu.

Xifeng Yan is a Ph.D. candidate in computer science at the University of Illinois at Urbana-Champaign. He can be reached at xyan@uiuc.edu.

Philip S. Yu is a manager of software tools and techniques at IBM T. J. Watson Research Center specializing in data mining and database systems. He can be reached at psyu@us.ibm.com.

Chapter 7

Efficient Data-Reduction Methods for On-Line Association Rule Discovery

Hervé Brönnimann, Bin Chen, Manoranjan Dash,
Peter Haas, and Peter Scheuermann

The volume of electronically accessible data in warehouses and on the internet is growing faster than the speedup in processing times predicted by Moore's Law (Winter and Auerbach 1998). Consequently, classical data mining algorithms that require one or more computationally intensive passes over the entire database are becoming prohibitively slow, and this problem will only become worse in the future. The scalability of mining algorithms has therefore become a major research topic. One approach to the scalability problem is to run data mining algorithms on a small subset of the data, sometimes called a *synopsis* or *sketch*. This strategy can yield useful approximate results in a fraction of the time required to compute the exact solution, thereby speeding up the mining process by orders of magnitude.

A number of synopses have been proposed in the literature (Gibbons and Matias 1999) but many of them require one or more expensive passes over all of the data. Using a sample of the data as the synopsis is a popular technique that can scale well as the data grows. Another nice property of sampling methods is that it is often possible to explicitly trade off processing speed and accuracy of results. Recent work in the area of approximate aggregation processing (Acharya, Gibbons, and Poosala 2000; Manku and Motwani 2002) shows that the benefits of sampling are most fully realized when the sampling technique is tailored to the specific problem at hand. In this spirit we investigate sampling methods that are designed to work with mining algorithms for *count* datasets, that is, datasets in which there is a base set of "items" and each data element is a vector of item counts — here "items" may correspond to physical items, responses on a survey, income levels, and so forth. As a first step, we present and compare two novel data-reduction methods in the context of the most well-studied mining problem defined on count data: the discovery of association rules in large transaction databases.

The two algorithms that we consider are similar in that both attempt to produce a sample whose "distance" from the complete database is minimal. The algorithms differ greatly, however, in the way they greedily search through the exponential number of possible samples. As we will soon discuss, the choice of which algorithm to use depends on the desired tradeoff between speed of computation and accuracy of results, the amount of available memory, and other factors. The first algorithm, finding association rules from sampled transactions (FAST) was recently presented in Chen, Haas, and Scheuermann (2002). FAST starts with a large random sample and trims away "outlier" transactions to produce a small final sample that more accurately reflects the entire database. The second algorithm, epsilon approximation (EA), is new. The EA algorithm repeatedly and deterministically halves the data to obtain the final sample. Unlike FAST, the EA algorithm provides a guaranteed upper bound on the distance between the sample and the entire database.

After presenting and comparing the FAST and EA algorithms, we will show how the EA approach can potentially be adapted to provide data-reduction schemes for streaming data systems. The proposed schemes favor recent data while still retaining partial information about all of the data seen so far.

This chapter is organized as follows. The FAST and EA algorithms are described and compared in section 7.1, and guidelines are given for their usage. In section 7.2 we discuss a possible approach for applying the EA data-reduction method to streaming data. Section 7.3 contains our conclusions and directions for future work.

7.1 Sampling-Based Association Rule Mining

Agrawal, Imielinski, and Swami (1993) proposed association rules as a means of identifying relationships among sets of items, which can be used to evaluate business trends, identify purchasing patterns, and classify customer groups.

Two measures, called *support* and *confidence*, are introduced by Agrawal, Imielinski, and Swami (1993) in order to quantify the significance of an association rule. The mining of association rules from a set of transactions is the process of identifying all rules having support and confidence greater than specified minimum levels; such rules are said to have "minimum confidence and support." We focus on the problem of finding the "frequent" itemsets, i.e., the itemsets having minimum support, because this operation is by far the most expensive phase of the mining process. We assume that the reader is familiar with the basic Apriori algorithm, introduced in Agrawal, Imielinski, and Swami (1993), for identifying frequent itemsets. A variety of modifications have been proposed to reduce the computational burden — see, for example, the papers and references therein by Agarwal, Agarwal, and Prasad (2000) and Han, Pei, and Yin (2000) — but with few exceptions all current algorithms require at least one expensive pass over the data.

Throughout this section, we assume that the contents of the transactional database do not change during the mining process. We also assume that the database is very large. Denote by D the database of interest, by S a simple random sample drawn without replacement from D, and by I the set of all items that appear in D. Also denote by $\mathcal{I}(D)$ the collection of itemsets that appear in D; a set of items A is an element of $\mathcal{I}(D)$ if and only if the items in A appear jointly in at least one transaction $t \in D$. If A contains exactly k (≥ 1) elements, then A is sometimes called a k-itemset. The collection $\mathcal{I}(S)$ denotes the itemsets that appear in S; of course, $\mathcal{I}(S) \subseteq \mathcal{I}(D)$. For $k \geq 1$ we denote by $\mathcal{I}_k(D)$ and $\mathcal{I}_k(S)$ the collection of k-itemsets in D and S, respectively. Similarly, $L(D)$ and $L(S)$ denote the frequent itemsets in D and S, and $L_k(D)$ and $L_k(S)$ the collection of frequent k-itemsets in D and S, respectively. For an itemset $A \subseteq I$ and a set of transactions T, let $n(A; T)$ be the number of transactions in T that contain A and let $|T|$ be the total number of transactions in T. Then the support of A in D and in S is given by $f(A; D) = n(A; D)/|D|$ and $f(A; S) = n(A; S)/|S|$, respectively.

7.1.1 FAST

Given a specified minimum support p and confidence c, the FAST algorithm for data reduction proceeds as follows:

1. Obtain a simple random sample S from D.

2. Compute $f(A; S)$ for each 1-itemset $A \in \mathcal{I}_1(S)$.

3. Using the supports computed in step 2, obtain the final small sample S_0 from S.

4. Run a standard association-rule mining algorithm against S_0 — with

minimum support p and confidence c — to obtain the final set of association rules.

Steps 1, 2, and 4 are straightforward. The drawing of a sample in Step 1 can be performed with a computational cost of $O(|S|)$ and a memory cost of $O(|S|)$. The computational cost of step 2 is at most $O(T_{\max} \cdot |S|)$, where $T_{\max}$ denotes the maximal transaction length. From a computational point of view, because the cost of step 2 is relatively low, the sample S can be relatively large, thereby helping to ensure that the estimated supports are accurate. Step 4 computes the frequent itemsets using a standard association rule mining algorithm such as Apriori (Agrawal and Srikant 1994).

The crux of the algorithm is step 3. Two approaches (trimming and growing) for computing the final small sample S_0 from S are given in Chen, Haas, and Scheuermann (2002). In this chapter, we discuss only the trimming method, which removes the "outlier" transactions from the sample S to obtain S_0. In this context an outlier is defined as a transaction whose removal from the sample maximally reduces (or minimally increases) the difference between the supports of the 1-itemsets in the sample and the corresponding supports in the database D. Since the supports of the 1-itemsets in D are unknown, we estimate them by the corresponding supports in S as computed in step 2. To make the notion of difference between 1-itemset supports precise we define a distance function, based on the symmetric set difference, by setting

$$Dist_1(S_0, S) = \frac{|L_1(S) - L_1(S_0)| + |L_1(S_0) - L_1(S)|}{|L_1(S_0)| + |L_1(S)|} \qquad (7.1)$$

for each subset $S_0 \subseteq S$. In accordance with our previous notation, $L_1(S_0)$ and $L_1(S)$ denote the sets of frequent 1-itemsets in S_0 and S. Observe that $Dist_1$ takes values in $[0, 1]$, and that it is sensitive to both false frequent 1-itemsets and missed frequent 1-itemsets. Our goal is to trim away transactions from S so that the distance from the final sample S_0 to the initial sample S is as small as possible. Other definitions of distance are possible, for example based on the L_2 metric between the frequency vectors:

$$Dist_2(S_0, S) = \sum_{A \in \mathcal{I}_1(S)} \left(f(A; S_0) - f(A; S) \right)^2. \qquad (7.2)$$

The basic FAST-TRIM algorithm is given in figure 7.1. By choosing a value of k between 1 and $|S|$, the user can strike a balance between ineffective but cheap "oblivious" trimming and very effective but very expensive "pure greedy" trimming. For more details on different aspects of FAST such as distance functions, variants of FAST, stopping criteria, detailed algorithm, and complexity analyses see Chen, Haas, and Scheuermann (2002). In addition, the addendum gives some previously unpublished implementation details and complexity analyses for the trimming step.

obtain a simple random sample S from D;
compute $f(A; S)$ for each item A in S;
set $S_0 = S$;
while $(|S_0| > n)$ { //trimming phase
    divide S_0 into disjoint groups of $\min(k, |S_0|)$
      transactions each;
    for each group G {
      compute $f(A; S_0)$ for each item A in S_0;
      set $S_0 = S_0 - \{t^*\}$, where
        $Dist(S_0 - \{t^*\}, S) = \min_{t \in G} Dist(S_0 - \{t\}, S)$;
    }
}
run a standard association-rule algorithm against S_0
    to obtain the final set of association rules;

Figure 7.1: The FAST-TRIM algorithm.

7.1.2   Epsilon Approximation

The epsilon approximation method is similar to FAST in that it tries to find a small subset having 1-itemset supports that are close to those in the entire database. The "discrepancy" of any subset S_0 of a superset S (that is, the distance between S_0 and S with respect to the 1-itemset frequencies) is computed as the L_∞ distance between the frequency vectors:

$$Dist_\infty(S_0, S) = \max_{A \in \mathcal{I}_1(S)} \left| f(A; S_0) - f(A; S) \right| \tag{7.3}$$

where A is an 1-itemset. The sample S_0 is called an ε-approximation of S if its discrepancy is bounded by ε. Obviously there is a trade-off between the size of the sample and ε: the smaller the sample, the larger the value of ε. For literature on ε-approximations, see, for example, *The Discrepancy Method* by Chazelle (2000).

The Halving Method

We now explain how we compute the approximations. At the heart of the epsilon approximation method is a method that computes a subset S_0 of approximately half the size. We use a variant due to Chazelle and Matoušek of the hyperbolic cosine method. (See, for example, chapter 15 of *The Probabilistic Method* by Alon and Spencer [1992], and chapter 1 of Chazelle's *The Discrepancy Method* [2000]). To start with, S is D, the entire database. The method scans sequentially through the transactions in S, and for each one makes the decision to color that transaction blue or red. At the beginning all transactions are grey (i.e., uncolored); at the end, all the transactions are colored, with the red transactions forming a set S_r and the blue a set S_b. Both sets have approximately the same size, so choosing either one as S_0 will do. Repeated iterations of this halving procedure results in the smallest subset S_0 for which $Dist_\infty(S_0, S) \leq \varepsilon$. Thus, while FAST terminates when it reaches a sample of a desired size, the epsilon approximation terminates when it detects that further subdivision will cause the distance to exceed the upper bound ε.

Specifically, let $m = |\mathcal{I}_1(S)|$ be the number of items. For each item A_i we define a penalty Q_i as follows. Intuitively this penalty will shoot up when the item is under- or over-sampled; how quickly depends on a constant $\delta_i \in (0, 1)$, whose value is given by (7.6) below. Denote by S^i the set of all transactions that contain item A_i and suppose that we have colored the first j transactions. Then the penalty Q_i is given by

$$Q_i = Q_i^{(j)} = (1 + \delta_i)^{r_i}(1 - \delta_i)^{b_i} + (1 - \delta_i)^{r_i}(1 + \delta_i)^{b_i} \tag{7.4}$$

where $r_i = r_i^{(j)}$ and $b_i = b_i^{(j)}$ are the numbers of red and blue transactions in S^i. Initially, $r_i = b_i = 0$ for each i, and so $Q_i = Q_i^{(0)} = 2$. In order to decide how to color transactions, we introduce the global penalty $Q = \sum_{1 \leq i \leq m} Q_i$. Assuming that the colors of the first j transactions have been chosen, there are two choices for the $(j + 1)^{th}$ transaction. Coloring it red yields $Q_i^{(j\|r)} = (1 + \delta_i)^{r_i+1}(1 - \delta_i)^{b_i} + (1 - \delta_i)^{r_i+1}(1 + \delta_i)^{b_i}$ while coloring it blue yields $Q_i^{(j\|b)} = (1 + \delta_i)^{r_i}(1 - \delta_i)^{b_i+1} + (1 - \delta_i)^{r_i}(1 + \delta_i)^{b_i+1}$. It is readily verified that $Q_i^{(j)} = \frac{1}{2}(Q_i^{(j\|r)} + Q_i^{(j\|b)})$. Summing over all items, we get $Q^{(j)} = \frac{1}{2}(Q^{(j\|r)} + Q^{(j\|b)})$, where $Q^{(j\|r)}$ and $Q^{(j\|b)}$ denote the global penalties incurred for coloring a transaction red or blue, respectively. Hence, there is one choice of color c for $(j + 1)^{th}$ transaction such that $Q^{(j\|c)} \leq Q^{(j)}$, and this is the color chosen for the transaction. At the end of the coloring, we have $Q^{final} \leq Q^{init} = 2m$. Since all the Q_i's are positive, this implies that, for each item, we have also $Q_i^{final} \leq 2m$. If $r_i = r_i^{(n)}$ and $b_i = b_i^{(n)}$ denote the final numbers of red and blue transactions in S^i, we have $r_i + b_i = |S^i|$. Hence

$$2m \geq (1 + \delta_i)^{r_i}(1 - \delta_i)^{b_i}$$
$$\geq (1 + \delta_i)^{r_i - b_i}(1 - \delta_i^2)^{|S^i|}$$

and the same bound holds when exchanging r_i and b_i, from which it follows that

$$|r_i - b_i| \leq \frac{\ln(2m)}{\ln(1 + \delta_i)} + \frac{|S^i| \ln(1/(1 - \delta_i^2))}{\ln(1 + \delta_i)}. \tag{7.5}$$

We can choose the value of δ_i to make the right side of equation (7.5) small. The first (resp., second) term in the sum is decreasing (resp. increasing) in δ_i, and so a reasonable choice is to balance the two terms, leading to

$$\delta_i = \sqrt{1 - \exp\left(-\frac{\ln(2m)}{|S^i|}\right)}. \qquad (7.6)$$

Since $x = \ln(2m)/|S^i|$ is typically very small whenever $|S^i|$ is reasonably large, substituting the approximations $1 - \exp(-x) \approx x$ into (7.6) and $\ln(1 + x) \approx x$ into (7.5) implies that $|r_i - b_i| = O\left(\sqrt{|S^i|\log(2m)}\right)$. Note that if $|S^i|$ is not too small, the latter quantity is much less than $|S^i|$. Hence, there are about as many red as blue transactions in S^i for each item. Since $r_i + b_i = |S^i|$, this also means that

$$\left|r_i - |S^i|/2\right| = O\left(\sqrt{|S^i|\log(2m)}\right). \qquad (7.7)$$

In order to guarantee that there are about as many transactions in S_r as in S_b, we can add a (fictitious) item A_0 that is contained in all transactions. In that case, $|S_r| - |S_b|$ is also $O\left(\sqrt{n\ln(2m)}\right)$, and this implies that $|S_r| = n/2 + O\left(\sqrt{n\ln(2m)}\right)$. Dividing equation (7.7) by S_r (or by $n/2$), we get that for each i,

$$|f(A_i; S_r) - f(A_i; S)| \leq \varepsilon(n, m) = O\left(\sqrt{\ln(2m)/n}\right).$$

In practice, the halving method will work with any choice of δ_i, but the bounds on $|f(A_i; S_r) - f(A_i; S)|$ will not necessarily be guaranteed. In the implementation, we have found that setting

$$\delta_i = \sqrt{1 - \exp\left(-\frac{\ln(2m)}{n}\right)}$$

is very effective. The advantage is that if the defining parameters of the database, i.e., the number n of transactions and number m of items, are already known then the halving method requires a single scan of the database.

The implementation works as follows: first it initializes all the r_i, b_i, δ_i and Q_i as indicated. Then it performs the scan, for each transaction deciding whether to color it red or blue as given by the penalties. In order to update the penalties, it is better to store both terms of Q_i separately into two terms $Q_{i,1}$ and $Q_{i,2}$. The penalties are then updated according to equation (7.4) and the color chosen for the transaction. The red transactions are added to the sample, and the blue are forgotten. The memory required by the halving method is

for each $i = 1$ to m {
    set $\delta_i = \left(1 - \exp(-\ln(2m)/n)\right)^{1/2}$
    set $Q_{i,1} = Q_{i,2} = 1$
}
for each transaction j do {
    for each item i contained in j {
        compute $Q_{i,1}^{(r)} = (1 + \delta_i)Q_{i,1}$, $Q_{i,2}^{(r)} = (1 - \delta_i)Q_{i,2}$;
        compute $Q_{i,1}^{(b)} = (1 - \delta_i)Q_{i,1}$, $Q_{i,2}^{(b)} = (1 + \delta_i)Q_{i,2}$;
    }
    set $Q^{(r)} = \sum_i Q_{i,1}^{(r)} + Q_{i,2}^{(r)}$ and $Q^{(b)} = \sum_i Q_{i,1}^{(b)} + Q_{i,2}^{(b)}$
    with the sum taken over those items i contained in j;
    if $Q^{(r)} < Q^{(b)}$ then
        color j red, and set $Q_{i,1} = Q_{i,1}^{(r)}$ and $Q_{i,2} = Q_{i,2}^{(r)}$
    else
        color j blue, and set $Q_{i,1} = Q_{i,1}^{(b)}$ and $Q_{i,2} = Q_{i,2}^{(b)}$;
}
return $S_0 = S_r$, the set of red transactions;

Figure 7.2: The EA-HALVING algorithm.

proportional only to the number $m = |\mathcal{I}_1(S)|$ of 1-itemsets, in order to store the penalties.

A further improvement in performance is obtained if we realize that only the penalties for the items contained in the current transaction need to be recomputed, not all m of them. Hence the halving method processes a transaction in time proportional to the number of items that it contains, and the entire halving takes time proportional to the size of the database (number of transactions), so that the worst-case total time complexity is $O(T_{\max} \cdot |S|)$, which is much smaller than $O(|\mathcal{I}_1(S)| \cdot |S|)$. The EA-halving method sketched above is summarized in figure 7.2; we assume in the figure that n and m are known.

Computing the Approximation

Having fixed ε, we compute an ε-approximation as follows. Note that the halving method computes an $\varepsilon(n, m)$-approximation of size $n/2$, where $\varepsilon(n, m) = O(\sqrt{\ln(2m)/n})$. (Note: $O(\sqrt{\ln(2m)/n})$ is a very small value when m is polynomially bounded in n and n is large). There is a key structural property that we can use to reduce the size of approximations (Chazelle 2000,

Lem. 4.2): if S_1 is an ε_1-approximation of S and S_2 an ε_2-approximation of S_1, then S_2 is an $(\varepsilon_1 + \varepsilon_2)$-approximation of S. Thus approximations can be *composed* by simply adding the discrepancies.

The repeated halving method starts with S, and applies one round of halving (as described in EA-HALVING) to get S_1, then another round of halving to S_1 to get S_2, etc. The sizes $n_1 \geq n_2 \geq \ldots$ of these samples decrease roughly geometrically by a factor of two—specifically, $n_1 \leq n\big(0.5 + \varepsilon(n, m)\big)$ and $n_{i+1} \leq n_i\big(0.5 + \varepsilon(n_i, m)\big)$. Note that by the above observation, S_t is an ε_t-approximation, where $\varepsilon_t = \sum_{k \leq t} \varepsilon(n_k, m)$. We stop the repeated halving for the maximum t such that $\varepsilon_t \leq \varepsilon$.

Implemented naively, the repeated halving method would require t passes over the database. However, observe that the halving process is inherently sequential in deciding the color of a transaction, and that either color may be chosen as the sample. Say we always choose the red transactions as our sample. In a single pass, we may store all the penalties of each halving method and proceed for each transaction as follows: based on the penalties of the first halving method, we decide whether to color that transaction red or not in the first sample. Should this transaction be red, we again compute the penalties of the second halving method, etc. until either the transaction is colored blue in a sample, or it belongs to the sample S_t. (Since the samples are expected to decrease by half at each level, setting $t = \log n$ will do.) Thus all the repeated halving methods can be run simultaneously, in a single pass. The memory required by this algorithm is thus $O(m \log n) = O(|\mathcal{I}_1(s)| \log |S|)$.

7.1.3 Comparison of FAST and EA

In this section we present an experimental comparison between FAST and EA. To compare FAST and EA, we used both synthetic and real-world databases in our experiments; we restrict ourselves here to reporting the results for the synthetic database and the trimming version of FAST. The synthetic database was generated using code from the IBM QUEST project (Agrawal and Srikand 1994). The parameter settings for synthetic data generation are similar to those written by (Agrawal and Srikand 1994): the total number of items was set to 1000, the number of transactions was set to 100,000, the number of maximal potentially frequent itemsets was set to 2000, the average length of transactions was 10, and the average length of maximal potentially frequent itemsets was 4. We used a minimum support value of 0.77%, at which level there are a reasonable number of frequent itemsets, and the length of the maximal frequent itemset is 6.

In addition to EA and FAST, we also performed experiments with simple random sampling (denoted SRS in the figures) in order to relate the current results to those previously reported by Chen, Haas, and Scheuermann (2002).

These latter results showed that FAST achieves the same or higher accuracy (between 90-95%) using a final sample that is only a small fraction (15 -35%) of a simple random sample.

To make a fair comparison between the three algorithms we used Apriori in all cases to compute the frequent itemsets and used a common set of functions for performing I/O. We used a publicly available implementation of Apriori written by Christian Borgelt.[1] This implementation, which uses prefix trees, is reasonably fast and has been incorporated into a commercial data mining package. FAST was implemented using distance functions $Dist_1$ and $Dist_2$. A 30% simple random sample was chosen as S. For the parameter k, the group size in the FAST-TRIM algorithm, we chose a value of 10 since this was shown to be a reasonable choice in Chen, Haas, and Scheuermann (2002). As EA cannot achieve all the sample sizes (because the halving process has a certain granularity), in each iteration we first ran EA with a given ϵ value, and then used the obtained sample size to run FAST and SRS. EA is not independent of the input sequence, so to account for any difference due to the particular input sequence the results of EA are computed as an average over 50 runs, each one corresponding to a different shuffle of the input. In order to estimate the expected behavior of FAST and SRS, the results of these algorithms are also averaged over 50 runs, each time choosing a different simple random sample from the database.

Our primary metrics used for the evaluation are accuracy and execution time. Accuracy is defined as follows:

$$accuracy = 1 - \frac{|L(D) - L(S)| + |L(S) - L(D)|}{|L(S)| + |L(D)|} \qquad (7.8)$$

where, as before, $L(D)$ and $L(S)$ denote the frequent itemsets from the database D and the sample S, respectively. Notice that this metric is similar to $Dist_1$, except that accuracy is based on the set difference between all frequent itemsets generated from D and S, while $Dist_1$ is based only on frequent 1-itemsets. The execution time is the total time that includes the time required for I/O, and that for finding the final sample and running Apriori.

Results

All the experiments were performed on a SUN Sparc Ultra workstation with a 333 megahertz processor and 256MB memory. The sampling ratios output by EA were 0.76%, 1.51%, 3.02%, 6.04%, 12.4%, and 24.9%. figure 7.3 (a) displays the accuracy of FAST-TRIM, EA and SRS on the synthetic database as a function of the sampling ratio, and figure 7.3 (b) depicts the execution time of the above mentioned algorithms versus the sampling ratio.

---

[1] http://fuzzy.cs.uni-magdeburg.de/borgelt/software. html

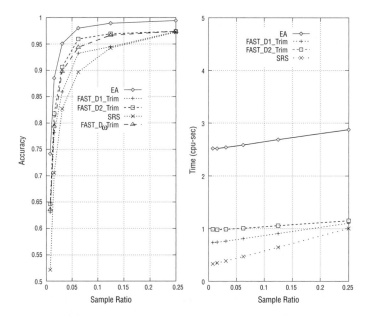

Figure 7.3: Results for synthetic dataset. *Left:* Accuracy versus sampling ratio. *Right:* Time versus sampling ratio.

From figure 7.3 (a) we observe that EA achieves very good accuracy even for small sample sizes. Thus, even for a sample size of 1.51% it could achieve close to 89% accuracy, while FAST-TRIM with distance functions $Dist_2$ and $Dist_\infty$ achieves only 82% and 79.4% accuracies respectively. For larger sample sizes, the differences in accuracy between EA and FAST-TRIM are smaller. For example, for a sample size of 12.4%, EA achieves close to 99% accuracy, versus 96.9% and 96.7% for FAST-TRIM with $Dist_2$ and $Dist_\infty$ respectively. On the other hand, as shown in figure 7.3 (b), EA is more time-consuming than FAST. When using a final sample size of 12.4%, for example, FAST-TRIM has an execution time about 1.5 times longer than SRS, while EA's time is approximately 4 times that of SRS. The trimming operation performed in FAST is substantially faster than the repeated halving method. Of course, the performance gains for either data-reduction method are more pronounced if the cost of producing the sample is amortized over multiple mining tasks.

We have not reported execution results for FAST-TRIM with $Dist_\infty$, because use of this distance function instead of $Dist_1$ or $Dist_2$ causes FAST-TRIM to run 8 times slower. The reasons for this discrepancy are detailed in the addendum to this chapter.

We observe here that Toivonen's (1996) sampling-based association rule algorithm requires a complete database scan like the EA algorithm. But while the EA algorithm examines each transaction only so far as to decide how to color it, Toivonen's algorithm uses each scanned transaction to update a large number of count statistics and in addition requires an expensive step to eliminate false itemsets. In Chen, Haas, and Scheuermann (2002) we have shown that Toivonen's method is very accurate, but 10 times slower than FAST.

7.2 Data Stream Reduction

In this section, we will present a streaming data analysis and discuss data stream reduction.

7.2.1 Streaming Data Analysis

Unlike finite stored databases, streaming databases grow continuously, usually rapidly, and potentially without bound. Examples include stock tickers, network traffic monitors, point-of-sale systems, and phone conversation wiretaps (for intelligence analysis). Unlike data processing methods for stored datasets, methods for analyzing streaming data require timely response and the use of limited memory to capture the statistics of interest. In addition, network management and stock analysis demand the real-time processing of the most recent information.

Manku and Motwani (2002) investigated the problem of approximately counting frequencies on streaming data. They proposed two algorithms, called "Sticky Sampling" and "Lossy Counting," to identify frequent singleton items over a stream. They mention many applications, including "Iceberg Queries" (Fang, Shivakumar, Garcia-Molina, Motwani, and Ullman 1998), "Iceberg Cubes" (Rebey and Ramakrishnan 1999; Han, Pei, Dong, and Wang 2001), "Apriori" (Agrawal and Srikand 1994), and "Network Flow Identification" (Estan and Verghese 2001).

Sticky Sampling uses a fixed-size buffer and a variable sampling rate to estimate the counts of incoming items. The first t incoming items are sampled at rate $r = 1$ (one item selected for every item seen); the next $2t$ items are sampled at rate $r = 2$ (one item selected for every two items seen); the next $4t$ items are sampled at rate $r = 4$, and so on, where t is a predefined value based on frequency threshold, user specified error, and the probability of failure. The approach is equivalent to randomly selecting the same number of items from an enlarging moving window that keeps doubling itself to include twice as many items as before. While Sticky Sampling can accurately maintain the statistics of items over a stable data stream in which patterns change slowly, it fails to address the needs of important applications, such as network traffic control and pricing, that require information about the entire stream but with emphasis on the most recent data. Indeed, the enlarging window and the increasing sampling rate make the statistics at hand less and less sensitive to the changes in recent data.

Lossy Counting is deterministic, and stores the observed frequency and the estimated maximal frequency error for each frequent (or potentially frequent) item in a set of logical buckets. New items are continually added to the buckets while less frequent items are removed. Although the worst-case space complexity of Lossy Counting exceeds that of Sticky Sampling, experiments showed that the former algorithm performs much better than the latter one when streams have random arrival distributions. The authors have extended Lossy Counting Algorithm to identify frequent itemsets. The idea is to virtually divide a stream into chunks based on the order of the arrival data and then identify the frequent itemsets from each chunk. Similarly to Sticky Sampling, Lossy Counting and its extension can be effective when the goal is to find frequent itemsets over a stable data stream. These algorithms, however, may not be effective for drastically changing data. Moreover, the computation of frequent itemsets from each chunk in the extension of Lossy Counting can be prohibitively expensive for high speed data streams, such as network traffic and words in phone conversations.

7.2.2   DSR: Data Stream Reduction

In this section, we propose an EA-based algorithm, data stream reduction (DSR), to sample data streams. Our goal is to generate a representative sample of a given data stream such that the sample carries information about the entire stream while favoring the recent data. Unlike static databases, a data stream, D_S, can be constantly changing. Therefore, its sample, S_S, should also be regularly adjusted to reflect the changes. Moreover, maintaining a dynamically changing sample of a data stream, rather than merely tracking count statistics, offers users more flexibility in choosing the information to be summarized from the sample, such as frequent itemsets, joint distributions or moments, principal component analysis and other statistical analysis, and so forth.

We discuss the data reduction problem for streaming data within a relatively simple context: each element of the data stream is a transaction consisting of a set of items and represented as a 0-1 vector. The resulting algorithm, DSR, is potentially applicable to other more complicated data streams.

First consider the following idealized algorithm for generating an N_S-element sample, S_S, of a data stream, D_S, where the sampling mechanism puts more weight on recent data. To construct S_S, temporarily "freeze" the data stream after observing $m_s \cdot (N_S/2)$ transactions. Assign the transactions into m_s logical buckets of size $N_S/2$ such that bucket 1 contains the oldest $N_S/2$ transactions, bucket 2 contains the next oldest $N_S/2$ transactions, etc., so that bucket m_s contains the most recent data. Next, for $k = 1, 2, \cdots, m_s$, halve bucket k exactly $m_s - k$ times as in the EA algorithm, and denote the resulting subset of bucket k by s_k. As discussed in section 7.1.2, each s_k is a reasonably good representative of the original contents of bucket k. The union $\bigcup_k s_k$ can therefore be viewed as a good reduced representation of the data stream; this representation contains approximately N_S transactions in total and favors recent data. In contrast to Sticky Sampling, which samples less and less frequently as time progresses, our approach samples more and more frequently, selecting, e.g., all of the $N_S/2$ transactions from the most recent bucket.

In reality, it can be prohibitively expensive to map the transactions into logical buckets and compute the representative subset of each bucket whenever a new transaction arrives. The idea behind DSR is to approximate the preceding idealized algorithm while avoiding frequent halving. To this end, a working buffer that can hold N_S transactions is utilized to receive and generate the reduced representative of the data stream. The buffer size N_S should be as large as possible. Initially, the buffer is empty. If one or more new data items arrive when the buffer contains N_S transactions, then the buffer is halved using EA and the new data items are inserted to the buffer. Observe that the older the data in the buffer, the more halvings by EA they have experienced. Whenever a user requests a sample of the stream, all of the transactions in the buffer are returned to the user.

7.2.3   Discussion of DSR

The advantages of DSR include the following. First, representative tuples are selected from a data stream at variable rates that favor recent data. Therefore DSR is more sensitive to recent changes in the stream than Sticky Sampling or Lossy Counting.

Second, unlike traditional tools on streaming data, DSR maintains a representative sample, rather than merely a collection of summary statistics such as counts. In this way, we offer more flexibility since users can decide what operations they would like to perform on the representative subset.

Third, when applying DSR to frequent-itemset identification, it suffices to generate frequent itemsets only when specifically requested by the user, thereby avoiding the need for ongoing periodic generation of frequent itemsets as in the extension of Lossy Counting.

Finally, since the data is more represented in the recent past, DSR supports well queries that deal with the recent past, such as slide-window queries. But unlike other sliding-window schemes, since the entire stream is represented, the size of the window is not fixed and the user can query further into the past as required by the data. Intuitively, the accuracy degrades as the size of the window increases.

A potential problem with DSR concerns the stability of analytical results computed from the sample. After the working buffer is halved, the number of transactions in the buffer changes from N_S to $N_S/2$. Two users who request data immediately prior to and after the halving operation, respectively, could receive data that vary dramatically and hence get very different analytical results even when the actual data stream remains stable. We can use a variant of DSR, called *continuous* DSR, to solve this problem. Unlike DSR, where the buffer is halved when it is filled, continuous DSR halves a smaller chunk of the buffer at a time, as follows. After the buffer is filled with N_S transactions, the transactions are sorted in increasing order of arrival and divided into $N_S/(2n_s)$ chunks, with each chunk containing $2n_s$ transactions. After n_s new transactions arrive, where $n_s \ll N_S$ and is a predefined fixed number, EA is called to halve the chunk containing the oldest $2n_s$ transactions. The n_s new transactions then replace the n_s old transactions that are evicted. When another n_s new transactions come, the second chunk is halved and the new transactions replace the newly evicted transactions. The procedure continues until all $N_S/(2n_s)$ chunks are halved. At this time, $N_S/2$ of the transactions in the buffer have been replaced by new transactions. Then all transactions in the buffer are re-assigned evenly and in arrival order to $N_S/(2n_s)$ chunks. This cycle continues so that, except for the initial warm-up period, the buffer is always full. Because $n_s \ll N_S$, no matter how close in time two users request the data, their results will not be drastically affected by the fluctuations caused by halving operations.

There are some open issues surrounding the choice of discrepancy function to use in the DSR context. On a static database, our experiments have indicated that in many cases the discrepancy function based on single item frequencies leads to acceptable error on the frequencies of higher level itemsets. However, in the case of streaming data, it is also not entirely clear how to evaluate the goodness of a representative subset obtained by DSR. Recall that our goal is to favor recent data, hence recent data is well represented, while old data is sampled more coarsely. How to approximate frequencies in that case? An intuitive way is to introduce a weight per element of the sample (initially 1), and double this weight each time the sample undergoes a halving; thus the weight roughly represents the number of elements of the stream that the sample stands for. Let us call that the "doubling weighted" scheme. But the error introduced by EA will likely accumulate and therefore the ε-bound degrades with the size of the data stream. More generally, we might want to put continuously decreasing weights on the data (say exponentially decreasing with age, of which the doubly weighted scheme is a coarse discretization). The measurement of the error associated with the reduced data stream should reflect the weighting scheme. We are currently investigating appropriate measurements for such weighted stream reduction.

If the user is allowed to limit the query to the recent past, or to a given time window as suggested in the fourth point in the above discussion, then the error bound of the doubly weighted scheme actually depends on the size of the window and may be quite reasonable for queries into the recent past.

7.3 Conclusion and Future Directions

In this chapter we have proposed and compared two algorithms for sampling-based association mining. Both algorithms produce a sample of transactions which is then used to mine association rules, and can be engineered to perform a single pass on the data. There are more accurate algorithms for solving this particular problem (e.g., Toivonen's algorithm which is probabilistic and has a higher accuracy, or Manku and Motwani's adaptation of lossy counting which makes one pass and identifies all the frequent itemsets), but our sampling approach is computationally less expensive (we only construct the higher-level itemsets for the sample, not for the original data as is the case for both Toivonen's and Manku and Motwani's algorithms) and has nevertheless a good accuracy.

We are currently modifying EA so that it need keep in memory at any time only the transactions that belong to the final sample. Such a modification would make EA an even more attractive alternative for extremely large databases. We are also exploring other modifications that would give the user finer control over the final sample size.

Overall, the FAST and EA data-reduction methods provide powerful, complementary tools for scaling existing mining algorithms to massive databases. Our results provide the user with new options for trading off processing speed and accuracy of results.

We conclude this chapter with a short list of challenges and future directions in sampling and data reduction.

7.3.1 Future Directions in Sampling

Data reduction is concerned with reducing the volume of the data while retaining its essential characteristics. As such, sampling provides a general approach which scales well and offers more flexibility than merely tracking count statistics. Moreover, the sample can later be used for training purposes or for further statistical analysis.

For the full benefit of sampling, however, it is best to tailor the sampling procedure to the problem at hand. For instance, we have adapted our sampling to reflect the frequent itemset accuracy (FAST) or 1-itemset frequencies (EA). A challenging problem is to adapt sampling to perform well with other subsequent processing of the data. High-level aggregates (such as frequencies, sums or averages, and higher moments) are especially suitable and have been well explored. Computing samples for more expensive processing (such as association and correlation rules, data cube queries, or even more involved statistical analyses such as principal components analysis) is still in need of more theory and experiments.

Sampling has its limitations, and does not perform well for some problems (notably, estimating join sizes) and other techniques may perform far better as shown in Gibbons and Matias (1999). Nevertheless, sampling serves a general purpose which is useful when the subsequent processing of the reduced data is not known or simply would be not feasible on the original data. Integrating both approaches and combining the strengths of each (e.g., keep a sample as well as other synopses, and use all in conjunction to speed up a problem more efficiently or more accurately) is a likely subject for future research.

7.3.2   Future Directions in Data Stream Reduction

A number of data-mining operations become more challenging in data streams. In addition, there are challenges in handling novel query types (such as various aggregates over a sliding window or continuous queries) and distributed data streams (for example, large web sites like Yahoo! may gather statistics coming from many servers). The algorithm community has responded very well to this new problematic. See the survey by Babcock, Dabu, Datar, Motwani, and Widom (2002) for models and challenges.

We have proposed some extensions of the EA algorithm to permit maintenance of a sample of streaming data. The resulting algorithm, DSR, is able to answer queries in windows in the past, where the size of the window is variable and determines the accuracy of the answer. The theoretical bounds are not easy to derive and are likely not very good in the worst case, but what can be said if items are coming from a stable distribution in random order?

One challenging problem is to detect changes in the stream distribution. For instance, one may want to adapt the sampling rate, or readjust some parameters (such as reducing a sliding window size to maintain a given level of accuracy). This is relevant with any method, not just DSR. If one analyses the sample created by DSR, it may be possible to take advantage of this and perhaps flush the buffer when a change in distribution is detected. We have not experimented with DSR enough to say if it is an effective method to detect changes in the distribution.

The sample obtained by DSR is well suited to frequency estimation and association rules, but there are other problems that are highly relevant for data streams. For instance, identifying and sampling extreme or unusual data has application to network intrusion detection. Sensor data streams introduce new and challenging problems, such as calibration, recovering from missing values, outlier detection, and distribution change. Data reduction is likely to bring order-of-magnitude improvements, but it remains to be seen if it can be done in a manner compatible with the problem at hand.

7.4 Addendum: Implementation of Trimming in FAST

In this addendum, we provide a detailed description of the trimming step in FAST. Both the trimming computations and the resulting computational cost of the trimming step depend critically on the choice of distance function. We give implementation details and complexity results for the three distance functions $Dist_1$, $Dist_2$, and $Dist_\infty$.

Denote by S the initial sample and by S_0 the current sample. Suppose that S_0 contains $N_0 + 1$ transactions and we are about to trim a specified group of transactions $\mathcal{G} = \{T_1, T_2, \ldots, T_K\} \subseteq S_0$ by removing an outlier, that is, by removing the transaction that will lead to the greatest decrease (or least increase) in the distance function.[2] Formally, we remove transaction T_{i^*}, where

$$i^* = \operatorname*{argmin}_{1 \le i \le K} Dist(S'_{0,i}, S).$$

In the above expression, $S'_{0,i} = S_0 - \{T_i\}$ and $\operatorname*{argmin}_{x \in U} f(x)$ denotes the element of the set U that minimizes the function f. We now discuss methods for identifying i^* when $Dist$ is equal to $Dist_1$, $Dist_2$, or $Dist_\infty$. With a slight abuse of notation, we use the symbol "A" to denote both an item A and the 1-itemset that contains item A. At each step, the FAST algorithm maintains the quantity $N_0 + 1$ standing for the number of transactions in S_0, and N standing for the number of transactions in S. FAST also maintains the quantities $M_A = n(A; S)$ and $M'_A = n(A; S_0)$ for each $A \in \mathcal{I}_1(S)$, where, as before, $n(A; U)$ denotes the number of transactions in the set U that contain item A.

---

[2] For ease of exposition, we assume that there is a unique outlier transaction. In general, if there are multiple outlier transactions, then we arbitrarily select one of them for removal.

7.4.1   Trimming With $Dist_1$

When $Dist = Dist_1$, we have

$$
\begin{aligned}
i^* &= \operatorname*{argmin}_{1 \le i \le K} Dist_1(S'_{0,i}, S) \\
&= \operatorname*{argmin}_{1 \le i \le K} \frac{|L_1(S) - L_1(S'_{0,i})| + |L_1(S'_{0,i}) - L_1(S)|}{|L_1(S'_{0,i})| + |L_1(S)|}.
\end{aligned}
\tag{7.9}
$$

Exact determination of i^* is expensive, because we need to calculate $Dist_1$ $(S'_{0,i}, S)$ for each $T_i \in \mathcal{G}$. Calculation of $Dist_1(S'_{0,i}, S)$ requires that we determine for each $A \in \mathcal{I}_1(S)$ whether A is frequent in $S'_{0,i}$; depending on this determination, we may then increment one or more of three counters that correspond to the terms $|L_1(S) - L_1(S'_{0,i})|$, $|L_1(S'_{0,i}) - L_1(S)|$, and $|L_1(S'_{0,i})|$ that appear in (7.9). Thus the cost of trimming the outlier is $O\big(K \cdot |\mathcal{I}_1(S)|\big)$, where typically $|\mathcal{I}_1(S)| \gg 0$.

To alleviate this cost problem, we observe that both $|L_1(S'_{0,i})|$ and $|L_1(S)|$ are typically very large, and compute

$$
i^{**} = \operatorname*{argmin}_{1 \le i \le K} \frac{|L_1(S) - L_1(S'_{0,i})| + |L_1(S'_{0,i}) - L_1(S)|}{|L_1^\dagger(S_0)| + |L_1(S)|}
$$

as an approximation to i^*. In the above formula, $L_1^\dagger(S_0)$ is the set of 1-itemsets that are frequent in S_0 when the support of each 1-itemset A is computed as $n(A; S_0)/(|S_0| - 1)$ rather than by the usual formula $n(A; S_0)/|S_0|$. Using the fact that, in general,

$$
\operatorname*{argmin}_{x \in U} f(x) = \operatorname*{argmin}_{x \in U} cf(x) + d
\tag{7.10}
$$

for any positive constant c and real number d, we can write

$$
i^{**} = \operatorname*{argmin}_{1 \le i \le K} \Delta_i^{(1)} + \Delta_i^{(2)},
$$

where

$$
\Delta_i^{(1)} = |L_1(S) - L_1(S'_{0,i})| - |L_1(S) - L_1^\dagger(S_0)|
$$

and

$$
\Delta_i^{(2)} = |L_1(S'_{0,i}) - L_1(S)| - |L_1^\dagger(S_0) - L_1(S)|].
$$

For each i, the quantities $\Delta_i^{(1)}$ and $\Delta_i^{(2)}$ can be calculated as follows:

$$\text{set } \Delta_i^{(1)} = \Delta_i^{(2)} = 0;$$
$$\text{for each item } A \in T_i \ \{$$
$$\quad \text{if } A \in L_1^{\dagger}(S_0) \text{ and } A \notin L_1(S_{0,i}') \ \{$$
$$\quad \quad \text{if } A \in L_1(S)$$
$$\quad \quad \quad \text{set } \Delta_i^{(1)} = \Delta_i^{(1)} + 1$$
$$\quad \quad \text{else}$$
$$\quad \quad \quad \text{set } \Delta_i^{(2)} = \Delta_i^{(2)} - 1;$$
$$\quad \}$$
$$\}$$

It is easy to see that the worst-case cost of computing i^{**} is $O(K \cdot T_{\max})$ which is usually much less than $O(K \cdot |\mathcal{I}_1(S)|)$.

Trimming With $Dist_2$

In this case, we need to compute

$$i^* = \operatorname*{argmin}_{1 \le i \le K} Dist_2(S_{0,i}', S) = \operatorname*{argmin}_{1 \le i \le K} \sum_{A \in \mathcal{I}_1(S)} \left(\frac{M_{A,i}"}{N_0} - \frac{M_A}{N} \right)^2,$$

where $M_{A,i}" = n(A; S_{0,i}')$. Observe that

$$M_{A,i}" = \begin{cases} M_A' - 1 & \text{if } A \in T_i; \\ M_A' & \text{if } A \notin T_i. \end{cases}$$

As with $Dist_1$, a naive computation incurs a cost of $O(K \cdot |\mathcal{I}_1(S)|)$. Appealing to (7.10), however, we can write

$$i^* = \operatorname*{argmin}_{1 \le i \le K} \sum_{A \in \mathcal{I}_1(S)} \left(\left(M_{A,i}" - \frac{M_A}{N} N_0 \right)^2 - \left(M_A' - \frac{M_A}{N} N_0 \right)^2 \right)$$

$$= \operatorname*{argmin}_{1 \le i \le K} \sum_{A \in T_i} \left(1 - 2M_A' + 2\frac{M_A}{N} N_0 \right).$$

It is clear from the above representation of i^* that the worst-case cost can be reduced from $O(K \cdot |\mathcal{I}_1(S)|)$ to $O(K \cdot T_{\max})$.

7.4.2 Trimming With $Dist_\infty$

We need to compute

$$i^* = \operatorname*{argmin}_{1 \le i \le K} Dist_\infty(S_{0,i}', S) = \operatorname*{argmin}_{1 \le i \le K} \max_{A \in \mathcal{I}_1(S)} \left| \frac{M_{A,i}"}{N_0} - \frac{M_A}{N} \right|.$$

As with the other distance functions, a naive approach to trimming incurs a cost of $O\big(K \cdot |\mathcal{I}_1(S)|\big)$. Denote by G_1 the collection of 1-itemsets having positive support in $\mathcal{G}$. It is not hard to show that computing i^* is equivalent to computing

$$i' = \operatorname*{argmin}_{1 \leq i \leq K} \max_{A \in G_1} \left| \frac{M_{A,i}"}{N_0} - \frac{M_A}{N} \right|.$$

Since $|G_1| \leq K \cdot T_{\max}$, the worst-case cost is reduced to $O(K^2 \cdot T_{\max})$. Although this cost is typically much less than $O\big(K \cdot |\mathcal{I}_1(S)|\big)$, the cost incurred by using $Dist_\infty$ is clearly much greater than the worst-case cost of $O(K \cdot T_{\max})$ that is incurred by using either $Dist_1$ or $Dist_2$.

Hervé Brönnimann is an assistant professor of computer and information sciences at Polytechnic University. His research interests are in computational geometry and algorithms. He can be reached at hbr@poly.edu.

Manoranjan Dash is an assistant professor in the School of Computer Engineering at Nanyang Technological University, Singapore. His research interests include data mining and machine learning. He can be reached at asmdash@ntu.edu.sg.

Peter J. Haas is a research staff member at the IBM Almaden Research Center, San Jose, California. His interests include novel methods for exploration and mining of massive datasets. He can be reached at www.almaden.ibm.com/cs/people/peterh.

Peter Scheuermann is a professor in the Department of Electrical and Computer Engineering at Northwestern University. His research interests are in database systems, data mining and distributed computing. He can be reached at peters@ece.northwestern.edu.

Chapter 8

Discovering Recurrent Events in Multichannel Data Streams Using Unsupervised Methods

Milind R. Naphade, Chung-Sheng Li, and Thomas S. Huang

There is an underlying structure in most broadcast videos available to viewers including movies, sports, talk shows, news, and so on. A related phenomenon is the recurrence of certain semantically well-defined temporal events that often act as anchors in the structural syntax of such videos. Obvious examples such as the news-anchor in news videos come to mind. In sports, a similar anchor could be the pitching event in a baseball game, which initiates a series of related events that also recur. In a talk show such an anchor might be the narration of a joke, which triggers laughter or applause. If detected, such anchor events can help detect the overall structure. Similarly, the detection of recurring events can aid summarization, similarity search, and enhanced browsing capabilities. All these applications assume importance in the wake of an increasingly digital broadcasting environment and entertainment enhancers such as TiVo.

Finding the semantic structure in videos is difficult. The one problem that has been addressed elaborately has been the detection of visual shots (Naphade, Mehrotra, Ferman, Warnick, Huang, and Tekalp 1998), (Srinivasan, Ponceleon,

Amir, and Petkovic 2000). There have been efforts to find low-level syntactic structure in videos by combining several shots into scenes. Recent work in structure detection for motion pictures includes that of Sundaram and Chang (2000). Statistical models like the hidden Markov models (HMM) have been used to impose structure on videos (Wolf 1997; Ferman and Tekalp 1999). The use of multimodal cues to improve the detection of shots and scenes has also been studied (Nam, Cetin, and Tewfik 1997); (Srinivasan, Ponceleon, Amir, and Petkovic 2000; Nakamura and Kanade 1997; Adams, Dorai, and Venkatesh 2001). Sundaram and Chang (2000) apply the rules of film production to detect scenes such as dialogues. Similar rules of film production and short and long term memory have been applied by Kender and Yeo (1998). More recently Liu and Kender (2000) use hidden Markov models for structuring documentaries through supervised classification of cues such as fade, zoom, and so on. Liu, Huang, and Wang (1998) in fact use an ergodic hidden Markov model and utilize statistical properties to classify TV programs into types of sports, news, weather, and so forth.

In this chapter we propose a novel unsupervised approach to detect recurring events and structure in videos. The novel aspect of our algorithm is its ability to account for short term as well as longer term continuity and its ability to detect recurring patterns automatically without supervision. The algorithm attempts to perform temporal clustering and segmentation. It can be recursively applied and can thus operate in a hierarchical mode. We apply this algorithm to detect recurring events in movies. The domain of motion pictures presents much more variability than that of sports or news or television documentaries. In motion pictures, our algorithm succeeds in discovering interesting audiovisual events such as "explosion." In television production such as talk shows it succeeds in discovering events such as "laughter," "applause," "speech," etc.

This chapter is organized as follows: In section 8.1 we present a probabilistic framework for temporal clustering. In section 8.2 we apply this algorithm to motion picture sequences as well as talk shows and demonstrate its discovering abilities.

8.1   Unsupervised Clustering of Recurring Temporal Events

We now present a probabilistic architecture for discovering recurring temporal patterns in the time series feature representations of multimedia content.

Our approach to the detection of recurring patterns in video is motivated by the unsupervised clustering algorithm proposed by Poritz (1982) that was extended to large vocabulary speech recognition by Levinson (1989).

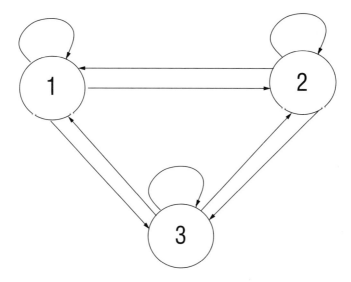

Figure 8.1: A 3 state ergodic HMM.

The idea is to use an ergodic hidden Markov model whose state transitions are illustrated in figure 8.1 to cluster the signal into as many stationary patterns as the number of states in the HMM. Each state ends up representing a type of the signal with particular stationary properties. Liu, Huang, and Wang (1998) have applied this same model to audio . A by product is the use of transitions between states to denote transitions in the signal. The problem with most such approaches used in the past is that the cluster can model only short term statistics in the signal. We are interested in the relatively long term temporal statistics as well. To give a textual analogy, if the traditional Poritz model can detect recurring patterns and clusters in alphabets we are interested in recurring strings of such alphabets. In this chapter we present a natural extension to overcome this challenge.

The architecture is shown in figure 8.2.

The time series is assumed to have been produced by a generative model emitting observations at each time/sample instance. Similar to the assumptions typical in an HMM setting, the observation at any given time is supposed to be dependent only on an unobserved state and the current state dependent on the state in the previous time instant. Figure 8.2 then illustrates the transition graph of the states in the proposed architecture. The framework can be thought of as a number of nonergodic hidden Markov models embedded within a hierarchical ergodic hidden Markov model. To make the connection between the models in figure 8.1 and 8.2, one could visualize each state in figure 8.1 being replaced

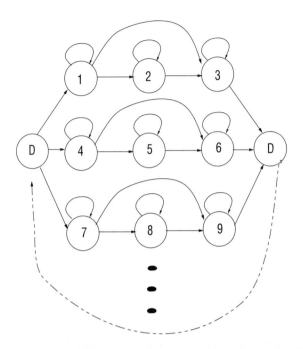

Figure 8.2: Imposing Structure using several nonergodic hidden Markov models embedded in a hierarchical ergodic configuration. States labeled D are dummy states that do not emit any observations. Each branch is a nonergodic HMM.

by a nonergodic HMM. This is exactly what is illustrated in figure 8.2 with states labeled D acting as dummy states without emitting any observations.

The exact number of nonergodic branches and the number of states within each branch is a matter of domain dependent experimental selection. What can be expected of the proposed model is that the time series can now be though of as being generated by a series of temporal events. If it is believed that there are N possible event types within a waveform, with sufficient data, it can be expected that these are learned automatically without the need for manual annotation. The model can thus significantly improve the modeling of the long term statistics of a piece-wise stationary signals. As a by-product the segmentation of the signal can now be analyzed at the level of states in the nonergodic chains. The signal can also be analyzed at the coarser temporal granularity that is offered by the detection of each branch in figure 8.2. The model is trained using the expectation maximization (EM) algorithm (Dempster, Laird, and Rubin 1977).

We believe that this offers the ability to discover structure in the audio and visual signals in multimedia content such as sports, motion pictures, news talk shows, etc. If this model is applied to a data set that is characterized by frequent recurring occurrences of a finite set of events, we can hope to capture them through the branches in the figure 8.2. Examples include talk shows, sports with regular structure like baseball, etc. On the other hand if this model is applied to diverse content with variability like movie clips, we hope that the model will discover at least some of the inherent recurring patterns. We test this hypotheses using content from movies as well as that from talk shows.

8.2   Experiments

Having described the model and the procedure for discovering the recurring patterns using an unsupervised approach, we now apply this algorithm to two different domains. In both domains we extract commonly used audiovisual features. All videos used for experiments have a 29.97 frame rate and a screen size of 352 by 240 pixels.

8.2.1   Features

We extract commonly used audio and visual features. In case of visual features, the image sequence may be downsampled to reduce processing and avoid redundancy.

Global Color Histogram: A linearized HSV histogram (Naphade, Mehrotra, Ferman, Warnick, Huang, and Tekalp 1998) is extracted from each frame of the image sequence. The number of bins for hue saturation and intensity were chosen to be 6,6 and 12 respectively.

Global Structure: A 24 bin edge direction (Naphade, Wang, and Huang 2001) histogram is extracted to represent the structure in each frame within the image sequence.

Audio Features: We represent audio by 15 mel frequency cepstral coefficients, 15 delta coefficients and 2 energy coefficients extracted by using a 33 ms window width. The window is deliberately chosen to equal the duration of 1 visual frame. While not the main motivation behind the choice of width, this helps synchronization between the two streams.

8.2.2   Movie Videos

We chose ten video clips from an action thriller that has several examples of interesting audiovisual events such as "explosion." For the audio feature stream we applied the proposed model with 6 possible nonergodic branches each with 3 hidden states. Each state emits observations using a Gaussian mixture model

(GMM) with 5 mixture components. Convergence was reached after 50 iterations of the EM algorithm. The GMM in each state of the proposed model was assumed to have a diagonal covariance matrix for the sake of computational convenience. For the visual stream we experimented with distinct models for color distribution, and structure as well as a model for the combined visual feature set. In each case we used 5 nonergodic branches.

We noticed very interesting results at the end of the iterations. One of the nonergodic HMM chains in the model picked up all the auditory events of explosion and crashlike sounds. Another picked up male speech while a third picked up a recurring musical theme that is played in different styles in the movie. The visual models also similarly converged to events such as the evolution of a fire and smoke, outdoor locales, indoor locales with people and faces, etc.

Figure 8.3 shows the different shots for which the same chain was active. All shots correspond to the audio event explosion.

8.2.3   Talk Shows

A similar application of the model to more regular video data like a talk show indicates its promise to detect recurring temporal patterns that can serve as anchors. For example, on applying this model to late night talk shows, one of the nonergodic chains picked up all the clapping and laughter of the audience response, one picked up all the female speech and yet another picked up all such scenes where speech and laughter were present jointly.

8.3   Biosurveillance

With certain extensions similar algorithms can be used for data mining for temporal patterns in other domains such as biosurveillance, where the multimodal sensor streams may be comprised of traditional and nontraditional data sources. An important modification in this case for the presented algorithms would have to be the ability to perform such learning and detection in an incremental and online fashion rather than an offline approach that works for the digital media content. We are actively investigating the application of such temporal and feature-based clustering techniques for features that are computed from nontraditional data streams for the advance detection and warning of bioterrorist attacks.

Figure 8.3: Key-frames from the explosion event detected across all clips by one of the nonergodic branches. This branch is active whenever there is an explosion or a loud crashing sound.

8.4 Concluding Remarks

In this chapter we have presented a novel probabilistic graphical model for discovering the recurring temporal patterns in audiovisual features. Applying a number of left to right hidden Markov models embedded in a hierarchical ergodic framework, we are able to learn the characteristic temporal patterns without any supervision. Interesting events such as explosion, music, speech, laughter, etc. were automatically picked up by the learned models consistently across the data set. The clustering as well as temporal segmentation was highly accurate. Such detection can be used for content based retrieval, browsing and structuring of video data. Future research will attempt to apply such unsupervised methods for discovering interesting and recurring patterns in more structured videos like baseball game videos. Future research will also involve the repeated application of this model at coarser granularity to find long term structure. With certain extensions similar algorithms can be used for data mining for temporal patterns in other domains such as biosurveillance, where the multimodal sensor streams may be comprised of traditional and nontraditional data sources.

Milind R. Naphade is a research staff member in the Business Informatics Department at IBM Thomas J. Watson Research Center, Hawthorne, New York. He specializes in multimedia learning and information extraction and can be reached at (914) 784-7032.

Chung-Sheng Li is a senior manager for the E-commerce and Data Management Department at IBM T. J. Watson Research Center. He has numerous inventions and patent application awards and holds 18 patents.

Thomas S. Huang is the William L. Everitt Distinguished Professor in the Department of Electrical and Computer Engineering at the University of Illinois, Urbana Illinois and a research professor at the Coordinated Science Laboratory, and head of the Image Formation and Processing Group at the Beckman Institute for Advanced Science and Technology.

Counterterrorism, Privacy,
and Data Mining

Chapter 9

Data Mining for Counterterrorism

Bhavani Thuraisingham

Data mining is the process of posing queries and extracting useful patterns or trends, often previously unknown, from large amounts of data using various techniques such as those from pattern recognition and machine learning. Today the technology is being used for a wide variety of applications, from marketing and finance to medicine and biotechnology to multimedia and entertainment. Recently there has been interest in using data mining for counterterrorism applications. For example, data mining can be used to detect unusual patterns, terrorist activities, and fraudulent behavior. While all these data mining applications can be of benefit and save lives, they can also threaten our privacy. Data mining tools are freely available, and even naïve users can use them to extract information from data stored in various databases and files, and in so doing sometimes violate the privacy of the individual. To carry out effective data mining and extract useful information for counterterrorism and national security, we need to gather all kinds of information about individuals. However, misuse of this information could threaten individuals' privacy and civil liberties.

In this chapter I will provide an overview of the application of data mining to counterterrorism. At the Next Generation Data Mining (NGDM) Workshop, a panel was conducted on data mining for counterterrorism. The panel raised many interesting technical challenges. In section 9.1 of this chapter I will discuss some of them. To understand how data mining could be applied to counterterrorism, we need a good understanding of what those threats might be. I've grouped the threats into several categories and will discuss them in section 9.2. The application of data mining techniques to counterterrorism will be the subject of section 9.3. There have been many discussions recently regarding the potential for invasion of privacy tprobhat could occur as a result of data mining. In section 9.4 I address the privacy issue, and also discuss data mining solutions that attempt to detect and prevent terrorism while at the same time maintaining some level of privacy. The chapter is concluded in section 9.5.

9.1   Research Challenges

Data mining technologies are now being applied to many applications. However, are they ready to detect and/or prevent terrorist activities? Can we completely eliminate false positives and false negatives? False positives could be disastrous to the affected individuals. False negatives could increase terrorist activities. Our challenge is to find the "needle in the haystack." We need knowledge-directed data mining to eliminate false positives and false negatives as much as possible.

Mining data in real time is another challenge. We now have tools that can detect credit-card and calling-card violations in real time. However can we build models in real time? The general view among the research community is that such real-time model building is still quite difficult. Furthermore, to detect counterterrorism activities, we need good training examples. How can we get such examples—especially in an unclassified setting?

Multimedia data mining is a third challenge. While we now have tools that can mine structured and relational databases, mining unstructured databases is still quite difficult. Do we extract structure from unstructured databases and then mine the structured data or do we apply mining tools directly on the unstructured data? Furthermore, although we have made progress in text mining, further work on audio and video as well as image mining is needed.

Other directions being taken include graph and pattern mining. Here, the challenge is to connect all the dots. Essentially, a graph structure is built, based on the information available. If multiple agencies are working on a problem, each agency will have its own graph. The challenge is to make inferences about missing nodes and links in the graph. The graph might be very large. How can we reduce the graph to a more manageable size?

Finding unclassified data to test is still a major challenge. How can we get unclassified data? Is it possible to scrub and clean classified data and produce reasonable data at an unclassified level? How can we find large data sets consisting of multimedia data types? Is it possible to develop a test-bed where one can apply various data mining tools to determine their efficiency?

Detecting unusual patterns is a challenge for web mining. In some ways web mining encompasses data mining, as one has to mine all the data on the web as well as structure and usage patterns. By mining usage patterns one could get patterns, such as "there are an unusual number of visits to a federal web site from Paris around 3 AM in the morning." Data on the web is can be either structured or unstructured. Therefore the tools developed for data mining also apply to web mining. We need tools that can mine the structure of the web as well as usage patterns.

Privacy is a major challenge for counterterrorism data mining. The challenge is to extract useful information while, at the same time, maintaining privacy. Several efforts are under way that attempt to preserve privacy during data mining. The idea is that various techniques, such as randomization, cover stories, or multiparty policy enforcement, can be used to preserve privacy while data mining. While there is some progress in this area, the effectiveness of such techniques needs further evaluation.

These are some of the challenges of counterterrorism data mining that were discussed at the NGDM workshop. Thus, although data mining can become a useful tool in the effort to counter terrorism, there are still many challenges that must be addressed. They include mining multimedia data, graph mining, building models in real time, knowledge-directed data mining to eliminate false positives and false negatives, web mining, and privacy sensitive data mining. Research is progressing in the right direction. However, there is still much to be done (for more discussion, see Thuraisingham [2003c]).

In the next three sections I will provide some more details on counterterrorism data mining.

9.2   Some Information on Terrorism, Security Threats, and Protection Measures

A critical application of data mining technologies is *counterterrorism*–the development of countermeasures to threats occurring from terrorist activities. In this section I focus on the various types of threats that can occur.

My discussion of counterterrorism is rather preliminary. I am not a counterterrorism expert. The information on terrorist threats presented here has been obtained entirely from unclassified newspaper articles and news reports. My focus, instead, is to illustrate how data mining can help combat terrorism. Data mining won't solve all the problems but, because it can extract patterns and trends (often previously unknown) we should certainly explore the application of data and web data mining technologies to counterterrorism efforts.

Web data mining goes beyond data mining in that it only includes data mining techniques but also focuses on web traffic and usage mining as well as web structure. There are additional challenges to web data mining that are not present in ordinary data mining. Furthermore, web data mining also includes structured as well as unstructured data mining. Because much of the data will eventually be on the web, whether in public networks such as the internet or in private, corporate, or classified intranets, the study of web data mining must include data mining as well.

Before discussing counterterrorism, we must first examine the *types* of threats faced. Such threats could be malicious and due to terrorist attacks, or nonmalicious and caused by inadvertent errors. While my primary focus in this chapter is on malicious attacks, I also cover some caused by inadvertent errors, as the solutions to both are often similar. The types of terrorist threats discussed include noninformation-related terrorism, information-related terrorism, bioterrorism, and chemical attacks. "Noninformation-related terrorism" includes people attacking others with weapons like bombs and guns. To combat this kind of threat, we need to find out who these people are by analyzing their connections and then developing counterterrorism solutions. "Information-related threats" are threats using computer systems and networks, such as unauthorized intrusions and viruses as well as computer-related vandalism. "Information-related terrorism" is essentially cyberterrorism. "Bioterrorism, chemical, and nuclear attacks" are terrorist attacks caused by biological substances and chemical or nuclear weapons. There are certainly other types of threats that exist but my examination will be limited to these. I will discuss how data mining can be used to help prevent and detect attacks caused by such threats.

9.2.1 Natural Disasters and Human Errors

Threats occur due to many reasons, including natural disasters, human errors, as well as malicious attacks. While the emergency responses to such attacks in the near term may not be that different, the method used to combat such threats in the longer term is likely to be quite different.

By "natural disasters" I mean disasters due to hurricanes, earthquakes, fires, power failures, or accidents. Some of these disasters may be caused by human error, such as pressing the wrong button in a process plant and causing the plant to explode. Data mining could help detect some natural disasters. By analyzing massive amounts of geological data, a data mining tool might be able to predict an earthquake, thus enabling a timely evacuation of the affected population. Similarly, by analyzing weather data, a data mining tool might be able to predict that a hurricane is about to occur.

Whether a building caught on fire through natural disasters or by terrorist attack, emergency response would probably not be too different. In both cases, there will be panic, although if a bomb was the cause the panic might be more intense and the collapse more rapid. Effective emergency response teams are needed to handle such attacks. Data mining could be used to analyze previous attacks, train various tools, and provide advice on how to handle the emergency situation. To accomplish this goal, we need training examples. If they do not exist, it may be necessary to train with hypothetical scenarios and simulated examples.

The long-term measures that need to be taken for natural disasters may be quite different those required for terrorist attacks. Earthquakes are rare occurrences, even in the most earthquake-prone regions. Hurricanes are rare even in the most hurricane-prone regions. Thus there is time to plan and react. This does not mean that natural disasters are easier manage. They are often devastating and take many human lives. Nevertheless, we usually plan for such disasters primarily on the basis of past experience.

Human errors are also a source of major concern. We need to continually train personnel and instruct them to be cautious and alert. We need to take proper actions when we have been careless. Human errors should never be treated lightly. That way, humans will be cautious and perhaps less prone to making such errors.

Terrorist attacks are quite different because they are much less predictable. We do not know when an attack will happen nor how it will happen. Most of us could never have imagined that airplanes would be used as weapons of mass destruction. Nor do we know what the next attack may be. Will the next attack be caused a suicide bomber or chemical weapons or cyberterrorism? The measures taken to prevent and detect terrorist attacks may be quite intense.

To develop effective techniques, data mining specialists must work together with counterterrorism experts—we cannot employ effective techniques without a good understanding of what the threats might be. Therefore, it is essential that those interested in applying data mining techniques to solve real world problems and terrorist attacks work with counterterrorism specialists. In the next few subsections I will discuss various types of terrorism and counterterrorism measures.

9.2.2 Noninformation-Related Terrorism

By "information-related terrorism" I mean attacks essentially on computers and networks that damage electronic information. Noninformation-related terrorism, on the other hand, is terrorism due to other means such as terrorist attacks, car bombings, and vandalism, such as setting fires.

Terrorist Attacks and External Threats

When I hear the word "terrorism" external threats are what come to mind. My earliest recollection of terrorism are riots where one ethnic group attacks another ethnic group, killing, looting, setting fires to houses, and committing other acts of terrorism and vandalism. Then later on, airplane hijackings occurred, where groups of terrorists hijacked airplanes and then made demands on governments, such as releasing political prisoners who were also possibly potential terrorists. Next came suicide bombings, where the terrorists carried bombs and blew themselves up as well as others nearby. Such attacks usually occurred in crowded places. More recently, airplanes have been used to blow up buildings.

While the above acts are all terrorist attacks, the news reports almost daily about shootings and killings where neither party belongs to a gang or terrorist group. In a way, this is also terrorism, but these acts are more difficult to detect and prevent because there are always what are called "crazy people" in our society. While the technologies I discuss may be able to detect and prevent such attacks, this chapter focuses on how to detect attacks from people belonging to terrorist groups.

So far, all the threats I have discussed are external threats—threats occurring from the outside. In general, terrorists are usually neither friends nor acquaintances of their victims. But there is another kind of threat as well—insider threats. I will discuss insider threats next.

Insider Threats

"Insider threats" are threats from people inside an organization who attack others around them usually using not bombs and airplanes but rather other sinister mechanisms. For example, one kind of insider threat might involve a person from a corporation who gives proprietary information to the corporation's competitor. Another example might be an agent from an intelligence agency who commits espionage. A third example might be a threat coming from one's own family. For example, a spouse, who has insider information about family assets gives the information to a competitor in order to secure some advantage. Insider threats can occur at all levels and all walks of life. They are often quite dangerous and sinister because you never know who these terrorists are. The might involve your so-called "best friend" or even your spouse or sibling.

People from the inside could also use guns to shoot the people around them. We have all heard about office shootings. But these shootings are not, in general, insider threats, because they do not happen in a sinister way. Instead, such shootings are a kind of external threat, even though they originate from people within the organization. So too are instances of domestic abuse and violence, such as husbands shooting wives or vice versa. These, too, also external threats even though they occur from the inside. Insider threats are threats where others around are totally unaware of the threat until something that is perhaps quite dangerous occurs. Espionage, for example, can go on for years before someone gets caught. While both insider threats and external threats are very serious and potentially devastating, insider threats can be even more dangerous because one never knows who these terrorists are.

Transportation and Border Security Violations

Now let's examine border threats, and then discuss threats to transportation.

Safeguarding borders is critical to ensure the security of a nation. Border threats include illegal immigration, gun, drug, and even human trafficking, as well as terrorists entering a country. Note that I do not mean to imply that illegal immigrants are dangerous or that they are terrorists, only that they have entered a country without the proper papers and that could be a major issue for the country, causing problems for the country's economy, or violating human rights by encouraging exploitation of undocumented workers.

Legal immigration gives some assurance that proper procedures have been followed. For official immigration into the USA, for example, one needs to go through interviews at a US embassy, undergo a thorough medical checkup that screens for diseases such as tuberculosis, undergo a background check and many more things. Entering a country legally does not always mean that a person is not a threat. Sometimes terrorists enter countries legally. However, with legal immigration, there is some assurance that some checks have been made.

Drug trafficking often occurs at borders. Drugs are a danger to society. They can cripple a nation, corrupt its children, cause havoc in families, and damage the education system. It is therefore critical that we protect the borders from drug trafficking as well as other types of trafficking, including firearms and human slaves. Other threats at borders include prostitution and child pornography, which are also serious threats to decent living. Safeguarding the border does not necessarily mean that everything is safe inside the country and that these problems are only at borders. Nevertheless we have to protect our borders so that there are no additional problems to our nations.

Transportation system security violations can also cause serious problems. Buses, trains, and airplanes are vehicles that can carry tens or hundreds of people at the same time and any security violation could cause serious damage— even death. A bomb exploding in an airplane or a train or a bus could be devastating. Transportation systems also provide the means for terrorists to escape once they have committed crimes. Therefore transportation systems must be secure. A key aspect of transportation systems security is port security. Ports are responsible for navy ships. Since these ships are at sea throughout the world, terrorists have many opportunities to attack these ships and their cargo. Therefore, we need security measures to protect the ports, cargo, and our military bases. In section 9.2.6 I will discuss various counterterrorism measures for the threats I have discussed here. The next three subsections will discuss additional types of terrorism.

9.2.3   Information-Related Terrorism

Now let's look at information-related terrorism. By "information related terrorism," I mean cyberterrorism as well as security violations through access control and other means. Trojan horses as well as viruses are also information-related security violations, which I group into information-related terrorism activities.

Cyberterrorism, Insider Threats, and External Attacks

Cyberterrorism is one of the major terrorist threats we face today. Because so much of our information is now available electronically, and much of it is on the web, attacks on our computers and networks, databases, and the internet can be devastating to businesses. It is estimated that cyberterrorism could cause billions of dollars worth of damage to businesses. For example, consider the banking system. If terrorists attack such a bank's information system and deplete accounts of the funds, the bank could lose millions if not billions of dollars. By crippling the bank's computer system millions of hours of productivity could be lost. Even a simple power outage at work through some accident could cause several hours of productively loss and result in a major financial loss. It is therefore critical that our information systems be secure.

Next let's look at the various types of cyberterrorist attacks, such as viruses and Trojan horses that can wipe away files and other important document, or intrusions into computer networks, (which I will discuss later). Information security violations, such as access control violations as well as a discussion of various other threats such as sabotage and denial of service will be given later.

Threats can occur both outside and inside the organization. Outside attacks are attacks on computers from someone outside the organization, such as hackers breaking into an organization's computer systems and causing havoc. There are also hackers who start spreading viruses that, in turn, cause great damage to the files in various computer systems. A more sinister problem, however, is the insider threat. Just as with noninformation-related attacks, insider threats can occur with information-related attacks. There are people inside organizations who have studied their company's business practices and have developed schemes that can cripple the organization's information assets.

These people might be regular employees or even those working at computer centers. The problem is quite serious as someone might masquerade as someone else and cause all kinds of damage.

In the next few sections I will examine how data mining could detect and perhaps prevent such attacks.

Malicious Intrusions

I have already discussed some types of malicious intrusions. Such intrusions could involve networks, web clients, servers, databases, operating systems, and so forth. Many of the cyberterrorist attacks that I have discussed in the previous sections are examples of malicious intrusions. I will revisit them here.

In a network intrusion, intruders try to tap into a network and intercept information that is being transmitted. The intruders might be human, or they might be Trojan horses set up by humans. Intrusions can also happen on files. For example, a person masquerading as someone else might log onto someone else's computer system and access their files. Intrusions can also occur on databases. Intruders posing as legitimate users can pose queries, such as SQL queries, and access data that they are not authorized to see.

Essentially, cyberterrorism includes malicious intrusions as well as sabotage through malicious intrusions or otherwise. Cybersecurity consists of security mechanisms that attempt to provide solutions to cyberattacks or cyberterrorism. When we discuss malicious intrusions or cyberattacks, we need to think about the noncyberworld—that is, noninformation-related terrorism—and then translate those attacks to attacks on computers and networks. For example, a thief could enter a building through a trap door. In the same way, a computer intruder could enter the computer or network through some sort of a trap door that has been intentionally built by a malicious insider and left unattended through careless design. Another example might be a thief wearing a mask, entering a bank, and stealing the bank's money. The analogy here is to an intruder masquerading as someone else, legitimately entering the system and taking all the information assets. Money in the real world translates to information assets in the cyberworld. There are many parallels between noninformation-related attacks and information-related attacks, and we must develop countermeasures for both types of attacks. Such countermeasures are discussed in section 9.2.7.

Credit Card Fraud and Identity Theft

We hear a lot these days about credit-card fraud and identity theft. In credit-card fraud, a thief gets hold of a person's credit card and makes one or more unauthorized purchases. By the time the owner of the card finds out about the unauthorized activity, it may be too late. The thief may have left the country by then. A similar problem occurs with telephone calling cards. In fact this type of attack happened once to me. Perhaps while I was making phone calls using my company's calling card at an airport, someone must have noticed the dial tones or numbers I was punching on the telephone, copied them, and and then used my calling card for their own calls. Fortunately our telephone company detected the problem and informed my company. The problem was dealt with immediately.

A more serious theft is identity theft. Here one assumes the identity of another person by obtaining a person's personal information (usually including their social security number) and essentially carrying out all types of transactions under the other person's name. This type of theft can, in extreme cases, even include selling real estate and depositing the income in a fraudulent bank account. By the time, the owner finds out it is often far too late—the victims may already have have lost millions of dollars due to the identity theft.

We need to explore the use of data mining both for credit card fraud detection as well as for identity theft. There have been some efforts in detecting credit card fraud. We need to start working actively on detecting and preventing identity thefts.

Information Security Violations

Now I will provide an overview of the various information security violations. Such violations do not necessarily occur because of cyberattacks or cyberterrorism. They could occur as a result of bad security design or faulty practices. Nevertheless I include this discussion for completion.

Information security violations typically occur due to access control violations. That is, users are granted access depending on their roles (called "role-based access control") or their clearance level (called "multilevel access control") or on a need-to-know basis. Access controls are violated usually because of either poor design or designer errors. For example, suppose John does not have access to salary data. By some error this rule is not enforced and John gains access to salary values. Access control violations can also occur because of malicious attacks. In a malicious attack, a person might enter the system by pretending to be the system administrator, then delete the access control rule that John does not have access to salaries. Another way is for a Trojan horse to operate on behalf of the malicious user. In this scenario, each time John makes a request, the malicious code could ensure that the access control rule is bypassed.

Security Problems for the Web

Since the web is a major means of information transportation, web security threats merit special consideration.[1] As we've already learned, there are numerous security attacks that can occur on the web. I discuss some of the web security threats in this section. Ghosh (1998) has provided an excellent introduction to web security and various threats the web poses. Although I focus on web threats here, the threats discussed are applicable to any information system, including networks, databases, and operating systems. These threats include access control violations, integrity violations, sabotage, fraud, denial of service, and infrastructure attacks.

Traditional access control violations, for example, can be extended to the web. Users may access unauthorized data across the web. There is so much data in so many places on the web that controlling access poses quite a challenge. Data on the web may also be subject to unauthorized modifications. This makes it easier to corrupt the data. Also, data can originate from anywhere. Consequently, producers of the data may not be trustworthy. Incorrect data can cause serious damages such as incorrect bank accounts, which might result in incorrect transactions. We have all heard of hackers breaking into systems and posting inappropriate messages. With so much business and commerce being carried out on the web without proper controls, internet fraud can cause businesses to loose millions of dollars. Intruders can obtain the identity of legitimate users and might empty bank accounts. Even infrastructures like the telecommunication system, the power system, and the heating system can be brought down by hackers. These systems are controlled by computers and often accessed through the Internet. Such attacks would cause denials of service.

Other threats include violations to confidentiality, authenticity, and no repudiation. Confidentiality violations enable intruders to listen in on messages. Authentication violations include using passwords without permissions, and nonrepudiation violations enable a person to deny that he or she sent a given message. The web threats discussed here occur because of insecure clients, servers, and networks. To have complete security, one needs end-to-end security; that means secure clients, secure servers, secure operating systems, secure databases, secure middleware, and secure networks.

9.2.4   Bioterrorism, Chemical and Nuclear Attacks

The previous two sections discussed noninformation-related as well as information-related terrorist attacks. Note that by "information-related" attacks I

---

[1]An excellent book on web security discussing various threats and solutions is the one by Ghosh (1998). I also discuss some of the cyberthreats and countermeasures in Thuraisingham (2003).

mean "cyberattacks." "Noninformation-related attacks" mean everything else. However I have separated bioterrorism and chemical weapons attacks from noninformation-related attacks. I have also given special consideration to critical infrastructure attacks. That is, the noninformation-related attacks are essentially attacks due to bombs, explosions, and other similar activities.

While bioterrorism and chemical/nuclear weapons attacks have been discussed at least for several decades, it was only after September 11, 2001 that the general public began paying a lot of attention to these discussions. The anthrax attacks that occurred during the latter part of 2001 have resulted in increased fear and awareness of the potential dangers of bioterrorism attacks and chemical/nuclear weapons attacks. Such attacks could kill several million people within a short space of time. More recently there is increasing awareness of the dangers due to bioterrorism attacks resulting in the spread of infectious diseases such as smallpox, yellow fever, and similar diseases. These diseases are so infectious that it is critical that their spread is detected as soon as they occur. Preventing such attacks would be the ultimate goal. One option is to carry out mass vaccination but this would mean some health hazards to various groups of people. Our challenge is to use technology to prevent and detect such deadly attacks. Technologies would include sensor technology and data mining and data management technologies.

Attacks using chemical weapons are equally deadly. One could spray poisonous gas and other chemicals into the air, water and food supplies. For example, various dangerous chemical agents could be sprayed from the air on plants and crops. These plants and crops could get into the food supply and kill millions. We have to develop technologies to detect and prevent such deadly attacks.

Another form of deadly attacks is the nuclear attacks. Such attacks could wipe out the entire population in the world. There are various nations developing nuclear weapons when they do not have the authorization to develop them. That is, these weapons are being developed illegally. This is what makes the world very dangerous. We have to develop technologies to detect and prevent such deadly attacks.

I have only briefly mentioned the various biological, chemical and nuclear attacks. There are some good books that are being written about such terrorist activities.[2] As I have stressed, I am not a counterterrorism expert. My goal is to examine various data mining techniques and see how they could be applied to detect and prevent such deadly terrorist attacks.

Data mining for counterterrorism will be discussed in sections 9.3 and 9.4. First, however, let's look at attacks on critical infrastructures and nonreal-time threats versus real-time threats.

---

[2] See Ellison 1999 and *The Counterterrorism Handbook: Tactics, Procedures, and Techniques*

9.2.5 Attacks on Critical Infrastructures

Attacks on critical infrastructures could cripple a nation and its economy. Infrastructure attacks include attacking the telecommunication lines, the electronic, power, gas, reservoirs and water supplies, food supplies and other basic entities that are critical for the operation of a nation.

Attacks on critical infrastructures could occur during any type of attacks whether they are noninformation-related, information-related or bioterrorism attacks. For example, one could attack the software that runs the telecommunications industry and close down all the telecommunications lines. Similarly software that rues the power and gas supplied could be attacked. Attacks could also occur through bombs and explosives. That is, the telecommunication lines could be attacked through bombs. Attacking transportation lines such as highways and railway tracks are also attacks on infrastructures.

As I mentioned earlier, infrastructures could also be attacked by natural disaster such as hurricanes and earthquakes. The primary interest here is attacks on infrastructures through malicious attacks—both information related and noninformation related. The goal is to examine data mining and related data management technologies to detect and prevent infrastructure attacks.

9.2.6 Nonreal-time Threats Versus Real-time Threats

The threats that I have discussed so far can be grouped into two categories; nonreal-time threats or real-time threats. In a way all threats are real-time as we have to act in real time once the threats have occurred. However, some threats are analyzed over a period of time while some others have to be handled immediately. I discuss the various threats here.

Consider for example biological, chemical and nuclear threats. Such threats have to be handled in real time because the response to these threats have timing constraints. If smallpox virus is being spread maliciously, vaccinations must start immediately. Similarly if networks for critical infrastructures are being attacked, the response has to be immediate; otherwise we could loose millions of lives and/or millions of dollars.

There are some other threats that do not have to be handled in real time. For example consider the behavior of suspicious people such as those belonging to a certain terrorist organization who enroll in flight schools. Although it is likely that such people are also planning terrorist attacks, in some cases, even they do not know when they will be ordered to attack. Therefore, such people must be monitored, their behavior must be analyzed, and their actions predicted. While there are timing constraints for such threats, the urgency is not as great as the spread of the smallpox virus. Nevertheless, we should be vigilant about nonreal-time threats.

In general there is no way to say that A is a real-time threat and B is a nonreal-time threat. A nonreal-time threat could turn into a real-time threat. For example, once the terrorists had hijacked the airplanes on September 11, 2001, the threat became a real-time threat as action to thwart the attack had to be taken within about an hour.

9.2.7 Aspects of Counterterrorism

Now that I have provided some discussion on various types of terrorist attacks including noninformation-related terrorism, information related terrorism, and bioterrorism, I will discus what counterterrorism is all about. Counterterrorism is a collection of techniques used to combat, prevent, and detect terrorism. In this section I will briefly discuss what counterterrorism means in the context of the terrorist attacks discussed in the previous sections. This discussion will include methods of protection from noninformation-related terrorism; protection from information-related terrorism (in particular, I will discuss various web security measures as well as other aspects such as intrusion detection and access control); protecting from bioterrorism and chemical attacks and nuclear attacks; and protecting the critical infrastructures. Finally, I will analyze counterterrorism measures for nonreal-time threats as well as for real-time threats.

Protecting from Noninformation-Related Terrorism

As I have stated, noninformation-related counterterrorism includes protecting from bombings, explosions, vandalism, and other kinds of terrorist attacks not involved with computers. For example, hijacking an airplane and attacking buildings with airplanes is a case of noninformation related terrorist activity. How we do protect against such terrorist attacks?

First we need to gather information about various scenarios and examples. We need to identify all the kinds of terrorist acts that have occurred in history, starting from airplane hijacking to bombing of buildings. We also need to gather information about those under suspicion. All of the data that we have gathered needs to be analyzed to see if any patterns emerge.

We also need to ensure there are physical safety measures. For example, we need to check the identity at airports or other places. We need to check for identity randomly in trains as well as routinely at checkpoints. We need to check the belongings of a person either randomly, routinely, or, if that person arouses suspicions, to see if there are dangerous weapons or chemicals in his/her belongings. We should also use sniffing dogs and sensor devices to see if there are potentially hazardous materials. We need surveillance cameras to see who is entering the building. These cameras should also capture facial expressions of various people. The data gathered from the cameras should be analyzed further for suspicious behavior. We also need to enforce access control measures at military bases and seaports.

In summary, several counterterrorism measures have to be taken to combat noninformation-related terrorism. These include information gathering and analysis, surveillance, physical security and various other mechanisms. In the next few sections I will examine the data mining techniques and see how they can detect and prevent such terrorist attacks.

Protecting from Information-Related Terrorism

Essentially, protecting from information-related terrorism is involved with detecting and preventing malicious attacks and intrusions. These attacks could be attacks due to viruses or spoofing or masquerading and stealing information assets. These attacks could also be attacks on databases and malicious corruption of data. That is, terrorist attacks are not necessarily stealing and accessing unauthorized information. They could also include malicious corruption and alteration of the data so that the data will be of little or no use. Terrorist attacks also include credit card frauds and identity thefts.

Various data mining techniques are being proposed for detecting intrusions as well as credit card fraud. I will discuss them in later sections. Preventing malicious attacks is more challenging. We need to design systems in such a way that malicious attacks and intrusions are prevented. When an intruder attempts to attack the system, the system would figure this out and alert the security officer. There is research being carried out on secure systems design so that such intrusions are prevented. However there is more focus on detecting such intrusions than prevention.

Enforcing appropriate access control techniques is also a way to enforce security. For example, users may have certificates to access the information they need to carry out the jobs that they are assigned to do. The organization should give the users no more or no less privileges. There is much research on managing privileges and access rights to various types of systems.

Next let's explore security solutions for the web in more detail. Note that there are also additional problems such as the inference problem where users pose sets of queries and infer sensitive information. This is also an attack. I will visit the inference problem later when I discuss privacy.

Security Solutions for the Web

We need end-end-end security and therefore the components include secure clients, secure servers, secure databases, secure operating systems, secure infrastructures, secure networks, secure transactions and secure protocols. One needs good encryption mechanisms to ensue that the sender and receiver communicate securely. Ultimately whether it be exchanging messages or carrying out transactions, the communication between sender and receiver or the buyer and the seller has to be secure. Secure client solutions including securing the browser, securing the Java virtual machine, securing Java applets, and incorporating various security features into languages such as Java. Note that Java is not the only component that has to be secure. Microsoft has come up with a collection of products including ActiveX and these products have to be secure also. Securing the protocols include secure HTTP, the secure socket layer. Securing the web server means the server has to be installed securely as well as it has to be ensured that the server cannot be attacked. Various mechanisms that have been used to secure operating systems and databases may be applied here. Notable among them are access control lists, which specify which users have access to which web pages and data. The web servers may be connected to databases at the back end and these databases have to be secure. Finally various encryption algorithms are being implemented for the networks and groups such as OMG (Object Management Group) are envisaging security for middleware such as ORB (Object Request Brokers).

One of the challenges faced by the web mangers is implementing security policies. One may have policies for clients, servers, networks, middleware, and databases. How do you integrate these policies? How do you make these policies work together? Who is responsible for implementing these policies? Is there a global administrator or are there several administrators that have to work together? Security policy integration is an area that is currently being examined by researchers.

Finally, one of the emerging technologies for ensuring that an organization's assets are protected is firewalls. Various organizations now have web infrastructures for internal and external use. To access the external infrastructure one has to go through a firewall. Firewalls examine the information that comes into and out of an organization. This way, the internal assets are protected and inappropriate information may be prevented from coming into an organization. We can expect sophisticated firewalls to be developed in the future. Other security mechanism includes cryptography.

Protection from Bioterrorism and Chemical Attacks

I discussed biological, chemical, and nuclear threats in section 9.2.4. Now let's look at counterterrorism measures. Unlike noninformation-related terrorism where bombing and shootings are fairly explicit, bioterrorism and chemical attacks are not immediately obvious. Suppose. for example, that a terrorist spreads the smallpox virus. It takes a few days before symptoms appear, and few more days before a diagnosis can be made. By then it may be too late to prevent the spread of the virus, as millions of people might have been infected in trains and planes and at large gatherings and meetings. The challenge, therefore, is to prevent as well as detect such attacks as soon as possible.

Preventing such attacks could mean developing special sensors to sense that certain viruses are in the air. Such sensors might also have to detect the type of virus, because a cold virus may not be as harmful as a smallpox virus. If the disease has spread, then quick action has to be taken to determine who and how many to vaccinate. Chemical weapons may require similar treatment. One needs sensors to detect who has the chemical weapons. Once dangerous chemicals have been spilled, we need to determine what agents must be sprayed to limit the damage caused by the chemicals. For example an acidic material spill can be countered by washing with soap-based materials.

In the case of nuclear attacks, we need to determine what nuclear weapons have been used and then decide what actions to take. How do we evacuate the affected people in an organized fashion? What medications do we give them? These are very difficult challenges for researchers. Investigative activities are proceeding, but it will take a very long time to find viable solutions.

Critical Infrastructure Protection

Now I'd like to discuss critical infrastructure protection. Our critical infrastructures include telecommunication lines, networks, water, food, gas electric lines, and so forth. Attacking any of these critical infrastructures could cripple businesses and the country. We need to determine what measures to take when infrastructures are attacked.

Essentially, countermeasures include those developed for noninformation-based terrorism as well as information-based terrorism. For example, a terrorist might bomb the telecommunication lines or create viruses that would affect the telecommunications software. Either attack might cripple communication through telephones as well as computer communications that occurs through telephone lines. The countermeasures developed for noninformation-related terrorism as well as for information related terrorism could be applied in this case. We need to gather information about terrorist groups and extract patterns. We also need to detect any unauthorized intrusions. Our ultimate goal is to prevent such disastrous acts.

Biological, chemical, and nuclear weapons could also be used to attack the infrastructure of the nation. For example our food supplies, water supplies, and hospitals could be damaged by biological warfare. Consequently, we need to examine counterterrorism measures for biological, chemical, and nuclear attacks and apply them here.

Protecting from Nonreal-time and Real-time Threats

As I have mentioned, it is difficult to differentiate between these kinds of threats because, over time, a nonreal-time threat could become a real-time threat. Real-time threats, such as a release of the smallpox virus, must be handled in real time.

When it comes to countermeasures for handling such threats, we must develop techniques that meet timing constraints to handle real-time threats. For example, if data mining is to be used to detect and prevent malicious intrusions into corporate networks, then the data mining techniques must give results in real time, whereas, in the case of nonreal-time threats, the data mining techniques could analyze the data and make predictions that certain threats might occur at some future date.

Next let's revisit nonreal-time threats and real-time threats from a data mining perspective. While real-time threats need immediate response, both types are potentially deadly and must be taken seriously.

9.3 Data Mining Applications in Counterterrorism

In this section I will provide a high-level overview of how web data mining as well as data mining could help to counter terrorism. As I have argued, data mining could make a contribution in counterterrorism efforts, because the ability to extract hidden patterns and trends from large quantities of data is very important in detecting and preventing terrorist attacks.

9.3.1 Data Mining for Handling Threats

In section 9.2 I grouped threats in different ways. One grouping was made on the basis of whether the threat was information or noninformation related. This grouping was somewhat artificial, because we need information on all types of threats. However, information-related threats are threats dealing with computers; some of these threats might be real time while others might be nonreal-time. Even this grouping is somewhat arbitrary, since, as we have already seen, nonreal-time threats can become real-time threats. For example, we might suspect that a group of terrorists will eventually perform some act of terrorism. The threat is nonreal time. However, once we determine that the terrorist act is likely to occur within, say, three months, the threat becomes a real-time one, and actions must be taken immediately. If threat and we have to take actions immediately. If the time bounds are even tighter–within two days–then we cannot afford to make any mistakes in our response.

Now let us examine both the nonreal-time threats and real-time threats and see how data mining in general and web data mining in particular could handle such threats. Some very good articles on data mining for counterterrorism were been presented at the Security Informatics Workshop held in June 2003, and I refer the reader to them for additional information (see Chen 2003).

Nonreal-time Threats

Nonreal-time threats are threats that do not have to be handled in real time. That is, they had no timing constraints. For example, we might need to collect data over a period of months, analyze the data, and then detect and/or prevent some terrorist attack, which might or might not occur. How can data mining help prevent such threats and attacks? As I noted in Thuraisingham (2003c), we need good data to carry out data mining and obtain useful results. We also need to reason with incomplete data. This is a big challenge, as most organizations are often not prepared to share the data. Consequently, data mining tools have to make assumptions about the data belonging to other organizations or, as an alternative, carry out federated data mining under a federated administrator. For example, in the U.S., the Homeland security department could serve as the federated administrator and ensure that the various agencies have autonomy but at the same time collaborate when needed.

Next, what data should we collect? We need to start gathering information about various people. The question is, what people? Everyone in the world? Clearly that is impossible. Nevertheless we need to gather information about as many people as possible; because sometimes even those who seem most innocent may have ulterior motives. One possibility is to group people, depending on where they come from, what they are doing, who their relatives are, and so on. Some people may have more suspicious backgrounds than others. If we know, for example, that someone has a criminal record, we might need to be more vigilant about that person.

To have complete information about people, we must gather all kinds of information about them, including their behavior, where they have lived, their religion, their ethnic origin, their relatives and associates, their travel records, and so forth. In gathering such information, we violate personal privacy and civil liberties but what alternative do we have? If we omit information, we may not have a complete picture. We also need complete data, not only about individuals, but also about various events and entities.

For example, suppose I drive a particular vehicle and information is being gathered about me. It should also include information about my vehicle, how long I have driven, any other hobbies or interests I might have, such as flying airplanes, whether I enrolled in flight schools, and if I told the instructor that I would like to learn to fly an airplane, but do not care learning take-offs or landings.

Once the data is collected, it has to be formatted and organized. It may be necessary to build a warehouse to analyze the data. Data may be structured or unstructured. It is likely that some of the warehoused data may not be of much use. For example, the fact that I like ice cream may not help the analysis a great deal. Therefore, the data can be segmented in terms of whether it is critical or noncritical.

Once the data has been gathered and organized, the next step is to mine it. We then need to ask what mining tools should be used and what outcomes should be found. Do we want to find associations or clusters? This will determine what our goal is. We may want to find anything that is suspicious. For example, the fact that I want to learn flying without caring about take-offs or landings should raise a red flag as, in general, most student pilots are interested in those critical components of flying. Once we determine the outcomes we want, we then determine the mining tools to use and start the mining process.

Then comes the very hard part. How do we know that the mining results are useful? There could be false positives and false negatives. For example, the tool might incorrectly produce the result that John is planning to attack the Empire State Building on July 1. As a result, law enforcement officials might arrest John. The consequences could be disastrous. The tool might also incorrectly produce a false negative result, concluding that James is innocent when he is, in fact, guilty. In this case law enforcement might not pay much attention to James. Again, the consequence could be disastrous.

Thus, as I have already stated, we need intelligent mining tools. At present, we also need human specialists who can work with the mining tools. If the tool states that John could be a terrorist, the specialist will have to do some more checking before released a result that might lead to John's arrest. On the other hand, if the tool states that James is innocent, the specialist should do some additional checking in this case as well.

In the case of nonreal-time threats, we have time to gather data and build profiles of (for example) terrorists, analyze the data and then take actions. However, nonreal-time threats can become real-time threats. The data mining tool might state, for instance, that there could be some potential terrorist attacks. But after a while, and with the input of additional information, the tool might conclude that the attacks will occur between September 10, 2001 and September 12, 2001.

At this point, the threat changes to a real-time threat. The challenge then becomes to determine exactly what the attack will be. Will it be an attack on the World Trade Center or will it be an attack on the Tower of London or will it be an attack on the Eiffel Tower?

We need data mining tools that can continue with the reasoning process as new information comes in. That is, as new data comes in, the warehouse must be updated and, in turn, the mining tools should be dynamic and take that new data and information into consideration during the mining process.

Real-time Threats

In the case of nonreal-time threats, we have time to handle the threats. Real-time threats, in contrast, have timing constraints and might require immediate response. Such a threat might be the spread of smallpox virus, a chemical attack, a nuclear attack, a network intrusion, or the bombing of a building before 9 AM in the morning. What type of data mining techniques do we need for real-time threats?

By definition, data mining works on data that has been gathered over a period of time. The goal is to analyze the data and make deductions and predict future trends. Ideally it is used as a decision support tool. However, in responding to a real-time threat, the situation is entirely different. We need to rethink the way we do data mining so that out tools can give out results in real time.

For data mining to work effectively, we need many examples and patterns. We use known patterns and historical data and then make predictions. Often, however, for real-time data mining—as well as terrorist attacks—we have no prior knowledge. For example, the attack on the World Trade Center came as a surprise to many of us—we could never have imagined that those buildings would be attacked by airplanes. So how do we train data mining tools, such as neural networks, without historical data? Here we need to use hypothetical data as well as simulated data. We need to work with counterterrorism specialists and get as many examples as possible. Once we gather the examples and start training the neural networks and other data mining tools, what kinds models do we build? Often, models for data mining are built before hand. Such models are not dynamic. To handle real-time threats, we the models have to change dynamically. This poses a big challenge.

Data gathering is also a challenge for real-time data mining. In the case of nonreal-time data mining, we can collect data, clean it, format it, build a warehouse and then carry out mining. None of these tasks may be possible for real-time data mining because of time constraints. Therefore what tasks are critical and what tasks are not? Do we have time to analyze the data? Which data do we discard? How do we build profiles of terrorists for real-time data mining? We need real-time data management capabilities for real-time data mining.

It is clear that there is a great deal of work yet to be done before we can effectively carry out real-time data mining. Some have argued that there is no such thing as real-time data mining and that it will be impossible to build models in real time. Some others have argued that without real world examples and historical data we cannot do effective data mining. These arguments may be true, in which case our challenge is to then to redefine data mining and figure out ways to handle real-time threats.

As I have already pointed out, there are many situations that require management in real time, including the spread of smallpox, network intrusions, and even analyzing data emanating from sensors, like the surveillance cameras placed in shopping centers, subways, and in front of embassies. The data emanating from such sensors must be analyzed, in many cases, in real time to detect and or prevent attacks. For example, in analyzing the data, we might find that there are some individuals at a mall carrying bombs. We then have to alert law enforcement officials so that they can take actions. However, this scenario also raises the questions of privacy and civil liberties. What alternatives do we have? Should we sacrifice privacy to protect the lives of millions of people? As stated in Thuraisingham (2003a) we need technologists, policy makers, and others to work together to come up with viable solutions. I will revisit the privacy issue in section 9.4.

9.3.2 Analyzing Techniques

As I mentioned previously, applying data mining for real-time threats is a major challenge because the goal of data mining is to analyze data and make predictions and trends. Current tools are not capable of making the predictions and trends in real time, although there are some real-time data mining tools emerging and some of them have been listed in KDD Nuggets.[3] The challenge is to develop models in real time as well as get patterns and trends based on real world examples.

Now let's look at various data mining outcomes and discuss how they could be applied for counterterrorism. Note that the outcomes include making associations, link analysis, forming clusters, classification and anomaly detection. The techniques that result in these outcomes are techniques based on neural networks, decisions trees, market basket analysis techniques, inductive logic programming, rough sets, link analysis based on the graph theory, and nearest neighbor techniques. As I stated in an earlier work (Thuraisingham 2003c), the methods used for data mining are top down reasoning where we start with a hypothesis and then determine whether the hypothesis is true or bottom up reasoning where we start with examples and then come up with a hypothesis.

Let us start with association techniques. Examples of these techniques are market basket analysis techniques. The goal is to find which items go together. For example, we may apply a data mining tool to data that has been gathered and find that John comes from Country X and he has associated with James who has a criminal record. The tool also outputs the result that an unusually large percentage of people from Country X have performed some form of terrorist attacks. Because of the associations between John and Country X, as

---

[3]http://www.kdnuggets.com.

well as between John and James, and James and criminal records, one may need to conclude that John has to be under observation. This is an example of an association.

Link analysis is closely associated with making associations. While association-rule based techniques are essentially intelligent search techniques, link analysis uses graph theoretic methods for detecting patterns. With graphs (i.e. node and links), one can follow the chain and find links. For example A is seen with B and B is friends with C and C and D travel a lot together and D has a criminal record. The question is what conclusions can we draw about A? Link analysis is becoming a very important technique for detecting abnormal behavior. Therefore, I will discuss this technique in a little more detail in the next section.

Next let us consider clustering techniques. One could analyze the data and form various clusters. For example, people with origins from country X and who belong to a certain religion may be grouped into Cluster I. People with origins from country Y and who are less than 50 years old may form another Cluster II. These clusters are formed based on their travel patterns or eating patterns or buying patterns or behavior patterns. While clustering divides the population not based on any pre-specified condition, classification divides the population based on some predefined condition. The condition is found based on examples. For example, we can form a profile of a terrorist. He could have the following characteristics: Male less than 30 years of a certain religion and of a certain ethnic origin. This means all males under 30 years belonging to the same religion and the same ethnic origin will be classified into this group and could possibly be placed under observation.

Another data mining outcome is anomaly detection. A good example here is learning to fly an airplane without wanting to learn to takeoff or land. The general pattern is that people want to get a complete training course in flying. However there are now some individuals who want to learn flying but do not care about take off or landing. This is an anomaly. Another example is John always goes to the grocery store on Saturdays. But on Saturday October 26, 2002 he goes to a firearms store and buys a rifle. This is an anomaly and may need some further analysis as to why he is going to a firearms store when he has never done so before. Is it because he is nervous after hearing about the sniper shootings or is it because he has some ulterior motive? If he is living in the Washington DC area, then one could understand why he wants to buy a firearm, possibly to protect him. But if he is living in Socorro, New Mexico, then his actions may have to be followed up further.

All of the discussions on data mining for counterterrorism have consequences when it comes to privacy and civil liberties. What are our alternatives? How can we carry out data mining and at the same time preserve privacy? I will revisit privacy in section 9.4.

9.3.3 Link Analysis

Link analysis is a particular data mining technique that is especially useful for detecting abnormal patterns. There have been many discussions in the literature on link analysis. In fact, one of the earlier books on data mining by Berry and Linoff (1997) discussed link analysis in some detail. As mentioned in the previous section, link analysis uses various graph theoretic techniques. It is essentially about analyzing graphs. Note that link analysis is also used in web data mining, especially for web structure mining. With web structure mining the idea is to mine the links and extract the patterns and structures about the web. Search engines such as Google use some form of link analysis for displaying the results of a search.

As mentioned in Berry and Linoff (1997), the challenge in link analysis is to reduce the graphs into manageable chunks. As in the case of market basket analysis, where one needs to carry out intelligent searching by pruning unwanted results, with link analysis one needs to reduce the graphs so that the analysis is manageable and not combinatorially explosive. Therefore results in graph reduction need to be applied for the graphs that are obtained by representing the various associations. The challenge here is to find the interesting associations and then determine how to reduce the graphs. Various graphs theoreticians are working on graph reduction problems. We need to determine how to apply the techniques to detect abnormal and suspicious behavior.

Another challenge on using link analysis for counterterrorism is reasoning with partial information. For example, agency A may have a partial graph, agency B another partial graph and agency C a third partial graph. The question is how do you find the associations between the graphs when no agency has the complete picture? One would ague that we need a data miner that would reason under uncertainty and be able to figure out the links between the three graphs. This would be the ideal solution and the research challenge is to develop such a data miner. The other approach is to have an organization above the three agencies that will have access to the three graphs and make the links. One can think of this organization to be the Homeland security agency. In the next section as well as in some of the ensuing sections I will discuss various federated architectures for counterterrorism.

We need to conduct extensive research on link analysis as well as on other data and web data mining techniques to determine how they can be applied effectively for counterterrorism. For example, by following the various links, one could perhaps trace the financing of the terrorist operations to the president of country X. Another challenge with link analysis as well with other data mining techniques is having good data. However for the domain that we are considering much of the data could be classified. If we are to truly get the benefits of the techniques we need to test with actual data. But not all of the researchers have the clearances to work on classified data. The challenge is to find unclassified data that is a representative sample of the classified data. It is not straightforward to do this, as one has to make sure that all classified information, even through implications, is removed. Another alternative is to find as good data as possible in an unclassified setting for the researchers to work on. However, the researchers have to work not only with counterterrorism experts but also with data mining specialists who have the clearances to work in classified environments. That is, the research carried out in an unclassified setting has to be transferred to a classified setting later to test the applicability of the data mining algorithms. Only then can we get the true benefits of data mining.

9.4 A Note on Privacy

There has been much debate recently among the counterterrorism experts and civil liberties unions and human rights lawyers about the privacy of individuals. That is, gathering information about people, mining information about people, conduction surveillance activities and examining e-mail messages and phone conversations are all threats to privacy and civil liberties. However, what are the alternatives if we are to combat terrorism effectively? Today we do not have any effective solutions. Do we wait until privacy violations occur and then prosecute or do we wait until national security disasters occur and then gather information? What is more important? Protecting nations from terrorist attacks or protecting the privacy of individuals? This is one of the major challenges faced by technologists, sociologists and lawyers. That is, how can we have privacy but at the same time ensure the safety of nations? What should we be sacrificing and to what extent?

The challenge is to provide solutions to enhance national security but at the same time ensure privacy. There is now research at various laboratories on privacy enhanced sometimes called privacy sensitive data mining (e.g., Agrawal at IBM Almaden, Gehrke at Cornell University and Clifton at Purdue University); see for example Agrawal and Srikant (2000), Clifton, Kantarcioglu, and Vaidya (2002), Gehrke (2002). The idea here is to continue with mining but at the same time ensure privacy as much as possible. For example, Clifton has proposed the use of the multiparty security policy approach for carrying out privacy sensitive data mining. While there is some progress we still have a long way to go. Some useful references are provided in Clifton, Kantarcioglu, and Vaidya (2002) (see also Evfimievski, Srikant, Agrawal, and Gehrke 2002).

An approach I am proposing is to process privacy constraints in a database management system. Note that one mines the data and extracts patterns and trends. The privacy constraints determine which patterns are private and to what extent. For example, suppose one could extract the names and health-care records. If we have a privacy constraint that states that names and healthcare records are private then this information is not released to the general public. If the information is semi-private, then it is released to those who have a need to know. Essentially the inference controller approach I discussed in an earlier paper (Thuraisingham and Ford 1995) is one solution to achieving some level of privacy. It could be regarded to be a type of privacy sensitive data mining. In Thuraisingham (2003b) I proposed an approach to handle privacy constraints during query, update and database design operations. Also recently IBM Almaden Research Center is developing a similar approach to privacy management. They call their approach "hypocritical databases."

Note that not all approaches to privacy enhanced data mining are the same. Researchers are taking different approaches to such data mining. Some have argued that privacy enhanced data mining may be time consuming and may not be scalable. However we need to investigate this area more before we can come up with viable solutions.

9.5 Directions

Data mining and web data mining technologies will have a significant impact on counterterrorism. Detecting and preventing terrorist attacks is a major concerns of the USA today. It is also becoming a goal for many nations in the world. We need to examine data mining and web mining technologies to see how they can be adapted for counterterrorism. We also need to develop special web mining techniques for counterterrorism. We expect much of the data to be on the internet or intranets. Analysts will have to collaborate via the web within an agency or between agencies. In the US, the new Homeland security department may have an impact on how data mining will be carried out.

In addition to improving data mining and web mining techniques and adapting them for counterterrorism, we also need to focus on federated data mining. We can expect agencies to collaboratively work together. They will have to share data as well as mine it collaboratively. We can expect to see an increased interest in federated data mining. In this chapter I have discussed high-level ideas. We need to explore the details.

Another areas of interest is multilingual data mining. Terrorism is not confined to one country—it has no borders. There is terrorism everywhere. It is carried out by many people from many different countries speaking many different languages. We need technologies that can not only understand the various languages but mine the text in a given language as well. We also need translators that can translate one language to another before mining. We also need language experts who can work with technologists for multilingual data management and mining. Terrorists may come from different countries and speak different languages. We need to understand their language without any ambiguity.

As I stressed in Thuraisingham (2003c), we cannot forget about privacy. National security measures may violate privacy and civil liberties. We cannot abandon our quest for eliminating terrorism. However, we must also be sensitive to the privacy need of individuals. This is a major challenge. We need to develop techniques for privacy sensitive data sharing and data mining.

Disclaimer

The views and conclusions expressed in this chapter are those of the author and do not reflect the policies or procedures of the MITRE Corporation or the National Science Foundation.

Bhavani Thuraisingham is at the National Science Foundation (NSF) on IPA from the MITRE Corporation. She is the Director of the Cyber Trust Initiative at NSF.

Chapter 10

Biosurveillance and Outbreak Detection

Paola Sebastiani and Kenneth D. Mandl

Our national security, threatened by asymmetrical warfare against military and civilian targets, has become increasingly dependent on quick acquisition, processing, integration and interpretation of massive amounts of data. In the mid 1990s, the White House and U.S. Department of Defense (DOD) identified bioterrorism directed against civilian populations as a substantial risk (U.S. Centers for Disease Control and Prevention 2000), and then stepped up efforts to prevent mass civilian casualties after the anthrax attacks in fall 2001 (Jernigan, Stephens, Ashford, Omenaca, Topiel, Galbraith, Fisk, Zaki, Popovic, Meyer, Quinn, Harper, Fridkin, Sejvar, Shepard, Guarner, Gerberding, and Hughes 2001). Early detection of bioterrorism requires both real time data and real time interpretation. Toward this goal, the biomedical, public health, defense, law enforcement, and and intelligence communities all endeavor to develop new means of communication and novel sources of data. Public health surveillance is defined as "the ongoing, systematic collection, analysis, interpretation, and dissemination of data regarding a health-related event for use in public health action to reduce morbidity and mortality and to improve health" (U.S. Center for Disease Control and Prevention 2001).

In response to this need, a new information infrastructure to support active, real time surveillance is emerging, (see Kohane 2002; Koplan 2001; Lober,

Karras, Wagner, Overhage, Davidson, Fraser, Trigg, Mandl, Espino, and Tsui 2002; O'Toole 2001; Teich, Wagner, Mackenzie, and Schafer 2002; and Yasnoff, Overhage, Humphreys, LaVenture, Goodman, Gatewood, Ross, Reid, Hammond, Dwyer, Huff, Gotham, Kukafka, Loonsk, and Wagner 2001). In fact, real time surveillance systems are now in place in several cities including Boston (Reis, Pagano, and Mandl 2003), Washington D.C. (Lombardo, Burkom, Elbert, Magruder, Lewis, Loschen, Sari, Sniegoski, Wojcik, and Pavlin 2003), Pittsburgh (Tsui, Espino, Dato, Gesteland, Hutman, and Wagner 2003), and New York (Greenko, Mostashari, Fine, and Layton 2003). These new systems, along with direct environmental monitoring (Miller 2003) are expected to form the basis of a national surveillance network.

While developing technologies will support not only bioterrorism surveillance but also the tracking and understanding of natural outbreaks, it is the lethality and rapidity of effect of biological warfare agents that most strongly compel the need for a real time infrastructure. The Centers for Disease Control and Prevention (CDC) classifies biological warfare agents in terms of how easily they could be disseminated to large numbers of people with the potential for causing mass casualties. The most threatening agents are classified as "category A" and include anthrax (bacillus anthracis), botulism, plague, smallpox, tularemia, and the viral hemorrhagic fevers.

The biological features of category A agents and the clinical effects on their victims require that urgent efforts be focused on developing of methods for early detection and monitoring. The case of an anthrax attack is illustrative. Anthrax is a spore forming bacterium. Spores are dormant cells that can reactivate under the right conditions. From the time that a person is first exposed to anthrax, the incubation period is one to six days until symptoms appear. The first signs and symptoms resemble those of influenza and include fever, malaise and fatigue. Within two to three days, patients become severely ill and develop respiratory distress, overwhelming blood infection, and in about half of the cases, meningitis, or infection of the fluid and tissues surrounding the brain and spinal cord. If antibiotic treatment is not initiated prior to the onset of the acute, severe phase of the illness, survival is unlikely. However, antibiotic prophylaxis at the time of exposure or treatment during the early phase of the disease is very effective (U.S. Army Medical Research Institute of Infectious Diseases 2001).

10.1 Detection

It is reasonable to assume that a biological attack on a civilian population will be carried out covertly. Hence, the first indication of an attack may be large numbers or smaller clusters of people developing an influenzalike illness between one and six days after the attack. Ideally, if this surge in people with influenzalike illness were detected at the early possible moment, a large scale public health response would be mobilized to initiate treatment of all those exposed. Epidemiological models presented in a Defense Department Jasons report project that fatalities resulting from a covert anthrax attack on the New York City subway system would be reduced by a factor of seven if an active surveillance system were in place. Such a system would reduce mortality by seven orders of magnitude for a communicable, highly contagious disease such as smallpox. An infrastructure to support fundamental change in the health care system must therefore include real time information about regional disease patterns, health care processes, and health related behaviors. Current health information systems fall far short of this capability (Fernandez 1999), despite readily available information technology to process patient data. The Federal focus on preparedness for bioterrorism (U.S. Center for Disease Control and Prevention 2000), which was sharpened after the 2001 anthrax mailings (Jernigan, Stephens, Ashford, Omenaca, Topiel, Galbraith, Fisk, Zaki, Popovic, Meyer, Quinn, Harper, Fridkin, Sejvar, Shepard, Guarner, Gerberding, and Hughes 2001), has thrown into greater relief the problems we face when providing health care and protecting the public health in the absence of real time information (Henderson 1999).

The state of the art for detecting abnormalities in surveillance data is primitive. Analyses are typically manual, and even when the data are available, the methods often involve simply comparing a count to an expected value and alarming when the count is too high.

10.2   Approaches to Surveillance

The goal of biosurveillance is to identify biological weapons before they are used or as soon as possible after release. The major targets for monitoring include the environment, animals, agriculture, the citizenry, or patient populations. Once an attack has occurred, surveillance of the environment provides the earliest possible warning of a biological release into, for example, the ventilation system of an office building. Detection systems such as those employing laser-induced fluorescence and immunologically based bioelectric sensors have been shown to be highly sensitive to biological releases (Primmerman 2000). Animals and agriculture are prime targets for bioterrorism. The extensive outbreak of foot and mouth disease in Great Britain (Ferguson, Donnelly, and Anderson 2001) illustrates the devastating economic and social impact that such an attack could have. The citizenry may be observed, polled, or examined. Telemarketing and the emerging field of consumer informatics enable surveillance of the ever growing population of Internet users (Mandl, Feit, Pena, and Kohane 2000).

Behaviors of the citizenry, when their health is affected, may leave imprints on certain data sets. The principal underlying premise of these systems is that the first signs of a covert biological warfare attack will be clusters of victims who change their behavior because they begin to feel ill. When people become sick, they may make purchases such as facial tissue, orange juice, and over-the-counter cold remedies (Goldenberg, Shmueli, Caruana, and Fienberg 2002), and rates of absenteeism will rise. They may stay home from school or work. The next phase of detectable activity is likely to be encounters with the health care system. Patients may phone in to nurses or physicians. They may visit primary care settings (Lazarus, Kleinman, Dashevsky, Adams, Kludt, De-Maria, and Platt 2002), and emergency departments (Lober, Karras, Wagner, Overhage, Davidson, Fraser, Trigg, Mandl, Espino, and Tsui 2002). They may be hospitalized. Some may die. All of this activity may precede the first confirmed diagnosis of a biological warfare victim.

10.3   Syndromic Surveillance

One recent approach to the problem of how to recognize an attack as soon as possible has been the development of syndromic surveillance systems. Syndromic surveillance relies on data that are available before the diagnosis of the individual patient and would precede recognition that there has been an attack. One approach to syndromic surveillance of emergency department populations has been drop-in surveillance as practiced by the CDC. Drop-in surveillance was implemented by the CDC at the World Trade Organization Ministerial (Seattle, Washington) in 1999, and at the Super Bowl (Tampa, Florida) and World Trade Center attacks (New York, NY) in 2001 (U.S. Center for Disease Control and Prevention 2002b). Drop-in surveillance is accomplished by staffing the emergency departments around an area thought to be at high risk of an attack. Health care providers use a paper form to indicate whether each patient fits a particular syndrome of concern. At the World Trade Center, the syndromes tracked were anxiety, asthma, botulismlike, death, gastrointestinal, inhalation, neurological, rash, respiratory, sepsis, and trauma. There are limitations to drop-in surveillance as it has recently been practiced. The very nature of the method assumes that the time and location of an attack can be predicted. Furthermore, reliance on manual processes produces incomplete and at times inaccurate data. Designing automated systems and interpreting their output, however, poses substantial methodological challenges.

10.4   Outbreak Detection

One approach to identify clusters of patients infected by biological warfare agents is to set up a detection system that distinguishes abnormal from normal

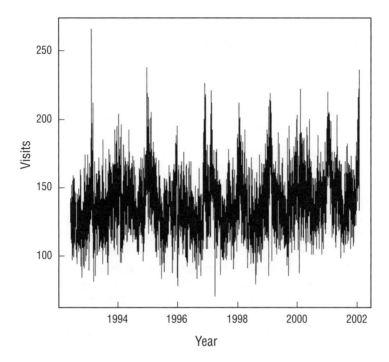

Figure 10.1: Number of daily visits at the emergency department of Children's Hospital, Boston, over the last 10 years.

patterns. The goal of such a detection system is to signal an alarm whenever the observed pattern departures from the expected normal pattern.

The most straight forward approach builds a control chart, such as CuSUM described for example in Basseville and Nikiforov (1993), in which cumulative differences between observed and expected data in a time window are compared to a threshold. In traditional CuSUM, the expected value is a theoretical mean describing, for example, the average number of hospital visits, and it is constant over time. A suspicious increase in the observed data over the theoretical mean is potentially indicative of an emerging outbreak and, to allow for sampling variability, the threshold of the maximum difference between observed and expected values is typically some multiple of the standard error of the sample mean. Because many health care datasets show regular periodicities (annual, seasonal, monthly, daily) the theoretical mean needs to change over time (Lewis, Pavlin, Mansfield, O'Brien, Boomsma, Elbert, and Kelley 2002; Reis, Pagano, and Mandl 2003). Figure 10.1, which shows the number of daily emergency department visits at Children's Hospital Boston between

June 1992 and February 2002, demonstrates such periodicity. The CuSUM method was corrected for seasonal and daily variations and is implemented in the CDC's early aberration reporting systems (EARS).

10.4.1 Temporal Modeling

Model-based detection approaches attempt to detect outbreaks by comparing the observation y_t with the predictions $\hat{y}_t$ generated by a model describing the normal pattern. More advanced multi-day temporal filters (Reis, Pagano, and Mandl 2003) compare a weighted prediction of multiple days at once to a threshold. This, in effect lessens the effects of the large variability of hospital visit rates and improve both the timeliness and sensitivity of detection.

Crucial choices in model-building are how to characterize the normal patterns and at what threshold to signal an alarm. Threshold values may be a multiple κ of the standard error s_t of the prediction. Generally κ is set between 2 and 3.5 to ensure that the false alarm rate is below 5%. An alarm is signaled whenever the observation y_t is outside the interval $\hat{y} \pm \kappa s_t$. Adjustment to take into account multiple comparisons can be based on Bonferroni's correction, or randomization procedures as those implemented in the RODS system (Tsui, Espino, Wagner, Gesteland, Olszewski, Liu, Zeng, Chapman, Wong, and Moore 2002; Wagner, Tsui, Espino, Dato, Sittig, Caruana, McGinnis, Deerfield, Druzdzel, and Fridsma 2001).

To establish normal patterns of temporal relationships among patients, it is helpful to have a few years of historical data at the surveillance sites that include regular recurrence of cyclic diseases, such as influenza. These historical data naturally contain local variations as well as trends in local population density and shifting referral patterns. Data normalization can help to reduce the effect of some of these factors.

Figure 10.2 a) shows the weekly number of death for pneumonia and influenza in New England between January 1996 and April 2002 (U.S. Center for Disease Control and Prevention 2002a). The data are published by the CDC as part of its national influenza surveillance effort. Figure 10.2 b) shows the weekly proportion of deaths for pneumonia and influenza after normalization with the number of deaths for all causes. The apparent increasing trend may be part of a secular trend with cyclic episodes of severe influenza epidemics (Simenson, Fukuda, Schonberg, and Cox 2000). Modeling normal patterns of disease or visit rates may rely on regression type models (Serfling 1963), classical autoregressive moving average models ($ARIMA$) (Box and Jenkins 1976) or a combination of both methods. Serfling's method monitors the normal pattern of susceptibility to death for pneumonia and influenza when there

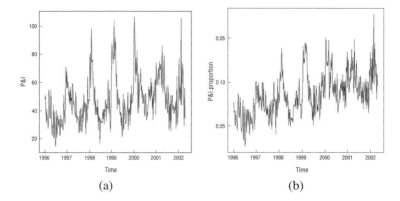

(a) (b)

Figure 10.2: Left: Weekly number of deaths for pneumonia and influenza in New England between January 1996 and April 2002. Right: Weekly proportion of deaths for pneumonia and influenza in New England between January 1996 and April 2002, after normalization with the number of deaths for all causes. Source: *CDC, Morbidity and Mortality Weekly Report* (http://wonder.cdc.gov/mmwr/mmwrmort.asp).

is not epidemic, and the objective is to determine an epidemic threshold. The method uses the cyclic regression equation

$$y_t = \mu_0 + \theta t + \alpha \sin(2\pi t/52) + \beta \cos(2\pi t/52) + \epsilon_t \qquad (10.1)$$

to model the weekly number y_t of people susceptible to death from pneumonia and influenza when there is no epidemic. The model consists of the linear component θt describing the secular trend and the sine-wave component $\alpha \sin(2\pi t/52) + \beta \cos(2\pi t/52)$ describing the periodic recurrence of influenza epidemics. Assuming that the weekly numbers of deaths are normally distributed and uncorrelated, the standard least squares method is used to estimate the model parameters from nonepidemic data, and to compute the predicted values $\hat{y}_t$. This model can be easily expanded to monitor hospital visit data for influenza (Simenson, Fukuda, Schonberg, and Cox 2000; Tsui, Espino, Wagner, Gesteland, Olszewski, Liu, Zeng, Chapman, Wong, and Moore 2002), to describe different secular trends by changing the linear component, and it can be adapted to include exogenous variables such as weather or pollution indicators and to model daily or monthly data, by changing the sine-wave component.

Serfling's method is the standard approach to detect epidemic thresholds for influenza and, in principle, it could be adapted to detect epidemic thresholds for other cyclic diseases. Its use requires a clear definition of the disease, the selection of data to identify a normal pattern of susceptible individuals, and the assumption that the normal pattern is periodical. However, to be able to detect an outbreak determined by a bioterrorism attack, recurrent incidence of cyclic diseases should be part of the "normal pattern of diseases" that underlies, for example, the dynamics of hospital visits rates. Furthermore, the assumption that the data are independent may be violated by hospital visits rates that may be dependent upon the past. Traditional time series models, such as $ARIMA$, seem to be more adequate to describe historical visits rates and can account for temporal dependency, trends corresponding to secular changes in the populations, and seasonal effects due, for example, to annual recurrence of influenza epidemics. An $ARIMA(p, d, q)$ model describes a nonstationary time series in which the series of differences $x_t = y_t - y_{t-d}$ is stationary and is described by an $ARMA(p, q)$ model. The $ARMA(p, q)$ model consists of two components: (1) an autoregressive component of order p, and (2) a moving average component of order q. The autoregressive component of order p describes explicitly the dependency of x_t on a linear combination of the past p points, whereas the moving average component uses an average of the past q uncorrelated errors to "shock" the process mean. Both the autoregressive and moving average orders can be chosen to get the best fitting from historical data, although large orders may compensate for recent trends and miss timely departures from normal patterns. Goodness of fit criteria such as the Akaike or the Schwarz information criteria (Shumway and Stoffer 2000) can be used to select the best orders p, q by trading off goodness of fit and model complexity, thus limiting the risk of over fitting. $ARIMA$ models can be extended to account for seasonality, by either decomposing the time series into a trend, a seasonal component and the residual, and by fitting an $ARMA(p, q)$ model to the residual component, or by fitting all components simultaneously (Box and Jenkins 1976). $ARIMA$ models to fit time series of patients with respiratory syndromes are described in Reis and Mandl (2003).

$ARIMA$ models are standardly used to fit time series data that do not exhibit a clear pattern, although many historical data at surveillance sites show clear periodicities. The regression type model in equation 10.1 describes periodicities of the mean by the sine wave component, but it does not take into account temporal correlation. A combination of the two models would give the advantage of an explicit description of important components such as periodicity and secular trends and, at the same time, it could account for the serial correlation.

Other approaches to model the normal pattern use hidden Markov models (LeStrat and Carrat 1999; Rabiner 1989; Rath, Carreras, and Sebastiani 2003) by using a hidden state that describes the presence or absence of epidemic of a particular disease, and a model of the data conditional on the epidemic status. Closely related to hidden Markov models are change point algorithms to detect changes in a baseline model describing the normal pattern (Basseville and Nikiforov 1993). A potential use of change-point algorithms is to automatically identify the historical data most relevant for modeling the normal pattern. When massive data at the surveillance sites are available, it is important to decide whether all data should be used to formulate a model for the normal pattern. Often, changes in the data collection or in population demographics determine a change of the dynamics underlying the normal pattern and not all the historical data should be used to have the best prediction. For example, modeling data from influenza mortality surveillance has shown that more accurate forecasts are based on five years historical data, and the CDC syndromic surveillance practice is to use at least five years historical data (Farrington, Andrews, Beale, and Catchpole 1996; Hutwagner, Maloney, Bean, Slutsker, and Martin 1997; Stern and Lightfoot 1999). The choice of the amount of historical data is an open issue and the availability of data will vary.

10.4.2 Spatial and Temporal Clustering Methods

Several traditional methods are available for cluster analysis in time, once a suspect location is identified. Methods as the scan test in Naus (1965) or the method in Ederer, Myers, and Mantel (1964) testing for temporal clustering using a cell-occupancy approach. In the scan test, the maximum number of cases observed in an interval of fixed length is found by scanning all intervals of the same length in a time period. The method in Ederer, Myers, and Mantel (1964) compares the distribution of cases into k disjoint subintervals with the distribution one would expect under the null hypothesis of no clustering. The difference between the two approaches is that the scan test uses overlapping intervals, compared to the disjoint intervals used in Ederer, Myers, and Mantel (1964).

Methods for spatial clustering can be grouped according to whether they use information about individuals or aggregate data. Our work has focused on detection of perturbations in the distribution of mutual distances among all individual cases in a geographical region to identify clusters. We find substantially increased power using this measure of geographical clustering compared with using relying on counts alone (Olson and Mandl 2002b).

The nearest-neighbor method examines the distribution of interpoint distances of infected individuals. The method of Ohno (Ohno, Aoki, and Aoki 1978) is a simple test for spatial clustering that uses rates for geographic areas rather than data for individual cases. The test assesses whether the rates in adjacent areas are more similar than would be expected under the null hypothesis of no clustering. More advanced Bayesian models for detection of spatial clusters of disease—known as Bayesian disease mappings—are described in Elliott, Wakefield, Best, and Briggseds (2000), and the extension of hidden

Markov models to detect small clusters in space is in Green and Richardson (2002). A potential limitation of Bayesian methods to disease mapping is their computational burden. This may make them unfeasible for monitoring rapidly shifting distributions of patients within an ill-defined window of hours to days. Furthermore, one of the fundamental steps in spatial analysis based on aggregate data is the definition of geographical areas to aggregate point data into groups. Geographical information systems are used to form spatial groups by aggregating small area units into larger, contiguous areas that can be given a particular classification. A common problem with spatial clustering procedures is that the scale of the area units chosen for the aggregation can have dramatic effects on the results of the classification. This effect is known as the modifiable area unit problem (MAUP) and a solution to this problem was proposed in Hobbs (1996). Most of the methods described for spatial clustering work retrospectively, whereas on line surveillance system need to process observations sequentially. Statistical methods for on-line surveillance are described by Rogerson (1997).

Detection of clusters in space and time is a much harder problem, and fewer methods are available. Knox method (Knox 1964) is a standard epidemiology approach to monitor the temporal-spatial spread of a disease by examining the distribution of geographical and temporal distances of affected individuals. The method works by classifying the pairs of cases as close in space and time, close in space only, close in time only, or close in neither space nor time. The limitation is the choice of time and space parameters to classify pairs as close or not, and it is overcome by temporal-spatial scan statistics (Kulldorf 2001) that identify "suspect clusters" by using a window that moves in time and space. In each window, the number of reported cases for a particular disease is compared to the number expected under the hypothesis that there is no cluster, and the window with largest evidence of cluster is identified. The K-nearest neighbor test by Jacquez (1996) uses a randomized test to assess the statistical significance of a potential space-time interaction process. Because most data at surveillance sites are count data, such as number of chief complaints for respiratory problems (Lazarus, Kleinman, Dashevsky, Adams, Kludt, DeMaria, and Platt 2002), one can use generalized linear models to compute the expected number of cases of a particular syndrome in a particular time and location. The expected number is compared with the observed number and an unusually large incidence of a particular syndrome is used to detect a cluster of illness.

10.5 Challenges

The process of syndromic surveillance can be broken down into five stages. First, there is the data acquisition stage, in which data are acquired from their sources. Next, in the syndromic grouping stage, data are processed, according to a scheme that allows each the assignment of each patient to a syndromic group (such as influenzalike illness, or gastrointestinal illness). Next is the modeling stage, in which historical data, ideally reaching back from one to several years, are analyzed to establish a model of the normal temporal pattern. Fourth, in the detection stage, the expected values (for example, daily frequencies of patients presenting in each syndromic group) are compared against observed values collected in the field in order to determine abnormal activity is occurring. Finally, in the alarms stage, thresholds are set for evaluation of whether or not the unusual patterns warrant notification. Each stage has its own particular set of challenges.

10.5.1 Data Acquisition Stage

A problem that plagues health care information technology generally, and bioterrorism surveillance specifically, is a lack of universal standards for storage and communication of medical information (Kohane, Fackler, Cimino, Kilbridge, Murphy, Rind, Safran, Barnett, and Szolovits 1996). Much medical data, even when stored electronically, exists as free text and requires natural language processing.[1] Even when the chief complaints are encoded, the classification schema have often been developed locally. Sharing information across systems requires a standardized method for describing data and their organization. Models for data exchange are being developed for health care (Beeler 1998), emergency medicine (Pollock and Lowery 2001; Barthell, Cordell, Moorhead, Handler, Feied, Smith, Cochrane, Felton, and Collin 2002), and public health. The public health information network (PHIN) is a standards-based approach to connect public health and clinical medicine.[2] As its implementation proceeds, PHIN will help standardize and facilitate the transfer of information needed for public health from clinical information systems.

Another issue is the timeliness of the data. To support real time detection, data must be available immediately. This requirement eliminates many otherwise useful data sources and sometimes precludes entire institutions from participation. The quality of the data used in automated systems varies. Establishing new manual data entry processes to collect data (effectively, relying on human intelligence) is difficult and costly. Therefore, the most successful surveillance systems to date rely on information already collected for other purposes. There are also important issues with the quality of geographical location data. Geographical information system (GIS) software can translate an

---

[1] The RODS Laboratory at the University of Pittsburgh has made a Bayesian language classifier available for this purpose at http://www.health.pitt.edu/rods/sw/default.htm.

[2] http://www.cdc.gov/phin/index.htm.

address into precise latitude and longitude coordinates. In general, in the health care system, the only address reliably collected is the home address. Ideally, a surveillance system should have access to data about where each individual works, goes to school, and has been recently. If an attack were to occur at a baseball game, for example, the home address may not be the most salient geographical feature of the patients, but rather a cluster of patients who had attended the game might be identified. The home address may be entered inaccurately, making geocoding a challenging task. In hospital information systems, new patient addresses may permanently overwrite older ones, making the historical geographical patient distributions difficult to reconstruct. Also, the accuracy of geocoding results is far from perfect (Krieger, Waterman, Lemieux, Zierler, and Hogan 2001; Olson and Mandl 2002).

10.5.2   Syndromic Grouping Stage

Since the data are automatically collected and were not originally designed to group patients into syndromes, they may not be ideally suited to the purpose of surveillance. The mapping of each case onto a syndrome is imprecise. The degree of imprecision is, however, measurable against a gold standard such as a physician chart review of the case (Espino and Wagner 2001; Beitel and Mandl 2002).

10.5.3   Modeling Stage

A common problem when establishing a new surveillance system, is that data may only be available going forward, making the modeling of normality impossible before a few years have elapsed. If these data are available, then the long term and local periodicities must be known or discovered in order to model the baseline. Such modeling is often based on an assumption that the data do not contain the signal of interest. While one can reasonably assume that a historical data set of, say, daily emergency department syndromic data, does not contain signal from a biological attack, it may well contain signal from nonperiodically recurring events such as a food-borne outbreak of gastrointestinal disease.

10.5.4   Detection Stage

The detection performance of a syndromic surveillance system can be evaluated by measuring its ability to detect signal (disease outbreak) against a background of noise (normal variation in baseline disease rates in the region). To benchmark performance, training and validation data containing signal and noise are required. A major problem is the lack of training data. Fortunately, few people have been infected with biological warfare agents although there are notable exceptions such as the people of Sverdlovsk (Meselson, Guillemin, Hugh-Jones, Langmuir, Popova, Shelokov, and Yampolskaya 1994) exposed in 1979 during an accidental release of anthrax from a weapons plant, and those involved in the Florida, New York, and Washington D.C. mail attacks in 2001. However, with few actual cases, syndromic surveillance systems cannot "learn" to detect bioterrorism with real world data. Nor can systems be bench-marked by their ability to detect actual attacks. These systems must be trained with nonbioterror-related events or simulated events instead. Training and validation data sets can be samples of authentic regional data, synthetic data, or a combination of both (semisynthetic data).

Detecting abnormal clusters of syndromic cases in space/time poses substantial challenges. Consideration of the temporal-spatial distribution of syndrome cases may facilitate the detection of a bioterrorism attack, when cases are distributed over space and/or time in a different manner from the normal pattern. In classical cluster detection for public health and epidemiology, a specific cluster is often being investigated, and the goal is to identify a point source, such as a toxic waste dump causing an excess number of cases of leukemia (Waller 2000). In automated bioterrorism detection, the location of the cluster is not known in advance and the temporal window in which cases are grouped is constantly forward moving and may be only a few days wide.

Attacks may produce signals in the data that have different shapes. For example, in a syndromic surveillance system that tracked the daily emergency department rates illustrated in figure 10.1, an attack might be characterized by a short high spike, a sustained low and flat signal, or an exponentially increasing high amplitude signal. Different methods, and different applications of methods, such as using varying temporal filters, may strongly influence detection capabilities (Reis, Pagano, and Mandl 2003). Therefore, a host of distinct methods may ultimately need to be simultaneously applied to the same data streams to enable the detection of all possible forms of attack.

10.5.5   Alarm Stage

Establishing appropriate thresholds is a nontrivial task. Obviously, a detection system with poor sensitivity, one that fails to detect most attacks, is not acceptable. However, in determining alarm thresholds, one must trade off sensitivity against specificity, ensuring that most alarms are real. Consequently, the more attacks one aims to detect, the more false alarms one must accept. The costs of false alarms are difficult to quantify but if a graded response is developed, news of a false alarm need not filter out to the public. In the case of bioterrorism, the cost of a missed signal might be astronomical. Decision analytic approaches are needed to estimate the human and economic implications across a range of alarm thresholds.

Using more than one signal stream may help to reduce false alarms. For example, if visits for influenza syndrome increase, but so do actual cases of influenza, there may not be a cause for alarm. If the two signal streams diverge, however, there may be more cause for concern. Ideally, a regional or national command center would act based upon an interpretation of multiple streams of data, whether they come from completely different sources (e.g. hospital visits, school absenteeism, sales of over-the-counter medication) or from different models of a single data source. Substantial work is needed to develop methods for such signal integration. Integration must be accomplished for signals from same data using multiple methods, signals from separate but potentially correlated data streams, signals from overlapping geographical regions, and signals from remote geographical regions.

10.6   Conclusions

The precise role and efficacy of biosurveillance in public health has yet to be determined. Syndromic surveillance systems as they existed to date in the New York City and Washington D.C. areas failed to detect the anthrax attacks of 2001. While these attacks affected only a small number of people, they nonetheless are a cause for humility for anyone attempting to predict with certainty when, where, and how bioweapons will be used. Astute clinicians will always play a role in the accurate diagnosis and treatment of patients as well as in the identification of public health emergencies. However, biosurveillance is another modality that clearly has the ability to detect certain kinds of events. The work to be done over the coming months and years is to build our data integration infrastructure, develop and refine our methods, and estimate to the best of our ability, the promise and limits of our technology.

Acknowledgements

This work was supported by the Agency for Health Care Quality and Research, contract # 290-00-0020, and the National Institutes of Health through a grant from the National Library of Medicine R01LM07677-01.

Paola Sebastiani is associate professor in biostatistics at the Boston University School of Public Health. Her web page is people.bu.edu/sebas

Kenneth D. Mandl, M.D. is an assistant professor at Harvard Medical School. His research is at the intersection of medical informatics and epidemiology.

Chapter 11

MINDS — Minnesota Intrusion Detection System

Levent Ertöz, Eric Eilertson,
Aleksandar Lazarevic, Pang-Ning Tan,
Vipin Kumar, Jaideep Srivastava, and Paul Dokas

Traditional methods for intrusion detection are based on extensive knowledge of attack signatures that are provided by human experts. The signature database has to be manually revised for each new type of intrusion that is discovered. A significant limitation of signature-based methods is that they cannot detect novel attacks. In addition, once a new attack is discovered and its signature developed, often there is a substantial latency in its deployment. These limitations have led to an increasing interest in intrusion detection techniques based upon data mining (Barbara, Wu, and Jajodia 2001; Bloedorn, Christiansen, Hill, Skorupka, Talbot, and Tivel 2001; Lee and Stolfo 1998; Luo 1999; Manganaris, Christensen, Zerkle, and Hermiz 1999), which generally fall into one of two categories: misuse detection and anomaly detection.

In misuse detection, each instance in a data set is labeled as "normal" or "intrusive" and a learning algorithm is trained over the labeled data. Research in misuse detection has focused mainly on detecting network intrusions using various classification algorithms (Barbara, Wu, and Jajodia 2001; Ghosh and Schwartzbard 1999; Lee and Stolfo 1998; Lippmann and Cunningham 2000;

Luo 1999; Chris Sinclair 1999), rare class predictive models (Joshi, Kumar, and Agarwal 2001; Joshi, Agarwal, and Kumar 2002; Joshi, Agarwal, and Kumar 2001; Joshi and Kumar 2003; Lazarevic, Chawla, Hall, and Bowyer 2002), association rules (Barbara, Wu, and Jajodia 2001; Lee and Stolfo 1998; Manganaris, Christensen, Zerkle, and Hermiz 1999) and cost sensitive modeling (Fan, Stolfo, Zhang, and Chan 1999; Joshi, Agarwal, and Kumar 2001). Unlike signature-based intrusion detection systems, models of misuse are created automatically, and can be more sophisticated and precise than manually created signatures. In spite of the fact that misuse detection models have high degree of accuracy in detecting known attacks and their variations, their obvious drawback is the inability to detect attacks whose instances have not yet been observed. In addition, labeling data instances as normal or intrusive may require enormous time for many human experts.

Anomaly detection algorithms build models of normal behavior and automatically detect any deviation from it (Denning 1987; Javitz and Valdes 1993). The major benefit of anomaly detection algorithms is their ability to potentially detect unforeseen attacks. In addition, they may be able to detect new or unusual, but nonintrusive, network behavior that is of interest to a network manager. A major limitation of anomaly detection systems is a possible high false alarm rate. There are two major categories of anomaly detection techniques, namely supervised and unsupervised. In supervised anomaly detection, given a set of normal data to train on, and given a new set of test data, the goal is to determine whether the test data is "normal" or anomalous. Recently, there have been several efforts in designing supervised network-based anomaly detection algorithms, such as ADAM (Barbara, Wu, and Jajodia 2001), PHAD (Mahoney and Chan 2001), NIDES (Anderson, Lunt, Javitz, Tamaru, and Valdes 1995), and other techniques that use neural networks (Ryan, Lin, and Miikkulainen 1997), information theoretic measures (Lee and Xiang 2001), network activity models (Cabrera, Ravichandran, and Mehra 2000), etc. Unlike supervised anomaly detection where the models are built only according to the normal behavior on the network, unsupervised anomaly detection attempts to detect anomalous behavior without using any knowledge about the training data. Unsupervised anomaly detection approaches are based on statistical approaches (Staniford, Hoagland, and McAlerney 2002), (Yamanishi, Takeuchi, Williams, and Milne 2000), (Ye and Chen 2001), clustering (Eskin, Arnold, Prerau, Portnoy, and Stolfo 2002), outlier detection schemes (Aggarwal and Yu 2001; Breunig, Kriegel, Ng, and Sander 2000); Knorr and Ng 1998; Ramaswamy, Rastogi, and Shim 2000), state machines (Sekar, Gupta, Frullo, Shanbhag, Tiwari, Yang, and Zhou 2002), etc.

In this chapter, we introduce the Minnesota Intrusion Detection System (MINDS), which uses a suite of data mining techniques to automatically detect attacks against computer networks and systems. While the long-term objective of MINDS is to address all aspects of intrusion detection, in this chapter we present details of two specific contributions: (1) an unsupervised anomaly detection technique that assigns a score to each network connection that reflects how anomalous the connection is, and (2) an association pattern analysis based module that summarizes those network connections that are ranked highly anomalous by the anomaly detection module.

We also provide an evaluation of our anomaly detection and association summarization schemes in the context of real life network data at the University of Minnesota. In the absence of labels of network connections (normal vs. intrusive), we are unable to provide any estimate of detection rate, but nearly all connections that are ranked highly by our anomaly detection algorithms are found to be interesting by the network security analyst on our team. In particular, during the past few months our techniques have been successful in automatically detecting several novel intrusions. In fact, many of these attacks have been reported on the CERT/CC (Computer Emergency Response Team/Coordination Center) list of recent advisories and incident notes. Finally, experiments on real network data demonstrate that association pattern analysis is successful in creating useful summaries of many novel attacks detected by our anomaly detection algorithms.

11.1   The Minnesota Intrusion Detection System Project

The Minnesota intrusion detection system (MINDS) is a data mining based system for detecting network intrusions. Figure 11.1 illustrates the process of analyzing real network traffic data using the system. Input to MINDS is Netflow version 5 data collected using flow-tools.[1] Flow-tools only capture packet header information (i.e., it does not capture message content), and build one way sessions (flows). We are working with Netflow data instead of tcpdump data because we currently do not have the capacity to collect and store the tcpdump. Netflow data for ten-minute windows, which typically results in 1–2 million flows, are stored in flat files. The analyst uses MINDS to analyze these 10-minute data files in a batch mode. The reason the system is running in a batch mode is not due to the time it takes to analyze these files, but because it is convenient for the analyst to do so. Running the system on a ten-minute file takes less than three minutes on a typical desktop computer. Before data is fed into the anomaly detection module, a data filtering step is performed by the analyst to remove network traffic that the analyst is not interested in analyzing. For example, data filtered may include traffic from trusted sources or

---

[1] http://www.splintered.net/sw/flow tools.

The MINDS System

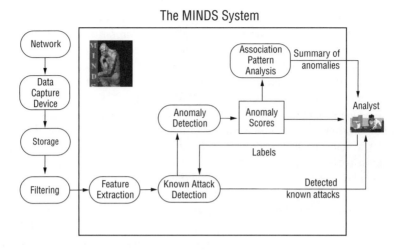

Figure 11.1: MINDS system.

unusual/anomalous network behavior that is known to be intrusion free.

The first step in MINDS is extracting features that are used in the data mining analysis. Basic features include source and destination IP addresses, source and destination ports, protocol, flags, number of bytes and number of packets. Derived features include time-window and connection-window based features. Time-window based features are constructed to capture connections with similar characteristics in the last T seconds. These features are especially useful in separating sources of high volume connections per unit time from the rest of the traffic such as fast scanning activities. A similar approach was used for constructing features in KDD Cup 1999 data (Lee and Stolfo 1998). Table 11.1 summarizes the time-window based features.

"Slow" scanning activities, i.e., those that scan the hosts (or ports) and use a much larger time interval than a few seconds, e.g. one touch per minute or even one touch per hour, cannot be separated from the rest of the traffic using time-window based features. To do so, we also derive connection-window based features that capture similar characteristics of connections as time-window based features, but are computed using the last N connections originating from (arriving at) distinct sources (destinations). The connection-window based features are shown in table 11.2.

After the feature construction step, the known attack detection module is used to detect network connections that correspond to attacks for which signatures are available, and then to remove them from further analysis. For results reported in this chapter, this step is not performed.

Next, the data is fed into the MINDS anomaly detection module that uses

Feature name	Feature description
count-dest	Number of flows to unique destination IP addresses inside the network in the last T seconds from the same source
count-src	Number of flows from unique source IP addresses inside the network in the last T seconds to the same destination
count-serv-src	Number of flows from the source IP to the same destination port in the last T seconds
count-serv-dest	Number of flows to the destination IP address using same source port in the last T seconds

Table 11.1: Time-window based features.

Feature name	Feature description
count-dest-conn	Number of flows to unique destination IP addresses inside the network in the last N flows from the same source
count-src-conn	Number of flows from unique source IP addresses inside the network in the last N flows to the same destination
count-serv-src-conn	Number of flows from the source IP to the same destination port in the last N flows
count-serv-dest-conn	Number of flows to the destination IP address using same source port in the last N flows

Table 11.2: Connection-window based features.

an outlier detection algorithm to assign an anomaly score to each network connection. A human analyst then has to look at only the most anomalous connections to determine if they are actual attacks or other interesting behavior.

MINDS association pattern analysis module summarizes network connections that are ranked highly anomalous by the anomaly detection module. The analyst provides a feedback after analyzing the summaries created and decides whether these summaries are helpful in creating new rules that may be used in the known attack detection module.

11.2 MINDS Anomaly Detection Module

In this section, we only present the density based outlier detection scheme used in our anomaly detection module. For more detailed overview of our research in anomaly detection, the reader is referred to Lazarevic, Ertöz, Ozgur, Kumar, and Srivastava (2003).

MINDS anomaly detection module assigns a degree of being an outlier to each data point, which is called the *local outlier factor* (LOF) (Breunig, Kriegel, Ng, and Sander 2000). The outlier factor of a data point is local in the sense that it measures the degree of being an outlier with respect to its neighborhood. For each data example, the density of the neighborhood is first computed. The LOF of a specific data example p represents the average of the ratios of the density of the example p and the density of its neighbors. To illustrate the advantages of the LOF approach, consider a simple two-dimensional data set given in figure 11.2. It is apparent that the density of cluster C_2 is significantly higher than the density of cluster C_1. Due to the low density of cluster C_1, for most examples q inside cluster C_1, the distance between the example q and its nearest neighbor is greater than the distance between the example p_2 and its nearest neighbor, which is from cluster C_2, and therefore example p_2 will not be considered as outlier.

Hence, the simple nearest neighbor approach based on computing the distances fail in these scenarios. However, the example p_1 may be detected as an outlier using the distances to the nearest neighbors. On the other hand, LOF is able to capture both outliers due to the fact that it considers the density around examples.

LOF requires the neighborhood around all data points be constructed. This involves calculating pairwise distances between all data points, which is an $O(n^2)$ process, which makes it computationally infeasible for millions of data points. To address this problem, we sample a training set from the data and compare all data points to this small set, which reduces the complexity to $O(n* m)$ where n is the size of the data and m is the size of the sample. Apart from achieving computational efficiency by sampling, anomalous network behavior will not be able to match enough examples in the sample to be called normal. This is because rare behavior will not be represented in the sample.

11.3   Evaluation of MINDS Anomaly Detection Results on Real Network Data

This section reports results of applying MINDS anomaly detection module on live network traffic at the University of Minnesota. When describing results on real network data, we are not able to report the detection rate and false alarm rate due to difficulty in obtaining the complete labeling of network connections.

The network security analyst at the University of Minnesota has been using MINDS to analyze the network traffic since August 2002. During this pe-

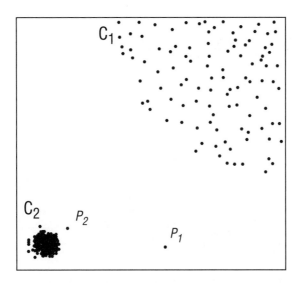

Figure 11.2: 2-D outlier example.

riod, MINDS has been successful in detecting many novel network attacks and
emerging network behavior that could not be detected using signature based
systems such as SNORT. In general, MINDS is able to routinely detect various suspicious behavior (e.g. policy violations), worms, as well as various
scanning activities. In the following, we first show how the analyst analyzes
the output of the MINDS anomaly detection module on a specific data set.
We then follow with few examples of each of the different types of attacks
identified by MINDS.

Figure 11.3 shows top ranked connections produced by the MINDS anomaly detection module for a 10-minute window on January 27, two days after
the Slammer / Sapphire worm started. The output contains the original netflow
data along with the anomaly score and relative contributions of each of the 16
attributes used by the anomaly detection algorithm. Note that most of the top
ranked connections shown belong to the Slammer / Sapphire worm. This is
despite the fact that for this period network connections due to the worm were
only about 2% of the total traffic. This shows the effectiveness of the MINDS
anomaly detection scheme in identifying connections due to worms. The connections due to the worm are highlighted in light gray. It can be observed that
the highest contributions to the anomaly score for these connections were due
to features 9 and 11. This was due to the fact that the infected machines outside our network were still trying to communicate with many machines inside
our network. In figure 11.3, it can also be observed that during this time in-

score	srcIP	sPort	dstIP	dPort	protocol	flags	packets	bytes	1	2	3	4	5	6	7	8	9	10	11	12	13	14	15	16
37674.69	63.150.X.253	1161	128.101.X.29	1434	17	16	[0,2)	[0,1829)	0	0	0	0	0	0	0	0	0.81	0	0.59	0	0	0	0	0
26676.62	63.150.X.253	1161	160.94.X.134	1434	17	16	[0,2)	[0,1829)	0	0	0	0	0	0	0	0	0.81	0	0.59	0	0	0	0	0
24323.55	63.150.X.253	1161	128.101.X.185	1434	17	16	[0,2)	[0,1829)	0	0	0	0	0	0	0	0	0.81	0	0.58	0	0	0	0	0
21169.49	63.150.X.253	1161	160.94.X.71	1434	17	16	[0,2)	[0,1829)	0	0	0	0	0	0	0	0	0.81	0	0.58	0	0	0	0	0
19525.31	63.150.X.253	1161	160.94.X.19	1434	17	16	[0,2)	[0,1829)	0	0	0	0	0	0	0	0	0.81	0	0.58	0	0	0	0	0
19235.39	63.150.X.253	1161	160.94.X.80	1434	17	16	[0,2)	[0,1829)	0	0	0	0	0	0	0	0	0.81	0	0.58	0	0	0	0	0
17679.10	63.150.X.253	1161	160.94.X.220	1434	17	16	[0,2)	[0,1829)	0	0	0	0	0	0	0	0	0.81	0	0.58	0	0	0	0	0
8183.58	63.150.X.253	1161	128.101.X.108	1434	17	16	[0,2)	[0,1829)	0	0	0	0	0	0	0	0	0.82	0	0.58	0	0	0	0	0
7142.98	63.150.X.253	1161	128.101.X.223	1434	17	16	[0,2)	[0,1829)	0	0	0	0	0	0	0	0	0.82	0	0.57	0	0	0	0	0
5139.01	63.150.X.253	1161	128.101.X.142	1434	17	16	[0,2)	[0,1829)	0	0	0	0	0	0	0	0	0.82	0	0.57	0	0	0	0	0
4048.49	142.150.X.101	0	128.101.X.127	2048	1	16	[2,4)	[0,1829)	0	0	0	0	0	0	0	0	0.83	0	0.56	0	0	0	0	0
4008.35	200.250.X.20	27016	128.101.X.116	4629	17	16	[2,4)	[0,1829)	0	0	0	0	0	0	0	0	0	0	0	0	0	0	1	0
3657.23	202.175.X.237	27016	128.101.X.116	4148	17	16	[2,4)	[0,1829)	0	0	0	0	0	0	0	0	0	0	0	0	0	0	1	0
3450.90	63.150.X.253	1161	128.101.X.62	1434	17	16	[0,2)	[0,1829)	0	0	0	0	0	0	0	0	0.82	0	0.57	0	0	0	0	0
3327.60	63.150.X.253	1161	160.94.X.223	1434	17	16	[0,2)	[0,1829)	0	0	0	0	0	0	0	0	0.82	0	0.57	0	0	0	0	0
2796.13	63.150.X.253	1161	128.101.X.241	1434	17	16	[0,2)	[0,1829)	0	0	0	0	0	0	0	0	0.82	0	0.57	0	0	0	0	0
2693.88	142.150.X.101	0	128.101.X.168	2048	1	16	[2,4)	[0,1829)	0	0	0	0	0	0	0	0	0.83	0	0.56	0	0	0	0	0
2683.05	63.150.X.253	1161	160.94.X.43	1434	17	16	[0,2)	[0,1829)	0	0	0	0	0	0	0	0	0.82	0	0.57	0	0	0	0	0
2444.16	142.150.X.236	0	128.101.X.240	2048	1	16	[2,4)	[0,1829)	0	0	0	0	0	0	0	0	0.83	0	0.56	0	0	0	0	0
2385.42	142.150.X.101	0	128.101.X.45	2046	1	16	[2,4)	[0,1829)	0	0	0	0	0	0	0	0	0.83	0	0.56	0	0	0	0	0
2114.41	63.150.X.253	1161	160.94.X.183	1434	17	16	[0,2)	[0,1829)	0	0	0	0	0	0	0	0	0.82	0	0.57	0	0	0	0	0
2057.15	142.150.X.101	0	128.101.X.161	2048	1	16	[2,4)	[0,1829)	0	0	0	0	0	0	0	0	0.83	0	0.56	0	0	0	0	0
1919.54	142.150.X.101	0	128.101.X.99	2048	1	16	[2,4)	[0,1829)	0	0	0	0	0	0	0	0	0.83	0	0.56	0	0	0	0	0
1634.38	142.150.X.101	0	128.101.X.219	2048	1	16	[2,4)	[0,1829)	0	0	0	0	0	0	0	0	0.83	0	0.56	0	0	0	0	0
1596.26	63.150.X.253	1161	128.101.X.160	1434	17	16	[0,2)	[0,1829)	0	0	0	0	0	0	0	0	0.82	0	0.57	0	0	0	0	0
1513.96	142.150.X.107	0	128.101.X.2	2048	1	16	[2,4)	[0,1829)	0	0	0	0	0	0	0	0	0.83	0	0.56	0	0	0	0	0
1389.09	63.150.X.253	1161	128.101.X.30	1434	17	16	[0,2)	[0,1829)	0	0	0	0	0	0	0	0	0.82	0	0.57	0	0	0	0	0
1315.88	63.150.X.253	1161	128.101.X.40	1434	17	16	[0,2)	[0,1829)	0	0	0	0	0	0	0	0	0.82	0	0.57	0	0	0	0	0
1279.75	142.150.X.103	0	128.101.X.202	2048	1	16	[0,2)	[0,1829)	0	0	0	0	0	0	0	0	0.83	0	0.56	0	0	0	0	0
1237.96	63.150.X.253	1161	160.94.X.32	1434	17	16	[0,2)	[0,1829)	0	0	0	0	0	0	0	0	0.82	0	0.57	0	0	0	0	0
1180.82	63.150.X.253	1161	128.101.X.61	1434	17	16	[0,2)	[0,1829)	0	0	0	0	0	0	0	0	0.82	0	0.57	0	0	0	0	0
1107.78	63.150.X.253	1161	160.94.X.154	1434	17	16	[0,2)	[0,1829)	0	0	0	0	0	0	0	0	0.82	0	0.57	0	0	0	0	0

Figure 11.3: Most anomalous connections found by the MINDS anomaly detection module in a 10-minute window, two days after the "slammer worm" started (January 27, 2003).

terval, there is another scanning activity (ping scan, highlighted in dark gray) that was detected mostly due to features 9 and 11. The two nonshaded flows are replies from "half-life game servers," which were flagged anomalous since those machines were talking to only port 27016/udp. For web connections, it is common to talk only on port 80, and it is well represented in the normal sample. However, since half-life connections did not match any normal samples with high counts on feature 15, they became anomalous.

Worm Detection

On October 10, 2002, our anomaly detection module detected two activities of the slapper worm that were not identified by SNORT since they were variations of an existing worm code. Once a machine is infected with the worm, it communicates with other machines that are also infected and attempts to infect other machines. The most common version of the worm uses port 2002 for communication, but some variations use other ports. Our anomaly detector flagged these connections as anomalous for two reasons. First, the source or destination ports used in the connection may not have been rare individually but the source-destination port pairs were very rare (the anomaly detector does not keep track of the frequency of pairs of attributes; however, while building the neighborhoods of such connections, most of their neighbors will not have the same source-destination port pairs, which will contribute to the distance). Second, the communication pattern of the worm looks like a slow scan causing the value of the variable that corresponds to the number of connections from the source IP to the same destination port in the last N connections to become large. SNORT has a rule for detecting worm that uses port 2002 (and a few other ports), but not for all possible variations. A single general SNORT rule can be written to detect the variations of the worm at the expense of a higher false positive rate.

Scanning and DoS Activities

On August 9 2002, CERT/CC issued an alert for "widespread scanning and possible denial of service activity targeted at the Microsoft-DS service on port 445/TCP" as a novel Denial of Service (DoS) attack. In addition, CERT/CC also expressed "interest in receiving reports of this activity from sites with detailed logs and evidence of an attack." Network connections due to this type of scanning were found to be the top ranked outliers on August 13, 2002, by our anomaly detection module in its regular analysis of University of Minnesota traffic. The port scan module of SNORT could not detect this attack, since the port scanning was slow. A rule to catch this type of attack was added later in September 2002.

On August 13, 2002, our anomaly detection module detected "scanning for an Oracle server" by ranking connections associated with this attack as the second highest ranked block of connections (top ranked block of connections belonged to the DoS activity targeted at the Microsoft-DS service on port 445/TCP). This type of attack is difficult to detect using other techniques, since the Oracle scan was embedded within a much larger web scan, and the alerts generated by web scan could potentially overwhelm the analysts. On June 13, CERT/CC had issued an alert for the attack.

Policy Violations

On August 8 and 10, 2002, our anomaly detection techniques detected a machine running a Microsoft PPTP VPN server, and another one running a FTP server on nonstandard ports, which are policy violations. Both policy violations were the top ranked outliers. Our anomaly detector module flagged these servers as anomalous since they are not allowed, and therefore very rare.

On February 6, 2003, unsolicited ICMP echo reply messages to a computer previously infected with Stacheldract worm (a DDoS agent) were detected by our anomaly detection techniques. Although the infected machine has been removed from the network, other infected machines outside our network were still trying to talk to the previously infected machine from our network.

11.3.1 SNORT Versus MINDS Anomaly Detection Module

In this section, we present a comparison of MINDS and SNORT in terms of types of attacks they are able to detect. Particularly, we compare their effectiveness on three categories of anomalous network behavior: content-based attacks, scanning activities, and policy violations.

Content-Based Attacks

Content-based attacks are out of scope for our anomaly detection module since the current version of MINDS does not make use of content based features. Therefore SNORT is superior in identifying those attacks. However, SNORT is able to detect only those content-based attacks that have known signatures/rules. Despite the fact that SNORT is more capable in detecting the content based attacks, it is important to note that once a computer has been attacked successfully, its behavior could become anomalous and therefore detected by our anomaly detection module, as seen in previous examples. This type of anomalous behavior will be further discussed in the Policy Violations subsection.

Scanning Activities

When detecting various scanning activities SNORT and MINDS anomaly detection module may have similar performance for certain types of scans, but they have very different detection capabilities for other types. In general there are two types of scans: (1) an inbound scan when an attacker outside the network is scanning for vulnerabilities within the monitored network, and (2) an outbound scan, when someone within the monitored network is scanning outside. There are two categories of inbound scanning activities, where SNORT and our anomaly detection module might have different detection performance: (1) fast (regular) scans, and (2) slow scans.

When detecting regular inbound scans from an outside source, SNORT portscan module keeps track of the number of destination IP addresses accessed by each source IP address in a given time window (default value is 3 seconds). Let's denote this variable count-dest, already defined in table 11.1. Whenever the value of count-dest is above a specified threshold (SNORT default value is 4), SNORT raises an alarm, thus indicating a scan by the source IP address. Our anomaly detection module is also able to assign high anomaly score to such network connections, since for most normal connections the value of count-dest is low. In addition, connections from many types of scanning activities tend to have other features that are unusual (such as very small payload), which make additional contributions to the anomaly score.

An inbound scan can be detected by SNORT provided the scan is fast enough for chosen time window (default value is 3 seconds) and count threshold (default value is 4). If a scanning activity is not fast enough (outside specified parameters), it will not be detected by SNORT. However, SNORT can still detect such activities by increasing the time window and/or decreasing the number of events counted within the time window, but this will tend to increase false alarm rate. On the other hand, our anomaly detection module is more suitable for detecting slow scans since it considers both time-window based and connection-window based features (as opposed to SNORT that uses only time-window based features).

SNORT is unable to detect outbound scans simply because it does not examine them. Contrary, our anomaly detection module is able to detect both inbound and outbound scans. Reversing the inputs to the portscan module will allow SNORT to detect outbound scans as well. However, this will increase the memory requirements, and SNORT will still have the same problem with slow outbound scans as it has with slow inbound scans.

Policy Violations

MINDS anomaly detection module is much more capable than SNORT in detecting policy violations (e.g. rogue and unauthorized services), since it looks for unusual network behavior. SNORT may detect these policy violations only if it has a rule for each of these specific activities. Since the number and variety of these activities can be very large and unknown, it is not practical to incorporate them into SNORT for the following reasons. First, processing of all these rules will require more processing time thus causing the degradation in SNORT performance. It is important to note that it is desirable for SNORT to keep the amount of analyzed network traffic small by incorporating as specific rules as possible. On the other hand, very specific rules limit the generalization capabilities of a typical rule based system, i.e., minor changes in the characteristics of an attack might cause the attack to be undetected.

Second, SNORT's static knowledge has to be manually updated by human analysts each time a new suspicious behavior is detected. In contrast, MINDS anomaly detection module is adaptive in nature, and it is particularly successful in detecting anomalous behavior originating from a compromised machine (e.g. attacker breaks into a machine, installs unauthorized software and uses it to launch attacks on other machines). Such behavior is often undetected by SNORT's signatures.

11.4 MINDS Module for Summarizing Anomalous Connections Using Association Rules

In the past decade, mining association rules has been the subject of extensive research in data mining. Techniques for mining association rules were originally developed to analyze sales transaction data, where analysts are interested to know what items are frequently bought together in the same transaction. In general, an association rule is an implication expression of the form $X \Rightarrow Y$, where X and Y are sets of binary features. An association rule can be used to predict the occurrence of certain features in a record given the presence of other features. For example, the rule $\{Bread, Butter\} \Rightarrow \{Milk\}$ indicates that most of the transactions that contain bread and butter also involve the purchase of milk. The sets of items or binary features are known as item sets in association rule terminology.

Given a set of records, the objective of mining association rules is to extract all rules of the form $X \Rightarrow Y$ that satisfy a user-specified minimum support and minimum confidence thresholds. Support measures the fraction of transactions that obey the rule while confidence is an estimate of the conditional probability $P(Y|X)$. For example, suppose 10% of all transactions contain bread and butter, and 6% of the transactions contain bread, butter, and milk. For this example, the support of the rule $\{Bread, Butter\} \Rightarrow \{Milk\}$ is 6% and its confidence is $6\%/10\% = 60\%$. If the minimum support threshold is chosen to be 1% and the minimum confidence threshold is 50%, then this rule would be extracted by the association rule mining algorithm. In this example, the set $\{Bread, Butter, Milk\}$ is also referred to as a frequent item set.

Association patterns, often expressed in the form of frequent item sets or association rules, have been found to be valuable for analyzing network traffic data (Lee and Stolfo 1998; Barbara, Wu, and Jajodia 2001; Manganaris, Christensen, Zerkle, and Hermiz 1999). These patterns can be used for the following purposes.

First, to construct a summary of anomalous connections detected by the IDS. Often times, the number of anomalous connections flagged by an IDS can be very large, thus requiring analysts to spend a large amount of time interpreting and analyzing each connection that has a high anomaly score. By applying association pattern discovery techniques, analysts can obtain a high-level summary of anomalous connections. For example, scanning activity for a particular service can be summarized by a frequent set:

srcIP=X, dstPort=Y

If most of the connections in the frequent set are ranked high by the anomaly detection algorithm, then the frequent set may be a candidate signature for addition to a signature-based system.

Second, to construct a profile of the normal network traffic behavior in anomaly detection systems (Barbara, Wu, and Jajodia 2001; Manganaris, Christensen, Zerkle, and Hermiz 1999). As previously noted, an anomaly detection system requires some information about how the normal network traffic behaves in order to ascertain the anomalous connections. Association patterns can provide the necessary information by identifying sets of features that are commonly found in the normal network traffic data. For example, a web browsing activity, (almost always on port 80 and uses the TCP protocol with a small number of packets) could generate the following frequent set:

protocol=TCP, dstPort=80, NumPackets=3...6

In addition, association patterns generated at different time frames can be used to study the significant changes in the network traffic at various periods of time (Lee and Stolfo 1998)

Third, recurrent patterns in normal or anomalous connections can serve as secondary features to be augmented to the original data in order to build better predictive models of the network traffic data.

Mining association patterns in network traffic data is a challenging task due to the following reasons.

Imbalanced class distribution. Standard association pattern discovery techniques rely on a user-specified minimum support threshold to eliminate patterns that occur infrequently in the data. For network intrusion data, the proportion of network traffic that corresponds to an attack is considerably smaller than the proportion of normal traffic. As a result, one has to apply a very low minimum support threshold to detect patterns involving the attack class. This will degrade the performance of association pattern discovery algorithms considerably and produces an overwhelmingly large number of patterns for the normal class.

Connections that have high anomaly scores are mostly likely to be attacks and those with low anomaly scores are most likely to be normal traffic. For association pattern analysis, we choose connections that appear in the top few percentage of anomaly scores to be the attack class and the bottom few percentage of anomaly scores to be the normal class. Connections with intermediate anomaly scores will be ignored. We then mine the frequent patterns for each class separately using different minimum support thresholds, depending on the number of connections that belong to each class. If the class is small, then a low minimum support threshold is chosen. Finally, a vertical association rule mining algorithm (Lee and Stolfo 1998; Zaki and Gouda 2001) is applied to efficiently discover frequent patterns of each class.

Binarization and grouping of attribute values. The network intrusion data contains several continuous attributes such as number of packets, number of bytes, and duration of each connection. These attributes must be transformed into binary features first before applying standard association pattern algorithms. The transformation can be performed using a variety of supervised and unsupervised discretization techniques. Using the output scores of the anomaly detector as its ground truth, MINDS employs a supervised binning strategy to discretize the attributes. Initially, all distinct values of a continuous attribute is

Class	v_1	v_2	v_3	v_4	v_5	v_6	v_7	v_8	v_9
Anomalous	0	0	20	10	20	0	0	0	0
Normal	150	100	0	0	0	100	100	150	100
	bin1		bin2			bin3			

Table 11.3: Discretization of a continuous attribute.

put into one bin. Worst bin in terms of purity is selected for partitioning until the desired number of bins is reached. Gini index is used to determine the best split. Binning for a continuous attribute is illustrated in table 11.3.

In addition, the source and destination IP addresses can be grouped together by applying varying sizes of net-masks. For example, the group 160. 94.*.* represents the class B address for all IP addresses whose first two octets are 160 and 94. However, by doing so, an IP address will now belong to multiple groups, which may give rise to multiple patterns describing similar types of connections. For example, if the pattern (SourceIP = $IP1$, Protocol=TCP) is frequent, then the pattern (SourceIP = $IP1'$, Protocol=TCP) where $IP1' = IP1 \& mask$ given a net-mask size, must also be frequent.

Pruning the redundant patterns. Although association patterns can detect sets of features that occur frequently in the network traffic data, the number of patterns extracted can be quite large, depending on the choice of minimum support threshold. Some of the patterns are redundant because they correspond to the subsets of other patterns. For example, given two frequent sets:

Protocol=TCP, DstPort=8888,TCPflags=SYN
DstPort=8888,TCPflags=SYN

the first one is more descriptive than the second. If the support of these two item sets is very close, then the second rule is redundant. MINDS applies a flexible pruning scheme to eliminate redundant patterns by comparing the support and confidence of patterns that share similar features. If the support and confidence of such patterns are almost identical, the more descriptive pattern is retained.

Finding discriminating patterns. Eventually, the goal of mining association patterns is to discover patterns that occur regularly in the normal class or anomaly class, but not both. To do this, we need a measure that can rank the patterns according to their discriminating power. MINDS allows the users to rank the discovered patterns according to various measures, as illustrated in figure 11.4.

Consider a set of features X that occur $c1$ times in the anomalous class and $c2$ times in the normal class. Also, let $n1$ and $n2$ be the number of anomalous and normal connections in the data set respectively. Assuming that we are only interested in finding profiles of the anomalous class, the ratio $c1/n1$

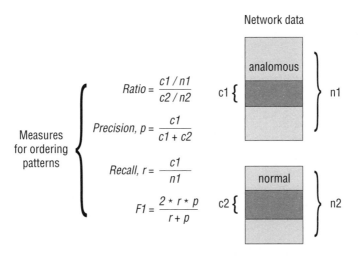

Figure 11.4: Measures for ordering patterns.

to $c2/n2$ would indicate how well the pattern could discern anomalous connections from normal connections. If the proportion of samples in each class is the same, i.e., $n1 = n2$, then the ratio measure is a monotone function of precision. Ratio or precision alone is insufficient because they often characterize only a small number of anomalous connections. In the extreme case, a rare pattern that is observed only once in the anomalous class and does not appear in the normal class will have a maximum value of ratio and precision, and yet, may not be significant. To account for the significance of a pattern, the recall measure can be used as an alternative. Unfortunately, a pattern that has high recall may not necessarily be discriminating. The F1-measure, which is the harmonic mean of precision and recall, provides a good trade-off between the two measures.

Grouping the discovered patterns. It is worth noting that some of the extracted patterns can describe a similar set of anomalous connections. For example, a probe or scan may give rise to multiple patterns that are very similar to each other (e.g., these patterns may involve the same source IP address and port number, but different destination IP addresses). Thus, it is useful to group together the related patterns before presenting them to the analysts.

The overall architecture of our association analysis module is shown in figure 11.5. As previously noted, MINDS would use the anomaly scores of the connections to determine whether a connection belongs to the normal or attack class. In our experiments, we choose connections that have the top 10% anomaly score to be the anomaly class and the bottom 30% anomaly score to be the normal class. Connections with intermediate anomaly scores are ig-

Anomaly Scores

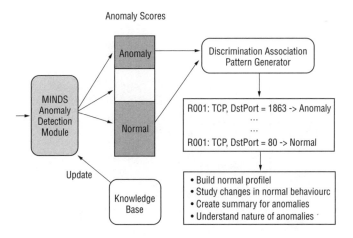

Figure 11.5: MINDS association analysis module.

nored. Next, the association pattern generator is applied to each class and the patterns are ranked according to the various measures described above. The extracted patterns can be used to create summaries and profiles for normal and anomalous connections.

Once the profile for the attack class is created, a follow-up analysis is often performed to study the nature of the anomalous connections. A typical follow-up analysis involves connecting via telnet to the suspected computer at the specific port and examining the returned information. Another possibility of analyzing the suspected computer is to start capturing packets on that machine at the particular port and to investigate the contents of the packets.

11.4.1 Evaluation of Attack Summaries on Real Network Data

In this section, we report some of the highest ranked (most discriminative) patterns generated by the our association pattern analysis module. These patterns represent a summary of the most frequently occurring and discriminating anomalous traffic flagged by MINDS anomaly detection module.

A typical output of the summarization module for a 10-minute window on May 21st is shown in figure 11.6. In addition to the information reported by the anomaly detection module, the summarizer has two additional columns c_1 and c_2, which are used to evaluate the quality of rules discovered. Given a rule, c_1 denotes how many times this rule occurred among anomalous connections, while c_2 denotes how many times this rule occurred in normal connections.

score	c1	c2	src IP	sPort	dst IP	dPort	protocol	flags	packets	bytes	1	2	3	4	5	6	7	8	9	10	11	12	13	14	15	16
31.17	-	-	218.1.9.x.168	5002	134.84.x.129	4182	6	27	(5,6)	[0,2045)	0	0.01	0.01	0.03	0	0	0	0	0	0	0	0	0	0	1	0
3.04	135	12	64.156.x.74	---	xx.xx.xx.xx	---	xxx	4	(0,2)	[0,2045)	0.12	0.44	0.26	0.58	0	0	0	0	0.07	0.27	0	0	0	0	0	0
15.41	-	-	218.1.9.x.168	5002	134.84.x.129	4896	6	27	(5,6)	[0,2045)	0.01	0.01	0.01	0.06	0	0	0	0	0	0	0	0	0	0	1	0
14.44	-	-	134.84.x.129	4770	218.1.9.x.168	5002	6	27	(5,6)	[0,2045)	0.01	0.01	0.05	0.01	0	0	0	0	0	1	0	0	0	0	0	0
7.81	-	-	134.84.x.129	3890	218.1.9.x.168	5002	6	27	(5,6)	[0,2045)	0.01	0.02	0.09	0.02	0	0	0	0	0	1	0	0	0	0	0	0
3.09	4	1	xx.xx.xx.xx	4729	xx.xx.xx.xx	---	6	---	---	0.14	0.13	0.17	0.47	0	0	0	0	0	0.2	0	0	0	0	0	0	
2.41	64	4	xx.xx.xx.xx	---	200.75.x.2	---	6			[0,2045)	0.13	0.27	0.21	0.49	0	0	0	0	0	0	0.3	0.25	0.01	0		
6.64	-	-	218.1.9.x.168	5002	134.84.x.129	3676	6	27	(5,6)	[0,2045)	0.03	0.03	0.03	0.15	0	0	0	0	0	0	0	0	0.99	0		
5.6	-	-	218.1.9.x.168	5002	134.84.x.129	4626	6	27	(5,6)	[0,2045)	0.03	0.03	0.03	0.17	0	0	0	0	0	0	0	0	0.98	0		
2.7	12	0	xx.xx.xx	---	xx.xx.xx	113	6	2	(0,2)	[0,2045)	0.25	0.09	0.15	0.15	0	0	0	0	0.08	0	0.8	0.15	0.01	0		
4.39	-	-	218.1.9.x.168	5002	134.84.x.129	4571	6	27	(5,6)	[0,2045)	0.04	0.05	0.05	0.26	0	0	0	0	0	0	0	0	0.96	0		
4.34	-	-	218.1.9.x.168	5002	134.84.x.129	4572	6	27	(5,6)	[0,2045)	0.04	0.05	0.05	0.23	0	0	0	0	0	0	0	0	0.97	0		
4.07	8	0	160.94.x.114	51827	64.8.x.60	119	6	24	[483,-)	[84,24,-)	0.09	0.26	0.16	0.24	0	0.01	0.9	0	0	0	0	0	0	0		
3.49	-	-	218.1.9.x.168	5002	134.84.x.129	4525	6	27	(5,6)	[0,2045)	0.06	0.06	0.06	0.35	0	0	0	0	0	0	0	0	0.93	0		
3.48	-	-	218.1.9.x.168	5002	134.84.x.129	4524	6	27	(5,6)	[0,2045)	0.06	0.06	0.07	0.35	0	0	0	0	0	0	0	0	0.93	0		
3.34	-	-	218.1.9.x.168	5002	134.84.x.129	4159	6	27	(5,6)	[0,2045)	0.06	0.07	0.07	0.37	0	0	0	0	0	0	0	0	0.92	0		
2.46	51	0	200.75.x.2	---	xx.xx.xx.xx	21	6	2		[0,2045)	0.19	0.64	0.35	0.32	0	0	0	0	0.18	0.44	0	0	0	0		
2.37	42	5	xx.xx.xx.xx	21	200.75.x.2	---	6	20		[0,2045)	0.35	0.31	0.22	0.57	0	0	0	0	0	0	0	0.2	0.28	0.01	0	
2.45	58	0	200.75.x.2	---	xx.xx.xx.xx	21	6			[0,2045)	0.19	0.63	0.35	0.32	0	0	0	0	0.18	0.44	0	0	0	0		

Figure 11.6: Output of MINDS summarization module.

Single network connections that are not part of a summary have dashes in these columns.

In figure 11.6, light gray colored connections, including the top ranked connection with a score of 31.17, correspond to a University of Minnesota computer connecting to a remote FTP server, which happens to be running on port 5002. Further investigation of the local machine showed that it is also running multiple peer-to-peer file sharing applications. These connections were not summarized because a large number of similar connections had low scores. The second line is a summary of 150 TCP reset packets received from 64.156.X.74. Further analysis indicated that this computer has been the victim of a DoS attack, and we were observing backscatter, i.e. replies to spoofed packets. The next summary of 5 connections on port 4729 appears to be a false alarm. The dark gray lines are summaries of 72 connections involved in an FTP scan from a computer in Columbia (200.75.X.2). The summary of 12 connections involving destination port 113 represents IDENT lookups, where a remote computer is trying to get the username of a user. The next summary of 8 connections with destination port 119, corresponds to a USENET server transferring a large amount of data.

In the following paragraphs, we present several additional association patterns found by the MINDS summarization module on different days.

- **Example 1**
  srcIP=IP1, dstPort=80, Protocol=TCP, Flag=SYN, NumPackets=3, NumBytes=120. . . 180 (c1=256, c2=1)
  srcIP=IP1, dstIP=IP2, dstPort=80, Protocol=TCP, Flag=SYN, NumPackets=3, NumBytes=120. . . 180 (c1=177, c2=0)

  The first rule indicates that the source of the anomalous connections originates from IP1, the destination port is 80, the protocol used is TCP with tcpflags set to SYN, the number of packets is 3, and the total number of bytes is between 120 and 180. Furthermore, this pattern is observed 256 times (c1 = 256) among the anomalous connections and only once (c2=1) in the normal connections. Therefore, it has a high ratio and precision, which is why it is ranked among the top few patterns found by the system.

At first glance, the first rule indicates a web scan since it appears mostly in the anomaly class with a fixed source IP address but not with a fixed destination IP address. However, the second rule suggests that an attack was later launched to one of the specific machines since the pattern originates from the same source IP address but has a specific destination IP address and covers only anomalous connections. Further analysis confirms that a scan has been performed from the source IP address IP1, followed by an attack on a specific machine that was previously identified by the attacker to be vulnerable.

- **Example 2**
  dstIP= IP3, dstPort=8888, Protocol=TCP (c1=369, c2=0)
  dstIP= IP3, dstPort=8888, Protocol=TCP, Flag=SYN (c1=291, c2=0)

  This pattern indicates a high number of anomalous TCP connections on port 8888 to a specific machine. Follow-up analysis of the connections covered by the pattern indicates possible existence of a machine that is running a variation of the KaZaA file-sharing protocol. KaZaA file sharing software is typically used for sharing audio, video, and software files, which are very often illegal copies.

- **Example 3**
  srcIP=IP4, dstPort=27374, Protocol=TCP, Flag=SYN, NumPackets=4, NumBytes=189200 (c1=582, c2=2)
  srcIP= IP4, dstPort=12345, NumPackets=4, NumBytes=189200 (c1=580, c2=3)
  srcIP= IP5, dstPort=27374, Protocol=TCP, Flag=SYN, NumPackets=3, NumBytes=144 (c1=694, c2=3)

  The patterns above indicate a number of scans on port 27374 (which is a signature for the SubSeven worm) and on port 12345 (which is a signature for the NetBus worm). Further analysis has shown that there are no fewer than five machines scanning for one or both of these ports within an arbitrary time window.

11.5   Future Directions

The overall objective of the MINDS project is to develop on-line and scalable data mining algorithms and tools for detecting attacks and threats against computer systems. Although our techniques developed to date are very promising and successful in detecting many computer attacks that could not be detected by state of the art intrusion detection systems, they need to be improved due to various challenges. First, data generated from network traffic monitoring tends to have very high volume, dimensionality and heterogeneity, and there is a need for high performance data mining algorithms that will scale to very large network traffic data sets. Second, network data is temporal (streaming) in nature, and development of algorithms for mining data streams is necessary for building real-time intrusion detection system. Third, low frequency of computer attacks requires modification of standard data mining algorithms for their detection. Fourth, cyber attacks may be launched from several different locations and targeted to many different destinations, thus creating a need to analyze network data from several network locations in order to detect these distributed attacks. Therefore, development of a cooperative and distributed intrusion detection system for correlating suspicious events among multiple participating network sites to detect coordinated attacks will be one of the key components of this project. Finally, converting network traffic data into useful features is a complex task. We plan to aggregate information from different sources (e.g., tcpdump data, syslog data, alarms from various IDSs) in order to obtain more comprehensive set of features that will be used in data mining algorithms. In addition to these challenges that define possible directions in our future research, MINDS also will have a visualization tool for providing a graphical user interface that will help security analysts to better comprehend the anomalous events and patterns extracted.

A number of applications outside of intrusion detection have similar characteristics, e.g. detecting credit card and insurance frauds, early signs of potential disasters in industrial process control, early detection of unusual medical conditions - e.g. cardiac arrhythmia, etc. We plan to explore the use of our techniques to such problems.

Acknowledgments

We are grateful to Yongdae Kim and Zhi-li Zhang for their comments and feedback on the general architecture of MINDS. This work was supported by Army High Performance Computing Research Center contract number DAAD19-01-2-0014. The content of the work does not necessarily reflect the position or policy of the government and no official endorsement should be inferred. Access to computing facilities was provided by the AHPCRC and the Minnesota Supercomputing Institute.

Levent Ertöz is a Ph.D. student in computer science at the University of Minnesota.

Eric Eilertson is a Ph.D. student in computer science at the University of Minnesota.

Aleksandar Lazarevic is a research associate at the Army High Performance Computing Research Center, Computer Science Department, University of Minnesota.

Pang-Ning Tan is an assistant professor in the Department of Computer Science and Engineering at Michigan State University.

Vipin Kumar is the director of the Army High Performance Computing Research Center and a professor of computer science and engineering at the University of Minnesota.

Jaideep Srivastava is a professor of computer science at the University of Minnesota.

Paul Dokas is a staff member at the Office of Information Technology Security and Assurance at the University of Minnesota.

Chapter 12

Marshalling Evidence Through Data Mining in Support of Counter Terrorism

Daniel Barbará, James J. Nolan,
David Schum, and Arun Sood

As the events of September 11, 2001 clearly illustrated, our technologies for collecting, transmitting, and archiving intelligence information have far outstripped our capabilities for processing it into useful information. This has severely limited our ability to put this information to inferential use in generating productive hypotheses and in drawing defensible and persuasive conclusions. One major discovery of this event is that we failed to aggregate items of intelligence information that, taken together, would allow us to suggest important and often surprising hypotheses that should be taken seriously. Unfortunately, due to the volume of data the intelligence community is currently burdened with, this is probably a more common occurrence than anyone would like to admit. The major contributions in this chapter concern techniques for marshaling or organizing intelligence information. Our thesis can be stated quite succinctly: How well we marshal or organize existing evidence influences how well we humans are able to generate new hypotheses as well as new evidential tests of all hypotheses we are considering. The process of marshaling or organizing evidence is a crucial step in the process of discovery or investigation. Commonly, new hypotheses or possibilities spring to our awareness only when we consider information items taken in combination.

In this chapter, we present a data-centered approach to marshaling evidence, which allows us to create, justify, or negate hypotheses. This is accomplished through the creation of intelligent agents that act as conceptual magnets that attract trifles[1] (or atomic pieces) of evidence. This attraction is triggered in one of three ways: (1) the evidence justifies an existing hypothesis, (2) the evidence negates an existing hypothesis, or (3) the evidence suggests that a new hypothesis be formed, which in turn becomes a new conceptual magnet. We propose a novel use of data mining, information retrieval, software agent, and distributed computing technologies to enable this innovation.

In this chapter we describe an architecture that facilitates the marshalling of the enormous volume of evidence that an intelligence analyst has available. We are currently working on building a prototype based on this architecture. A crucial point in our design is that of *not* automating the process of hypothesis generation. We believe that no system that generates hypotheses automatically is flexible enough to capture the dynamics of this problem. Such a system would miss novel threats and therefore lose much of its usefulness. Humans, in contrast, have an amazing capacity of adaptation to new situations, and are capable of thinking of scenarios that have not occurred before. We are, however, incapable of marshalling and organizing such a huge amount of evidence to corroborate or negate our hypothesis, and that is where our system strength resides. The central piece of our design is the support for queries, both ad-hoc and long standing, that act as "magnets" attracting the relevant evidence that a human needs to estimate the validity of her hypothesis.

The remainder of this chapter is as follows. In section 12.1 we present our technical approach. Section 12.2 outlines a narrative scenario to which the architecture could be applied. Section 12.3 presents the agent-based system that is utilized as the platform to implement the technical approach. Section 12.4 summarizes and concludes.

12.1 Technical Approach

In this section we present the technical approach to achieving the innovations mentioned above. This approach is incorporated into our collaborative, distributed, agent-based system for imagery and geospatial computing called the

---

[1]The term "trifle," borrowed from Sherlock Holmes's works, refers to any singular detail that is observed by any human source or sensing device. Trifles can become evidence in intelligence analyses when their relevance to hypotheses is established.

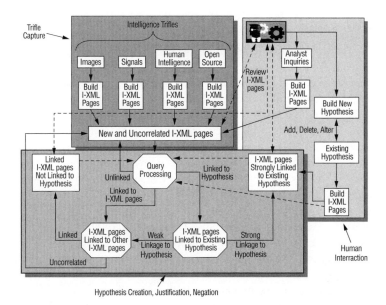

Figure 12.1: System architecture.

agent-based imagery and geospatial computing architecture (AIGA).[2] AIGA has produced several useful results which assist in the current research: (1) a novel architecture for distributed computing (Simon, Nolan, and Sood 2002), (2) a semantic approach to discovering widely distributed resources (Nolan, Simon, and Sood 2001b) that has been shown to scale to support hundreds of thousands of agents (Nolan, Sood, and Simon 2002), and an ontology and agent communication language that supports all of the above (Nolan, Simon, and Sood 2001a). To summarize, the AIGA architecture is prototyped in Java, using Jini to enable distributed computing, incorporates a novel representation schema for imagery and geospatial intelligence data called "I- XML," enables collaboration through a novel approach to strategy reuse, and provides a graphical interface allowing users to construct task-driven metaagents from low-level, atomic agents available on the network.

The architecture of the system is shown in figure 12.1. As shown in this figure, the architecture can be grouped into three primary areas: (1) trifle capture, (2) hypothesis creation, justification, or elimination, and (3) human interaction. This figure serves as the template for our work; we will walk through the technical details in each box in this chapter.

---

[2]A description of this project, API documentation, and downloadable papers can be found at http://aiga.cs.gmu.edu.

12.1.1 Intelligence Trifle Representation

Before going into the details of our technical approach, we need to define a trifle as it forms the fundamental piece of evidence that will be used in hypothesis processing. Examples of trifles, or pieces of evidence, with which the intelligence community is currently inundated are: (1) an object identified in an image, (2) information in an intelligence report, (3) information in an open-source document (e.g., online newspaper article), or (4) a video clip (e.g., from Al-Jazeera or CNN). These trifles are captured, or extracted using a variety of techniques that can be automated, semiautomated, or manual. For example, objects in images can be extracted using feature extraction algorithms or delineated by a human analyst; information from text sources can be extracted using natural language processing techniques; and video clips can be extracted using video segmenting algorithms. These trifles could be stored in a structured database or found from some unstructured location (e.g., web, Intelink). These trifles must be marshaled to support an existing query (e.g., Is chemical plant X producing weapons of mass destruction?) or to direct the analyst to perhaps consider a new hypothesis. In this part of our approach, we present an extension of I-XML to represent intelligence data. In AIGA, I-XML serves several purposes: representing metadata, communication sessions between intelligent agents, and allowing human analysis to be added regarding the data referenced in the I-XML page. In addition to the XML standard, I-XML also incorporates other industry and government standards for data representation. These standards include: OpenGIS's geography markup language (GML) and the DoD's VPF formats for feature data and NITF for image data. In our approach, we have extended I-XML to include textual, signal, human, and other kinds of intelligence information. In our model, there are five high levels of information captured in the intelligence trifle:

1. *Trifle storage location* is the trifle storage address, so as to facilitate the recovery of the source document. The trifles are expected to be stored in a distributed storage. We expect that a distributed file system or distributed database will be used to store the trifle.

2. *Page descriptors* contain general information regarding the intelligence trifle including: the source of the information, the location of the source (e.g., a URL or other location where the information was obtained), and the date and time of the trifle.

3. *Page contents* includes the geographic location(s) to which the intelligence trifle refers, any chronological information, individuals that are referenced, keywords that are matched in our current dictionary, potential keywords that should be added to the dictionary, a textual description

(if available), and linkages to other trifle, hypothesis and query I-XML pages.

4. *Analyst input* includes any analysis that may have been input against this trifle. This could be one of two things: (1) any inquiries (or hypotheses) that have been attracted to this trifle, and (2) any analysis that has been written regarding the trifle.

5. *Credibility index* includes information on the credibility of a trifle including: the credibility of the source and an analyst's assessment of the credibility of the individual trifle.

12.1.2 Human, Hypothesis, or Trifle Interaction

The key innovation of this chapter results in a new way for intelligence analysts to interact with the intelligence data stream and can be described by the following. Intelligence analysts are currently overwhelmed with the amount of data that they must analyze. Most of this data is never analyzed at all, potentially leaving key pieces of information out of the analysis process. Our ability to collect data will only grow, further accentuating the problem. Our approach allows the analyst to interact with the intelligence stream in a novel way. This interaction can be viewed as a triangle with the human, hypotheses, and trifles at each vertex. The interaction is not isolated at each vertex of the triangle however, and the interaction with all three is the key to the analyst making informed analysis that supports the intelligence decision-making process. In this view, the human interacts with hypotheses: she generates them, determines if they should be validated or negated, and refines them. The human also interacts with the trifles, not arbitrarily, but as a result of the hypothesis processing discussed in section 12.1.3. From this processing, trifles are accumulating, forming a critical mass that may require the attention of the analyst. Perhaps a new hypothesis should be considered as a result of this, for example. In the remainder of this section, we discuss how the user interacts with the system, illustrating how the analyst generates hypotheses and supports their analysis with the results the system provides.

Our approach is to support a variety of query and hypothesis types in terms of their *durability and complexity* (note: we will use the term "query" and "hypothesis" interchangeably here). The *durability* of a query refers to its lifetime in the system. For example, queries that continue to attract trifles are highly durable; those that fail to attract many trifles over time are less durable. *Complexity* refers primarily to the structure of the query: formatted, unformatted, or rich queries. This section discusses these topics and their importance in our approach. The approach uses an agent-based system to formulate queries, these

are built using existing atomic and composite queries as we have developed in
Nolan, Simon, and Sood (2001b).

As we stated previously, the analyst interacts with the system for one of
three reasons: (1) the evidence justifies an existing hypothesis, (2) the evidence negates an existing hypothesis, or (3) the evidence suggests that a new
hypothesis be formed, which in turn becomes a new conceptual magnet. We
use agents to do the processing and provide the interaction with the system.
There are two types of agents in the system: *Analyst agents*—agents that are
created by a human analyst, and *processing agents*—agents that are monitoring the archived and current trifle stream, and reacting to requests from analyst agents. In other words, when an analyst creates a query or hypothesis, an
I-XML document is created by manually entering a hypothesis. After complet-
ing this, it is submitted to the system, whereby an analyst agent is created to
represent that document. This agent will then begin working through the system, communicating with other agents to determine trifles that may support or
negate the hypothesis.

We now turn our attention to the types of queries our system will handle:
standing and ad hoc queries to reflect *durability* of the query, and formatted,
unformatted and rich queries that have different complexities.

Durability of Queries: Standing and Ad-hoc Queries

In terms of durability, we distinguish between two kinds of queries: standing
and ad-hoc queries. *Standing queries,* or as they are commonly referred to in
the data base community, continuous queries, are long duration queries that
are registered by the analyst to continuously monitor the system for arrival of
new trifles that fit the query's condition.

Once an analyst registers a standard query, an agent is created to control
it. As we described in section 12.1.3, the agent finds the trifles that are already
in the system and that satisfy the standing query. This is done through agent
communication between the analyst agent and other agents that represent the
trifle base: *cluster agents* who represent trifles that have been clustered based
on a similarity measurements, and *classification agents* that have classified trifles based on a schema. The standard query is registered at the cluster agents
and classification agent that control groups where the query has found "target" trifles that are responsive to the query. These group agents (representing
cluster and classification agents) will be responsible for keeping track of new
trifles that are of potential interest to the registered standing query. Since new
trifles are assigned to group agents by an incremental, scalable process, the
support for standard queries is guaranteed to scale with the continuously arriving stream of trifles. Ad-hoc queries, as opposed to standing queries, are
snapshots, or immediate views of the trifle base. Their targets are found the

same way that the original targets for standing queries are found, but no effort is made to track future trifles that may satisfy the ad-hoc query. Of course, the analyst may choose to convert the ad-hoc query into a standing one by registering it in the system. Like standard queries, agents are used to build ad-hoc queries.

Query Complexity: Formatted, Unformatted, and Rich Queries

In terms of complexity, we distinguish between three classes of queries: unformatted, formatted, and rich. Here we discuss these types and how our approach will address the difficulties with each.

Unformatted queries are posed by taking a piece of a trifle and using it as an example. The aim is to find trifles that most resemble the example. To do this, one can use a similarity-based approach. As we explain in section 12.1.3 the query is transformed into a vector of features that its similarity measured (by using some metric) with respect to the vector representing a trifle. (Both, the vectors of the query and trifle have to contain exactly the same features.) When looking for similar trifles, one can use the clusters obtained by the techniques described in section 12.1.3 to find the most likely set of similar trifles to the query vector. As we shall see in that section, this requires the transformation of the query and trifles in the system into vectors of features. An unformatted query will be implemented in our system by the instantiation of an agent responsible for gathering the identifiers of the trifles in the target of the query and for displaying the trifles to the analyst.

Formatted queries are a list of keywords (which define classes, as we will explain in section 12.1.3) joined by Boolean operators. For instance, the analyst may be interested in finding trifles that satisfy the query: "Iraq and (weapons of mass destruction)." This query will be answered by looking at trifles in the classes defined by the keywords Iraq and Weapons of mass destruction jointly, following a process described in section 12.1.3 As with unformatted queries, formatted ones lead to the creation of agents in charge of the queries.

Richer queries have the highest degree of complexity in our system. These are the queries aimed to support hypotheses verification. In fact, a hypothesis can always be expressed as a rich query. Examples of such queries are the following:

> Find cases in which a riot in a city has been followed by the kidnapping of an American citizen in the vicinity of that city.

> Is there any change in the trend of money transfers to Saudi Arabian students in the US during the last 6 months?

Notice that both examples can be thought of as enquires to find out evidence about a train of thought the analyst is following (suspicion of a correlation between riots and kidnappings; suspicion of heavy money transfers to a group of students). The answer to these queries provides the evidence (or lack of it) to this train of thought. More elaborate queries can then be posed by combining those already posed or by expressing higher-level concepts. Moreover, by registering these queries as standing queries, the analyst can keep track of potentially dangerous situations (a riot occurring at a given time may forewarn a kidnapping; a huge transfer of money to a student in a particular group can forewarn a terrorist activity). The complexity of richer queries is only limited by the capability of the system in solving them. For instance, the examples shown need to be supported by the execution of two data mining tasks: mining frequent episodes and finding outliers in time series.

Mining frequent episodes: An episode is a sequence of events (described by trifles). Streams of trifles can be mined to obtain information about frequent sequences of events. Sequences of events that occur relatively close to each other in a given partial order are called "episodes," and can be a good method of obtaining knowledge. The mining of such episodes has been studied in Mannila, Toivonen, and Verkamo (1996).

Finding outliers in time series: Time series are temporal sequences of measures that can be mined for information. One of the important tasks in the extraction of information from time series is that of finding sudden unusual movements, or outliers. Some initial approaches to this task can be found in Martin and Yohai (2001).

As with the other types of queries, the posing of a richer query leads to the creation of an agent responsible for this query. The agent is an incarnation of the data mining process that the query needs for its support. Notice that in this way, the capabilities of the system can grow incrementally with the incorporation of new types of agents capable of managing different richer queries.

12.1.3 Hypothesis Processing

Our approach centers on taking the normalized trifles discussed previously and marshalling them to support the hypothesis creation, justification, and negation process (figure 12.1). Hypotheses (or conjectures) are generated by the human analyst for one or more reasons and input into the system as described above. For example: there could be an area the analyst is monitoring for a particular reason (e.g., Could chemical plant X be producing WMD?), or there could be a body of evidence (a collection of trifles) that suggests a certain hypotheses, or world events may simply warrant that certain hypotheses be considered.

There are two approaches to marshalling evidence to support hypothesis processing: the *hypothesis driven* approach or the *data driven* approach. In the hypothesis driven case, the analyst creates a hypothesis, submits it to the system, and incoming intelligence trifles are used to support or negate it. This approach is good at handling incoming trifles, but requires a hypothesis creation mechanism (or a reason for the analyst to come up with the hypothesis in the first place) to back it up. In the data driven approach, incoming trifles are analyzed with respect to the other trifles in the system and linked appropriately. This approach is good at reducing the historical bias, but leads to an explosion of the data set. Since the processed data set is itself very large, this approach further accentuates the problem. We propose an approach that integrates the best elements of the two approaches. Further, it is our thesis that the intelligence data handling is a complex task and the tools likely to be available in the next five years are unlikely to be effective in identifying imminent threats—for this reason our approach assumes a key role for the human-in-the-loop.

Our approach makes use of the metaphor of conceptual "magnets" whose function is to attract interesting and productive combinations of intelligence trifles that should be considered. There may be different magnets we can employ, each representing a different strategy for marshaling or organizing intelligence information. Note that these "magnets" can be simply viewed as queries that retrieve relevant trifles. Some of these queries will be standing queries (i.e., queries that continuously monitor new entries to the system, updating the answers accordingly otherwise known in the literature as continuous queries (Barbará 1999; Babu and Wido 2001), and ad-hoc queries, posed by an analyst in a one-time attempt to gather evidence for an evolving hypothesis. We believe that the query process is a key part of the process of investigation and discovery, something more than simple search. Such investigations also require informed and productive strategies for inquiry, the asking of questions.

The marshaling strategies we have in mind are designed in part to stimulate the process of inquiry on the part of the human analyst. If we do not ask appropriate and useful questions, no inferential strategy will save us. It turns out that different questions we may be prompted to ask will serve, in their turn, as new magnets. The conceptual framework for this approach has been discussed in a series of articles by D. A. Schum (1999, 2001a, b). To create the conceptual magnets described, it is necessary to develop techniques that create relationships between, or "link" the trifles in some fashion. In our approach, we develop data driven approaches for determining linkages between the trifles. We call these linkages "cues" or linkages of data that should be examined by analyst. A cue may need attention for one of two reasons: (1) it is related to a currently existing hypothesis, or (2) it may represent a new hypothesis (that the analyst should consider).

The cues are developed using several methods including: clustering, classification, and a "small worlds" concept we will present. For each of the cues we

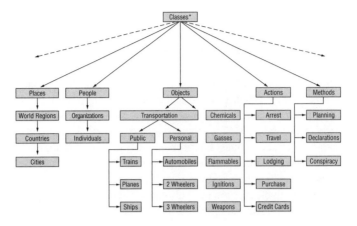

Figure 12.2: Example of a set of classes defined by the analyst.

suggest the need for a quantitative and a qualitative assessment, what we call a "result confidence index" (RCI). We then systematically increase the quantitative measure as more and more data is received. This update is likely to be dependent on the number and variety of linkages, frequency of occurrence of the linkages, geographical dispersion of the cues, etc. After a threshold is crossed, the information is brought to the attention of the analyst. The analyst assesses the need to add a hypothesis to the existing set of hypotheses, and if necessary formulates a hypothesis. In summary, in this part of our research we focus on techniques in data mining, and information retrieval. In summary, the hypothesis creation, justification and negation process relies on two automated functions: query processing, and linking and grouping of trifles. In the following sections we discuss our approach to these two functions.

Grouping and Querying Trifles

To develop the cues for the analyst, it is necessary to employ techniques to group trifles, and determine trifle-to-trifle links and trifle-to-hypothesis links. The hypotheses and the analyst queries are presented to the system and are processed using an approach similar to the trifles normalization. An I-XML page is generated for each hypothesis and query. Thereafter the trifles, hypotheses and queries are linked and grouped, and the strength of the linkage and associations is established. Figure 12.1 emphasizes that the results of these processes are made available to the analyst, and is potentially used to formulate additional queries. We note that, intelligence resources are allocated to analysis of hard targets (large share of resources), tracking concerns (some resources), and global watch (least resources). An essential step in building

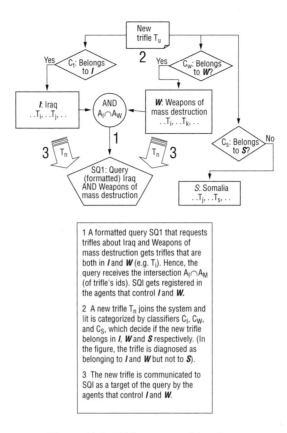

Figure 12.3: Trifles grouped by class.

support for queries is the grouping of trifles using some criteria of similarity among them. Grouping the trifles is accomplished through three distinct mechanisms. These mechanisms are not mutually exclusive and together serve as a powerful support for answering the queries posed by the analyst.

Supervised Learning

The first way to group trifles is to classify them into groups according to a predefined set of classes. An example of a predefined set of classes is shown in figure 12.2. Once such a set has been defined, the job is to classify trifles into those groups, by using their contents. Figure 4 provides an example of the application of this approach. This process is otherwise known as text categorization (recall that although not all trifles are text-based, their resulting I-XML pages are), that is, the ability to label documents with thematic cate-

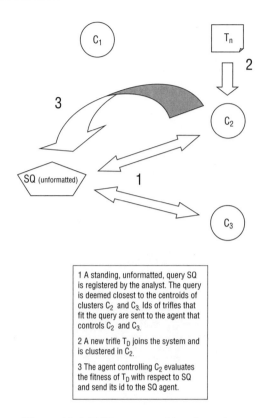

1 A standing, unformatted, query SQ is registered by the analyst. The query is deemed closest to the centroids of clusters C_2 and C_3. Ids of trifles that fit the query are sent to the agent that controls C_2 and C_3.

2 A new trifle T_D joins the system and is clustered in C_2.

3 The agent controlling C_2 evaluates the fitness of T_D with respect to SQ and send its id to the SQ agent.

Figure 12.4: Trifles grouped by clustering.

gories from a predefined set. Text categorization is an active area of research with many applications in areas such as information retrieval and natural language processing (Sebastiani 2002). It is widely recognized that the best way to perform text categorization is to devote efforts toward the construction of an automatic builder of classifiers (a classifier is a system that learns to classify objects into predetermined classes). Several steps are necessary to perform text categorization:

Step one—document indexing: Since text cannot be directly given to a classifier, a succinct representation is needed. So, an indexing step that maps the document into a vector of features is needed. The choice of features depends on what is regarded as important and meaningful. In our case, the production of this succinct representation is helped by the tags used in the I-XML pages, since the data bracketed by these tags can also be viewed as features of the document. Values of the features can be binary (presence or absence of a keyword), or multi-valued (e.g., number of times a keyword appears in the document). The selection of features plays, of course, an important role in the effectiveness of the classifier.

Step two—dimensionality reduction: The result of the previous step are vectors with a large number of features. High dimensionality usually poses a problem for classification methods, so performing dimensionality reduction is advisable. (A survey of methods can be found in Barbará [1997]). Dimensionality reduction is also beneficial since it tends to reduce overfitting (a phenomenon by which a classifier is biased towards the specific characteristics of the data used to train it). Techniques such as term selection using information-theoretical functions, and latent semantic indexing have been used effectively for this step.

Step three—building of classifiers: There exist a variety of techniques to produce classifiers. However, their application relies on the availability of an initial corpus of preclassified documents. This set (or part of it) is used to train the classifier. (Usually part of the set is reserved for testing the effectiveness of the trained classifier.) So, in the context of trifle classification, there are three roadblocks that need to be addressed:

(1) The absence or at least the limited availability of an initial corpus of preclassified trifles. This is likely to be the case at least in the initial stages of the system, since the initial classification of documents can be a labor-intensive process. This problem can be alleviated by using clustering techniques such as the one described in Barbará, Couto, and Li (2002). Taking an initial, small seed of preclassified trifles, one can use clustering to divide them in groups. If the clustering is effective, each group will contain only trifles of a class. Then one can add trifles to the groups by incrementally clustering (for which the technique described in Barbará, Couto, and Li (2002) is well suited), thereby labeling the newly clustered trifles with the labels of the groups they join. Other methods have been used (at small scale) for training classifiers without training data. Concretely, in Fellegi and Sunte (1969), the authors use a method to automatically estimate the needed probabilities to implement text classification using a technique called record linkage. To do this, certain implicit assumptions about the structure of the data are required. Other work that becomes relevant is that of Tom Mitchell in using unlabeled data for classification (Mitchell 1999),(Nigam, McCallum, Thrun, and Mitchel 2000)

(2). The dynamic nature of the trifles: Classifiers trained with an initial corpus may be rendered ineffective as time goes by. The nature of the new trifles joining the system may change, so, insisting on using the same classifiers may result in a lot of misclassification and reduced effectiveness in helping the analyst in gathering clues. So, classifiers evolve as the stream of new trifles arrives, continuously monitoring their effectiveness and modifying the models as needed. Initial work on evolving classifiers has been published in Domingos,

Hulten, and Spencer (2001). We plan to develop monitoring methods based on the techniques we have developed in Barbará and Chen (2001) for tracking clusters. In effect, tracking how the new trifles cluster fit in existing clusters (see section 12.1.3), and the relation of the clusters with respect to the pre-defined classes, will suggest the need to adjust the classifiers and perhaps to define new classes for trifles.

Clustering

A second way to group trifles is by using an unsupervised learning technique such as clustering. This way, the trifles are not placed in predefined classes, but rather they are grouped according to the similarities that their descriptions (vectors) show. In particular, we want to use the highly scalable, incremental technique that we have developed and presented in Barbará, Couto, and Li (2002) to cluster trifles.

Our technique, based in information theory is well suited to cluster vectors of categorical features such as words. The technique is designed to work with data streams, making it ideal for the environment of continuously arriving trifles, as depicted in figure 12.4. Additionally, the groups found by this technique can be characterized in their composition with respect to the predefined classes used in text categorization. That way, our techniques that aim to track the evolution of clusters can also help in determining whether the classifiers built for those classes need to change. Our approach here focused on determining what reduced set of features can be most effective for clustering (dimensionality reduction using the information theoretical framework of our algorithm), and the incorporation of missing values in the vector (again, by using the framework of our algorithm).

Finding Extra Links

Using similarity comparison (between the query and centroids, or between the query and the individual trifles) it is possible to miss important trifles. Consider for instance the recent news about the possibility that Cuba may be exporting chemical weapons. If a trifle with that information enters the system, it may not be targeted by a standing query that is trying to find trifles related to Iraq. This could be because the query targets the predefined class Iraq (and no other), or because the query finds as similar centroids those of groups in which the trifle about Cuba is not contained. However, by enhancing the system including links between trifles of different groups, one can increase the effectiveness of query processing.

In figure 12.5, we show how trifles are related through the standing queries. In it, trifles Ti and Tj are a target for standing query SQ1, while trifles Tj and

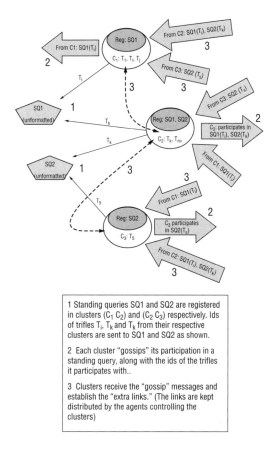

Figure 12.5: How the extra links are formed.

Tk are a target for the standing query SQ2. One can say that Ti and Tj (and Tj and Tk) are "related" (they "work" together in the solution of SQ1—or SQ2 in the case of Tj and Tk), while there are two degrees of separation between Ti and Tk (Ti works with some trifle, namely Tj, that in turn works with Tj in another query). In this way we anticipate the discovery of interesting extra links, which may provide cues to new hypothesis. In figure 12.6 we show how the extra links would be used to support a new standing query (SQ3). Finding extra links is a complex task—this is not surprising, after all trifle marshalling is a complex problem. However, we believe that this complexity can be successfully managed because of the small world phenomenon and our ability to control the degree of separation, and the success of sharing information through gossiping with neighbors in Gnutellalike peer-to-peer systems.

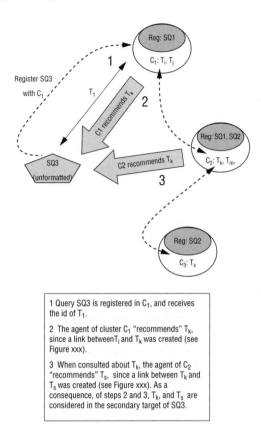

1 Query SQ3 is registered in C_1, and receives the id of T_1.

2 The agent of cluster C_1 "recommends" T_k, since a link between T_i and T_k was created (see Figure xxx).

3 When consulted about T_k, the agent of C_2 "recommends" T_s, since a link between T_k and T_s was created (see Figure xxx). As a consequence, of steps 2 and 3, T_k, and T_s are considered in the secondary target of SQ3.

Figure 12.6: How the extra links help enhancing the answer.

This phenomenon is also the paradigm that is used in the "Kevin Bacon" game,[3] where actors are linked by their common participation in a movie. (B. Tjaden, a member of the computer-science faculty at the University of Virginia made the claim that Bacon was at the center of the movie universe). For instance, if you take an actor like Patrick Stewart, his "Bacon number" (degrees of separation to K. Bacon) is two since Stewart worked with Steve Martin in *Prince of Egypt,* and Martin, in turn, worked with Bacon in *Novocaine.* The claim is that every actor has a Bacon number less than or equal to 4. This game is simply an instantiation of the "small world" phenomenon (amply discussed in Watts (1999). The study of small worlds is firmly based in probabilistic graph theory and statistics. In our case, the small world will is composed of a network of trifles that are connected to each other by their

---

[3] See for example, http://www.cs.virginia.edu/oracle/.

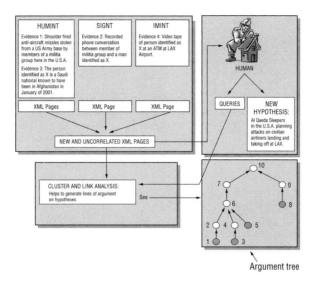

Figure 12.7: Example scenario.

participation in standing (or ad-hoc) queries. Of course, the network starts having a few connections found by the initial seed of standing queries, but it can quickly (demonstrably) grow to become an "small world." How does this help the query answering process? While query processing, the system should look not only at trifles in clusters similar to the query, but should also look at other trifles connected to those in the initial target by a limited degree of separation. In other words, we enhance the query answering process in the following way: (1) For a given query, look at the trifles in groups whose centroids (or classes) are closest to the query description. Call these trifles the primary target. (2) For those trifles in the primary target, look at all the trifles within a predefined degree of separation from them, and place them in the secondary target. (3) Offer trifles in both primary and secondary targets as answers to the query.

In our example, the trifle about Cuba might not be in the primary target of a query about Iraq, but standing queries about biological agents and unconventional weapons, might link the Cuba trifle with another trifle T' and this trifle T' with one in the class of Iraq trifles, so the enhanced version of the answering process will capture the Cuba trifle in the secondary target.

12.2 Narrative Scenario

An example scenario for our approach is shown in figure 12.7 with detailed evidence presented in the table of figure 12.8. In this example, four pieces of

Event	Description
1	Evidence 1: Shoulder fired anti-aircraft missiles stolen from a US Army base by member of a militia group in USA
2	The militia group has shoulder-fired AA missiles
3	Evidence 2: Phone conversation between X and a member of the militia group.
4	The conversation involved the sale of stolen weapons.
5	Evidence 3: X is a Saudi national known to have been in Afghanistan in January, 2001
6	X has obtained shoulder-fired AA missiles from the militia group.
7	The shoulder-fired AA missiles that will be delivered to the L. A. area.
8	Evidence 4: Photo of X at an ATM at LAX.
9	X is now in LA area.
10	Hypothesis: Al Qaeda sleepers in the USA are planning attacks on civilian airliners landing and taking off at LAX.

Figure 12.8: Detailed listing of evidence.

evidence are received by the analyst—evidence 1, 2, 3 and 4, corresponding to events 1, 3, 5 and 8. The development of the argument is shown in the argument tree of figure 12.7. For example, evidence 1 (event 1) prompts the analyst to formulate hypothesis 2; evidence 2 (event 3) leads to 4. These hypothesis along with evidence 3 (event 5) yields hypothesis 6 and so on. Our approach automates this process of clustering, linking and argument generation. In this way the analyst can experiment with more hypotheses.

12.3 Prototype: Human/Agent Interaction

As mentioned previously, the evidence marshaling architecture is built upon the agent-based imagery and geospatial processing architecture (AIGA). Details of this architecture can be found in Simon, Nolan, and Sood (2002). One of the key contributions of this architecture is a scalable, text-based, agent discovery and composition mechanism (Nolan, Sood, and Simon 2002). The approach, termed SADISCO, allows agents and clients to discover agents for processing utilizing keyword-based queries, and link or compose them together to solve complex problems. SADISCO is a distributed search space that is formed over a network and has been shown to scale to support up to 100,000 agents on the network.

The prototype is built in Java and uses Jini for the middleware. The agents implemented in the prototype include: (1) image processing—ninety-six agents that perform low level image processing functions provided by the Java Ad-

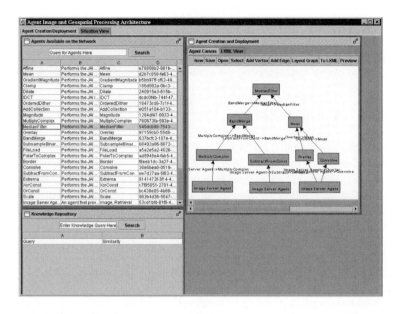

Figure 12.9: Discovering, composing, and deploying agents in AIGA.

vanced Imaging API. (2) Geospatial processing—ten agents that perform low-level geospatial processing provided by the OpenMap API.[4] (3) Information extraction—two agents that perform information extraction and parts-of-speech tagging provided by the GATE API.[5] (4) Clustering and classification—twenty-one agents that perform clustering and classification as provided by the WEKA API[6] (5) Information retrieval—an algorithm that implements Salton's SMART algorithm for information retrieval. (6) Client agent—and agent that represents the human user to the agent system.

In figure 12.9, we show the the client interface to the agent system. Here the user can search for agents, select agents from the network, link them together, edit their parameters, and deploy them as a new, metaagent. In the upper left quadrant of the screenshot is the agent list panel. This panel gives a list of all agents available on the network, or a user can search for a specific agent by typing in a textual description. In the lower left quadrant is the Knowledge List Panel. This panel allows the user to search the knowledge repository and see how and what agents have been used to solve particular queries. Users can view the agent composition, even down to the detail of the parameters and their setting for each agent composition. In the upper right quadrant of the screen-

---

[4]http://openmap.bbn.com.
[5]http://gate.ac.uk.
[6]http://www.cs.waikato.ac.nz/ml/weka.

shot is the agent canvas. From the agent list panel, users can drag agents onto this canvas, link them together, and create a new metaagent for processing. Additionally, users can select a scheduling mechanism to distribute the agents across multiple processors on the network.

12.4   Conclusions

We have presented in this chapter an architecture for marshalling the large volume of evidence that an intelligence analyst may have at her disposition. The crucial concept on this architecture is that the analyst preserves the capability of thinking and generating hypothesis that can be automatically tested by posing queries to the system. These queries are supported by a variety of data mining techniques that allow the system to obtain the pieces of evidence required for the query. The architecture is integrated with AIGA, an agent-based distributed system for query resolution.

Daniel Barbara is an associate professor at George Mason University, specializing in data mining and its applications. He can be reached at dbarbara@gmu.edu

David Schum, is a professor of law at George Mason University.

James J. Nolan is a senior scientist at Decisive Analytics Corporation in Arlington, Virginia.

Arun Sood is a professor and chair of the Computer Science Department of George Mason University. His research interests include multi-agent systems, modelling and image and multimedia computing. He can be reached at asood(at)gmu.edu.

Chapter 13

Relational Data Mining with Inductive Logic Programming for Link Discovery

Raymond J. Mooney, Prem Melville
Lappoon Rupert Tang, Jude Shavlik,
Inês de Castro Dutra, David Page,
and Vítor Santos Costa

Since the events of September 11, 2001, the development of information technology that could aid intelligence agencies in their efforts to detect and prevent terrorism has become an important focus of attention. The Evidence Extraction and Link Discovery (EELD) program of the Defense Advanced Research Projects Agency (DARPA) is one research project that attempts to address this issue. The establishment of the EELD program for developing advanced software for aiding the detection of terrorist activity predates the events of September 11. The program had its genesis at a preliminary DARPA planning meeting held at Carnegie Mellon University after the opening of the Center for Automated Learning and Discovery in June of 1998. This meeting discussed the possible formation of a new DARPA research program focused on novel knowledge-discovery and data mining (KDD) methods appropriate for counter-terrorism.

The scope of the new program was subsequently expanded to focus on three related subtasks in detecting potential terrorist activity from numerous large information sources in multiple formats. *Evidence extraction* (EE) is the task of obtaining structured evidence data from unstructured, natural-language documents. EE builds on information extraction technology developed under DARPA's earlier message understanding conference (MUC) programs (Lehnert and Sundheim 1991; Cowie and Lehnert 1996) and the current automated content extraction (ACE) program at the National Institute of Standards and Technology (NIST).[1] *Link discovery* (LD) is the task of identifying known, complex, multirelational patterns that indicate potentially threatening activities in large amounts of relational data. It is therefore a form of pattern-matching that involves matching complex, multirelational "patterns of interest" against large amounts of data. Some of the input data for LD comes from EE applied to news reports and other unstructured documents, other input data comes from existing relational databases on financial and other transactions. Finally, *pattern learning* (PL) concerns the automated discovery of new relational patterns for potentially threatening activities. Since determining and authoring a complete and accurate set of formal patterns for detecting terrorist activities is a difficult task, learning methods may be useful for automatically acquiring such patterns from supervised or unsupervised data. Learned patterns can then be employed by an LD system to improve its detection of threatening activities. The current EELD program focused on these three subtopics started in the summer of 2001. After September 11, it was incorporated under the new Information Awareness Office (IAO) at DARPA.

The data and patterns used in EELD include representations of people, organizations, objects, and actions and many types of relations between them. The data is perhaps best represented as a large graph of entities connected by a variety of relations. The areas of link analysis and social network analysis in sociology, criminology, and intelligence (Jensen and Goldberg 1998; Wasserman and Faust 1994; Sparrow 1991) study such networks using graph-theoretic representations. Data mining and pattern learning for counter terrorism therefore requires handling such multirelational, graph-theoretic data.

Unfortunately, most current data mining methods assume the data is from a single relational table and consists of flat tuples of items, as in market-basket analysis. This type of data is easily handled by machine learning techniques that assume a "propositional" ("feature vector" or "attribute value") representation of examples (Witten and Frank 1999). *Relational data mining* (RDM) (Džeroski and Lavrač 2001b), on the other hand, concerns mining data from multiple relational tables that are richly connected. Given the style of data needed for link discovery, pattern learning for link discovery requires rela-

---

[1] http://www.nist.gov/speech/tests/ace/.

tional data mining. The most widely studied methods for inducing relational patterns are those in *inductive logic programming* (ILP) (Muggleton 1992; Lavrač and Džeroski 1994). ILP concerns the induction of Horn-clause rules in first-order logic (i.e., logic programs) from data in first-order logic. This chapter discusses our on-going work on applying ILP to pattern learning for link discovery as a part of the EELD project.

13.1   Inductive Logic Programming (ILP)

ILP is the study of learning methods for data and rules that are represented in first-order predicate logic. Predicate logic allows for quantified variables and relations and can represent concepts that are not expressible using examples described as feature vectors. A relational database can be easily translated into first-order logic and be used as a source of data for ILP (Wrobel 2001). As an example, consider the following rules, written in Prolog syntax (where the conclusion appears first), that define the uncle relation:

```
uncle(X,Y)  :- brother(X,Z),parent(Z,Y).
uncle(X,Y)  :- husband(X,Z),sister(Z,W),parent(W,Y).
```

The goal of *inductive logic programming* (ILP) is to infer rules of this sort given a database of background facts and logical definitions of other relations (Muggleton 1992; Lavrač and Džeroski 1994). For example, an ILP system can learn the above rules for uncle (the *target predicate*) given a set of positive and negative examples of uncle relationships and a set of facts for the relations parent, brother, sister, and husband (the *background predicates*) for the members of a given extended family, such as:

```
uncle(tom,frank), uncle(bob,john),
not uncle(tom,cindy), not uncle(bob,tom)
parent(bob,frank), parent(cindy,frank), parent(alice,john),
parent(tom,john), brother(tom,cindy), sister(cindy,tom),
husband(tom,alice), husband(bob,cindy).
```

Alternatively, rules that logically define the brother and sister relations could be supplied and these relationships inferred from a more complete set of facts about only the "basic" predicates: parent, spouse, and gender.

If-then rules in first-order logic are formally referred to as *Horn clauses*. A more formal definition of the ILP problem follows:

Given:

- Background knowledge, B, a set of Horn clauses.

- Positive examples, P, a set of Horn clauses (typically ground literals).

- Negative examples, N, a set of Horn clauses (typically ground literals).

Find: A hypothesis, H, a set of Horn clauses such that:

- $\forall p \in P : H \cup B \models p$ (completeness)

- $\forall n \in N : H \cup B \not\models n$ (consistency)

A variety of algorithms for the ILP problem have been developed (Džeroski and Lavrač 2001a) and applied to a variety of important data mining problems (Džeroski 2001; Houstis, Catlin, Rice, Verykios, Ramakrishnan, and Houstis 2000). Nevertheless, relational data mining remains an under-appreciated topic in the larger KDD community. For example, recent textbooks on data mining (Han and Kamber 2001; Witten and Frank 1999; Hand, Mannila, and Smyth 2001) hardly mention the topic. An increasing number of applications require handling complex, structured data types, including bioinformatics, web and text mining, and engineering. Therefore, we believe it is an important topic for "next generation" data mining systems. In particular, it is critical for link discovery applications in counter-terrorism.

One of the standard criticisms of ILP methods from a data mining perspective is that they do not scale to large amounts of data. Since the hypothesis space of possible logic programs is extremely large and since just testing individual hypotheses requires potentially complex automated deduction, ILP methods can have difficulty processing large amounts of data. We have developed methods to help address both of these aspects of computational complexity. First, we have developed methods for controlling the number of hypotheses tested by developing new search methods that use stochastic search to more efficiently explore the space of hypotheses (Zelezny, Srinivasan, and Page 2002) or that combine aspects of existing top-down and bottom-up methods (see section 13.2.2). Second, we have developed methods for automatically optimizing learned clauses by inserting cuts[2] in the Prolog code so that deduction is more efficient (Santos Costa, Srinivasan, and Camacho 2000). However, as discussed in section 13.3, scaling ILP to very large data sets is a significant area for future research.

13.2   Initial Work on ILP for Link Discovery

We tested several ILP algorithms on various EELD datasets. The current EELD datasets pertain to two domains that were chosen as "challenge problems" in

---

[2]In Prolog, cuts (!) are procedural operators that prevent potentially computationally expensive backtracking where the programmer determines it is unnecessary.

link discovery that have many of the underlying properties of the counter-terrorism problem—nuclear smuggling and contract killing. The contract-killing domain is further divided into natural (real world) data manually collected and extracted from news sources and synthetic (artificial) data generated by simulators. Section 13.2.1 presents our experimental results on the natural smuggling and contract-killing data, while section 13.2.2 presents results on the synthetic contract-killing data.

13.2.1 Experiments on Natural Data

In this subsection, we present the data on nuclear smuggling and natural contract-killing, and discuss the ILP results on the natural data.

The Nuclear-Smuggling Data

The nuclear-smuggling dataset consists of reports on Russian nuclear materials smuggling (McKay, Woessner, and Roule 2001). The chronology of nuclear and radioactive smuggling incidents is the basis for the analysis of patterns in the smuggling of Russian nuclear materials. The information in the chronology is based on open-source reporting, primarily World News Connection (WNC) and Lexis-Nexis. There are also some articles obtained from various sources that have been translated from Italian, German and Russian. The research from which the chronology grew began in 1994 and the chronology itself first appeared as an appendix to a paper by Williams and Woessner in 1995 (Williams and Woessner 1995a, Williams and Woessner 1995b). The continually evolving chronology then was published twice as separate papers in the same journal as part of the recent events section (Woessner 1995; Woessner 1997). As part of the EELD project, the coverage of the chronology was extended to March 2000 and grew to include 572 incidents.

The data is provided in the form of a relational database. This database contains objects (described in rows in tables), each of which has attributes of differing types (i.e., columns in the tables), the values of which are provided by the source information or the analyst. The objects are of different types, which are denoted by prefixes (E_, EV_, and LK_), and consist of the following:

- Entity objects (E_....): these consist of E_LOCATION, E_MATERIAL, E_ORGANIZATION, E_PERSON, E_SOURCE, and E_WEAPON;

- Event objects (EV_....): these currently consist of the generic EV_EVENT;

- Link objects (LK_....): used for expressing links between/among entities and events,

The database has over 40 relational tables. The number of tuples in a relational table varies from as many as 800 to as little as 2 or 3.

As a representative problem, we used ILP to learn rules for determining which events in an incident are *linked*. Such rules could be used to construct larger knowledge structures that could be recognized as threats. Hence, the ILP system is given positive training examples of known "links" between events. We assume all other events are unrelated and therefore compose a set of negative examples. We also provide background knowledge that the *linked* relation is commutative. Our training set consists of 140 positive examples and 140 distinct negative examples randomly drawn from a full set of 8,124 negative pairs of events. The linking problem in the nuclear-smuggling data is thus quite challenging in that it is a heavily relational learning problem over a large number of relations, whereas traditional ILP applications usually require a small number of relations.

The Natural Contract-Killing Data

The dataset of contract killings was first compiled by O'Hayon and Cook (2000) in response to research on Russian organized crime that encountered frequent references to contract killings. The dataset was subsequently expanded by the authors with funding from the EELD program through Veridian Systems Division (Williams 2002). The database consists of a chronology of incidents each described using information drawn from one or more news articles. As in the nuclear-smuggling dataset, information in the chronology is based on open-source reporting, especially Foreign Broadcast Information Service (FBIS) and Joint Publications Research Service (JPRS) journals, and subsequently both FBIS on-line and the on-line version World News Connection (WNC). These services and Lexis-Nexis were the main information sources.

The data is organized in relational tables in the same format as the Nuclear-Smuggling data described in the previous section. The dataset used in our experiments has 48 relational tables. The number of tuples in a relational table varies from as many as 1,000 to as few as 1. Each killing was categorized according to one of three possible motivations: "rival," "obstacle," or "threat." The ILP task was to determine whether the motivation for a killing was categorized as "rival" or not. The motivation for this learning task was to recognize patterns of activity that indicate an underlying motive, which in turn contributes to recognizing threats. The number of positive examples in this dataset is 38, while the number of negative examples is 34.

ILP Results on the Natural Data

Aleph. We used the ILP system ALEPH (Srinivasan 2001) to learn rules for the natural datasets. By default, ALEPH uses a simple greedy set covering procedure that constructs a complete and consistent hypothesis one clause at a time.

```
linked(A,E) :-
lk_event_person(_,EventA,PersonC,_,RelationB,RelationB,DescriptionD),
lk_event_person(_,EventF,PersonC,_,RelationB,RelationB,DescriptionD),
lk_material_location(_,MaterialG,_,EventE,_,_,_,_,_),
lk_event_material(_,EventF,MaterialG,_,_,_,_).
```

Figure 13.1: Nuclear-smuggling data: sample learned rule.

In the search for any single clause, ALEPH selects the first uncovered positive example as the seed example, *saturates* this example, and performs an admissible search over the space of clauses that subsume this saturation, subject to a user-specified clause length bound. Further details about our use of ALEPH in these experiments are available from Dutra, Page, Costa, and Shavlik (2002).

Ensembles aim at improving accuracy through combining the predictions of multiple classifiers in order to obtain a single classifier. In contrast with previous approaches (Quinlan 1996; Hoche and Wrobel 2001), each classifier is a logical theory generated by ALEPH. Many methods have been presented for ensemble generation (Dietterich 1998). We use *bagging* (Breiman 1996a), a popular method that is known to frequently create a more accurate ensemble. Bagging works by training each classifier on a random sample from the training set. Bagging has the important advantage that it is effective on "unstable learning algorithms" (Breiman 1996b), where small variations in the input data can cause large variations in the learned theories. Most ILP algorithms are unstable in this sense. A second advantage is that the bagging algorithm is highly parallel (Dutra, Page, Santos, Shavlik, and Waddell 2003). Further details about our approach to bagging for ILP, as well as our experimental methodology, can be found in Dutra, Page, Costa, and Shavlik (2002). Our experimental results are based on a five-fold cross-validation, where five times we train on 80% of the examples and then test what was learned on the remaining 20% (in addition, each example is in one and only one test set).

For the task of identifying linked events in the nuclear-smuggling dataset, ALEPH produces an average testset accuracy of 85%. This is an improvement over the baseline case (majority class—always guessing two events are not linked), which produces an average accuracy of 78%. Bagging (with 25 different sets of rules) increases the accuracy to almost 90%.

An example of a rule with good accuracy found by the system is shown in figure 13.1. This rule covers 43 of the 140 positive examples and no negative examples. According to this rule, two smuggling events A and E are related if event A involves a person C who is also involved in another event F. Event F involves some material G that appears in event E. In other words, a person C in event A is involved in a third event F that uses material from event E. Person C played the same role B, with description D, in events A and F.

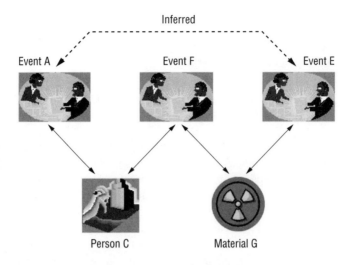

Figure 13.2: Pictorial representation of a learned rule.

```
rivalKilling(EventA) :-
lk_event_event(_,EventB,EventA,RelationC,EventDescriptionD),
lk_event_event(_,EventB,EventE,RelationC,EventDescriptionD),
lk_event_event(_,EventE,EventF,_,EventDescriptionD),
lk_org_org(_,_,_,EventF,_,_,_,_,_).
```

Figure 13.3: Natural contract-killing data: sample learned rule.

The "_" symbols mean that those arguments were not relevant for that rule. Figure 13.2 illustrates the connections between events, material and people involved. Solid lines are direct connections shown by the literals in the body of the clause. The dotted line corresponds to the newly learned concept that describes a connection between two events.

The task of identifying the underlying motive in the contract-killing data set is much more difficult, with ALEPH's accuracy at 59%, compared with the baseline accuracy of 52%. Again, bagging improves the accuracy, this time to 69%. The rule in figure 13.3 shows one logical clause the ILP system found for this dataset. The rule covers 19 of the 38 positive examples and a single negative example. The rule says that event *A* is a killing by a rival if we can follow a chain of events that connects event *A* to event *B*, event *B* to event *E*, and event *E* to an event *F* that relates two organizations. Events *A* and *E* have the same kind of relation, *RelationC*, to *B*. All events in the chain are subsets of the same incident *D*.

13.2.2   Experiments on Synthetic Data

The ease of generating large amounts of data and privacy considerations have led the EELD program to use synthetic data generated by simulators. Next, we describe the results we obtained from simulated data for the CK problem. This data was generated from a run of a task-based (TB) simulator developed by Information Extraction and Transport Incorporated (IET). The TB simulator outputs case files, which contain complete and unadulterated descriptions of murder cases. These case files are then filtered for observability, so that facts that would not be accessible to an investigator are eliminated. To make the task more realistic, the simulator output is corrupted, for example, by misidentifying role players or incorrectly reporting group memberships. This filtered and corrupted data form the evidence files. In the evidence files, facts about each event are represented as ground facts, such as:

```
murder(Murder714)
perpetrator(Murder714, Killer186)
crimeVictim(Murder714, MurderVictim996)
deviceTypeUsed(Murder714, PistolCzech)
```

The synthetic dataset that we used consists of 632 murder events. Each murder event has been labeled as either a positive or negative example of a murder-for-hire. There are 133 positive and 499 negative examples in the dataset. Our task was to learn a theory to correctly classify an unlabeled event as either a positive or negative instance of murder-for-hire. The amount of background knowledge for this dataset is extremely large; consisting of 52 distinct predicate names, and 681,039 background facts in all.

Scaling to large datasets in data mining typically refers to increasing the *number* of training examples that can be processed. Another measure of complexity that is particularly relevant in relational data mining is the *size* of individual examples, i.e. the number of facts used to describe each example. To our knowledge, the challenge problems developed for the EELD program are the largest ILP problems attempted to date in terms of the number of facts in the background knowledge. In order to more effectively process such large examples, we have developed a new ILP method that reduces the number of clauses that are generated and tested.

BETH

The two standard approaches to ILP are bottom-up and top-down (Lavrač and Džeroski 1994). Bottom-up methods like ALEPH start with a very specific clause (called a *bottom clause*) generated from a seed positive example and generalize it as far as possible without covering negative examples. Top-down methods like FOIL (Quinlan 1990) and mFOIL (Lavrač and Džeroski 1994) start with the most general (empty) clause and repeatedly specialize it until it no longer covers negative examples. Both approaches have problems scaling to large examples. When given large amounts of background knowledge, the bottom clause in bottom-up methods becomes intractably large and the increased branching factor in top-down methods greatly impedes their search.

Since top-down and bottom-up approaches have both strengths and weaknesses, we developed a hybrid method that helps reduce search when learning with large amounts of background knowledge. It does not build a bottom clause using a seed example *before* searching for a good clause. Instead, after a random seed example is chosen, it generates literals in a top-down fashion (i.e. guided by heuristic search), except the literals generated are constrained to cover the seed example. Based on this idea, we have developed a system called "bottom-clause exploration through heuristic-search" (BETH) in which the bottom clause is not constructed in advance but "discovered" during the search for a good clause. Details of the algorithm are given in Tang, Mooney, and Melville (2003).

Results and Discussion

The performance of ALEPH, mFOIL, and BETH was evaluated using 6-fold cross-validation. The data for each fold was generated by separate runs of the TB simulator. The facts produced by one run of the simulator only pertain to the entities and relations generated in that run; hence the facts of each fold are unrelated to the others. For each trial, one fold is set aside for testing, while the remaining data is *combined* for training. The total number of Prolog atoms in the data is so large that running more than six folds is not feasible.[3] To test performance on varying amounts of training data, learning curves were generated by testing the system after training on increasing subsets of the overall training data. Note that, for different points on the learning curve, the background knowledge remains the same; only the number of positive and negative training examples given to the system varies.

We compared the three systems with respect to accuracy and training time. Accuracy is defined as the number of correctly classified test cases divided by the total number of test cases. The training time is measured as the CPU time consumed during the training phase. All the experiments were performed on a 1.1 gigahertz Pentium with dual processors and 2 gigabytes of RAM. BETH and mFOIL were implemented in Sicstus Prolog version 3.8.5 and ALEPH was implemented in Yap version 4.3.22. Although different Prolog compilers were used, the Yap Prolog compiler has been demonstrated to outperform the Sicstus Prolog compiler, particularly in ILP applications (Santos Costa 1999).

---

[3]The maximum number of atoms that the Sicstus Prolog compiler can handle is approximately a quarter million.

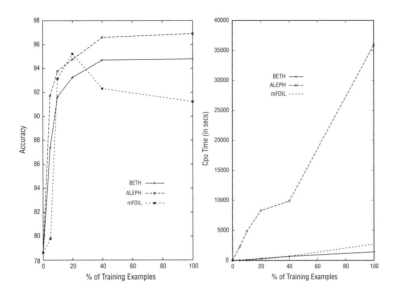

Figure 13.4: Learning curves for accuracy and training speed.

The following is a sample rule learned by BETH:

```
murder_for_hire(A):- murder(A), eventOccursAt(A,H),
geographicalSubRegions(I,H), perpetrator(A,B),
recipientOfinfo(C,B), senderOfinfo(C,D), socialParticipants(F,D),
socialParticipants(F,G), payer(E,G), toPossessor(E,D).
```

This rule covered 9 positive examples and 3 negative examples. The rule can be interpreted as: A is a murder-for-hire, if A is a murder event, which occurs in a city in a subregion of Russia, and in which B is the perpetrator, who received information from D, who had a meeting with and received some money from G.

The results of our experiments are summarized in figure 13.4. A snapshot of the performance of the three ILP systems given 100% of the training examples is shown in table 13.1. On the full training set, BETH trains 25 times faster than ALEPH while losing only 2 percentage points in accuracy and it trains twice as fast as mFOIL while gaining 3 percentage points in accuracy. Therefore, we believe that its integration of top-down and bottom-up search is an effective approach to dealing with the problem of scaling ILP to large examples. The learning curves for training time further illustrate that although BETH and mFOIL appear to scale linearly with the number of training examples, ALEPH's training-time growth is super-linear.

Systems like BETH and ALEPH construct literals based on actual ground atoms in the background knowledge, guaranteeing that the specialized clause

System	Accuracy	CPU Time (mins)	# of Clauses	Bottom Clause Size
BETH	94.80% (+/- 2.3%)	23.39 (+/- 4.26)	4483	34
ALEPH	96.91% (+/- 2.8%)	598.92 (+/- 250.00)	63334	4061
mFOIL	91.23% (+/- 4.8%)	45.28 (+/- 5.40)	112904	n/a

Table 13.1: Results on classifying *murder-for-hire* events given all the training data. *# of clauses* is the total number of clauses tested; and *bottom clause size* is the average number of literals in the bottom clause constructed for each clause in the learned theory. The 90% confidence intervals are given for test *accuracy* and *CPU time*.

covers at least the seed example. On the other hand, mFOIL generates more literals than necessary by enumerating all possible combination of variables. Some such combinations make useless literals; adding any of them to the body of the current clause makes specialized clauses that do not cover any positive examples. Thus, mFOIL wastes CPU time constructing and testing these literals. Since the average predicate arity in the EELD data was small (2), the speedup over mFOIL was not as great, although much larger gains would be expected for data that contains predicates with higher arity.

13.3 Current and Future Research

An under-studied issue in relational data mining is scaling algorithms to very large databases. Most research on ILP and RDM has been conducted in the machine learning and artificial intelligence communities rather than in the database and systems communities. Consequently, there has been insufficient research on systems issues involved in performing RDM in commercial relational-database systems and scaling algorithms to extremely large datasets that will not fit in main memory. Integrating ideas from systems work in data mining and deductive databases (Ramamohanarao and Harland 1994) would seem to be critical in addressing these issues.

On the issue of scaling, in addition to the BETH system discussed in section 13.2.2, we are currently working on efficiently learning complex relational concepts from large amounts of data by using stochastic sampling methods. A major shortcoming of ILP is the computational demand that results from the large hypothesis spaces searched. Intelligently sampling these large spaces can provide excellent performance in much less time (Srinivasan 1999; Zelezny, Srinivasan, and Page 2002).

We are also developing algorithms that learn more robust, probabilistic relational concepts represented as stochastic logic programs (Muggleton 2003) and variants. This will enrich the expressiveness and robustness of learned concepts. As an alternative to stochastic logic programs, we are working on learning clauses in a constraint logic programming language where the constraints are Bayesian networks (Page 2000; Costa, Page, Qazi, and Cussens 2003).

One approach that we plan to investigate further is the use of approximate prior knowledge to induce more accurate, comprehensible relational concepts from fewer training examples (Richards and Mooney 1995). The use of prior knowledge can greatly reduce the burden on users; they can express the "easy" aspects of the task at hand and then collect a small number of training examples to refine and extend this prior knowledge.

We also plan to use active learning to allow our ILP systems to select more effective training examples for interactively learning relational concepts (Muggleton, Bryant, Page, and Sternberg 1999). By intelligently choosing the examples for users to label, better extraction accuracy can be obtained from fewer examples, thereby greatly reducing the burden on the users of our ILP systems.

Another important issue related to data mining for counter-terrorism is privacy preservation. DARPA's counter-terrorism programs have attracted significant public and media attention due to concerns about potential privacy violations (e.g. Clymer 2003). Consequently, privacy-preserving data mining (Gehrke 2002) is another very significant "next generation" issue in data mining.

13.4 Related Work

Although it is the most widely studied, ILP is not the only approach to relational data mining. In particular, other participants in the EELD program are taking alternative RDM approaches to pattern learning for link discovery. This section briefly reviews these other approaches.

13.4.1 Graph-based Relational Learning

Some relational data mining methods are based on learning structural patterns in graphs. In particular, SUBDUE (Cook and Holder 1994, 2000) discovers highly repetitive subgraphs in a labeled graph using the minimum description length (MDL) principle. SUBDUE can be used to discover interesting substructures in graphical data as well as to classify and cluster graphs. Discovered patterns do not have to match the data exactly since SUBDUE can employ an inexact graph-matching procedure based on graph edit-distance. SUBDUE has been successfully applied to a number of important RDM problems in molecular biology, geology, and program analysis. It is also currently being applied to discover patterns for link discovery as a part of the EELD project.[4] Since relational data for LD is easily represented as labeled graphs, graph-based RDM methods like SUBDUE are a natural approach.

13.4.2 Probabilistic Relational Models

Probabilistic relational models (PRM's) (Koller and Pfeffer 1998) are an extension of Bayesian networks for handling relational data. Methods for learning Bayesian networks have also been extended to produce algorithms for inducing PRM's from data (Friedman, Getoor, Koller, and Pfeffer 1999). PRM's have the nice property of integrating some of the advantages of both logical and probabilistic approaches to knowledge representation and reasoning. They combine some of the representational expressivity of first-order logic with the uncertain reasoning abilities of Bayesian networks. PRM's have been applied to a number of interesting problems in molecular biology, web-page classification, and analysis of movie data. They are also currently being applied to pattern learning for link discovery as a part of the EELD project.

13.4.3 Relational Feature Construction

One approach to learning from relational data is to first "flatten" or "propositionalize" the data by constructing features that capture some of the relational information and then applying a standard learning algorithm to the resulting feature vectors (Kramer, Lavrač, and Flach 2001). *Proximity* (Neville and Jensen 2000) is a system that constructs features for categorizing entities based on the categories and other properties of other entities to which it is related. It then uses an interactive classification procedure to dynamically update inferences about objects based on earlier inferences about related objects. *Proximity* has been successfully applied to company and movie data. It is also currently being applied to pattern learning for link discovery as a part of the EELD project.

13.5   Conclusions

Link discovery is an important problem in automatically detecting potential threatening activity from large, heterogeneous data sources. DARPA's EELD program is a U.S. government research project exploring link discovery as an important problem in the development of new counter-terrorism technology. Learning new link-discovery patterns that indicate potentially threatening

---

[4]For details see http://ailab.uta.edu/eeld/.

activity is a difficult data mining problem. It requires discovering novel relational patterns in large amounts of complex relational data. In this work we have shown that ILP methods can extract interesting and useful rules from link-discovery data-bases containing up to hundreds of thousands of items. To do so, we improved search efficiency and computation time per node over current ILP systems.

Most existing data mining methods assume flat data from a single relational table and are not appropriate for link discovery. Relational data mining techniques, such as inductive logic programming, are needed. Many other problems in molecular biology (Srinivasan, Muggleton, Sternberg, and King 1996), natural-language understanding (Zelle and Mooney 1996), web page classification (Craven, DiPasquo, Freitag, McCallum, Mitchell, Nigam, and Slattery 2000), information extraction (Califf and Mooney 1999; Freitag 1998), and other areas also require mining multirelational data. However, relational data mining requires exploring a much larger space of possible patterns and performing complex inference and pattern matching. As a result, current RDM methods are not sufficiently scalable to very large databases. Consequently, we believe that relational data mining is one of the major research topics in the development of the next generation of data mining systems, particularly those in the area of counter-terrorism.

Acknowledgments

This research is sponsored by the Defense Advanced Research Projects Agency and managed by Rome Laboratory under contract F30602-01-2-0571. The views and conclusions contained in this document are those of the authors and should not be interpreted as necessarily representing the official policies, either expressed or implied of the Defense Advanced Research Projects Agency, Rome Laboratory, or the United States Government.

Vítor Santos Costa and Inês de Castro Dutra are on leave from COPPE / Sistemas, Federal University of Rio de Janeiro and were partially supported by CNPq. Many thanks to Hans Chalupksy's group at ISI, in particular to André Valente, who gave us support on using the Task-based simulator. We would like to thank the Biomedical Computing Group support staff and the Condor Team at the Computer Sciences Department of the University of Wisconsin, Madison, for their invaluable help with Condor. We also would like to thank Ashwin Srinivasan for his help with the ALEPH system.

Raymond J. Mooney is a professor of computer sciences at the University of Texas at Austin. His interests include machine learning, text mining, and natural-language processing. More information is available at www.cs.utexas.edu/users/mooney.

Prem Melville is a Ph.D. candidate in the Department of Computer Sciences at the University of Texas at Austin. His interests include machine learning, recommender systems, and relational data mining. For details see www.cs.utexas.edu/users/melville.

Lappoon Rupert Tang earned his Ph.D. at the University of Texas at Austin and is currently a post-doctoral fellow at the University of Delaware. His interests include relational data mining and bioinformatics. He can be reached at ltang@cis.udel.edu.

Jude Shavlik is a professor of computer sciences and of biostatistics and medical informatics at the University of Wisconsin - Madison. His research interests include machine learning and computational biology. For more details see www.cs.wisc.edu/~shavlik

Inês Dutra is a professor of computer science at Federal University of Rio de Janeiro. Her interests include relational data mining and parallel processing. She can be reached at ines@cos.ufrj.br.

C. David Page, Jr. is an associate professor in the Department of Biostatistics and Medical Informatics and the Department of Computer Sciences at the University of Wisconsin Medical School. For more details see www.cs.wisc.edu/~dpage.

Vítor Santos Costa is a professor of computer science at Universidade Federal do Rio de Janeiro, Brazil. His interests include logic programming,compilers and machine learning. He can be reached as vitor@cos.ufrj.br

Chapter 14

Defining Privacy for Data Mining

Chris Clifton, Murat Kantarcıoğlu, and Jaideep Vaidya

There has recently been a surge in interest in privacy preserving data mining (Agrawal and Srikant 2000; Agrawal and Aggarwal 2001; Muralidhar, Sarathy, and Parsa 2001; Kantarcioglu and Clifton 2002; Vaidya and Clifton 2002; Evfimievski, Srikant, Agrawal, and Gehrke 2002; Rizvi and Haritsa 2002; Clifton and Estivill-Castro 2002; KDD Explorations 2003; Vaidya and Clifton 2003). Even the popular press has picked up on this trend (Hamblen 2002; Eisenberg 2002). However, the concept of what is meant by privacy isn't clear. In this chapter we outline some of the concepts that are addressed in this line of research, and provide a roadmap for defining and understanding privacy constraints.

Generally when people talk of privacy, they say "keep information about me from being available to others." This doesn't match the Webster's dictionary definition: "freedom from unauthorized intrusion." It is this intrusion, or use of personal data in a way that negatively impacts someone's life, that causes concern. As long as data is not misused, most people do not feel their privacy has been violated. The problem is that once information is released, it may be impossible to prevent misuse. Utilizing this distinction—ensuring that a data mining project won't enable *misuse* of personal information—opens opportunities that "complete privacy" would prevent. To do this, we need technical and social solutions that ensure data will not be released.

The same basic concerns also apply to collections of data. Given a collection of data, it is possible to learn things that are not revealed by any individual data item. An individual may not care about someone knowing their birth date, mother's maiden name, or social security number, but knowing all this information enables identity theft. This type of privacy problem arises with large, multi-individual collections as well. A technique that guarantees no individual data is revealed may still release information describing the collection as a whole. Such "corporate information" is generally the goal of data mining, but some results may still lead to concerns (often termed a "secrecy" rather than "privacy" issue.) The difference between such corporate privacy issues and individual privacy is not that significant. If we view disclosure of knowledge about an entity (information about an individual) as a potential individual privacy violation, then generalizing this to disclosure of information about a subset of the data captures both views.

In section 14.3 we will give real-world examples of collection privacy problems. Section 14.2 discusses approaches to dealing with individual privacy. First, however, we give background on the two main classes of privacy preserving data mining.

14.1 Approaches to Privacy Preserving Data Mining

Two papers entitled "Privacy Preserving Data Mining" appeared in 2000. Although both addressed a similar problem, constructing decision trees from private training data, the concepts of privacy were quite different. One was based on *data obscuration*, i.e., modifying the data values so real values are not disclosed (Agrawal and Srikant 2000). The other used secure multiparty computation (SMC) to "encrypt" data values (Lindell and Pinkas 2000), ensuring that no party learns anything about another's data values. We first describe SMC, then give additional background on data obscuration. We also discuss a problem that has received little attention: How do we constrain data mining if it is possible that the results alone violate privacy?

14.1.1 Secure Multiparty Computation

The idea of secure multiparty computation (SMC) (Yao 1986; Goldreich, Micali, and Wigderson 1987) is that the parties involved learn nothing but the results. Informally, imagine we have a trusted third party to which all parties give their input. The trusted party computes the output and returns it to the parties.

SMC enables this without the trusted third party. There may be considerable communication between the parties to get the final result, but the parties don't learn anything from this communication. The computation is secure if given just one party's input and output from those runs, we can *simulate* what would be seen by the party. In this case, to simulate means that the distribution of what is actually seen and the distribution of the simulated view over many runs are computationally indistinguishable. We may not be able to exactly simulate every run, but over time we cannot tell the simulation from the real runs.

Since we could simulate the runs from knowing only our input and output, it makes sense to say that we don't learn anything from the run other than the output. It has been shown that any output that can be represented as a Boolean circuit (effectively anything we can compute) can be computed securely (Goldreich, Micali, and Wigderson 1987). The key idea is that each party divides each bit of its input to the circuit into two shares, such that the exclusive or of the shares is the real input. One (randomly chosen) share is given to the other party. This share is equally likely to be a 0 or 1, so the other party learns nothing. (I.e., if the real value is a 1, each is equally likely to get the 1 or the 0. If the real value is 0, both will get a 0 or both a 1.) For each gate, the two parties carry out a protocol that gives them each a random share of the output of that gate. The shares propagate through the system; at the end the parties combine their shares to get the result. No party learns anything from the intermediate steps, since the random share is equally likely to be 0 or 1.

The protocol to be carried out for each gate is straightforward in the case of an XOR gate: Each computes the xor of its shares (see figure 14.1.) Since no information is shared, there is clearly no security breach.

Securely computing an AND gate is more complex, and involves a cryptographic technique known as oblivious transfer. One party chooses a random value as its share of the output, and constructs a table that gives the other party's share of the output (table 14.1.) The other party looks in the appropriate table entry based on their inputs to find their share of the AND gate output. The key is that the table entry is done with an oblivious transfer: The second party only gets to look at one entry in the table, and the first party doesn't know which one. Several protocols for oblivious transfer exist (see Naor and Pinkas [2001] for one). Party A gains no information, and since the value seen by party B is randomly determined by A's choice of c_1, it learns nothing from the oblivious transfer.

While this construction shows the *possibility* of secure distributed data mining, it is not practical for data mining-sized inputs. The definitions, standards, and technique of SMC have been used for practical privacy preserving

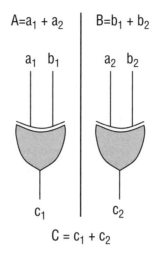

$A=a_1 + a_2$ | $B=b_1 + b_2$

a_1 b_1 | a_2 b_2

c_1 | c_2

$C = c_1 + c_2$

Figure 14.1: Securely computing shares of XOR.

Value of a_2, b_2	0 0	0 1	1 0	1 1
Share	$c_1 + a_1 b_1$	$c_1 + a_1 \overline{b_1}$	$c_1 + \overline{a_1} b_1$	$c_1 + \overline{a_1} \overline{b_1}$

Table 14.1: Table of share of AND gate output.

data mining algorithms (Lindell and Pinkas 2000; Du and Atallah 2001a; Du and Atallah 2001b). We must be careful when using SMC to define privacy. For example, suppose we use a SMC technique to build a decision tree from databases at two sites (Lindell and Pinkas 2000), classifying people into high and low risk for a sensitive disease. Assume that the nonsensitive data is public, but the sensitive data (needed as training data to build the classifier) cannot be revealed. The SMC computation won't reveal the sensitive data, but the resulting classifier will enable all parties to estimate the value of the sensitive data. It isn't that the SMC was "broken," but that the result itself violates privacy.

14.1.2 Obscuring Data

Another approach to privacy is to obscure data: making private data available, but with enough noise added that exact values (or approximations sufficient to allow misuse) cannot be determined. One approach, typically used in census data, is to aggregate items. Knowing the average income for a neighborhood is not enough to determine the actual income of a resident of that neighborhood.

An alternative is to add random noise to data values, then mine the distorted data. While this lowers the accuracy of data mining results, research has shown that the loss of accuracy can be small relative to the loss of ability to estimate an individual item. We can reconstruct the original distribution of a collection of obscured numeric values, enabling better construction of decision trees (Agrawal and Srikant 2000; Agrawal and Aggarwal 2001). This would enable data collected from a web survey to be obscured at the source—the correct values would never leave the respondent's machine—ensuring that exact (misusable) data doesn't exist. Techniques have also been developed for association rules, enabling valid rules to be learned from data where items have been randomly added to or removed from individual transactions (Evfimievski, Srikant, Agrawal, and Gehrke 2002; Rizvi and Haritsa 2002).

14.1.3 Perfect Privacy

One problem with the above is the tradeoff between privacy and accuracy of the data mining results. SMC does better, but at a high computational and communication cost. In the "web survey" example, the respondents could engage in a secure multiparty computation to obtain the results, and reveal no information that is not contained in the results. However, getting thousands of respondents to participate synchronously in a complex protocol is impractical. While useful in the corporate model, it is not appropriate for the web model. Here we present a solution based on moderately trusted third parties—the parties are not trusted with exact data, but trusted only not to collude with the "data receiver."

Assume the existence of k *untrusted, noncolluding* sites.

> *Untrusted* implies that none of these sites should be able to gain any useful information from any of the inputs of the local sites.

> *Noncolluding* implies that none of these sites should collude with any other sites to obtain information beyond the protocol.

Then, all of the local parties can split their local inputs into k random shares which are then split across the k untrusted sites. Each of these random shares are meaningless information by themselves. However, if any of the parties combined their data, they would gain some meaningful information from the combined data. For this reason, we require that the sites be noncolluding. We believe this assumption is not unrealistic. Each site combines the shares of the data it has received using a secure protocol to get the required data mining result.

The following is a brief description of this approach. Every party is assumed to have a single bit of information x_i, identified by some key i. Each party locally generates a random number r_i and then sends $(i, \bar{x}_i = x_i \oplus r_i)$ to one site and (i, r_i) to the second site. Note that neither site will be able to predict the x_i. Due to the xor operation $\oplus$, the input they see is indistinguishable from any uniformly generated random sequence. Given any data mining task(f) defined on $X = [x_1, x_2, \ldots, x_n]$, it suffices to evaluate $f(\bar{X} \oplus R) = f(X)$ since $R = [r_1, r_2, \ldots, r_n]$ and $\bar{X} \oplus R = [\bar{x}_1 \oplus r_1, \bar{x}_2 \oplus r_2, \ldots, \bar{x}_n \oplus r_n]$. It is a known fact that with the assumption of existence of trapdoor permutations (RSA is assumed to be a trapdoor permutation), any functionality g, $(g : \{0, 1\}^* \times \{0, 1\}^* \mapsto \{0, 1\}^* \times \{0, 1\}^*)$ can be evaluated privately in the semihonest model (Goldreich, Micali, and Wigderson 1987). Since the initial xor operation can be easily represented as a circuit, given functionality f, we can define a functionality $g(X, R) = f(\bar{X} \oplus R)$. Thus, any data mining functionality can be evaluated privately without revealing any information other than the final result. (For a more complete treatment, see Kantarcioglu and Vaidya [2002].)

While this solution is not especially efficient, indeed not even necessarily very practical for large quantities of data, it does demonstrate a method of maintaining perfect privacy while computing the required data mining function.

14.1.4   Limitations on Results

How can we constrain the results of data mining? There has been work in this area, addressing specific problems such as hiding specific association rules (Atallah, Bertino, Elmagarmid, Ibrahim, and Verykios 1999; Saygin, Verykios, and Clifton 2001) or limiting confidence in *any* data mining (Clifton 2000). While these provide some specific techniques, the means available to constrain results are limited. What is needed is a general way to specify what is and is not allowed.

One possible approach is constraint-based data mining (Bayardo 2002). This line of research is concerned with improving the efficiency of algorithms and understandability of results through providing up-front constraints on what results would be of interest. Would the languages used to describe these constraints also serve to define what results are acceptable from a privacy standpoint? While the current methods do not *enforce* that nothing outside the constraints can be learned, they could provide a starting point for further research.

The remainder of this chapter provides some specific suggestions for methods to specify privacy constraints in ways that still allow data mining. We start with a discussion of individual privacy. We then discuss corporate privacy, or constraining what is disclosed about subsets of the entire data. We conclude with several orthogonal metrics for defining and measuring privacy.

14.2   Individual Privacy

Most legal efforts have been directed to protecting data of the individual. For example, the European Community regulates *personal data* (Official Journal of the European Communities 1995):

> "personal data" shall mean any information relating to an identified or identifiable natural person ("data subject"); an identifiable person is one who can be identified, directly or indirectly, in particular by reference to an identification number or to one or more factors specific to his physical, physiological, mental, economic, cultural or social identity;

and specifies that data can be

> kept in a form which permits identification of data subjects for no longer than is necessary for the purposes for which the data were collected or for which they are further processed. Member States shall lay down appropriate safeguards for personal data stored for longer periods for historical, statistical or scientific use.

The key element here is "identifiable": As long as the data cannot be traced to an individual, the regulations do not apply. The U.S. HIPAA rules (U.S. Federal Register 2001) are similar—they apply to *protected health information*, defined as individually identifiable health information:

> *Individually identifiable health information* is information that is a subset of health information, including demographic information collected from an individual, and: (1) is created or received by a health care provider, health plan, employer, or health care clearinghouse; and (2) relates to the past, present, or future physical or mental health or condition of an individual; the provision of health care to an individual; or the past, present, or future payment for the provision of health care to an individual; and (a) that identifies the individual; or (b) with respect to which there is a reasonable basis to believe the information can be used to identify the individual.

Any information that cannot be traced to a specific individual falls outside the scope of most privacy laws. This provides one solution to privacy and data mining projects: As long as the data used is not individually identifiable, there should be no problems.

Another factor in individual data is how the data is collected and held. The U.S. HIPAA rules assume that data is created and held by a healthcare provider. This gives a *corporate* model—individually identifiable information first "appears" within a collection held by someone other than the individual.

An alternative is the "world wide web" model, where individuals provide the data in electronic form themselves. These models lead to different solutions. We first look at some generally applicable solutions, then discuss some that are only relevant in the corporate model.

Data obscuration is effective both in the web and corporate model. Obscuration can be done by the individual (if the receiver isn't trusted), or by the holder of data (to reduce concerns about breached security.) However, obscuring data falls into a legal gray area. Rules such as EC 95/46 and HIPAA would probably view individually identifiable data with values obscured as protected, even if the exact values are unknowable. However, obscuration could be as or more effective at protecting actual data values than the aggregation methods used on publicly available census data. Demonstrating the effectiveness of data obscuration in comparison with census data could improve public acceptance, and lead to changes in legal standards.

Data obscuration techniques could also be used to ensure that otherwise identifiable data isn't individually identifiable. Reidentification experiments have shown that data that might be viewed as nonidentifiable, such as birth date and postal code, can in combination allow identification of an individual (Sweeney 2001). Obscuring the data could make reidentification impossible, thus meeting both the spirit and letter of privacy laws.

14.3 Collection Privacy

Protecting individual data items may not be enough—we may need to protect against learning about subsets of a collection. Such issues are common in a data warehousing environment, where data from multiple sources is combined for analysis (see figure 14.2). This requires that the warehouse be trusted to maintain the privacy of all parties—since it knows the source of data, it learns site-specific information as well as global results. Even techniques that prevent disclosure of individual data items may reveal rules, trends, or patterns about individual sites. This may reveal trade secrets, or embarrassing or damaging information. In a sense this is a scaled-up version of the individual privacy problem, however it is an area where the SMC approach is more likely to be applicable.

Addressing these issues requires understanding the reasons behind them. We now discuss two issues that lead to privacy concerns in collections of data, and ways to understand those that enable data mining to proceed.

14.3.1 Secrecy

Individual privacy concerns can lead to corporate privacy concerns. The holder of a collection of individual data may be trusted by those individuals, but if

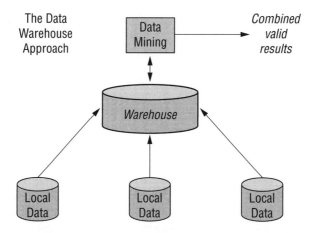

Figure 14.2: The data warehouse approach to mining distributed sources.

that data is revealed, this trust (often protected contractually) is broken. The collection holder may be willing to participate in a distributed data mining project, but only if it can ensure that its own data items are not revealed. Secure Multiparty Computation would seem to provide a solution to this, however the problem of results revealing private information still remains.

Another issue is protecting the data holder. Even if we assume that (1) individual data items can be disclosed, or are protected by the privacy preserving methods; and (2) global data mining results do not violate the privacy/secrecy concerns, problems may still arise. Knowledge about a subset of the combined data set (as separable from the global results) may reveal secrets of one of the data holders.

As an example, a medical study may want to use data mining to establish overall trends from hospital data. Even if the techniques used protect patient privacy, they may reveal hospital-specific information. Rules establishing conditions that lead to a high complication rate for a particular operation would be useful study results. However, if these conditions are tied to a particular hospital, there may be liability or public relations implications. Such implications may limit willingness to participate in such a study. We can develop efficient techniques for data mining that protect such study (Kantarcioglu and Clifton 2002).

In other cases, participants in the data mining project may have specific secrets they wish to withhold, such as trade secrets. An industry consortium may want to mine data to find ways that all members can use to improve their processes. However, learning a particular member's trade secret, and sharing that with the rest of the consortium, is inappropriate. The ability to protect secrets while otherwise participating in a data mining exercise will expand the applicability of data mining.

14.3.2 Limitations on Collaboration

At other times, it may not be the participants that are concerned about sharing data, but external parties. As an example, U.S. antitrust regulations limit the ability of companies to collaborate. The basic premise is protecting the consumer: collaborations that harm the consumer (such as price-fixing cartels) are illegal. The problem is establishing that collaboration *is* to the consumers' benefit. If the chief executive officers of Ford and General Motors meet privately, the public doesn't know if there is illegal collaboration, likely triggering an investigation. Privacy preserving data mining techniques provide a solution to this. If we can prove that no information is shared other than the results, it is easier to justify that the collaboration is for legal purposes. As we discuss in the next section, this leads to a "need to know" criteria for determining acceptable information sharing.

14.4 Measures of Privacy Preservation

We have discussed some issues imposing privacy constraints on data mining. How do we translate these into solutions that address the issues? The key is an ability to measure privacy. Since privacy has many meanings, we require a set of metrics. Several suggestions are given in this section.

14.4.1 Bounded Knowledge

The data obscuration approach leads to a *bounded knowledge* metric. Bounded knowledge implies that some information about a protected attribute may be revealed, but the actual value can only be estimated. This may be based on hard bounds (e.g., by adding noise from a random variable uniformly distributed within the bounds), or probabilistic estimates (e.g., by adding noise from a gaussian distribution).

A good measure for quantifying privacy based on such bounded estimation is given by Agrawal and Aggarwal (2001). They propose a measure based on the *differential entropy* of a random variable. The differential entropy $h(A)$ is a measure of the uncertainty inherent in A. Their metric for privacy is $2^{h(A)}$. Specifically, if we add noise from a random variable A, the privacy is:

$$\Pi(A) = 2^{-\int_{\Omega_A} f_A(a) log_2 f_A(a) da}$$

where Ω_A is the domain of A.

This metric has several nice features. It is intuitively satisfying for simple cases. For noise generated from A, a uniformly distributed random variable between 0 and a, $\Pi(A) = a$. Thus this privacy metric is exactly the width of the unknown region. Furthermore, if a sequence of random variables A_i converges to B, then $\Pi(A_i)$ converges to $\Pi(B)$. For most random variables, e.g., a gaussian, the notion of width of the unknown region does not make sense. However, we can calculate Π for such random variables, and the above properties allow us to make the case that the privacy is equivalent to having no knowledge of the value except that it is within a region of width Π. This gives an intuitively satisfying way of comparing the privacy of different methods of adding random noise.

The authors extend this definition to *conditional privacy*, capturing the possibility that the inherent privacy from obscuring data may be reduced by what we can learn from a collection. The conditional privacy $\Pi(A|B)$ follows from the definition of conditional entropy:

$$\Pi(A|B) = 2^{-\int_{\Omega_{A,B}} f_{A,B}(a,b) log_2 f_{A|B=b}(a) da\, db}$$

They show how this can be applied to measure the actual privacy after reconstructing distributions of the original data to improve the accuracy of decision trees build on the obscured data (Agrawal and Srikant 2000; Agrawal and Aggarwal 2001). The result is that data obscuration techniques in Agrawal and Srikant (2000) do not provide as much privacy as we might naïvely expect, as the ability to use them to produce valid data mining results also decreases the effectiveness of adding noise. Similar analyses on other data obscuration techniques would provide an effective way to compare those techniques.

Another use of this metric is to evaluate the inherent loss of privacy caused by data mining results. The use of conditional privacy enables us to estimate how much privacy is lost by knowing the data mining results, even with a "perfect" privacy-preserving technique such as secure multiparty computation. The literature has not yet addressed this issue; the assumption has generally been that the data mining results do not of themselves violate privacy.

14.4.2 Need to Know

The *need to know* concept is well established in controlling access to data. In the U.S., access to classified data requires both a security clearance and a justification of why the data should be accessed. The same concept appears in the EC95/46 directive:

> Member States shall provide that personal data may be processed only if: (a) the data subject has unambiguously given his consent; or (b) processing is necessary for the performance of a contract

> to which the data subject is party or in order to take steps at the request of the data subject prior to entering into a contract; or ...

Note clause (b): It is acceptable to use individual data if it is needed to achieve a result requested by the individual.

This same standard also applies to corporate privacy problems. A need to know standard can be used to decide if collaboration between companies falls afoul of antitrust regulations. For example, airlines in the United States make their fares available on shared reservation systems used by travel agents (Sabre, Apollo). This allows easy comparison of prices by both consumers and the airlines—and a quick check will show that the airlines generally offer the same prices on the same routes. Airlines used to put out a notice of proposed prices, and if other airlines didn't match the price the notice would be removed. This gives the appearance of colluding to fix prices, illegal under U.S. antitrust law. The airlines were found to engage in such price fixing, and ordered to stop.

Operations today are similar—the shared reservations systems exist and prices are the same on the same routes. The only change is that the proposed prices no longer exist. Instead, an airline must actually change its prices, then see if other airlines go along. Why is this allowed, even though the end result is the same?

The key is that the current system provides two key benefits to consumers: (1) price competition among the airlines—they are *allowed* to offer as low a price as they want; and (2) easy comparison shopping—consumers can check prices, and take the lowest.

The first benefit cannot be accomplished without allowing airlines to change their prices. The second, giving consumers the ability to see and compare prices, also enables the airlines to see and compare prices. Sharing currently available prices thus meets the *need to know* standard. The previous "notice of proposed pricing" approach did not, as this information was not shared with or useful to consumers. The information sharing that did not meet the "need to know" standard, the notice of proposed pricing, was found to be illegal.

Secure multipath computation (SMC) (Yao 1986; Goldreich, Micali, and Wigderson 1987) provides a basis for data mining that meets a need to know standard. If the results of the data mining are required to accomplish an allowable task, then learning those results should be allowed under the "need to know" standard under which most privacy regulations allow release of information. Data mining approaches that are SMCs can be proven not to disclose anything except the results. However, SMC-based techniques are not sufficient. We still need to ensure that the data mining results do fall under the need to know standard. Complicating matters is the fact that we do not know the results in advance, so we must demonstrate that any possible data mining results fall under need to know. Alternatively we can define a limited subset of data mining results that are acceptable, and ensure that the computation termi-nates without releasing information (other than the lack of results) if the results do not fall in this subset. This requires that the computation be customized for each data mining project.

Need to know is interesting in that it is a binary measure. A result is ei-ther acceptable (it is required to accomplish the end goal), or unacceptable. It is also difficult in that it can apply to a collection of results rather than a single result; two different result sets may each be sufficient to achieve a goal (either alone meets the need to know standard), but knowing both result sets exceeds need to know. Formal definitions of this criteria are probably domain specific, however the legal and social acceptability of this "measure" suggests that further research is warranted.

14.4.3   Protected from Disclosure

Another problem is when we have specific items we want to protect. This may be individual data items, specific rules we don't want disclosed, or even gen-eral classes of knowledge that must be protected. The database security com-munity has developed effective techniques for inference prevention (Delugach and Hinke 1996; Hinke, Delugach, and Wolf 1997; Yip and Levitt 1998). This work is for "provable facts," or inferences that are always true. Data mining finds inferences that are interesting, but do not always hold. Methods have been proposed to alter data to bring the support or confidence of specific rules below a threshold (Atallah, Bertino, Elmagarmid, Ibrahim, and Verykios 1999; Saygin, Verykios, and Clifton 2001), but choice of an appropriate threshold is still difficult. Alternatively, we may want to protect against association rules that involve a particular outcome (e.g., any rules that pertain to equipment fail-ures), but the problem of defining when a rule is considered strong enough to violate privacy concerns is still a problem.

One option is to use classification as a measure. Many data mining prob-lems can be expressed in terms of classification, e.g., association rules can be used as decision rules. If the ability to classify is limited, many other types of data mining will be limited as well. This idea has been used to evaluate the risk posed by data mining when the knowledge to be protected is not known (Clifton 2000). However, this assumes the goal is prevention of *any* data mining. Use of classification as a metric to prohibit learning specific facts is ripe for exploration. For example, we could state "it should be impossible to learn a classifier from the data that can predict a person having AIDS with $P(false\ hit) < .9$"—any classifier suggesting someone had AIDS would be wrong at least 90% of the time. This would alleviate concerns that even if in-dividually identifiable data didn't contain the protected attribute (has AIDS), the data might enable someone to *learn* that attribute.

14.4.4 Anonymity

While protecting against learning a particular attribute may address some concerns, it requires that we know the potentially misused attribute in advance. It may also over-constrain the problem—learning statistics that apply to an entire population allows us to better predict those statistics for an individual, but need not violate the standards of use of "individually identifiable data." What is needed is a result-independent method of stating that data mining results do not violate individual privacy, even if they allow us to learn something that can be applied to an individual.

One method for protecting individual privacy is k-anonymity (Samarati and Sweeney 1998). The goal of k-anonymity is to only release data where for all possible queries, at least k results will be returned. To achieve this result, generalization and suppression techniques are used. In generalization techniques, some attributes are replaced with more general values so that k people will be found with any attribute value. For example, exact ages are replaced by some age ranges. In suppression techniques, data points that may cause too much generalization may be eliminated or a column that has identifying information can be deleted. Although this approach works well for individual data, it is not directly applicable to restricting privacy-preserving data mining results.

We propose the following definition of individual privacy that maintains the spirit of k-anonymity, but protects against data mining results that can be used to predict information about an individual.

Definition 14.4.1 *Two records that belonging to different individuals I_1, I_2 are p-indistinguishable given data X if for every polynomial-time function $f : I \mapsto \{0, 1\}$*

$$|Pr\{f(I_1) = 1|X\} - Pr\{f(X_2) = 1|X\}| \leq p$$

where $0 < p < 1$.

Informally this means that given a set of (privacy preserving) data, we are unable to learn any classifier that would distinguish between two individuals based on the data we've seen about those individuals. This doesn't necessarily mean we can't learn a good classifier, only that we can't use it to distinguish between the individuals.

From this, we can define a privacy preserving data mining process as one that does not enable us to distinguish between any individuals based solely on that data mining process.

Definition 14.4.2 *A data mining process said to be p-individual privacy preserving if using all of the information X seen during the data mining process, any two individual records are p-indistinguishable.*

Example: Assume that we are using the model described in section 14.1.3 to find the count of particular attribute value, e.g., we want to know the number of people that have a particular cancer type where this information is represented as binary attribute. User i sends $(i, X_i \oplus r_i)$ to one noncolluding site and (i, r_i) to a second noncolluding site, where r_i is a random bit and $\oplus$ is the xor operation. Clearly the data gathering process is individual privacy preserving, because what both sites see about individuals is indistinguishable from random data. So the probability of predicting that each individual has the cancer is the same. Now let us find the count of the individuals who have the cancer. To do this, assume the noncolluding sites add $\frac{d(1-p)}{p}$ noisy data items to actual data (d is number of actual data entries). The sites then count the support including the noise items. (Details of this procedure can be found in Kantarcioglu and Vaidya [2002].) Due to potential reuse of the data actual id's i are replaced by random permutation and fake data is randomly distributed among the original data. When one site receives the count, it subtracts the amount of fake support and learns the actual result. A third noncolluding site joins the $(i_j, X_i \oplus r_i)$ with (i_j, r_i). Clearly, the first two noncolluding sites do not learn anything from this process. After the process, the probability that any given individual has the cancer is the same, even though there may be huge difference between prior and posterior probabilities.

We now show that p-indistinguishability holds for any two data entries on the third (join) site. Assume that the join site compares two randomly ordered data items. Since with probability p any item compared is fake, the probability that any statement is true is less than p. In other words, $Pr\{f(X_{org}) = 1 | X_{seen}\} = p * Pr\{f(X_{org}) = 1 | X_{seen} \text{ is true}\} + (1 - p) * 0 \leq p$. We can see that $|Pr\{f(X_1) = 1 | X_1 \text{ is seen}\} - Pr\{f(X_2) = 1 | X_2 \text{ is seen}\} \leq p$. (In the worst case, one probability will be zero and one will be p.) Since p-indistinguishability is satisfied for any given data item pairs on the join site, we can conclude that the data mining process is individual privacy preserving assuming no collusion.

14.5   Conclusions

Privacy preserving data mining has the potential to increase the reach and benefits of data mining technology. However, we must be able to justify that privacy is preserved. For this, we need to be able to communicate what we mean by "privacy preserving." The current mixture of definitions, with each paper having its own definition of what privacy is maintained, will lead to confusion among potential adopters of the technology.

We have presented some suggestions for defining, measuring, and evaluating privacy preservation. We showed how these relate to both privacy policy and practice in the wider community, and to techniques in privacy preserving data mining. The key point to remember is that privacy preserving data mining is possible. Technology has been, and is being, developed to allow data mining without disclosing private information. There are legal and historical definitions of privacy that can be used to justify that this technology does preserve privacy.

This is by no means the definitive word on the subject. While some measures, such as the differential entropy metric of Agrawal and Aggarwal (2001), have clear mathematical foundations and applications, others (such as using classification accuracy as a means of protecting rules from disclosure) have strong potential for further development. Adopting a common framework for discussion of privacy preservation will enable next generation data mining technology to make substantial advances in alleviating privacy concerns.

Chris Clifton is an associate professor of computer science at Purdue University, working in data mining, databases, and their associated privacy and security issues. He can be reached at www.cs.purdue.edu/people/clifton

Murat Kantarcioglu is a Ph.D. candidate at Purdue University. His research interests include privacy aspects of data mining and processing. He can be reached at kanmurat@cs.purdue.edu

Jaideep Vaidya is a Ph.D. candidate in the Department of Computer Sciences at Purdue University. His interests lie at the confluence of privacy, security, and data mining. He can be reached at jsvaidya@cs.purdue.edu.

Scientific
Data Mining

Chapter 15

Mining Temporally-Varying Phenomena in Scientific Datasets

*Raghu Machiraju, Srinivasan Parthasarathy, John Wilkins,
David S. Thompson, Boyd Gatlin, David Richie,
Tat-Sang S. Choy, Ming Jiang, Sameep Mehta,
Matthew Coatney, Stephen A. Barr, and Kaden Hazzard*

The physical and engineering sciences increasingly study large, complex ensembles seeking to understand the underlying phenomena. These studies require analysis of the data generated by either experiments or computational simulations. In this chapter, we focus on the latter and provide motivation using applications from two disparate fields—numerical simulations of fluid flow and molecular dynamics. Computational fluid dynamics (CFD) seeks to understand flow patterns to enhance, for instance, drug delivery schemes for pulmonary treatments for asthma. Similarly, molecular dynamics (MD) seeks to understand the evolution of material defects that affect the properties or performance of industrial materials. In these data, patterns of interest arise and evolve over time as a result of the unsteady nature of the phenomenon under consideration.

Scientific discoveries are often best understood visually—from Galle seeing Neptune in 1846 to Binnig and Rohrer seeing atoms on a surface in the twentieth century. Both discoveries were not surprises in the sense that previous analysis had convinced most of their reality. However, each discovery stimulated future work more dramatically than any analysis might have done.

Unfortunately, the size of simulation datasets significantly challenges our abilities to explore and comprehend effectively the generated data. Analysis via interactive visualization sessions is tantamount to searching for the proverbial "needle in a haystack." Currently, a well-trained individual may need several days or even weeks to analyze the data generated by an MD simulation and create a list of viable defect structures. Similarly, in the extremely large datasets generated by simulations of complex fluid flows, locating and tracking relevant features are daunting tasks. In both cases, phenomena occur on multiple length and time scales. Some features persist sufficiently to have gross macroscopic effects. Other short-lived transients are precursor events central to the unsteady (in the temporal domain) behavior of the system. An additional complication is that currently available hardware does not have the prowess yet to provide even near real-time visualizations.

Therefore, we believe it is crucial that some degree of automation be incorporated into the exploration process for large datasets. One such successful approach is described in Machiraju, Fowler, Thompson, Soni, and Schroeder (2001) and is based on a representational scheme that facilitates ranked access to macroscopic features in the dataset. However, other than identifying, denoising, and ranking the features, no attempt is made to extract information about the features or track and catalog them.

An alternative approach would be to apply traditional data mining algorithms to these scientific datasets. However, it is our contention that existing data mining techniques, applied in isolation, are simply too general. Embedding domain expertise (i.e., via understanding the science) in the data mining process is critical to its success especially for the datasets characteristic of large-scale simulations. Moreover the application of existing data mining techniques may not be the most efficient of solutions, particularly for analyzing complex simulation data.

Thus, there is a paucity of general approaches that facilitate meaningful analysis of large and complex data describing physical phenomena. There is a need to explore a larger space of solutions that are based on the underlying physics and are enabled by computer science techniques from visualization, data analysis, and data mining. By incorporating application-specific physics into the mining effort, we can develop characterizations of physically-relevant features. In this chapter, we describe one such approach that we call feature mining.

The remainder of this chapter is organized as follows. In section 15.1 we describe the two important applications that motivate this work. In section 15.2 we describe the system and identify the key components. Section 15.3 documents the preliminary results we have for the two application domains, while section 15.4 describes previous work conducted by other groups. Finally we provide conclusions and future directions in section 15.5.

15.1 Example Applications

We now provide some background information on the two science drivers we have chosen—respiratory flow in multi-generational bronchial trees and defect evolution in materials. While our two science drivers would seem significantly different, we contend that a common framework can facilitate effective exploration for both problems.

15.1.1 Computational Simulation of Biomedical Fluid Flows

Respiration—specifically, airflow through the network of lung airways—produces surprisingly complex flow fields. Although the flow is laminar through much of the bronchial tree, secondary currents can be dominant, particularly transverse vortex pairs that form due to axial curvature of the tubes and wall shear. These vortices migrate downstream and interact with new ones generated by repeated branching. These secondary flows are critical to the efficient filtering of inhaled air: aerosols, entrained in their trajectories, impact mucus-lined walls from which they can be expelled from the lungs through the action of cilia or coughing.

The analysis of these secondary flows is complex, both because of their not yet understood persistence and their branching into multiple vortices. Much of the computational modeling of flow through small airway bifurcations is that due to Gatlin, Hammersley, and colleagues (Hammersley, Olson, Reddy, Arab-shahi, and Gatlin 1993; Gatlin, Cuicchi, Hammersley, Olsen, Reddy, and Burn-side 1995; Gatlin, Cuicchi, Hammersley, Olsen, Reddy, and Burnside 1997a; Gatlin, Cuicchi, Hammersley, Olsen, Reddy, and Burnside 1997b). When dealing with datasets generated by simulations of complex temporally varying fluid flows, it is challenging to locate and track relevant features. Existing techniques for vortex detection are typically based on local, flow-field parameters such as the velocity gradient tensor. The generation of new features and destruction of existing features present challenges for feature correspondence algorithms.

Potential Impact

New data mining techniques relevant to computed respiration flow data not only can enhance the understanding of known flow characteristics, but also may discover previously undetected features, just as visualization techniques revealed the long unknown secondary structures in the flow. Of particular interest are the longevity of vortex pairs generated by bifurcation and the mechanisms of interaction between vortices. Additionally, the detection of regions of flow separation are important for understanding the impaction of entrained particles and the interruption of laminar flow. Improved understanding of these flows has two important applications: (1) the health hazard posed by the inhalation of carcinogenic, disease-bearing, or lung-damaging aerosols and (2) the clinical delivery of both local and systemic aerosolized drugs through the lungs. While the depth of penetration into the tubular network of the lungs depends on the nature and concentration of particles, the aerodynamics of respiration plays a critical role.

15.1.2 Molecular Dynamics Simulations of Defect Evolution

The key complexity of real materials used in commercial applications is not that they are defected in the trivial sense of being imperfect or impure, but rather that their material properties depend critically on their nonideality. As an example, the enhanced diffusion of dopants in the presence of extended {311} defects in silicon is a limiting factor in the fabrication of shallow junction devices (Cowern, Mannino, Stolk, Roozeboom, Huizing, van Berkum, Cristiano, Claverie, and Jaraiz 1999). The growth of such extended defects involves the diffusion, capture and dissociation of silicon point defects (Arai, Takeda, and Kohyama 1997; Kim, Kirchhoff, Aulbur, Wilkins, and Khan 1999; Kim, Kirchhoff, Wilkins, and Khan 2000). This example can be repeated with variations in every material essential to current high technology.

Molecular dynamics simulations can track the nucleation and growth of defects but realistic time scales exceed computing technology. Emerging acceleration techniques (Montalenti, Sørensen, and Voter 2001; Sørensen and Voter 2000; Voter 1997; Voter 1998) can achieve realistic simulation times. Wavelet techniques (Richie, Kim, and Wilkins 2001) can dramatically reduce the molecular dynamics data and detect persistent defect structures. The challenge is to identify and classify these structures and track their evolution and interactions.

Potential Impact

New data mining techniques can not only uncover fundamental defect nucleation and growth processes but also provide essential parameters for modeling macroscopic properties of materials. This need is well recognized in the the semiconductor industry in its "silicon roadmap" that identifies the short- and long-range problems necessary to continually pack more transistors on a chip. In structural materials used, for example, in turbine engines, there is a growing need to connect the microscopic and macroscopic scales. Indeed the phrase "multiscale methods" recognizes the wide spread importance of connecting complex microscopic processes to the design and optimization of materials properties.

15.2   Generalized Framework

Essentially, there is a need to deduce the presence of features and derive their shape characteristics from a large data repository that describes some time-varying, evolutionary phenomenon. In this context, shape refers to the salient characteristics of a feature including kinematical and dynamical characteristics along with a geometrical description. This abstract notion of shape allows us to apply more general data mining algorithms to the extracted features and their characteristics. It is our claim that a "shape-based" data-mining paradigm will prove fruitful in the analysis of complex unsteady phenomena. Kamath also makes similar remarks about the utility of feature-based approaches (Kamath 2001).

Figure 15.1 illustrates our generalized framework applied to processing of physically-based simulation data. We contend that a common framework can compactly store and analyze data of evolutionary phenomena. We assume that certain locally computable quantities can detect precursor events. Our approach is novel in its flexibility and applicability across disciplines. The shape-based analysis converts the task of data management and analysis into one of choosing robust shape descriptors and being able to index features from a catalog. The descriptors will be derived from the application.

In addition to feature detection algorithms, aggregation or segmentation, tracking and characterization algorithms must be utilized in conjunction with traditional data mining algorithms to facilitate cataloging detected structures and expediting searches to gain scientific insights. Our framework synergistically brings to bear these techniques to address the problems associated with analyzing large datasets generated by simulations of physical phenomena. We now describe the key elements of our framework.

Spatial Partitioning to Exploit Locality

Fine spatial resolutions are often used to resolve features in computational simulations. Tracking features over the entire spatial domain is not viable and

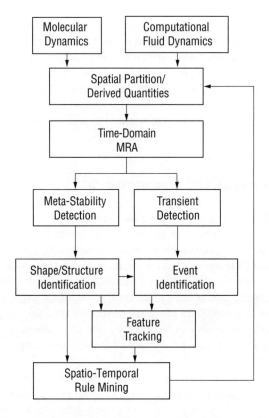

Figure 15.1: Generalized feature mining framework.

meaningful. Hence, through a process of partitioning, smaller subdomains are considered for shape and feature evolution. This process is tantamount to dividing the bale of hay into smaller bales to search for the proverbial needle. Thus regular and irregular sized subdomains derived from either just the domain or function values can be considered.

Multiscale Event and Feature Detection

A feature at a given temporal scale can be stable, metastable, or transient. The birth, evolution and death of a feature is often triggered by precursor events. It is therefore crucial to identify when such events occur. We have chosen a "trigger-based" multi-resolution analysis (MRA) using wavelets for event detection. Thus, a single derived quantity or a trigger is monitored for events at multiple time scales. For instance this quantity is *swirl* in a CFD simulation. In an MD simulation this quantity is *potential* or *energy* or *dislocations* of atoms. Multiscale trigger monitoring is needed given the range of feature lifetimes. Wavelet techniques are effective here and are already successfully working in molecular dynamics simulations (Richie, Kim, and Wilkins 2001; Richie, Kim, Hazzard, Hazzard, Barr, and Wilkins 2002) .

Feature Mining

A systematic approach to feature mining (Thompson, Machiraju, Jiang, Nair, Craciun, and Venkata 2002), i.e., the process of detecting, characterizing and tracking relevant features, is being developed. Our intent is to exploit the physics of the problem at hand to develop highly discriminating, application-dependent feature detection algorithms and then use data mining algorithms to classify, cluster, and categorize the identified features. Our work parallels that of Yip and Zhao (1996) in some ways. It should be noted that our work relies on more physics-based understanding of features and exploits the underlying physics to a greater extent.

The most basic aspect of feature mining is *feature detection*. The output of any detection algorithm is a collection of many regions-of-interest (ROIs). The underlying physics is exploited to locate features using local operators or sensors to detect and nonlocal or global operators to verify. Verification is need in some cases to confirm that a given ROI indeed represents a feature. We consider defects at quenched states and finite temperatures for MD simulations and shocks and vortices for CFD.

A second component of feature mining is *shape-based feature characterization and categorization* in which the "shape" of a feature is described by characteristics, such as shape and structure, and kinematical and dynamical properties in an abstract *multidimensional shape space*. The descriptors for a MD simulation can include the number of atoms involved, their orientations, the connectivity between atoms, the trajectory, and history of its evolution. In a CFD simulation, vortices, the type of feature of importance for respiratory flows, can be characterized by their strength and sense of rotation as well as obvious geometrical parameters such as position, shape, and extent. These features can be categorized by notions of similarity. Shape categories enable synergistic understanding of events and features in the MD and CFD domains. To compute the similarity between shapes or structures we rely on spatial geometric hashing (Wolfson and Rigotsos 1997) and clustering algorithms (Jain and Dubes 1988). To categorize the structures we rely on classification algorithms (Quinlan 1996) using the generalized shape descriptors as input to the classifiers. For CFD data we employ a generalized shape descriptor for swirling regions and propose hierarchical shape matching algorithms.

A third component of feature mining is *corresponding and tracking of fea-*

tures over time. The generation of new features and destruction of existing features pose major challenges to effective, feature-tracking algorithms. The essential problem is to determine how the position of a particular feature changes during a given time interval. In our datasets, this is nontrivial since fissures and fusions of features are extremely common. Furthermore, the structural descriptors of the same feature may change over time. Tracking and correspondence complete the construction of the multi-dimensional shape space for a given application. Relevant related work in feature tracking was reported in Samtaney, Silver, Zabusky, and Cao (1994) and Silver and Wang (1997). Shapes were not considered therein and the method is, in general, expensive. Similarly in Reinders, Post, and Spoelder (1999) and Reinders, Jacobson, and Post (2000) the skeleton or an approximate medial axis was computed for vortices. However, this representation is very *crisp* and does not allow tangible matching and tracking. In Thampy (2003), a predictive algorithm was developed that utilized the evolution of selected kinematical and dynamical properties to enhance confidence in the correspondence algorithm.

Mining for Spatial and Spatio-Temporal Patterns

Over any time interval in a simulation, we need techniques that can identify important spatial patterns efficiently. Some patterns can be complex and not necessarily sequential. The aim is to derive predictive rules: combinations of features resulting in certain events, (e.g., fusion or fissure). To derive such rules requires identifying frequently occurring spatial patterns. Clustering, association (Agrawal, Mannila, Srikant, Toivonen, and Verkam 1996), and sequential pattern analysis (Parthasarathy, Zaki, Ogihara, and Dwarkadas 1999), and spatio-temporal analysis (Vlachos, Kollios, and Gunopulos 2002) will be used to determine the important patterns. Our eventual goal is to correlate information from a shape categorization together with transition detection mechanisms to help discover novel axioms relating to the evolution of shapes over time. An example of such an axiom could be "a type-A feature evolves into a type-B feature through some particular mechanism." Such rules can be found using event-based sequential and association pattern analysis. Equally important is to identify those axioms that dominate the particular simulation type. These data mining algorithms will operate on the shape space constructed in an earlier step and produce explanations of feature behavior and evolution.

Generality

The large-data exploration methodology we describe is appropriate for any data that can be transformed to a multiscale representation and consists of features that can be extracted through local operators and aggregated in spatial, scale, and temporal dimensions. Thus, one can consider domains in addition to CFD and MD.

15.3   Current Efforts

In the previous sections we described our vision for the generalized framework and described our motivating applications. In this section we describe current and ongoing work toward realizing our vision. The methods described below will partially construct the shape space for a given application. Work on tracking and correspondence is ongoing and is not described. We also do not describe our approach to conducting data mining tasks in the shape space as it is a work in progress.

15.3.1   Feature Mining

In this section, we focus on one component of feature mining and describe two distinct feature detection paradigms (Thompson, Machiraju, Jiang, Nair, Craciun, and Venkata 2002). The common thread is that both are bottom-up feature constructions with underlying physically-based criteria. The two perform essentially the same steps, but in different orders. As will become evident, it is unlikely that nonphysics-based techniques would provide the fidelity needed to locate complex flow field (CFD) or defect (MD) structures.

In general, a feature is a pattern occurring in a dataset that is of interest and that manifests correlation relationships among various components of the data. For instance, a shock in a supersonic fluid flow would be considered a significant feature: when such a shock occurs, the pressure increases abruptly in the direction of the flow, and the fluid velocity decreases in a prescribed manner. A significant feature also has spatial and temporal scale coherence.

For many applications, generic data mining techniques such as clustering, association, and sequencing can reveal statistical correlations between various components of the data. Returning to the shock example, we could use statistical mining to ferret out associations, but it might be difficult to attach precise spatial associations for the rules discovered. A fluid dynamicist, however, would like to locate features with a rather high degree of certainty. Such qualitative assertions alone will not suffice. This is where our approach to feature mining comes in: we take advantage of the fact that, for simulations of physical phenomena, the field variables satisfy certain physical laws. We can exploit these kinematic and dynamic considerations to locate features of interest.

The fidelity improvements garnered by tailoring these highly discriminating feature detection algorithms to the particular application far outweigh any loss of generality. The state of the art in feature detection and mining in simulation data is similar to what existed for image processing when edge detection methods were the main techniques. Much more is now understood, and mining for image data is often done in terms of the features, namely edges. This suggests that a blend of data- and feature-mining methods might have the potential to reduce the burdensome chore of finding features in large datasets.

Point Classification Techniques

The first feature detection paradigm, which we call *point classification,* requires several operations in sequence:

- Detection by application of a local operator at each point in the domain

- Binary classification of each point based on some criteria

- Aggregation of contiguous regions of similarly classified points

- Denoising to eliminate aggregates that are of insufficient extent, strength, etc.

- Ranking based on feature saliency

- Tracking identified features

This approach identifies individual points as belonging to a feature and then aggregates them to identify regions that are features. The points are obtained from a tour of the discrete domain and can be in many cases the grid points of a physical grid (CFD) or a lattice (MD). The operator used in the detection step and the criteria used in the classification step embody physically based point-wise characteristics of the feature of interest. In this context, classification accords membership of a discrete point in the dataset to a feature.

Aggregate Classification Techniques

We can best incorporate the global information needed to define a vortex into our second feature detection paradigm, the aggregate classification approach. Aggregate classification follows a somewhat different sequence of operations:

- Detection by application of a local operator at each point in the domain

- Aggregation of contiguous regions of probable candidate points

- Binary classification (or verification) of each aggregate based on some criteria

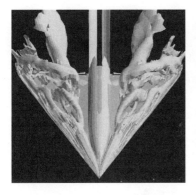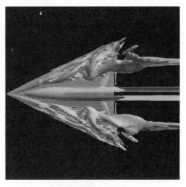

Figure 15.2: The results of our point classification algorithm applied to a delta wing dataset. The front and top views respectively are shown. The yellow regions indicate regions of swirling flow. There exist several regions which are falsely classified.

- Denoising to eliminate aggregates that are of insufficient extent, strength, etc.

- Ranking based on feature saliency

- Tracking identified features

This approach identifies individual points as being the probable candidate points in a feature and then aggregates them. The classification algorithm is applied to the aggregate using physically based regional criteria to determine whether the candidate points constitute a feature. Thus, the operator deployed towards point classification can be efficient but less accurate. False positives generated at the earlier stages can be eliminated later in the verification stage. Classification in this context confirms that an aggregated subset of a domain indeed forms a relevant feature.

15.3.2   Fluid Dynamics

We now present two examples of feature detection algorithms as applied to CFD datasets. Although algorithms have been developed for other features, we focus on those for vortices because of the critical role they play in the bronchial airflow. Additionally, the vortex provides a direct way to contrast the two different feature detection paradigms.

CFD Example 1—Vortex Detection Using Point Classification: The first technique we consider uses the eigenvalues of the local velocity gradient ten-

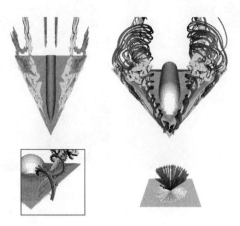

Figure 15.3: The results of our aggregate classification technique applied to the delta wing dataset. (left) All candidate core regions are shown. The verified cores are shown in yellow while the spurious ones are shown in green. (middle) Streamline tracing around verified cores. (right) The top image shows the verification algorithm at work through seeding and tracing, while the bottom image shows illustrates the use of projections and angles to verify vortices.

sor. In regions of swirling flow, the eigenvalues of the velocity gradient tensor are complex. Berdahl and Thompson (1993) defined a swirl parameter that estimates the tendency for the fluid to swirl about a given point. The swirl has a nonzero value in regions containing vortices and attains a local maximum in the core region. In this point classification algorithm, the detection step consists of computing the eigenvalues of the velocity gradient tensor at each field point. The classification step consists of checking for complex eigenvalues and assigning a swirl value if they exist. The aggregation step then agglomerates contiguous grid points where the swirl parameter exceeds a threshold value into vortical regions. This method's primary shortcoming is that it–and all eigenvalue-based vortex detection techniques–can generate false positives. An example of this method is shown in figure 15.2. Its local nature makes it unable to discriminate between locally curved streamlines and closed streamlines characteristic of a vortex. Other features, such as shocks, are more amenable to the point classification framework.

CFD Example 2—Vortex Detection Using Aggregate Classification: We recently developed an aggregate classification-type vortex detection technique. We based its detection step on an idea derived from a lemma in combinatorial topology. Specifically, velocity vectors around core regions exhibit certain flow patterns unique to vortices, and it is precisely these flow patterns that we search for in the computational grid. Not surprisingly, our approach is related to critical point theory. However, critical points alone are not sufficient to detect a vortex. For each grid point, our algorithm examines its immediate neighbors to see whether the neighboring velocity vectors point in three or more direction ranges. The novelty of this method is its relative insensitivity to core direction. Therefore, very approximate core directions may be used in the detection step.

Our technique segments candidate core regions by aggregating points identified from the detection phase. We then classify (or verify) these candidate core regions based on the existence of swirling streamlines surrounding them. (For features that lack a formal definition, such as the vortex, we must choose the verification criteria so that it concurs with the intuitive understanding of the feature. In this case, verifying whether a candidate core region is a vortex core region requires checking for any swirling streamlines surrounding it.) Checking for swirling flow in three dimensions is a nontrivial problem since vortices can bend and twist. The technique we developed essentially checks to see if the local tangent to the streamline, when projected onto the plane normal to the local core tangent, spans 2π. The aggregate nature of this classification step is apparent. Checking for swirling streamlines is a global (or aggregate) approach to feature classification (or verification) because swirling is measured with respect to the core region, not just individual points within the core region. Figure 15.3 describes all steps of this paradigm.

15.3.3   Molecular Dynamics Simulations of Defect Evolution

The challenge of detecting features during an ongoing MD simulation was met with the application of multiresolution analysis (MRA) techniques. Wavelet analysis is exploited in the time domain to analyze dynamics. For each atom, its sequence of positions are projected on a wavelet basis, with the expansion coefficients generated incrementally using components supplied by the STORMRT scientific wavelet package (Richie, Kim, and Wilkins 2001). These components treat streaming data more efficiently than more conventional "fast" wavelet transform (FWT) techniques.

The same feature mining procedures that worked well for CFD data work for MD too. In any persistent structure, "defect" atoms must be distinguished from "bulk" atoms. While this task might seem more challenging at finite temperature due to the thermal noise, a *single* rule works for all structures: thermal and quenched. For a bulk atom, precisely four atoms have bonds (with the bulk atom) less than 2.6 Å and the angles between any two bonds lie within 90-130 degrees. Any other atom is a defect. Similar definitions can be formulated for other systems. Atoms near the surface of a periodically repeated cell don't "see" the other atoms though. This problem is solved by padding the cell with a layer of periodic material.

Here, we illustrate how point classification procedures can be employed toward the defects in the quenched (cooled state) and finite thermal temperatures respectively. Each atom site is visited and the atom is tested for membership in a defect ensemble. The classification operator for this application is as follows. We define two conditions C_1 (bond angle as above) and C_2 (number of bonds as above) to accurately classify bulk atoms. The *conjunction* of the above two conditions as well as the *disjunction* are evaluated for all atom sites. The atom sites which satisfy the conjunction are the ones which definitely belong to the bulk. Those that satisfy the disjunction will with some likelihood belong to the bulk. The remaining atom sites are definitely part of the defect. Such atoms are referred to as *defect atoms*. The defect atoms are then spatially clustered to aggregate these into possible defect structures. We empirically verified that this method works well even on noisy data. Figure 15.4a shows a persistent structure at 1000 K. The black atoms are those identified as defect atoms. Figure 15.4b shows the same structure quenched with a first-principles approach; the quenching removes thermal noise at a heavy computational cost. The same atoms are marked in both structures which demonstrates this method works on nonquenched structures.

In a large scale simulation the challenge is to isolate separate defect clusters. A line is drawn connecting all defect atoms that lie within 4 Å of each other. Thus, a cluster is comprised of connected defect atoms, a computationally fast process. Figure 15.5 shows two defects embedded in a 512 atom lattice.

The deployment of aggregate classification techniques for MD data is far from clear. This is still an active area of research. The large number of resulting identified structures (from the detection phase) must be sorted into a smaller set of distinct types. Quenching solves this problem but is computationally expensive. In addition, some structures are stable only at high temperatures. Through quenching, these structures are lost. Identifying time averaged structures is a great challenge. Occasionally with noisy data too many or too few atoms are marked. Figure 15.6 demonstrates this problem. These two structures have different numbers of defect atoms marked, yet when quenched are the same. Additionally, we are still exploring robust and viable shape descriptors and matching algorithms for MD data.

15.4 Related Work

The framework described here is related to the work being conducted by Marusic and his associates (Marusic, Chandler, Interrante, Subbareddy, and Moss

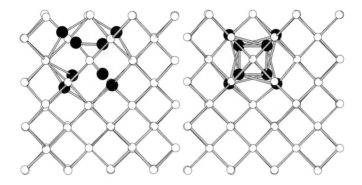

Figure 15.4: Black atoms are defect atoms. Left is a structure identified at 1000K. Right is the same structure quenched using first principles. Even though the atoms in the top structure are displaced due to thermal noise, the same atoms are marked as defect in both structures.

2001). Event time-series tracking is employed to detect turbulent bursts which are then analyzed and tracked. However, they do not consider the detection and cataloging of features at multiple temporal scales.

Knowledge discovery and data mining (KDD) refers to the overall process of discovering new patterns or building models from a given dataset. Fundamental KDD research in the last decade has primarily focused on:(1) new techniques to preprocess, mine and evaluate the data, (2) efficient algorithms that implement these techniques, and (3) applications of above techniques on business applications.

More recently, researchers have started tackling the problem of mining scientific datasets. In particular approaches for mining astronomical (Burl, Asker, Smyth, Fayyad, Perona, Aubele, and Crumple 1998), physical (fluid flow) (Han, Karypis, and Kumar 2001), biological (Wang, Wang, Shasha, Shapiro, Dikshitulu, Rigoutsos, and Zhang 1997; Li and Parthasarathy 2001; Parthasarathy and Coatney 2002) and chemical (Dehaspe, Toivonen, and King 1998) datasets have been recently proposed by various researchers. Few of the above methods actually account for the structural or spatial properties of the data. A straight-forward application of well-known data-mining techniques does not always yield the most efficient algorithms.

Computational fluid datasets have received more scrutiny from visualization and data-mining researchers than other computational domains. Significant progress has been made in the area of identifying regions of swirling flow. Algorithms described in Berdahl and Thompson (1993), Banks and Singer (1995), Jeong and Hussain (1995), Portela (1997), Sujudi and Haimes (1995),

Figure 15.5: Two separated defects: black atoms are one cluster, grey atoms are different cluster.

Jiang, Machiraju, and Thompson (2002a and b) demonstrate the ability to identify regions of swirling flow in complex three-dimensional flow fields.

Consideration of time-varying data introduces additional complexity — through the need for tracking of features. According to Samtaney, Silver, Zabusky, and Cao (1994), five distinct evolutionary events can occur to features in scientific simulations: continuation, creation, dissipation, bifurcation, and amalgamation. Each of these processes must be accounted for in the tracking algorithm.

15.5   Summary

The steady increase in computing power available for science and engineering problems challenges our ability to learn new science from the massive data. We have proposed and are developing a generalized framework that facilitates the analysis of large-scale simulation data for time-varying, evolutionary phenomena. The key component of our approach is an abstract shape-based description of the relevant features. This abstract notion of shape allows us to apply more general data mining algorithms to the extracted features and their characteristics.

Our flexible approach is motivated by two disparate applications—respiratory flow and material defect simulation. Both drivers raise *central* issues that

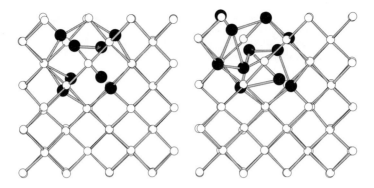

Figure 15.6: These two structures have a different number of defect atoms marked. When quenched however they are the same structure.

the components of the framework will necessarily address (1) multiscale event detection; (2) feature mining, (3) shape-based feature characterization and categorization, (4) correspondence and tracking of features over time; and (5) mining for spatial and spatio-temporal patterns It should be noted that both science drivers have commonalities that are exploited by the techniques listed above.

Preliminary results have been very encouraging. However, more remains to be done to realize the complete unified framework. A systematic approach to feature mining was conceived to locate both local and global features. Currently, tracking features in a time-varying dataset is being investigated. Similarly, we are conceiving a comprehensive framework that will allow one to derive appropriate associations between the occurrence of transitionary events and the change in feature demographics. This framework will also include environmental parameters such as the underlying geometry. Also, of interest is the creation of tools which will control both the feature- and data-mining exercises. It is our belief that our proposed framework is likely to garner new insights from massive simulation datasets and allow for a better understanding of the underlying physical phenomena.

Raghu Machiraju is an associate professor in the Department of Computer and Information Science, The Ohio State University

Srinivasan Parthasarathy (Ph.D. 2000, University of Rochester), is an sssistant professor of computer science and engineering at The Ohio State University. His research interests are in data mining and parallel and distributed computing systems. For more information: dmrl.cis.ohio-state.edu or www.cis.ohio-state.edu/ srini

John Wilkins is a professor in the Department of Physics at The Ohio State University.

David S. Thompson is an associate professor in the Department of Aerospace Engineering at Mississippi State University.

Boyd Gatlin is a professor in the Department of Aerospace Engineering at Mississippi State University.

David A. Richie is a scientist with High Performance Technologies, Inc., Reston, Virginia.

Tat-Sang S. Choy is a postdoctoral researcher in the Department of Physics at The Ohio State University.

Ming Jiang is a graduate research associate in the Department of Computer and Information Science, The Ohio State University.

Sameep Mehta is a Ph.D. student in the Department of Computer and Information Science at The Ohio State University.

Matthew Coatney (MS 2003, The Ohio State University) is a senior systems analyst at Bearing Point Inc. His research interests are in data mining and bioinformatics. For more information, see dmrl.cis.ohio-state.edu University.

Stephen A. Barr is a student in the Department of Physics at The Ohio State University.

Kaden Hazzard is a research student in the Department of Physics at The Ohio State University.

Chapter 16

Methods for Mining
Protein Contact Maps

Mohammed J. Zaki, Jingjing Hu, and Chris Bystroff

Bioinformatics is the science of storing, extracting, organizing, analyzing, interpreting, and utilizing information from biological sequences and molecules. It has been mainly fueled by advances in DNA sequencing and genome mapping techniques. Genome sequencing projects have resulted in rapidly growing databases of genetic sequences, while the Structural Genomics Initiative is doing the same for the protein structure database. New techniques are needed to analyze, manage and discover sequence, structure and functional patterns or models from these large sequence and structural databases. High performance data analysis algorithms are also becoming central to this task.

Bioinformatics is an emerging field, undergoing rapid and exciting growth. Knowledge discovery and data mining (KDD) techniques will play an increasingly important role in the analysis and discovery of sequence, structure and functional patterns or models from large sequence databases. One of the grand challenges of bioinformatics still remains, namely the protein folding problem.

Proteins fold spontaneously and reproducibly (on a time scale of milliseconds) into complex three-dimensional globules when placed in an aqueous solution, and, the sequence of amino acids making up a protein appears to completely determine its three dimensional structure (Branden and Tooze 1991).

Given a protein amino acid sequence *(linear structure)*, determining its three dimensional folded shape, *(tertiary structure)*, is referred to as the *structure prediction problem*; it is widely acknowledged as an open problem, and a lot of research in the past has focused on it.

Traditional approaches to protein structure prediction have focused on detection of evolutionary homology (Altschul, Madden, Schaffer, Zhang, Zhang, Miller, and Lipman 1997), fold recognition (Bryant 1996; Sippl 1996), and where those fail, ab initio simulations (Skolnick, Kolinski, and Ortiz 2000) that generally perform a conformational search for the lowest energy state (Simons, Kooperberg, Huang, and Baker 1997). However, the conformational search space is huge, and, if nature approached the problem using a complete search, a protein would take longer to fold than the age of the universe, while proteins are observed to fold in milliseconds. Thus, a structured folding pathway (time ordered sequence of folding events) must play an important role in this conformational search. Strong experimental evidence for pathway-based models of protein folding has emerged over the years, for example, experiments revealing the structure of the "unfolded" state in water (Mok, Kay, Kay, and Forman-Kay 1999), burst-phase folding intermediates (Colon and Roder 1996), and the kinetic effects of point mutations ("phi-values") (Nolting, Golbik, Neira, Soler-Gonzalez, Schreiber, and Fersht 1997). These pathway models indicate that certain events always occur early in the folding process and certain others always occur later.

It appears that the traditional approaches, while having provided considerable insight into the chemistry and biology of folding, are still struggling when it comes to structure prediction (Bonneau and Baker 2001; Honig 1999), hence, a novel approach is called for, for example, using data mining. Mining from examples is a data driven approach that is generally useful when physical models are intractable or unknown, however, data representing the process is available. Thus, our problem appears to be ideally suited to the application of mining—physical models of folding are either intractable or not well understood, and data in the form of a protein data base exists.

16.1 Modeling Protein Folding

It is well known that proteins fold spontaneously and reproducibly to a unique 3D structure in aqueous solution (Branden and Tooze 1991). Despite significant advances in recent years, the goal of predicting the three dimensional structure of a protein from its one-dimensional sequence of amino acids, without the aid of evolutionary information, remains one of greatest and most elusive challenges in bioinformatics. The current state of the art in structure prediction provides insights that guide further experimentation, but falls far short of replacing those experiments.

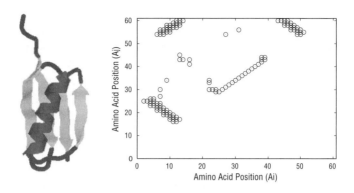

Figure 16.1: *Left:* 3D structure for protein G (PDB file 2igd, sequence length 61). *Right:* Contact map for protein G—circles indicate residue contacts, while noncontacts are represented by empty space. Only the upper triangle of the matrix is shown, since the contact map is symmetric. Clusters of circles indicate certain secondary structures, for example, the cluster along the main diagonal is an α-helix, and the clusters parallel and antiparallel to the diagonal are parallel and antiparallel β-sheets, respectively.

Today we are witnessing a paradigm shift in predicting protein structure from its known amino acid sequence $(a_1, a_2, \cdots, a_n)$. The traditional or Ab initio folding method employed first principles to derive the 3D structure of proteins. However, even though considerable progress has been made in understanding the chemistry and biology of folding, the success of ab initio folding has been quite limited. See Hardin, Pogorelov, and Luthey-Schulten (2002) and Bonneau and Baker (2001) for recent surveys on ab initio methods.

Instead of simulation studies, an alternative approach is to employ learning from examples using a database of known protein structures. For example, the Protein Data Bank (PDB) records the 3D coordinates of the atoms of thousands of protein structures. Most of these proteins cluster into around 700 fold-families based on their similarity. It is conjectured that there will be on the order of 1000 fold-families for the natural proteins (Wolf, Grishin, and Koonin 2000). The PDB thus offers a new paradigm to protein structure prediction by employing data mining methods like clustering, classification, association rules, hidden Markov models, etc. See Rost (2001), Moult (1999), and Schonbrun, Wedemeyer, and Baker (2002) for a review of existing structure prediction methods.

The ability to predict protein structure from the amino acid sequence will do no less than revolutionize molecular biology. All genes will be interpretable as three-dimensional, not one-dimensional, objects. The task of assigning a predicted function to each of these objects (arguably a simpler problem than protein folding) would then be underway. In the end, combined with proteomics data (i.e. expression arrays), we would have a flexible model for the whole cell, potentially capable of predicting emergent properties of molecular systems, such as signal transduction pathways, cell differentiation, and the immune response.

16.1.1 Protein Contact Maps

A *contact map* is a particularly useful two dimensional representation of a protein's tertiary structure. An example is shown in figure 16.1. Two residues (or amino acids) a_i and a_j in a protein are in *contact* if their 3D distance is less than some threshold value t (we used $t = 7\text{Å}$). Using this definition, every pair of amino acids is either in contact or not. Thus, for a protein with N residues, this information can be stored in an NxN binary symmetric matrix C, called the contact map. Each element, C_{ij}, of the contact map is called a contact, and is 1 if residues a_i and a_j are in contact, and 0 otherwise. The contact map provides a host of useful information. For example, clusters of contacts represent certain secondary structures: α-Helices appear as bands along the main diagonal since they involve contacts between one amino acid and its four successors; β-Sheets appear as thick bands parallel or antiparallel to the main diagonal. Tertiary structure may also be obtained by reverse projecting into 3D space using the MAP algorithm (Vendruscolo, Kussell, and Domany 1997).

16.1.2 Protein Folding Pathways

Proteins are chains of amino acids having lengths ranging from 50 to 1000 or more residues. The early work of Levinthal (1968) and Anfinsen (Anfinsen and Scheraga 1975) established that a protein chain folds spontaneously and reproducibly to a unique three dimensional structure when placed in aqueous solution. The sequence of amino acids making up the polypeptide chain contains, encoded within it, the complete building instructions. Levinthal also proved that the folding process cannot occur by random conformational search for the lowest energy state, since such a search would take millions of years, while proteins fold in milliseconds. As a result, Anfinsen proposed that proteins must form structure in a time-ordered sequence of events, now called a "pathway." The nature of these events, whether they are restricted to "native contacts" (defined as contacts that are retained in the final structure) or whether they might include nonspecific interactions, such as a general collapse in size at the very beginning, were left unanswered. Over time, the two main theories for how proteins fold became known as the "molten globule" or "hydrophobic

Protein Folding   Pathway Tree

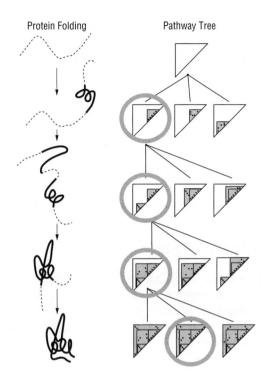

Figure 16.2: Folding pathway and tree search. Large triangles represent the contact map, initially empty. Each branch defines a region of the contact map (gray) by setting pairs of amino acids to be in contact (dots) or not (space). Each node in the tree corresponds uniquely to a three dimensional structure (left), where the dotted lines represent segments of the chain that have undefined structure.

collapse" (invoking nonspecific interactions) and the "framework" or "nucleation/condensation" model (restricting pathways to native contacts only).

Over the years, the theoretical models for folding have converged somewhat, in part due to a better understanding of the structure of the so-called "unfolded state" and due to a more detailed description of kinetic folding intermediates. The "folding funnel" model (Nolting, Golbik, Neira, Soler-Gonzalez, Schreiber, and Fersht 1997) has reconciled hydrophobic collapse with the nucleation-condensation model by envisioning a distorted, funicular energy landscape and a "minimally frustrated" pathway. The view remains of a gradual, counter-entropic search for the hole in the funnel as the predominant barrier to folding.

It is natural to define a *pathway* as a time-series of possible folding events, i.e., a sequence of contacts or sets of contacts (which we call blocks). A *folding pathway* will then be a pathway along with an assignment of 1 or 0 to each contact. Starting from an unfolded protein, the set of possible folding pathways can be represented on a tree, as is illustrated in figure 16.2. A path from the root to a leaf is a particular folding pathway. Each branch defines a region of the contact map by setting pairs of amino acids to be in contact or not. Each set of contacts is physically realizable. The left column in the figure shows how each (circled) node in the tree corresponds uniquely to a three dimensional structure, where the dotted lines represent segments of the chain that have undefined structure. The final nodes of the tree represent complete, physical contact maps, which may be projected back into three dimensions using the MAP algorithm (Vendruscolo, Kussell, and Domany 1997).

16.1.3   Protein Data Bank

Since we are using a data driven learning approach, we take a moment to discuss our data source. The protein data bank (PDB) records the 3D coordinates of the atoms of thousands of protein structures. The set of all known, globular proteins cluster into around 700 families based on their sequence similarity (PDBselect (Hobohm and Sander 1994)). It is conjectured that there will be on the order of 1000-2000 fold-families for the natural proteins. Thus from the PDB we can extract a set of proteins along with their known contact maps. These contact maps form the "learning data," which will be used to mine for association rules and contact map patterns. Part of this data set will be used for learning meaningful patterns, and a part will be set aside for validation.

16.1.4   Contributions

In this chapter we describe how data mining can be used to extract valuable information from contact maps. More specifically we focus on the following tasks: (1) Given a database of protein sequences and their 3D structure in the form of contact maps, build a model to predict if pairs of amino acids are likely to be in contact or not. (2) Use contact maps to discover an extensive set of nonlocal dense patterns and compile a library of such nonlocal interactions. (3) Cluster these patterns based on their similarities and evaluate the clustering quality. We further highlight promising directions of future work. For example, how mining can help in generating heuristic rules of contacts, and how one can generate plausible folding pathways in contact map conformational space.

The protein folding problem will be solved gradually, by many investigators who share their results at the biannual CASP (critical assessment of protein structure prediction) meeting (Moult, Pedersen, Judson, and Fidelis 1995), that offers a world-wide blind prediction challenge. Here, we will investigate how mining can uncover interesting knowledge from contact maps.

16.2   Mining Contacts Using Local Structure

We used a generalized hidden Markov model (HMM) called HMMSTR based on the I-sites library (Bystroff, Thorsson, and Baker 2000) to model statistical interactions between adjacent motifs on the chain, and were thus able to model the local propagation of structure. I-sites (or initiation sites) are local sequence motifs that tend to fold the same way across protein families independent of the context. A rule-based method for predicting tertiary contacts in proteins, using HMMSTR as a preprocessor has already been developed (Zaki, Jin, and Bystroff 2000) and can be extended to sequentially output probabilities for subsets of contacts.

Sequences from the database of 700 nonredundant proteins with less than 25% sequence similarity (the PDBselect dataset (Hobohm and Sander 1994)) were pre-processed using HMMSTR. The associated structures were converted to contact maps. The whole dataset was then mined to find common association rules for tertiary contacts. The rules were tested on a subset not used in the data mining.

The database of known proteins was divided into a training set and a test set. Each protein sequence was submitted to Psi-Blast (Altschul, Madden, Schaffer, Zhang, Zhang, Miller, and Lipman 1997) to generate a sequence family, from which a sequence profile was summed, and backbone angles were discretized (Bystroff, Thorsson, and Baker 2000). For the training set, the amino acid profile and the backbone angle regions were the input data for the forward/backward calculation (Rabiner 1989), which produced a "gamma" matrix of position-dependent HMMSTR Markov state probabilities. For the test set, only the amino acid profile was used to generate the gamma matrix. A contact map was calculated for each member of the training set using a alpha-carbon distance cutoff of 7Å. From these data, a database of "item sets" was constructed. One entry corresponds to an ij residue pair, where $|i - j| > 4$, and consists of the amino acid pair and two sets of Markov state identifiers. Markov state identifiers were included as "items" associated with the ij contact if the position-dependent probability of the state was greater than twice the *a priori* probability of that state. Each entry had a label "1" meaning i and j were in contact in the structure, or "0" if they were not. All items are discrete symbols.

Association rule data mining (Agrawal, Mannila, Srikant, Toivonen, and Verkamo 1996; Zaki 2000) was applied to the database of item sets to extract rules which were predictive of contacts. A rule has the form: "item1" +

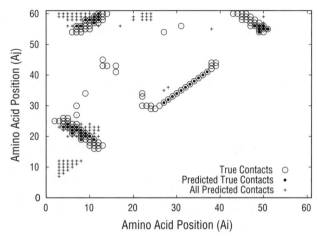

Figure 16.3: Predicted contact map (PDB protein 2igd). We were able to predict parts of the major structures.

"item2" $+ \ldots \Rightarrow C$, where C is 1 or 0. Items may be amino acids, predicted or observed secondary structure symbols, predicted or observed Markov state identifiers, or sequence separation ranges. Prediction of contacts in the test set was carried out by comparing the rule support for contact prediction with the rule support for noncontact prediction. The ratio of these values for all ij pairs in a given protein was sorted, and the top N pairs were predicted to be in contact, where N is the expected number of contacts, which depends on the sequence length. We shall call our method HMMassoc for later reference. Figure 16.3 shows an example contact map prediction. Previous work on contact prediction has employed Neural Networks (Fariselli and Casadio 1999), and statistical techniques based on correlated mutations (Olmea and Valencia 1997; Thomas, Casari, and Sander 1996). Recent work by Vendruscolo (Vendruscolo, Kussell, and Domany 1997) has also shown that it is possible to recover the 3D structure from even corrupted contact maps. Our recent results (Zaki, Jin, and Bystroff 2000) show that our model obtains around 20% accuracy and coverage over the set of all proteins; the model is also 5.2 times better than a random predictor. We can significantly enhance coverage to over 40% if we sacrifice accuracy (13%). For short proteins (length< 100) we get 30% accuracy and coverage (4.5 times better than random); if we lower accuracy to 26% we can get coverage up to 63%. While these results are better than (or equal to) those reported previously, we have still a long way to go before the goal of protein structure prediction is fully realized. Generating three-dimensional structure from the predicted contact maps is now a subject of our investigations.

16.3   Other Methods for Contact Map Prediction

In this section we review some previous work on contact map prediction. It has been shown that neural networks score higher than statistical approaches for contact map prediction (Fariselli and Casadio 1999). We will thus briefly review the statistical approaches and then focus more on the neural network based methods.

16.3.1   Statistical Approaches

A number of earlier methods for contact predictions have relied on correlated mutation (CM) analysis (Gobel, Sander, Schneider, and Valencia 1994; Shindyalov, Kolchanov, and Sander 1994; Thomas, Casari, and Sander 1996; Olmea and Valencia 1997), which compares multiple members of a protein family and detects residues that remain constant or mutate together. The basic idea is to note the distance between residues that appear at a given position in a multiple sequence alignment. Next the correlation coefficient between pairs of positions in an alignment of n proteins is computed as follows:

$$r_{ij} = \frac{1}{n^2} \sum_{k=1}^{n} \sum_{l=1}^{n} \frac{(s_{ikl} - \mu_i)(s_{jkl} - \mu_j)}{\sigma_i \sigma_j}$$

where s_{ikl} is the similarity between residues k and l, μ_i is the mean similarity, and σ_i the standard deviation of the similarity at position i in the alignment. Completely conserved positions or those with gaps over 10% are ignored.

Olmea and Valencia (1997) used correlated mutations and other information like sequence conservation, alignment stability, contact occupancy, etc. to improve the accuracy. The prediction results from their approach (CC) are shown in table 16.1; they did not report the result for all proteins. Another correlated mutation based approach to contact map prediction was presented in Thomas, Casari, and Sander (1996), they obtained an accuracy of 13%.

Recent work by Singer, Vriend, and Bywater (2002) has also suggested use of a contact likelihood matrix derived from PDB to improve correlated mutation analysis to predict contacts. Work by Zhao and Kim (2000) examined pairwise amino acid interactions in the context of secondary structural environments; they reported a set of residue contact energies for a 20×3 (α, β, coil) = 60 residue alphabet. They also tested the use of these environment-dependent contact energies (ERCE) for contact predictions. The predictive accuracy results from the ERCE method are shown in table 16.1.

16.3.2   Neural Networks

Fariselli and Casadio (1999) were the first to apply a neural network (NN) to predict pair-wise residue contacts. They also trained on the PDBselect dataset (Hobohm and Sander 1994) (an older version with 608 proteins). They used a classical feed-forward NN with a standard back-propagation algorithm (Rumelhart, Hinton, and Williams 1986). The network architecture consisted of one output neuron for contact propensity between an amino-acid pair, one hidden layer with two neurons, and an input layer with variable number of neurons depending on the input encoding. They implemented five different networks with increasing input complexity.

Given residues at position i and j, every network had 2 fixed input neurons: one input neuron for the normalized sequence separation $i - j$, and another for the normalized sequence length. The different networks tried included the following:

Net1 uses only the amino acids for prediction. Each input neuron encodes a particular ordered pair of residue types, contributing $\binom{20}{2} = 190$ input neurons for distinct pairs (e.g., A-G) and 20 input neurons for pairs of same residue type (e.g., A-A). The input neuron for the pair (a_i, a_j) is set to 1 while the remaining 209 input neurons are set to 0. With the 2 fixed neurons, there are 212 input neurons.

Net2 incorporates, in addition to the amino acids, the hydrophobicity scale for each reside (averaged over a window of 7 consecutive residues); it thus has 214 input neurons.

Net3 encodes (in addition to information from Net1 and Net2) evolutionary information obtained from the multiple sequence alignment (MSA) of the protein to other similar proteins taken from the HSSP database (Sander and Schneider 1991). For the positions i and j, they count the different residue types that occur in those positions in the MSA. The normalized pair counts are used as input to the NN. Two additional neurons record how well positions i and j are conserved in the MSA. The total input neurons is thus 216.

Net4 tries to capture the sequence context for each residue. They center a window of length 3 at positions i and j and consider the 5 possible pairings of residues (parallel and antiparallel) ($210 \times 5 = 1050$ neurons). With hydrophobic values for each position, it has 1054 input neurons.

Net5 is Net4 augmented with evolutionary information as in Net3.

The accuracy of prediction for proteins of various lengths and on the entire testing set are shown in table 16.1. It appears that all the additional information is helpful in the prediction. Net5 performs the best overall and it incorporates the hydrophobicity values, evolutionary information, and sequence context.

The recent neural networks proposed in Fariselli, Olmea, Valencia, and Casadio (2001) improve upon the work by Fariselli and Casadio (1999). One factor is that they have a more recent and larger version of the PDBselect dataset with 822 nonredundant proteins. Another factor is that the new NNs incorporate more information. The basic architecture consists of one output, 8 hidden, and variable input layer neurons. The different NNs trained were:

Method	$N < 100$	$100 \leq N < 170$	$170 \leq N < 300$	$N \geq 300$	All
AA	13	6	4.5	2	8.5
CM	13	13	11	3	-
CC	19	12	9	4	-
ERCE	19.6	12.1	7.2	-	13.5
Net1	18	16.1	13.3	12.7	14.4
Net2	18	16.4	13.6	13.1	14.7
Net3	19	16.9	13.8	13.2	15
Net4	18	16.7	14.1	13.7	15.1
Net5	19	18	14.9	*14.4*	16
NETCSS	*26*	*21*	*15*	11	*21*
HMMassoc	*26*	*21.5*	13	9.7	19

Table 16.1: Comparative prediction accuracy for different methods.

- NET: same as Net4 above.

- NETC: same as NET with three additional inputs: two for residue conservation values for i and j and third for the correlated mutation between them.

- NETCW: same as NETC but with 6 residue conservation values and 9 correlated mutation values for the length 3 window around i and j.

- NETCSEP: same as NETC, but with an additional neuron coding for sequence separation.

- NETCSS: adds secondary structure information (3 states: α-helix, β-sheet, and coil) to NETC. For each of the 3 positions around i and j (6 total), add an input assigning the residues to one of 3 states, i.e., 18 extra inputs.

They found NETCSS to perform the best. Generally the more information used by the NN the better it performed. The accuracy values for NETCSS are shown in table 16.1.

16.3.3 Comparative Performance

A summary of known results on contact map prediction accuracy is shown in table 16.1. AA (using amino acids only) and HMMassoc (HMMSTR with association mining) values are taken from Zaki, Jin, and Bystroff (2000), CM (correlated mutation) and CC (correlation + conservation) from Olmea and Valencia (1997), ERCE (environment dependent contact energy) is taken from Zhao and Kim (2000), Net1-Net5 from Fariselli and Casadio (1999), NETCSS from Fariselli, Olmea, Valencia, and Casadio (2001). We add as a caveat that direct comparison is not possible, since previous works used a different (and smaller) PDBselect databases for training and testing. One draw back of these previous approaches is that they do not report any coverage values, so it is not clear what percentage of contacts are correctly predicted. Having said that it is still possible to draw some overall conclusions.

The best results in each column are highlighted in italics. The proteins have been separated into bins based on sequence length N. It can be seen that the NN-based methods and HMMassoc outperform other statistically-based methods. Among the NN methods, NETCSS is the best. NETCSS and HM-Massoc perform the same on proteins up to 170 residues long, with NETCSS having an advantage of about 2% for longer proteins. It should be noted that while NETCSS explicitly incorporates the evolutionary information, sequence context, hydrophobicity, etc., HMMassoc does so implicitly in the HMM state output in the form of the "gamma" matrix. We plan to add more explicit information to the association mining approach to test its efficacy.

Also, it has been reported that postprocessing the predicted contact maps by filtering out overpredicted contacts can help improve the accuracy (Olmea and Valencia 1997; Fariselli, Olmea, Valencia, and Casadio 2001). The results shown above are without such postfiltering.

16.3.4 Other Advances

There has been some recent work by Pollastri and Baldi (2002) on using recurrent neural network architectures for contact prediction. Their PDBselect dataset is even larger, consisting of 1484 proteins, and the inputs consist of an orthogonal encoding of pairs of amino acids (pairs of binary vectors of length 20), evolutionary information in terms of profiles, correlated mutations, specific secondary structural features (α, β, coil), and relative solvent accessibility (buried, exposed). They report an overall accuracy of 27% for all proteins, which would make it the best current method. They concluded that the use of secondary structure and solvent accessibility is more useful than profiles and correlated profiles.

Support vector machines (SVM) have also been used by Zhao and Karypis (2003) for contact map mining. They trained 15 different SVMs using a different number of features. The possible features included sequence conservation values for i and j, sequence separation, correlated mutation values, predicted secondary structure values, and sequence profiles (for evolutionary information). The best SVM method used all of the available features to give an overall accuracy of 22.4%. However, it should be noted that they used a different set of only 177 proteins, and not the nonredundant set from PDBselect.

16.4 Characterizing Contact Maps

Proteins are self-avoiding, globular chains. A contact map, if it truly represents a self-avoiding and compact chain, can be readily translated back to the three-dimensional structure from which it came. But, in general, only a small subset of all symmetric matrices of ones and zeros have this property. Previous work (Zaki, Jin, and Bystroff 2000) has generated a method to output a contact map that both satisfies the geometrical constraints and is likely to represent a low-energy structure. Interactions between different subsequences of a protein are constrained by a variety of factors. The interactions may be initiated at several short peptides (initiation sites) and propagate into higher-order intra- or inter-molecular interactions. The properties of such interactions depend on (1) the amino acid sequence corresponding to the interactions, (2) the physical geometry of all interacting groups in three dimensions, and (3) the immediate contexts (linear, and secondary components for tertiary structural motifs) within which such interactions occur.

We describe below the method that we use for mining frequent dense patterns or structural motifs in contact maps. All protein sequences used are from Protein Data Bank (PDB). Briefly, there are four major stages in our approach: (1) mining dense patterns,(2) pruning mined patterns, (3) clustering the dense patterns, and (4) integration of these patterns with biological data.

16.4.1 Mining Dense Patterns in Contact Maps

To enumerate all the frequent 2D dense patterns we scan the database of contact maps with a 2D sliding window of a user specified size. Across all proteins in the database, any submatrix under the window that has a minimum "density" (the number of '1's or contacts) is captured. For a $N \times N$ contact map (N is the length of the protein), using a 2D $W \times W$ window, there are $(N - W) \times (N - W)/2$ possible submatrices. We have to tabulate those which are dense, using different window sizes. We choose window sizes from 5 to 10 to capture denser contacts close to the diagonal (i.e., short-range interactions), as well as the sparser contacts far from the diagonal (i.e., long-range interactions).

Counting Dense Patterns

As we slide the $W \times W$ window, the submatrix under the window will be added to a dense pattern list if its density exceeds the *min_d* threshold. However, we are interested in those dense patterns that are frequent, i.e., when adding a new pattern to the list of dense patterns we need to check if it already exists in the list. If yes, we increase the frequency of the pattern by one, and if not, we add it to the list initialized with a count of one.

The main complexity of the method stems from the fact that there can be a huge number of candidate windows. For instance, with a window size of $W = 5$, and for $N = 60$, we have 1485 windows per contact map. This translates to roughly 28 million possible windows for a database with 18,455 contact maps (equal to the number of proteins stored in the PDB database). Of these windows only relatively few will be dense, since the number of contacts is a lot less than the number of noncontacts. Still we need an efficient way of testing if two submatrices are identical or not. We assume that P is the number of current dense patterns of size $W \times W$. The naive method to add a new pattern is to check equality against all P patterns, where each check takes $O(W^2)$ time, giving a total time of $O(W^2 P)$ per equality check. A better approach is to use a hash table of dense patterns instead of a list. This can cut down the time to $O(W^2)$ per equality check if a suitable hash function is found. We will describe below how we can further improve the time to just $O(W)$ per check.

Counting Dense Patterns via Hashing

For fast hashing and equality checking, we will encode each submatrix in the following way: each row of the contact map, i.e., the $\{0, 1\}$ sequence, will be converted into a number corresponding to the binary value represented by the sequence, and all the numbers computed this way will be concatenated into a string. For example the 5×5 submatrix below is encoded as the string: 0.12.8.8.0.

```
submatrix, binary value of row
00000  0
01100  12
01000  8
01000  8
00000  0
stringId(concatenate row values) = 0.12.8.8.0
Hashing of a Dense Pattern
```

According to our submatrix encoding scheme, each dense $W \times W$ window M is encoded as the string $stringId(M) = v_1.v_2.\cdots.v_W$, where v_i is the value of the row treated as a binary string. For fast counting we will employ a 2-level hashing scheme. For the first level we use the sum of all the row values as the hash function:

$$h_1(M) = \sum_{i=1}^{W} v_i$$

The second level hashing uses the *stringId* as the hash key and therefore is an

Contact Threshold	# Patterns	# Clusters	Cluster Quality
5 Å	2508	83	0.8931
6 Å	9929	99	0.8633
7 Å	21231	367	0.8367

Table 16.2: Clustering of dense patterns.

exact hashing, i.e., $h_2(M) = stringId(M)$. The use of this 2-level hashing scheme allows us to avoid many unnecessary checks. The first level hashing (h_1) narrows the potential matching submatrices to a very small number. Then the second level hashing (h_2) computes the exact matches. Computing h_1 and h_2 both take $O(W)$ time; thus the equality check of a submatrix takes $O(W)$ time.

After all dense areas are hashed into the second level slot, the support counts for each unique *stringId* of the dense patterns are collected, and those patterns that have support counts more than a user specified *minSupport* will be considered frequent dense patterns and will be output for further analysis.

After a pruning step to remove redundant patterns (Hu, Shen, Shao, Bystroff, and Zaki 2002), we generated the possible dense patterns with *minSupport* 1, i.e., the exhaustive set of dense patterns that appear in our database. We also varied the amino acid contact threshold while creating the contact map (recall that two amino acids are in contact if they are at most t distance apart in 3D; we used $t = 5,6$ and 7 Å in our experiments). When using sliding window size less than 5, the dense patterns generated are trivial and didn't show enough structural meaning. With window size 6 and above, we generated only slightly more dense patterns than with window size 5. We consider 5 an important window size to generate existing dense patterns. In the following study, only data with sliding window size 5 will be listed. An example dense pattern with associated information is shown below (its support count is 5 and its volume, the number of 1's, is 10):

```
Sup:5 Str:0.28.12.15.1. Vol:10
00000
11100
01100
01111
00001
a dense pattern example
```

The numbers of nonredundant dense patterns extracted using different contact thresholds is shown in the second column of table 16.2 (it also shows other clustering information which will be explained in the next section).

16.4.2 Clustering Dense Patterns

In the mining step, a large number of possible dense patterns are generated even after pruning. Instead of analyzing these nonlocal patterns directly it is beneficial to group them into groups of similar interactions. To characterize all the dense patterns that we have mined, clustering provides an effective way to obtain a gross view.

There are two main approaches to clustering: partition-based clustering and hierarchical clustering. Partition-based clustering tries to divide the data of N objects into k partitions or groups using heuristic search or iterative methods (e.g., k-means clustering). Hierarchical clustering comes in two flavors: (1) Agglomerative clustering technique starts with each object in its own cluster; at each step pairs of clusters with minimum distance between them are successively merged; and (2) divisive clustering takes the opposite approach, it starts with all the records in one cluster, and then successively splits clusters into small pieces.

In this chapter, we used agglomerative clustering to group the mined dense patterns to find the dominant nonlocal interactions, using the methodology described below.

Calculating Distance

First, the distance between every pair of patterns is calculated using the formula:

$$Distance(M_i, M_j) = \sum_{k=1}^{W^2} |M_i[k] - M_j[k]| \qquad (16.1)$$

where M_i and M_j are dense patterns, and k is the position in the $W \times W$ matrix taken as a linear array (top left corner is position 0 and bottom right is $W \times W$). Thus $M_i[k]$ is either 0 or 1, indicating a noncontact and contact, respectively. The smaller the distance between two patterns, the more likely the two patterns are similar to each other.

We also need to define the distance between two clusters, say c_1 and c_2. Let the size of c_1 be n and the size of c_2 be m patterns. Then the distance between the pair of clusters is given as: $\sum_{i=1}^{n} \sum_{j=1}^{m} Distance(M_i, M_j)$ (with pattern $M_i \in c_1$ and $M_j \in c_2$), i.e., the sum of all pair-wise distances between patterns in a cluster.

Clustering

Before we start the clustering, we need to determine a threshold distance for a cluster, namely, the maximum average distance among the patterns in one

cluster. Once this is done, the procedure is as follows: (1) Compare all pairs
of clusters and mark the pair that is closest. (2) The distance between this
closest pair of clusters is compared to the threshold value. If the distance is
less than the threshold distance, these clusters become linked and are merged
into a single cluster. Return to Step 1 to continue the clustering. If the distance
between the closest pair is greater than the threshold, the clustering stops. If
the threshold value is too small, there will still be many groups present at the
end, and many of them will be singletons. Conversely, if the threshold is too
large, objects that are not very similar may end up with the same cluster. We
used distance 4 as the threshold for clustering.

```
Cluster No.1, Count = 59
Contact Probabilities: Representative:
0:0.05 1:0.05 2:0.68 3:0.85 4:0.71      | 00111
5:0.03 6:0.02 7:0.14 8:0.07 9:0.09      | 00000
10:0.05 11:0.05 12:0.12 13:0.09 14:0.03 | 00000
15:0.03 16:0.05 17:0.15 18:0.27 19:0.85 | 00001
20:0.25 21:0.10 22:0.59 23:0.92 24:0.83 | 00011
```

After the agglomerative clustering step, for each cluster, we need a way
to compactly describe the dominant interactions represented by all members
of the cluster. For this we calculated the contact probability at each of the
$W \times W$ positions in the submatrix. Assume that there are n patterns grouped
in cluster c. Contact probability at position k is defined as the ratio of the
number of contacts at that position divided by the cluster cardinality, and is
given as $p_k^c = (1/n) \times \sum_{i=1}^{n} M_i[k]$. Based on these probability values, a
representative contact pattern is generated for each cluster. In a representative
contact pattern, we record a '1' at position k whenever p_k^c is greater than some
probability threshold r and a '0' otherwise. An example cluster is shown below
with associated information. Count is the number of patterns in the cluster and
the notation 0:0.05 means that the probability of contact at position 0 is 0.05.
The representative contact pattern for the cluster with a probability threshold
$r = 0.65$ is also shown.

The number of clusters generated using different amino acid contact threshold are listed in table 16.2, column 2 (with clustering threshold of 4 and window size 5). For instance at 6Å contact threshold we obtained 99 clusters from
the 9929 mined patterns.

Evaluating Clustering Quality

After clustering is finished, we need a method to evaluate how effective it is.
One way is to define an objective notion of clustering quality. While this may
be hard in general, the contact probabilities for a cluster gives a good indication

about how good the cluster is. For example, a cluster with very high values at some positions and very low values at some positions is a good cluster, while a cluster that has contact probabilities close to 0.5 is not very good. In other words, if a majority of the cluster members agree on a position (mostly 0's or mostly 1's), that indicates a good clustering.

We use the formula below to generate the sum of contact probabilities at each position in the window within a cluster c:

$$S_c^1 = \sum_{k=1}^{W^2} p_k^c, \text{ if } p_k^c > 0.5 \tag{16.2}$$

$$S_c^0 = \sum_{k=1}^{W^2} (1 - p_k^c), \text{ if } p_k^c \leq 0.5 \tag{16.3}$$

The quality of a cluster c is then given by the sum $Q_c = S_c^1 + S_c^0$. A high Q_c value close to 1 indicates a good cluster, while a value close to 0.5 indicates a poor cluster.

The final clustering quality across all the clusters is given as the weighted sum of individual cluster quality values, as shown in the formula below:

$$Q = \frac{\sum_{i=1}^{|C|} |c_i| \times Q_{c_i}}{N}, (0.5 \leq Q \leq 1) \tag{16.4}$$

where C is the set of clusters, $|C|$ is the number of clusters, $c_i \in C$ is one cluster in the set, $|c_i|$ is the numbers of patterns in the cluster, and N is the total number of patterns. Note how the clustering quality Q varies from 0.5 to 1, with a higher value suggests better clustering quality because it clusters patterns which share similar occurrence positions for '1's and '0's. A cluster with the same contact pattern has a $Q = 1$. The clustering quality corresponding to clusters generated in our experiments is listed in table 16.2, column 3 (with clustering threshold of 4 and window size 5). For example, given window size of 5, contact distance threshold of 6 Å and clustering threshold of 4, the clustering quality of the 99 clusters is 0.865753.

16.4.3 Integration and Visualization

After dense patterns are found and clustered, the final step is to incorporate the protein sequence/structure information with them. That is, for each dense pattern and its occurrences in the different contact maps (that is in different protein segments in PDB), we note the protein id, the start positions of the window (given as (X, Y) coordinates of the top left corner), and the type of interaction. This information is then used to visualize the mined patterns or interactions. An example of a dense pattern with associated information is shown below. This pattern with 11 contacts, occurs only once in PDB file with id $1vjs\_.1$, at position $(134, 109)$, i.e., it represents a nonlocal interaction between protein segment at positions 134-138 (the X axis) and the protein segment at positions 109-113 (the Y axis), in this case an interaction between two beta-strands.

```
Sup:1 Str:1.5.31.24.16 Vol:11
00001
00101
11111
11000
10000
pdb- x_start y_start interaction
1vjs_.1 134 109 beta strand-beta strand
```

16.4.4 Experimental Results

We used a nonredundant set of 2702 proteins from the PDB for our experiments. Preliminary distance maps for protein were produced based on the 3D coordinates of the α-Carbon atoms of each amino acid Based on these distance maps, binary contact maps were generated using several contact thresholds As described previously, we discovered 9929 dense patterns when using a sliding window of size 5, maximum amino acid contact threshold of $6\overset{\circ}{A}$ and a minimum density of 0.125. When agglomerative clustering is applied, 99 clusters are generated using a clustering threshold of 4. The clustering quality is 0.8633. Two example clusters with their four associated patterns and corresponding interactions are given in figure 16.4.

Figure 16.4 shows an example of the structures of four different patterns from one of the mined clusters. Beta strand interacting with beta strand is the dominant nonlocal motif in this cluster. In other clusters, different dominant interactions were discovered. These interactions can be further divided into subclasses according to the number of contacts involved in each component, multiplicity of interacting atoms (one to one, one to many, or many to many), sequence specificities, and the linear/secondary structural contexts of the interaction.

These experiments shows that we efficiently clustered patterns according to their similarities both in submatrix level and structure level. With our clustering method, we can compile a library of possible dense patterns for further application in extracting valuable information to improve the accuracy of protein structure and pathway prediction. For instance the exhaustive collection of mined patterns can be used in a post-processing step to filter out over predicted

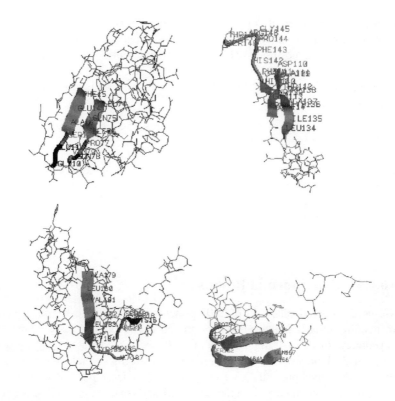

Figure 16.4: Secondary structures of four different patterns from one cluster–beta strand versus beta strand.

contacts, similar to the approach in Olmea and Valencia (1997) and Fariselli, Olmea, Valencia, and Casadio (2001).

16.5 Future Directions

Many interesting questions still remain to be answered in the context of contact map mining. The ultimate goal is to use the mined results for better structure prediction.

16.5.1 Improving Prediction of Contact Maps

As mentioned above we applied a hybrid method based on hidden Markov Models and association rule mining to predict the contact map for a given protein sequence (see Zaki, Jin, and Bystroff [2000] for details). Figure 16.3

shows the predicted contact map for the protein $2igd$ from figure 16.1. We got 35% accuracy and 37% coverage for this protein. The figure shows the true contacts, the contacts correctly predicted, and all the contacts predicted (correctly or incorrectly). Our prediction was able to capture true contacts representing portions of all the major interactions. For example, true contacts were found for the alpha helix, the two antiparallel beta sheets and the parallel beta sheet. However, some spurious clusters of contacts were also discovered, such as the triangle in the lower left corner or the block of contacts in top left and middle regions of the contact map. Using the extensive library of nonlocal motifs, one can eliminate such false contacts by recognizing the fact that they never occur in real proteins, and thus these blocks of contacts are physically impossible. In future work we will study the effectiveness of this post-processing approach (by filtering out physically impossible blocks) in improving the prediction of contact maps.

16.5.2 Mining Heuristic Rules for "Physicality"

Simple geometric considerations may be encoded into heuristics that recognize physically possible and protein-like patterns within contact maps, C. For example, we may consider the following to be rules that are never broken in true protein structures: a) If $C(i, j) = 1$ and $C(i + 2, j + 2) = 1$, then $C(i, j+2) = 0$, and $C(i+2, j) = 0$. b) If $C(i+2, j) = 1$ and $C(i, j+2) = 1$), then $C(i, j) = 0$, and $C(i + 2, j + 2) = 0$. These rules encode the observation that a beta sheet (contacts in a diagonal row) is either parallel or antiparallel (respectively), but not both.

Another example may be drawn from contacts with alpha helices: If $C(i, i+4) = 1$ and $C(i, j) = 1$ and $C(i+4, j) = 1$, then $C(i+2, j) = 0$. This follows from the fact that $i + 2$ lies on the opposite side of the helix from i to $i + 4$, and therefore cannot share contacts with nonlocal residue j. Local structures may be used in the definition of the heuristics. For example, if an unbroken set of $C(i, i + 4) = 1$ exists, the local structure is a helix, and therefore, for all $|j - i| > 4$ in that segment, $C(i, j) = 0$. The question is whether one can mine these rules automatically.

One approach is to discover "positional" rules, i.e., the heuristic geometric rules by considering an appropriate neighborhood around each contact $C(i, j)$ and noting down the relative coordinates of the other contacts and noncontacts in the neighborhood, conditional on the local structure type(s). For instance, consider a lower 1-layer (denoted LL1) neighborhood for a given point, $C(i, j)$. LL1 includes all the coordinates within $i + 1$ and $j + 1$, i.e. each point has 3 other points in its LL1 neighborhood, namely $C(i, j+1)$, $C(i+1, j)$ and $C(i + 1, j + 1)$. From the LL1 region around each point we obtain a database which can be mined for frequent combinations. Other rules can be found by defining an appropriate neighborhood and by incorporating sequence information. We are currently developing techniques to mine such heuristic rules of contact automatically.

16.5.3 Rules for Pathways in Contact Map Space

Currently, there is no strong evidence that specific nonnative contacts (i.e., those that are not present in the final 3D structure) are required for the folding of any protein. Many simplified models for folding, such as lattice simulations, tacitly assume that nonnative contacts are "off pathway" and are not essential to the folding process. Therefore, we choose to encode the assumption of a "native pathway" into our algorithmic approaches. This simplifying assumption allows us to define potential folding pathways based on a known three-dimensional structure. We may further assume that native contacts are formed only once in any given pathway.

A pathway in contact map space consists of a time-ordered series of contacts. The pathway is initiated by high-confidence Initiation-sites (Bystroff, Thorsson, and Baker 2000), and thereafter it follows a tree-search format (see figure 16.2). We may impose a "condensation rule" onto our pathway model by assuming that any new contact must occur within S_{max} residues of a contact that is already formed. In other words we assume that $U(i,j) \leq S_{max}$, where $U(i,j)$ is the number of "unfolded" residues between i and j. Intervening residues are "folded" when a contact forms. Each level of the tree is the addition of a contact that satisfies the condensation rule. A maximum of k branches can be selected based on the energy. In addition, contacts that are not physically possible can be rejected, using the mined clusters of dense patterns or using the heuristics rules for physicality. Identical branches (same set of contacts, different order) can of course be merged.

We believe that the rules for folding in contact map space are consistent with the accepted biophysical theories of folding, while confining the search to a greatly simplified and reduced space. We are currently developing methods to discover the folding pathways in the contact map space. It is worth observing that while the structure prediction problem has attracted a lot of attention, the pathway prediction problem has received almost no attention. However, the solution of either task would greatly enhance the solution of the other, hence it is natural to try to solve both of these problems within a unifying framework. Our current work is a step toward this unified approach.

16.6 Conclusions

In this chapter we described how data mining can be used to extract valuable information from contact maps. More specifically we focused on the following tasks: (1) Given a database of protein sequences and their 3D structure in the form of contact maps, build a model to predict if pairs of amino acids are likely to be in contact or not. (2) Use contact maps to discover an extensive set of nonlocal dense patterns and compile a library of such nonlocal interactions. We reviewed previous methods for contact map predictions and we highlighted some promising directions of future work. For example, how mining can help in generating heuristic rules of contacts, and how one can generate plausible folding pathways in contact map conformational space.

Acknowledgements

This work was supported in part by NSF CAREER Award IIS-0092978, DOE Early Career Award DEFG02- 02ER25538, NSF grant EIA0103708, and RPI Exploratory Seed Grant

Mohammed J. Zaki is an associate professor of computer science at Rensselaer Polytechnic Institute, specializing in data mining and its applications in bioinformatics. He can be reached at zaki@cs.rpi.edu.

Jingjing Hu received her M.S. degree in computer science at Rensselaer Polytechnic Institute in 2003. Her interest are in data mining and its applications in bioinformatics. She can be reached at huj5@cs.rpi.edu.

Christopher Bystroff is an assistant professor of biology at Rensselaer Polytechnic Institute. His research centers on protein structure prediction using bioinformatics. He can be reached at bystrc@rpi.edu

Chapter 17

Mining Scientific Data Sets using Graphs

*Michihiro Kuramochi, Mukund Deshpande,
and George Karypis*

Data mining is the process of automatically extracting new and useful knowledge hidden in large datasets. This emerging discipline is becoming increasingly important as advances in data collection have lead to the explosive growth in the amount of available data. To date, the majority of the research has been focused on developing algorithms for datasets arising in various business, information retrieval, and financial applications. However, the success of data mining techniques in these fields has sparked an interest of applying such analysis techniques to various scientific and engineering fields, such as fluid dynamics, astronomy, ecosystem modeling, structural mechanics, and biological sciences. This is illustrated by the large number of workshops in scientific data mining that were recently held at various data mining conferences, research centers, and NSF-funded centers. Early results of applying various data mining techniques in scientific and engineering applications have shown that data mining holds the promise of being an effective tool for analyzing and understanding such complex and diverse datasets.

The characteristics of the datasets arising in scientific applications, quite often, differ significantly from those arising in commercial and business settings. Scientific datasets tend to have a strong temporal, sequential, spatial, topological, geometric, and/or relational nature. Most of the existing data mining algorithms (e.g., pattern discovery, clustering, and classification) expect the data to be described either as a set of transactions (e.g., market-basket data), a sequence of such transactions (e.g., historical market-basket data), or as multi-dimensional vectors (e.g., demographic characteristics, document vectors). Sometimes it is easy to transform scientific datasets in these types of frameworks (Weir, Fayyad, and Djorgovski 1995; Stolorz and Dean 1996; Fayyad, Haussler, and Stolorz 1996; Han, Karypis, and Kumar 2001); however, quite often such transformations are either impossible or it can only be done with a substantial loss in the amount of information.

We believe that developing data mining algorithms that operate on a representation that accurately models the key characteristics of the original datasets, holds the promise of further increasing the usefulness of such techniques in scientific applications. In recent years, labeled graphs (either topological or geometric) have emerged as a promising abstraction to capture the characteristics of these datasets (Holder, Cook, and Djoko 1994a; Yoshida and Motoda 1995; Inokuchi, Washio, and Motoda 2000; Kuramochi and Karypis 2001; Kuramochi and Karypis 2002a). In this approach, each object to be mined is represented via a separate graph or the entire set of objects and their relations are represented via a single large graph. The vertices of these graphs correspond to the entities in the objects and the edges correspond to the relations between them. This graph-based modeling allows us to directly capture many of the sequential, topological, geometric, and other relational characteristics of scientific datasets, that cannot currently be modeled by existing approaches.

For example, graphs can be used to directly model the key topological and geometric characteristics of chemical structures (e.g., chemical compounds, protein molecules, etc.). Vertices in these graphs will correspond to different atoms or amino acids and the edges will correspond to atoms connected via bonds, or amino acids that are connected in the protein's backbone or are connected via noncovalent bonds (i.e., contact points) in their 3D structure. Similarly, graphs can be used to model the relevant characteristics of datasets generated by various numerical simulations. For instance, data generated from turbulent fluid-flow simulations can be represented via a graph whose vertices will model the vortices and edges will model various relations between them such as relative distance and/or orientation.

The key advantage of graph modeling is that it allows us to solve problems that we could not easily solve previously. For instance, consider the problem of mining chemical compounds to find recurrent substructures. We can achieve that using a graph-based pattern discovery algorithm by creating a graph for each one of the compounds and then mine recurrent substructures across different compounds by finding frequently occurring subgraphs. Similarly, we can organize a set of proteins into fold-families and/or discovery novel structural motifs by modeling them via geometric graphs and use clustering algorithm to group together graphs that are geometrically similar. Finally, we can develop computationally efficient algorithms for high-throughput screening of millions of chemical compounds—a critical step in rational drug design—by using graphs to model the topology and structure of compounds that have been shown (either experimentally or via computationally expensive molecular dynamic calculations) to be promising and then use classification algorithms to build predictive models by reasoning directly about the graph (sub)structure of the various objects.

The added power provided by graph-modeling can only be realized if computationally efficient and scalable algorithms for many of the classical data-mining tasks, such as frequent pattern discovery, clustering, and classification, become available. Developing such algorithms poses a number of challenges as relatively trivial operations such as inclusion and identity-checking map to nontrivial operations of subgraph and graph isomorphisms. In the rest of this chapter we review some of our research on developing algorithms for finding frequently occurring patterns and building predictive models for graph datasets, and outline various promising research directions.

17.1 Definitions and Notation

A *graph* $g = (V, E)$ is made of two sets, the set of vertices V and the set of edges E. Each vertex $v \in V$ has a label $l(v) \in L_V$, and each edge $e \in E$ is an unordered pair of vertices uv where $u, v \in V$. Each edge also has a label $l(e) \in L_E$. L_E and L_V denote the sets of edge and vertex labels respectively. Those edge and vertex labels are not necessarily to be unique. That means more than one distinct edges or vertices may have the same label. If $|L_E| = |L_V| = 1$, then we call it an *unlabeled graph*. If each vertex $v \in V$ of the graph has coordinates associated with it, in either the two or three dimensional space, we call it a *geometric graph*. We will denote the coordinates of a vertex v by $c(v)$.

Two graphs $g_1 = (V_1, E_1)$ and $g_2 = (V_2, E_2)$ are *isomorphic*, denoted by $g_1 \sim g_2$, if they are topologically identical to each other, i.e., there is a bijection $\phi : V_1 \mapsto V_2$ with $e = xy \in E_1 \leftrightarrow \phi(x)\phi(y) \in E_2$ for every edge $e \in E_1$ where $x, y \in V_1$. In the case of labeled graphs, this mapping must also preserve the labels on the vertices and edges, that means for every vertex $v \in V, l(v) = l(\phi(v))$ and for every edge $e = xy \in E, l(xy) = l(\phi(x)\phi(y))$. A graph $g = (V, E)$ is called *automorphic* if g is isomorphic to itself via a nonidentity mapping. Given two graphs $g_1 = (V_1, E_1)$ and $g_2 = (V_2, E_2)$, the problem of *subgraph isomorphism* is to find an isomorphism between g_2 and

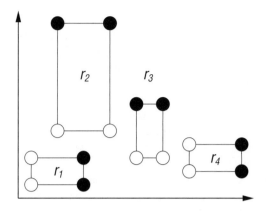

Figure 17.1: Geometrically isomorphic graphs.

a subgraph of g_1, i.e., to determine whether or not g_2 is included in g_1.

The notion of isomorphism and automorphism can be extended for the case of geometric graphs as well. A simple way of defining geometric isomorphism between two geometric graphs g_1 and g_2 is to require that there is an isomorphism ϕ that in addition to preserving the topology and the labels of the graph, to also preserve the coordinates of every vertex. However, since the coordinates of the vertices depend on the particular reference coordinate axes, the above definition is of limited interest. Instead, it is more natural to define geometric isomorphism that allows homogeneous transforms on those coordinates, prior to establishing a *match*. For this reason, we consider three basic types of geometric transformations: rotation, scaling and translation, as well as, their combination. In light of that, we define that two geometric graphs g_1 and g_2 are *geometrically isomorphic*, if there exists an isomorphism ϕ of g_1 and g_2 and a homogeneous transform $\mathcal{T}$, that preserves the coordinates of the corresponding vertices, i.e., $\mathcal{T}(c(v)) = c(\phi(v))$ for every $v \in V$. In this case, ϕ is called a *geometric isomorphism* between g_1 and g_2. Geometric automorphism is defined in an analogous fashion. Figure 17.1 shows some examples illustrating this definition. There are four geometric graphs drawn in this two dimensional example, each of which is a rectangle. Edges are unlabeled and vertex labels are indicated by their colors. The graphs $r_1 \sim r_2$ if all of the rotation, scaling and translation are allowed, and $r_1 \sim r_3$ if both rotation and translation are allowed, and $r_1 \sim r_4$ if translation is allowed.

One of the challenges in using the above definition of geometric graph isomorphism is that it requires an exact match of the coordinates of the various vertices. Unfortunately, equivalence of the two sets of coordinates is not straightforward. Geometric graphs derived from physical datasets may contain

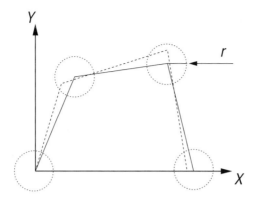

Figure 17.2: Tolerance r.

small amounts of error, and in many cases, we are interested in find geometric patterns that are similar to, but slightly different from each other. To accommodate these requirements, we allow a certain amount of tolerance r when we establish a match between coordinates. That is, if $\| \mathcal{T}(c(v)) - c(\phi(v)) \| \leq r$ for every $v \in V$, we regard ϕ as a valid geometric isomorphism. We will refer to the parameter r as the *coordinate matching tolerance*. A two dimensional example is shown in figure 17.2. We can think of an imaginary circle or sphere of a radius r centered at each vertex. After aligning the local coordinate axes of the two geometric graphs with each other, if a corresponding vertex in another graph is inside this circle or sphere, we consider that the two vertices are located at the same position. We will refer to these isomorphisms as *r-tolerant geometric isomorphisms*, and will be the type of isomorphisms that will assume for the rest of this chapter.

A graph is *connected* if there is a path between every pair of vertices in the graph. Given a graph $g = (V, E)$, a graph $g_s = (V_s, E_s)$ will be a *subgraph* of g if and only if $V_s \subseteq V$ and $E_s \subseteq E$. In a way similar to isomorphism, the notion of subgraph can be extended to *r-tolerant geometric subgraphs* in which the coordinates match after a particular homogeneous transform $\mathcal{T}$.

The *canonical label* of a graph $G = (V, E)$, $\mathrm{cl}(G)$, is defined to be a unique *code* (e.g., string) that is invariant on the ordering of the vertices and edges in the graph (Read and Corneil 1977; Fortin 1996; McKay 1990). As a result, two graphs will have the same canonical label if they are isomorphic. Canonical labels allow us to quickly compare two graphs and to establish a total ordering of graphs, regardless of the original vertex and edge ordering.

17.2   Discovering Frequent Patterns

The problems of finding frequently occurring patterns in topological and geometric graph datasets are identical to that of finding all frequently occurring subgraphs and can be formally defined as follows:

> **Topological Subgraph Discovery.** Given a set of graphs D, each of which is an undirected labeled graph and a parameter σ such that $0 < \sigma \leq 1.0$, find all connected undirected graphs that are subgraphs in at least $\sigma|D|\%$ of the input graphs.

> **Geometric Subgraph Discovery.** Given a set of graphs D, each of which is an undirected labeled geometric graph, a parameter σ such that $0 < \sigma \leq 1.0$, a set of allowed geometric transforms out of rotation, scaling and translation, and a coordinate matching tolerance r, find all connected undirected geometric graphs that have an r-tolerant geometric subgraph in at least $\sigma|D|\%$ of the input graphs.

We will refer to each of the graphs in D as a *(geometric) graph transaction* or simply a *transaction* when the context is clear, to D as the (geometric) graph transaction database, to σ as the *support* threshold, and each of the discovered patterns as the either the *frequent subgraph* or the *r-tolerant frequent geometric subgraph*, depending on the context.

There are four key aspects in the above problem statements. First, we are only interested in (geometric) subgraphs that are connected. This is motivated by the fact that the resulting frequent subgraphs will be encapsulating relations (or edges) between some of the entities (or vertices) of various objects. Within this context, connectivity is a natural property of frequent patterns. An additional benefit of this restriction is that it reduces the complexity of the problem, as we do not need to consider disconnected combinations of frequent connected subgraphs.

Second, we allow the graphs to be labeled, and as discussed in section 17.1, each graph (and discovered pattern) can contain vertices and/or edges with the same label. This greatly increases our modeling ability, as it allow us to find patterns involving multiple occurrences of the same entities and relations, but at the same time makes the problem of finding such frequently occurring subgraphs nontrivial (Kuramochi and Karypis 2001). In such cases, any frequent subgraph discovery algorithm needs to correctly identify how a particular subgraph maps to the vertices and edges of each graph transaction, that can only be done by solving many instances of the subgraph isomorphism problem, which has been shown to be in NP-complete (Garey and Johnson 1979).

Third, in the case of geometric subgraph discovery, we allow homogeneous transforms when we find instances of them in transactions. That is, a pattern can appear in a transaction in a shifted, scaled or rotated fashion. This greatly increases our ability to find interesting patterns. For instance in many chemical datasets, common substructures are at different orientation from each other, and the only way to identify them is to allow for translation and rotation invariant patterns. However, this added flexibility comes at a considerable increase in the complexity of discovering such patterns, as we need to consider all possible geometric configurations (a combination of rotation, scaling and translation) of a single pattern.

Fourth, we allow for some degree of tolerance when we try to establish a matching between the vertex-coordinates of the geometric pattern and its supporting transaction. Even though this significantly improves our ability to find meaningful patterns and deal with measurement errors and errors due to floating point operations (that are occurred by applying the various geometric transforms), it dramatically changes the nature of the problem for the following reason. In traditional pattern discovery problems such as finding frequent itemsets, sequential patterns, and/or frequent topological graphs there was a clear definition of what was the pattern given its set of supporting transactions. On the other hand, in the case of r-tolerant geometric subgraphs, there are many different geometric representations of the same pattern (all of which will be r-tolerant isomorphic to each other). The problem becomes not only that of finding a pattern and its support, but also finding the right representative of this pattern. Note that this representative can be either an actual instance, or a composite of many instances. The selection of the right representative can have a serious impact on correctly computing the support of the pattern. For example, given a set of subgraphs that are r-tolerant isomorphic to each other, the one that corresponds to an *outlier* will tend to have a lower support than the one corresponding to the *center*. Thus, the exact solution of the problem of discovering all r-tolerant geometric subgraphs involves a *pattern optimization* phase whose goal is to select the right representative for each pattern, such that it will lead to the largest number of frequent patterns.

17.2.1 Related Research

Over the years, a number of different algorithms have been developed to find frequent patterns corresponding to frequent subgraphs in topological graph databases. Developing such algorithms is particularly challenging and computationally intensive, as graph and/or subgraph isomorphisms play a key role throughout the computations. For this reason, a considerable amount of work has been focused on approximate algorithms (Holder, Cook, and Djoko 1994a; Yoshida and Motoda 1995; Srinivasan, King, Muggleton, and Sternberg 1997b; Muggleton 1999; Gonzalez, Holder, and Cook 2001; Kramer, De Raedt, and Helma 2001) that used various heuristics to prune the search space. Some of them employ heuristic shrinking of input datasets to speedup the overall computation (Holder, Cook, and Djoko 1994a; Yoshida and Motoda 1995; Gonzalez, Holder, and Cook 2001), others approximate graphs as sequences of vertices and edges (Kramer, De Raedt, and Helma 2001), and others (Srinivasan, King, Muggleton, and Sternberg 1997b; Muggleton 1999) are based on Inductive Logic Programming (ILP) and prune the search space by focusing only on subgraphs that are well-suited for a particular task (e.g., classification). However, a number of exact algorithms have also been developed (Dehaspe, Toivonen, and King 1998; Inokuchi, Washio, and Motoda 2000; Kuramochi and Karypis 2001; Inokuchi, Washio, Nishimura, and Motoda 2002; Ghazizadeh and Chawathe 2002; Kuramochi and Karypis 2002b; Yan and Han 2002; Borgelt and Berthold 2002) that are guaranteed to find all subgraphs that satisfy certain minimum support or other constraints. Among them, algorithms developed in the last few years (Kuramochi and Karypis 2001; Inokuchi, Washio, Nishimura, and Motoda 2002; Ghazizadeh and Chawathe 2002; Kuramochi and Karypis 2002b; Yan and Han 2002; Borgelt and Berthold 2002), have been shown to achieve reasonably good performance and scalability. The enabling factors to the computational efficiency of these recent schemes have been (1) the development of efficient candidate subgraph generation schemes that reduce the number of times the same candidate subgraph is being generated, (2) the use of efficient canonical labeling schemes to represent the various subgraphs; and (3) the use of various techniques developed by the data-mining community to reduce the number of times subgraph isomorphism computations need to be performed.

Relatively little research has been done for finding frequent subgraphs in geometric graph databases. The most notable exception is the work by Jason T. L. Wang et al., that have published a series of papers on finding geometric patterns from graph datasets (Wang, Wang, Shasha, Shapiro, Dikshitulu, Rigoutsos, and Zhang 1997; Wang and Wang 2000; Wang, Ma, Shasha, and Wu 2001; Wang, Wang, Shasha, Shapiro, Rigoutsos, and Zhang 2002). In their most recent publication (Wang, Wang, Shasha, Shapiro, Rigoutsos, and Zhang 2002), they propose an algorithm to find frequent substructures from a set of three dimensional graphs. Their approach starts with identifying blocks, or nondecomposable rigid substructures, and counts the frequency of them by geometric hashing (Wolfson and Rigoutsos 1997). By restricting the definition of a pattern to just those blocks, they do not have to perform any candidate generation. However, this approach is not complete, as it will not find arbitrary frequent geometric subgraphs. Moreover, depending on the application domain, the assumption that the frequent subgraphs will have such block-based structure may not be applicable. Recently Parthasarathy and Coatney proposed an algorithm to find substructures from a geometric graph dataset (Parthasarathy and Coatney 2002). Their approach is to represent frequent geometric subgraphs as a set of vertex pairs with their distances and to find frequent subsets made of those pairs using an Apriorilike method. Moreover, they allow approximate matching for comparing distances, which greatly improves the practicality of the algorithm.

17.2.2 FSG—Discovering Topological Patterns

Our topological frequent subgraph discovery algorithm (FSG), initially presented in Kuramochi and Karypis (2001), with subsequent improvements presented in Kuramochi and Karypis (2002b); Kuramochi and Karypis (2002c), uses a breadth-first approach to discover the lattice of frequent subgraphs. It starts by enumerating small frequent graphs consisting of one and two edges and then proceeds to find larger subgraphs by joining previously discovered smaller frequent subgraphs. The size of these subgraphs is grown by adding one-edge-at-a-time. The lattice of frequent patterns is used to prune the set of candidate patterns, and it only explicitly computes the frequency of the patterns which survived this downward closure pruning.

Despite the inherent complexity of the problem, FSG employs a number of sophisticated techniques to achieve high computational performance. It uses a canonical labeling algorithm that fully makes use of edge and vertex labels for fast processing, and various vertex invariants to reduce the complexity of determining the canonical label of a graph. These canonical labels are then used to establish the identity and total order of the frequent and candidate subgraphs, a critical step of redundant candidate elimination and downward closure testing. It uses a sophisticated scheme for candidate generation (Kuramochi and Karypis 2002c) that minimizes the number of times each candidate subgraph gets generated and also dramatically reduces the generation of subgraphs that fail the downward closure test. Finally, for determining the actual frequency of each subgraph, FSG reduces the number of subgraph isomorphism operations by using TID-lists (Dunkel and Soparkar 1999; Shenoy, Haritsa, Sundarshan, Bhalotia, Bawa, and Shah 2000) ,(Zaki 2000; Zaki and Gouda 2001) to keep track of the set of transactions that supported the frequent patterns discovered at the previous level of the lattice. For every candidate, FSG takes the intersection of TID-lists of its parents, and performs the subgraph isomorphism only on the transactions contained in the resulting TID-list.

Performance

Table 17.1 is an example to show the performance of FSG. The input datasets contain chemical compounds which are available from the Developmental

Support	Total Number of Transactions $|D|$										
σ	$|D| = 10,000$			$|D| = 20,000$			$|D| = 50,000$			$|D| = 100,000$		
[%]	t[sec]	l	#f	t[sec]	l	#f	t[sec]	l	#f	t[sec]	l	#f
5.0	24	12	989	48	12	1001	120	12	1017	255	12	1068
4.0	29	12	1528	57	12	1468	144	13	1523	311	13	1676
3.0	37	14	2599	73	13	2639	184	14	2705	392	14	2810
2.0	52	14	5096	104	14	5201	260	14	5295	561	14	5633
1.0	115	16	16811	261	17	18505	656	16	19373	1451	16	20939

Table 17.1: Runtimes in seconds for the DTP chemical compound data sets. The column "Support." shows the used minimum support (%), the column with t is the running time in seconds, the column with l shows the size of the largest frequent subgraph discovered, and the column with #f is the total number of discovered frequent patterns.

Therapeutics Program (DTP) at National Cancer Institute (NCI).[1] This set of experiments was designed to evaluate the scalability of FSG with respect to the number of input graph transactions. We created four datasets with 10,000, 20,000, 50,000 and 100,000 transactions. Each graph transaction was randomly chosen from the original dataset of 223,644 compounds. The average transaction size (the number of edges in a transaction) is 22 for all datasets.

Looking at these results we can see that FSG is able to effectively operate in datasets containing over 100,000 graph transactions, and discover all subgraphs that occur in at least 1% of the transactions in approximately 25 minutes. Moreover, with respect to the number of transactions, we can see that the runtime of FSG scales linearly. For instance, for a support of value 2%, the amount of time required for 10,000 transactions is 52 seconds, whereas the corresponding time for 100,000 transactions is 561 seconds; an increase by a factor of 10.8. Also, as the support decreases up to 1%, the amount of time required by FSG increases gradually, mirroring the increase in the number of frequent subgraphs that exist in the dataset. For instance, for 100,000 transactions, the running time for the support 1% is 2.6 times longer than that for the support of 2%, while there are 3.7 times more frequent subgraphs with 1% support.

17.2.3 gFSG—Discovering Geometric Patterns

Our geometric frequent subgraph discovery algorithm (gFSG) presented in Kuramochi and Karypis (2002a) follows a similar breadth-first approach as FSG, but it differs in a number of ways as it uses the geometric information to prune the space of frequent subgraphs and speedup a number of key operations. First, gFSG does not use canonical labels to check if two graphs are

---

[1] ftp://dtpsearch.ncifcrf.gov/jan02_2d.bin.

identical or not. Instead, it uses geometric graph isomorphisms whose time complexity is in P. Second, to reduce the amount of time spent during geometric isomorphism (which can be rather high due to various geometric transformations), gFSG uses various *graph signatures* such as the set of vertex and edge labels, the sum of the distances to the medoid vertex of the graph, and the set of angles between the edges in the graph (edge-angles), that are (or can be made to be via normalization) translation, scaling, and rotation invariant. The idea is that if two graphs are geometrically isomorphic, then their signatures should match, and thus quickly eliminate graphs that are not geometrically isomorphic. Third, a similar graph signature-based approach is employed to speedup the frequency counting phase. Instead of directly checking whether a geometric subgraph is embedded in a transaction by geometric subgraph isomorphism, it checks the set of edge-angles T_ϕ of the graph transaction with the corresponding set for the subgraph pattern P_ϕ, and performs the geometric subgraph isomorphism only when $P_\phi \subset T_\phi$. The additional advantage of this is that gFSG does not need to use TID-lists during frequency counting.

Performance

Table 17.2 shows the scalability of gFSG with respect to the number of input transactions. We used the same dataset shown in table 17.1, although this time, each vertex has its two-dimensional coordinates. There are three main observations that can be made from these results. First, gFSG scales linearly with the database size. For most values of support, the amount of time required on the database with 20,000 transactions is 15-30 times larger than the amount of time required for 1,000 transactions. Second, as with any frequent pattern discovery algorithm, as we decrease the support the runtime increases and the number of frequent patterns increases. The overall increase in the amount of time tends to follow the increase in the number of patterns, indicating that the complexity of gFSG scales well with the number of frequent patterns. Third, comparing the scale invariant with the scale variant results, we can see that the latter is faster by almost a factor of two. This is because the number of discovered patterns is usually smaller, and each pattern has fewer supporting transactions, reducing the amount of time to compute their frequency.

17.3 Classifying Chemical Compounds

Identifying potentially toxic compounds or compounds that can inhibit the active sites of viruses in the early phase of drug discovery is becoming an appealing strategy with pharmaceutical companies (Durham and Pearl 2001). However, determining the suitability of a chemical compound to a particular

Scaling	Support	Total Number of Transactions D								
		$D = 5000$			$D = 10000$			$D = 20000$		
	%	t[sec]	l	#f	t[sec]	l	#f	t[sec]	l	#f
No	3.0	32	6	177	69	6	187	109	4	143
	2.0	62	6	321	128	6	321	216	5	269
	1.0	161	8	795	423	8	874	839	7	826
	0.5	622	9	2177	1514	9	2281	2465	7	2091
	0.25	2224	10	6112	5351	9	6090	8590	10	5649
Yes	3.0	73	7	236	126	6	217	321	6	224
	2.0	124	7	404	205	7	352	522	7	359
	1.0	460	9	1189	1107	8	1295	1974	8	1019
	0.5	2108	10	3593	4621	9	3869	9952	9	3354
	0.25	8972	12	11103	17421	9	10929	41895	11	11177

Table 17.2: Running times in seconds for chemical compound data sets which are randomly chosen from the DTP dataset. The column "Support."shows the used minimum support (%), the column with t is the running time in seconds, the column with l shows the size of the largest frequent subgraph discovered, and the column with #f is the total number of discovered frequent patterns.

biological state is not a very viable solution—mainly for two reasons. First, the number of chemical compounds in the repository and those that can be generated by combinatorial chemistry is extremely large. Second, experimentally determining the suitability of a compound using bio-assays (*in vivo*) techniques is an expensive and time consuming process. For these reasons, there is a great need to develop reliable computational techniques (*in silico*), based on classification, that can quickly screen thousands of compounds and identify the compounds that display the highest levels of the desired property.

A chemical compound consists of different atoms being held together via bonds adopting a well-defined geometric configuration. Figure 17.3(a) represents the chemical compound Flucytosine from the DTP AIDS repository[2] it consists of a central benzene ring and other elements like N, O and F. There are many different ways to represent such chemical compounds. The simplest representation is the molecular formula that lists the various molecules making up the compound; the molecular formula for Flucytosine is $C_4H_4FN_3O$. A more sophisticated representation can be achieved using SMILES (Weininger 1988) that besides the atoms also represents the bonds between different atoms. The SMILES representation for Flucytosine is Nc1nc(O)ncc1F. In addition to these topological representations, the actual 3D coordinates of the various atoms can also be supplied.

The key challenges in developing classification techniques for chemical compounds stems from the fact that their properties are strongly related to their chemical structure. However, traditional machine learning techniques

---

[2]http://dtp.nci.nih.gov

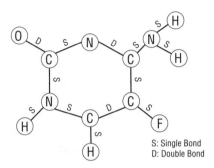

(a) NSC 103025 Flucytosine

S: Single Bond
D: Double Bond

(b) Graph Representation

Figure 17.3: Chemical and graphical representation of Flucytosine.

are suited to handle datasets represented by multidimensional vectors or sequences, and cannot handle the relational nature of the chemical structures.

17.3.1 Related Research

In recent years number of techniques have been proposed for classifying chemical compounds. These techniques can be broadly categorized into two groups. The first group consists of techniques that rely on physico-chemical properties of the compounds to predict its chemical activity. The second set of techniques discover a discriminatory set of substructures from the chemical compound dataset, these substructures are then used as features for building the classifier.

In the early 1960s, the pioneering work of Hansch, Maolney, Fujita, and Muir (1962) and Hansch, Muir, Fujita, Maloney, and Streich (1963) demonstrated that the biological activity of a chemical compound is a function of its physico-chemical properties. Most of these physico-chemical properties are derived from the structure of a chemical compound and are called quantitative structure-activity relationships (QSAR). QSARs could be as simple as the molecular weight, molecule size, or could be quite complex as linear free energy (LFE), or electronic properties requiring many parameters to compute. The discussion of different QSARs that can be used for classifying chemical compounds beyond the score of this chapter, here we will restrict ourselves to the techniques used for classification of chemical compounds once the QSAR attributes have been computed. This classification approach can be though of as representing each chemical with vector of numeric attribute values, and then learning a classifier on these numeric attributes. Historically, regression techniques (Hansch, Maolney, Fujita, and Muir 1962; Frank and Friedman 1993) have been most commonly used on these datasets. An and Wang (2001) study the performance of different classification techniques and report the best performance for decision tree classifiers. Andrea and Kalayeh (1991) study the classification problem using using a neural networks approach. It is worth noting that QSAR approach does not capture the specific structural constraints present in the chemical compound dataset and assumes that the QSAR properties will be able to discriminate among different classes, therefore the task of selecting the appropriate QSAR attributes requires significant expertise as well as a good understanding of the classification problem.

The second set of techniques attempt to capture the structural constraints present in the chemical compound datasets. Since the chemical compounds are not amenable to be represented in attribute value (propositional) format, needed for traditional machine learning algorithms, inductive logic programming (ILP) techniques were used (King, Muggleton, Lewis, and Sternberg 1992; King, Muggleton, Srinivasan, and Sternberg 1996; King, Srinivasan, and Dehaspe 2001; Sriniviasan and King 1999; Srinivasan, Kind, Muggleton, and Sternberg 1997a). For ILP-based approach each chemical compound was expressed using first order logic, a vertex and edge is represented as a predicate. The substructure discovered by the ILP algorithm is nothing but a conjunction of such predicates. One of the advantages of ILP-based approaches is that it allows the users to make use of any prior knowledge while generating the final hypothesis. Though ILP-based techniques are quite powerful they are limited in the size of substructures and the amount of dataset that they can handle (King, Srinivasan, and Dehaspe 2001).

A more heuristic base approach to discover subgraphs was taken by the SUBDUE system (Holder, Cook, and Djoko 1994b). The SUBDUE system discovers subgraphs based on the subgraph's ability to compress the original graph dataset, it then replaces all such subgraphs with a single new vertex. Though such approach cannot discover all possible subgraphs, the computational complexity is significantly reduced. For classifying chemical compounds a new heuristic is used, in this a substructure (subgraph) is selected if it displays a high confidence on the positive examples of the dataset, this approach is referred as the SUBDUE-CL (Gonzalez, Holder, and Cook 2001). Though SUBDUE can handle much larger datasets than the ILP based approaches the time required to discover discriminatory substructures is still quite large.

In 1997 and 2000 two competitions to predict the toxicity of a chemical compounds were arranged (Srinivasan, King, Muggleton, and Sternberg 1997c; Christoph, King, Kramer, and Srinivasan 2001). A dataset consisting of chemical compounds with known toxicity was released and the competitors were required to build classification model on this dataset. At a later date a set of compounds were released and the competitors were required to predict the toxicity of these compounds. The evaluation of the prediction results suggests that the task of correctly classifying a chemical compound is still quite challenging and significant advances are required before such computational techniques can be used extensively (Srinivasan, King, Muggleton, and Sternberg 1997c).

17.3.2 Feature-Based Classification Methodology

The overall outline of our approach is shown in figure 17.4. Initially, each of the chemical compound is represented using a graph. The vertices of these graphs correspond to the various atoms, and the edges correspond to the bonds between the atoms. Each one of the vertices and edges has a label associated with it. The labels on the vertices correspond to the type of atoms, and the labels on the edges correspond to the type of bond. The graph representation of Flucytosine is shown in figure 17.3(b). Then, FSG (or gFSG) is used to mine these graphs and find all subgraphs that occur in a nontrivial fraction of the compounds. Each of these subgraphs then becomes a candidate feature, and various feature selection algorithms are used to obtain a smaller set of discriminatory and nonredundant features. The remaining subgraphs are then used to create a feature space such that each of the selected feature corresponds to a dimension, and each compound is represented as a boolean vector based on the particular set of features (i.e., subgraphs) that it contains. Finally, these feature vector representation of the chemical compounds are supplied into a traditional classifier to learn the appropriate classification model. In our experiments, we performed the actual classification using the SVM classifier (Vapnik 1998).

Our approach shares some of the characteristics with earlier approaches for chemical compound classification based on substructure discovery (Wang, Wang, Shasha, Shapiro, Dikshitulu, Rigoutsos, and Zhang 1997), (An and Wang 2001), but it has a number of inherent advantages. First, unlike previous approaches that used restricted definitions of what constitutes a substructure (e.g., induced subgraphs (Inokuchi, Washio, and Motoda 2000), or blocks (Wang, Wang, Shasha, Shapiro, Dikshitulu, Rigoutsos, and Zhang 1997), we use the most generic model possible that of connected subgraphs. Moreover,

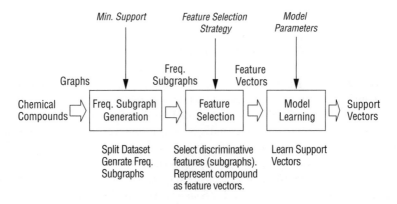

Figure 17.4: Graph classification flowchart.

unlike the approaches based on approximate matching (Chittimoori, Holder, and Cook 1999), the structure discovery algorithm that we use is guaranteed to find all subgraphs that satisfy the user-supplied minimum support constraint. Consequently, our approach can be used to mine chemical compounds with very little domain knowledge. Second, our approach decouples the processes of feature discovery from the actual classification process, and can be used with any existing (and future developed) classification algorithm. Third, since the classifier is built on the transformed feature-space, the above approach can easily incorporate any additional nongraphical features that may be available for the compounds such as molecular weight, surface area, etc., by simply adding them as additional dimensions in the feature-space.

17.3.3   Experimental Evaluation

We experimentally evaluated our approach for classifying chemical compounds on two different datasets: aids and anthrax.

AIDS dataset: This dataset is obtained from the National Cancer Institute's DTP AIDS antiviral screen program(Kramer, De Raedt, and Helma 2001). [3] Each compound in the dataset is evaluated for evidence of anti-HIV activity. The screen utilizes a soluble formazan assay to measure protection of human CEM cells from HIV-1 infection (Weislow, Kiser Fine, Bader, Shoemaker, and Boyd 1989). Compounds able to provide at least 50% protection to the CEM cells were re-tested. Compounds that provided at least 50% protection on retest were listed as *moderately active* (CM, confirmed moderately active). Compounds that reproducibly provided 100% protection were listed

---

[3]http://dtp.nci.nih.gov/docs/aids/aids_data.html.

as *confirmed active* (CA). Compounds neither active nor moderately active were listed as *confirmed inactive* (CI). We have formulated three classification problems on this dataset, in the first problem we consider only confirmed active (CA) and moderately active (CM) compounds and then build a classifier to separate these two compounds; this problem is referred as *CA/CM*. For the second problem we combine moderately active (CM) and confirmed active (CA) compounds to form one set of active compounds, we then build a classifier to separate these active and confirmed inactive compounds; this problem is referred as *(CA+CM)/CI*. The dataset for the third classification problem contains only the compounds that are confirmed active (CA) and confirmed inactive (CI), this classification problem is referred as (CA/CI). The dataset contains total of 42,389 compounds out of which 40,891 are confirmed inactive (CI), 822 are confirmed active and 1,076 are moderately active. The average number of vertices in this dataset is 46, and the average number of edges is 47.

Anthrax dataset: This dataset was obtained from the Center of Computational Drug Discovery's anthrax project at the University of Oxford (Richards 2002). The goal of this project was to discover small molecules that would bind with the heptameric protective antigen (PA) component of the anthrax toxin, and prevent it from spreading its toxic effects. A library of small sized chemical compounds was screened to identify a set of chemical compounds that could bind with the anthrax toxin. The screening was done by computing the binding free energy for each compound using numerical simulations. The screen identified a set of 12,376 compounds that could potentially bind to the anthrax toxin and a set of 22,460 compounds that were unlikely to bind to the chemical compound. The average number of vertices in this dataset is 25 and the average number of edges is also 25. The classification problem for this dataset was given a chemical compound classify it in to one of these two classes, i.e, will the compound bind the anthrax toxin or not.

Evaluation Methodology

Since the classification problem for both datasets is cost sensitive i.e., the misclassification cost for each class label could be different. As a result, the traditional *accuracy* metric is not sufficiently broad to provide a complete assessment of a classifier. For this reason, to get a better understanding of the classifier's performance for different cost settings we plot the ROC curve (Provost and Fawcett 2001) for each classifier. ROC curve plots the false positive rate (X axis) versus the true positive rate (Y axis) of a classier; it displays the performance of the classifier regardless of class distribution or error cost. Two classifiers are compared by comparing their ROC curves, if the ROC curve of one classifier completely subsumes the other ROC curve, then that classifier

	Aids			Anthrax
	CA/CM	(CA+CM)/CI	CA/CI	
QSAR	0.642	0.586	0.669	0.521
FSG	0.807	0.765	0.844	0.816
gFSG	0.812	0.784	0.896	0.825
FSG+gFSG	0.813	0.786	0.864	0.823
FSG+gFSG+QSAR	0.812	0.786	0.860	0.823
SUBDUE-CL	0.726	0.500	0.482	0.715

Table 17.3: Results on the different classification problems. Each entry corresponds to the area under the ROC curve that was obtained by our classification framework using the particular set of features.

has superior performance for any cost model of the problem. Another qualitative way to compare the performance is to compare the area under the ROC curve for each classifier. The area under the ROC curve will be the measure that we will use in our experiments, since due to space limitations it is infeasible to plot ROC curves for all the classification results that we present.

Results

Table 17.3 displays the results obtained using our classification methodology for six sets of features on the two datasets (four classification problems). Specifically, we evaluated features obtained from various QSAR parameters, FSG, gFSG, and different combinations of the three. In addition, we also evaluated the features obtained from the SUBDUE-CL algorithm that used the class information to guide/focus the discovery of the frequent subgraphs (Gonzalez, Holder, and Cook 2001).

From table 17.3 we can infer that the classification performance achieved by the schemes that use subgraph features (FSG, gFSG, SUBDUE-CL), significantly outperform the QSAR features. Comparing the performance achieved using the features obtained by FSG and gFSG we observe that gFSG significantly outperforms FSG on the CA/CI classification problem, whereas for the remaining problems the performance of gFSG is marginally better. Also, combining different sets of features gives no significant improvement over directly using the subgraph features. Finally, the results show that the classifiers that are based on the features of FSG and gFSG substantially outperform the classifier that uses the features discovered by SUBDUE-CL—clearly illustrating that there is a definite advantage in using all possible frequent subgraphs during classification.

17.4   Conclusion and Directions for Future Research

Graphs provide a powerful new representation for modeling diverse scientific datasets. However the flexibility offered by this representation increases the computational complexity of mining such datasets. In this chapter we presented two techniques for finding patterns in graph databases and presented a framework that uses these patterns to build graph-based classifiers. These results illustrate both the computational feasibility of graph-mining as well as its potential as an effective tools for analyzing and understanding scientific datasets.

However, there are a number of problems that still need to be addressed, creating exciting areas for further research. For example, despite the recent research that led to the development of efficient frequent subgraph discovery algorithms, there are a number of open issues associated with developing similar computationally efficient and scalable algorithms that find approximate subgraphs or subgraphs that occur many times within one single large graph. These problems pose their own unique challenges because depending on the precise problem definition they can lead to instances that are either nondownward close or their solution will require to solve other NP-complete problems.

Similarly, new graph-based classification algorithms need to be developed that incorporate information about the position within the structures that each of the pattern occurs and their relative location. Within the context of classifying chemical compounds, the overall performance can be improved by developing methods that take into account the potentially multiple 3D conformations of each compound. Moreover, even though the substructure-based approach significantly outperforms those based on QSAR, our analysis showed that there is a significant difference as to which compounds are correctly classified by these two approaches, suggesting that better results can be potentially obtained by combining them.

In addition, graph datasets provide a number of challenges as well as opportunities in developing scalable algorithms for other data-mining tasks such as clustering, deviation detection, and trend-analysis, especially for dynamic graphs. Finally, the problem of graph mining needs to be extended from graphs to hypergraphs as the latter provide an effective and sparse mechanism by which to capture set relations between entities.

Michihiro Kuramochi is a graduate student in computer science at University of Minnesota. He can be reached at kuram@cs.umn.edu.

Mukund Deshpande is a graduate student in computer science at the University of Minnesota, Minneapolis.

George Karypis is an assistant professor in the Department of Computer Science and Engineering at the University of Minnesota, Twin Cities Campus.

Chapter 18

Challenges in Environmental Data Warehousing and Mining

Nabil R. Adam, Vijayalakshmi Atluri,
Dihua Guo, and Songmei Yu

In the area of environmental and earth sciences, we are concerned with the collection, assimilation, cataloging and dissemination or retrieval of a vast array of environmental data. Environmental and Earth science computer systems receive their input from various types of devices, such as satellite imagery of different resolutions captured by different sensors, aerial photos, radar and other monitoring networks. Furthermore, the input to the environmental databases also includes models of the topography and spatial attributes of the landscape such as roads, rivers, parcels, schools, zip code areas, city streets and administrative boundaries (all exist in topographic maps), census information that describes the socio-economic and health characteristics of the population, processed digital terrain models into a new information product in the form of three-dimensional visualizations of digital terrain models projected as video "fly-bys," and finally information transmitted (almost in real-time) from ground monitoring stations.

As an example, at the Meadowlands Environment Research Institute (MERI), which is a collaboration between the New Jersey Meadowlands Commission and Rutgers CIMIC, we have developed a "digital meadowlands," where a wide variety of environmental data is collected, processed, analyzed and disseminated. The primary goal of MERI is to conduct and sponsor research to support the restoration, preservation and improvement of the ecological and human health and welfare in the Meadowlands district, an estuarine system in northeastern New Jersey. To accomplish this, it conducts monitoring and assessment throughout the district, including ad-hoc biologic, sediment and water studies, quarterly water quality monitoring, and an expanding continuous, automated water, air and weather monitoring network, with data available via the WWW in near real-time. The research draws expertise from biologists, ecologists, geologists, environmental scientists, hydrological modelers, remote sensing and geographic information systems experts, as well as computer scientists. The scientific content of these studies need to be disseminated to the scientific community and the various government agencies including local municipalities, and have to be transformed into educational exhibits to be delivered to local schools.

At MERI, we download 6-9 AVHRR images from NOAA satellites (NOAA12, NOAA14, and NOAA15) daily, 2–3 from each satellite. The AVHRR images have 5 bands and the resolution is 1km. We also have LANDSAT images with 7 bands, whose resolution is 30-meter. 14-bands ASTER images for the interest district are available every day to every other day. The ASTER images consist of three visible and Infrared bands with 15-meter resolution, six short wave infrared bands with 30-meter resolution and five thermal infrared bands with 90-meter resolution. We also receive the 36-band MODIS data, available every day or every other day, whose spatial resolutions range from 250m to 1000m. The AISA sensor image datasets that we collect cover the portions of the USGS 7.5' quadrangles, including Weehawken, Jersey City, Elizabeth and Orange of New Jersey, and have 2.5m resolution with 34 bands. We also plan to collect images from the RADARSAT, IKONOS and QUICKBIRD sensors. The RADARSET sensor three-meter resolution data will be the highest resolution commercially available SAR data. The IKONOS sensor, launched by Space Imaging, collects 1m resolution panchromatic images and 4m resolution 4 bands multispectral images; while the QUICKBIRD sensor, from DigitalGlobe, offers 70-centimeter panchromatic and 2.8-meter 4 bands multispectral images. Figure 18.1 depicts the input sources and the output generated from the digital meadowlands.

Traditional database technology provides some analysis capabilities, where a user can query, browse and retrieve spatial and nonspatial environmental data with queries specified by sensor type, geographical location, time of acquisition, and some image features. However, we lack effective methods for exploiting and analyzing the heterogeneous spatial datasets for knowledge discovery,

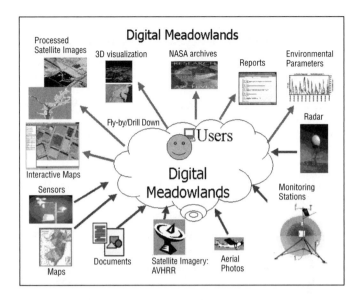

Figure 18.1: Input and output environmental data at Digital Meadowlands.

hypothesis testing and modeling. Some examples of the challenges encountered at MERI are discussed below (Barrett 2002).

Motivating Examples

One of the major concerns in the Meadowlands is to monitor changes in the wetlands that could affect the ecological system. This in turn requires identifying natural disturbance affecting wetland vegetation. Such a disturbance could be triggered by fire, pathogen infestation or wilting caused by drought. To distinguish the changes caused by these different events we need a series of satellite images over time (at least a few years), calculated soil and vegetation indices for these images, digital elevation models, series of precipitation records for during this time interval, and zoning designation for the observed area. For instance, from the vegetation and soil indices, we may notice that some areas have sudden drops in the vegetation index (NDVI) in a year, say 1998. At the same time the soil index may be classified to bare mineral soil. From these two, we can learn that something unusual may have happened in that region during 1998. However, this information is not sufficient to conclude whether this unusual event is due to a fire, a pathogen infestation, a severe wilt or a flood? We can refer to the digital elevation models and might discard the possibility of flood, if the elevation of that particular area is above the sea level. By referring to the precipitation record, we can see if there is a long severe drought, which can cause the fast propagation of some insects, or not. As can be seen, data sets have to be selectively chosen and analyzed to make intelligent conclusions.

Observing the behavior of birds and finding the bird-resting patterns along the eastern seaboard migration corridor is another measure of the ecological health, and therefore is of concern to MERI as well. We have the extent of ecosystems that support invertebrates along the migration corridor and the availability of invertebrates in water and sediments through the migrating period. As related to the availability of food at each rest stop and the changes of the food availability, it is possible for observers to deduct the number of birds and birds based on the trends found using the historical records. It is also feasible to detect abnormal bird populations (low or high), which are not explained by the availability of food at specific resting stops.

Other questions MERI wants to probe include determining and predicting the marsh sediment movement and accumulation according to global and local climate models, and affect of urbanization on the Meadowlands. The storm intensity/frequency and the sea level rise, and increased human impacts (e.g. development, nonpoint source pollution, and dredge) have been identified as affecting coastal wetlands related to climate variability and change. Pertaining to the Meadowlands, people would want to know more about ecosystems' changes led by the change of climate and human activities. Other questions include What will be the water and sediment discharge from the Hackensack and Passaic rivers into the Newark? What will be the sea level off the Atlantic coast in response to climate changes? Will the more urban pavements and increasing surface albedo *(reflection of the sun light from the earth/ice/water surface)* cause more storm runoff and less ground water recharge? To answer these questions, data need to be collected from a variety of aspects, including climate, river, coast, and estuarine data.

There are many interesting phenomena that deserve more investigation in every aspect of environmental research. While at MERI, we focus on a small geographical region and a more specific set of issues, in this chapter, we identify and provide motivation for data mining and warehousing research using more general environmental examples.

For example, to investigate the associations between changes in forest cover and illegal exploitation of protected tropical forest would help people find and manage the major factors causing deforestation. With the satellite images/maps, it is possible to calculate deforestation rates using NDVI indices. Also, based on the available data on truck movement, records on ship movements from local ports, data on migrant worker camps, we might be able to relate deforestation rate to new road construction, truck/ship traffic in areas where the topography and local ecosystems support exotic tropical trees.

The developments in data collection and data processing technologies, for the first time, provide opportunities for identifying possible trends, thereby enabling preventing of the future potential problems or try to arrive at a feasible solution. Each of the queries listed above requires a careful analysis by a domain expert. Therefore, it is essential to provide users who typically are policy makers, general public or even students that do not necessarily posses the domain expertise, with analysis tools to help them obtain useful information quickly and accurately. Such analysis tools require knowledge discovery from vast array of heterogeneous multi dimensional datasets. Discovering knowledge from environmental data has its own unique challenges, out of which, those in the areas of data warehousing and mining are outlined in this chapter. Although there are some efforts on spatial data warehouse and spatial data mining, it is still in its infancy (Koperski, Adhikary, and Han 1996; Miller and Han 2001).

18.1 Challenges in Data Warehousing

An environmental data warehouse (EDW) is a typical example of spatial data warehouse, which needs to provide, among others, flexible image extraction functionalities, such as hyper-spectral channel extraction, overlaying, and ad-hoc thematic coloring (Bosques, Rodriguez, Rondon, and Vasquez 1997). Such data warehouses are intended to serve the evaluation and formulation of environmental policies by enabling users, including management and researchers to query various critical parameters such as ambient air and water quality and visualize the results in a graphical form. In addition to serving decision makers and researchers, these systems are intended to also serve the citizens, thus, enabling any citizen of any given district or a state to look at his/her county, community, home and be able to obtain relevant information on such issues as environment, health, and infrastructure, among others. They should also facilitate effective knowledge discovery in a manner tailored to the changing needs and abilities of users, both intellectual and technological.

When compared to a traditional data warehouse, an EDW poses many challenging requirements with respect to the design of appropriate spatial data model, and the execution of spatial on-line analytical processing (OLAP) along the spatial dimension hierarchies. In the following, we elaborate these challenges and suggest some new OLAP operators that need to be exploited to accommodate the complex spatial queries.

18.1.1 Data Modeling Challenges

One of the challenges in data modeling for an EDW is the multidimensional nature of each dimension itself. In a traditional data warehouse the various dimensions contributing to the warehouse data are simple in nature, each having different attributes. For example, sales amount, which is a numeric measure with several dimensions including region, time and product. On the other hand, the different dimensions in a spatial data warehouse comprise of different types of data, each of which is multidimensional. The various raster images such as satellite downloads, images generated from these satellite images describing various parameters including land-use, water, temperature have multiple dimensions including the geographic extent and coordinates of the image, the time and date of its capture, and resolution, among others. Other such examples include aerial photographs. The regional maps represented as vector data also have a temporal dimension as they change over time. The streaming data collected from various sensors placed at different geographic locations that sense temperature, air quality, atmospheric pressure, water quality, dissolved oxygen, mineral contents, salinity, again have both spatial and temporal dimensions. Other dimensions include demographic data, census data, traffic patterns, and many such as these.

Data models such as the star schema, fact constellation schema, snowflake schema or the multidimensional model can be used to represent the traditional data warehouse. Since these models are not adequate to represent the different dimensions in a spatial data warehouse that comprise of different types of data, where each of which is multidimensional in nature, in Adam, Atluri, Yu, and Yesha (2002), a *cascaded star model* has been proposed. Under the cascaded star model, each multidimensional attribute in the dimension table can be implemented, in which it explicitly provides support for attribute hierarchies, where the single fact table is joined with several dimension tables, and each dimension table is a star schema by itself.

Although, at a first glance, the cascaded star model may appear similar to a snowflake schema, it differs in that in the snowflake model, each dimension is normalized, whereas in the cascaded star model each dimension is multidimensional. For example, the fact table may comprise of various dimensions of the spatial data, which include land-use, temperature, water and vector maps. Each of these dimensions in turn is multidimensional, represented as a star. For example, the land-use dimension may comprise of a fact table of its own with dimensions time, spatial and attributes, where the time dimension can be comprised of attributes year, date and time of capture of the image; the spatial dimension can be comprised of the x, y coordinates of the lower left hand and corner and the upper right hand corner of the region covered by the image, and the resolution; the attributes dimension can be comprised of the amount of vegetation, developed, barren, forested upland, etc., in the image. Similar to land-use, themes and water dimensions can also be multidimensional in nature.

Note that, the cascaded dimension structures are different from the spatial dimension with multiple hierarchies proposed by Papadias, Tao, Kalnis, and Zhang (2001). Specifically, a cascaded dimension means each dimension itself is multidimensional, i.e., each dimension has its own attributes or subdimensions, and the dimension and its subdimensions have certain hierarchy structures for performing aggregated operations. On the other hand, a single spatial dimension may have multiple hierarchies based on multiple grouping standards. For example, a simple dimension called "city roads" may have a grouping based on the areas of responsibility of each police station, and another grouping based on the areas covered by each fire station, but do not have multidimensional feature for this simple dimension. We could integrate the multiple hierarchy structure into our proposed cascaded dimension structures if there is a need for multiple groupings of certain single dimensions.

18.1.2 Spatial OLAP Challenges

The second challenge is due to the nature of the queries posed to the environmental data warehouses. Generally speaking, these queries involve complex spatial aggregation processes in accessing multiple dimensions, each of which in itself is multidimensional. We illustrate with two examples:

Example 1: A user may want to look at the changes in the vegetation pattern over a certain region during the past 10 years, and see their effects on the regional maps over that time period. This involves layering the images representing the vegetation patterns with those of the maps whose time intervals of validity overlap, and then traverse along this temporal dimension with the overlaid image. In the traditional data warehouse sense, this amount to first constructing two data cubes along the time dimensions for each of the vegetation images and maps, and then fusing these two cubes into one. One may envision fusing of multiple cubes. For example, if the user also wants to observe the changes in the surface water, population, etc., due the changes in the vegetation pattern over the years, fusion of such multiple cubes is needed.

Example 2: Another user may want to simulate a fly-by over a certain region starting with a specific point and elevation, and traverse the region on a specific path with reducing elevation levels at a certain speed, and reaching a destination, effectively traversing a 3-dimensional trajectory. This query involves retrieving images that span adjacent regions that overlap the spatial trajectory, but with increasing resolution levels to simulate the effect of reduced elevation level. Another important aspect of satisfying such a query additionally requires the additional requirements of controlling the speed at which they are displayed to match the desired velocity of the fly-by.

We identify two basic research issues involved in the execution of the spatial OLAP in an EDW: spatial aggregation operations and spatial dimension hierarchies. The following is a brief discussion of each.

Spatial Aggregation Operations

There is a need for certain spatial operators that enable us to perform spatial aggregation, such as "overlay" in the fly-by example above. Therefore, the traditional aggregate functions such as "sum" are not applicable in this context, and we need to find new ways to create aggregated spatial views in a hierarchical way utilizing existing spatial operators.

In traditional data warehouses, one can simply create hierarchical views using traditional aggregate functions such as distributive functions (count, sum, average), algebraic functions (standard_deviations), and holistic functions (median). For example, one can first aggregate the sales amount in a given day, then aggregate on a month using the result of the first step, then aggregate on a year using the result of the second step, and so on. The same process can apply to the region (city-state-country) dimension. In this way, we can create aggregate views hierarchically, and users can roll-up or drill-down to view different aggregation results. Here we assume the aggregation function being "sum." We need to apply a similar process to extend it to the case of spatial operators thus, being able to create spatial hierarchical views for query processing. Several questions arise in this regard: Can we use the preoverlaid images to overlay another image, or can we use preunion result of geometries to union more geometries? Does this apply to all spatial operators or only a subset, if so, what are the common attributes of these operators?

There exists considerable research on efficient image operation techniques such as spatial join, spatial union and intersect (Mamoulis and Papdias 2001; Patel 2000; Open GIS Consortium 1998). How such operations would work in a spatial data warehouse in the context of creating hierarchical spatial aggregation still needs further investigation. Moreover, there are quite a number of spatial operations dealing with a variety of spatial analyses (e.g., map overlay and buffer) using spatial operators. As we know, spatial operators are used to capture all the relevant geometric properties of objects embedded in the physical space and the relations between them, as well as perform spatial analysis. Open GIS categorizes the spatial operators based on the applied primitive geometric data types (points, lines, and regions), or derived data types (e.g. networks). Although spatial operators form the foundation for the spatial aggregate functions, they alone, however, cannot create spatial views in a hierarchical way. Using the motivating example above (example 2), we have a spatial analysis operator named "Overlay," which takes two given geometries and returns the overlaying result specified on some conditions such as coordinating systems. We may use this operator to overlay population and vegetation maps during the spatial measure aggregation process, however, as noted above, this operator alone cannot capture the essence of the entire aggregation process in terms of N-dimensional cube computations. We have to first operate within a small cube, i.e., on a subcube of vegetation, traverse the time dimension to get the changing vegetation patterns, then expand to the bigger cube to traverse along this subcube to get the changing population distributions, and finally overlay the two maps to see the impact of vegetation on population. We may overlay more maps to see the interactive influences among several factors such as surface water, soil, or oil distribution. This process implies an aggregate function F in which there exists a function G such that the value of F for an N-dimensional cube can be computed by applying G to the value of F for M dimensional subcubes, which means this operation aggregates the computed regions of the subset, then computes the final result by using the result from the subset. We cannot use only a spatial binary operation to describe this process, and we need to develop a new set of spatial aggregation functions based on spatial operators to create hierarchical views for query processing in a spatial data warehouse.

To our knowledge, as of to date there is no published work in this area. There is substantial work on image processing techniques dealing with spatial operations, but we are more interested in how to utilize spatial operators to perform aggregation functions in a spatial data warehouse, i.e., how to construct spatial views in a hierarchical way to process the queries in a spatial data warehouse.

Spatial Dimension Hierarchies

Essentially, all of the OLAP operations are processes on dimension hierarchies, which allow data to be handled at varying levels of abstraction and provide users flexibility to view data from different perspectives. A number of OLAP data cube operations exist to facilitate this process, e.g., roll-up, drill-down, slice-and-dice, and pivot, and normally they are used in a single star schema. Hierarchy is fundamental to data warehouse and OLAP environment. In a traditional data warehouse, the dimension hierarchies are obvious and can be easily constructed. They are also static and preknown and thus preset in advance. We normally do aggregation on these hierarchies by different group-bys, or just as simple as CUBE to derive different levels of aggregations. For instance, various types of products dimension for which we want aggregated statistical information, or time dimension where at the finer granularity is date are grouped by day so that users can ask queries involving grouping by week, month and year. In order to accelerate such queries, all or some of these results can be precalculated and materialized. Extending this to the spatial domain, we could have, for example, preaggregated results for specific regions of interest, e.g., cities, states, countries and so on.

The positions and the ranges of spatial query windows usually do not conform to predefined hierarchies such as city-state-country. Moreover, in some spatial cases, these hierarchies are often not known in advance. A typical example is the coordinates dimension. Users may issue an ad-hoc query regarding the vegetation pattern in a specific region of interest, which may cross several preset coordinates-based query windows depending on their interests. The problem is that the positions and the ranges of spatial query windows usually do not conform to predefined hierarchies, and are not known at the design time. Furthermore, in some applications, the spatial dimensions may be volatile, for example, the city boundary may evolve as time goes by due to the administrative policies. Hence this dynamic behavior calls for the complicated spatiotemporal combined dimension hierarchy structures (Papadias, Tao, Kalnis, and Zhang 2002).

Numerous indexes have been proposed for indexing spatial databases. The most popular being the R-tree and the R*-tree. Historical R-tree (HR-tree) (Nascimento 1998) was developed to index dynamic data at different time stamps However, all of these techniques were not constructed for use in a data warehouse, i.e., they are not well suited for hierarchical aggregation. For the purpose of data warehouses, we need to have a hierarchical structure to store aggregated views at different levels. Recently, Papadias, Tao, Kalnis, and Zhang (2001) proposed aggregate R-trees (aR-trees) which augment the tree nodes with summarized data about the subbranch under them in order to answer aggregated queries. By traversing the index, a rough approximation is obtained from the values at the higher levels, which is progressively refined as the search continues towards the leaves. They have also studied the spatial-temporal combination structure for a spatial dimension by extending R-tree and B-tree in an aggregated way (Papadias, Tao, Kalnis, and Zhang 2001), (Papadias, Tao, Kalnis, and Zhang 2002). However, these approaches focus only on simple aggregate functions such as "sum" or "count." In a spatial data warehouse, we are concerned with more complex situations where the aggregation process may involve complicated spatial operations and the corresponding indexing structures must be able to handle this with associated query mechanism. Unfortunately, none of the above structures can meet these requirements. In summary, all traditional techniques to build dimension hierarchy for a data warehouse have one of three basic limitations when applied directly to spatial data warehouse: (1) no support for ad-hoc hierarchies, unknown at the design time (2) lack of spatiotemporal indexing methods, therefore limited provision for dimension versioning and volatile regions, and (3) no capability to store and handle complex spatial aggregate results and operations.

Aggregation Operator

A crucial aspect of OLAP is the ability to support highly efficient cube computations since we model data in a multidimensional way in a data warehouse. In

SQL terms, we have used the well-known CUBE operation to define and compute aggregates over all subsets of the dimensions specified in the operation. However, CUBE is not well suited for our case since it is working only with a single star schema and cannot handle aggregates across multilevels within one dimension. In the motivating example 1, we have to first CUBE on time intervals to see changes of population maps, then CUBE again on aggregated population changes to see corresponding changes of vegetation patterns, hence we have to CUBE twice and cannot express the user's query within one statement. If a spatial dimension turns out to be more than two-level multidimensional, more CUBEs will have to be invoked. Thus, it is not an efficient processing technique. One need to have efficient operators to execute certain OLAP operations in a spatial data warehouse, such as the CUBE operator for a traditional warehouse, which can represent the nature of the spatial data in a cascaded star model while doing spatial aggregations.

Recently, Map Cube, a visualization tool for analyzing data in a spatial data warehouse was proposed (Han and Kamber 2001), which organizes the album of generated maps using the given aggregation hierarchy to support browsing via roll-up, drill-down, and other operators on aggregation hierarchies. However, Map Cube has been developed for a single star model with given dimension hierarchies, which cannot handle either ad-hoc hierarchy structures or a spatial dimension with cascaded star features. Therefore, a new operator needs to be developed, which in general is an aggregate operator based on conventional data cube operator but extended for the spatial domains where each dimension is multidimensional by itself, and it may include either preset hierarchy structures or ad-hoc hierarchies. It should allow users to aggregate either spatial or nonspatial measures across multiple levels of each dimension within one SQL-like statement and generalize the histograms, cross-tabulation, roll-up, drill-down, and subtotal constructs upon users' group-by interests. In the most simple case, if we assume the cascaded star model is on only two levels, the proposed new operator would be $N * M$ (N dimensions with each dimension has M subdimensions) dimensional generalization of complex aggregate functions.

18.1.3 Implementation Challenges

The most significant challenge faced when building an EDW is the support for efficient storage and retrieval of image data. Databases, typically, do not offer the same level of support on large images, e.g., raster data. Usually image files are copied into database byte streams called BLOBs (binary large objects), which have no associated semantics (pixel type, dimension, extent). Consequently, no semantically adequate query support is possible, such as "retrieve the region bounded by the (closed) polygon P and give the percentage of vegetation." (This is one of the core reasons why databases are not used for earth observation data today. Instead, file-based solutions prevail, or a combination of databases (for metadata) and files (for raster data).

Han, Altman, Kumar, Mannila, and Pregibon (2002) and Han and Kamber (2000) have proposed spatial data cube construction based on approximation and selective precomputation spatial OLAP operations, such as merging of a number of spatially connected regions. The precomputation involves spatial region merge, spatial map overlay, spatial join, and intersection between lines and regions. The Microsoft TerraServer (Barclay and Slutz 2000) stores aerial, satellite, and topographic images of the earth in a database available via the Internet, where users are provided with intuitive spatial and text interfaces to the data. Basically terabytes of "internet unfriendly" geospatial images are scrubbed and edited into hundreds of millions of "internet friendly" image tiles and loaded into a data warehouse. Users can search the data warehouse by coordinates and place names, and can easily view the images with different resolutions by simply clicking on it. The application logic responds to the HTTP requests and interacts with the back end database to fetch the results. The database is an SQL server 7.0 RDBMS containing all images and meta-data of images that are preprocessed and stored, for example, all levels of the image pyramid (7 is maximum) are precomputed and stored. However, this system does not provide powerful and comprehensive image preprocessing tools such as spatial OLAP for advanced spatial data analysis. Moreover, the RDBMS integration with image repository has inherent problems, as SQL server 7 stores imagery in JPEG or GIF format which does not have much flexibility in handling spatial data. Other commercial products include ESRI ArcSDE, which is an application server for RDBMS to manage data with spatial attributes including maps. Through standard SQL query engine, it allows users to insert, retrieve and manipulate images. However, the manipulation is at the coverage level (such as trimming, zoom in, zoom out, etc), but not at the pixel level. Pixel level queries, such as "The average NDVI for location x/y" and "The maximum NDVI at time T within location $(x0, y0), (x1, y1)$" that can be supported by RasDaMan (Baumann 2001; Baumann and Widmann 1997). RasDaMan is the outcome of a European basic research project extending standard SQL (RasQL) with multidimensional image processing expressions. Currently, we have adopted RasDaMan for implementing the image database at Rutgers CIMIC. Both the above queries can be expressed in RasQL as follows:

select avg_cells(ndvi[x, y, *:*])   from ndvi

select max_cells(ndvi[x0:x1, y0:y1, T])   from landsat

A more complex query, for example, is "NDVI from landsat for date D, region R (bounded by (x0, y0)/(x1, y1)), threshold at 65%" can be expressed in RasQL as:

select abs((landsat.near_infrared -landsat.red) / (landsat.near-infrared +
landsat.red)) [x0:x1, y0:y1, D] > .65 from landsat.

The query result is a Boolean matrix indicating for every pixel whether the threshold is exceeded or not. However, none of the above work provides the necessary primitives for the specification and execution of OALP queries for the cascaded star such as roll-up, drill-down, slicing, dicing, pivoting, and zoom-in, zoom-out, and aggregation of views.

Furthermore, an additional related challenge is rendering the query output in an EDW. This part is mainly determined by users' requirements since most of the queries are decision-support type of queries that are more complex than OLTP queries and make extensive use of aggregation and other OLAP operations. In addition, most users need some specific visualization results such as fly-by over a certain region starting with a specific point and elevation and traversing the region on a specific path with reducing elevation levels at a certain speed, and reaching a destination—effectively traversing a 3-dimensional trajectory. Therefore, representing the spatial output in a visualized and dynamic way is a complex process which is different from query output in a traditional data warehouse.

18.2 Environmental Data Warehousing and Mining

At this point, it is important to recognize that, one of the distinguishing features in building certain views in an EDW, when compared to those of a traditional data warehouses, is that they require data mining. For example, consider a query: "identify a natural disturbance affecting wetland vegetation such as fire, pathogen infestation or wilting by drought in New Jersey meadowlands." Several steps are involved in processing this query: first, a time series of satellite images for a few years need to be gathered and stored in EDW; second, soil and vegetation indices for these images need to be computed and stored; third, the digital elevation models (DEM) of meadowlands region, precipitation record for time series and zoning designation for area being observed have to brought together and stored; fourth, sudden drop in the vegetation index (NDVI) in areas where NDVI has been consistently high through time to be identified; fifth, areas where suddenly the soil index is high due to the exposure of bare mineral soil must be determined, and finally combine high soil index with low NDVI and precipitation record to reflect the occurrence of vegetation disturbance. This typical process makes building an EDW interleaved with data mining procedures such as outlier detection, classification and characterization, and the results of these procedures must be materialized and stored back in the data warehouses for further usage. On the other hand, construction of views in traditional data warehouses does not require data mining. Basically this interleaved process forms the backbone of decision support systems for complex data analysis and decision making procedures.

18.3 Challenges in Data Mining

Environmental data mining encompasses mining both spatial and nonspatial data. Although spatial data mining attracted the attention of a number of researchers (see for example Miller and Han 2001; Roddick, Hornsby, and Spiliopoulou 2001; Koperski, Adhikary, and Han 1996; Koperski and Han 1995; Shekhar, Chawla, Ravada, Fetterer, Liu, and tien Lu 1999; Shekhar and Huang 2001; and Shekhar, Lu, and Zhang 2001), it is due to the unique characteristics of spatial data that many challenges are yet to be addressed. We start by first presenting a brief discussion of some of the challenges with respect to mining environmental data in general. This is followed by a discussion of some of the challenges faced when applying specific data mining techniques to spatial data.

18.3.1 Mining Environmental Data

The unique characteristics of environmental data, including the large data size and the complexity of the spatial data pose unique challenges with respect to data mining. Below is a brief discussion of some of these challenges.

Diverse Data Format

The challenge here lies in converting the diverse datasets from various sources that are represented in different formats, into proper representation that data mining algorithms can deal with. As we know, traditional data mining techniques manipulate categorical and numeric data stored in relational databases. On the other hand, the inputs to environmental data mining algorithm includes satellite imagery, census data, reports, maps, etc., with heterogeneous data types including vector, raster, and multimedia data. Data mining techniques cannot be applied directly to such a collection of data; preprocessing is necessary. For example, suppose we need to discover the association between the NDVI and precipitation, we would not directly mine the NDVI maps at pixel level. Instead, we would rather divide the raster NDVI maps into small regions, and mine the association between the regions and the precipitation records. Therefore, the challenge here is how to map the input data into proper format that data mining algorithms can work without any loss of semantic information contained in original data.

Auto-Correlation Among Spatial Data

One of the distinguishing characteristics of spatial data, as compared to traditional data is the presence of auto-correlation (Miller and Han 2001), meaning that objects are influenced by their nearby objects. Most data mining techniques are based on statistical methods that assume statistical independence among input data. The presence of spatial autocorrelation violates this assumption. Also, as identified by Chawla, Shekhar, Wu, and Ozesmi (2001), the dominant feature of geography is that the closer the objects, the more related they are. To solve the side effect of autocorrelation of spatial objects on statistical mining, researchers have proposed several approaches including Markov random field (MRF) and spatial autoregression (SAR) models, as summarized in Shekhar Schrater, Vatsavai, Wu, and Chawla (2002).

Spatial Relationships Among Objects

Environmental data mining is also different from traditional data mining since it must take spatial relationships into consideration, including topological and direction relationships. Unlike traditional data where relationships among objects are identified and explicitly stored, identifying and storing all spatial relationships when dealing with spatial data is infeasible because of space and maintenance requirements. Identifying spatial relationships among objects correctly and efficiently, and representing them properly is a research topic.

Data Granularity

In relational databases, objects are disjoint. While in environmental dataset, the input data are not always represented in a disjoint way. For example, raster imagery, is one of the major inputs for environmental data mining. Though image pixels are disjoint, dealing with pixel is computationally intensive. A natural way of dealing with this problem is to divide the images into small areas. However, the challenge here is how to decide on the proper area size for a continuous raster image. On one hand, working with high level of granularity may result in missing some interesting information. On the other hand, very fine granularity may result in sacrificing the efficiency of the data mining algorithms. Therefore, determining the proper neighborhood in the continuous (nondisjoint) datasets is a research topic because it would directly affect the quality and efficiency of data mining techniques.

18.3.2   Data Mining Techniques and Spatial Data

In the following list, we present some examples of queries and discuss the data mining techniques suitable to address each query, and then identify their limitations in directly employing them for spatial data.

1. How can we link the changes in NDVI to changes in the hydrologic condition? — *association rule mining*

2. Can we distinguish between the changes due to various factors, such as inter-annual climate variability and human action impact — *spatiotemporal trend detection and characterization*

3. Is it possible to distinguish between variabilities related to inter-annual and long-term trends? — *spatiotemporal trend detection*

4. Is there a correlation between NDVI variations and ecoregion, or between NDVI with other parameters, such as climate, physiography, topography or hydrology? — *association rule mining*

5. Are the trends confined to certain region? Is the nature of the variability and trend different in different regions? — *clustering*

6. Can we identify the abnormal changes in NDVI or the abnormal changes of a particular species of vegetation. — *outlier detection*

For each of the data mining technique identified above, we discuss, below, some of the limitations and challenges arise when applied to spatial data.

Clustering

Spatial data clustering algorithms can be classified into four groups (Miller and Han 2001): partitioning algorithms, hierarchy algorithms, density-based algorithms and grid-based algorithms. In this chapter, we discuss only a representative set of spatial clustering techniques.

CLARANS (Ng and Han 1994), a k-medoid algorithm, is a representation of partitioning algorithm. It starts from an arbitrary point, by checking a sample of the neighbors of the node to search for the best point as the medoids to represent the cluster. This algorithm suffers from the main drawback of all partitioning algorithms: the result is affected by the selection of initial point. Also, the computation time makes it infeasible for large data sets, which is one of the main characteristics of environmental data.

DBSCAN, GDBSCAN (Sander, Ester, Kriegel, and Xu 1998) and AUTOCLUST (Estivill-Castro and Lee 2000) are examples of density-based algorithms. The basic idea of DBSCAN is that it uses as input parameters *Eps* that defines the diameter of the neighborhood of each point in a cluster, and *MinPts* that defines the minimum number of points. For each point of a cluster its *Eps*-neighborhood for some given *Eps*>0 has to contain at least a minimum number of points, *MinPts* (Sander, Ester, Kriegel, and Xu 1998). GDBSCAN generalized the DBSCAN algorithms from two aspects: the definition of neighbor, and the cardinality of the neighbor (Sander, Ester, Kriegel, and Xu 1998). The major limitations with this are that the input parameters, *Eps* and

MinPts, are highly depend on the dataset, and the time complexity is O(N log N). AUTOCLUST focuses on dealing with massive point data automatically by eliminating the parameter tuning. It fulfills the automatic determination of the parameters by extracting boundaries based on Varonoi modeling and Delaunay Diagrams. Although it is efficient and does not require human input, and is able to detect clusters of different densities, the efficiency of the algorithm was shown only for two dimensional data (O(N log N)) and unknown for higher dimensions.

BIRCH (Zhang, Ramakrishnan, and Livny 1996) uses a hierarchical data structure called "clustering-feature (CF) tree. The CF vector is a triple ($CF = N, LS, SS$), where N is the number of data points, LS the linear sum of the N data points, and SS is the square-sum of the N data points. CF values are organized in a balanced tree, which using nonleaf node represents a cluster consisting of all the subclusters represented by its children. The challenge of this approach is that it is hard to find the distance in nonnumerical space. It uses a centroid-based method to form the clusters once the initial scan is done. This would result in the inaccuracy caused by the abnormality of the shape.

STING (Wang, Yang, and Muntz 1997) is a grid-based approach, which equally divides the spatial area into small areas at different resolutions. This grid-based algorithm is query-independent and facilitates parallel processing (Miller and Han 2001). However, it can only answer several specific types of region-related queries and moreover, the granularity is a critical parameter, which affects the result of the clustering.

Challenges: Based on the above brief discussion, we observe that there is no single clustering technique that is readily available and well suited to address question 5, above. Clustering the trends or the variability at different region, is not just a simple high dimensional vector clustering. How to generalize the variabilities or trends, and cluster them is a challenge. For example, if we want to find whether the correlations between two parameters are different from area to area, say time and NDVI over different spots, the output of the regression analysis is a collection of lines and it is not clear how to cluster these lines. The problem can be generalized as how to cluster a set of the regression lines. The proper selection of the distance function or representation of the regression lines is application dependent. Also the distance between lines is much complicated than distances between points. Currently, most of the spatial data mining techniques do not provide an answer for this problem.

Association Rule Mining

Spatial association rule mining has been explored in Koperski and Han (1995), Shekhar and Huang (2001), Malerba and Lisi (2001), Malerba, Esposito, and Lisi (2001), and Li, Deogun, and Harms (2003). In Koperski and Han (1995), the spatial association rules are acquired by searching through the concept hierarchy whenever frequent occurrences of interesting objects can be observed. Malerba and Lisi (2001) and Malerba, Esposito, and Lisi (2001) proposed SPADA, which uses similar approach to mine spatial related census data, employs inductive logic programming, which relies on an augmented expressive power to help represent spatial relationships and symbolic background knowledge in an elegant way. However, using concept hierarchy is too rigid. In Koperski and Han (1995), the concept hierarchy is defined according to the size of the objects, which only reflects one characteristic of an object. In other words, to find the association rules related to other aspects of a spatial object, there is a need to build other hierarchies. Another limitation is that sometimes it is not reasonable to divide the continuous spatial data into disjoint sets. For example, it is difficult to decide on how to divide a smoothly changing NDVI map into separate regions.

To address these issues, Shekhar and Huang (2001) have proposed an algorithm that can find the spatial colocation pattern. It has chosen neighborhood approach to overcome the problem of hard to identify disjoint transactions from continuous spatial data. It uses the coLocation Miner algorithm to find the local colocation pattern and spatial colocation pattern based upon the coexistence by extending the neighborhood. To define the coexistence relationship between two events, the algorithm has to determine the neighbors of each event first. Also, it deals only with Boolean spatial features. By quantifying some of the features, the association rule mining may be able to find other rules than colocation. Li, Deogun, and Harms (2003) proposed an interpolation technique for geo-spatial association rule mining. By integrating two basic interpolation methods, IDW and Kriging, they can discover relationships between environmental variables from datasets. IDW algorithm is a preinterpolation method, while the Kriging is a postinterpolation method, in terms of interpolation done before or after rule finding. Although the proposed method is trying to improve the correctness of the rule finding, it does not contribute much to spatial data mining.

Challenges: One of the challenges is how to mine both the vector data and the raster data. As we have already seen from the literature, part of the work is based on the assumption that all the data can be divided into disjoint transactions, which does not hold most of the time in environmental data mining. For example, in question 4, the NDVI is represented by raster data, which is an example of continuous data. How to divide the NDVI map into disjoint areas properly needs investigation.

Although Shekhar and Huang (2001) presents a good solution for finding the colocation rules, it only targets a small portion of the association rule mining problems. First, colocation is just one type of association rules that could be found. There are other associations related to spatial relationships, especially when we categorize the geo-spatial relationships among arbitrary spatial objects, i.e. points, lines, and polygons. According to Egenhofer, Mark, and Herring (1994) there are five topological relations between two polygons: *disjoint, intersect, subset, subset with partial boundary overlap, coincide*, 33 relationships between two simple lines, and 20 relationships between a region and a line. Second, colocation detection deals with binary spatial features. Nevertheless, to summarize the features into binary features is subjective. For example, how to determine that object A is *close_to* object B? There is a need to investigate quantitative association rule mining, which would avoid the problems binary features have.

Third, the association rule should be concluded based on the frequent datasets, which is the basic assumption of association rule mining. If the dataset does not contain frequent occurrences, the two evaluation parameters *support* and *confidence* are not reliable because of the small sample size. However, there are some events that do not occur very often or are hard to obtain information about, such as the disturbance in meadowlands. Consequently, the dataset is limited. If we are interested in identifying the factor(s) causing the disturbance, we actually have to determine if there is any association relation between the disturbance and the potential causing events. Due to the limited amount of information on this kind of disturbance, using association rule mining is not a convincing alternative due to the small sample size. What we actually do is rare pattern mining. It is important to note that rare pattern mining is different from outlier detection, because even though the events do not happen frequently, they are not deviations from normal trends. There is not much research in the area of rare pattern mining pertaining to spatial data. Therefore, how could we mine the rare patterns from environmental datasets is another challenge.

Trends Detection

Trends detection algorithms can be classified into three groups: temporal trends detection, spatial trends detection (Ester, Kriegel, Sander, and Xu 1997; Ester, Frommelt, Kriegel, and Sander 1998) and spatiotemporal trends detection (Schoenberg, Peng, Huang, and Rundel 2003; Kitamoto 2002; Wang, Yang, and Muntz 1997; Wang, Yang, and Muntz 2000). Temporal data mining is concerned with the changes of environmental-related objects or features over one or more dimensions of time. Spatial trends detection, on the other hand is concerned with the pattern of objects along the spatial dimension. Spatiotemporal trends detection integrates the changes on both dimensions. Since we believe that environmental data mining is an extension of spatial data mining, we focus our research on spatial and spatiotemporal trends detection. Early attempts of spatial trends mining can be found in Ester, Kriegel, Sander, and

Xu (1997), and Ester, Frommelt, Kriegel, and Sander (1998). Spatial trends describe a regular change of nonspatial attributes when moving away from a start object. They use neighborhood path of an object to find the evolution of nonspatial attributes. Here the challenge is to find the neighborhood path in a continuous dataset. Spatiotemporal trends detection has been explored by Roddick, Hornsby, and Spiliopoulou (2001), Kitamoto (2002), and Wang, Yang, and Muntz (2000).

Challenges: In order to answer questions 2 and 3, we need a large amount of satellite images as well as other GIS information over a long period of time. The reality is that, over the long period, the devices we use to acquire data have evolved dramatically. For example, consider the LandSAT series remote sensors, both the resolution and available bands have increased substantially. Landsat 1, 2, and 3 gathered multispectral scanner data with 80-meter ground resolution, while Landsat7 gathers both multispectral scanner data and thematic mapper data with 30-meter ground resolution.

Consequently, to discover spatiotemporal trends, one has to cope with different kinds of images. However, none of the current spatiotemporal techniques take this into account, instead using images from the same sensor or database. Also, dealing with the satellite images or other thematic maps over a period of time brings extremely heavy computation burden. It is obvious that we should guarantee the algorithms focus on the meaningful patterns. Though some algorithms (Wang, Yang, and Muntz 2000) made efforts in this direction, further research in data filtering is still necessary under the condition that a nonspecialist does not have much environmental prior knowledge.

Outlier Detection

Outlier detection is to find an observation, which is inconsistent with the known trends or segmentation. Question 6 is trying to find the abnormal changes of NDVI or some vegetation. The outlier detection techniques can be classified according to different criteria, for example, in Ng (2001) the outlier detection techniques are categorized as distribution-based, distance-based and depth-based. Regardless of those categorizations, there are two approaches to find the abnormal patterns. The first one is to find the normal distribution first, then the outliers are those which are not conforming to the distribution. The second method tries to cluster the data first. After clustering, the data elements that do not belong to any cluster are automatically identified as outliers. Thus it can be seen that outlier detection builds on the efforts of other techniques.

18.4   Conclusions

Environmental data comprises of both traditional and spatial data, collected from multiple, possibly heterogeneous, autonomous, distributed databases and other information sources. An environmental data warehouse (EDW) is required for the purpose of complex querying, analysis and decision support. We have recognized that, one of the distinguishing features in building certain views in an EDW, when compared to those of a traditional data warehouses, is that they require data mining. The unique characteristics of environmental data, including its large data size, multidimensional nature and the complexity of the spatial data pose unique challenges with respect to data warehousing and mining. In this chapter, we have provided a review of the state of art and identify major research challenges. In particular, with respect to the EDW we address the issues regarding the data model, the spatial OLAP operations, and we have pointed out some implementation challenges that make building an EDW a more complex task than building a traditional data warehouse. With respect to data mining we have discussed the challenges encountered in mining environmental data in general, and then identify the challenges faced when applying specific data mining techniques to spatial data. In particular, we have considered clustering, association rule mining, trends detection and outlier detection, as they are relevant for spatial data mining.

Acknowledgement

This work is partially sponsored by the Meadowlands Environment Research institute (MERI).

Nabil R. Adam is a professor of comptuer and information systems at Rutgers, The State University of New Jersey, and director of the Rutgers Center for Information Management, Integration and Connectivity (CIMIC).

Vijayalakshmi Atluri is an associate professor of computer information systems at Rutgers, The State University of New Jersey, and research director of the Rutgers Center for Information Management, Integration and Connectivity (CIMIC).

Dihua Guo is a Ph.D. student in the Center for Information Management, Integration and Connectivity at Rutgers, The State University of New Jersey.

Songmei Yu is a Ph.D. student in the Center for Information Management, Integration and Connectivity at Rutgers, The State University of New Jersey

Chapter 19

Trends in Spatial Data Mining

*Shashi Shekhar, Pusheng Zhang, Yan Huang,
and Ranga Raju Vatsavai*

The explosive growth of spatial data and widespread use of spatial databases emphasize the need for the automated discovery of spatial knowledge. Spatial data mining (Roddick and Spiliopoulou 1999, Shekhar and Chawla 2002) is the process of discovering interesting and previously unknown, but potentially useful patterns from spatial databases. The complexity of spatial data and intrinsic spatial relationships limits the usefulness of conventional data mining techniques for extracting spatial patterns. Efficient tools for extracting information from geospatial data are crucial to organizations that make decisions based on large spatial datasets, including NASA, the National Imagery and Mapping Agency (NIMA), the National Cancer Institute (NCI), and the United States Department of Transportation (USDOT). These organizations are spread across many application domains including ecology and environmental management, public safety, transportation, earth science, epidemiology, and climatology.

General purpose data mining tools, such as Clementine, See5/C5.0, and Enterprise Miner, are designed to analyze large commercial databases. Although these tools were primarily designed to identify customer-buying patterns in market basket data, they have also been used in analyzing scientific and engineering data, astronomical data, multimedia data, genomic data, and web data. Extracting interesting and useful patterns from spatial data sets is more difficult than extracting corresponding patterns from traditional numeric and categorical data due to the complexity of spatial data types, spatial relationships, and spatial autocorrelation.

Specific features of geographical data that preclude the use of general purpose data mining algorithms are: (1) rich data types(e.g., extended spatial objects) (2) implicit spatial relationships among the variables, (3) observations that are not independent, and (4) spatial autocorrelation among the features. In this chapter we focus on the unique features that distinguish spatial data mining from classical data mining in the following four categories: data input, statistical foundation, output patterns, and computational process. We present major accomplishments of spatial data mining research, especially regarding output patterns known as predictive models, spatial outliers, spatial colocation rules, and clusters. Finally, we identify areas of spatial data mining where further research is needed.

19.1   Data Input

The data inputs of spatial data mining are more complex than the inputs of classical data mining because they include extended objects such as points, lines, and polygons. The data inputs of spatial data mining have two distinct types of attributes: nonspatial attribute and spatial attribute. Nonspatial attributes are used to characterize nonspatial features of objects, such as name, population, and unemployment rate for a city. They are the same as the attributes used in the data inputs of classical data mining. Spatial attributes are used to define the spatial location and extent of spatial objects (Bolstad 2002). The spatial attributes of a spatial object most often include information related to spatial locations, e.g., longitude, latitude and elevation, as well as shape.

Relationships among nonspatial objects are explicit in data inputs, e.g., arithmetic relation, ordering, is_instance_of, subclass_of, and membership_of. In contrast, relationships among spatial objects are often *implicit*, such as overlap, intersect, and behind. One possible way to deal with implicit spatial relationships is to materialize the relationships into traditional data input columns and then apply classical data mining techniques (Quinlan 1993, Barnett and Lewis 1994, Agrawal and Srikant 1994, Jain and Dubes 1988). However, the materialization can result in loss of information. Another way to capture implicit spatial relationships is to develop models or techniques to incorporate spatial information into the spatial data mining process. We discuss a few case studies of such techniques in section 19.3.

Nonspatial Relationship (Explicit)	Spatial Relationship (Often Implicit)
Arithmetic	Set-oriented: union, intersection, membership, $\cdots$
Ordering	Topological: meet, within, overlap, $\cdots$
Is_instance_of	Directional: North, NE, left, above, behind, $\cdots$
Subclass_of	Metric: e.g., distance, area, perimeter, $\cdots$
Part_of	Dynamic: update, create, destroy, $\cdots$
Membership_of	Shape-based and visibility

Table 19.1: Relationships among nonspatial eata and spatial data.

19.2 Statistical Foundation

Statistical models (Cressie 1993) are often used to represent observations in terms of random variables. These models can then be used for estimation, description, and prediction based on probability theory. Spatial data can be thought of as resulting from observations on the stochastic process $Z(s)$: $s \in D$, where s is a spatial location and D is possibly a random set in a spatial framework. Here we present three spatial statistical problems one might encounter: point process, lattice, and geostatistics.

Point process: A point process is a model for the spatial distribution of the points in a point pattern. Several natural processes can be modeled as spatial point patterns, e.g., positions of trees in a forest and locations of bird habitats in a wetland. Spatial point patterns can be broadly grouped into random or nonrandom processes. Real point patterns are often compared with a random pattern(generated by a Poisson process) using the average distance between a point and its nearest neighbor. For a random pattern, this average distance is expected to be $\frac{1}{2*\sqrt{density}}$, where density is the average number of points per unit area. If for a real process, the computed distance falls within a certain limit, then we conclude that the pattern is generated by a random process; otherwise it is a nonrandom process.

Lattice: A lattice is a model for a gridded space in a spatial framework. Here the lattice refers to a countable collection of regular or irregular spatial sites related to each other via a neighborhood relationship. Several spatial statistical analyses, e.g., the spatial autoregressive model and Markov random fields, can be applied on lattice data.

Geostatistics: Geostatistics deals with the analysis of spatial continuity and weak stationarity (Cressie 1993), which is an inherent characteristics of spatial data sets. Geostatistics provides a set of statistics tools, such as kriging (Cressie 1993) to the interpolation of attributes at unsampled locations.

One of the fundamental assumptions of statistical analysis is that the data samples are independently generated: like successive tosses of coin, or the

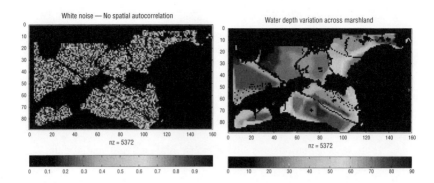

Figure 19.1: Attribute values in space with independent identical distribution and spatial autocorrelation.

rolling of a die. However, in the analysis of spatial data, the assumption about the independence of samples is generally false. In fact, spatial data tends to be highly self correlated. For example, people with similar characteristics, occupation and background tend to cluster together in the same neighborhoods. The economies of a region tend to be similar. Changes in natural resources, wildlife, and temperature vary gradually over space. The property of like things to cluster in space is so fundamental that geographers have elevated it to the status of the first law of geography: "Everything is related to everything else but nearby things are more related than distant things" (Tobler 1979). In spatial statistics, an area within statistics devoted to the analysis of spatial data, this property is called *spatial autocorrelation*. For example, figure 19.1 shows the value distributions of an attribute in a spatial framework for an independent identical distribution and a distribution with spatial autocorrelation.

Knowledge discovery techniques that ignore spatial autocorrelation typically perform poorly in the presence of spatial data. Often the spatial dependencies arise due to the inherent characteristics of the phenomena under study, but in particular they arise due to the fact that the spatial resolution of imaging sensors are finer than the size of the object being observed. For example, remote sensing satellites have resolutions ranging from 30 meters (e.g., the Enhanced Thematic Mapper of the Landsat 7 satellite of NASA) to one meter (e.g., the IKONOS satellite from SpaceImaging), while the objects under study (e.g., urban, forest, water) are often much larger than 30 meters. As a result, per-pixel-based classifiers, which do not take spatial context into account, often produce classified images with *salt and pepper* noise. These classifiers also suffer in terms of classification accuracy.

The spatial relationship among locations in a spatial framework is of-

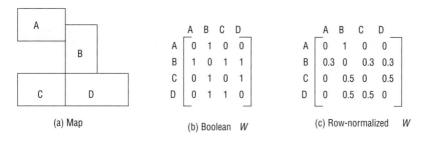

Figure 19.2: A spatial framework and its four-neighborhood contiguity matrix.

ten modeled via a contiguity matrix. A simple contiguity matrix may represent a neighborhood relationship defined using adjacency, Euclidean distance, etc. Example definitions of neighborhood using adjacency include a four-neighborhood and an eight-neighborhood. Given a gridded spatial framework, a four-neighborhood assumes that a pair of locations influence each other if they share an edge. An eight-neighborhood assumes that a pair of locations influence each other if they share either an edge or a vertex.

Figure 19.2(a) shows a gridded spatial framework with four locations, A, B, C, and D. A binary matrix representation of a four-neighborhood relationship is shown in figure 19.2(b). The row-normalized representation of this matrix is called a contiguity matrix, as shown in figure 19.2(c). Other contiguity matrices can be designed to model neighborhood relationships based on distance. The essential idea is to specify the pairs of locations that influence each other along with the relative intensity of interaction. More general models of spatial relationships using cliques and hypergraphs are available in the literature (Warrender and Augusteijn 1999). In spatial statistics, spatial autocorrelation is quantified using measures such as Ripley's K-function and Moran's I (Cressie 1993).

19.3 Output Patterns

In this section, we present case studies of four important output patterns for spatial data mining: predictive models, spatial outliers, spatial colocation rules, and spatial clustering.

19.3.1 Predictive Models

The prediction of events occurring at particular geographic locations is very important in several application domains. Examples of problems that require location prediction include crime analysis, cellular networking, and natural

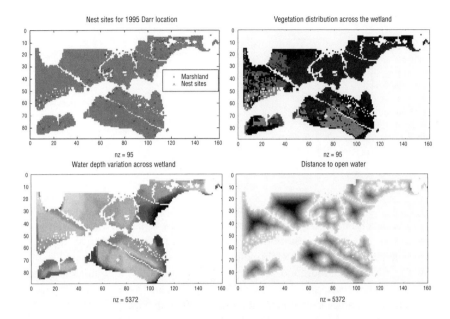

Figure 19.3: *Top left:* Learning dataset: The geometry of the Darr wetland and the locations of the nests. *Top right:* The spatial distribution of *vegetation durability* over the marshland. *Bottom left:* The spatial distribution of *water depth*. *Bottom right:* The spatial distribution of *distance to open water.*

disasters such as fires, floods, droughts, vegetation diseases, and earthquakes. In this section we provide two spatial data mining techniques for predicting locations, namely the spatial autoregressive model (SAR) and Markov random fields (MRF).

An Application Domain

We begin by introducing an example to illustrate the different concepts related to location prediction in spatial data mining. We are given data about two wetlands, named Darr and Stubble, on the shores of Lake Erie in Ohio USA in order to *predict* the spatial distribution of a marsh-breeding bird, the red-winged blackbird (*Agelaius phoeniceus*). The data was collected from April to June in two successive years, 1995 and 1996.

A uniform grid was imposed on the two wetlands and different types of measurements were recorded at each cell or pixel. In total, the values of seven attributes were recorded at each cell. Domain knowledge is crucial in deciding which attributes are important and which are not. For example, *vegetation durability* was chosen over *vegetation species* because specialized knowledge about the bird-nesting habits of the red-winged blackbird suggested that the choice of nest location is more dependent on plant structure, plant resistance to wind, and wave action than on the plant species.

An important goal is to build a model for predicting the location of bird nests in the wetlands. Typically, the model is built using a portion of the data, called the learning or training data, and then tested on the remainder of the data, called the testing data. In this study we build a model using the 1995 Darr wetland data and then tested it 1995 Stubble wetland data. In the learning data, all the attributes are used to build the model and in the training data, one value is hidden, in our case the location of the nests. Using knowledge gained from the 1995 Darr data and the value of the independent attributes in the test data, we want to predict the location of the nests in 1995 Stubble data.

Modeling Spatial Dependencies Using the SAR and MRF Models

Several previous studies (Jhung and Swain 1996; Solberg, Taxt, and Jain 1996) have shown that the modeling of spatial dependency (often called context) during the classification process improves overall classification accuracy. Spatial context can be defined by the relationships between spatially adjacent pixels in a small neighborhood. In this section, we present two models to model spatial dependency: the spatial autoregressive model (SAR) and Markov random field(MRF)-based Bayesian classifiers.

Spatial Autoregressive Model

The spatial autoregressive model decomposes a classifier $\hat{f}_C$ into two parts, namely spatial autoregression and logistic transformation. We first show how spatial dependencies are modeled using the framework of logistic regression analysis. In the spatial autoregression model, the spatial dependencies of the error term, or, the dependent variable, are directly modeled in the regression equation (Anselin 1988). If the dependent values y_i are related to each other, then the regression equation can be modified as

$$y = \rho W y + X\beta + \epsilon. \tag{19.1}$$

Here W is the neighborhood relationship contiguity matrix and ρ is a parameter that reflects the strength of the spatial dependencies between the elements of the dependent variable. After the correction term $\rho W y$ is introduced, the components of the residual error vector ϵ are then assumed to be generated from independent and identical standard normal distributions. As in the case of classical regression, the SAR equation has to be transformed via the logistic function for binary dependent variables.

We refer to this equation as the spatial autoregressive model (SAR). Notice that when $\rho = 0$, this equation collapses to the classical regression model. The benefits of modeling spatial autocorrelation are many: The residual error will have much lower spatial autocorrelation (i.e., systematic variation). With the proper choice of W, the residual error should, at least theoretically, have no systematic variation. If the spatial autocorrelation coefficient is statistically significant, then SAR will quantify the presence of spatial autocorrelation. It will indicate the extent to which variations in the dependent variable (y) are explained by the average of neighboring observation values. Finally, the model will have a better fit, (i.e., a higher R-squared statistic).

Markov Random Field-based Bayesian Classifiers

Markov random field-based Bayesian classifiers estimate the classification model $\hat{f}_C$ using MRF and Bayes' rule. A set of random variables whose interdependency relationship is represented by an undirected graph (i.e., a symmetric neighborhood matrix) is called a Markov random field (Li 1995). The Markov property specifies that a variable depends only on its neighbors and is independent of all other variables. The location prediction problem can be modeled in this framework by assuming that the class label, $l_i = f_C(s_i)$, of different locations, s_i, constitutes an MRF. In other words, random variable l_i is independent of l_j if $W(s_i, s_j) = 0$.

The Bayesian rule can be used to predict l_i from feature value vector X and neighborhood class label vector L_i as follows:

$$Pr(l_i|X, L_i) = \frac{Pr(X|l_i, L_i)Pr(l_i|L_i)}{Pr(X)} \tag{19.2}$$

The solution procedure can estimate $Pr(l_i|L_i)$ from the training data, where L_i denotes a set of labels in the neighborhood of s_i excluding the label at s_i, by examining the ratios of the frequencies of class labels to the total number of locations in the spatial framework. $Pr(X|l_i, L_i)$ can be estimated using kernel functions from the observed values in the training dataset. For reliable estimates, even larger training datasets are needed relative to those needed for the Bayesian classifiers without spatial context, since we are estimating a more complex distribution. An assumption on $Pr(X|l_i, L_i)$ may be useful if the training dataset available is not large enough. A common assumption is the uniformity of influence from all neighbors of a location. For computational efficiency it can be assumed that only local explanatory data $X(s_i)$ and neighborhood label L_i are relevant in predicting class label $l_i = f_C(s_i)$. It is common to assume that all interaction between neighbors is captured via the interaction in the class label variable. Many domains also use specific parametric probability distribution forms, leading to simpler solution procedures.

In addition, it is frequently easier to work with a Gibbs distribution specialized by the locally defined MRF through the Hammersley-Clifford theorem (Besag 1974).

Comparison of the Methods

A more detailed theoretical and experimental comparison of these methods can be found in Shekhar, Vatsavai, Wu, and Chawla (2002). Although MRF and SAR classification have different formulations, they share a common goal, estimating the posterior probability distribution: $p(l_i|X)$. However, the posterior for the two models is computed differently with different assumptions. For MRF the posterior is computed using Bayes' rule. On the other hand, in logistic regression, the posterior distribution is directly fit to the data. One important difference between logistic regression and MRF is that logistic regression assumes no dependence on neighboring classes. Logistic regression and logistic SAR models belong to a more general exponential family. The exponential family is given by $Pr(u|v) = e^{A(\theta_v)+B(u,\pi)+\theta_v^T u}$ where u, v are location and label respectively. This exponential family includes many of the common distributions such as Gaussian, Binomial, Bernoulli, and Poisson as special cases.

Experiments were carried out on the Darr and Stubble wetlands to compare classical regression, SAR, and the MRF-based Bayesian classifiers. The results showed that the MRF models yield better spatial and classification accuracies over SAR in the prediction of the locations of bird nests. We also observed that SAR predictions are extremely localized, missing actual nests over a large part of the marshlands.

19.3.2   Spatial Outliers

Outliers have been informally defined as observations in a dataset that appear to be inconsistent with the remainder of that set of data (Barnett and Lewis 1994), or that deviate so much from other observations so as to arouse suspicions that they were generated by a different mechanism (Hawkins 1980). The identification of global outliers can lead to the discovery of unexpected knowledge and has a number of practical applications in areas such as credit card fraud, athlete performance analysis, voting irregularity, and severe weather prediction. This section focuses on spatial outliers, i.e., observations that appear to be inconsistent with their neighborhoods. Detecting spatial outliers is useful in many applications of geographic information systems and spatial databases, including transportation, ecology, public safety, public health, climatology, and location-based services.

A spatial outlier is a spatially referenced object whose nonspatial attribute

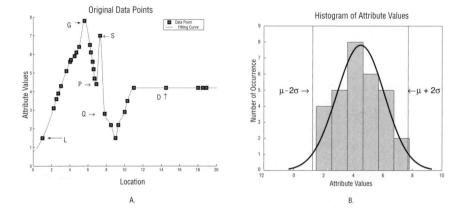

Figure 19.4: A dataset for outlier detection. (a) An example dataset. (b) Histogram of attribute values.

values differ significantly from those of other spatially referenced objects in its spatial neighborhood. Informally, a spatial outlier is a local instability (in values of nonspatial attributes) or a spatially referenced object whose nonspatial attributes are extreme relative to its neighbors, even though the attributes may not be significantly different from the entire population. For example, a new house in an old neighborhood of a growing metropolitan area is a spatial outlier based on the nonspatial attribute house age.

Illustrative Examples

We use an example to illustrate the differences among global and spatial outlier detection methods. In figure 19.4(a), the X-axis is the location of data points in one-dimensional space; the Y-axis is the attribute value for each data point. Global outlier detection methods ignore the spatial location of each data point and fit the distribution model to the values of the nonspatial attribute. The outlier detected using this approach is the data point G, which has an extremely high attribute value 7.9, exceeding the threshold of $\mu + 2\sigma = 4.49 + 2 * 1.61$ = 7.71, as shown in figure 19.4(b). This test assumes a normal distribution for attribute values. On the other hand, S is a spatial outlier whose observed value is significantly different than its neighbors P and Q.

Tests for Detecting Spatial Outliers

Tests to detect spatial outliers separate spatial attributes from nonspatial attributes. Spatial attributes are used to characterize location, neighborhood, and

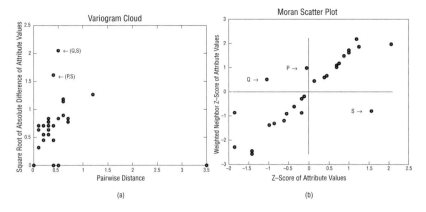

Figure 19.5: Variogram cloud and moran scatterplot to detect spatial outliers. (a) Variogram cloud. (b) Moran scatter plot.

distance. Nonspatial attribute dimensions are used to compare a spatially referenced object to its neighbors. Spatial statistics literature provides two kinds of bi-partite multidimensional tests, namely graphical tests and quantitative tests. Graphical tests, which are based on the visualization of spatial data, highlight spatial outliers. Example methods include variogram clouds and Moran scatterplots. Quantitative methods provide a precise test to distinguish spatial outliers from the remainder of data. Scatterplots (Luc 1994) are a representative technique from the quantitative family.

A variogram-cloud (Cressie 1993) displays data points related by neighborhood relationships. For each pair of locations, the square-root of the absolute difference between attribute values at the locations versus the Euclidean distance between the locations are plotted. In datasets exhibiting strong spatial dependence, the variance in the attribute differences will increase with increasing distance between locations. Locations that are near to one another, but with large attribute differences, might indicate a spatial outlier, even though the values at both locations may appear to be reasonable when examining the dataset nonspatially. Figure 19.5(a) shows a variogram cloud for the example dataset shown in figure 19.4(a). This plot shows that two pairs (P, S) and (Q, S) on the left hand side lie above the main group of pairs, and are possibly related to spatial outliers. The point S may be identified as a spatial outlier since it occurs in both pairs (Q, S) and (P, S). However, graphical tests of spatial outlier detection are limited by the lack of precise criteria to distinguish spatial outliers. In addition, a variogram cloud requires nontrivial post-processing of highlighted pairs to separate spatial outliers from their neighbors, particularly when multiple outliers are present, or density varies greatly.

A Moran scatterplot (Luc 1995) is a plot of normalized attribute value $(Z[f(i)] = \frac{f(i)-\mu_f}{\sigma_f})$ against the neighborhood average of normalized attribute values $(W \cdot Z)$, where W is the row-normalized (i.e., $\sum_j W_{ij} = 1$) neighborhood matrix, (i.e., $W_{ij} > 0$ iff neighbor(i, j)). The upper left and lower right quadrants of figure 19.5(b) indicate a spatial association of dissimilar values: low values surrounded by high value neighbors(e.g., points P and Q), and high values surrounded by low values (e.g,. point S). Thus we can identify points(nodes) that are surrounded by unusually high or low value neighbors. These points can be treated as spatial outliers.

A scatterplot (Luc 1994) shows attribute values on the X-axis and the average of the attribute values in the neighborhood on the Y-axis. A least square regression line is used to identify spatial outliers. A scatter sloping upward to the right indicates a positive spatial autocorrelation (adjacent values tend to be similar); a scatter sloping upward to the left indicates a negative spatial autocorrelation. The residual is defined as the vertical distance (Y-axis) between a point P with location (X_p, Y_p) to the regression line $Y = mX + b$, that is, residual $\epsilon = Y_p - (mX_p + b)$. Cases with standardized residuals, $\epsilon_{standard} = \frac{\epsilon - \mu_\epsilon}{\sigma_\epsilon}$, greater than 3.0 or less than -3.0 are flagged as possible spatial outliers, where μ_ϵ and σ_ϵ are the mean and standard deviation of the distribution of the error term ϵ. In figure 19.6(a), a scatterplot shows the attribute values plotted against the average of the attribute values in neighboring areas for the dataset in figure 19.4(a). The point S turns out to be the farthest from the regression line and may be identified as a spatial outlier.

A location (sensor) is compared to its neighborhood using the function $S(x) = [f(x) - E_{y \in N(x)}(f(y))]$, where $f(x)$ is the attribute value for a location x, $N(x)$ is the set of neighbors of x, and $E_{y \in N(x)}(f(y))$ is the average attribute value for the neighbors of x (Shekhar, Lu, and Zhang 2001). The statistic function $S(x)$ denotes the difference of the attribute value of a sensor located at x and the average attribute value of $x's$ neighbors.

Spatial statistic $S(x)$ is normally distributed if the attribute value $f(x)$ is normally distributed. A popular test for detecting spatial outliers for normally distributed $f(x)$ can be described as follows: Spatial statistic $Z_{s(x)} = |\frac{S(x)-\mu_s}{\sigma_s}| > \theta$. For each location x with an attribute value $f(x)$, the $S(x)$ is the difference between the attribute value at location x and the average attribute value of $x's$ neighbors, μ_s is the mean value of $S(x)$, and σ_s is the value of the standard deviation of $S(x)$ over all stations. The choice of θ depends on a specified confidence level. For example, a confidence level of 95 percent will lead to $\theta \approx 2$.

Figure 19.6(b) shows the visualization of the spatial statistic method described above. The X-axis is the location of data points in one-dimensional

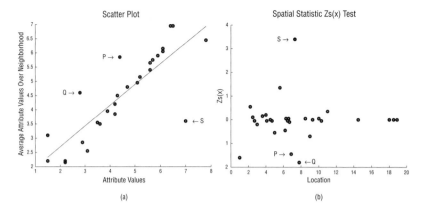

Figure 19.6: Scatterplot and spatial statistic $Z_{s(x)}$ to detect spatial outliers. (a) Scatter plot. (b) Spatial statistics $Z_{s(x)}$.

space; the Y-axis is the value of spatial statistic $Z_{s(x)}$ for each data point. We can easily observe that point S has a $Z_{s(x)}$ value exceeding 3, and will be detected as a spatial outlier. Note that the two neighboring points P and Q of S have $Z_{s(x)}$ values close to –2 due to the presence of spatial outliers in their neighborhoods.

19.3.3 Spatial Colocation Rules

Boolean spatial features are geographic object types that are either present or absent at different locations in a two dimensional or three dimensional metric space, e.g., the surface of the earth. Examples of Boolean spatial features include plant species, animal species, road types, cancers, crime, and business types. Colocation patterns represent the subsets of the boolean spatial features whose instances are often located in close geographic proximity. Examples include symbiotic species, e.g., Nile crocodile and Egyptian plover in ecology, and frontage roads and highways in metropolitan road maps.

Colocation rules are models to infer the presence of Boolean spatial features in the neighborhood of instances of other Boolean spatial features. For example, "Nile Crocodiles → Egyptian Plover" predicts the presence of Egyptian Plover birds in areas with Nile crocodiles. Figure 19.7(a) shows a dataset consisting of instances of several Boolean spatial features, each represented by a distinct shape. A careful review reveals two colocation patterns, i.e., ('+','×') and ('o','*').

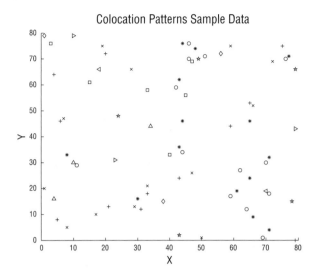

Figure 19.7: Illustration of point spatial colocation patterns. Shapes represent different spatial feature types. Spatial features in sets {'+', '×'} and {'o', '*'} tend to be located together.

Colocation rule discovery is a process to identify colocation patterns from large spatial datasets with a large number of Boolean features. The spatial colocation rule discovery problem looks similar to, but, in fact, is very different from the association rule mining problem (Agrawal and Srikant 1994) because of the lack of transactions. In market basket datasets, transactions represent sets of item types bought together by customers. The support of an association is defined to be the fraction of transactions containing the association. Association rules are derived from all the associations with support values larger than a user given threshold. The purpose of mining association rules is to identify frequent item sets for planning store layouts or marketing campaigns. In the spatial colocation rule mining problem, transactions are often not explicit. The transactions in market basket analysis are independent of each other. Transactions are disjoint in the sense of not sharing instances of item types. In contrast, the instances of Boolean spatial features are embedded in a continuous space and share a variety of spatial relationships (e.g., neighbor) with each other.

Colocation Rule Approaches

Approaches to discovering colocation rules in the literature can be categorized into three classes, namely spatial statistics, association rules, and the event

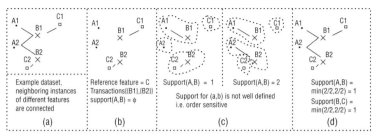

Figure 19.8: Example to illustrate different approaches to discovering colocation patterns (a) Example dataset. (b) Data partition approach. Support measure is ill-defined and order sensitive. (c) Reference feature centric model. (d)
Event centric model.

centric approach. Spatial statistics-based approaches use measures of spatial
correlation to characterize the relationship between different types of spatial
features using the cross K function with Monte Carlo simulation and quadrat
count analysis (Cressie 1993). Computing spatial correlation measures for all
possible colocation patterns can be computationally expensive due to the exponential number of candidate subsets given a large collection of spatial Boolean
features.

Association rule-based approaches focus on the creation of transactions
over space so that an apriorilike algorithm (Agrawal and Srikant 1994) can
be used. Transactions over space can use a reference-feature centric(Koperski
and Han 1995) approach or a data-partition (Morimoto 2001) approach. The
reference feature centric model is based on the choice of a reference spatial
feature and is relevant to application domains focusing on a specific Boolean
spatial feature, e.g., incidence of cancer. Domain scientists are interested in
finding the colocations of other task relevant features (e.g., asbestos) to the
reference feature. A specific example is provided by the spatial association
rule presented in Koperski and Han (1995). Transactions are created around
instances of one user-specified reference spatial feature. The association rules
are derived using the a priori (Agrawal and Srikant 1994) algorithm. The rules
found are all related to the reference feature. For example, consider the spatial dataset in figure 19.8(a) with three feature types, A, B and C. Each feature type has two instances. The neighbor relationships between instances are
shown as edges. Colocations (A, B) and (B, C) may be considered to be frequent in this example. Figure 19.8(b) shows transactions created by choosing
C as the reference feature. Colocation (A, B) will not be found since it does
not involve the reference feature.

Defining transactions by a data-partition approach (Morimoto 2001) defines transactions by dividing spatial datasets into disjoint partitions. There

Model	Items	Transactions defined by	Interest measures for $C_1 \to C_2$	
			Prevalence	Conditional probability
reference feature centric	predicates on reference and relevant features	instances of reference feature C_1 and C_2 involved with	fraction of instance of reference feature with $C_1 \cup C_2$	$Pr(C_2$ is true for an instance of reference features given C_1 is true for that instance of reference feature)
data partitioning	Boolean feature types	a partitioning of spatial dataset	fraction of partitions with $C_1 \cup C_2$	$Pr(C_2$ in a partition given C_1 in that partition)
event centric	Boolean feature types	neighborhoods of instances of feature types	participation index of $C_1 \cup C_2$	$Pr(C_2$ in a neighborhood of $C_1)$

Table 19.2: Interest measures for different models.

may be many distinct ways of partitioning the data, each yielding a distinct set of transactions, which in turn yields different values of support of a given colocation. Figure 19.8 (c) shows two possible partitions for the dataset of figure 19.8 (a), along with the supports for colocation (A, B).

The event centric model finds subsets of spatial features likely to occur in a neighborhood around instances of given subsets of event types. For example, let us determine the probability of finding at least one instance of feature type B in the neighborhood of an instance of feature type A in figure 19.8 (a). There are two instances of type A and both have some instance(s) of type B in their neighborhoods. The conditional probability for the colocation rule is: *spatial feature A at location l $\to$ spatial feature type B in neighborhood is 100%*. This yields a well-defined prevalence measure(i.e., support) without the need for transactions. Figure 19.8 (d) illustrates that our approach will identify both (A, B) and (B, C) as frequent patterns.

Prevalence measures and conditional probability measures, called *interest measures,* are defined differently in different models, as summarized in table 19.2. The reference feature centric and data partitioning models "materialize" transactions and thus can use traditional support and confidence measures. The event centric approach defined new transaction free measures, e.g., the participation index (see Shekhar and Huang [2001] for details).

19.3.4   Spatial Clustering

Spatial clustering is a process of grouping a set of spatial objects into clusters so that objects within a cluster have high similarity in comparison to one another, but are dissimilar to objects in other clusters. For example, clustering is used to determine the "hot spots" in crime analysis and disease tracking. Hot spot analysis is the process of finding unusually dense event clusters across time and space. Many criminal justice agencies are exploring the benefits provided by computer technologies to identify crime hot spots in order to take preventive strategies such as deploying saturation patrols in hot spot areas.

Spatial clustering can be applied to group similar spatial objects together; the implicit assumption is that patterns in space tend to be grouped rather than randomly located. However, the statistical significance of spatial clusters should be measured by testing the assumption in the data. The test is critical before proceeding with any serious clustering analyses.

Complete Spatial Randomness, Cluster, and Decluster

In spatial statistics, the standard against which spatial point patterns are often compared is a completely spatially random point process, and departures indicate that the pattern is not distributed randomly in space. *Complete spatial randomness* (CSR) (Cressie 1993) is synonymous with a homogeneous Poisson process. The patterns of the process are independently and uniformly distributed over space, i.e., the patterns are equally likely to occur anywhere and do not interact with each other. However, patterns generated by a nonrandom process can be either cluster patterns(aggregated patterns) or decluster patterns(uniformly spaced patterns).

To illustrate, figure 19.9 shows realizations from a completely spatially random process, a spatial cluster process, and a spatial decluster process (each conditioned to have 80 points) in a square. Notice in figure 19.9 (a) that the complete spatial randomness pattern seems to exhibit some clustering. This is not an unrepresentative realization, but illustrates a well-known property of homogeneous Poisson processes: event-to-nearest-event distances are proportional to χ_2^2 random variables, whose densities have a substantial amount of probability near zero (Cressie 1993). Spatial clustering is more statistically significant when the data exhibit a cluster pattern rather than a CSR pattern or decluster pattern.

Several statistical methods can be applied to quantify deviations of patterns from a complete spatial randomness point pattern (Cressie 1993). One type of descriptive statistics is based on quadrats (i.e., well defined area, often rectangle in shape). Usually quadrats of random location and orientations in the quadrats are counted, and statistics derived from the counters are computed. Another type of statistics is based on distances between patterns; one

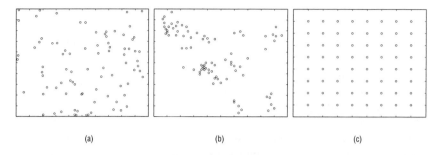

(a)   (b)   (c)

Figure 19.9: Illustration of CSR, cluster, and decluster patterns. (a) CSR pattern. (b) Cluster pattern. (c) Decluster pattern.

Generic	Spatial Data Mining
Divide-and-Conquer	Space Partitioning
Filter-and-Refine	Minimum-Bounding-Rectangle(MBR)
Ordering	Plane Sweeping, Space Filling Curves
Hierarchical Structures	Spatial Index, Tree Matching
Parameter Estimation	Parameter estimation with spatial autocorrelation

Table 19.3: Algorithmic strategies in spatial data mining.

such type is Ripley's K-function (Cressie 1993).

After the verification of the statistical significance of the spatial clustering, classical clustering algorithms (Han, Kamber, and Tung 2001) can be used to discover interesting clusters.

19.4   Computational Process

Many generic algorithmic strategies have been generalized to apply to spatial data mining. For example, as shown in table 19.3, algorithmic strategies, such as divide-and-conquer, filter-and-refine, ordering, hierarchical structure, and parameter estimation, have been used in spatial data mining.

In spatial data mining, spatial autocorrelation and low dimensionality in space(e.g., 2-3) provide more opportunities to improve computational efficiency than classical data mining. NASA earth observation systems currently generate a large sequence of global snapshots of the earth, including various atmospheric, land, and ocean measurements such as sea surface temperature, pressure, precipitation, and net primary production. Each climate attribute in a location has a sequence of observations at different time slots, e.g., a collection of monthly temperatures from 1951-2000 in Minneapolis. Finding locations where climate attributes are highly correlated is frequently used to retrieve interesting relationships among spatial objects of earth science data. For example, such queries are used to identify the land locations whose climate is severely affected by El Nino. However, such correlation-based queries are computationally expensive due to the large number of spatial points, e.g., more than 250k spatial cells on the earth at a 0.5 degree by 0.5 degree resolution, and the high dimensionality of sequences, e.g., 600 for the 1951-2000 monthly temperature data.

A spatial indexing approach proposed by Zhang, Huang, Shekhar, and Kumar (2003) exploits spatial autocorrelation to facilitate correlation-based queries. The approach groups similar time series together based on spatial proximity and constructs a search tree. The queries are processed using the search tree in a filter-and-refine style at the group level instead of at the time series level. Algebraic analyses using cost models and experimental evaluations showed that the proposed approach saves a large portion of computational cost, ranging from 40% to 98% (see Zhang, Huang, Shekhar, and Kumar [2003] for details).

19.5   Research Needs

In this section, we discuss some areas where further research is needed in spatial data mining.

Comparison of classical data mining techniques with spatial data mining techniques: As we discussed in section 19.1, relationships among spatial objects are often implicit. It is possible to materialize the implicit relationships into traditional data input columns and then apply classical data mining techniques (Quinlan 1993, Barnett and Lewis 1994, Agrawal and Srikant 1994, Jain and Dubes 1988). Another way to deal with implicit relationships is to use specialized spatial data mining techniques, e.g., the spatial autoregression and colocation mining. However, existing literature does not provide guidance regarding the choice between classical data mining techniques and spatial data mining techniques to mine spatial data. Therefore new research is needed to compare the two sets of approaches in effectiveness and computational efficiency.

Modeling semantically rich spatial properties, such as topology: The spatial relationship among locations in a spatial framework is often modeled via a contiguity matrix using a neighborhood relationship defined using adjacency and distance. However, spatial connectivity and other complex spatial topological relationships in spatial networks are difficult to model using the continuity matrix. Research is needed to evaluate the value of enriching the continuity matrix beyond the neighborhood relationship.

Statistical interpretation models for spatial patterns: Spatial patterns, such

	Classical Data Mining	Spatial Data Mining
Predictive Model	Classification accuracy	Spatial accuracy
Cluster	Low coupling and high cohesion in feature space	Spatial continuity, unusual density, boundary
Outlier	Different from population or neighbors in feature space	Significant attribute discontinuity in geographic space
Association	Subset prevalence, $Pr[B \in T \mid A \in T, T : a\,transaction]$ Correlation	Spatial pattern prevalence $Pr[B \in N(A) \mid N : neighborhood]$ Cross K-Function

Table 19.4: Interest measures of patterns for classical data mining and spatial data mining.

as spatial outliers and colocation rules, are identified in the spatial data mining process using unsupervised learning methods. There is a need for an independent measure of the statistical significance of such spatial patterns. For example, we may compare the colocation model with dedicated spatial statistical measures, such as Ripley's K-function, characterize the distribution of the participation index interest measure under spatial complete randomness using Monte Carlo simulation, and develop a statistical interpretation of colocation rules to compare the rules with other patterns in unsupervised learning.

Another challenge is the estimation of the detailed spatial parameters in a statistical model. Research is needed to design effective estimation procedures for the continuity matrices used in the spatial autoregressive model and Markov random field-based Bayesian classifiers from learning samples.

Spatial interest measures: The interest measures of patterns in spatial data mining are different from those in classical data mining, especially regarding the four important output patterns shown in table 19.4.

For a two-class problem, the standard way to measure classification accuracy is to calculate the percentage of correctly classified objects. However, this measure may not be the most suitable in a spatial context. *Spatial accuracy*—how far the predictions are from the actuals—is equally important in this application domain due to the effects of the discretizations of a continuous wetland into discrete pixels, as shown in figure 19.10. Figure 19.10(a) shows the actual locations of nests and 19.10(b) shows the pixels with actual nests. Note the loss of information during the discretization of continuous space into pixels. Many nest locations barely fall within the pixels labeled "A" and are quite close to other blank pixels, which represent "no-nest." Now consider two predictions shown in figure 19.10(c) and 19.10(d). Domain scientists prefer prediction 19.10(d) over 19.10(c), since the predicted nest locations are closer on average to some actual nest locations. However, the classification accuracy measure cannot distinguish between 19.10(c) and 19.10(d) since spatial accu-

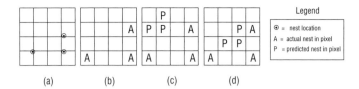

(a)   (b)   (c)   (d)

Figure 19.10: (a)The actual locations of nests. (b) Pixels with actual nests. (c) Location predicted by a model. (d) Location predicted by another model. Prediction (d) is spatially more accurate than (c).

racy is not incorporated in the classification accuracy measure. Hence, there is a need to investigate proper measures for location prediction to improve spatial accuracy.

Effective visualization of spatial relationships: Visualization in spatial data mining is useful to identify interesting spatial patterns. As we discussed in section 19.1, the data inputs of spatial data mining have both spatial and nonspatial features. To facilitate the visualization of spatial relationships, research is needed on ways to represent both spatial and nonspatial features.

For example, many visual representations have been proposed for spatial outliers. However, we do not yet have a way to highlight spatial outliers within visualizations of spatial relationships. For instance, in variogram cloud (figure 19.5 (a)) and scatterplot (figure 19.6 (b)) visualizations, the spatial relationship between a single spatial outlier and its neighbors is not obvious. It is necessary to transfer the information back to the original map in geographic space to check neighbor relationships. As a single spatial outlier tends to flag not only the spatial location of local instability but also its neighboring locations, it is important to group flagged locations and identify real spatial outliers from the group in the post-processing step.

Improving computational efficiency: Mining spatial patterns is often computationally expensive. For example, the estimation of the parameters for the spatial autoregressive model is an order of magnitude more expensive than that for the linear regression in classical data mining. Similarly, colocation mining algorithm is more expensive than the apriori algorithm for classical association rule mining (Agrawal and Srikant 1994). Research is needed to reduce the computational costs of spatial data mining algorithms by a variety of approaches including the classical data mining algorithms as potential filters or components.

Preprocessing spatial data: Spatial data mining techniques have been widely applied to the data in many application domains. However, research on the preprocessing of spatial data has lagged behind. Hence, there is a need for preprocessing techniques for spatial data to deal with problems such as treat-

	Classical Data Mining	Spatial Data Mining
Input	Simple types Explicit relationship	Complex types Implicit relationships
Statistical Foundation	Independence of samples	Spatial autocorrelation
Output	Set-based interest measures e.g., classification accuracy	Spatial interest measures, e.g., spatial accuracy
Computational Process	Combinatorial optimization, Numerical Algorithms	Computational efficiency opportunity Spatial autocorrelation, plane-sweeping New complexity: SAR, colocation

Table 19.5: Difference between classical data mining and spatial data mining.

ment of missing location information and imprecise location specifications, cleaning of spatial data, feature selection, and data transformation.

19.6 Summary

In this chapter we have presented the features of spatial data mining that distinguish it from classical data mining in the following four categories: input, statistical foundation, output, and computational process as shown in table 19.5. We have discussed major research accomplishments and techniques in spatial data mining, especially those related to four important output patterns: predictive models, spatial outliers, spatial colocation rules, and spatial clusters. We have also identified research needs for spatial data mining.

Acknowledgments

This work was supported in part by the Army High Performance Computing Research Center under the auspices of the Department of the Army, Army Research Laboratory cooperative agreement number DAAD19-01-2-0014, the content of which does not necessarily reflect the position or the policy of the government, and no official endorsement should be inferred.

We are particularly grateful to our collaborators Prof. Vipin Kumar, Prof. Paul Schrater, Dr. Sanjay Chawla, Dr. Chang-Tien Lu, Dr. Weili Wu, and Prof. Uygar Ozesmi for their various contributions. We also thank Xiaobin Ma, Hui

Xiong, Jin Soung Yoo, Qingsong Lu, Baris Kazar, and anonymous reviewers for their valuable feedbacks on early versions of this chapter. We would also like to express our thanks to Kim Koffolt for improving the readability of this chapter.

Shashi Shekhar, a computer science professor at the University of Minnesota, was elected an IEEE fellow for contributions to spatial database storage methods, data mining, and geographic information systems. He can be reached at www.cs.umn.edu/~shekhar..

Pusheng Zhang is a Ph.D. candidate at the University of Minnesota, specializing in spatial databases, data mining, and temporal databases. He can be reached at pusheng@cs.umn.edu.

Yan Huang is an assistant professor of computer science at the University of North Texas. Her interests include spatial databases, data mining, and geographic information systems. She can be reached at www.cs.unt.edu~huangyan.

Ranga Raju Vatsavai is a Ph.D. candidate at the University of Minnesota, specializing in spatial databases, data mining, and geographic information systems. He can be reached at vatsavai@cs.umn.edu.

Chapter 20

Challenges in Scientific Data Mining
Heterogeneous, Biased, and Large Samples

Zoran Obradovic and Slobodan Vucetic

Observing a phenomenon followed by creating and testing a hypothesis and developing and refining a model is a scientific paradigm shared across disciplines (Mjoslness and DeCoste 2001). Temporal studies where observations of past outcomes of a phenomenon are used to anticipate its future behavior are very common in science (Drossu and Obradovic 2000). Furthermore, sequence studies are often performed in biosciences where the objective is to explain certain property characterizing a given sequence or its specific position by observing and analyzing similar sequences or neighboring positions in a given sequence (Vucetic, Brown, Dunker, and Obradovic 2003). In a large number of scientific disciplines including geosciences, astronomy, and biology, spatial studies are carried out where observations at certain locations in space are used to understand the process at the same or other locations at different points in time (Vucetic, Fiez, and Obradovic 2000). In spatial-temporal scientific studies temporal and spatial aspects are considered together with an objective of understanding certain spatiotemporal patterns (Pokrajac, Hoskinson, and Obradovic 2003).

Data analysis techniques supporting traditional scientific processes were aimed at handling a fairly small amount of low dimensional data through a hypothesize-and-test paradigm. These extremely labor intensive techniques are becoming infeasible for analysis of enormous scientific datasets obtained at much higher speed and lower cost using improved or novel data collection technologies. In recent years astronomers, geoscientists, biochemists, high energy physicists and other scientists collect huge and high dimension datasets using advanced telescope technologies (Brunner, Djorgovski, Prince, and Szalay 2002), multi-spectral remote sensors on satellites (Nasa 1999), integrating global positioning systems with high resolution sensors on ground (Vucetic and Obradovic 2000), developing massively parallel instruments like microarrays that generate gene expressions for entire organisms at once (Brown, Grundy, Lin, Cristianini, Sugnet, Furey, Ares, and Haussler 2000), and employing other advanced technologies (Han, Altman, Kumar, Mannila, and Pregibon 2002).

For example, in earth sciences, in addition to a network of geostationary and polar orbiting weather and meteorological satellites, novel series of satellites have been recently introduced that provide steady data stream from multiple sensors to accomplish deeper understanding of climate and environmental changes (Barrett and Curtis 1999 Drury 1998). In particular, NASA Earth Observation System (Nasa 1999) consisting of several low-altitude satellites is the first observing system to offer integrated measurements of the earth's processes. It supports a coordinated series of polar-orbiting and low-inclination satellites for long-term global observations of the land surface, biosphere, solid earth, atmosphere, and oceans. Its Landsat 7 instrument has a data rate of 150 megabytes per second (Nasa 2002), while Terra instrument produces data in order of one terabyte daily (Nasa 1999).

Another source of large datasets in science is the result of using fast computational facilities in simulations of astrophysics, fluid dynamics, structural mechanics, chemical engineering, climate modeling and other fields. For example, the Reanalysis Project, jointly pursued by the National Center for Environmental Prediction and the National Center for Atmospheric Research, has a goal to produce new atmospheric analyses using historical data as well as to produce analyses of the current atmospheric state (Kalnay 1996). This effort results with 55 gigabytes per year of processed data, containing several temporal climate and weather attributes at a regular 3D spatial grid for 50+ years of atmospheric fields. The data has been employed in various domains including climatology, forestry and environmental sciences (Nogues-Paegle, Mo, and Paegle 1998) as well to create snapshot annual CD- ROMs containing digests of raw reanalysis data.

In principle, data mining provides an opportunity for a shift from a traditional hypothesize-and-test scientific paradigm to a partial automation of the entire process including hypothesis generation, model construction and experimentation (Mjoslness and DeCoste 2001. Some data mining techniques developed initially for automation of a business decision making process were quickly adopted to large scale scientific domains. For example, a general-purpose text mining technique of searching for co-occurrences of predefined terms was successfully applied to problems from bioscience for extracting known protein-protein interactions or gene names from Medline abstracts (Jenssen, Laegreid, Komorowski, and Hovig 2001; Marcotte, Xenarios, and Eisenberg 2001) and for finding similarities among abstracts (Han, Vucetic, and Obradovic 2003; Shatkay, Edwards, Wilbur, Boguski, Genes 2000).

Also, innovative data mining methods were developed to address certain aspects of specific scientific problems that are distinct from typical business applications and were employed at other scientific domains (Kamath 2002). At the 1996 report of the Workshop on Scientific Data Management, Mining, Analysis and Assimilation it was emphasized that regardless of a particular domain, scientific data sets share a lot of common properties and need a unified approach to efficiently solve numerous common problems involving data storage, organization, access, and knowledge discovery (Grossman and Moore 1996). Terrabyte scale problems were proposed for evaluating scientific data mining technologies at this workshop. For example, one of the reported applications was aimed at analysis of 3 terabytes of radio astronomy data for determining size and distribution of objects. To analyze this data in five minutes would require a data handling system with an access rate of 10 gigabytes per second to the stored data. In more recent scientific data mining workshops (Grossman and Moore 1996; Grossman, Kamatch, Kumar, Namburu 2000; Burl, Kamatch, Kumar, Namburu 2001; Burl, Kamatch, Kumar, Namburu, 2001; Kumar, Burl, Kamatch, and Namburu 2002) and elsewhere (Nasa 1999; Kamath 2002; Kargupta and Joshi 2002) testbed problems were increased to petabytes of data (Grossman, Creel, Harinath, Mazzucco, Reinhart, and Turinskiy 2000; Szalay, Gray, and Vandenberg 2002) distributed among multiple locations (Kargupta and Joshi 2002; Lazarevic and Obradovic 2002).

In spite of significant advances in data mining and in related fields of remote sensing, databases, machine learning, temporal, spatial and spatial-temporal statistics (Roddick and Spiliopoulou 1999), there is an urgent need for additional scientific data mining activities in order to make a genuine paradigm shift in science a reality (Han, Altman, Kumar, Mannila, and Pregibon 2002). Challenges that need more attention are numerous. Some of important scientific data mining issues that will not be considered at this article include: learning with prior knowledge (Abu-Mostafa 1995; Niyogi, Girosi, and Poggio 1998; incremental learning (Domingos and Hulten 2000); handling short observation history (Pokrajac, Hoskinson, and Obradovic 2003); integrating information from many sources (Hall and Llinas 2001;, Kargupta and Joshi 2002; Lazarevic and Obradovic 2002); and performing effective data registration to relate information from various subjects (Lester and Arridge 1999).

Our discussion will focus on the following scientific data mining challenges: (1) understanding heterogeneous phenomena with local relationships in observed attributes; (2) handling spatial, temporal and sequence correlation in data; (3) learning from small and biased labeled samples; (4) exploiting large unlabeled datasets; and (5) reducing data with controllable information loss for efficient analysis.

Some of our techniques proposed for handling these problems will be described and their application will be illustrated on several scientific data mining problems currently studied at our laboratory.

20.1   Mining of Heterogeneous Data

In the section, we discuss heterogeneous spatial data and nonstationary time series, the partitioning algorithm, the mining of heterogeneous spatial data (application 1), mining of nonstationary time series (application 2), and mining of heterogeneous sequence data (application 3).

20.1.1   Heterogeneous Spatial Data and Nonstationary Time Series

Real-life spatial data are often heterogeneous, such that at different spatial locations the dependencies between observed attributes and the response are different. Heterogeneity could be caused by presence of unobserved or very noisy spatial attributes. If it is possible to partition heterogeneous spatial data into spatial regions with homogeneous distributions, specialized models could be learned on each homogeneous region separately. This would result in better overall prediction accuracy as compared to constructing a single model on all data.

Similarly, real-life time series are often nonstationary with data distribution changing over time. Piece-wise stationary time series consisting of time intervals that could be considered stationary are common in practice. Union of all intervals of a piece-wise stationary time series with approximately the same stationary distribution is called a regime. In general, the number of regimes and their switching dynamics is not known in advance. Fitting a global regression model to such data would fail to capture the underlying relationships and would result in learning an averaged behavior of its regimes.

Let us denote each data point as a pair $(\mathbf{x}_s, y_s)$, where s represents its spatial or time location, $\mathbf{x}_s$ is a vector of attributes, and y_s is a real-valued response variable. Let us also denote each homogeneous region/regime as S_j, $j = 1, \ldots, J$, where J is a number of homogeneous regions/regimes, and $s \in S_j$ means that data point s belongs to region/regime S_j. The relationship between attributes and response in region/regime S_j can be expressed as $y_s = f_j(\mathbf{x}_s) + \epsilon_s$, where f_j is a regression function, and ϵ_s is the error term representing the unexplained variance. The task of mining of heterogeneous spatial and time data can now be stated as:

1. Discovering homogeneous regions/regimes S_j, their number J, and their location in space/time

2. Analyzing each of the regions/regimes separately by estimating regression function f_j on each of them

Both space and time domains are characterized by a significant degree of correlation where data points close in space/time are more likely to have similar properties and, therefore, to belong to the same homogeneous region/regime. This fact can be used to improve the mining of heterogeneous data. In our previous work (Vucetic and Obradovic 2000; Vucetic, Obradovic, and Tomsovic 2001) we proposed an algorithm for mining of heterogeneous spatial and time data that: (1) determines whether the data set is heterogeneous; (2) discovers an appropriate partitioning into more homogeneous subsets; and (3) constructs specialized regression model on each identified homogeneous subset. This algorithm is based on partitioning of heterogeneous data through a competition of regression models for data points using information about spatial/temporal correlation to stabilize the partitioning process.

20.1.2   Partitioning Algorithm

The proposed partitioning algorithm relies on the competition among regression models for each part of a given data set S_0. The algorithm starts by learning a global regression model on the complete data set. Next, the dataset is split randomly into two equal sized disjoint subsets and separate regression models are trained on each of them. The two models then compete for each data point such that a given point is assigned to the model achieving higher accuracy. This competition procedure iterates until a stable partitioning of data into two regions/regimes is obtained.

Subsequently, the accuracy obtained by such a partition is compared to the accuracy of the global model. If the improvement is not sufficiently large, the algorithm is stopped and it is concluded that the data set is homogeneous. If using two regression models is better than one global model, the algorithm proceeds by partitioning data into three regions/regimes in an attempt to further increase the prediction accuracy. The procedure continues by adding new models into the competition until it is concluded that further partitioning does not improve prediction accuracy. Partitioning algorithm for heterogeneous spatial and temporal data is described next.

Partitioning Algorithm

- Learn a single model on complete data set S_0 and calculate its accuracy.

- Split S_0 into disjoint equal size sets $S_{1,2}^0$ and $S_{2,2}^0$. Denote $S_2^0 = \{S_{1,2}^0, S_{2,2}^0\}$.

- Modify S_2^0 through **the competition procedure** and calculate the overall accuracy achieved by the obtained partitioning $S_2 = \{S_{1,2}, S_{2,2}\}$.

- Terminate the algorithm if the accuracy is not improved — data is homogeneous.

- L=2.
  repeat
      for $i = 1$ to L

         – Split $S_{i,L}$ into two disjoint subsets of the same sizes, $S_{i,L}'$ and $S_{i,L}''$, to obtain the initial partitioning $S_{L+1,i}^0 = \{S_L/S_{i,L}, S_{i,L}', S_{i,L}''\}$.
         – Modify $S_{L+1,i}^0$ through the competition procedure and calculate the accuracy achieved by the obtained partitioning $S_{L+1,i}$.

      end

         – Out of L partitions, $S_{L+1,i}$, $i = 1, \ldots, L$, choose the partitioning achieving the best accuracy as the new partitioning, $S_{L+1} = \{S_{1,L+1}, \ldots, S_{L+1,L+1}\}$.
         – $L \leftarrow L + 1$

      until there is improvement in accuracy

- Output: $L - 1$ homogeneous subsets defined by partitioning S_{L-1}.

The competition procedure used in partitioning consists of the following steps.

Competition Procedure

- Start from a partitioning into L subsets S_L^0 and set $n = 0$.
  repeat
  - Learn L models using L subsets of S_L^n, $S_i, i = 1, \ldots, L$.
  - Filter errors of all models over space/time.
  - If model M_j gives the best accuracy on data point s assign it to subset S_j.
  - Form a new partitioning, S_L^{n+1}, from reassignments.
  - $n \leftarrow n + 1$

  until convergence to a stable solution

One of the most important mechanisms for efficient partitioning is competition of regression models with assigning a data point to the model achieving the highest accuracy. If data is characterized by a significant level of noise, the probability of incorrectly assigning a data point could become significant. The convergence of the competition and accuracy of partition can be aided by an error-filtering step that tends to assign data points close in space/time to the same homogeneous region. Following the construction of predictors in the competition step absolute prediction errors are filtered using a corresponding spatial/temporal filter. The coverage of spatial/temporal filter should correspond to the range over which spatial/temporal correlation of absolute prediction errors exists, and it could be easily determined experimentally.

In Vucetic and Obradovic(2000a and b) we showed that, when two homogeneous regions/regimes characterize the data heterogeneity, the partitioning algorithm converges and the quality of partitioning increases with the appropriate use of error filtering.

20.1.3 Application 1: Mining of Heterogeneous Spatial Data

We performed an extensive study on synthetic spatial data to characterize the partitioning algorithm (Vucetic and Obradovic 2000). The results confirmed that convergence is very fast and that in the presence of unexplained variance in spatial data, incorporating error filtering to the competition procedure can significantly improve the partitioning accuracy.

We also performed an experiment on a real-life scientific database containing a grid of 8 topographic attributes and winter wheat yield from a 220 ha field. The goal was to predict wheat yield as a function of terrain attributes derived from USGS 30 m DEM data mapped to a 10 x 10 m grid, where the majority of the terrain attributes were continuous and non-Gaussian. The crop yield values were collected with a combine mounted yield monitor and a global positioning system. There were 24,592 data points in the entire data set.

From the previous results (Vucetic, Fiez, and Obradovic 1999), it was known that topographical attributes alone could explain just a small part of crop yield variance. A global neural network with 5 hidden nodes achieved R^2 of only 0.11 on test data. The partitioning algorithm was applied in order to examine if the field was heterogeneous such that possible homogeneous regions could be treated differently. Using the advances in precision agriculture, this would allow farmers to apply different practices on each of the homogeneous regions to obtain larger profits as compared to treating the whole field uniformly.

From the correlogram of prediction errors of a global neural network achieving the range at about 150 meters, the error filter size was set to 150 meters. The partitioning algorithm discovered 3 homogeneous regions such that the achieved accuracy was improved to $R^2 = 0.31$. A brief analysis of discovered regions showed that the largest homogeneous region corresponded to the high-yielding low-slope part of the field, while the smaller two regions corresponded to the low-yielding higher-slope parts oriented toward south and north, respectively. This illustrated the benefits of careful mining of heterogeneous spatial scientific databases.

20.1.4 Application 2: Mining of Nonstationary Time Series

We applied the partitioning algorithm to characterize recent price behavior in the California electricity market (Vucetic, Obradovic, and Tomsovic 2001). Publicly available data on day-ahead forecasted load l_t was known before trading and market clearing prices p_t of day-ahead market in the period from April 1, 1998 until September 30, 1999, were used in the experiments (first two plots from figure 20.1). A total of 12,952 data points were constructed from hourly data covering this period. Since the relationship between price and generated power for thermal power generators is usually expressed as quadratic function, we have decided to model the relationship between $\{p_t\}$ and $\{l_t\}$ as $p_t = y(l_t, \beta) = \beta_0 + \beta_1 l_t + \beta_2 l_t^2 + \beta_3 l_t^3$, and used this functional form to construct competing price predictors in the partitioning algorithm. The length of error filter was set to 168 (representing a period of two weeks).

The partitioning algorithm discovered 4 specific regimes in the data (third plot from figure 20.1). The mean squared error of four specialized price predictors was 61.6 representing a significant improvement over 93.9 achieved with a single price predictor. We observed that the four regimes differ significantly in price-load relationships (different price for the same load) as well as in price volatility. Regimes with relatively high prices indicated periods of ex-

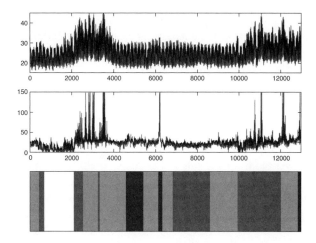

Figure 20.1: Plot of hourly load, hourly MCP between April 1, 1998 and September 30, 1999 as well as the four regimes discovered by the partitioning algorithm (Vucetic, S., Tomsovic, K. and Obradovic, Z., IEEE Transactions on Power Systems, vol. 16, no. 2, pp. 280-286, 2001)(©2001 IEEE, reproduced with permission).

ercising the market power with large suppliers possibly withholding a portion of generation and causing a price increase. The regime appearing during the nine weeks of May and June of 1998 was characterized by extremely low price and low volatility apparently caused by high hydro generation and relatively low load. Extremely high prices and high price volatility with a relatively low load characterize regime which appeared during the five weeks of October and November in 1998, one week at the end of December of 1998, and the last week of September of 1999. We speculated that this was caused by scheduled maintenance and lower hydro availability but a definitive answer depends on data not publicly available. As a conclusion, the partitioning algorithm proved as a potentially very valuable tool in analyzing price behavior and inefficiencies in electricity markets.

20.1.5 Application 3: Mining of Heterogeneous Sequence Data

We also modified our partitioning algorithm for mining of heterogeneous sequence data (Vucetic, Brown, Dunker, and Obradovic 2003). Our interest in this problem originated from the study of protein disorder property. Briefly, protein disorder is a biological concept that refers to regions in protein sequence that do not have unique 3D structure under physiological conditions (Dunker, Brown, Lawson, Lakoucheva, and Obradovic 2002). Our previous studies suggested that predictors of protein disorder trained on disorder from one type of protein achieve poor accuracy on other disordered proteins, indicating the existence of different types, or flavors, of disorder. Therefore, our objective was to determine if disordered proteins could be partitioned in a systematic manner into a number of groups with distinct statistical and biological properties.

To a certain extent, the partitioning problem could be formulated as clustering. However, with a large number of relevant attributes and strong influence of unobserved effects, applying of-the-shelf clustering software results in clusters with low biological significance. So, we modified the described partitioning algorithm such that S_0 corresponds to the set of all disordered proteins and each model is learned to classify between a given subset of S_0 versus examples of protein sequences that are ordered.

The proposed algorithm (Vucetic, Brown, Dunker, and Obradovic 2003) starts by fitting a global classifier based on all available disordered proteins and an equal number of examples of protein order. Next, disordered proteins are divided randomly into two disjoint subsets of equal size and separate classifiers are trained using each of them. The two classifiers then compete for each disordered protein such that a given protein is assigned to the predictor achieving the highest accuracy. This step is related with the error filtering since each protein is represented as a set of data points whose number equals protein length and each protein is assigned exclusively to a single flavor. The competition iterates until a stable partitioning is obtained. Subsequently, the overall accuracy obtained by such a partitioning is compared to the accuracy of the global classifier. The algorithm proceeds by gradually partitioning disordered proteins into more subsets in an attempt to further improve the accuracy.

Data sets with 145 nonredundant disordered protein regions and about equal number of ordered proteins of similar length were used in the experiment. For each position in a protein sequence we extracted 18 amino acid frequencies, flexibility, and sequence complexity calculated over a sliding window of length 41. By employing the proposed partitioning algorithm we concluded that 3 disorder flavors exist where accuracy of the global classifier of 71% was improved to 84% when 3 specialized classifiers were used. This difference in the accuracy of 3 flavor-specific predictors versus a global predictor was significant enough to validate the claim that disorder flavors indeed exist. The 3 flavors, denoted as V, C and S, contained 52, 39 and 54 disordered proteins, respectively. A comparison of amino acid compositions revealed that the flavors have statistically significant differences where flavor C was very different from both the other two flavors and ordered proteins, while flavors V and S were more similar.

Experiments on 28 complete genomes revealed that 5 of the 6 *archaea* genomes were biased towards flavor V and 12 of 18 *eubacteria* genomes were biased towards flavor S (4 *eubacteria* have affinity towards flavor C and 2 toward flavor V), while all 4 *eukaryote* genomes were biased towards flavor S. We also used flavor-specific predictions on SwissProt data bank to assess flavor-function relationships. The flavor V predictor gave the strongest prediction of disorder for helical regions. We have shown previously that disordered domains that become ordered helices upon binding to other proteins are compositionally distinct from other types of disorder. The flavor C predictor gave strong predictions of disorder for poly-and oligosaccharide binding domains. The flavor S predictor strongly predicted leucine rich regions such as leucine zippers to be disordered.

The partitioning was based exclusively on sequence statistics, whereas, post hoc, we found relationships between discovered flavors and function. This gives a strong indication that the proposed modification of the partitioning algorithm was very successful in discovering a biologically valid partition of disordered proteins and thus giving a novel insight into properties of protein disorder.

20.2   Learning from Biased Data

In this section we describe learning from biased data. We will discuss biased labeled data, reestimating the class distribution, classification with biased class distribution (application 4), contrast classifiers for learning from biased data, and using contrast classifiers in bioinformatics (application 5).

20.2.1   Biased Labeled Data

A common assumption made in machine learning is that labeled data used for training a classifier and unlabeled new data can be considered as samples from the same underlying distribution. In such a case one could apply a standard machine learning procedure to learn a classifier from labeled data (e.g., logistic regression, decision trees, neural networks), estimate its accuracy (e.g., directly from training set, using cross-validation), and apply it on unlabeled examples in a straightforward manner. However, this assumption is often violated with labeled and/or unlabeled data obtained by biased sampling from an underlying distribution. If class distribution on labeled data is different from that of unlabeled data, a classifier trained on labeled data can cause incorrect inference and produce suboptimal classification on unlabeled data.

Large quantities of unlabeled data are often available in data-rich scientific domains such as remote sensing or bioscience. Predictive data mining, with a few exceptions, typically relies on labeled data without exploiting a much larger source of available unlabeled data. In this section we illustrate two approaches that exploit unlabeled data for more effective mining on biased data.

20.2.2   Reestimating the Class Distribution

The problem of learning from data with biased class distribution can be defined as the construction of a classifier using labeled data S_L with class probabilities $P_L[y = j]$, $j = 1, \ldots, c$, where c is the number of classes, for accurate prediction on unlabeled data S_U with unknown class probabilities $P_U[y = j]$. This problem can be addressed by (*step 1*) estimating the class distribution $P_U[y = j]$, followed by (*step 2*) using this estimate to construct a desired classifier. We proposed a bootstrap methodology to estimate distribution of $P_U[y = j]$ based on (*step 1.a*) an estimate of a classifier's accuracy obtained on labeled data, and (*step 1.b*) an estimate of a classifier's class predictions on unlabeled data (Vucetic and Obradovic 2001).

Given a predictor, by $p_j = P_U[y = j]$ we denote the class probability on S_U, by $p(k|j) = P[\hat{y} = k|y = j]$ the probability of predicting class k if the true class is j, and by $q_k = P_U[\hat{y} = k]$ the probability of predicting class k on S_U. Using the law of total probability, q_k can be calculated as $q_k = \sum p(k|j) \times p_j$, or in the matrix form as $\mathbf{q} = \mathbf{P} \times \mathbf{p}$, where $\mathbf{q} = \{q_k\}$, $\mathbf{P} = \{p(k|j)\}$, $\mathbf{p} = \{p_j\}$. Therefore, the true class probability p_j can be calculated as $\mathbf{p} = \mathbf{P}^{-1} \times \mathbf{q}$ in the matrix form, under the assumption that values of q_j and $p(k|j)$ are known with certainty. This can occur only if S_L and S_U are very large. However, the size of available data sets is always limited and so q_k and $p(k|j)$ can be considered as random variables whose properties should be estimated first.

For statistical inference suitable for estimating the distribution of p_j from estimates of q_k and $p(k|j)$, we adopted a powerful bootstrap simulation methodology (Efron and Tibshirani 1993). Given an original sample X with n examples the bootstrap sample X^* is obtained by randomly sampling n examples from X with replacement. Briefly, bootstrap samples S_L^* and S_U^* are repeatedly taken and used to estimate $p^*(k|j)$ from S_L^* and q_j^* from S_U^*. ¿From these two estimates p_j are be calculated. Bootstrap estimate of p_j can be obtained as an average p_j^* over B bootstrap rounds. It should be noted that that estimates $\mathbf{p}^* = \{p_i^*\}$ can be unfeasible if $\mathbf{P}^* = \{p^*(j|i)\}$ is noninvertible or if elements of $\mathbf{p}^* = (\mathbf{P}^*)^{-1}\mathbf{q}^*$ are negative. Such bootstrap estimates are rejected.

20.2.3 Application 4: Classification with Biased Class Distribution

If a classifier could estimate posterior class probabilities $P(j|\mathbf{x})$ when presented with a new example $\mathbf{x}$, then it can be directly adjusted without the need for retraining according to estimated class probabilities p_j on S_U. For example, a neural network with a large hidden layer and c outputs (representing each of the c classes) trained by minimizing the mean squared error is known to be able to approximate posterior class probabilities. Adjusted posterior class probabilities $P_{adjust}(j|\mathbf{x})$ can be calculated as $P_{adjust}[j|x] = CP[j|x]P_U[y=j]/P_L[y=j]$, where $P_L[y=j]$ is class j probability on labeled data S_L and C is a normalization constant.

Retraining a predictor based on an estimate of class probability p_i on unlabeled data S_U is another choice for improving classification. In this case, labeled data S_L is resampled according to estimated p_j and a predictor is learned on the resampled data set. This simple procedure can be iterated several times by estimating p_j based on the improved predictor, resampling S_L, and learning a new predictor.

Our preliminary evaluation of the proposed bootstrap algorithm on synthetic data of various statistical properties showed that it accurately estimates the class probabilities on unlabeled data (Vucetic and Obradovic 2001). In another experiment on a 3-class benchmark dataset called Waveform (Breiman, Friedman, Olshen, and Stone 1984) the S_L was constructed with balanced classes, while we experimented with different class distributions p_j on S_U. It was shown that for balanced classes $\mathbf{p} = [1/3, 1/3, 1/3]$ the original predictor had slightly higher accuracy then adjusted or retrained predictor for small data sets ($n_L = n_U = 500$), while all 3 strategies resulted in similar accuracy for larger data sets ($n_L = n_U > 1000$). For unbalanced classes, $\mathbf{p} \neq [1/3, 1/3, 1/3]$, our methodology with predictor adjusting or retraining resulted in significant accuracy improvement over original predictors. Moreover, retrained predictors were superior over adjusted predictors for large data. Bootstrap estimates of p_j were sufficiently accurate even for small data sets while this accuracy increased with the size of data sets.

20.2.4 Contrast Classifiers for Learning from Biased Data

Recently, we proposed use of contrast classifiers trained to discriminate between labeled and unlabeled examples for mining of biased data (Peng, Vucetic, Han, Xie, and Obradovic 2003). The name contrast classifier comes from the meaning of their outputs - they represent difference, or contrast, of a given example from the underlying distribution of labeled data. Given this explanation, it is apparent that contrast classifiers could be used in a number of important data mining applications including outlier detection and learning on biased data.

Given an unlabeled dataset representative of the underlying distribution and a K-class labeled sample that might be biased, our approach is to learn K contrast classifiers $cc_k(\mathbf{x})$, $k = 1, \ldots, K$, each trained to discriminate a certain class of labeled data from the unlabeled population. If an employed contrast classifier learned on a balanced set of labeled and unlabeled data points is able to approximate posterior class probabilities it can be shown that contrast classifiers can be used to construct the maximum a posteriori classifier for the K-classification problem with the optimal decision obtained as

$$\hat{c} = \arg \max_j \frac{1 - cc_j(\mathbf{x})}{cc_j(\mathbf{x})} \times p_j,$$

where p_j is prior probability for unlabeled data with class j.

Moreover, for a test data point $\mathbf{x}$ the ratio $(1 - cc_j(\mathbf{x}))/cc_j(\mathbf{x})$ measures difference from class j of labeled data, thus providing a mechanism for detection of unlabeled points under-represented in labeled data. Prediction on such uncharacteristic points can be expected to be less accurate since it corresponds to the extrapolation to less explored parts of the attribute space. Therefore, contrast classifiers are characterized by the ability to provide optimal classification on the explored portion of the attribute space, while detecting data points from the less-explored regions. This allows achieving an appropriate tradeoff between classification accuracy and prediction coverage.

Experiments on the Waveform data confirmed that contrast classifiers achieve accuracy comparable to standard classifiers in the case of unbiased labeled data, while they are significantly more efficient when the labeled data is biased. This approach is also shown to be more accurate than alternatives such as kernel density estimation that rely solely on a distribution of a positive class. Contrast classifiers are very robust to a small labeled data size and a high dimensional space with many irrelevant attributes.

20.2.5 Application 5: Using Contrast Classifiers in Bioinformatics

In recent work (Peng, Vucetic, Han, Xie, and Obradovic 2003) we applied contrast classifiers to identify proteins in large sequence repositories that are statistically underrepresented in our labeled database of known ordered and disordered proteins. Understanding biological properties of these outliers could lead to more effective studies of protein disorder.

We were given a nonredundant labeled data (sequence identity less than 25%) consisting of 152 proteins with disordered regions longer than 30 consecutive residues, and 290 completely ordered proteins. In addition, we had access to 17,676 nonredundant unlabeled protein sequences derived from the SwissProt database (Boeckmann, Bairoch, Apweiler, Blatter, Estreicher, Gasteiger, Martin, Michoud, O'Donovan, Phan, Pilbout, and Schneider 2003) by grouping homologues (similar sequences) to the ProtoMap clusters (Yona, Linial, Linial 1999).

Two class-specific contrast classifiers were constructed, one for contrasting disordered class from unlabeled data and another for contrasting order class from unlabeled data. A disordered predictor constructed from two contrast classifiers achieved accuracy of 84% that is practically identical to our currently most accurate disorder predictor (Obradovic, Peng, Vucetic, Radivojac, Brown, and Dunker 2003) thus confirming the effectiveness of contrast classifiers.

The two contrast classifiers were used for selection and evaluation of underrepresented SwissProt proteins. From the unlabeled dataset we first selected a set we call *SWISS* consisting of 6,964 sequences similar in length to our labeled sequences (200 to 500 amino-acids long). To detect proteins that are overall the most different from ordered and disordered proteins, we summarized each protein in *SWISS* according to the average predictions of the two contrast classifiers over its sequence. Sequences with the largest average contrast with respect to both classes of labeled data (ordered and disordered proteins) were denoted as *OUTLIERS* consisting of 1,259 sequences. For comparison we also derived from the SwissProt database 539 homologues to ordered proteins from the training data and 356 homologues of confirmed disordered proteins. For each of the 4 identified data sets we calculated the frequency of each of the 840 protein function keywords listed in SwissProt database. By comparing these frequencies we were able to observe significant differences between biological functions of proteins in the 4 groups.

The most interesting result was that frequency of glycoprotein, Inner membrane, membrane, transmembrane and transport proteins in *OUTLIERS* was extremely high as compared to the other three data sets. They are all members of a large family of membrane proteins known to be structurally and functionally diverse and are highly underrepresented among our labeled order and disorder sequences. This is also consistent with the results of our control study where outliers were identified by learning class-conditional distribution models of ordered and disordered protein sequences (Vucetic, Pokrajac, Xie, and Obradovic 2003). In fact, we found that the contrast for membrane proteins was so high that it is likely that most of the bias in our labeled data comes from this group. This interesting result is very important for the more efficient study of protein disorder and it also illustrates the promise of using contrast classifiers in scientific data mining on biased data.

20.3   Performance-Controlled Data Reduction

Much of machine learning research has concentrated on induction and model validation from limited data sets. However, in a number of scientific domains the data sets are extremely large, distributed over a number of locations, and dynamically increasing with time. While large data sets are desirable regarding the resolution of potentially extractable knowledge, they can easily cause computational and storage problems. Most approaches that can accomplish efficient transfer and storage include lossless attribute compression (Memon, Sayood, and Magliveras 1994) or lossy attribute compression using vector quantization (Ryan and Arnold 1997).

An important knowledge discovery problem is to establish a reasonable bound on the size of data sets needed for their accurate and efficient analysis. For example, for many applications a 10-fold increment of the data set size for a potential accuracy gain of 1% cannot be justified due to huge additional computational costs. Reducing large data sets into more compact representative subsets while retaining essentially the same extractable knowledge could speed up learning and reduce storage requirements.

20.3.1   Downsampling and Quantization Methods

We proposed an effective data reduction procedure (Vucetic and Obradovic 2000) that, for a user-specified allowed accuracy loss, (1) applies down-sampling to identify a minimal representative random sample size, and follows it by (2) determining an appropriate quantization for each continuous attribute and performing compression of attributes and the target.

Assume a data set is given with N examples, each represented by a set of K attributes and the corresponding target variable. The task is to obtain a reduced data set with a minimal size that, using the same learning algorithm, allows knowledge extraction with accuracy reduced for at most α [%]. To achieve this goal we proposed the following two-phase method: (1) reduce the sample size from N to n_{min} while allowing accuracy loss α_D to achieve a data compression ratio $C_D = N/n_{min}$, and (2) perform proper quantization of continuous attributes in such down-sampled data set allowing accuracy loss α_Q, followed by Huffman coding (Huffman 1952) of discretized attributes to achieve compression ratio C_Q. Assuming that total accuracy loss α is close to zero, it follows that $\alpha \approx \alpha_D + \alpha_C$ with the achieved total compression ratio $C = C_D \times C_Q$.

A learning curve for least squares predictors depicts the dependence of the predictor accuracy measured as mean squared error (MSE) on the training set size n. This curve consists of two regions: (1) the initial region characterized by fast drop of the mean squared error (MSE) with the increasing sample size, and (2) the convergence region where addition of new samples into the training set does not significantly improve prediction accuracy. In our studies we used the idea of progressive sampling (Provost, Jensen, Oates 1999) to efficiently span the available range of sampling sizes and estimate the parameters of learning curve in search for the n_{min}.

Uniform quantization, where the range of a continuous attribute is split into equal subintervals (bins), was applied with subsequent Huffman coding of discretized values. Attributes on which the response has less sensitivity can be allowed higher distortion (the coarser quantization) and vice versa. To estimate the influence of attributes quantization on model prediction quality, we proposed the sensitivity analysis of a prediction model obtained on the down-sampled data set. This analysis allowed developing heuristics for proper quantization levels of all attributes in an efficient manner.

20.3.2 Application 6: Reduction of Spatially Correlated Data

We performed a number of down-sampling and quantization experiments (Vucetic and Obradovic 2000) on several large data sets including Covertype Data Set. This set is currently one of the largest databases in the University of California, Irvine's Database Repository (Murphy, Aha, and Robinson 1992) containing 581,012 examples with 54 attributes and 7 target classes and representing the forest cover type at 30×30 meter grid, obtained from U.S. Forest Service Region 2 Resource Information System (Blackard 1998).

The data was transformed into 12 attributes, 10 of which were continuous. In its raw form the data set has 60MB and can be compressed 6 times by gzip software. We examined data reduction when neural networks are used as nonlinear least square estimators. Our experiments showed that the convergence region of the learning curve corresponded to sample sizes larger than 1,000, that asymptotic accuracy of a neural network is 70.1%, and that for allowed accuracy loss of $\alpha_C = 1\%$ the size of reduced dataset can be 3,600. To properly estimate the learning curve it was needed to train less than 20 neural networks on increasing sample sizes where the total number of data points used was around 30,000. Therefore, this learning effort was order of magnitude smaller than training a single neural network on the complete Covertype data. Quantization of the 10 continuous attributes with accuracy loss $\alpha_Q = 1\%$ allowed their representation with around 20 bits that compares favorably with 320 bits when standard double precision representation is used. To perform the quantization step around 20 neural networks were trained on the reduced data set with 3,600 data points. By properly combining the down-sampling and quantization steps we were able to reduce the size of Covertype data to 25kB, 12kB, and 5kB for user-specified accuracy loss of $\alpha = 1, 2,$ and 5%, respectively.

Considering the original data size of 60 megabytes it is evident that reduction of more than 3 orders of magnitude are possible for a small acceptable prediction accuracy loss. This result indicates potentially huge benefits of the performance controlled data reduction in data-rich scientific data mining.

20.4 Discussion

Detection, understanding, and managing heterogeneity in large spatial or temporal scientific datasets with attributes that are noisy, collected with different resolutions, or even missing is a critical task of scientific data mining. Its success will depend on integration and extension of techniques from statistics (Cressie 1993; Hamilton 1994) and data mining (Roddick and Spiliopoulou 2002). The partitioning algorithm described in section 20.2.1 and successfully applied to spatial and temporal domains as reported in sections 20.2.2 and 20.2.3 resembles a large class of expectation-maximization (EM) algorithms (Dempster, Laird, and Rubin, 1977), and, more particular, the mixture-of-experts approach (Jacobs, Jordan, Nowlan, and Hinton 1991; Weigend, Mangeas, and Srivastava 1995), annealed competition (Pawelzik, Kohlmorgen, and Muller 1996), and Markov switching models (Hamilton 1990). It is based on iterative improvements of the partitions and their corresponding specialized predictors where the overall goal is maximizing the accuracy of the specialized predictors.

The success of our algorithm could be attributed to error filtering that stabilizes partitioning by utilizing the spatial/temporal correlations existing in the data. This property is especially useful when unobserved or very noisy attributes are present, i.e. when attribute spaces of the corresponding homogeneous regions or regimes overlap. Additional advantage of our algorithm on scientific data mining domains is "hard" assignment of a data point to a single region or regime. This improves the robustness of the partitioning algorithm to the deviations from the assumed distribution, such as existence of non-Gaussian error terms.

Sequence mining is an active research area with its most prominent application in bioinformatics. A large body of research in computational biology concentrates on effective algorithms for similarity search among biological sequences. The basic thrust behind this line of research is the fact that biological molecules with similar sequences tend to share structural and functional properties. Most available algorithms (Altschul, Madden, Schaffer, Zhang, Zhang, Miller, and Lipman 1997; Hofmann 1999; Sonnhammer, Eddy, Birney, Bateman, and Durbin 998 are rather conservative: given a query sequence they select only a subset of sequences within a limited region of sequence space that guarantees their relatedness in a statistical sense. However, different biological properties tend to exist over a large number of families with unrelated sequences. Hence, important open problems of bioinformatics are inferring properties of sequences without well-studied homologues as well as increasing knowledge about certain insufficiently studied properties of the molecules. Thus, one would like to use more aggressive algorithms that generalize over a larger region of sequence space while handling an increased level of prediction error. The representatives of these algorithms are various predictors of structure (Jones 1999) or function (King, Karwath, Clare, and Dehaspe 2000) from sequence data.

Partitioning of heterogeneous sequence data by our approach (subsection 20.2.4) is based on sequence representation through a set of representative attributes. Examples from the negative class were used to provide partitioning based on the most relevant attributes, arguably, the ones that are helpful in classification between data points from the positive and the negative class. Based on this notion, we successfully modified our original partition algorithm to incorporate competition of specialized classifiers learned to discriminate between negative data and homogeneous subsets of positive data.

Learning from Biased Data

The biased labeled data problem discussed in section 20.3 is common in science. It has been known in statistics as sample selection bias, and a partial solution for its correction even led to a Nobel prize in economy (Heckman 1979). It is also a topic of active research in machine learning and data mining. The EM-based algorithms, used to iteratively estimate the model parameters and assign soft labels to unlabeled examples by treating the unknown labels as missing data and assuming generative model such as mixture of Gaussians, have been widely used in areas such as text document classification (Nigam, McCallum, Thrun, and Mitchell 2000), image retrieval (Wu, Tian, and Huang 2000), and multispectral data classification (Shahshahani and Landgrebe 1994). Cotraining (Blum and Mitchell 1998) provides another popular strategy of incorporating the unlabeled data if the data can be described in two different sufficient views, or sets of attributes. However, it is often observed that these approaches could also degrade performance due to violated model assumption or convergence to local maxima (Seeger 2001). Partially supervised classification (Liu, Lee, Yu, and Li 2002) provides a notable solution to one-class classification problems that utilizes unlabeled data; it initially assumes that all unlabeled examples are from negative class, and then applies the EM algorithm to refine the assumption.

Although very effective, it should be noted that the methodology for reestimating the class distribution described in section 20.3.2 is applicable only to the sampling bias in class distribution (as was the case in section 20.3.3).

Therefore, some theoretical or empirical evidence about sampling bias in labeled and unlabeled data should be provided to validate the algorithm application. The goal of our work in progress is to derive statistical tests that could determine (1) if class distribution is biased, and (2) if there are other types of sampling bias in data.

Use of contrast classifiers for mining on biased data, described in section 20.3.4, is related to partially supervised classification (Liu, Lee, Yu, and Li 2002). Contrast classifiers provide a framework for utilizing unlabeled data on a larger class of problems than the previously proposed solutions for the partially supervised classification. The positive results obtained in a bioinformatics problem (section 20.3.5) indicate that unlabeled data, if available in large amount, should be considered as an integral part of data mining process and, therefore, should not be ignored. This is particularly the case in biased data scenarios. An appropriate use of unlabeled data could be greatly beneficial to improvement of scientific data mining quality.

Performance-Controlled Data Reduction

Data reduction is an active area of research in data mining. Common approaches include mining on down-sampled data or building predictors on progressively increasing samples until no significant improvement in accuracy is achieved (Provost, Jensen, Oates 1999). One could choose to take a random sample from available large dataset or perform weighted sampling to increase the utility of reduced data. Examples of such weighted sampling include editing and condensing (Devijver and Kittler 1982) or boosting-like methods (Freund and Schapire 1996) that concentrate on difficult-to-learn regions of attribute space. Our approach was based on random sampling since the goal was obtaining a representative sample of available data that could be reused in different incremental or distributed learning scenarios.

It is likely that modification of our methodology providing an appropriate weighted sampling could allow more efficient data reduction. It is worth noting that data reduction is similar to active sampling (Cohn, Ghahramani, and Jordan, 1996) where the goal is to maximize learning accuracy with the minimum amount of labeled data. It would be interesting to explore if the ideas of active sampling could be used in providing more efficient data reduction. Correlations existing in large spatial and temporal scientific datasets provide another dimension for data reduction. Starting from the preliminary results herein, further research is likely to result in efficient procedures specialized to performance controlled data reduction in spatial-temporal domains.

Overall Summary

Applications briefly described at this article were drawn from important domains of precision agriculture, electric power systems and biochemistry. In many ways these areas are very different. However, they all have a common need for a partial automation of a scientific or engineering process due to a huge amount of collected data that prohibits a low capacity approach of a traditional hypothesize-and-test paradigm.

Common challenges for data mining in these areas considered in this article include efficient handling of heterogeneous data distributions, biased labeled samples and large unlabeled databases. The proposed techniques for addressing these challenges provide preliminary evidence in support of a claim that data mining methods can facilitate a shift in scientific methodology towards a more automatic hypothesis generation, model construction and experimentation in science. The current techniques for addressing the scientific data mining problems are far from comprehensive solutions. Therefore, a lot of work in this area is still needed.

Acknowledgements

We thank C. J. Brown, A. K. Dunker, T. Fiez, B. Han, K. Peng, D. Pokrajac, P. Radivojac, K. Tomsovic and H. Xie for collaboration on scientific studies used to illustrate benefits of data mining methods described at this article. These projects were supported in part by NIH grant 1 R01 LM06916-01 to A.K. Dunker and Z. Obradovic, NSF grant IIS-9711532 to Z. Obradovic and A.K. Dunker, NSF grant ECS-9988626 to K. Tomsovic and Z. Obradovic and NSF grant IIS-0219736 to Z. Obradovic and S. Vucetic.

Zoran Obradovic is director of the Information Science and Technology Center at Temple University. Funded by NSF, NIH, DOE and industry, he contributed to about 160 refereed articles in data mining, bioinformatics, and machine learning. For more details see www.ist.temple.edu/~zoran.

Slobodan Vucetic is an assistant professor of computer and information sciences at Temple University specializing in data mining, machine learning, and bioinformatics. He can be reached at vucetic@ist.temple.edu.

Web, Semantics,
and Data Mining

Chapter 21

Web Mining — Concepts, Applications, and Research Directions

Jaideep Srivastava, Prasanna Desikan, and Vipin Kumar

Web mining is the application of data mining techniques to extract knowledge from web data, including web documents, hyperlinks between documents, usage logs of web sites, etc. A panel organized at ICTAI 1997 (Srivastava and Mobasher 1997) asked the question "Is there anything distinct about web mining (compared to data mining in general)?" While no definitive conclusions were reached then, the tremendous attention on web mining in the past five years, and a number of significant ideas that have been developed, have certainly answered this question in the affirmative in a big way. In addition, a fairly stable community of researchers interested in the area has been formed, largely through the successful series of WebKDD workshops, which have been held annually in conjunction with the ACM SIGKDD Conference since 1999 (Masand and Spiliopoulou 1999; Kohavi, Spiliopoulou, and Srivastava 2001; Kohavi, Masand, Spiliopoulou, and Srivastava 2001; Masand, Spiliopoulou, Srivastava, and Zaiane 2002), and the web analytics workshops, which have been held in conjunction with the SIAM data mining conference (Ghosh and Srivastava 2001a, b). A good survey of the research in the field (through 1999) is provided by Kosala and Blockeel (2000) and Madria, Bhowmick, Ng, and Lim (1999).

Two different approaches were taken in initially defining web mining. First was a "process-centric view," which defined web mining as a sequence of tasks (Etzioni 1996). Second was a "data-centric view," which defined web mining in terms of the types of web data that was being used in the mining process (Cooley, Srivastava, and Mobasher 1997). The second definition has become more acceptable, as is evident from the approach adopted in most recent papers (Madria, Bhowmick, Ng, and Lim 1999; Borges and Levene 1998; Kosala and Blockeel 2000) that have addressed the issue. In this chapter we follow the data-centric view of web mining which is defined as follows,

> **Web mining** is the application of data mining techniques to extract knowledge from web data, i.e. web content, web structure, and web usage data.

The attention paid to web mining, in research, software industry, and web-based organization, has led to the accumulation of significant experience. It is our goal in this chapter to capture them in a systematic manner, and identify directions for future research.

The rest of this chapter is organized as follows: In section 21.1 we provide a taxonomy of web mining, in section 21.2 we summarize some of the key concepts in the field, and in section 21.3 we describe successful applications of web mining. In section 21.4 we present some directions for future research, and in section 21.5 we conclude the chapter.

21.1 Web Mining Taxonomy

Web mining can be broadly divided into three distinct categories, according to the kinds of data to be mined. Figure 21.1 shows the taxonomy.

21.1.1 Web Content Mining

Web content mining is the process of extracting useful information from the contents of web documents. Content data is the collection of facts a web page is designed to contain. It may consist of text, images, audio, video, or structured records such as lists and tables. Application of text mining to web content has been the most widely researched. Issues addressed in text mining include topic discovery and tracking, extracting association patterns, clustering of web documents and classification of web pages. Research activities on this topic have drawn heavily on techniques developed in other disciplines such as Information Retrieval (IR) and Natural Language Processing (NLP). While there exists a significant body of work in extracting knowledge from images in the fields of image processing and computer vision, the application of these techniques to web content mining has been limited.

21.1.2   Web Structure Mining

The structure of a typical web graph consists of web pages as nodes, and hyperlinks as edges connecting related pages. Web structure mining is the process of discovering structure information from the web. This can be further divided into two kinds based on the kind of structure information used.

Hyperlinks

A hyperlink is a structural unit that connects a location in a web page to a different location, either within the same web page or on a different web page. A hyperlink that connects to a different part of the same page is called an *intra-document hyperlink*, and a hyperlink that connects two different pages is called an *inter-document hyperlink*. There has been a significant body of work on hyperlink analysis, of which Desikan, Srivastava, Kumar, and Tan (2002) provide an up-to-date survey.

Document Structure

In addition, the content within a Web page can also be organized in a tree-structured format, based on the various HTML and XML tags within the page. Mining efforts here have focused on automatically extracting document object model (DOM) structures out of documents (Wang and Liu 1998; Moh, Lim, and Ng 2000).

21.1.3   Web Usage Mining

Web usage mining is the application of data mining techniques to discover interesting usage patterns from web usage data, in order to understand and better serve the needs of web-based applications (Srivastava, Cooley, Deshpande, and Tan 2000). Usage data captures the identity or origin of web users along with their browsing behavior at a web site. web usage mining itself can be classified further depending on the kind of usage data considered:

Web Server Data

User logs are collected by the web server and typically include IP address, page reference and access time.

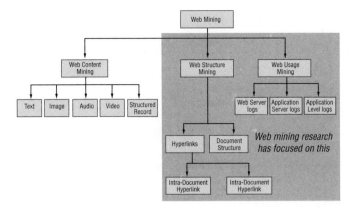

Figure 21.1: Web mining Taxonomy

Application Server Data

Commercial application servers such as Weblogic,[1,2] StoryServer,[3] have significant features to enable E-commerce applications to be built on top of them with little effort. A key feature is the ability to track various kinds of business events and log them in application server logs.

Application Level Data

New kinds of events can be defined in an application, and logging can be turned on for them — generating histories of these events.

It must be noted, however, that many end applications require a combination of one or more of the techniques applied in the above the categories.

21.2 Key Concepts

In this section we briefly describe the new concepts introduced by the web mining research community.

21.2.1 Ranking Metrics—for Page Quality and Relevance

Searching the web involves two main steps: *Extracting the pages relevant to a query* and *ranking them according to their quality*. Ranking is important as it

---

[1]http://www.bea.com/products/weblogic/server/index.shtml
[2]http://www.bvportal.com/.
[3]http://www.cio.com/sponsors/110199_vignette_story2.html.

helps the user look for "quality" pages that are relevant to the query. Different metrics have been proposed to rank web pages according to their quality. We briefly discuss two of the prominent ones.

PageRank

PageRank is a metric for ranking hypertext documents based on their quality. Page, Brin, Motwani, and Winograd (1998) developed this metric for the popular search engine Google[4] (Brin and Page 1998). The key idea is that a page has a high rank if it is pointed to by many highly ranked pages. So, the rank of a page depends upon the ranks of the pages pointing to it. This process is done iteratively until the rank of all pages are determined. The rank of a page p can be written as:

$$PR(p) = d/n + (1 - d) \sum_{(q,p) \in G} (\frac{PR(q)}{Outdegree(q)})$$

Here, n is the number of nodes in the graph and $OutDegree(q)$ is the number of hyperlinks on page q. Intuitively, the approach can be viewed as a stochastic analysis of a random walk on the web graph. The first term in the right hand side of the equation is the probability that a random web surfer arrives at a page p by typing the URL or from a bookmark; or may have a particular page as his/her home page. Here d is the probability that the surfer chooses a URL directly, rather than traversing a link[5] and $1 - d$ is the probability that a person arrives at a page by traversing a link. The second term in the right hand side of the equation is the probability of arriving at a page by traversing a link.

Hubs and Authorities

Hubs and authorities can be viewed as "fans" and "centers" in a bipartite core of a web graph, where the "fans" represent the hubs and the "centers" represent the authorities. The hub and authority scores computed for each web page indicate the extent to which the web page serves as a hub pointing to good authority pages or as an authority on a topic pointed to by good hubs. The scores are computed for a set of pages related to a topic using an iterative procedure called HITS (Kleinberg 1999). First a query is submitted to a search engine and a set of relevant documents is retrieved. This set, called the "root set," is then expanded by including web pages that point to those in the "root set" and are pointed by those in the "root set." This new set is called the "base set." An adjacency matrix, A is formed such that if there exists at least one

---

[4]http://www.google.com.
[5]The parameter d, called the dampening factor, is usually set between *0.1* and *0.2* (Brin and Page 1998).

hyperlink from page i to page j, then $A_{i,j} = 1$, otherwise $A_{i,j} = 0$. HITS algorithm is then used to compute the hub and authority scores for these set of pages.

There have been modifications and improvements to the basic page rank and hubs and authorities approaches such as SALSA (Lempel and Moran 2000), topic sensitive page rank, (Haveliwala 2002) and web page reputations (Mendelzon and Rafiei 2000). These different hyperlink based metrics have been discussed by Desikan, Srivastava, Kumar, and Tan (2002).

21.2.2 Robot Detection and Filtering—Separating Human and Nonhuman Web Behavior

Web robots are software programs that automatically traverse the hyperlink structure of the web to locate and retrieve information. The importance of separating robot behavior from human behavior prior to building user behavior models has been illustrated by Kohavi (2001). First, e-commerce retailers are particularly concerned about the unauthorized deployment of robots for gathering business intelligence at their web sites. Second, web robots tend to consume considerable network bandwidth at the expense of other users. Sessions due to web robots also make it difficult to perform click-stream analysis effectively on the web data. Conventional techniques for detecting web robots are based on identifying the IP address and user agent of the web clients. While these techniques are applicable to many well-known robots, they are not sufficient to detect camouflaged and previously unknown robots. Tan and Kumar (2002) proposed a classification based approach that uses the navigational patterns in click-stream data to determine if it is due to a robot. Experimental results have shown that highly accurate classification models can be built using this approach. Furthermore, these models are able to discover many camouflaged and previously unidentified robots.

21.2.3 Information Scent—Applying Foraging Theory to Browsing Behavior

Information scent is a concept that uses the snippets of information present around the links in a page as a "scent" to evaluate the quality of content of the page it points to, and the cost of accessing such a page(Chi, Pirolli, Chen, and Pitkow 2001). The key idea is to model a user at a given page as "foraging" for information,and following a link with a stronger "scent." The "scent" of a path depends on how likely it is to lead the user to relevant information, and is determined by a network flow algorithm called spreading activation. The snippets, graphics, and other information around a link are called "proximal cues."

The user's desired information need is expressed as a weighted keyword vector. The similarity between the proximal cues and the user's information need is computed as "proximal scent." With the proximal cues from all the links and the user's information need vector, a "proximal scent matrix" is generated. Each element in the matrix reflects the extent of similarity between the link's proximal cues and the user's information need. If enough information is not available around the link, a "distal scent" is computed with the information about the link described by the contents of the pages it points to. The proximal scent and the distal scent are then combined to give the scent matrix. The probability that a user would follow a link is then decided by the scent or the value of the element in the scent matrix.

21.2.4 User Profiles — Understanding How Users Behave

The web has taken user profiling to new levels. For example, in a "brick-and-mortar" store, data collection happens only at the checkout counter, usually called the "point-of-sale." This provides information only about the final outcome of a complex human decision making process, with no direct information about the process itself. In an on-line store, the complete click-stream is recorded, which provides a detailed record of every action taken by the user, providing a much more detailed insight into the decision making process. Adding such behavioral information to other kinds of information about users, for example demographic, psychographic, and so on, allows a comprehensive user profile to be built, which can be used for many different purposes (Masand, Spiliopoulou, Srivastava, and Zaiane 2002).

While most organizations build profiles of user behavior limited to visits to their own sites, there are successful examples of building web-wide behavioral profiles such as Alexa Research[6] and DoubleClick[7]. These approaches require browser cookies of some sort, and can provide a fairly detailed view of a user's browsing behavior across the web.

21.2.5 Interestingness Measures — When Multiple Sources Provide Conflicting Evidence

One of the significant impacts of publishing on the web has been the close interaction now possible between authors and their readers. In the preweb era, a reader's level of interest in published material had to be inferred from indirect measures such as buying and borrowing, library checkout and renewal, opinion surveys, and in rare cases feedback on the content. For material published on the web it is possible to track the click-stream of a reader to observe the exact

---

[6]http://www.alexa.com.
[7]http://www.doubleclick.com/.

path taken through on-line published material. We can measure times spent on each page, the specific link taken to arrive at a page and to leave it, etc. Much more accurate inferences about readers' interest in content can be drawn from these observations. Mining the user click-stream for user behavior, and using it to adapt the "look-and-feel" of a site to a reader's needs was first proposed by Perkowitz and Etzioni (1999).

While the usage data of any portion of a web site can be analyzed, the most significant, and thus "interesting," is the one where the usage pattern differs significantly from the link structure. This is so because the readers' behavior, reflected by web usage, is very different from what the author would like it to be, reflected by the structure created by the author. Treating knowledge extracted from structure data and usage data as evidence from independent sources, and combining them in an evidential reasoning framework to develop measures for interestingness has been proposed by several authors (Padmanabhan and Tuzhilin 1998, Cooley 2000).

21.2.6 Preprocessing—Making Web Data Suitable for Mining

In the panel discussion referred to earlier (Srivastava and Mobasher 1997), preprocessing of web data to make it suitable for mining was identified as one of the key issues for web mining. A significant amount of work has been done in this area for web usage data, including user identification and session creation (Cooley, Mobasher, and Srivastava 1999), robot detection and filtering (Tan and Kumar 2002), and extracting usage path patterns (Spiliopoulou 1999). Cooley's Ph.D. dissertation (Cooley 2000) provides a comprehensive overview of the work in web usage data preprocessing.

Preprocessing of web structure data, especially link information, has been carried out for some applications, the most notable being Google style web search (Brin and Page 1998). An up-to-date survey of structure preprocessing is provided by Desikan, Srivastava, Kumar, and Tan (2002).

21.2.7 Identifying Web Communities of Information Sources

The web has had tremendous success in building communities of users and information sources. Identifying such communities is useful for many purposes. Gibson, Kleinberg, and Raghavan (1998) identified web communities as "a core of central authoritative pages linked together by hub pages. Their approach was extended by Ravi Kumar and colleagues (Kumar, Raghavan, Rajagopalan, and Tomkins 1999) to discover emerging web communities while crawling. A different approach to this problem was taken by Flake, Lawrence, and Giles (2000) who applied the "maximum-flow minimum cut model" (Jr and Fulkerson 1956) to the web graph for identifying "web communities." Imafuji and Kitsuregawa (2002) compare HITS and the maximum flow approaches and discuss the strengths and weakness of the two methods. Reddy and Kitsuregawa (2002) propose a dense bipartite graph method, a relaxation to the complete bipartite method followed by HITS approach, to find web communities. A related concept of "friends and neighbors" was introduced by Adamic and Adar (2003). They identified a group of individuals with similar interests, who in the cyberworld would form a "community." Two people are termed "friends" if the similarity between their web pages is high. Similarity is measured using features such as text, out-links, in-links and mailing lists.

21.2.8 Online Bibiliometrics

With the web having become the fastest growing and most up to date source of information, the research community has found it extremely useful to have online repositories of publications. Lawrence observed (Lawrence 2001) that having articles online makes them more easily accessible and hence more often cited than articles that are offline. Such online repositories not only keep the researchers updated on work carried out at different centers, but also makes the interaction and exchange of information much easier.

With such information stored in the web, it becomes easier to point to the most frequent papers that are cited for a topic and also related papers that have been published earlier or later than a given paper. This helps in understanding the state of the art in a particular field, helping researchers to explore new areas. Fundamental web mining techniques are applied to improve the search and categorization of research papers, and citing related articles. Some of the prominent digital libraries are Science Citation Index (SCI),[8] the Association for Computing Machinery's ACM portal,[9], the Scientific Literature Digital Library (CiteSeer),[10] and the DBLP Bibliography.[11]

21.2.9 Visualization of the World Wide Web

Mining web data provides a lot of information, which can be better understood with visualization tools. This makes concepts clearer than is possible with pure textual representation. Hence, there is a need to develop tools that provide a graphical interface that aids in visualizing results of web mining.

---

[8]http://www.isinet.com/isi/products/citation/sci/.
[9]http://portal.acm.org/portal.cfm.
[10]http://citeseer.nj.nec.com/cs
[11]http://www.informatik.uni-trier.de/ ley/db/.

Analyzing the web log data with visualization tools has evoked a lot of interest in the research community. Chi, Pitkow, Mackinlay, Pirolli, Goss-weiler, and Card (1998) developed a web ecology and evolution visualization (WEEV) tool to understand the relationship between web content, web structure and web usage over a period of time. The site hierarchy is represented in a circular form called the "Disk Tree" and the evolution of the web is viewed as a "Time Tube." Cadez, Heckerman, Meek, Smyth, and White (2000) present a tool called WebCANVAS that displays clusters of users with similar navigation behavior. Prasetyo, Pramudiono, Takahashi, Toyoda, and Kitsuregawa developed Naviz, an interactive web log visualization tool that is designed to display the user browsing pattern on the web site at a global level, and then display each browsing path on the pattern displayed earlier in an incremental manner. The support of each traversal is represented by the thickness of the edge between the pages. Such a tool is very useful in analyzing user behavior and improving web sites.

21.3 Prominent Applications

Excitement about the web in the past few years has led to the web applications being developed at a much faster rate in the industry than research in web related technologies. Many of these are based on the use of web mining concepts, even though the organizations that developed these applications, and invented the corresponding technologies, did not consider it as such. We describe some of the most successful applications in this section. Clearly, realizing that these applications use web mining is largely a retrospective exercise. For each application category discussed below, we have selected a prominent representative, purely for exemplary purposes. This in no way implies that all the techniques described were developed by that organization alone. On the contrary, in most cases the successful techniques were developed by a rapid "copy and improve" approach to each other's ideas.

21.3.1 Personalized Customer Experience in B2C E-commerce—Amazon.com

Early on in the life of Amazon.com,[12] its visionary CEO Jeff Bezos observed,

> "In a traditional (brick-and-mortar) store, the main effort is in getting a customer to the store. Once a customer is in the store they are likely to make a purchase — since the cost of going to another store is high — and thus the marketing budget (focused on getting

[12]http://www.amazon.com.

the customer to the store) is in general much higher than the in-store customer experience budget (which keeps the customer in the store). In the case of an on-line store, getting in or out requires exactly one click, and thus the main focus must be on customer experience in the store."[13]

This fundamental observation has been the driving force behind Amazon's comprehensive approach to personalized customer experience, based on the mantra "a personalized store for every customer" (Morphy 2001). A host of web mining techniques, such as associations between pages visited and click-path analysis are used to improve the customer's experience during a "store visit." Knowledge gained from web mining is the key intelligence behind Amazon's features such as "instant recommendations," "purchase circles," "wish-lists," etc.

21.3.2 Web Search—Google

Google[14] is one of the most popular and widely used search engines. It provides users access to information from over 2 billion web pages that it has indexed on its server. The quality and quickness of the search facility makes it the most successful search engine. Earlier search engines concentrated on web content alone to return the relevant pages to a query. Google was the first to introduce the importance of the link structure in mining information from the web. PageRank, which measures the importance of a page, is the underlying technology in all Google search products, and uses structural information of the web graph to return high quality results.

The Google toolbar is another service provided by Google that seeks to make search easier and informative by providing additional features such as highlighting the query words on the returned web pages. The full version of the toolbar, if installed, also sends the click-stream information of the user to Google. The usage statistics thus obtained are used by Google to enhance the quality of its results. Google also provides advanced search capabilities to search images and find pages that have been updated within a specific date range. Built on top of Netscape's Open Directory project, Google's web directory provides a fast and easy way to search within a certain topic or related topics.

The advertising program introduced by Google targets users by providing advertisements that are relevant to a search query. This does not bother users with irrelevant ads and has increased the clicks for the advertising companies

---

[13]The truth of this fundamental insight has been borne out by the phenomenon of "shopping cart abandonment," which happens frequently in on-line stores, but practically never in a brick-and-mortar one.

[14]http://www.google.com.

by four to five times. According to BtoB, a leading national marketing publication, Google was named a top 10 advertising property in the Media Power 50 that recognizes the most powerful and targeted business-to-business advertising outlets[15].

One of the latest services offered by Google is Google News[16]. It integrates news from the online versions of all newspapers and organizes them categorically to make it easier for users to read "the most relevant news." It seeks to provide latest information by constantly retrieving pages from news site worldwide that are being updated on a regular basis. The key feature of this news page, like any other Google service, is that it integrates information from various web news sources through purely algorithmic means, and thus does not introduce any human bias or effort. However, the publishing industry is not very convinced about a fully automated approach to news distillation (Springer 2002).

21.3.3 Web-Wide Tracking—DoubleClick

"Web-wide tracking," i.e. tracking an individual across all sites he visits, is an intriguing and controversial technology. It can provide an understanding of an individual's lifestyle and habits to a level that is unprecedented, which is clearly of tremendous interest to marketers. A successful example of this is DoubleClick Inc.'s DART ad management technology[17]. DoubleClick serves advertisements, which can be targeted on demographic or behavioral attributes, to the end-user on behalf of the client, i.e. the web site using DoubleClick's service. Sites that use DoubleClick's service are part of The DoubleClick Network and the browsing behavior of a user can be tracked across all sites in the network, using a cookie. This makes DoubleClick's ad targeting to be based on very sophisticated criteria. Alexa Research[18] has recruited a panel of more than 500,000 users, who have voluntarily agreed to have their every click tracked, in return for some freebies. This is achieved through having a browser bar that can be downloaded by the panelist from Alexa's website, which gets attached to the browser and sends Alexa a complete click-stream of the panelist's web usage. Alexa was purchased by Amazon for its tracking technology.

Clearly web-wide tracking is a very powerful idea. However, the invasion of privacy it causes has not gone unnoticed, and both Alexa/Amazon and DoubleClick have faced very visible lawsuits.[19] Microsoft's Passport[20] technology

---

[15] http://www.google.com/press/pressrel/b2b.html

[16] http://news.google.com

[17] http://www.doubleclick.com/dartinfo/

[18] http://www.alexa.com.

[19] See http://www.wired.com/news/business/0,1367,36434,00.html.

[20] http://www.microsoft.com/netservices/passport/.

also falls into this category. The value of this technology in applications such as cyber-threat analysis and homeland defense is quite clear, and it might be only a matter of time before these organizations are asked to provide information to law enforcement agencies.

21.3.4   Understanding Web Communities—AOL

One of the biggest successes of America Online (AOL)[21] has been its sizeable and loyal customer base. A large portion of this customer base participates in various AOL communities, which are collections of users with similar interests. In addition to providing a forum for each such community to interact amongst themselves, AOL provides them with useful information and services. Over time these communities have grown to be well-visited waterholes for AOL users with shared interests. Applying web mining to the data collected from community interactions provides AOL with a very good understanding of its communities, which it has used for targeted marketing through advertisements and e-mail solicitation. Recently, it has started the concept of "community sponsorship," whereby an organization, say Nike, may sponsor a community called "Young Athletic TwentySomethings." In return, consumer survey and new product development experts of the sponsoring organization get to participate in the community, perhaps without the knowledge of other participants. The idea is to treat the community as a highly specialized focus group, understand its needs and opinions on new and existing products, and also test strategies for influencing opinions.

21.3.5   Understanding Auction Behavior—eBay

As individuals in a society where we have many more things than we need, the allure of exchanging our useless stuff for some cash, no matter how small, is quite powerful. This is evident from the success of flea markets, garage sales and estate sales. The genius of eBay's[22] founders was to create an infrastructure that gave this urge a global reach, with the convenience of doing it from one's home PC. In addition, it popularized auctions as a product selling and buying mechanism and provides the thrill of gambling without the trouble of having to go to Las Vegas. All of this has made eBay as one of the most successful businesses of the internet era. Unfortunately, the anonymity of the web has also created a significant problem for eBay auctions, as it is impossible to distinguish real bids from fake ones. eBay is now using web mining techniques to analyze bidding behavior to determine if a bid is fraudulent (Colet

---

[21] See http://www.aol.com.
[22] http://www.ebay.com.

2002). Recent efforts are geared towards understanding participants' bidding
behaviors/patterns to create a more efficient auction market.

21.3.6 Personalized Portal for the Web—MyYahoo

Yahoo[23] was the first to introduce the concept of a "personalized portal," i.e.
a web site designed to have the look-and-feel and content personalized to the
needs of an individual end-user. This has been an extremely popular concept
and has led to the creation of other personalized portals such as Yodlee[24] for
private information like bank and brokerage accounts. Mining MyYahoo usage
logs provides Yahoo valuable insight into an individual's web usage habits,
enabling Yahoo to provide personalized content, which in turn has led to the
tremendous popularity of the Yahoo web site.[25]

21.3.7 CiteSeer—Digital Library and Autonomous Citation Indexing

NEC ResearchIndex, also known as CiteSeer[26] (Bollacker, Lawrence, and Giles 1998) is one of the most popular online bibiliographic indices related to
computer science. The key contribution of the CiteSeer repository is its "Autonomous Citation Indexing" (ACI) (Lawrence, Giles, and Bollacker 1999).
Citation indexing makes it possible to extract information about related articles. Automating such a process reduces a lot of human effort, and makes it
more effective and faster.

CiteSeer works by crawling the web and downloading research related papers. Information about citations and the related context is stored for each of
these documents. The entire text and information about the document is stored
in different formats. Information about documents that are similar at a sen-
tence level (percentage of sentences that match between the documents), at a
text level or related due to cocitation is also given. Citation statistics for documents are computed that enable the user to look at the most cited or popular
documents in the related field. They also a maintain a directory for computer
science related papers, to make search based on categories easier. These documents are ordered by the number of citations.

---

[23]http://www.yahoo.com.
[24]See http://www.yodlee.com.
[25]Yahoo has been consistently ranked as one of the top web properties for a number of years
(See http://www.jmm.com/xp/jmm/press/mediaMetrixTop50.xml).
[26]See http://citeseer.nj.nec.com/cs.

21.4 Research Directions

Although we are going through an inevitable phase of irrational despair following a phase of irrational exuberance about the commercial potential of the web, the adoption and usage of the web continues to grow unabated. [27] As the web and its usage grows, it will continue to generate ever more content, structure, and usage data, and the value of web mining will keep increasing. Outlined here are some research directions that must be pursued to ensure that we continue to develop web mining technologies that will enable this value to be realized.

21.4.1 Web Metrics and Measurements

From an experimental human behaviorist's viewpoint, the web is the perfect experimental apparatus. Not only does it provide the ability of measuring human behavior at a micro level, it eliminates the bias of the subjects knowing that they are participating in an experiment, and allows the number of participants to be many orders of magnitude larger than conventional studies. However, we have not yet begun to appreciate the true impact of this revolutionary experimental apparatus for human behavior studies. The web Lab of Amazon[28] is one of the early efforts in this direction. It is regularly used to measure the user impact of various proposed changes, on operational metrics such as site visits and visit/buy ratios, as well as on financial metrics such as revenue and profit, before a deployment decision is made. For example, during Spring 2000 a 48 hour long experiment on the live site was carried out, involving over one million user sessions, before the decision to change Amazon's logo was made. Research needs to be done in developing the right set of web metrics, and their measurement procedures, so that various web phenomena can be studied.

21.4.2 Process Mining

Mining of market basket data, collected at the point-of-sale in any store, has been one of the visible successes of data mining. However, this data provides only the end result of the process, and that too decisions that ended up in product purchase. Click-stream data provides the opportunity for a detailed look at the decision making process itself, and knowledge extracted from it can be used for optimizing, influencing the process, etc. (Ong and Keong 2003). Underhill (2000) has conclusively proven the value of process information in

---

[27] See, for example, http://thewhir.com/marketwatch/ser053102.cfm.
[28] See http://www.amazon.com.

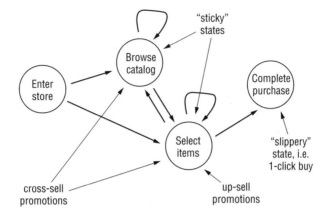

Overall goal:
- Maximize probability of reaching final state
- Maximize expected sales from each visit

Figure 21.2: Shopping pipeline modeled as state transition diagram.

understanding users' behavior in traditional shops. Research needs to be carried out in (1) extracting process models from usage data, (2) understanding
how different parts of the process model impact various web metrics of interest, and (3) how the process models change in response to various changes that
are made, i.e. changing stimuli to the user. Figure 21.2 shows an approach of
modeling online shopping as a state transition diagram.

21.4.3   Temporal Evolution of the Web

Society's interaction with the web is changing the web as well as the way people interact with each other. While storing the history all of this interaction in
one place is clearly too staggering a task, at least the changes to the web are being recorded by the pioneering internet archive project.[29] Research needs to be
carried out in extracting temporal models of how web content, web structures,
web communities, authorities, hubs, etc. evolve over time. Large organizations
generally archive usage data from their web sites. With these sources of data
available, there is a large scope of research to develop techniques for analyzing
of how the web evolves over time.

---

[29] See http://www.archive.org/.

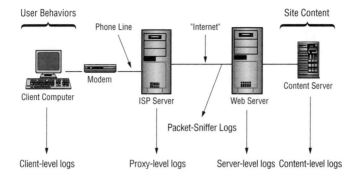

Figure 21.3: High level architecture of different web logs.

21.4.4   Web Services Performance Optimization

As services over the web continue to grow (Katz 2002), there will be a continuing need to make them robust, scalable and efficient. Web mining can be applied to better understand the behavior of these services, and the knowledge extracted can be useful for various kinds of optimizations. The successful application of web mining for predictive prefetching of pages by a browser has been demonstrated in Pandey, Srivastava, and Shekhar (2001). It is necessary to do analysis of the web logs for web services performance optimization as shown in figure 21.3. Research is needed in developing web mining techniques to improve various other aspects of web services.

21.4.5   Fraud and Threat Analysis

The anonymity provided by the web has led to a significant increase in attempted fraud, from unauthorized use of individual credit cards to hacking into credit card databases for blackmail purposes (Scarponi 2000). Yet another example is auction fraud, which has been increasing on popular sites like eBay. Since all these frauds are being perpetrated through the internet, web mining is the perfect analysis technique for detecting and preventing them. Research issues include developing techniques to recognize known frauds, characterize them and recognize emerging frauds. The issues in cyber threat analysis and intrusion detection are quite similar in nature (Lazarevic Dokas, Ertoz, Kumar, Srivastava, and Tan 2002).

21.4.6   Web Mining and Privacy

While there are many benefits to be gained from web mining, a clear drawback is the potential for severe violations of privacy. Public attitude towards privacy seems to be almost schizophrenic, i.e. people say one thing and do quite the opposite. For example, famous cases like those involving Amazon[30] and Doubleclick[31] seem to indicate that people value their privacy, while experience at major e-commerce portals shows that over 97% of all people accept cookies with no problems, and most of them actually like the personalization features that are provided based on it. Spiekerman, Grossklags, and Berendt (2001) have demonstrated that people were willing to provide fairly personal information about themselves, which was completely irrelevant to the task at hand, if provided the right stimulus to do so. Furthermore, explicitly bringing attention to information privacy policies had practically no effect. One explanation of this seemingly contradictory attitude towards privacy may be that we have a bi-modal view of privacy, namely that "I'd be willing to share information about myself as long as I get some (tangible or intangible) benefits from it, and as long as there is an implicit guarantee that the information will not be abused." The research issue generated by this attitude is the need to develop approaches, methodologies and tools that can be used to verify and validate that a web service is indeed using user's information in a manner consistent with its stated policies.

21.5 Conclusions

As the web and its usage continues to grow, so too grows the opportunity to analyze web data and extract all manner of useful knowledge from it. The past five years have seen the emergence of web mining as a rapidly growing area, due to the efforts of the research community as well as various organizations that are practicing it. In this chapter we have briefly described the key computer science contributions made by the field, a number of prominent applications, and outlined some areas of future research. Our hope is that this overview provides a starting point for fruitful discussion.

Acknowledgements

The ideas presented here have emerged in discussions with a number of people over the past few years — far too numerous to list. However, special mention must be made of Robert Cooley, Mukund Deshpande, Joydeep Ghosh, Ronny Kohavi, Ee-Peng Lim, Brij Masand, Bamshad Mobasher, Ajay Pandey, Myra Spiliopoulou, Pang-Ning Tan, Terry Woodfield, and Masaru Kitsuregawa discussions with all of whom have helped develop the ideas presented herein.

---

[30]http://www.ecommercetimes.com/perl/story/2467.html.
[31]http://www.wired.com/news/business/0,1367,36434,00.html.

This work was supported in part by the Army High Performance Computing Research Center contract number DAAD19-01-2-0014. The ideas and opinions expressed herein do not necessarily reflect the position or policy of the government (either stated or implied) and no official endorsement should be inferred. The AHPCRC and the Minnesota Super-Computing Institute provided access to computing facilities.

Jaideep Srivastava is a professor of computer science and engineering at the University fo Minnesota,specializing in databases, data mining, and multi-media computing. He can be'reached at www.cs.umn.edu/~srivasta.

 Prasanna Desikan is Ph.D student in the Department of Computer Science and Engineering at the University of Minnesota specializing in link analysis and web mining. He can be reached at www.cs.umn.edu/~desikan

 Vipin Kumar is currently director of the Army High Performance Computing Research Center'and a professor of computer science and engineering at the University of Minnesota specializing in high-performance computing and data mining. He can be reached at www.cs.umn.edu/~kumar

Chapter 22

Advancements in Text Mining Algorithms and Software

Svetlana Y. Mironova, Michael W. Berry,
Scott Atchley, and Micah Beck

The amount of textual-based information stored electronically, whether on our own computers or on the Web, is rapidly accumulating. Any desktop or laptop computer can accommodate huge amounts of data due to the advances in hardware storage devices. Although accumulating information is easy, finding relevant information on demand can be difficult. Constructing data structures (indices) to facilitate the retrieval of relevant information becomes problematic as the size of collections continue to escalate. In this chapter we discuss novel developments in the design of software for large-scale index creation. A more comprehensive survey of the field of text mining is available in the paper "Survey of Text Mining: Clustering, Classification, and Retrieval" (Berry 2003).

22.0.1 Software Advancement for Information Retrieval

Software companies develop products that may require megabytes of hard drive space. Without upgrading computers every few years, one cannot download favorite music, movies or play the most recent (popular) computer games.

Researchers and scientists involved in data mining and information retrieval are facing the same reality — an enormous amount of storage may be needed to run simulations and store their outputs. In creating the general text parser (GTP) with network storage capability, we are trying to address the needs of experts in information retrieval and modeling who deal with large text corpora on a daily basis but are subject to limited storage capabilities. This software allows a user to parse a large collection of documents and create a vector space information retrieval model for subsequent concept-based query processing.

GTP utilizes latent semantic indexing (LSI) for its information retrieval (IR) modeling (Berry and Browne 1990; Berry, Dumais, and O'Brien 1995; Berry, Drmač(c), and Jessup 1999). The user has the option of storing the model outputs on one of the available internet backplane protocol (IBP) servers or depots (Bassi, Beck, Fagg, Moore, Plank, Swany, and Wolski 2002; Plank, Bassi, Beck, Moore, Swany, and Wolski 2001) so that disk or memory space is shared over the network.

IBP is the foundation of the logistical networking testbed developed at the Logistical Computing and Internetworking (LoCI) Lab at the University of Tennessee. This infrastructure provides a scalably sharable storage service as a network resource for distributed applications (Beck, Moore, and Plank 2002).

The remainder of the chapter is organized as follows: in section 22.1, we provide an overview of the general text parser (GTP) and the GTPQUERY process. In section 22.2, we describe the network storage stack and its components which are used to implement the network storage utility within GTP. Section 22.3 details the GTP network storage implementation and usage. Section 22.4 discusses future work in the use of network storage for indexing. Concluding remarks for the chapter are provided in section 22.5.

22.1 General Text Parser

General text parser (GTP) is a software package developed at the University of Tennessee to facilitate text/document processing and parsing and to implement an underlying IR model based on sparse matrix data structures. GTP has the ability to parse any document: raw text, HTML document or any other tag separated document collection via tag filters. During the parsing process GTP creates a vector-space model in which the documents and queries are represented as vectors of the terms parsed. A term-by-document matrix is used to define the relationships between the documents in the collection and the parsed terms or keywords. The elements of the matrix are typically weighted/unweighted frequencies of terms (rows) with respect to their corresponding documents (columns) (Giles, Wo, and Berry 2003).

The underlying vector-space model exploited by the GTP is latent semantic indexing (LSI). LSI is an efficient IR technique that uses statistically derived conceptual indices rather than individual words to encode documents. Specifically, LSI uses the singular value decomposition (SVD) or semi-discrete decomposition (SDD) of the large sparse term-by-document matrix mentioned above to build a conceptual vector space (Berry and Browne 1990; Berry, Dumais, and O'Brien 1995). A lower-rank approximation to the original term-by-document matrix is used to derive vector encodings for both terms and documents in the same k-dimensional subspace. The clustering of term or document vectors in this subspace suggests an underlying (latent) semantic structure in the usage of terms within the documents.

22.1.1 Evolution of the General Text Parser

GTP is public domain software.[1] The original version was developed in C++ for both Solaris and Linux platforms. There also exists a parallel version of the SVD components used in GTP which is written in C++/MPI (message passing interface) (Snir, Otto, Huss-Lederman, Walker, Dongarra 1995). The C++ version was recently ported to Java to utilize more object-oriented features. The Java version has certain limitations compared to its C++ counterpart: it is slower and it does not accept custom filters, but it does provide an internal HTML filter.

22.1.2 Capabilities

GTP is characterized by the numerous options provided for the user. The options allow both novice and expert users to tune the software to their needs. Recently a graphical user interface has been developed to help keep track of all the options. Some options let the user change thresholds for document and global frequencies, specify custom filters and local or global weighting schemes, and indicate new document delimiters. For more detailed overview of the options see Giles, Wo, and Berry (2003).

Depending on the collection, the size of the above mentioned files (when deploying the SVD) can be very large varying from kilobytes to gigabytes. For 8-byte double precision storage, a k-dimensional LSI model requires $8k(t + d)$ bytes, where t and d are the number of terms and documents in the collection, respectively. Hence, a 300-dimensional vector space model for a text collection comprising 100,000 terms and 10,000 documents would require well over 250 megabytes. The user must also consider that in the course of their research he/she might need to repeat the process of parsing several times to achieve the desired IR model.

---

[1] It is available at http://www.cs.utk.edu/~lsi.

Using the internet backplane protocol (IBP) as described in section 22.3, one can successfully eliminate the storage bottleneck.

22.1.3   The GTPQUERY Process

GTP is not only capable of creating an index; it provides users with a GT-PQUERY module for querying, i.e., determining the similarities between a query and all documents in the collection. This query processing module requires several of the output files generated by GTP, namely *key*, *output*, and *LAST_RUN*. A cosine similarity measure between the query vector and document vectors is used to determine the relevance of any/all documents to the query. Query vectors are constructed as pseudo-document vectors thus allowing their projection into the original term-document vector space.

The result of the query process consists of files (one per query) with document ID and corresponding cosine similarity pairs ranked from the most relevant to the least relevant. The entire GTP and GTPQUERY process is summarized in figure 22.1.

22.2   Network Storage Stack

The network storage stack has been developed by the Logistical Computing and Internetworking Lab (LoCI) at the University of Tennessee.[2] As discussed by Bassi, Beck, Fagg, Moore, Plank, Swany, and Wolski (2002), the network storage stack is modeled after the Internet Protocol (IP) Stack, and is designed to add storage resources to the Internet in a sharable, scalable manner. Figure 22.2 shows the organization of the network storage stack.

22.2.1   Internet Backplane Protocol

The internet backplane protocol (IBP) is an essential part of the Network Storage Stack. IBP's purpose is to allow users to share storage resources across networks. Its design echoes the major advantages of Internet Protocol (IP): abstraction of the datagram delivery process, scalability, simple fault detection (faulty datagrams are dropped), and ease of access. These factors allow any participant in an IBP network to use any local storage resource available regardless of who owns it (Bassi, Beck, Fagg, Moore, Plank, Swany, and Wolski 2002). Using IP networking to access IBP storage creates a global storage service.

There are some limitations that arise from two underlying network problems. The first problem concerns a vulnerability of IP networks to denial of

---

[2]http://www.loci.cs.utk.edu.

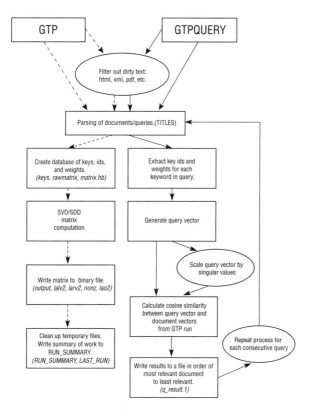

Figure 22.1: Flowchart of GTP and GTPQUERY processing; output files are listed in parentheses.

use (DoU). The free sharing of communication within a routed IP network leaves every local network open to being overwhelmed by traffic from the wide area network. A second concern lies in that traditionally, the storage service is based on processor-attached storage, which implies strong semantics: near-perfect reliability and availability. Such strong semantics are almost impossible to implement on the scale of the wide area networks (Bassi, Beck, Fagg, Moore, Plank, Swany, and Wolski 2002). These issues are resolved as follows:

- IBP storage is time limited. When the time expires the resources can be reused. An IBP allocation can also be refused by a storage facility (depot) if the user's request demands more resources than available.

- IBP is a best effort storage service (Bassi, Beck, Fagg, Moore, Plank,

Applications	
Logistical File System	
Logistical Tools	
L-Bone	**exNode**
IBP	
Local Access	
Physical	

Figure 22.2: Network storage stack.

Swany, and Wolski 2002). The semantics of IBP storage are weaker than the typical storage service. Since there are so many unpredictable and uncontrollable factors involved, network access to storage may become permanently unavailable (due to a network partition, for example).

IBP storage is managed by depots or servers used by a client to perform storage operations such as *allocate*, *load*, *store*, and *copy*. See the paper by S. Mironova (2003) for details on these and other storage operations.

22.2.2   ExNode

The management of several IBP capabilities can be complicated. The exNode library was created to help the user in this task and to automate most of the work. The exNode data structure is somewhat similar to the Unix inode, but at the same time it is fundamentally different.

The exNode makes it possible for the user to chain IBP allocations into a logical entity that resembles a network file (Bassi, Beck, and Moore 2001). Current IBP allocations have a limit of 2 gigabytes; the exNode though allows the user to aggregate up to 2 billion IBP allocations, which equals 4 exabytes (2^{62}) (Bassi, Beck, and Moore 2001).

The exNode consists of two major components: arbitrary metadata and mappings. The exNode library allows the user to create an exNode, attach a mapping to it, store IBP capabilities into the mapping and add metadata to the mapping. The exNode can also be serialized to XML, so that exNodes created on one platform can be recognized on other supported platforms. Each exNode can maintain multiple copies of the data that is stored in any allocation, which provides better fault-tolerance. If a depot becomes unavailable for some reason, the user can still retrieve data from the copies stored on other depots.

Figure 22.3: Over 150 worldwide depots of the L-Bone (computer and working lab 2003).

22.2.3 Logistical Backbone

The logistical backbone (L-Bone) is a resource discovery service that maintains a list of public depots and metadata about those depots (Bassi, Beck, Fagg, Moore, Plank, Swany, and Wolski 2002; Beck, Moore, and Plank 2002). The L-Bone also uses the Network Weather Service (NWS) (Wolski, Spring, and Hayes 1999) to monitor throughput between depots. As of March 2003, the L-Bone provides service of over 150 depots on five continents. Figure 22.3 shows the locations of the available IBP depots.

22.2.4 Logistical Runtime System

The next and final layer of the network storage stack (see figure 22.2) which we briefly mention is the logistical runtime system, or LoRS. The LoRS layer consists of a C API and a command line interface tool set that automate the finding of IBP depots via the L-Bone, creating and using IBP capabilities and creating and managing exNodes.[3] The LoRS library also provides flexible tools to deal with the lower levels of the network storage stack. Sample network file-based functions (Bassi, Beck, Fagg, Moore, Plank, Swany, and Wolski 2002) include: *Upload, download, augment, trim, refresh,* and *list*. LoRS supports checksums to ensure end-to-end correctness, multiple encryption algorithms since IBP depots are public, untrusted servers, and compression to reduce the amount of data transferred and stored.

---

[3]http://www.loci.cs.utk.edu.

22.3 The General Text Parser with Network Storage

In the process of developing GTP, we realized that parsing large collections generates numerous large files that take up a lot of valuable disk space. The logistical networking testbed developed at LoCI facilitated the temporary storage of these files on a remote network (Internet) along with immediate retrieval when needed.

In the course of creating an index for a document collection, new documents may get added to the collection or some documents may be deleted. In any case, before the final collection is created, several revisions are usually done and the user may need to parse the collection multiple times. In some cases the collection is dynamic, as is the case with web pages (HTML), so that parsing is done on a regular basis in order to monitor updates. If the user keeps all the files generated by GTP and GTPQUERY after each parsing, the subsequent output files will take up an excessive amount of local disk storage. Fortunately, the concept of network storage can alleviate this burden: the user can clean up his or her hard drive and store the information produced by the parser on a remote network. Since the storage provided by the internet backplane protocol (IBP) is temporary, if the user is not satisfied with the results, he will not choose to extend the time on the files stored on the IBP and the storage will be automatically reused. If, on the other hand, the user wants to store the results of the parser permanently, he can either make sure that the time limits do not expire or he can download the files back to his personal machine and then write them to other media, e.g., a CD-ROM.

22.3.1 Overview

The execution of GTP (see figure 22.1) creates two large files: *keys* (the database of the terms parsed) and *output* (a binary file, containing vector encodings generated by the SVD). These files are essential to the GTP and GTPQUERY. If the user chooses to use network storage, after the files keys and output are generated, they are automatically uploaded to IBP depot(s). When the user wants to query into the collection that has been created, these files are downloaded back to the user's space. The LoRS tools are used to facilitate upload and download processing.

22.3.2 The General Text Parser and Upload

The upload process requires as little or as much information from the user as he/she is willing to provide. This information helps to optimize the performance of the tools. The fields the user can specify are "location," "duration," "fragments," and "copies." We briefly describe them in the following para-graphs.

Location allows the user to enter keyword and value pairs to determine where they want storage and minimum environmental criteria. The user may specify as many or as few keyword/value pairs as the user wants. They may even leave location pointer equal to NULL if location and environment are unimportant. One can specify host name, zip, state, city, country and airport.

Duration is the maximum number of days that the user will need the space. The user can even specify partial day amounts. For example, if 0.5 is entered, data will be stored on the network for 12 hours. Each depot has the maximum number of days the data will be stored for. This information can be obtained from the L-Bone[4] If a longer time period is required, the user is currently responsible for extending the time of the allocation. A set of tools that will do this automatically is in development.

Fragments allows the user to subdivide a file into partitions of equal size and to store those partitions on different depots. Available depot space is used more efficiently and the performance of the download can be greatly improved.

Copies allows the user to specify how many copies of the original file to store. Users are encouraged to store several copies of the data. As was men-tioned in section 22.2.2, there is always a possibility that the data could be lost due to numerous uncontrollable circumstances. Subdividing the file into sev-eral fragments and storing multiple copies of the file can prevent an undesired loss of data. If during the download process some fragments cannot be found, LoRS tools will automatically check for all the copies of this fragment and will deliver the first available one.

If the upload is successful, LoRS tools will return to the user a file with .xnd extension. This file contains XML encoded information needed by the user and IBP to keep track of the file, retrieve the file and perform LoRS oper-ations described in section 22.2.4. GTP will store XML files (one per uploaded file) in a directory and will automatically delete the files being uploaded in or-der to conserve local disk storage. If on the other hand, the upload has failed, the files will be saved on the user's machine and the user will be notified of the failure.

22.3.3 Download and GTPQUERY

If IBP was used to store the GTP-generated index, a query into the document collection requires that the files keys and output be downloaded from the net-work. The download process solely depends on the XML files produced during the upload process. The .xnd files hold the key to the location of the user's data

---

[4]See http://loci.cs.utk.edu/lbone.

within IBP. If those files do not exist, download will fail and the recovery of the data will be impossible. The LoRS download tool uses multiple threads to retrieve small blocks of data and then it reassembles the blocks into the complete file at the client. LoRS uses an adaptive algorithm that retrieves more blocks from faster depots (depots with higher throughput to the client). If some depots are much slower than others, the download tool can automatically try getting lagging blocks from the other depots that have the same data (Plank, Atchley, Ding, and Beck 2002). The download tool is capable of starting from a specified offset and can process a prescribed byte count of data. All GTP output files, however, are downloaded in their entirety. After the download process is complete, the user will have the files necessary to perform any query on the collection. The progress of any upload or download is monitored by a special panel ("Network Storage Panel") provided in the GTP graphical user interface (GUI) (Mironova 2003).

22.3.4 Performance

Current benchmarks (see Mironova 2003) on a Foreign Broadcast Information Service (FBIS) subcollection from TREC-5 (Harman and Voorhees 1996) (size: 63 megabytes, 20,000 documents, 46,488 terms, *output* — 28 megabytes, *keys* — 5.8 megabytes) indicate that the additional time/overhead for upload is not significant compared to the total elapsed time. Table 22.1 shows the timing results for a GTP upload to France (FR), California (CA) and Tennessee (TN) with the server located in TN. The time of the upload depends on multiple factors: how far the location of the upload is from the user's location, network bandwidth, size of the file to be uploaded and the number of copies requested.

The GTP download process, on the other hand, is almost instantaneous. All the preprocessing is done by GTP during the parsing and construction of the model, so that the GTPQUERY process simply projects the query into the original term-document space. Table 22.1 demonstrates that most of the time of the download and query processing (GTPQUERY) is taken by the download. The three batch-mode ad hoc queries used to demonstrate this benchmark were *Yugoslavia Croatia*, *Russia embassy FIS*, and *Nissan Motor* (Mironova 2003).

22.4 Future Software Development

The network storage option implemented for the Java version of GTP presented some challenges, since all IBP and LoRS tools were originally implemented in C. The merge was possible due to a special LoRS server. Each time the IBP or LoRS tools were updated, GTP had to be tuned to adjust to the

Upload Performance (seconds)

	FR	CA	TN
GTP	320	320	320
Upload/IBP	270	23	78

Download Performance (seconds)

	FR	CA	TN
GTPQUERY	23	23	23
Download/IBP	113	38	34

Table 22.1: GTP Upload and download benchmarks for the FBIS subcollection (20,000 documents and 3 queries). FR = France, CA = California, and TN = Tennessee.

changes. Work to integrate network storage into the C++ and parallel versions of GTP is in progress.

In collaboration with the Computing and Working (LoCI) Laboratory,[5] refinements of the network storage procedure itself are underway. Upgrades include adding interactive maps and utilities to allow the user to see the information about the files stored on IBP, extending storage time with a click of a button, and the possibility of streaming the data directly from a LoRS Java (or C) client to IBP depots as it gets generated. Currently, streaming can only be performed using the LoRS C library or the UNIX command line tools. This would eliminate local file generation and greatly improve the overall performance of GTP.

GTP has the ability to parse and index large text collections through networking storage. Therefore, a variety of distributed data mining algorithms and data mining systems can use GTP for data collection.

22.5   Concluding Remarks

The object-oriented software environment GTP with network storage capability has been designed to provide a scalable solution to index growing and dynamic text collections. It allows IR professionals to create, store, and share an index via a remote network. The addition of network storage capability certainly addresses the problem of inadequate storage and file sharing over the network. GTP with network storage gives users an opportunity to create a user-specific IR model, place the files (index) generated by GTP on a sharable

---

[5]http://www.loci.cs.utk.edu

network so that all the participants in a project, no matter where they are located, can have access to them.

Acknowledgements

The research of S. Y. Mironova and M. W. Berry was supported in part by the National Science Foundation under grant CISE-EIA-99-72889, and that of S. Atchley and M. Beck was supported by the U.S. Department of Energy (Sci-DAC) under grant DE-FC02-01ER25465 and by the National Science Foundation under grant ANI-99-80293.

All the coauthors thank the anonymous referees for their helpful comments and suggestions for improving the chapter.

Scott Atchley is a research leader in computer science at the University of Tennessee. His interests include integrating storage and computation in the wide-area network. He can be reached at www.cs.utk.edu/~atchley.

Micah Beck is an associate professor of computer science and director of the Logistical Computing and Internetworking Laboratory at the University of Tennessee. His research interests include distributed/high performance/data intensive systems, network/infrastructure architecture, and language/middleware support for distributed applications. His website is www.cs.utk.edu/~mbeck.

Michael W. Berry is a professor and interim department head of computer science at the University of Tennessee. His research interests include bioinformatics, computational science, scientific computing, and parallel algorithms.

Svetlana Y. Mironova completed her Masters in computer science from the University of Tennessee, Knoxville in 2003. She is currently employed by the International Paper Company, and can be reached at mironova@cs.utk.edu.

Chapter 23

On Data Mining, Semantics, and Intrusion Detection

What to Dig for and Where to Find It

Anupam Joshi and Jeffrey L. Undercoffer

The field of data mining has been the object of considerable attention over the last decade. In its broadest sense, it has been defined as the extraction of "implicit, nontrivial knowledge" from data (Shapiro 1991). However, despite this definition, much of the data mining research has been more narrowly focused on mathematical or statistical methods, and has built on prior work in pattern recognition. Clustering, association (correlation) rules, and sequence analysis methods all typically operate by looking for "patterns" at the syntactic level.

Separate from the data mining work is a large body of work in logic, that in some sense attacks a similar problem wherein it "infers" new knowledge from given facts. While representing knowledge and reasoning over it have been extensively studied domains in artificial intelligence, recent applications of knowledge representation techniques to create the "semantic web" (Berners-Lee, James Hendler, and Ora Lassila 2002) have given it an added dimension. There are significant efforts to develop ontologies, (explicit formal specifications of the terms in a domain and the relations between them [Gruber 1992]), in the DARPA agent markup language plus ontology interface layer

(DAML+OIL) (Hendler 2000) for a variety of domains, and to mark up web documents with them.[1]

Given that both AI and KD domains seek to obtain knowledge and or information from data, it would be natural to explore if they can work together. Surprisingly, there is little effort in this direction. Han, Ng, Fu, and Dao (1998) explore building a hierarchical concept structure (essentially a taxonomy), using it to generalize association rules (e.g.: Coke and Sprite are kinds of soft drinks). More recently, Basu, Mooney, Pasupuleti, and Ghosh (2001) use WordNet to compute the average semantic distance between words in the antecedent and consequence of an association rule and then use it as a measure of rule novelty.

In this chapter, we assert that semantic descriptions and logical inferences can operate in synergy with syntax-based traditional data-mining techniques to make them more efficient. We make this case in the context of distributed data mining in general, although a similar case can be made for mining the semantic web itself (Gerd, Hotho, and Berendt 2002). Currently, much of the work in distributed data mining assumes that the data sources are predefined, and the key task is to be able to mine across the sources without moving the data to any centralized site. In other words, *where to dig* for information is known up front. However, in many critical applications, the sources to be mined will need to be dynamically selected based on several criterion, including what information we seek to obtain from the underlying data, and even patterns that are discovered in some initial data source. Moreover, with the proliferation of sensors and other information sources, a large amount of data and features may be available at a given location, not all of which would need to be mined. Again, the assumption in traditional distributed data mining is that *what to dig* is known up front. We claim that both the *what* and *where* questions can be dynamically decided using reasoning over domain models described in semantically rich languages such as DAML+OIL or the Web Ontology Language (OWL).[2] To illustrate our point, we will use distributed intrusion detection as an example application.

23.0.1   Intrusion Detection

Research in the field of intrusion detection has been ongoing for approximately 20 years. One of the earliest papers in the field is James Anderson's 1980 paper "Computer Security, Threat Monitoring, and Surveillance" (Anderson 1980). Seven years later, Dorothy Denning wrote "An Intrusion Detection Model" (Denning 1987), providing an initial framework for intrusion detection systems (IDS). Denning held that evidence of malicious activity would be re-

---

[1]For examples of such projects, see http://www.daml.org.
[2]Available at http://www.w3c.org/TR/owl-ref/

flected in the audit records of the affected host. The challenge has been to extract that evidence from those records.

Over the years many disciplines have been applied to the task of intrusion detection, including probabilistic models, hidden Markov models, expert systems, neural networks, and data mining. Given twenty years of research, one would think that IDSs would be well advanced, detecting and blocking intruders as they attempt to cross the perimeters of our networks or detect "insiders" as they attempt to abuse their system privileges; however, this is not the case. According to the Carnegie Mellon Software Engineering Institute's report, "State of the Practice of Intrusion Detection Technologies" (Allen, Christie, Fithen, McHugh, Pickel, and Stoner 2000), most commercial IDS systems use a signature-based approach and do not provide a complete intrusion detection solution. Moreover, the Carnegie Mellon report further states: "despite substantial research and commercial investments, IDS technology is immature, and its effectiveness is limited."

We argue that the somewhat ambiguous state of the art in intrusion detection is attributable to the current situation where research in the field has often been at too high a level, not digging deep enough, or from an approach that is too philosophical, incorrectly identifying where to dig. For data mining techniques to work well in the (distributed) intrusion detection domain, we need to create a model of the class intrusion. Accordingly, based upon empirical evidence, we have modeled computer attacks and have categorized them by the system component targeted, the means and consequence of attack, and the location of the attacker. Our model is represented as a *target-centric* ontology, where the structural properties of the classification scheme help infer where to dig. Moreover, these properties need to be in terms of features that are observable and measurable by an IDS, consequently specifying what to dig for. Once we have identified that data that is to be mined and where it is located we specify an IDS model that employs data mining and a backward chaining reasoner. Data mining techniques are used for preliminary hypothesis testing while our ontology, as asserted into the reasoning engine, is used to further evaluate events that are initially flagged as "abnormal."

23.1 Classification and Characterization Schemes

Traditionally, the characterization and classification of computer attacks and other intrusive behaviors have been limited to simple taxonomies. Taxonomies, however, lack the necessary and essential constructs needed by an intrusion detection system (IDS) to reason over an instance representative of the domain of a computer attack. Alternatively, ontologies, unlike taxonomies, provide powerful constructs that include machine interpretable definitions of the concepts within a domain and the relations between them. Ontologies provide software systems with the ability to share a common understanding of the information at issue, in turn enabling the software system with a greater ability to reason over and analyze this information.

Taxonomies, do however, play an integral part of an ontology. Whereas a taxonomy is a classification of terms, an ontology subsumes the taxonomy and defines the relationships that hold between those terms. There are numerous attack taxonomies proposed for use in intrusion detection research where the characteristics are classified from many differing perspectives. Often times these characteristics are not discernible by analyzing an instance of the intrusive event. As detailed by Julia Allen and her colleagues (Allen, Christie, Fithen, McHugh, Pickel, and Stoner 2000), and John McHugh (2000), the taxonomic characterization of intrusive behavior has typically been from the attacker's point of view, each suggesting that alternative taxonomies need to be developed. Allen and her colleagues state that intrusion detection is an immature discipline and has yet to establish a commonly accepted framework. McHugh suggests classifying attacks according to protocol layer or, as an alternative, whether or not a completed protocol handshake is required. Likewise, Biswaroop Guha (Guha and Mukherjee 1997) suggests an analysis of each layer of the TCP/IP protocol stack to serve as the foundation for an attack taxonomy.

We proceed by defining the characteristics of a sufficient taxonomy then state the reasons why a taxonomy is insufficient and needs to be "upgraded" to an ontology.

23.1.1   Characteristics of a Sufficient Taxonomy

A *taxonomy* is a *classification* system where the classification scheme conforms to a systematic arrangement into groups or categories according to established criteria (*Merriam-Webster's Collegiate Dictionary* 1993). Glass and Vessey (1995) contend that taxonomies provide a set of unifying constructs so that the area of interest can be *systemically* described and aspects of relevance may be interpreted. The overarching goal of any taxonomy, therefore, is to supply some predictive value during the analysis of an unknown specimen, while the classifications within the taxonomy offer an explanatory value.

According to George Gaylord Simpson (1961) classifications may be created either a priori or a posteriori. An a priori classification is created nonempirically whereas an a posteriori classification is created by empirical evidence derived from some data set. Simpson defines a taxonomic character as a feature, attribute or characteristic that is divisible into at least two contrasting states and used for constructing classifications. He further states that taxonomic characters should be observable from the object in question.

Edward Amoroso (1994), Ulf Lindqvist and Erland Jonsson (1997) and Ivan Krusl (1998) each have identified what they believe to be the requisite properties of a sufficient and acceptable taxonomy for computer security. Collectively, they have identified the following properties as essential to a taxonomy:

Mutually Exclusive A classification in one category excludes all others because categories do not overlap.

Exhaustive The categories, taken together, include all possibilities.

Unambiguous The category is clear and precise so that classification is not uncertain, regardless of who is classifying.

Repeatable Repeated applications result in the same classification, regardless of who is classifying.

Accepted The taxonomy should be logical and intuitive so that it can become generally approved.

Useful The taxonomy can be used to gain insight into the field of inquiry.

Comprehensible The taxonomy should be useful to those with less than expert knowledge.

Conforming The terminology of the taxonomy should comply with established security terminology.

Objectivity The features must be identified from the object under observation where the attribute being measured should be clearly observable.

Determinism There must be a clear procedure that can be followed to extract the feature.

Repeatability Several people independently extracting the same feature for the object must agree on the value observed.

Specificity The value for the feature must be unique and unambiguous.

Upon review of the above list we believe that a sufficient and acceptable taxonomy must be mutually exclusive, exhaustive, unambiguous, useful, objective, deterministic, repeatable and specific.

23.1.2 From Taxonomies to Ontologies: The Case for Ontologies

In the paper "Abstraction-based Intrusion in Distributed Environments," Peng Ning, Sushil Jajodia, and Xiaoyang Sean Wang (2001) propose a hierarchical model for attack specification and event abstraction using three concepts essential to their approach: *system view, misuse signature* and *view definition*. Their model is based upon a thorough examination of attack characteristics and attributes. However, their model is encoded within the logic of their proposed system. Consequently, it is not readily interchangeable and reusable by other systems.

Similarly, the Intrusion Detection Working Group of the Internet Task Force has defined the intrusion detection message exchange format data model (IDMEF) (Curry and Debar 2002) to describes a data model to represent information exported by IDS's and by individual components of distributed IDS's. Although the IDMEF specification states: "... the Intrusion Detection Message Exchange Format is intended to be a standard data format that automated intrusion detection systems can use to report alerts about events that they deem suspicious" it also specifies the architecture of an intrusion detection system and models some attacks. IDMEF uses the extensible mark-up language (XML) to encode the data model, consequently, due to XML's limitations, the data model is not contained within the XML declarations but rather in the logic of how the particular IDS interprets the XML declarations.

Because IDMEF is specified in an XML document type definition (DTD)[3] it does not convey the semantics, relationships, attributes and characteristics of the objects which it represents. Moreover, XML does not support the notion of inheritance.

In commenting on the IETF's IDMEF, Richard Kemmerer and Giovanni Vigna (1999) state "it is a but a first step, however additional effort is needed to provide a common ontology that lets IDS sensors agree on what they observe."

According to Randall Davis, Howard Shrobe, and Peter Szolovits (1993) knowledge representation is a surrogate or substitute for an object under study. In turn, the surrogate enables an entity, such as a software system, to reason about the object. Knowledge representation is also a set of *ontological* commitments specifying the terms that describe the essence of the object. In other words, *meta-data* or data about data describing their relationships.

Frame based systems are an important thread in knowledge representation. According to Daphne Koller and Avi Pfeffer (1998) frame based systems provide an excellent representation for the organizational structure of complex domains. Frame based languages, which support frame based systems, include RDF, and are used to represent ontologies. According to Chris Welty (2000), at its deepest level an ontology subsumes a taxonomy. Similarly, Natalya Noy and Deborah McGuinnes (1999) state the process of developing an ontology includes arranging classes in a taxonomic hierarchy.

The relationship among data objects may be highly complex, however at

---

[3] See the XML Schema Working Group, http://www.w3c.org/XML/Schema.

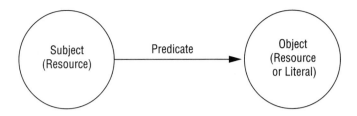

Figure 23.1: RDF Graph.

the   finest level of granularity, the knowledge representation of any object may be represented within a resource description framework schema (RDF-S), which formally defines the data model as:

1. A set called *resources*.

2. A set called *literals*.

3. A subset of resources called *properties*

4. A set called *Statements*, where each element is a triple of the form {*sub, pred, obj* } where *pred* is a member of properties, *sub* is a member of resources, and *obj* is either a member of resources or a member of literals.

Figure 23.1 graphically illustrates the basic RDF-S model. In addition to a graphical representation, the relationship between a set of objects may be described as a set of *N-triples*, or by a statement in an ontology representation language like RDFS (The World Wide Web Consortium 1999) or DAML+OIL.

In applying an ontology and semantic reasoning to the problem of intrusion detection its power and utility is not simply in representing the attributes of the attack, but rather because we can express the relationships between collected data and use those relationships to deduce that the particular data represents an attack of a particular type. We provide an example of this utility in section 23.4.

An ontology decouples the data model representing an intrusion from the logic of the intrusion detection system. The decoupling of the data model from the IDS logic enables nonhomogeneous IDS's to share data without a prior agreement as to the semantics of the data. To effect this sharing, the ontology is made available and if the recipient does not understand some aspect of the data it obtains the ontology in order to interpret and use the data.

Ontologies therefore, unlike taxonomies, provide powerful constructs that include machine interpretable definitions of the concepts within a specific domain and the relations between them. In our case the domain is that of a particular computer or a software system acting on the computer's behalf in order to detect attacks and intrusions. Ontologies may be utilized to not only provide IDS's with the ability to share a common understanding of the information at issue but also further enable the IDS with improved capacity to reason over and analyze instances of data representing an intrusion. Moreover, within an ontology characteristics such as cardinality, range and exclusion may be specified and the notion of inheritance is supported.

23.2 Target Centric Ontology Attributes of the Class Intrusion

In constructing our ontology, we relied upon an empirical analysis (Undercoffer and Pinkston 2002) of the features and attributes, and their interrelationships, of over 4,000 classes of computer attacks and intrusions. Figure 23.2, presents a high level view of our ontology. The attributes of each class and subclass (denoted by ellipses) are not shown because it would make the illustration unwieldy.

At the top most level we define the class *Host*. Host has the properties *Current State* which is defined by the class *System Component* and *Victim of* which is defined by the class *Attack*. As defined in section 23.1.2 the property, also called the predicate, defines the relationship between a subject and an object.

The System Component class is comprised of the three subclasses: Network, System, and Process.

Network. This class is inclusive of the network layers of the protocol stack. We have focused on TCP/IP therefore we only consider IP, TCP, and UDP subclasses. For example, and as will be later demonstrated, the TCP subclass includes the properties *TCP_MAX,* which defines the maximum number of TCP connections, *WAIT_STATE* defining the number of connections waiting on the final *ack* of the three-way handshake to establish a TCP connection, *THRESHOLD* specifying the allowable ratio between maximum connections and partially established connections and *EXCEED_T* a Boolean value indicating that the allowable ratio has been exceeded. It should be noted that these are only four of several network properties.

System. This class includes attributes representing the operating system of the host. It includes attributes representing overall memory usage (*MEM_TOTAL, MEM_FREE, MEM_SWAP*) and CPU usage (*LOAD_AVG*). The class also contains attributes reflective of the number of current users, disk usage, the number of installed kernel modules, and change in state of the interrupt descriptor and system call tables.

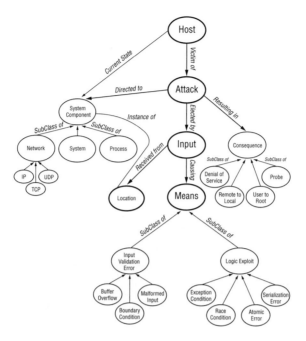

Figure 23.2: Target centric ontology.

Process. This class contains attributes representing particular processes that are to be monitored. These attributes include the current value of the instruction pointer (*INS_P*), the current top of the stack (*T_STACK*), a scalar value computed from the stream of system calls (*CALL_V*), and the number of child processes (*N_CHILD*).

The class *Attack* has the properties *Directed to, Effected by,* and *Resulting in.* This construction is predicated upon the notion that an attack consists of some input which is directed to some system component and results in some consequence. Accordingly, the classes *System Component, Input,* and *Consequence* are the corresponding objects. The class Consequence is comprised of several subclasses which include *Denial of Service, User Access, Root Access,* and *Probe.*

Denial of Service. The attack results in a denial of service to the users of the system. The denial of service may be because the system was placed into an unstable state or all of the system resources may be consumed by meaningless functions.

User Access. The attack results in the attacker having access to services on the target system at an unprivileged level.

Root Access. The attack results in the attacker being granted privileged access to the system, consequently having complete control of the system.

Probe. This type of an attack is the result of scanning or other activity wherein a profile of the system is disclosed.

Finally, the class *Input* has the the attributes *Received from* and *Causing* where *Causing* defines the relationship between the *Means* of attack and some input. We define the following two subclasses (Input Validation Error and Logic Exploits) for *Means* of attack:

Input Validation Error. An input validation error exists if some malformed input is received by a hardware or software component and is not properly bounded or checked. This class is further subclassed as:

1. Buffer Overflow. The classic buffer overflow results from an overflow of a static-sized data structure.

2. Boundary Condition Error. A process attempts to read or write beyond a valid address boundary or a system resource is exhausted.

3. Malformed Input. A process accepts syntactically incorrect input, extraneous input fields, or the process lacks the ability to handle field-value correlation errors.

Logic Exploits. Logic exploits are exploited software and hardware vulnerabilities such as race conditions or undefined states that lead to performance degradation and/or system compromise. Logic exploits are further subclasssed as follows:

1. Exception Condition. An error resulting from the failure to handle an exception condition generated by a functional module or device.

2. Race Condition. An error occurring during a timing window between two operations.

3. Serialization Error. An error that results from the improper serialization of operations.

4. Atomicity Error. An error occurring when a partially-modified data structure is used by another process; an error occurring because some process terminated with partially modified data where the modification should have been atomic.

23.3   Implementation

There are several reasoning systems that are compatible with DAML+OIL. According to their functionality, reasoning systems can be classified into two types, backward-chaining and forward-chaining. Backward-chaining reasoners process queries and return proofs for the answers they provide. Forward-chaining reasoners process assertions substantiated by proofs, and draw conclusions. Available reasoning systems include Stanford's Java Theorem Prover (Frank, Jenkins, and Fikes 2002), Drexel's DAMLJessKB (Kopena 2002) and the Renamed ABox and Concept Expression Reasoner (Haarslev and Moller 2001).

We have prototyped the logic portion of our system using the DAML-JessKB reasoning system, an extension to the Java expert system shell (JESS) (Friedman-Hill 1977. JESS is a Java implementation of the C language integrated production system (CLIPS) (Giarratano and Riley 1998). DAML-JessKB is employed to reason over instances of our data model that are considered to be suspicious. These suspicious instances are constrained according to our target-centric ontology and asserted into the knowledge base.

Upon initialization of DAMLJessKB we converted the DAML+OIL statements representing the ontology into *N-Triples* and assert them into a knowledge base as rules. The assertions are of the form:

```
(assert
(PropertyValue (predicate) (subject) (object)))
```

Once asserted, DAMLJessKB generates additional rules which include all of the chains of implication derived from the ontology.

Figures 23.2–23.8 illustrate the DAML+OIL encoding of selected class, subclasses and their respective properties, of our ontology.

Figure 23.3 lists the DAML+OIL statements defining the class *Attack* and its properties *Directed To, Resulting In* and *Effected By*. These properties correspond to the edges between the node labeled *Target* and the nodes labeled *System Component, Input* and *Consequence* respectively, in figure 23.2.

Figure 23.4 presents the DAML+OIL notation for the class *System Component*, its subclass *Network*, and Network's subclass *TCP*. Figure 23.5 lists the DAML+OIL notation for some of the attributes of the class *TCP*.

Figure 23.6 details the specification of the class *Consequence* while figures 23.7 and 23.8 show similar details for the specification of the classes *Denial of Service* and *Syn Flood*. The Syn Flood class, which is not shown in figure 23.2 illustrating our ontology, is a subclass of both Denial of Service and TCP and, as stated in the DAML+OIL notation, will only be instantiated when the threshold of pending TCP connections is exceeded.

23.3.1   Querying the Knowledge Base

Once the ontology is asserted into the knowledge base and all of the derived rules resulting from the chains of implication are generated, the knowledge

```
<rdfs:Class rdf:about="&IntrOnt;Attack"
rdfs:label="Consequence">
<rdfs:subClassOf rdf:resource="&rdfs;Resource"/>
</rdfs:Class>

<rdf:Property rdf:about="&IntrOnt;Directed_To" rdfs:label="Directed_To">
<rdfs:domain rdf:resource="&IntrOnt;Attack"/>
<rdfs:range rdf:resource="&IntrOnt;SysComp"/>
</rdf:Property>

<rdf:Property rdf:about="&IntrOnt;Resulting_In" rdfs:label="Resulting_In"
<rdfs:domain rdf:resource="&IntrOnt;Attack"/>
<rdfs:range rdf:resource="&IntrOnt;Conseq"/>
</rdf:Property>

<rdf:Property rdf:about="&IntrOnt;Effected_By" rdfs:label="Effected_By">
<rdfs:domain rdf:resource="&IntrOnt;Attack"/>
<rdfs:range rdf:resource="&IntrOnt;Input"/>
</rdf:Property>
```

Figure 23.3: DAML+OIL statements defining the class attack and its properties Directed To, Resulting In, and Effected By.

base is ready to receive instances of the ontology. Instances are asserted and de-asserted into/from the knowledge base as temporal events dictate. To query the knowledge base for the existence of an attack or intrusion, the query could be so granular that it requests an attack of a specific type, such as a Syn Flood:

```
(defrule isSynFlood

(PropertyValue
(p http://www.w3.org/1999/02/22-rdf-syntax-ns#type)
(s ?var)
(o http://security.umbc.edu/IntrOnt#SynFlood))

=>

(printout t ''A SynFlood attack has occurred." crlf
''with event number: '' ?var))
```

The query could be of a medium level of granularity, asking for all attacks of a specific class, such as denial of service. Accordingly, the following query will return all instances of an attack of the class Denial of Service.

```
(defrule isDOS

(PropertyValue
(p http://www.w3.org/1999/02/22-rdf-syntax-ns#type)
```

```
<daml:Class rdf:about="&IntrOnt;SysComp" rdfs:label="State">
<rdfs:subClassOf rdf:resource="&rdfs;Resource"/>
</daml:Class>

<daml:Class rdf:about="&IntrOnt;Network" rdfs:label="Network">
<rdfs:subClassOf rdf:resource="&IntrOnt;SysComp"/>
</daml:Class>

<daml:Class rdf:about="&IntrOnt;TCP" rdfs:label="Network">
<rdfs:subClassOf rdf:resource="&IntrOnt;Network"/>
</daml:Class>
```

Figure 23.4: DAML+OIL statements specifying the class system component and its subclass, Network and TCP.

```
rdf:Property rdf:about="&IntrOnt;TCP_Max" rdfs:label="TCP_Max">
<rdfs:domain rdf:resource="&IntrOnt;Network"/>
<rdfs:range rdf:resource="&rdfs;nonNegativeInteger"/>
</rdf:Property>

<rdf:Property rdf:about="&IntrOnt;Wait_State" rdfs:label="Wait_State">
<rdfs:domain rdf:resource="&IntrOnt;Network"/>
<rdfs:range rdf:resource="&rdfs;nonNegativeInteger"/>
</rdf:Property>

<rdf:Property rdf:about="&IntrOnt;Threshold" rdfs:label="Threshold">
<rdfs:domain rdf:resource="&IntrOnt;Network"/>
<rdfs:range rdf:resource="&rdfs;nonNegativeInteger"/>
</rdf:Property>

<rdf:Property rdf:about="&IntrOnt;Exceed_T" rdfs:label="Exceed_T">
<rdfs:domain rdf:resource="&IntrOnt;Network"/>
<rdfs:range rdf:resource="&IntrOnt;BooleanValue"/>
</rdf:Property>
```

Figure 23.5: DAML+OIL notation specifying attributes of the TCP subclass.

```
(s ?var)
(o http://security.umbc.edu/IntrOnt#DoS))

=>

(printout t ''A DoS attack has occurred." crlf
''with ID number: '' ?var))
```

Finally, the following rule will return instances of any attack, where the event numbers that are returned by the query need to be iterated over in order to discern the specific type of attack:

```
(defrule isConseq
```

```
<rdfs:Class rdf:about="&IntrOnt;Conseq" rdfs:label="Conseq">
<rdfs:subClassOf rdf:resource="&rdfs;Resource"/>
</rdfs:Class>
```

Figure 23.6: DAML+OIL specification of the class Consequence.

```
<rdfs:Class rdf:about="&IntrOnt;DoS" rdfs:label="DoS">
<rdfs:subClassOf rdf:resource="&IntrOnt;Conseq"/>
</rdfs:Class>
```

Figure 23.7: DAML+OIL statements specifying the Denial of Service sub-class.

```
(PropertyValue
(p http://www.w3.org/1999/02/22-rdf-syntax-ns#type)
(s ?var)
(o http://security.umbc.edu/IntrOnt#Conseq))

=>

(printout t ''An attack has occurred." crlf
''with ID number: '' ?var))
```

These varying levels of granularity are possible because of DAML+OIL's notion of classes, subclasses, and the relationships that hold between them. The variable *?var*, contained in each of the queries, is instantiated with the subject whenever a predicate and object from a matching triple is located in the knowledge base.

23.4 Using the Ontology to Detect Attacks: Use Case Scenarios

To test and experiment with our implementation we created instances of our ontology in DAML+OIL notation and asserted them into the knowledge base. We then ran our queries against the knowledge base.

23.4.1 Denial of Service — Syn Flood

The DAML+OIL representation of an instance of a *Syn_Flood* attack is illus-trate in figure 23.9. The first statement indicates that an event numbered 00035

```
<daml:Class rdf:about="&IntrOnt;Syn_Flood" rdfs:label="Syn_Flood">
<rdfs:subClassOf rdf:resource="&IntrOnt;DoS"/>
<rdfs:subClassOf rdf:resource="&IntrOnt;TCP">
<daml:Restriction>
<daml:onProperty rdf:resource="&IntrOnt;Exceed_T"/>
<daml:hasValue rdf:resource="#true"/>
</daml:Restriction>
</rdfs:subClassOf>
</daml:Class>
```

Figure 23.8: DAML+OIL Statements specifying the SynFlood subclass.

```
<Intrusion:Host rdf:about="&IntrOnt;00035"
Intrusion:IP_Address="130.85.112.231" rdfs:label="00035">
<Intrusion:resulting_in rdf:resource="&IntrOnt;00038"/>
</Intrusion:Host>

<Intrusion:Syn_Flood rdf:about="&IntrOnt;00038"
Intrusion:Exceed_T="true"
Intrusion:time="15:43:12"
Intrusion:date="02/22/2003" rdfs:label="00038"/>
```

Figure 23.9: DAML+OIL notation for an instance of a Syn Flood attack.

has occurred which has the *resulting_in* property instantiated to an instance of a Syn Flood that is uniquely identified as event number 00038.

When the knowledge base was queried for instances of Denial of Service (DoS) attacks, the following was returned:

```
The event number of the intrusion is:
http://security.umbc.edu/Intrusion#00038
The type of intrusion is:
http://security.umbc.edu/Intrusion#Syn_Flood
The victim's IP address is:
130.85.112.231
The time and date of the event:
15:43:12 hours on 02/22/2003
```

It is important to note that we only queried for the existence of a Denial of Service attack, we did not specifically ask for Syn Flood attacks. The instance of the Syn Flood attack was returned because it is a subclass of Denial of Service.

23.4.2   The Classic Mitnick Type Attack

This subsection provides an example of using our ontology as it operates within a coalition of distributed IDSs to detect the *Mitnick* attack. This particular attack is a distributed attack consisting of a Denial of Service attack, TCP sequence number prediction and IP spoofing.

The following example of a distributed attack illustrates the utility of our ontology.

The Mitnick attack is multi-phased, consisting of a Denial of Service attack, TCP sequence number prediction and IP spoofing. When this attack first occurred in 1994, a Syn Flood was used to effect the denial of service, however any denial of service attack would have sufficed.

In the following example, which is illustrated in figure 23.10, Host B is the ultimate target and Host A is trusted by Host B.

The attack is structured as follows:

1. The attacker initiates a Syn/Flood attack against Host A to prevent Host A from responding to Host B.

2. The attacker sends multiple TCP packets to the target, **Host B**, in order to be able to predict the values of TCP sequence numbers generated by Host B.

3. The attacker then pretends to be Host A by spoofing Host A's IP address, and sends a Syn packet to Host B in order to establish a TCP session between Host A and Host B.

4. Host B responds with a SYN/ACK to Host A. The attacker does not see this packet. Host A, since its input queue is full due to number of half open connections caused by the Syn/Flood attack, cannot send a *RST* message to Host B in response to the spurious Syn message.

5. Using the calculated TCP sequence number of Host B (recall that the attacker did not see the Syn/ACK message sent from **Host B** to Host A) the attacker sends an *Ack* with the predicted TCP sequence number packet in response to the *Syn/Ack* packet sent to Host A.

6. Host B is now in a state where it believes that a TCP session has been established with a trusted host Host A. The attacker now has a one way session with the target, Host B, and can issue commands to the target.

It should be noted that an intrusion detection system running exclusively at either host will not detect this multiphased and distributed attack. At best, Host A's IDS would see a relatively short lived Syn Flood attack, and Host B's IDS might observe an attempt to infer TCP sequence numbers, although this may not stand out from other nonintrusive but ill-formed TCP connection attempts.

The following example illustrates the utility of our ontology, as well as the importance of forming coalitions of IDSs. In our model, all of the IDSs share a

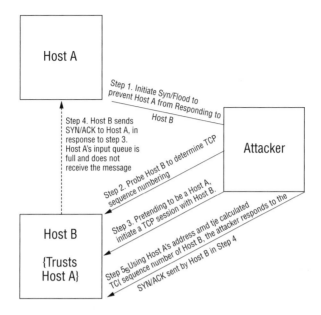

Figure 23.10: Illustration of the Mitnick attack.

common ontology and utilize a secure communications infrastructure that has been optimized for IDSs. We present such a communications infrastructure in Undercoffer, Perich, Cedilnik, Kagal, and Joshi (2002); Kagal, Undercoffer, Joshi, and Finin (2002); and Undercoffer, Perich, and Nicholas. 92002).

Consider the case of the instance of the Syn Flood attack presented in section 23.4.1 and that it was directed against Host A in our example scenario. As the IDS responsible for Host A is continually monitoring for anomalous behavior, asserting and deasserting data as necessary, it detects the occurence of an inordinate number of partially established TCP connections, and transmits the instance of the Syn Flood illustrated in figure 23.9 to the other IDSs in its coalition.

This instance is converted into a set of *N-Triples* and asserted into the knowledge base of each IDS in the coalition. (Note: those same *N-Triples* will be deasserted when the responsible IDS transmits a message stating that the particular host is no longer the victim of a Syn Flood attack.) As this situation, especially in conjunction with Host B being subjected to a series of probes meant to determine its TCP sequencing, are anomalous and may be the prelude to a distributed attack the, current and pending connections are also asserted into the knowledge base. Figure 23.11 lists the set of DAML+OIL statements describing those connections that were used in our experiments.

```
<IntrOnt:Connection rdf:about="&IntrOnt;00043"
IntrOnt:IP_Address="130.85.112.231"
IntrOnt:conn_time="15:42:59"
IntrOnt:conn_date="02/22/2003"
rdfs:label="00041"/>

<IntrOnt:Connection rdf:about="&IntrOnt;00043"
IntrOnt:IP_Address="130.85.112.231"
IntrOnt:conn_time="15:44:17"
IntrOnt:conn_date="02/22/2003"
rdfs:label="00043"/>

<IntrOnt:Connection rdf:about="&IntrOnt;00101"
IntrOnt:IP_Address="202.85.191.121"
IntrOnt:conn_time="15:12:21"
IntrOnt:conn_date="02/22/2003"
rdfs:label="00101"/>

<IntrOnt:Connection rdf:about="&IntrOnt;00102"
IntrOnt:IP_Address="68.54.101.78"
IntrOnt:conn_time="15:01:52"
IntrOnt:conn_date="02/22/2003"
rdfs:label="00102"/>
```

Figure 23.11: DAML+OIL notation for an instances of connections.

Figure 23.12 illustrates the DAML+OIL notation specifying the Mitnick attack. Notice that it is a subclass of both the class defining a denial of service attack and the TCP subclass, with a restriction on the property indicating that the target of the attack has established a connection with the victim of the denial of service (DoS) attack.

DAML+OIL, like any other notation language, does not have the functionality to perform mathematical operations. Consequently, when querying for the existence of a Mitnick type of attack, we must define a rule that tests for concomitance between the DoS attack and the establishment of the connection with the target of the DoS attack. The following query performs that test:

```
(defrule isMitnick

(PropertyValue
(p http://security.umbc.edu/IntrOnt#Mitnick )
(s ?eventNumber) (o "true"))

(PropertyValue
(p http://security.umbc.edu/IntrOnt#Int_time)
(s ?eventNumber) (o ?Int_Time))

(PropertyValue
```

```
<daml:Class rdf:about="&Intrusion;Mitnick"
rdfs:label="P\_Mitnick">
<rdfs:subClassOf>
<daml:Restriction>
<daml:onProperty rdf:resource="&IntrOnt;Victim"/>
<daml:hasValue rdf:resource="#true"/>
<daml:toClass rdf:resource="&IntrOnt;DoS"/>
</daml:Restriction>
</rdfs:subClassOf>
<rdfs:subClassOf>
<daml:Restriction>
<daml:onProperty rdf:resource="&IntrOnt;est_connections"/>
<daml:hasValue rdf:resource="#IP_Address"/>
<daml:toClass rdf:resource="&IntrOnt;TCP"/>
</daml:Restriction>
</rdfs:subClassOf>
</daml:Class>
```

Figure 23.12: DAML+OIL specification of the Mitnick attack.

```
(p http://security.umbc.edu/IntrOnt#Conn_time)
(s ?eventNumber) (o ?Conn_Time))

=>

(if (>= ?Conn_Time ?Int_Time) then
(printout t ''event number: ''
?eventnumber '' is a Mitnick Attack: crlf)))
```

This query makes the correlation between event Number 00043, the connection occurring at 15:44:17 with the host at IP address 130.85.112.23, and event number 00038, the Denail of Service attack. The query, in conjunction with the other queries, produced the following response:

```
The synflood attack is:
http://security.umbc.edu/Intrusion#00038
The dos attack is:
http://security.umbc.edu/Intrusion#00038
The event number of the connection is:
http://security.umbc.edu/Intrusion#00043
The mitnick attack is:
http://security.umbc.edu/Intrusion#genid21
A connection with 130.85.112.231 was
made at 15:44:17 on 02/22/2003
```

Where event number *genid21* was generated by the knowledge base based upon event number 00038 and event number 00043 and the specification of the Mitnick attack in the ontology.

At this point it is important to review the sequence of events leading up to the discovery of the Mitnick attack. Recall, that the IDS responsible for the victim of the Syn Flood attack queried its knowledge base for an instance of a *DoS* denial of service attack. The query returned an instance of a Syn Flood which was instantiated solely on the condition that a Syn Flood is a subclass of both the *DoS* and *Network* classes restricted to the value of *Exced_T* being true.

The instance (its properties) of the Syn Flood attack was transmitted in the form of a set of DAML+OIL statements to the other IDSs in the coalition. In turn, these IDSs converted the DAML+OIL notated instance, into a set of *N-Triples* and asserted them into their respective knowledge bases. As a Syn Flood is a precursor to a more insidious attack, instances of established and pending connections were asserted into the knowledge base. As the state of the knowledge base is dynamic due to the assertions and deassertions, the rule set of each IDS is continually applied to the knowledge base.

Finally, the instance of the Mitnick attack was instantiated by the knowledge base based upon the existence of both the instance of the TCP connection and the instance of the DoS attack.

23.4.3   Buffer Overflow Attack

The "C" strcpy() function is one of several functions that need to be bounded in order to prevent a buffer overflow attack. A buffer overflow attack occurs when deliberately constructed code is placed onto the stack frame, overwriting the return address from the current function. When a function is called, input parameters to the function, the frame pointer(ebp register) and the return address (the current eip + the length of the call instruction) are pushed onto the stack. Like all instructions, they are located in the *Text* address space of memory.

In the simplest of terms, the goal of the buffer overflow is to overrun a buffer that is contained on the stack,consequently overwriting the return address with an address that is within the stack. When finished, the function pops the return address from the stack, the instruction pointer now points to an instruction(s) that is/are within the stack. These spurious instructions are intended to provide the attacker with some heretofore unintended access to the machine. A unique characteristic of this attack is that the malicious instructions are not within the text area of memory, but in the stack. Because the text area has clearly delineated boundaries, we are able to test if the instruction pointer references an area with the Text section of the stack section of memory.

As previously stated, we have instrumented the Linux kernel and are able to intercept any given process at each system call, and examine the contents of its registers and stack frame. Consequently, we are able to define the charac-

```
<daml:Class rdf:about="&IntrOnt;Buff_OF" rdfs:label="Buff_OF">
<rdfs:subClassOf rdf:resource="&IntrOnt;R_to_L"/>
<rdfs:subClassOf rdf:resource="&IntrOnt;U_to_R">
<rdfs:subClassOf rdf:resource="&IntrOnt;Process">
<daml:Restriction>
<daml:onProperty rdf:resource="&IntrOnt;EIP_out_Txt"/>
<daml:hasValue rdf:resource="#true"/>
</daml:Restriction>
</rdfs:subClassOf>
</daml:Class>

<rdf:Property rdf:about="&IntrOnt;EIP_out_Txt"
rdfs:label="EIP_out_Txt">
<rdfs:domain rdf:resource="&IntrOnt;
Buff_OF"/>
<rdfs:range rdf:resource="&IntrOnt;
BooleanValue"/>
</rdf:Property>
```

Figure 23.13: DAML+OIL notation specifying the Buffer Overflow subclass.

teristics of a buffer overflow attack such that the instruction pointer references a memory location that is outside of the boundaries of the text segment. Figure 23.13 presents the DAML+OIL notation for the class *Buffer Overflow* and one of its properties.

Similar to the previous two examples, querying the knowledge base with the following will yield all instances of a buffer overflow.

```
(defrule isBufferOverflow

(PropertyValue
(p http://www.w3.org/1999/02/22-rdf-syntax-ns#type)
(s ?var)
(o http://security.umbc.edu/IntrOnt#Buff_OF))

=>

(printout t ''A Buffer Overflow has occurred." crlf
''with ID number: '' ?var))
```

23.5   Building an Intrusion Detection Model: What to Mine and Where to Find It

In the introduction to this chapter we posit that the lackluster performance of IDSs in general is attributable to research in the field being at too high a level, consequently not digging deep enough, or from an approach that is too philosophical, consequently incorrectly identifying where to dig. We now state where we "dig" and what we are "digging for."

IDSs are categorized according to scope — network-based or host-based, and method — signature (misuse) based or anomaly based. Typically, misuse detectors examine TCP/IP network traffic using pattern, expression or byte code matching to detect an actual or attempted intrusion. Signature based detectors use rule sets defining unacceptable behavior and raise an alarm whenever the event matches a pre-defined rule or signature. Consequently, there are several thousand rules that define the attacks and their variants that are discernible by examining network data. There are, however, numerous attacks that are indiscernible by network based IDSs.

To alleviate the situation wherein some attacks are undetectable due to the absence of information, we capture data concerning the global system state as well as data specific to applications that accept network connections. In other words, we expand the feature set over which the data mining algorithms used in any individual IDS would operate. It now consists of the data contained within following heterogeneous streams (from the kernel, network protocol stack and the network interface) on each node in the system:

1. Per process system calls, to include the system calls of child processes.

2. Per process kernel information. This includes page faults, memory usage, CPU usage, flags, signals, interrupts, and similar information on child processes.

3. Global system state to include memory usage, CPU statistics, and disk i/o information.

4. Network statistics. Including all available IP, ICMP, TCP, and UDP statistics.

5. Network flows. TCPDump information.

6. The state of neighboring information.

Accordingly, we are capturing 184 distinct elements in the IP statistics flow, 63 distinct elements per process kernel information flow, and 40 distinct elements in the global system information flow. TCPDump information is dependent upon the type of packet captured and the possible number of elements processed is the cumulative total of distinct fields in the various packet types. Per process system calls are distilled into a single metric that measures deviation from the process' established baseline. In all we capture and mine several hundred attributes.

Our purpose for mining this data is to construct a model of the quiescent (unattacked) state of the host. Due to the magnitude of variables, the first order

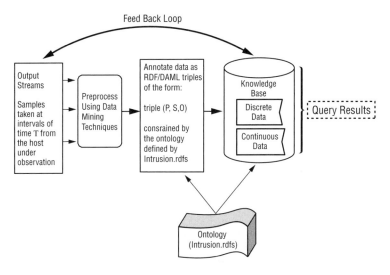

Figure 23.14: IDS Model using data mining for preliminary hypothesis testing.

of business is to attempt to reduce the dimensionality of the data set. In our own research we use *principal component analysis* (Jolliffe 1986) to obtain 12 features from the original 184. In future work, we plan to investigate other approaches such as random projections.

The best method to effectively and accurately construct the model is an ongoing part of our research. We used a fuzzy clustering based approach (Krishnapuram, Joshi, Nasraoui, and Yi 2001) that is highly robust, tolerant of noise and has linear complexity. Given the model, a system could mine the heterogeneous data streams emanating from the processes and system(s) under observations and detect "outliers" that signal a possible attack. Figure 23.14 shows our approach. We gather data from the logs, project them to the reduced space, and then construct clusters. Outliers are detected by computing how far away they are from the clusters that represent the unattacked state. While cluster construction is an offline process, we can detect the outliers from the stream in near real time. In preliminary results, we found that we could detect a wide variety of attacks against the apache server such as chunking, line feed, mime flood, cross site scripting etc. At present, we can detect an attack close to 100% of the time, with a false positive rate that ranges from 0 to 8 percent. we can also pick up attacks when they are mixed in with normal traffic to the server. We hope in the future to use ideas related to subsampling proposed by Paul Dokas, Levent Ertoz, Vipin Kumar, Aleksandar Lazarevic, Jaideep Srivastava, and Pang-Nig Tan (2002).

Information about the outliers is annotated into RDF/DAML triples and asserted into a knowledge base for further evaluation. Should the reasoning engine suspect that an attack is underway, it can then invoke more sophisticated data mining algorithms suitable for finding particular patterns in the underlying data stream. It can tell them *where* to look, and *what* features to mine. For instance, in the Mitnick attack case it would ask the data mining algorithm to look at the local (where) network interface data (what). The more sophisticated algorithms would thus only be deployed when needed, be looking at the right data streams and the right subset of possible features. These algorithms would either provide further evidence to support that the detected outlier is indeed an attack, or alternatively show it to be harmless. Notice that this need not be a single step process — the data mining algorithms invoked by the reasoner would provide it additional "facts" based on which it could decide to invoke yet another set of algorithms on a possibly different subset of the features at a possibly different location in the system.

In summary, we have shown how building a model of the attacks, describing it in semantically rich languages such as those being developed for the semantic web, and reasoning over "facts" provided by mining of system and network related data streams can be used to create a distributed IDS. Such a system is much more sophisticated than IDSs that use data mining or other syntactic level pattern recognition techniques since it can detect distributed attacks and variants thereof naturally. We argue that such an approach, which combines semantic and and syntactic approaches, can be applied to distributed data mining in general for dynamic selection of data sources and feature subsets.

Anupam Joshi is an associate professor in the Department of Computer Science and Electrical Engineering at the University of Maryland, Baltimore County.

Jeffrey L. Undercoffer is a retired Supervisory Special Agent of the United States Secret Service and a current Ph.D. student at the University of Maryland, Baltimore County.

Chapter 24

Usage Mining for and on the Semantic Web

Bettina Berendt, Gerd Stumme, and Andreas Hotho

Web usage mining is the application of data mining methods to the analysis of recordings of web usage, most often in the form of web server logs. One of its central problems is the large number of patterns that are usually found: among these, how can the *interesting* patterns be identified?

For example, an application of association rule analysis to a web log will typically return many patterns like the observation that 90% of the users who made a purchase in an online shop also visited the homepage — a pattern that is trivial because the homepage is the site's main entry point.

Statistical measures of pattern quality, like support and confidence, and measures of interestingness based on the divergence from prior beliefs, are a primarily syntactical approach to this problem. They need to be complemented by an understanding of what a site and its usage patterns are about, i.e. a semantic approach.

A popular approach for modeling sites and their usage is related to OLAP techniques: a modeling of the pages in terms of (possibly multiple) concept hierarchies, and an investigation of patterns at different levels of abstraction, i.e. a knowledge discovery cycle that iterates over various "roll-ups" and "drill-downs." Concept hierarchies conceptualize a domain in terms of taxonomies such as product catalogs, topical thesauri, etc. The expressive power of this form of knowledge representation is limited to is-a relationships. However, for many applications, a more expressive form of knowledge representation is desirable, for example *ontologies* that allow arbitrary relations between concepts.

A second problem facing many current analyses that take semantics into account is that the conceptualizations often have to be hand-crafted to represent a site that has grown independently of an overall conceptual design, and that the mapping of individual pages to this conceptualization may have to be established.

It would thus be desirable to have a rich semantic model of a site, of its content and its (hyperlink) structure, a model that captures the complexity of the manifold relationships between the concepts covered in a site, and a model that is "built into" the site in the sense that the pages requested by visitors are directly associated with the concepts and relations treated by it.

The semantic web is just this: today's web enriched by a formal semantics expressed as ontologies that captures the meaning of pages and links in a machine-understandable form. The main idea of the semantic web is to enrich the current web by machine-processable information in order to allow for semantics-based tools supporting the human user. In this chapter, we discuss how the semantic web can improve web usage mining, and, conversely, how usage mining can help to build up the semantic web.

After a short overview of the relevant areas of web mining in the next section, section 24.2 will describe this understanding of the semantic web in more detail. Section 24.3 then gives an overview of how semantics can enhance web usage mining, ranging to a mining of the semantic web itself. We also discuss how to incorporate knowledge about behavior in web hypermedia that transcends the semantics of sites in themselves.

Section 24.4 then illustrates how mining can contribute to the development of the semantic web by automatically extracting knowledge from web resources.

We use the term *semantic web mining* to denote these various methods of mining the semantic web and mining for the semantic web. Besides semantic web usage mining, semantic web mining also includes semantic web content and structure mining. Ideally, all methods addressed above should be combined to go from a site and its usage to its semantics and back. We discussed the overall view of semantic web mining and sketched this feedback loop in Berendt, Hotho, and Stumme (2002). In the current chapter, we will focus on more specific aspects of semantic web usage mining.

24.1   Web (Usage) Mining

Web mining is the application of data mining techniques to the content, structure, and usage of web resources. This can help to discover global as well as local structure within and between web pages. Like other data mining applications, web mining can profit from given structure on data (as in database tables), but it can also be applied to semistructured or unstructured data like free-form text. This means that web mining is an invaluable help in the transformation from human understandable content to machine understandable semantics.

A distinction is generally made between web mining that operates on the web resources themselves (often further differentiated into *content* and *structure* mining), and mining that operates on visitors' *usage* of these resources (Zaïane 1998; Kosala and Blockeel 2000; Srivastava, Cooley, Deshpande, and Tan 2000).

Web content mining is a form of text mining (for recent overviews, see Chakrabarti [2000] and Sebastiani [2002]). It concentrates on the content of individual pages, which is contained in the HTML, script, etc. code that generates a page. It can therefore take advantage of the semistructured nature of these types of text. The hyperlink structure between those pages is, on the one hand, a structure over and above the individual page. This is utilized in web structure mining approaches like the Google PageRank algorithm that determines the relevance of a page by how many other pages "cite" it (Page, Brin, Motwani, and Winograd [1998]; see also Kleinberg [1999]). On the other hand, hyperlinks are part of the textual content of a page. This is particularly true for pages in which hyperlinks, like other elements, are (semantically) marked up. In the following, we will therefore treat these two areas in an integrated fashion (Cooley, Mobasher, and Srivastava 1997). Web content and structure mining can be used, among other things, to extract information from web pages to determine keywords describing content, or even to assign web pages to a domain model, to detect events or track developments in time-varying series of web resources like newswire articles.

In *web usage mining*, the primary web resource that is being mined is a record of the requests made by visitors to a web site, most often collected in a web server log (for an overview, see chapter 21). The content and structure of web pages, and in particular those of one web site, reflect the intentions of the authors and designers of the pages and the underlying information architecture. The actual behavior of the users of these resources may reveal additional structure.

First, relationships may be induced by usage where no particular structure was designed. For example, in an online catalog of products, there is usually either no inherent structure (different products are simply viewed as a set), or one or several hierarchical structures given by product categories, manufacturers, etc. Mining the visits to that site, however, one may find that many of the users who were interested in product A were also interested in product B. Here, "interest" may be measured by requests for product description pages, or by the placement of that product into the shopping cart (indicated by the request for the respective pages). The identified association rules are at the center of cross-selling and up-selling strategies in e-commerce sites. When a new user shows interest in product A, she will receive a recommendation for product B (e.g., Mobasher, Cooley, and Srivastava 2000; Lin, Alvarez, and Ruiz 2002).

Second, relationships may be induced by usage where a different relationship was intended. For example, sequence mining may show that many of the users who visited page C later went to page D, along paths that indicate a prolonged search (frequent visits to help and index pages, frequent backtracking, etc.) (Cooley 2000; Kato, Nakayama, and Yamane 2000). This can be interpreted to mean that visitors wish to reach D from C, but that this was not foreseen in the information architecture, hence that there is at present no hyperlink from C to D. This insight can be used for static site improvement for all users (adding a link from C to D), or for dynamic recommendations personalized for the subset of users who go to C ("you may wish to also look at D").

It is useful to combine web usage mining with content and structure analysis in order to make sense of observed frequent paths and the pages on these paths. This can be done using a variety of methods. Many of these methods rely on a mapping of pages into an ontology. An underlying ontology and the mapping of pages into it may already be available, the mapping of pages into an existing ontology may need to be learned, and/or the ontology itself may have to be inferred first.

In the following sections, we will first investigate the notions of semantics (as used in the semantic web) and ontologies in more detail. We will then look at how the use of ontologies, and other ways of identifying the meaning of pages, can help to make web mining go semantic. Finally, we will investigate how web usage mining can contribute to the learning of ontologies and their instances.

24.2 Semantic Web

The semantic web is based on a vision of Tim Berners-Lee, the inventor of the WWW. The great success of the current world wide web leads to a new challenge: a huge amount of data is interpretable by humans only; machine support is limited. Berners-Lee suggests enriching the web by machine-processable information that supports the user in his tasks. For instance, today's search engines are already quite powerful, but still frequently return overly large or inadequate lists of hits. Machine-processable information can point the search engine to the relevant pages and can thus improve both precision and recall.

For instance, it is today almost impossible to retrieve information with a keyword search when the information is spread over several pages. Consider, for example, the query for web mining experts in a company intranet, where the only explicit information stored are the relationships between people and the courses they attended on one hand, and between courses and the topics they cover on the other hand. In that case, the use of a rule stating that people who attended a course which was about a certain topic have knowledge about that topic might improve the results.

The process of building the semantic web is today still under way. Its structure has to be defined, and this structure has then to be filled with life. In order to make this task feasible, one should start with the simpler tasks. The following steps show the direction where the semantic web is heading: (1) providing a common syntax for machine understandable statements, (2) establishing common vocabularies, (3) agreeing on a logical language, and (4) using the language for exchanging proofs.

Berners-Lee suggested a layer structure for the semantic web: (1) Unicode/URI, (2) XML/namespaces/XML Schema, (3) RDF/RDF Schema, (4) ontology vocabulary, (5) logic, (6) proof, (7) trust.[1] This structure reflects the steps listed above. It follows the understanding that each step alone will already provide added value, so that the semantic web can be realized in an incremental fashion.

On the first two layers, a common syntax is provided. *Uniform resource identifiers* (URIs) provide a standard way to refer to entities;[2] *Unicode* is a standard for exchanging symbols. The *Extensible Markup Language* (XML) fixes a notation for describing labeled trees, and XML schema allows one to define grammars for valid XML documents. XML documents can refer to different namespaces to make explicit the context (and therefore meaning) of different tags. The formalizations on these two layers are now widely accepted, and the number of XML documents is increasing rapidly.

The next three layers form the current core of the web enriched by formal semantics. These are the most important for our ensuing formalization of semantic web usage mining; we will therefore treat them in detail in section 24.2.1.

Proof and *trust* are the remaining layers. They follow the understanding that it is important to be able to check the validity of statements made in the (semantic) web. These two layers are rarely tackled today, but are interesting topics for future research.

---

[1] See http://www.w3.org/DesignIssues/Semantic.html

[2] URL (uniform resource locator) refers to a locatable URI such as an http://...address. It is often used as a synonym, although strictly speaking URLs are a subclass of URIs. See http://www.w3.org/Addressing.

24.2.1   Modeling the Semantics of the Web:
RDF (Metadata), Ontologies, and Logics

According to the W3C recommendation,[3] the *resource description framework*
(RDF) "is a foundation for processing metadata; it provides interoperability
between applications that exchange machine-understandable information on
the web." RDF documents consist of three types of entities: resources, properties, and statements. Resources may be web pages, parts or collections of web
pages, or any (real-world) objects that are not directly part of the world wide
web.

Resources are always addressed by URIs. Properties are specific attributes,
characteristics, or relations describing resources. A resource together with a
property having a value for that resource form an RDF statement. A value
is either a literal, a resource, or another statement. Statements can thus be
considered as object–attribute–value triples.

The middle part of figure 24.1 shows an example of RDF statements. Two
of the authors of the present chapter (their web pages) are represented as resources URI-GST and URI-AHO. The statement on the lower right consists of
the resource "URI-AHO" and the property "cooperates-with" with the value
"URI-GST," (which again is a resource). The resource "URI-SWMining" has
as value for the property "title" the literal "semantic web mining." This ontology will be used as a running example throughout the chapter.

The data model underlying RDF is basically a directed labeled graph.
RDF schema defines a simple modeling language on top of RDF that includes
classes, is-a relationships between classes and between properties, and do-
main/range restrictions for properties. RDF and RDF schema are noted with
the syntax of XML, but they do not employ the tree semantics of XML.

The next layers are the *ontology vocabulary* and *logic*. Today the semantic web community tends to consider these layers as one single layer because
most ontologies allow for logical axioms. Following Gruber (1993), an ontology is "an explicit formalization of a shared understanding of a conceptualization." This high-level definition is realized differently by different research
communities. However, most of them have a certain understanding in common, as most of them include a set of concepts, a hierarchy on them, and
relations between concepts. Most of them also include axioms in some specific logic. To give a flavor, we present here just the core of our own definition
(Stumme 2002b; Bozsak, Ehrig, Handschuh, Hotho, Maedche, Motik, Oberle,
Schmitz, Staab, Stojanovic, Stojanovic, Studer, Stumme, Sure, Tane, Volz, and
Zacharias 2002), whose modularity ensures that different needs can be fulfilled
by combining parts.

---

[3] See http://www.w3.org/TR/2004/REC-rdf-syntax-grammar-20040210/

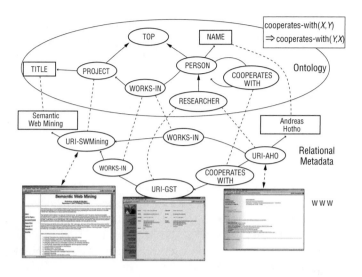

Figure 24.1: The relation between the world wide web, relational metadata, and ontologies.

Definition 24.2.1 *A core ontology with axioms is a tuple* $\mathcal{O} := (C, \leq_C, R, \sigma, \leq_R, \mathcal{A})$ *consisting of*

- *two disjoint sets C and R whose elements are called concept identifiers and relation identifiers, respectively,*

- *a partial order $\leq_C$ on C, called concept hierarchy or taxonomy,*

- *a function $\sigma: R \to C^+$ called signature (where C^+ is the set of all finite tuples of elements in C),*

- *a partial order $\leq_R$ on R, called relation hierarchy, where $r_1 \leq_R r_2$ implies $|\sigma(r_1)| = |\sigma(r_2)|$ and $\pi_i(\sigma(r_1)) \leq_C \pi_i(\sigma(r_2))$, for each $1 \leq i \leq |\sigma(r_1)|$, with π_i being the projection on the ith component, and*

- *a set $\mathcal{A}$ of logical axioms in some logical language $\mathcal{L}$.*

This definition constitutes a core structure that is quite straightforward, well-agreed upon, and that may easily be mapped onto most existing ontology representation languages. Step by step the definition can be extended by taking into account axioms, lexicons, and knowledge bases (Stumme 2002b).

As an example, have a look at the top of figure 24.1. The set C of concepts is the set {Top, Project, Person, Researcher, Literal}, and the concept hierarchy $\leq_C$ is indicated by the arrows with a bold head. The set R of relations is the set {works-in, cooperates-with, name}. The relation "works-in" has (Person, Project) as signature, the relation "name" has (Person, Literal) as signature.[4] In this example, the hierarchy on the relations is flat, i.e., $\leq_R$ is just the identity relation. The objects of the metadata level can be seen as instances of the ontology concepts. For example, "URI-SWMining" is an instance of the concept "Project," and thus by inheritance also of the concept "Top." Up until here, RDF schema would be sufficient for formalizing the ontology.

Often ontologies also contain logical axioms. By applying logical deduction, one can infer new knowledge, which is expressed implicitly, from the available information. For instance, the axiom in figure 24.1 states that the cooperates-with relation is symmetric. From it, one can infer that the person addressed by URI-AHO cooperates with the person addressed by URI-GST (and not only the other way around).

Apriori, any knowledge representation mechanism[5] can play the role of a semantic web language. Frame Logic (or F–Logic) (Kifer, Lausen, and Wu 1995), for instance, provides a semantically founded knowledge representation based on the frame and slot metaphor. Probably the most popular framework at the moment are description logics (DL). DLs are subsets of first order logic which aim at being as expressive as possible while still being decidable. The description logic $\mathcal{SHIQ}$ provides the basis for the web language DAML+OIL.[6] Its latest version has recently been released as a W3 Recommendation under the name OWL.[7]

Several tools are in use for the creation and maintenance of ontologies and metadata, as well as for reasoning within them. Our group has developed OntoEdit (Sure, Erdmann, Angele, Staab, Studer, and Wenke 2002; Sure, Staab, and Angele 2002), an ontology editor that is connected to Ontobroker (Fensel, Decker, Erdmann, and Studer 1998), an inference engine for F–Logic. It provides means for semantics-based query handling over distributed resources. Recently, the Karlsruhe Ontology Framework (KAON) (Bozsak, Ehrig, Handschuh, Hotho, Maedche, Motik, Oberle, Schmitz, Staab, Stojanovic, Stojanovic, Studer, Stumme, Sure, Tane, Volz, and Zacharias 2002)[8] has been set up as follow–up to OntoEdit. It is an open-source ontology management infrastructure targeted for business applications consisting of a comprehensive tool suite.

---

[4]It is a drawing convention to have relations with Literal as range drawn this way, as they are sometimes considered as attributes.

[5]See Studer, Benjamins, and Fensel (1998) for a general discussion.

[6]http://www.daml.org

[7]http://www.w3.org/TR/owl-features/

[8]http://kaon.semanticweb.org

KAON allows for easy ontology creation and management, as well as building ontology-based applications. A connection to the FaCT[9] inference engine for the description language $\mathcal{SHIQ}$ is planned.

24.3 Using Semantics for Usage Mining and Mining the Usage of the Semantic Web

Semantics can be utilized for web mining for different purposes. Some of the approaches presented in this section rely on a comparatively ad hoc formalization of semantics, while others exploit the full power of the semantic web. The semantic web offers a good basis to enrich web mining. The types of (hyper)links are now described explicitly, allowing the knowledge engineer to gain deeper insights in web structure mining and the contents of the pages come along with a formal semantics, allowing the engineer to apply mining techniques that require more structured input. Because the distinction between the use of semantics for web mining and the mining of the semantic web itself is all but sharp, we will discuss both in an integrated fashion.

24.3.1 Modeling the Semantics of Web Usage: Application Events

Web usage mining benefits from including semantics into the mining process for the simple reason that the application expert as the end user of mining results is interested in events in the application domain, in particular user behavior, while the base data — web server logs — are technically oriented sequences of HTTP requests. A central aim is therefore to map HTTP requests to meaningful events.

To achieve this, web usage mining needs to take a step that corresponds to the one that the semantic web takes to enrich the current web (figure 24.1): from (hyperlinked sets of) web pages to meaningful units that are the concepts and relations from an ontology, via a mapping established by RDF statements. In addition, the step to semantic web usage mining must consider what it takes to go from the web to web usage mining. The basic units of the web are (hyperlinked sets of) web pages, the basic units of web usage mining are web log entries that record requests for and, in response to these requests, deliveries of web pages. This adds two things to the meaning that these delivered pages would have when viewed in isolation: (a) user intentions and expectations, and (b) "is-related-to" structures induced by cohesive user activities like sessions.

---

[9]http://www.cs.man.ac.uk/~horrocks/FaCT

Combining these observations, one can say that the basic syntactic units of semantic web usage mining are requests for web pages, and the basic semantic units are *application events*: (a) atomic application events that mirror requests for individual pages, and (b) complex application events that mirror the structure inherent in a cohesive user activity. Again, the mapping from requests to application events can be noted in the form of RDF metadata.

In the following paragraphs, we will formalize these notions and use the result as a common framework to portray examples from a number of different studies. The studies themselves come from a variety of backgrounds and therefore construct and describe their formalizations in different ways.

Atomic Application Events

Atomic application events are the basic building blocks of web-usage behavior. They are modeled in terms of the content and service a web site offers. These, in turn, are represented in the content ontology $\mathcal{C}$ and the service ontology $\mathcal{S}$, respectively.

The ontology in figure 24.1 can be used to describe the content of web pages (as the metadata in the same figure show). In this way, it can serve as a content ontology. Information about one content item (e.g., a particular researcher) or about one content concept (e.g., "researchers") can be requested in different ways (such as in the "entry page" for researcher information, as a "list" of researchers' names, as a particular researcher's "personal home page," or in a "communication channel" addressing that researcher). These ways of requesting information are the services a page offers; they are the concepts of a service ontology.

The requested service should be distinguished from content because focusing on content only, one may often find requests for "meaningless" pages like "no items found in catalog" or even "404 page not found." Still, the observation that these were results of a "person search by search criterion project" can give important insights about user intentions, expectations, and behavior. (In fact, it may be argued that it is the inclusion of service that transforms page descriptions into event and thus behavior modeling.)

It is often useful to describe content or service in a structured way. Rather than simple statements like "page p is about content concept c," one may want to express "with respect to aspect d, page p is about content concept c" (analogously for service). We refer to these aspects as *information dimensions*. The values c for one dimension d are from a set of concepts from $\mathcal{C}$ (or $\mathcal{S}$); they may be hierarchically organized.

Based on this, we define:

Definition 24.3.1 *A site model $M := (\mathcal{S}, \mathcal{C}[, \mathcal{D}_\mathcal{S}][, \mathcal{D}_\mathcal{C}])$ is a tuple consisting*

Atomic application events

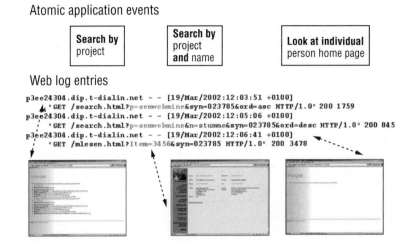

Figure 24.2: Atomic application events 1, 2, and 3 in the fictitious community portal (top), the web log with requests that are instances of these events (middle), and the web pages generated in response to the requests (bottom).

of a service ontology S, a content ontology C, and optionally tuples D_S and/or D_C consisting of the service/content information dimensions.

Definition 24.3.2 *An* atomic application event *for a site model* $M = (S, C[, D_S][, D_C])$ *is a tuple* $AAE := (S, C)$ *consisting of (1) S, the service: a concept or relation from the service ontology S, or (if and only if D_S is present in M) a tuple whose components are concepts/relations from S describing the service along the dimensions of D_S, and (2) C, the content: a concept or relation from the content ontology C, or (if and only if D_C is present in M) a tuple whose components are concepts/relations from C describing the service along the dimensions of D_C.*

In the running example, service may be described by the information dimensions $D_S = $ *[level of detail, search criterion, display language]*. A list page generated after a search specification corresponds to the requested service "list ... " (level of detail) "... by project ..." (search criterion) and "... in Italian" (display language). Each of these concepts can be part of a hierarchy; for example, the concept "by project" is a subconcept of "with one search parameter," and a super-concept of "by directed projects," "by projects participated in," etc. In addition to these three service information dimensions, there is also the dimension *type of entity*. This can be modeled as a fourth information dimension of service. What type of entity is the search for? Alternatively, it can be modeled as the content of the page. What type of entity is the returned page about? Further examples are given in example (3) below.

Figure 24.2 illustrates these ideas further. It demonstrates that one web page may be mapped to only one concept (event 1: service "by project," event 3: service "individual home page," event 3: content "person"), or mapped to several concepts (event 2: service "by project" and "by name"). If the mapping is clear from the context, it may also be disregarded (content "person" in events 1 and 2). In general, more than one page will be mapped onto one application event (e.g., a search by project ABC will be mapped to event 1, as will a search by project XYZ).

Altogether, there are four combinations of mapping (n web pages to 1 versus to m application event(s) – $n:1$ versus $n:m$) and application event structure (single concept versus tuple of concepts). These will be described referring to examples from the literature:

(1) *$n:1$ mapping to single-concept application events:* In an e-business site, n products and b stages of a canonical buying process give rise to $n \times b$ dynamically generated pages that are product views, product click-throughs, shopping cart insertions, purchases, etc. (service or merchandising function [Lee, Podlaseck, Schonberg, and Hoch 2001]) of book A, CD B, etc. (content). All n pages that are a product view will be mapped to one application event, product view (with whatever content) (Lee, Podlaseck, Schonberg, and Hoch 2001). Higher-level content concepts (such as books versus CDs) will be the content of pages delivering "category click-through service." Higher-level service concepts may aggregate activities like "information gathering," "interaction with a shopbot" (Berendt 2002a), "transaction," or "multi-channel" (Teltzrow and Günther 2003).

(2) *$n:m$ mapping to single-concept application events:* A page may be mapped to "requesting information" on the set of all content items it contains (Mobasher, Dai, Luo, Sun, and Zhu 2000).

This idea can also be transferred to an analysis of requested services. In Oberle, Berendt, Hotho, and Gonzalez (2003), a scheme for application server logging of user queries with respect to a full-blown ontology is presented. The ontology is a superset of the ontology shown in figure 24.1 (a "knowledge portal" in the sense of Hotho, Maedche, Staab, and Studer [2001]). A log entry is interpreted as showing "interest in" the set of all concepts and relations appearing in the query that generates the page.

(3) *$n:1$ mapping to tuple-of-concepts application events:* The example described in figure 24.2 follows the information dimensions for service proposed in Berendt and Spiliopoulou (2000). In Anderson, Domingos, and Weld (2002), pages are modeled by different content aspects (product view pages are described by the information dimensions product ID and stock level, e.g.).[10]

---

[10] Anderson, Domingos, and Weld (2002) point out that different page types — in our termi-

Structured modeling of content is an integral part of semantic web proposals like the LOM metadata standard for educational resources. [11] For example, "simulation" is a content concept that can describe the *learning resource type* information dimension, thus indicating an interactive simulation program. However, a learning resource could also be a text on simulation, making "simulation" (part of) the *description* dimension.

(4) *n:m mapping to tuple-of-concepts application events:* Individual information dimensions of an application event may be set-valued, implying that one page may be mapped to several concepts along this dimension. For example, a given educational resource embodied in a web page may be usable for both undergraduate students and postgraduate students (dimension *intended end user role*). The question is whether beyond that, one page can be mapped to several tuple-of-concepts application events. To our knowledge, no examples of this exist in the literature.

The ontologies of content and services of a web site as well as the mapping of pages into them may be obtained in various ways. At one extreme, ontologies may be hand-crafted ex post; at the other extreme, they may be the generating structure of the web site (in which case also the mapping of pages to ontology elements is already available). In most cases, mining methods must be called upon to establish the ontology (ontology learning) and/or the mapping (instance learning), for example by using methods of learning relations (e.g., Maedche and Staab 2000) and information extraction (e.g., Craven, DiPasquo, Freitag, McCallum, Mitchell, Nigam, and Slattery 2000; and Laender, Ribeiro-Neto, da Silva, and Teixeira 2002).

To reconstruct requested content and services, it is necessary that the required information has been recorded or can be reconstructed. In a site consisting only of static pages that do not change across the duration of the analysis, reconstruction is possible. When pages are dynamically constructed, URL stems (e.g., search.html in figure 24.2) plus query strings (e.g., p=semwebmine in figure 24.2) contain information about service and content. Query strings may be recorded in the web server log, or in an application server log. The analysis of query strings can be done in an automatic way; their structured nature yields good results in the classification of required services (Berendt and Spiliopoulou 2000; Oberle, Berendt, Hotho, and Gonzalez 2003). Some information about content may however be lost, for example, if the underlying database content and therefore the mapping from queries to returned content changes over time.

In general, the learning methods cannot operate fully automatically, but they are invaluable tools to gain overviews of large data sets and to generate

---

nology, events — may be described by different information dimensions. For simplicity, we have assumed here that information dimensions are uniform across events.

[11] http://ltsc.ieee.org

Complex application events

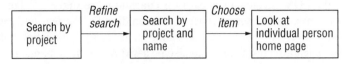

Figure 24.3: A complex application event in the fictitious community portal.

recommendations for semantics, such as for page classification into service and content concepts.

Complex Application Events

A requested web page, or rather, the activity/ies behind it, is generally part of a more extended behavior.

Definition 24.3.3 *A complex application event CAE is a nonempty (1) set, (2) sequence (i.e., order relation), or (3) another sequential structure (a regular expression, a context-free grammar, ...), whose elements are atomic application events.*

To specify complex application events, it is necessary to introduce background knowledge. This can be done in two ways: (a) *based on the site model* — referring to the site itself, i.e. to relations on its concepts that already exist in its content or service ontologies, or (b) *pattern-based* — referring to knowledge about, or expectations concerning, navigation patterns (whichever source they come from).

Examples of complex application events based on the site model include canonical activity sequences pertaining to the site type, e.g., catalog search / browse, choose, add-to-cart, pay in an e-commerce setting (Menascé, Almeida, Fonseca, and Mendes 1999; Berendt 2002a), or searching in on-line catalogs (Berendt and Spiliopoulou 2000).

Pattern-based complex application events are generally descriptions of behavior identified by application experts in exploratory data analysis. This includes problem-solving strategies consciously pursued by the user (e.g., to narrow down search by iteratively refining search terms [Berendt 2002b]). For example, figure 24.3 shows the complex application event "successful search with search refinement" as the sequence of atomic application events known from figure 24.2.

Another example is the distinction of four kinds of online shopping strategies by Moe (2002): *directed buying, search/deliberation, hedonic browsing,* and *knowledge building*. The first group is characterized by focused search patterns and immediate purchase. The second is more motivated by a future purchase and therefore tends to browse through a particular category of products rather than directly proceed to the purchase of a specific product. The third is entertainment- and stimulus-driven, which occasionally results in spontaneous purchases. The fourth also shows exploratory behavior, but for the primary goal of information acquisition as a basis for future purchasing decisions. In Moe (2002), these browsing patterns were characterized in terms of product and category pages visited on a web site.

In Spiliopoulou, Pohle, and Teltzrow (2002), the conceptualization was transferred to the analysis of a noncommercial information site. The authors formulated regular expressions that capture the behavior of search/deliberation and knowledge building, and used sequence mining to identify these behaviors in the site's logs. Search/deliberation corresponds to the regular expression (home, list, product, individual*), and knowledge building to the expression (home, list, individual*, list, list*, individual*). Referring back to figures 24.2 and 24.3, the first strategy would be instantiated by a search by project followed by requests for several of the individual-people pages hyperlinked on that list (e.g., URI-GST and then URI-AHO). Knowledge building, on the other hand, could involve repeated cycles through lists of various entities (people, projects, publications, ...) and individual pages.

24.3.2   Using Knowledge about
Application Events in Mining

Once requests have been mapped to concepts, the question arises how knowledge is gained from these transformed data. We will investigate the treatment of atomic and complex application events in turn.

Mining using multiple taxonomies is related to OLAP data cube techniques: objects (in this case, requests or requested URLs) are described along a number of dimensions, and concept hierarchies or lattices are formulated along each dimension to allow more abstract views (see, for example, Zaïane, Xin, and Han 1998; Kimball and Merx 2000; Huang, Ng, Ching, Ng, and Cheung 2002; Stumme 2002a).

For many mining applications, the analysis of data abstracted using taxonomies is essential to generate meaningful results: In a site with dynamically generated pages, each individual page will be requested so infrequently that no regularities may be found in an analysis of navigation behavior. Rather, regularities may exist at a more abstract level, leading to rules like "visitors who are interested in persons are also interested in publications." Second, patterns mined in past data are not helpful for applications like recommender systems when new items are introduced into product catalog, knowledge base, and/or

site structure: A publication P newly entered into the database cannot be recommended simply because it was not in the site before and thus could not co-
occur with any other item, be recommended by another user, etc. A knowledge
of regularities at a more abstract level could help to derive a recommendation
of P because it too deals with the topic "relational data mining" (and there are
criteria for recommending publications on that topic).

After the preprocessing steps in which access data have been mapped into
taxonomies, two main approaches are taken in subsequent mining steps. In
many cases, mining operates on concepts at a chosen level of abstraction. For
example, the sessions are transformed into points in a feature space (Mobasher,
Dai, Luo, Sun, and Zhu 2000), or on the sessions transformed into sequences
of content units at a given level of description (for example, association rules
can be sought between abstract concepts such as persons, projects, and publications). This approach is usually combined with interactive control of the
software, so that the analyst can re-adjust the chosen level of abstraction after
viewing the results (e.g., in the miner WUM; see Berendt and Spiliopoulou
[2000] for a case study).

Alternatively to this static approach, other algorithms identify the most
specific level of relationships by choosing concepts dynamically. This may
lead to rules like "visitors who are interested in projects tend to also request
information on the XYZ 2003 workshop." Srikant and Agrawal (1995) search
for associations in given taxonomies, using support and confidence thresholds
to guide the choice of level of abstraction. Dai and Mobasher (2002) present a
scheme for aggregating towards more general concepts when an explicit taxonomy is missing. They apply clustering to sets of sessions; this clustering
identifies related concepts at different levels of abstraction.

Semantic web usage mining for complex application events involves two
steps of mapping requests to events. As we previously discussed in section
24.3.1, complex application events are usually defined by regular expressions
in atomic application events (at some given level of abstraction in their respective hierarchies). Therefore, in a first step, URLs are mapped to atomic application events at the required level of abstraction. In a second step, a sequence
miner can then be used to discover sequential patterns in the transformed data.
The shapes of sequential patterns sought, and the mining tool used, determine
how much prior knowledge can be used to constrain the patterns identified:
They range from largely unconstrained first-order or k^{th} order Markov chains
(Borges and Levene 2000), to regular expressions that specify the atomic activities completely (the name of the concept) or partially (a variable matching a
set of concepts) (Spiliopoulou 1999; Baumgarten, Büchner, Anand, Mulvenna,
and Hughes 2000).

Examples of the use of regular expressions describing application-relevant
courses of events include search strategies (Berendt and Spiliopoulou 2000), a

segmentation of visitors into customers and noncustomers (Spiliopoulou and Pohle 2001), and a segmentation of visitors into different interest groups based on the customer buying cycle model from marketing (Spiliopoulou, Pohle, and Teltzrow 2002).

To date, few commonly agreed-upon models of semantic web behavior exist. The still largely exploratory nature of the field implies that highly interactive data preparation and mining tools are of paramount importance: They give the best support for domain experts working with analysts to contribute their background knowledge in an iterative mining cycle. A central element of interactive tools for exploration is visualization. Visualization allows the detection of further structure in sequential patterns (for a survey, see Berendt [2002a]).

However, with the increasing standardization of many web applications, and the increasing confluence of research in mining with application domains (e.g., marketing), the number of standard courses of events is likely to grow. Examples are the predictive schemes of e-commerce sites (see the example from Menascé, Almeida, Fonseca, and Mendes [1999] mentioned in section 24.3.1 above), and the description of browsing strategies given by Moe (2002).

24.4   Extracting Semantics from Web Usage

The effort behind the semantic web is to add semantic annotation to web documents in order to access knowledge instead of unstructured material. The purpose is to allow knowledge to be managed in an automatic way. Web mining can help to learn definitions of structures for knowledge organization (such as ontologies) and to provide the population of such knowledge structures. In Berendt, Hotho, and Stumme (2002), we have discussed how content, structure, and usage mining can be used for creating semantics. Here, we focus on the contribution of usage mining.

All approaches discussed here are semiautomatic. They assist the knowledge engineer in extracting the semantics, but cannot completely replace her. In order to obtain high-quality results, one cannot replace the human in the loop, as there is always a lot of tacit knowledge involved in the modeling process. A computer will never be able to fully consider background knowledge, experience, or social conventions. If this were the case, the semantic web would be superfluous, since then machines like search engines or agents could operate directly on conventional web pages. The overall aim of our research is thus not to replace the human, but rather to provide him or her with more and more support.

In the world wide web as in other places, much knowledge is socially constructed. This social behavior is reflected by the usage of the web. One tenet related to this view is that navigation is not only driven by formalized relationships or the underlying logic of the available web resources, but that it "is an information browsing strategy that takes advantage of the behavior of like-minded people" (Chen 1999, page 18). Recommender systems based on collaborative filtering have been the most popular application of this idea. In recent years, the idea has been extended to consider not only ratings, but also web usage as a basis for the identification of like-mindedness ("people who liked and/or bought this book also looked at ..."); see Mobasher, Cooley, and Srivastava (2000) for a recent mining-based system; see also Joachims, Freitag, and Mitchell (1997) for a classic application. Ratings and usage patterns can be interpreted as inducing a relation "is related to" on the objects described in these web pages, and on the pages themselves.

Extracting such relations from usage can be interpreted as a kind of ontology learning, in which binary relations on pages (and thus concepts) are learned. Can usage patterns reveal further relations to help build the semantic web? Put differently, the question is how usage patterns can help to learn ontological structure or classify instances better than the automated analysis of the pages' content and structure alone may do, because some content and structure is only defined after and through (frequent) usage. An illustrative selection of approaches will highlight the research questions in this current area of research.

The combination of implicit user input (usage) and explicit user input (search engine queries) can serve as a further generator of conceptual structure. User navigation has been employed to infer topical relatedness, i.e. the relatedness of a set of pages to a topic as given by the terms of a query to a search engine. Aggarwal (2002) refers to this as "collaborative crawling" and proposes it as a method for improving on focused and intelligent crawling, which uses only the information from page content and hyperlink structure. A classification of pages into "satisfying the user defined predicate" and "not satisfying the predicate" is thus learned from usage, structure, and content information. An obvious application is to mine user navigation to improve search engine ranking (Joachims 2002, Kemp and Ramamohanarao 2002).

Ypma and Heskes (2002) propose a method for learning content categories from usage. They model navigation in terms of hidden Markov models, with the hidden states being page categories, and the observed request events being instances of them. Their primary aim is to show that a meaningful page categorization may be learned simultaneously with the user labeling and intercategory transitions; semantic labels (such as "sports pages") must be assigned to a state manually. The resulting taxonomy and page classification can be used as a conceptual model for the site, or used to improve an existing conceptual model.

Yet another application uses mining techniques to learn a classification of site users' goals from their navigation patterns. Ed Chi and colleagues (Chi, Pirolli, and Pitkow 2000; Chi, Pirolli, Chen, and Pitkow 2001) identify frequent paths through a site. Based on the keywords extracted from the pages along the path, they compute the likely information scent followed, i.e. the intended goal of the path. The information scent is a set of weighted keywords, which can be inspected and labeled more concisely using an interactive tool. Thus, usage creates a set of information goals users expect the site to satisfy.[12] These goals may be used to modify or extend the content categories shown to the users, employed to structure the site's information architecture, or employed in the site's conceptual model.

Many approaches use a combination of content extraction techniques (like keyword analysis) and techniques for extracting patterns of usage to generate recommendations. For example, in content-based collaborative filtering, textual categorization of documents is used for generating pseudo-rankings for every user-document pair (Melville, Mooney, and Nagarajan 2001). In Parent, Mobasher, and Lytinen (2001), ontologies, IE techniques for analyzing single pages, and a user's search history together serve to derive recommendations for query improvement in a search engine.

To sum up, these examples show how techniques of web (usage) mining can help build up the semantic web.

24.5   Conclusion and Outlook

In this chapter, we have studied the combination of the two fast-developing research areas: semantic web and web mining, especially usage mining. We discussed how semantic web usage mining can improve the results of classical usage mining by exploiting the new semantic structures in the web, and how the construction of the semantic web can make use of web mining techniques. A truly semantic understanding of web usage needs to take into account not only the information stored in server logs, but also the *meaning* that is constituted by the sequences of web page accesses. The examples provided show the potential benefits of further research in this integration attempt.

One important focus is to make search engines and other programs able to better understand the content of web pages and sites. This is reflected in the wealth of research efforts that model pages in terms of an ontology of the content. Overall, three important directions for further interdisciplinary cooperation between mining and application experts in semantic web usage mining have been identified: (1) the development of ontologies of complex behavior, (2) the deployment of these ontologies in semantic web description and

---

[12] An empirical validation showed that this kind of content analysis does indeed group paths that have the same information goal (Chi, Rosien, and Heer 2002).

mining tools, and (3) continued research on methods and tools that allow the integration of both experts' and users' background knowledge into the mining cycle.

Web mining methods should increasingly treat content, structure, and usage in an integrated fashion in iterated cycles of *extracting* and *utilizing* semantics, to be able to understand and (re)shape the web.

Bettina Berendt is assistant professor of information systems at Humboldt University Berlin. Her research interests include knowledge discovery and representation, computational and empirical methods of analyzing web usage, visualization, and the semantic web. She can be reached at www.berendt.de.

Gerd Stumme is full professor of knowledge and data engineering at the University of Kassel. His research interests include knowledge discovery andrepresentation, semantic web and ontologies, and formal concept analysis. He can be reached at www.kde.cs.uni-kassel.de.

Andreas Hotho is a Ph.D. student at Karlsruhe University. His research interests include the application of data, text and web mining (especially text clustering with background knowledge), information retrieval, and semantic web mining. He can be reached at www.aifb.uni-karlsruhe.de/WBS/aho/.

Bibliography

Abdulghani, A.; Imielinski, T.; and Khachiyan, L. 2002. Cubegrades: Generalizing Association Rules. *Data Mining and Knowledge Discovery* 6(3): 219–258.

Abu-Mostafa, Y. S. 1995. Hints. *Neural Computation* 7(4): 639–671.

Acharya, S.; Gibbons, P. B.; and Poosala, V. 2000. Congressional Samples for Approximate Answering of Group-By Queries. In Proceedings of the ACM SIGMOD International Conference on Management of Data, 487–498. New York: Association for Computing Machinery, Special Interest Group on Management of Data.

Adam, N.; Atluri, V.; Yesha, Y.; and Yu, S. 2002. Efficient Storage and Management of Environmental Information. In Proceedings of the Eleventh Mass Storage Conference, 78–83. Piscataway, N.J.: The Institute of Electrical and Electronics Engineers, Inc.

Adamic, L.; and E. Adar. 2001. Friends and Neighbors on the Web. Palo Alto, Calif.: Xerox, Palo Alto Research Center.

Adams, B.; Dorai, C.; and Venkatesh, S. 2001. Automated Film Rhythm Extraction for Scene Analysis. In Proceedings of the IEEE International Conference on Multimedia and Expo, 216. Los Alamitos, Calif.: IEEE Computer Society.

Adams, C.; Dashevsky, I.; DeMaria, A.; Kleinman, K.; Kludt, P.; Lazarus, R.; and Platt, R. 2002. Use of Automated Ambulatory-Care Encounter Records for Detection of Acute Illness Clusters, Including Potential Bioterrorism Events. *Emergency Infectious Diseases* 8(8): 753–760.

Adhikary, J.; Han, J.; and Koperski, K. 1996. Spatial Data Mining: Progress and Challenges Survey Paper. Paper presented at the 1996 SIGMOD Workshop on Research Issues in Data Mining and Knowledge Discovery, Montreal, Canada, June.

Agarwal, C. C.; and Agrawal, D. 2001. On the Design and Quantification of Privacy Preserving Data Mining Algorithms. In Proceedings of the Twentieth ACM SIGACT-SIGMOD-SIGART Symposium on Principles of Database Systems, 247–255. New York: Association for Computing Machinery.

Agarwal, C. C.; and Yu, P. S. 2001. Outlier Detection for High Dimensional Data. In Proceedings of the ACM SIGMOD International Conference on Management of Data, 37–46. New York: Association for Computing Machinery, Special Interest Group on Management of Data.

Agarwal, R. C. 2002. Collaborative Crawling: Mining User Experiences for Topical Resource Discovery. In Proceedings of the Eighth ACM SIGKDD International Conference on Knowledge Discovery and Data Mining, 423–428. New York: Association for Computing Machinery, Special Interest Group on Knowledge Discovery and Data Mining.

Agarwal, R. C.; Agarwal, C. C.; and Prasad, V. V. V. 2000. Depth First Generation of Long Patterns. In Proceedings of the Sixth ACM SIGKDD International Conference on Knowledge Discovery and Data Mining, 108–118. New York: Association for Computing Machinery, Special Interest Group on Knowledge Discovery and Data Mining.

Agarwal, R. C.; Joshi, M. V.; and Kumar, V. 2001a. Evaluating Boosting Algorithms to Classify Rare Classes: Comparison and Improvements. In Proceedings of the 2001 IEEE International Conference on Data Mining, 257–264. Los Alamitos, Calif.: IEEE Computer Society.

Agarwal, R. C.; Joshi, M. V.; and Kumar, V. 2001b. Mining Needles in a Haystack: Classifying Rare Classes Via Two-Phase Rule Induction. In Proceedings of the ACM SIGMOD Conference on Management of Data, 91–102. New York: Association for Computing Machinery, Special Interest Group on Management of Data.

Agarwal, R. C.; Joshi, M. V.; and Kumar, V. 2002. Predicting Rare Classes: Can Boosting Make Any Weak Learner Strong? In Proceedings of the Eighth ACM SIGKDD International Conference on Knowledge Discovery and Data Mining, 297–306. New York: Association for Computing Machinery, Special Interest Group on Knowledge Discovery and Data Mining.

Agarwal, R. C.; Karypis, G.; Kumar, V.; and Shekhar, S. 1997. Multilevel Hypergraph Partitioning: Applications in VLSI Domain. Paper presented at the Thirty-Fourth Annual Design and Automation Conference, Anaheim, Calif., 9–13 June.

Agha, G. 1986. *ACTORS: A Model of Concurrent Computation in Distributed Systems.* Cambridge, Mass.: The MIT Press.

Agrawal, G. 2003. High-Level Interfaces for Data Mining: From Offline Algorithms on Clusters to Streams on Grids. Paper presented at the Workshop on Data Mining and Exploration Middleware for Distributed and Grid Computing, Minneapolis, Minn., 18–19 September.

Agrawal, R. 2002. Hypocritical Databases. In *Proceedings of the Twenty-Eighth International Conference on Very Large Data Bases.* San Francisco: Morgan Kaufmann Publishers.

Agrawal, R.; and Shafer, J. C. 1996. Parallel Mining of Association Rules. *IEEE Transactions on Knowledge and Data Engineering* 8(6): 962–969.

Agrawal, R.; and Srikant, R. 1994. Fast Algorithms for Mining Association Rules. In *Proceedings of the Twenty-Second International Conference on Very Large Data Bases,* 487–499. San Francisco: Morgan Kaufmann Publishers.

Agrawal, R.; and Srikant, R. 1995. Mining Sequential Patterns. In Proceedings of the International Conference Data Engineering, 3–14. Los Alamitos, Calif.: IEEE Computer Society.

Agrawal, R.; and Srikant, R. 2000. Privacy-Preserving Data Mining. In Proceedings of the ACM SIGMOD International Conference on Management of Data, 439–450. New York: Association for Computing Machinery, Special Interest Group on Management of Data.

Agrawal, R.; Evfimievski, A.; and Srikant, R. 2003. Information Sharing Across Private Databases. In Proceedings of the ACM SIGMOD Conference on Management of Data, 86–97. New York: Association for Computing Machinery, Special Interest Group on Management of Data.

Agrawal, R.; Evfimievski, A.; Gehrke, J.; and Srikant, R. 2002. Privacy Preserving Mining of Association Rules. In Proceedings of the Eighth ACM SIGKDD International Conference on Knowledge Discovery and Data Mining, 217–228. New York: Association for Computing Machinery, Special Interest Group on Knowledge Discovery and Data Mining.

Agrawal, R.; Imielinski, T.; and Swami, A. 1993. Mining Association Rules Between Sets of Items in Large Databases. In Proceedings of the ACM SIGMOD International Conference on Management of Data, 207–216. New York: Association for Computing Machinery, Special Interest Group on Management of Data.

Agrawal, R.; Mannila, H.; Srikant, R.; Toivonen, H.; and Verkamo, A. I. 1996. Fast Discovery of Association Rules. In *Advances in Knowledge Discovery and Data Mining,* eds. U. Fayyad, G. Piatetsky-Shapiro, and R. Uthurusamy, 307–328. Menlo Park, Calif.: The AAAI Press / The MIT Press.

Agrawal, S.; Arnold, D.; Blackford, S.; Dongarra, J.; Miller, M.; Sagi, K.; Seymour, K.; Shi, Z.; Vadhiyar, S. 2002. Users' Guide to NetSolve V1.4, Tech. Rep. ICL-UT-02-05, Dept. of Computer Science, Univ. of Tennessee. Knoxville, Tenn.

Aha, D.; Murphy, P.; and Robinson, G. 1992. Univ. of California at Irvine Repository of Machine Learning Databases: Machine-Readable Data Repository, Irvine, Calif.

Allen, J.; Christie, A.; Fithen, W.; McHugh, J.; Pickel, J.; and Stoner, E. 2000. State of the Practice of Intrusion Detection Technologies, Tech. Rep. CMU/SEI-99-TR-028, Carnegie Mellon— Software Engineering Institute, Pittsburgh, Penn.

Almeida, V.; Fonseca, R.; Menascé, D. A.; and Mendes, M. A. 1999. A Methodology for Workload Characterization of E-Commerce Sites. In Proceedings of the First ACM Conference on Electronic Commerce, 119–128. New York: Association for Computing Machinery.

Alon, N.; and Spencer, J. H. 1992. *The Probabilistic Method.* New York: Wiley Interscience.

Alon, N.; Matias, Y.; and Szegedy, M. 1996. The Space Complexity of Approximating the Frequency Moments. In Proceedings of the ACM Symposium on the Theory of Computing (STOC), 20–29. New York: Association for Computing Machinery.

Alpert, C. J.; and Kahng, A. B. 1995. Recent Directions in Netlist Partitioning: A Survey. *Integration: The VLSI Journal* 19(1): 1–18.

Alsabti, K.; Ranka, S.; and Singh, V. 1997. A One-Pass Algorithm for Accurately Estimating Quantiles for Disk-Resident Data. In *Proceedings of the Twenty-Third International Conference on Very Large Data Bases,* 346–355. San Francisco: Morgan Kaufmann Publishers.

Altman, R. B.; Han, J.; Kumar, V.; Mannila, H.; and Pregibon, D. 2002. Emerging Scientific Applications in Data Mining. *Communications of the ACM* 45(8): 54–58.

Altschul, S.; Lipman, D.; Madden, T.; Miller, W.; Schaffer, A.; Zhang, J.; and Zhang, Z. 1997. Gapped BLAST and PSI-BLAST: A New Generation of Protein Database Search Programs. *Nucleic Acids Research* 25(17): 389–402.

Alvarez, S. A.; Lin, W.; and Ruiz, C. 2002. Efficient Adaptive-Support Association Rule Mining for Recommender Systems. *Data Mining and Knowledge Discovery* 6(1): 83–105.

Amoroso, E. G. 1994. *Fundamentals of Computer Security Technology.* Upper Saddle River, N.J.: Prentice Hall.

An, A.; and Wang, Y. 2001. Comparisons of Classification Methods for Screening Potential Compounds. In Proceedings of the IEEE International Conference on Data Mining, 11–18. Los Alamitos, Calif.: IEEE Computer Society.

Anand, S. S.; Baumgarten, M.; Büchner, A. G.; Hughes, J. G.; and Mulvenna, M. D. 1999. User-Driven Navigation Pattern Discovery from Internet Data. In *Web Usage Analysis and User Profiling: International WEBKDD'99 Workshop,* Lecture Notes in Computer Science 1836, 74–91, eds. M. M. Brij and M. Spiliopoulou. New York: Springer-Verlag.

Ananthanarayan, A.; Grossman, R. L.; Levera, J.; Mazzucco, M.; and Rao, G.B. 2002. Merging Multiple Data Streams on Common Keys Over High Performance Networks. In Proceedings of the 2002 ACM / IEEE Conference on Supercomputing, 1–12. Los Alamitos, Calif.: IEEE Computer Society.

Anderson C. R.; Domingos, P.; and Weld, D. S. 2002. Relational Markov Models and Their Application to Adaptive Web Navigation. In Proceedings of the Sixth ACM SIGKDD International Conference on Knowledge Discovery and Data Mining, 143–152. New York: Association for Computing Machinery, Special Interest Group on Knowledge Discovery and Data Mining.

Anderson, D.; Javitz, H.; Lunt, T. F.; Tamaru, A.; and Valdes, A. 1995. Detecting Unusual Program Behavior Using the Statistical Component of the Next-Generation Intrusion Detection Expert System NIDES, Tech. Rep. SRI-CSL-95-06, Computer Science Laboratory, SRI International, Menlo Park, Calif.

Anderson, J. P. 1980. Computer Security, Threat Monitoring, and Surveillance, Tech. Rep., James P. Anderson, Co., Fort Washington, Penn.

Anderson, R. M.; Donnelly, C. A.; and Ferguson, N. M. 2001. The Foot-and-Mouth Epidemic in Great Britain: Pattern of Spread and Impact of Interventions. *Science* 292(5519): 1155–1160.

Andrea, T. A.; and Kalayeh, H. 1991. Applications of Neural Networks in Quantitative Structure-Activity Relationships of Dihydrofolate Reductase Inhibitors. *Journal of Medicinal Chemistry* 34(9): 2824–2836.

Andrews, N. J.; Beale, A. D.; Catchpole, M. A.; and Farrington, C. P. 1996. A Statistical Algorithm for the Early Detection of Outbreaks of Infectious Disease. *Journal of the Royal Statistical Society* Series A 159: 547–563.

Anfinsen, C.; and Scheraga, H. 1975. Experimental and Theoretical Aspects of Protein Folding. *Advances in Protein Chemistry* 29: 205–300.

Anselin, L. 1988. *Spatial Econometrics: Methods and Models.* Dortrecht, The Netherlands: Kluwer Academic Publishers.

Anselin, L. 1994. Exploratory Spatial Data Analysis and Geographic Information Systems. In EUROSTAT Third Report : New Tools for Spatial Analysis. Luxembourg: Statistical Office of the European Communities.

Anselin, L. 1995. Local Indicators of Spatial Association: LISA. *Geographical Analysis* 27(2): 93–115.

Aoki, K.; Aoki, N.; and Ohno, Y. 1978. A Test of Significance for Geographic Clusters of Disease. *International Journal of Epidemiology* 8(3): 273–281.

Apweiler, R.; Bairoch, A.; Blatter, M. C.; Boeckmann, B.; Estreicher, A.; Gasteiger, E.; Martin, M. J.; Michoud, K.; O'Donovan, C.; Phan, I.; Pilbout, S.; and Schneider M. 2003. The SWISS-PROT Protein Knowledgebase and Its Supplement TrEMBL. *Nucleic Acids Research* 31(1): 365–370.

Arabshahi, A.; Gatlin, B.; Hammersley, J. R.; Olson, D. E.; and Reddy, R. N. 1993. Computational Modeling of Airflows in the Smaller Airways. *American Review of Respiratory Diseases* 145: A32.

Arai, N.; Kohyama, M.; and Takeda, S. 1997. Self Interstitial Clustering in Crystalline Silicon. *Physical Review Letters* 78: 4265–4268.

Ares M. Jr.; Brown, M. P. S.; Cristianini, N.; Furey, T. S.; Grundy, W. N.; Haussler, D.; Lin, D.; and Sugnet, C. W. 2000. Knowledge-Based Analysis of Microarray Gene Expression Data by Using Support Vector Machines. *Proceedings of the National Academy of Science of the United States of America* 97(1): 262–267.

Arge, L.; Hinrichs, K. H.; Vahrenhold, J.; and Vitter, J. S. 2002. Efficient Bulk Operations on Dynamic R-Trees. *Algorithmica* 33(1): 104–128.

Arnold, A.; Eskin, E.; Portnoy, L.; Prerau, M.; and Stolfo, S. 2002. A Geometric Framework for Unsupervised Anomaly Detection: Detecting Intrusions in Unlabeled Data. In *Data Mining for Security Applications.* Dortrecht, The Netherlands: Kluwer Academic Publishers.

Aronis, J.; Buchanan, B.; Kolluri, V.; and Provost, F. 1997. The WORLD: Knowledge Discovery and Multiple Distributed Databases. Paper presented at the Tenth Florida Artificial Intelligence Research Symposium, Datona Beach, Fla., 12–14 May.

Arridge, S. R.; and Lester, H. 1999. A Survey of Hierarchical Non-Linear Medical Image Registration. *Pattern Recognition* 32(1): 129–149.

Ashford, D. A.; Fisk, T. L.; Fridkin, S. K.; Galbraith, M.; Gerberding, W.; Guarner, M. M. J.; Harper, S. A.; Hughes, J. M.; Jernigan, J. A.; Meyer, R. F.; Omenaca, C.; Popovic, T.; Quinn, C. P.; Sejvar, J. J.; Shepard, C. W.; Stephens, D. S.; Tapper, M.; Topiel, M. S.; Zaki, S.; and Members of the Anthrax Bioterrorism Investigation Team. 2001. Bioterrorism-related Inhalational Anthrax: The First 10 Cases Reported in the United States. *Emerging Infectious Diseases* 7(6): 933–944.

Asker, L.; Aubele, J.; Burl, M.; Crumpler, L.; Fayyad, U.; Perona, P.; and Smyth, P. 1998. Learning to Recognize Volcanoes on Venus. *Machine Learning* 30(2–3): 165–195.

ASME 1997. Proceedings of the ASME FLuids Engineering Division Summer Meeting, FEDSM 97. New York: American Society of Mechanical Engineers.

Atallah, M. J.; and Du, W. 2001. Secure Multi-Party Computation Problems and Their Applications: A Review and Open Problems. In Proceedings of the 2001 Workshop on New Security Paradigms, 13–22. New York: Association for Computing Machinery.

Atallah, M. J.; and Du, W. 2001a. Privacy-Preserving Cooperative Scientific Computations. In Proceedings of the Fourteenth IEEE Computer Security Foundations Workshop, 273–282. Piscataway, N.J.: The Institute of Electrical and Electronics Engineers, Inc.

Atallah, M. J.; and Du, W. 2001b. Privacy-Preserving Statistical Analysis. Paper presented at the Seventeenth Annual Computer Security Applications Conference, New Orleans, Louisiana, 10–14 December.

Atallah, M.; Bertino, E.; Elmagarmid, A.; Ibrahim, M.; and Verykios, V. 1999. Disclosure Limitation of Sensitive Rules. In Proceedings of the IEEE Knowledge and Data Engineering Exchange Workshop, 25–32. Los Alamitos, Calif.: IEEE Computer Society.

Aulbur, W.; Khan, F.; Kim, J.; Kirchhoff, F.; and Wilkins, J. 1999. Thermally Activated Reorientation of Di-Interstitial Defects in Silicon. *Physical Review Letters* 83(10): 1990.

Axen, U.; Carr, H.; and Snoeyink, J. 2000. Computing Contour Trees in All Dimensions. In Proceedings of the Eleventh ACM / SIAM Symposium on Discrete Algorithms, 918–926. Philadelphia, Penn.: Society for Industrial and Applied Mathematics.

Ayyagari R.; and Kargupta, H. 2002. A Resampling Technique for Learning the Fourier Spectrum of Skewed Data. Paper presented at the ACM SIGMOD Workshop on Research Issues in Data Mining and Knowledge Discovery, Madison, Wisc., June.

Babcock, B.; Babu, S.; Datar, M.; Motwani, R.; and Widom, J. 2002. Models and Issues in Data Stream Systems. In Proceedings of the ACM SIGACT-SIGMOD-SIGART Symposium on Principles of Database Systems (PODS), 1–16. New York: Association for Computing Machinery.

Babu, S.; and Widom, J. 2001. Continuous Queries Over Data Streams. *ACM SIGMOD Record* 30(3): 109–120.

Bacchus, F.; and Lam, W. 1994. Learning Bayesian Belief Networks: An Approach Based on The MDL Principle. *Computational Intelligence* 10(4): 262–293.

Bairoch, A.; Bucher, P.; Falquet, L.; and Hofmann, K. 1999. The PROSITE Database, Its Status in 1999. *Nucleic Acids Research* 27(1): 215–219.

Baker, D.; and Bonneau, R. 2001. Ab Initio Protein Structure Prediction: Progress and Prospects. *Annual Review of Biophysics and Biomolecular Structure* 30(1): 173–189.

Banks, D. C.; and Singer, B. A. 1995. A Predictor-Corrector Technique for Visualizing Unsteady Flow. *IEEE Transactions on Visualization and Computer Graphics* 1(2): 151–163.

Bannister, J.; Chien, A.; Faber, T.; Falk, A.; Grossman, R.; and Leigh, J. 2003. Transport Protocols for High Performance: Whither TCP? *Communications of the ACM* 46(11): 42–49.

Barbará, D.; Couto, J.; and Li. Y. 2002. COOLCAT: An Entropy-Based Technique to Cluster Categorical Data. Paper presented at the Eleventh ACM Conference on Information and Knowledge Management (CIKM), McLean, Va., November.

Barbará, D. 1999. The Characterization of Continuous Queries. *The International Journal of Cooperative Information Systems* 8(4): 295–323.

Barbará, D.; and Chen, P. 2001. Tracking Clusters in Evolving Data Sets. In *Proceedings of the Fourteenth International Florida Artificial Intelligence Research Society Conference,* 239–243. Menlo Park, Calif.: AAAI Press.

Barbará, D.; DuMouchel, W.; Faloutsos, C.; Haas, P. J.; Hellerstein, J. M.; Ioannidis, Y. E.; Jagadish, H. V.; Johnson, T.; Ng, R. T.; Poosala, V.; Ross, K. A.; and Sevcik, K. C. 1997. The New Jersey Data Reduction Report. *IEEE Bulletin of the Technical Committee on Data Engineering* 20(4): 3–45.

Barbara, D.; Jajodia, S.; and Wu, N. 2001. Detecting Novel Network Intrusions Using Bayes Estimators. In Proceedings of First SIAM Conference on Data Mining. Philadelphia, Penn.: Society for Industrial and Applied Mathematics.

Barclay, T.; and Slutz, D. 2000. Microsoft Terraserver: A Spatial Data Warehouse. In Proceedings of the ACM SIGMOD Conference on Management of Data, 307–318. New York: Association for Computing Machinery, Special Interest Group on Management of Data.

Barnett, J. 1981. Computational Methods for a Mathematical Theory of Evidence. In *Proceedings of the Seventh International Joint Conference on Artificial Intelligence,* 868–875. San Francisco: Morgan Kaufmann Publishers.

Barnett, O.; Cimino, C.; Fackler, J. C.; Kilbridge, P.; Kohane, I. S.; Murphy, S.; Rind, H. C. D.; Safran, C.; Szolovits, P.; and van Wingerde, F. J. 1996. Sharing Electronic Medical Records Across Multiple Heterogeneous and Competing Institutions. In *Proceedings of the Annual AMIA Fall Symposium,* 608–612. Philadelphia: Hanley and Belfus, Inc.

Barnett, V.; and Lewis, T. 1994. *Outliers in Statistical Data.* Third Edition. New York: John Wiley and Sons.

Barrett, E. C.; and Curtis, F. L. 1999. *Introduction to Environmental Remote Sensing.* Cheltenham, UK: Stanley Thornes Publishers Ltd.

Barthell, E. N.; Cochrane, D. G.; Collins, M. A.; Cordell, W. H.; Feied, C.; Felton, C. W.; Handler, J.; Moorhead, J. C.; and Smith, M. S. 2002. The Frontlines of Medicine Project: A Proposal for the Standardized Communication of Emergency Department Data for Public Health Uses Including Syndromic Surveillance for Biological and Chemical Terrorism. *Annals of Emergency Medicine* 39(4): 422–429.

Basseville, M.; and Nikiforov, I. 1993. *Detection of Abrupt Changes: Theory and Application.* Upper Saddle River, N.J.: Prentice Hall.

Bassi, A.; Beck, M.; and Moore, T. 2001. Mobile Management of Network Files. In Proceedings of the Third International Workshop on Active Middleware Services, 106. Los Alamitos, Calif.: IEEE Computer Society.

Bassi, A.; Beck, M.; Fagg, G.; Moore, T.; Plank, J.; Swany, M.; and Wolski, R. 2002. The Internet Backplane Protocol: A Study in Resource Sharing. In Proceedings of the Second IEEE / ACM International Symposium on Cluster Computing and the Grid (CCGRID 2002), 194. Piscataway, N.J.: The Institute of Electrical and Electronics Engineers, Inc.

Basu, S.; Ghosh, J.; Mooney, R. J.; and Pasupuleti, K. V. 2001. Evaluating the Novelty of Text-Mined Rules Using Lexical Knowledge. In Proceedings of the Seventh ACM SIGKDD International Conference on Knowledge Discovery and Data Mining, 233–238. New York: Association for Computing Machinery, Special Interest Group on Knowledge Discovery and Data Mining.

Bauer, E.; and Kohavi, R. 1999. An Empirical Comparison of Voting Classification Algorithms: Bagging, Boosting, and Variants. *Machine Learning* 36(1–2): 105–139.

Bauer, E.; Koller, D.; and Singer, Y. 1997. Update Rules for Parameter Estimation in Bayesian Networks. In *Proceedings of the Thirteenth Conference on Uncertainty in Artificial Intelligence,* 3–13. San Francisco: Morgan Kaufmann Publishers.

Baumann, P. 2001. Web-Enabled Raster GIS for Large Image and Map Databases. In *Proceedings of the International Conference on Database and Expert Systems Applications,* 870–874. Berlin: Springer-Verlag.

Baumann, P.; and Widmann, N. 1997. Towards Comprehensive Database Support for Geoscientific Raster Data. In *Proceedings of the Fifth ACM International Symposium on Advances in Geographic Information Systems,* 162–175. Berlin: Springer-Verlag.

Bean, N. H.; Hutwagner, L. C.; Maloney, E. K.; Martin, S. M.; and Slutsker, L. 1997. Using Laboratory-Based Surveillance Data for Prevention: An Algorithm for Detecting Salmonella Outbreaks. *Emerging Infectious Diseases* 3(3): 395–400.

Beck, M.; Moore, T.; and Plank, J. S. 2002. An End-To-End Approach to Globally Scalable Network Storage. In Proceedings of the 2002 Conference on Applications, Technologies, Architectures, and Protocols for Computer Communication, 339–346. New York: Association for Computing Machinery.

Beeler, G. W. 1998. HL7 Version 3—An Object-Oriented Methodology for Collaborative Standards Development. *International Journal of Medical Informatics* 48(1-3): 151–161.

Beitel, A. R. B.; and Mandl, K. D. 2002. Use of Emergency Department Chief Complaint and ICD9 Diagnostic Codes for Real Time Bioterrorism Surveillance Abstract. *Pediatric Research* 51(4, Pt. 2): 94a.

Belew, R. K.; and Menczer, F. 1998. Adaptive Information Agents for Distributed Textual Environments. In Proceedings of the Second International Conference on Autonomous Agents, 157–164. New York: Association for Computing Machinery.

Berdahl, C. H.; and Thompson, D. S. 1993. Education of Swirling Structure Using the Velocity Gradient Tensor. *American Institute of Aeronautics and Astronautics Journal* 31(1): 97–103.

Berendt, B. 2002a. Detail and Context in Web Usage Mining: Coarsening and Visualizing Sequences. In *Workshop on Web Knowledge Discovery and Data Mining* Lecture Notes in Computer Science 2703, 1–24. Berlin: Springer-Verlag.

Berendt, B. 2002b. Using Site Semantics to Analyze, Visualize and Support Navigation. *Data Mining and Knowledge Discovery* 6(1): 37–59.

Berendt, B.; and Spiliopoulou, M. 2000. Analysis of Navigation Behaviour in Web Sites Integrating Multiple Information Systems. *The Very Large Data Bases Journal* 9(1): 56–75.

Berendt, B.; Gonzalez, J.; Hotho, A.; and Oberle, D. 2003. Conceptual User Tracking. In *Proceedings of Web Intelligence, First International Atlantic Web Intelligence Conference, AWIC,* Lecture Notes in Artificial Intelligence 2663, 155–164. Berlin: Springer-Verlag.

Berendt, B.; Hotho, A.; and Stumme, G. 2002. Towards Semantic Web Mining. In *Proceedings of the First International Semantic Web Conference* Lecture Notes in Computer Science 2342, 264–278. Berlin: Springer-Verlag.

Berendt, B.; Hotho, A.; and Stumme, G. 2002. Using Mining for and on the Semantic Web. Paper presented at the National Science Foundation Next Generation Data Mining Techniques Workshop, Baltimore, Md., 1–3 November.

Berners-Lee, T.; Hendler, J.; and Lassila, O. 2001. The Semantic Web. *Scientific American* 284(5): 35–43.

Berry, M. W., ed. 2003. *Survey of Text Mining: Clustering, Classification, and Retrieval.* New York: Springer-Verlag.

Berry, M. W.; and Browne, M. 1990. *Understanding Search Engines: Mathematical Modeling and Text Retrieval.* Philadelphia, Penn.: Society for Industrial and Applied Mathematics.

Berry, M. W.; Drmač Z.; and Jessup, E. 1999. Matrices, Vector Spaces, and Information Retrieval. *SIAM Review* 41(2): 335–362.

Berry, M. W.; Dumais, S. T.; and O'Brien, G. W. 1995. Using Linear Algebra for Intelligent Information Retrieval. *SIAM Review* 37(4): 573–595.

Berry, M. W.; Giles, J. T.; and Wo, L. 2003. GTP (General Text Parser) Software for Text Mining. In *Statistical Data Mining and Knowledge Discovery,* ed. H. Bozdogan, 455–471. Boca Raton, Fla.: CRC Press.

Berry, M.; and Linoff, G. 1997. *Data Mining Techniques for Marketing, Sales, and Customer Support.* New York: John Wiley and Sons.

Berthold, M. R.; and Borgelt, C. 2002. Mining Molecular Fragments: Finding Relevant Substructures of Molecules. In Proceedings of the IEEE International Conference on Data Mining. Los Alamitos, Calif.: IEEE Computer Society.

Besag, J. 1974. Spatial Interaction and Statistical Analysis of Lattice Systems. *Journal of Royal Statistical Society* 36 (Series B): 192–236.

Best, N. G.; Briggseds, D.; Elliott, P.; and Wakefield, J. C. 2000. *Spatial Epidemiology: Methods and Applications.* Oxford: Oxford Univ. Press.

Beyer, K.; and Ramakrishnan, R. 1999. Bottom-Up Computation of Sparse and Iceburg Cubes. In Proceedings of the ACM SIGMOD International Conference on Management of Data, 359–370. New York: Association for Computing Machinery, Special Interest Group on Management of Data.

Beynon, M. D.; Catalyurek, U.; Chang, C.; Kurc, T.; Saltz, J.; and Sussman, A. 2001. Distributed Processing of Very Large Datasets with Datacutter. *Parallel Computing* 27(11): 1457–1478.

Bhargava, R.; Kargupta, H.; and Powers, M. 2003. Energy Consumption in Data Analysis for On-Board and Distributed Applications. Paper presented at the ICML'03 Workshop on Machine Learning Technologies for Autonomous Space Applications, Washington, D.C., 21–24 August.

Binder, J.; Kanazawa, K.; Koller, D.; and Russel, S. 1997. Adaptive Probabilistic Networks with Hidden Variables. *Machine Learning* 29(2–3): 213–244.

Blackard, J. 1998. Comparison of Neural Networks and Discriminant Analysis in Predicting Forest Cover Types. Ph.D. diss., Dept. of Computer Science, Colorado State Univ., Fort Collins, Colo.

Blockeel, H.; and Kosala, R. 2000. Web Mining Research: A Survey. *SIGKDD Explorations* 2(1): 1–16.

Bloedorn, E.; Christiansen, A. D.; Hill, W.; Skorupka, C.; Talbot, L. M.; and Tivel, J. 2001. Data Mining for Network Intrusion Detection: How to Get Started, Tech. Rep., The MITRE Corporation, McLean, Va.

Blum, A.; and Mitchell, T. 1998. Combining Labeled and Unlabeled Data with Cotraining. In Proceedings of the Eleventh Annual Conference on Computational Learning Theory, 92–100. New York: Association for Computing Machinery.

Bohanec, M.; Bratko, I.; Cestnik, B.; and Zupan, B. 1997. A Dataset Decomposition Approach to Data Mining and Machine Discovery. In *Proceedings of the Third International Conference on Knowledge Discovery and Data Mining,* 299–303. Menlo Park, Calif.: AAAI Press.

Boley, D.; Gini, M.; Gross, R.; Han, E.; Hastings, K.; Karypis, G.; Kumar, V.; Mobasher, B.; and Moore, J. 1999. Partitioning-Based Clustering for Web Document Categorization. *Decision Support Systems* 27(3): 329–341.

Bollacker, K. D.; and Ghosh, J. 1999. Effective Supra-Classifiers for Knowledge Base Construction. *Pattern Recognition Letters* 20(11–13): 1347–1352.

Bollacker, K.; Giles, C. L.; and Lawrence, S. 1998. CiteSeer: An Autonomous Web Agent for Automatic Retrieval and Identification of Interesting Publications. In Proceedings of the Second International Conference on Autonomous Agents, 116–123. New York: Association for Computing Machinery.

Bolstad, P. 2002. *GIS Foundamentals: A First Text on GIS.* Minneapolis, Minn.: Eider Press.

Bolz, F.; Dudonis, K. S.; and Schulz, D. P. 2001. *The Counterterrorism Handbook: Tactics, Procedures, and Techniques.* Second Edition. Boca Raton, Fla: CRC Press.

Bonetti, M.; Mandl, K. D.; Olson, K.; and Pagano, M. 2002. Enhanced Power to Detect Bioterrorism with Spatial Clustering (Abstract). *Pediatric Research* 5(4): 132.

Bonnet, P.; Gehrke, J.; and Seshadri, P. 2001. Towards Sensor Database Systems. In Proceedings of the International Conference on Mobile Data Management, 3–14. Los Alamitos, Calif.: IEEE Computer Society.

Boomsma, L. G.; Elbert, Y.; Kelley, P. W.; Lewis, M.; Mansfield, J.; O'Brien, S.; and Pavlin, J. 2002. Disease Outbreak Detection System Using Syndromic Data in the Greater Washington D.C. Area. *American Journal of Preventive Medicine* 23(3): 180–186.

Borges, J. L.; and Levene, M. 1999. Data Mining of User Navigation Patterns. In *Web Usage Analysis and User Profiling: International WEBKDD'99 Workshop,* Lecture Notes in Computer Science 1836, 92–111, eds. M. M. Brij and M. Spiliopoulou. New York: Springer-Verlag.

Borges, J.; and Levene, M. 1998. Mining Association Rules in Hypertext Databases. In *Knowledge Discovery and Data Mining,* ed. G. Piatetsky-Shapiro, 149–153. Menlo Park, Calif.: AAAI Press / The MIT Press.

Bosques, W.; Rodriguez, R.; Rondon, A.; and Vasquez, R. 1997. A Spatial Data Retrieval and Image Processing System for the World Wide Web. Paper presented at the Twenty-First International Conference on Computers and Industrial Engineering, San Juan, Puerto Rico, March 9–12.

Bowyer, K. W.; Chawla, N. V.; Hall, L. O.; and Lazarevic, A. 2002. Smoteboost: Improving the Prediction of Minority Class in Boosting, Tech. Rep. 2002-136, Army High Performance Computing Research Center, Minneapolis, Minn.

Box, G. E. P.; and Jenkins, G. M. 1976. *Time Series Analysis: Forecasting and Control.* Second Edition. San Francisco: Holden-Day.

Bozsak, E.; Ehrig, M.; Handschuh, S.; Hotho, A.; Maedche, A.; Motik, B.; Oberle, D.; Schmitz, C.; Staab, S.; Stojanovic, L.; Stojanovic, N.; Studer, R.; Stumme, G.; Sure, Y.; Tane, J.; Volz, R.; and Zacharias, V. 2002. Kaon—Towards a Large Scale Semantic Web. In *Proceedings of the Third International Conference on E-Commerce and Web Technologies* Lecture Notes in Computer Science 2455, 304–313, eds. K. Bauknecht, A. Min Tjoa; and G. Quirchmayr. Berlin: Springer-Verlag.

Bradley, P. S.; Fayyad, U. M.; and Reina, C. 1998. Initialization of Iterative Refinement Clustering Algorithms. In *Proceedings of the Fourth International Conference on Machine Learning,* 194–198. San Francisco: Morgan Kaufmann Publishers.

Branden, C.; and Tooze, J. 1991. *Introduction to Protein Structure.* New York: Garland Publishing.

Breiman, L. 1996a. Bagging Predictors. *Machine Learning* 24(2): 123–140.

Breiman, L. 1996b. Stacked Regressions. *Machine Learning* 24(1): 49–64.

Breiman, L. 1999. Pasting Small Votes for Classification in Large Databases and On-Line. *Machine Learning* 36(1–2): 85–103.

Breiman, L.; Friedman, J. H.; Olshen, R. A.; and Stone, C. J. 1984. *Classification and Regression Trees.* Belmont, Calif.: Wadsworth International Group.

Breitzman, A.; Cheney, M.; and Thomas, P. 2000. Technological Powerhouse or Diluted Competence: Techniques for Assessing Mergers Via Patent Analysis. Paper presented at the Society of Competitive Intelligence Technical Intelligence Symposium, San Francisco, 8–9 June.

Breunig, M.; Kriegel, H.-P.; Ng, R. T.; and Sander, J. 2000. LOF: Identifying Density-Based Local Outliers. In Proceedings of the ACM SIGMOD International Conference on Management of Data, 93–104. New York: Association for Computing Machinery, Special Interest Group on Management of Data.

Brill, E. 2000. Pattern-Based Disambiguation for Natural Language Processing. Paper presented at the Joint SIGDAT Conference on Empirical Methods in Natural Language Processing and Very Large Corpora, Hong Kong, 7–8 October.

Brin, S.; and Page, L. 1998. The Anatomy of a Large-Scale Hypertextual Web Search Engine. *Computer Networks and ISDN Systems* 30(1–7): 107–117, 1998.

Brown, C. J.; Dunker, A. K.; Lakoucheva, L. M.; Lawson, J. D; and Obradovic, Z. 2002. Intrinsic Disorder and Protein Function. *Biochemistry* 41(21): 6573–6582.

Brown, C.; Dunker, A. K.; Obradovic, Z.; Peng, K.; Radivojac, P.; and Vucetic, S. 2003. Predicting Intrinsic Disorder from Amino Acid Sequence. *Proteins: Structure, Function, and Genetics* 53(Supplement 6): 566–572.

Brunner, R. J.; Djorgovski, S. G.; Prince, T. A.; and Szalay, A. S. 2002. Massive Datasets in Astronomy. In *Handbook of Massive Datasets,* eds. J. Abello, P. Pardalos, and M. Resende, 931. Dortrecht, The Netherlands: Kluwer Academic Publishers.

Bryant, C.; Muggleton, S.; Page, C.; and Sternberg, M. 1999. Combining Active Learning with Inductive Logic Programming to Close the Loop In Machine Learning. Paper presented at the AISB 1999 Symposium on AI and Scientific Creativity, Edinburgh, Scotland, 8–9 April.

Bryant, S. 1996. Evaluation of Threading Specificity and Accuracy. *Proteins* 26(2): 172–85.

Buntine, W. 1991. Theory Refinement on Bayesian Networks. In *Proceedings of the Seventeenth Annual Conference on Uncertainty in Artificial Intelligence,* 52–60. San Francisco: Morgan Kaufmann Publishers.

Burkom, H.; Elbert, R.; Lewis, S. H.; Lombardo, J.; Loschen, W.; Magruder, S.; Pavlin, J.; Sari, J.; Sniegoski, C.; and Wojcik, R. 2003. A Systems Overview of the Electronic Surveillance System for the Early Notification of Community-Based Epidemics (ESSENCE II). *Journal of Urban Health* 80(2 Supplement 1): I32–I42.

Burl, M.; Kamatch, C.; Kumar, V.; and Namburu, R. eds. 2002. Papers of the Fifth Workshop on Mining Scientific Datasets, Second SIAM International Conference Data Mining. Philadelphia, Penn.: Society for Industrial and Applied Mathematics.

Burl, M.; Kamatch, C.; Kumar, V.; and Namburu, R. 2001. Fourth Workshop on Mining Scientific Datasets. In Proceedings of the Seventh ACM SIGKDD International Conference on Knowledge Discovery and Data Mining. New York: Association for Computing Machinery, Special Interest Group on Knowledge Discovery and Data Mining.

Burl, M.; Kamatch, C.; Kumar, V.; and Namburu, R. 2001. Third Workshop on Mining Scientific Datasets. In Proceedings of the First SIAM International Conference on Data Mining. Philadelphia, Penn.: Society for Industrial and Applied Mathematics.

Burnside, G. G.; Cuicchi, C. E.; Gatlin, B.; Hammersley, J. R.; Olsen, D. E.; and Reddy, R. N. 1995. Computational Simulation of Steady and Oscillating Flow in Branching Tubes. Paper presented at the 1995 ASME / JSME Fluids Engineering and Laser Anemometry Conference and Exhibition: Bio-Medical Fluids Engineering, Hilton Head, So. Car., August.

Burnside, G. G.; Cuicchi, C. E.; Gatlin, B.; Hammersley, J. R.; Olsen, D. E.; and Reddy, R. N. 1997a. Computation of Converging and Diverging Flow Through an Asymmetric Tubular Bifurcation. Paper presented at the ASME Summer Fluids Engineering Conference, Vancouver, Brit. Col., June.

Burnside, G. G.; Cuicchi, C. E.; Gatlin, B.; Hammersley, J. R.; Olsen, D. E.; and Reddy, R. N. 1997b. Particle Paths and Deposition Patterns for Laminar Flow Through a Branching Tube. Paper presented at the ASME Summer Fluids Engineering Conference, Vancouver, Brit. Col., June.

Byrne C.; and Edwards, P. 1995. Refinement in Agent Groups. In *Adaption and Learning in Multi-Agent Systems,* Lecture Notes in Artificial Intelligence 1042, 22–39, eds. G. Weiss and S. Sen. New York: Springer-Verlag.

Bystroff, C.; Hu, J.; Shao, Y.; Shen, X.; and Zaki, M. 2002. Mining Protein Contact Maps. Paper presented at the Second BIOKDD Workshop on Data Mining in Bioinformatics, Edmonton, Alberta, 23 July.

Bystroff, C.; Thorsson, V.; and Baker, D. 2000. HMMSTR: A Hidden Markov Model for Local Sequence-Structure Correlations in Proteins. *Journal of Molecular Biology* 301(1): 173–190.

Cabrera, J. B. D.; Mehra, R. K.; and Ravichandran, B. 2000. Statistical Traffic Modeling for Network Intrusion Detection. Paper presented at the Eighth International Symposium on Modeling, Analysis and Simulation of Computer and Telecommunication Systems, San Francisco, 29 August-1 September.

Cadez, I. V.; Heckerman, D.; Meek, C.; Smyth, P.; and White S. 2000. Visualization of Navigation Patterns on a Web Site Using Model-Based Clustering. In Proceedings of the the Sixth ACM SIGKDD International Conference on Knowledge Discovery and Data Mining, 2–23. New York: Association for Computing Machinery, Special Interest Group on Knowledge Discovery and Data Mining.

Califf, M. E.; and Mooney, R. J. 1999. Relational Learning of Pattern-Match Rules for Information Extraction. In *Proceedings of the Seventeenth National Conference on Artificial Intelligence,* 328–334. Menlo Park, Calif.: AAAI Press / The MIT Press.

Cannataro, M.; and Comito, C. 2003. A Data Mining Ontology for Grid Programming. In Paper presented at the First International Workshop on Semantics in Peer-To-Peer and Grid Computing (SemPGrid2003), Budapest, Hungary, 20 May.

Cannataro, M.; and Talia, D. 2003. The Knowledge Grid. *Communications of the ACM* 46(1): 89–93.

Cannataro, M.; and Talia, D. 2003. Towards the Next-Generation Grid: A Pervasive Environment for Knowledge-Based Computing. In Proceedings of the Fourth IEEE International Conference on Information Technology: Coding and Computing, 347–441. Los Alamitos, Calif.: IEEE Computer Society.

Cannataro, M.; Talia, D.; and Trunfio, P. 2001. KNOWLEDGE GRID: High Performance Knowledge Discovery on the Grid. In *Proceedings of the Second International Workshop on Grid Computing,* Lecture Notes in Computer Science 2242, 38–50, ed. C. A. Lee. Berlin: Springer-Verlag.

Card, S.K.; Chi, E. H.; Gossweiler, R.; Mackinlay, J.; Pirolli, P.; and Pitkow, J. 1998. Visualizing the Evolution of Web Ecologies. In *Proceedings of the SIGCHI Conference on Human Factors in Computing Systems,* 400–407. New York: ACM Press / Addison-Wesley Publishing Co.

Carmel, D.; and Markovitch, S. 1995. Opponent Modeling in Multi-Agent Systems. In *Adaption and Learning in Multi-Agent Systems,* Lecture Notes in Artificial Intelligence 1042, 40–52, eds. G. Weiss and S. Sen. New York: Springer-Verlag.

Carney, D.; Cetintemel, U.; Cherniack, M.; Convey, C.; Lee, S.; Seidman, G.; Stonebraker, M.; Tatbul, N.; and Zdonik, S. 2002. Monitoring Streams—A New Class of Data Management Applications. In *Proceedings of the Twenty-Eighth International Conference on Very Large Databases,* 215–226. San Francisco: Morgan Kaufmann Publishers.

Carrat, F.; and LeStrat, Y. 1999. Monitoring Epidemiologic Surveillance Data Using Hidden Markov Models. *Statistics in Medicine* 18(24): 3463–3478.

Caruana, R. A.; Fienberg, S. E.; Goldenberg, A.; and Shmueli, G. 2002. Early Statistical Detection of Anthrax Outbreaks by Tracking Over-the-Counter Medication Sales. *Proceedings of the National Academy of Sciences of the United States of America* 99(8): 5237–5240.

Casadio, R.; and Fariselli, P. 1999. A Neural Network Based Predictor of Residue Contacts in Proteins. *Protein Engineering* 12(1): 15–21.

Casadio, R.; Fariselli, P.; Olmea, O.; and Valencia, A. 2001. Prediction of Contact Maps with Neural Networks and Correlated Mutations. *Protein Engineering* 14(11): 835–843.

Catlin, A. C.; Houstis, C. E.; Houstis, E. N.; Ramakrishnan, N.; Rice, J. R.; and Verykios, V. S. 2000. PYTHIA-II: A Knowledge / Database System for Managing Performance Data and Recommending Scientific Software. *ACM Transactions on Mathematical Software* 26(2): 227–253.

Cetin, A.; Nam, J.; and Tewfik, A. 1997. Speaker Identification and Video Analysis for Hierarchical Video Shot Classification. In Proceedings of the IEEE International Conference on Image Processing 2, 550–555. Los Alamitos, Calif.: IEEE Computer Society.

Chakrabarti, S. 2000. Data Mining for Hypertext: A Tutorial Survey. *SIGKDD Explorations* 1(2): 1–11.

Chakraborty, D.; and Joshi A. 2001. Dynamic Service Composition: State-of-the-Art and Research Directions, Tech. Rep. TR-CS-01-19, Dept. of Computer Science, Univ. of Maryland, Baltimore County, Baltimore, Md.

Chan, P. K.; Fan, W.; Stolfo, S. J.; and Zhang, J. 1999. AdaCost: Misclassification Cost-Sensitive Boosting. In *Proceedings of the Sixteenth International Conference on Machine Learning,* 97–105. San Francisco: Morgan Kaufmann Publishers.

Chan, P.; and Kargupta, H. eds. 2000. *Advances in Distributed and Parallel Knowledge Discovery.* Menlo Park, Calif.: AAAI Press / The MIT Press.

Chan, P.; and Kargupta, H. eds. 2000. *Advances in Distributed and Parallel Knowledge Discovery.* Menlo Park, Calif.: AAAI Press / The MIT Press.

Chan, P.; and Stolfo, S. 1993a. Experiments on Multistrategy Learning by Meta-Learning. Paper presented at the Second International Conference on Information Knowledge Management, Washington D.C., November.

Chan, P.; and Stolfo, S. 1993b. Toward Parallel and Distributed Learning by Meta-Learning. In Knowledge Discovery in Databases: Papers from the AAAI Workshop, 227–240. Tech. Rep. WS-93-02, American Association for Artificial Intelligence, Menlo Park, Calif.

Chan, P.; and Stolfo, S. 1998. Toward Scalable Learning with Non-Uniform Class and Cost Distribution: A Case Study in Credit Card Fraud Detection. In *Proceeding of the Fourth International Conference on Knowledge Discovery and Data Mining,* 164–168. Menlo Park, Calif.: AAAI Press.

Chandler, G. V.; Interrante, V.; Marusic, I.; Moss, A.; and Subbareddy, P. K. 2001. Real Time Feature Extraction for the Analysis of Turbulent Flows. In *Data Mining for Scientific and Engineering Applications,* eds. R. L. Grossman; C. Kamath; P. Kegelmeyer; V. Kumar; and R. R. Namburu, 223–238. Dortrecht, The Netherlands: Kluwer Academic Publishers.

Chandrasekaran, S.; Cooper, O.; Deshpande, A.; Franklin, M. J.; Hellerstein, J. M.; Hong, W.; Krishnamurthy, S.; Madden, S. R.; Raman, V.; Reiss, F.; and Shah, M. A. 2003. TelegraphCQ: Continuous Dataflow Processing for an Uncertain World. In Proceedings of the First Conference on Innovative Data Systems Research (CIDR). Columbus, Ohio: Very Large Data Base Endowment, Inc.

Chandrasekaran, S.; Deshpande, A.; Franklin, M. J.; Hellerstein, J. M.; Hildrum, K.; Madden, S.; Raman, V.; and Shah, M. A. 2000. Adaptive Query Processing: Technology in Evolution. *IEEE Data Engineering Bulletin* 23(2): 7–18.

Chau, M.; Chen, H.; and Xu, J. J. 2002. Extracting Meaningful Entities from Police Narrative Reports. Paper presented at the National Conference for Digital Government Research, Los Angeles, Calif., 19–22 May.

Chaudhuri, S.; and Narasayya, V. R. 1997. An Efficient Cost-Driven Index Selection Tool for Microsoft SQL Server. In *Proceedings of the Twenty-Third International Conference on Very Large Databases,* 146–155. San Francisco: Morgan Kaufmann Publishers.

Chawathe, S.; and Ghazizadeh, S. 2002. SEuS: Structure Extraction Using Summaries. In *Proceedings of the Fifth International Conference on Discovery Science,* Lecture Notes in Computer Science 2534, 71–85, eds. S. Lange; K. Satoh; and C. H. Smith. Berlin: Springer-Verlag.

Chawla, S.; Ozesmi, U.; Shekhar, S.; and Wu, W. 2001. Modeling Spatial Dependencies for Mining Geospatial Data. In Proceedings of the First SIAM International Conference on Data Mining. Philadelphia, Penn.: Society for Industrial and Applied Mathematics.

Chazelle, B. 2000. *The Discrepancy Method.* Cambridge: Cambridge Univ. Press.

Chee, S.; Chen, J.; Chen, Q.; Cheng, S.; Chiang, J.; Han, J.; Gong, W.; Kamber, M.; Koperski, K.; Liu, G.; Lu, Y.; St-Fanovic, N.; Winstone, L.; Xia, B.; Zaiane, O.R.; Zhang, S.; and Zhu, H. 1997. Dbminer: A System for Data Mining in Relational Databases and Data Warehouses. Paper presented at Centre for Advanced Studies CASCON 1997 Conference: Meeting of Minds, Toronto, Canada, 10–13 November.

Cheeseman, P.; and Stutz, J. 1996 Bayesian Classification (Autoclass): Theory and Results. In *Advances in Knowledge Discovery and Data Mining,* eds. U. Fayyad; G. P. Shapiro; P. Smyth; and R. S. Uthurasamy, 153–180. Menlo Park, Calif.: AAAI Press.

Chelliah, M.; Collins, W.; Deaven, D.; Ebisuzaki, W.; Higgins, W.; Gandin, L.; Iredell, M.; Janowiak, J.; Jenne, R.; Joseph, D.; Kalnay, E.; Kanamitsu, M.; Kistler, R.; Leetmaa, A.; Mo, K. C.; Reynolds, R.; Ropelewski, C.; Saha, S.; Wang, J.; White, G.; Woollen, J.; and Zhu, Y. 1996. A Literature Network of Human Genes for High-Throughput Analysis of Gene Expression. *Bulletin of the American Meteorological Society* 76(3): 437–471.

Chen, B.; Haas, P.; and Scheuermann, P. 2002. A New Two-Phase Sampling Based Algorithm for Discovering Association Rules. In Proceedings of the Eighth ACM SIGKDD International Conference on Knowledge Discovery and Data Mining, 462–468. New York: Association for Computing Machinery, Special Interest Group on Knowledge Discovery and Data Mining.

Chen, C. 1999. *Information Visualisation and Virtual Environments.* Berlin: Springer-Verlag.

Chen, H.; Miranda, R.; Zeng, D. D.; Demchak, C.; and Madhusudan, T. 2003. *Intelligence and Security Informatics: Proceedings of the First National Science Foundation / NIJ Symposium.* Berlin: Springer-Verlag.

Chen, J.; DeWitt, D. J.; Tian, F.; and Wang, Y. 2000. Niagara CQ: A Scalable Continuous Query System for Internet Databases. In Proceedings of the ACM SIGMOD International Conference on Management of Data, 379–390. New York: Association for Computing Machinery, Special Interest Group on Management of Data.

Chen, K.; Chi, E. H.; Pirolli, P.; and Pitkow, J. E. 2001. Using Information Scent to Model User Information Needs and Actions and the Web. In Proceedings of the ACM CHI 2001 Conference on Human Factors in Computing Systems, 490–497. New York: Association for Computing Machinery.

Chen, R.; and Sivakumar, K. 2002. A New Algorithm for Learning Parameters of a Bayesian Network from Distributed Data. In Proceedings of the IEEE International Conference on Data Mining, 585–588. Los Alamitos, Calif.: IEEE Computer Society.

Chen R.; and Sivakumar, K.; and Kargupta, H. 2001a. An Approach to Online Bayesian Learning from Multiple Data Streams. Paper presented at the Workshop on Ubiquitous Data Mining: Technology for Mobile and Distributed KDD, Fifth European Conference, PKDD, Freiburg, Germany, September 2001.

Chen R.; Sivakumar, K.; and Kargupta, H. 2001b. Distributed Web Mining Using Bayesian Networks from Multiple Data Streams. In *Proceedings of the IEEE International Conference on Data Mining,* 75–82. Los Alamitos, Calif.: IEEE Computer Society.

Chen R.; and Sivakumar, K.; and Kargupta, H. 2003. Learning Bayesian Network Structure from Distributed Data. In Proceedings of the Third SIAM International Conference on Data Mining. Philadelphia, Penn.: Society for Industrial and Applied Mathematics.

Chen, Y.; Dong, G.; Han, J.; Wah, B. W.; and Wang, J. 2002. Multi-Dimensional Regression Analysis of Time-Series Data Streams. In *Proceedings of the Twenty-Eighth International Conference on Very Large Data Bases,* 323–334. San Francisco: Morgan Kaufmann Publishers.

Chervenak, A.; Foster, I.; Kesselman, C.; and Tuecke, S. 2000. Protocols and Services for Distributed Data-Intensive Science. Paper Presented at the Seventh International Workshop on Advanced Computing and Analysis Techniques in Physics Research (ACAT), Naperville, Ill., 16–20 October.

Chervenak, A.; Foster, I.; Kesselman, C.; Salisbury, C.; and Tuecke, S. 2000. The Data Grid: Towards an Architecture for the Distributed Management and Analysis of Large Scientific Datasets. *Journal of Network and Computer Applications* 23(3): 187–200.

Cheung, D. W.; Fu, A. W.; Fu, Y.; and Ng, V. T. 1996. Efficient Mining of Association Rules in Distributed Databases. *IEEE Transactions on Knowledge and Data Engineering* 8(6): 911–922.

Cheung, D.; Ching, W.-K.; Huang, J. Z.; Ng, J.; and Ng, M. 2001. A Cube Model for Web Access Sessions and Cluster Analysis. In *WEBKDD 2001—Mining Web Log Data Across All Customers Touch Points,* ed. R. Kohavi, B. M. Masand, M. Spiliopoulou, and J. Srivastava. Lecture Notes in Computer Science 2356. Berlin: Springer-Verlag.

Chi, E. H.; Heer, J.; and Rosien, A. 2002. Intelligent Discovery and Analysis of Web User Traffic Composition. In *Mining Web Data for Discovery Usage Patterns and Profiles: Workshop on Web Knowledge Discovery and Data Mining,* Lecture Notes in Computer Science 2703, 1–15. Berlin: Springer-Verlag.

Chi, E. H.; Pirolli, P.; and Pitkow, J. 2000. The Scent of a Site: A System for Analyzing and Predicting Information Scent, Usage, and Usability of a Web Site. In Proceedings of the ACM CHI 2000 Conference on Human Factors in Computing Systems, 161–168. New York: Association for Computing Machinery.

Chickering, D. M. 1996. Learning Equivalence Classes of Bayesian Network Structure. In *Proceedings of the Twelfth Conference on Uncertainty in Artificial Intelligence,* 150–157. San Francisco: Morgan Kaufmann Publishers.

Chickering, D. M.; and Heckerman, D. 1997. Efficient Approximation for the Marginal Likelihood of Incomplete Data Given a Bayesian Network. *Machine Learning* 29(2–3): 181–212.

Chittimoori, R. N.; Cook, D. J.; and Holder, L. B. 1999. Applying the Subdue Substructure Discovery System to the Chemical Toxicity Domain. In *Proceedings of the Twelfth International Florida Artificial Intelligence Research Society Conference,* 90–94. Menlo Park, Calif.: AAAI Press.

Cho, V.; and Wüthrich, B. 2002. Distributed Mining of Classification Rules. *Knowledge and Information Systems* 4(1): 1–30.

Christoph, H.; King, R. D.; Kramer, S.; and Srinivasan, A. 2001. The Predictive Toxicology Challenge 2000–2001. *Bioinformatics* 17(1): 107–108.

Clare, A.; Dehaspe, L.; Karwath, A.; and King, R. D. 2000. Genome Scale Prediction of Protein Functional Class from Sequence Using Data Mining. In Proceedings of the Sixth ACM SIGKDD International Conference on Knowledge Discovery and Data Mining, 384–389. New York: Association for Computing Machinery, Special Interest Group on Knowledge Discovery and Data Mining.

Clark, D.; Lambert, M.; and Zhang, L. 1987. NETBLT: A High Throughput Transport Protocol. In Proceedings of the ACM Workshop on Frontiers in Computer Communications Technology, 353–359. New York: Association for Computing Machinery Special Interest Group on Data Communication.

Claverie, A.; Cowern, N. E. B.; Cristiano, F.; Huizing, H. G. A.; Jaraiz, M.; Mannino, G.; Roozeboom, F.; Stolk, P. A.; and Van Berkum, J. G. M. 1999. Energetics of Self-Interstitial Clusters in Si. *Physical Review Letters* 82(22): 4460–4463.

Cleverdon, C. W. 1972. On the Inverse Relationship of Recall and Precision. *Journal of Documentation* 28: 195–201.

Clifton C.; Kantarcioglu, M.; and Vaidya, J. 2002. Defining Privacy for Data Mining, Tech. Rep., Dept. of Computer Science, Purdue Univ., West Lafayette, Ind.

Clifton, C. 2000. Using Sample Size to Limit Exposure to Data Mining. *Journal of Computer Security* 8(4): 281–307.

Clifton, C.; and Estivill-Castro, V., eds. 2002. In Proceedings of the Workshop on Privacy, Security and Data Mining, IEEE International Conference on Data Mining Workshop on Privacy, Security and Data Mining 14. Canberra, Australia: Australian Computer Society.

Clifton, C.; and Kantarcioglu, M. 2002. Privacy-Preserving Distributed Mining of Association Rules on Horizontally Partitioned Data. Paper presented at the ACM SIGMOD Workshop on Research Issues on Data Mining and Knowledge Discovery (DMKD'02), Madison, Wisc., 2 June.

Clifton, C.; and Kantarcioglu, M. 2002. Privacy-Preserving Distributed Mining of Association Rules on Horizontally Partitioned Data. Paper presented at the ACM SIGMOD Workshop on Research Issues on Data Mining and Knowledge Discovery, Madison, Wisc., 2 June.

Clymer, A. 2003. Pentagon Surveillance Plan Is Described as Less Invasive. *New York Times,* 7 May.

Cohen, P. R.; Oates, T.; and Schmill, M. D. 1997. Parallel and Distributed Search for Structure in Multivariate Time Series. In *Proceedings of the Ninth European Conference on Machine Learning,* Lecture Notes in Computer Science 1224, 191–198, eds. M. van Someren, and G. Widmer. New York: Springer-Verlag.

Cohn, D.; Ghahramani, Z.; and Jordan, M. 1996. Active Learning with Statistical Models. *Journal of Artificial Intelligence Research* 4: 129–145.

Colet, E. 2000. Using Data Mining to Detect Fraud in Auctions. *DSstar* 4(26).

Collier, N.; Nobata, C.; and Tsujii, J. 2000. Extracting the Names of Genes and Gene Products with a Hidden Markov Model. In *Proceedings of the Eighteenth International Conference on Computational Linguistics,* 201–207. San Francisco: Morgan Kaufmann Publishers.

Colon, W.; and Roder, H. 1996. Kinetic Intermediates in the Formation of the Cytochrome C Molten Globule. *Nature Structural Biology* 3(12): 1019–1025.

Congiusta, A.; Cannataro, M.; Talia, D.; and Trunfio, P. 2002. A Data Mining Toolset for Distributed High-Performance Platforms. In *Proceedings of the Third International Conference on Knowledge Discovery and Data Mining,* 41–50. Menlo Park, Calif.: AAAI Press.

Cook, D. J.; and Holder, L. B. 1994. Substructure Discovery Using Minimum Description Length and Background Knowledge. *Journal of Artificial Intelligence Research* 1: 231–255.

Cook, D. J.; and Holder, L. B. 2000. Graph-Based Data Mining. *IEEE Intelligent Systems* 15(2): 32–41.

Cook, D. J.; Djoko, S.; and Holder, L. B. 1994. Substructure Discovery in the SUBDUE System. In Knowledge Discovery in Databases: Papers from the AAAI Workshop, Tech. Rep. WS-94-03, American Association for Artificial Intelligence, Menlo Park, Calif.

Cook, D. J.; Gonzalez, J.; and Holder, L. B. 2001. Application of Graph-Based Concept Learning to the Predictive Toxicology Domain. Paper presented at the Predictive Toxicology Challenge Workshop, Freiburg, Germany, 3–7 September.

Cook, W. A.; and O'Hayon, G. B. 1998. A Chronology of Russian Killings. *Transnational Organized Crime* 4(2).

Cooley, R. 2000. Web Usage Mining: Discovery and Application of Interesting Patterns from Web Data. Ph.D. diss., Dept. of Computer Science, Univ. of Minnesota, Minneapolis, Minn.

Cooley, R.; Mobasher, B.; and Srivastava, J. 1997. Web Mining: Information and Pattern Discovery on the World Wide Web. In Proceedings of the Ninth IEEE International Conference on Tools with Artificial Intelligence. Los Alamitos, Calif.: IEEE Computer Society.

Cooley, R.; Mobasher, B.; and Srivastava, J. 1999. Data Preparation for Mining World Wide Web Browsing Patterns. *Knowledge and Information Systems,* 1(1): 5–32.

Cooley, R.; Mobasher, B.; and Srivastava, J. 2000. Automatic Personalization Based on Web Usage Mining. *Communications of the ACM* 43(8): 142–151.

Cooley, R.; Srivastava, J.; and Mobasher, B. 1997. Web Mining: Information and Pattern Discovery on the World Wide Web. In Proceedings of the Ninth IEEE International Conference on Tools with Artificial Intelligence. Los Alamitos, Calif.: IEEE Computer Society.

Cooper, G. F.; and Herskovits, E. 1992. A Bayesian Method for the Induction of Probabilistic Networks from Data. *Machine Learning* 9(4): 309–347.

Corkill, D. D.; Durfee, E.; and Lesser, V. R. 1989. Cooperative Distributed Problem Solving. In *The Handbook of Artificial Intelligence,* volume IV, eds. A. Barr, P. R. Cohen, and E. A. Feigenbaum, 83–147. Reading, Mass.: Addison-Wesley Publishing Co.

Cortes, C.; and Pregibon, D. 2001. Signature-Based Methods for Data Streams. *Data Mining and Knowledge Discovery* 5(3): 167–182.

Costa, V. S.; Cussens, J.; Page, D.; and Qazi, M. 2003. CLP(BN): Constraint Logic Programming for Probabilistic Knowledge. In *Proceedings of the Nineteenth International Conference on Uncertainty in Artificial Intelligence,* 517–524. San Francisco: Morgan Kaufmann Publishers.

Costa, V. S.; Dutra, I. C.; Page, D.; and Shavlik, J. W. 2002. An Empirical Evaluation of Bagging in Inductive Logic Programming. In *Proceedings of the Twelfth International Conference on Inductive Logic Programming,* Lecture Notes in Artificial Intelligence 2583, 48–65, eds. S. Matwin and C. Sammut. Berlin: Springer-Verlag.

Costa, V. S.; Dutra, I. C.; Page, D.; Shavlik, J. W.; and Waddell, M. 2003. Towards Automatic Management of Embarassingly Parallel Applications. In *Proceedings of Europar 2003,* Lecture Notes in Computer Science 2790, 509–516. Berlin: Springer-Verlag.

Coupet, P.; Hehenberger, M.; Huot, C.; and Stensmo, M. 1999. Text Mining of Chemical and Patent Literature. In *Proceedings of the 1999 International Chemical Information Conference.* Tetbury, England: Informatics, Ltd.

Cowie, J.; and Lehnert, W. 1996. Information Extraction. *Communications of the ACM* 39(1): 80–91.

Craven, M.; DiPasquo, D.; Freitag, D.; McCallum, A. K.; Mitchell, T.; Nigam, K.; and Slattery, S. 2000. Learning to Construct Knowledge Bases from the World Wide Web. *Artificial Intelligence* 118(1–2): 69–113.

Craven, M.; DiPasquo, D.; Freitag, D.; McCallum, A.; Mitchell, T.; Nigam, K.; and Slattery, S. 2000. Learning to Construct Knowledge Bases from the World Wide Web. *Artificial Intelligence* 118(1–2): 69–113.

Creel, E.; Grossman, R. L.; Harinath, S.; Mazzucco, M.; Reinhart, G.; and Turinskiy, A. 2000. Terabyte Challenge 2000: Project DataSpace. Paper presented at the Workshop on Mining Scientific Datasets, Minneapolis, Minn., 20–21 July.

Cressie, N. A. C. 1993. *Statistics for Spatial Data.* Revised Edition. New York: John Wiley and Sons.

Curry, D.; and Debar, H. 2002. Intrusion Detection Message Exchange Format Data Model and Extensible Markup Language (XML) Document Type Definition. (draft-ietf-idwg-xmlsmi-00.txt) June. Reston, Va.: The Internet Society.

Da Silva, A. S.; Laender, A. H. F.; Ribeiro-Neto, B. A.; and Teixeira, J. S. 2002. A Brief Survey of Web Data Extraction Tools. *SIGMOD Record* 31(2): 84–93.

Dai H.; and Mobasher, B. 2002. Using Ontologies to Discover Domain-Level Web Usage Profiles. Paper presented at the Second Semantic Web Mining Workshop at PKDD 2002, Helsinki, Finland, August.

Dai, H.; Luo, T.; Mobasher, B.; Sun, Y.; and Zhu, J. 2000. Integrating Web Usage and Content Mining for More Effective Personalization. In *Proceedings of the First International Conference on Electronic Commerce and Web Technologies,* Lecture Notes in Computer Science 1875, 165–176, eds. K. Bauknecht; S. K. Madria; and G. Pernul. Berlin: Springer-Verlag.

Dao, S.; Fu, Y.; Han, J. J.; and Ng, R. T. 1998. Dealing with Semantic Heterogeneity by Generalization-Based Data Mining Techniques. In *Cooperative Information Systems: Current Trends and Directions,* eds. M. P. Papazoglou and G. Schlageter, 207–231. San Diego, Calif.: Elsevier.

Darlington, J.; Guo, Y.; Sutiwaraphun, J.; and To, H. W. 1997. Parallel Induction Algorithms for Data Mining. Paper presented at the Second International Symposium on Intelligent Data Analysis (IDA-97), London, 4–6 August.

Das, A.; Gehrke, J.; and Riedewald, M. 2003. Approximate Join Processing Over Data Streams. In Proceedings of the ACM SIGMOD International Conference on Management of Data, 40–51. New York: Association for Computing Machinery, Special Interest Group on Management of Data.

Dasarathy, B. 1994. Decision Fusion. Los Alamitos, Calif: IEEE Computer Society.

Datar, M.; Gionis, A.; Indyk, P.; and Motwani, R. 2002. Maintaining Stream Statistics Over Sliding Windows. In Proceedings of the ACM-SIAM Symposium on Discrete Algorithms (SODA), 635–644. Philadelphia, Penn.: Society for Industrial and Applied Mathematics.

Datta, S.; Kargupta, H.; Sivakumar, K.; and Wang, Q. 2003. On the Privacy Preserving Properties of Random Data Perturbation Techniques. In Proceedings of the IEEE International Conference on Data Mining, 99–106. Los Alamitos, Calif.: IEEE Computer Society.

Davidson, A. J.; Espino, J. U.; Fraser, H.; Karras, B. T.; Lober, W. B.; Mandl, K. D.; Overhage, J. M.; Trigg, L. J.; Tsui, C. F.; and Wagner, M. M. 2002. Roundtable on Bioterrorism Detection: Information System-Based Surveillance. *Journal of the American Medical Informatics Association* 9(2): 105–115.

Davies, R.; and Smith, R. G. 1983. Negotiation as a Metaphor for Distributed Problem Solving. *Artificial Intelligence* 20(1): 63–108.

Davis, R.; Shrobe, H.; and Szolovits, P. 1993. What Is Knowledge Representation? *AI Magazine* 14(1): 17–33.

De Raedt, L.; Helma, C.; and Kramer, S. 2001. Molecular Feature Mining in HIV Data. In Proceedings of the Seventh ACM SIGKDD International Conference on Knowledge Discovery and Data Mining, 136–143. New York: Association for Computing Machinery, Special Interest Group on Knowledge Discovery and Data Mining.

Decker, S.; Erdman, M.; Fensel, D.; and Studer, R. 1998. Ontobroker in a Nutshell. In *Proceedings of the Second European Conference on Research and Advanced Technology for Digital Libraries,* 663–664, Berlin: Springer-Verlag.

DeCoste, D.; and Mjoslness, E. 2001. Machine Learning for Science: State of the Art and Future Prospects. *Science* 293(14 September): 2051–2055.

Dehaspe, L.; King, R. D.; and Srinivasan, A. 2001. Warmr: A Data Mining Tool for Chemical Data. *Journal of Computer Aided Molecular Design* 15(2): 173–181.

Dehaspe, L.; King, R. D.; and Toivonen, H. 1998. Finding Frequent Substructures in Chemical Compounds. In *Proceedings of the Fourth International Conference on Knowledge Discovery and Data Mining,* 30–36. Menlo Park, Calif.: AAAI Press.

Delugach, H. S.; and Hinke, T. H. 1996. Wizard: A Database Inference Analysis and Detection System. *IEEE Transactions on Knowledge and Data Engineering* 8(1): 56–66.

Delugach, H. S.; Hinke, T. H.; and Wolf, R. P. 1997. Protecting Databases from Inference Attacks. *Computers and Security* 16(8): 687–708.

Dembeck C.; and Greenberg, P. A. 2000. Amazon: Caught Between a Rock and a Hard Place. *E-Commerce Times*. Feb. 8.

Dempster, A. P.; Laird, N. M.; and Rubin, D. B. 1977. Maximum Likelihood from Incomplete Data Via the EM Algorithm. *Journal of the Royal Statistical Society* B(39): 1–38.

Denning, D. E. 1987. An Intrusion-Detection Model. *IEEE Transactions on Software Engineering* 13(2): 222–232.

Deogun, J.; Harms, S.; and Li, D. 2003. Interpolation Techniques for Geo-Spatial Association Rule Mining. In *Proceedings of the Ninth International Conference on Rough Sets, Fuzzy Sets, Data Mining and Granular Computing, RSFDGrC2003*, Lecture Notes in Computer Science 2639, 573–580, eds. Q. Liu, A. Skowron, G. Wang, and Y. Yao. New York: Springer-Verlag.

Desikan, P.; Kumar, V.; Srivastava, J.; and Tan, P. N. 2002. Hyperlink Analysis-Techniques and Applications, Tech. Rep. 2002-152, Army High Performance Computing Research Center, Minneapolis, Minn.

Devijver, P.; and Kittler, J. 1982. *Pattern Recognition: A Statistical Approach*. Upper Saddle River, N.J.: Hall.

DeWitt, D. J.; and Patel, J. M. 2000. Clone Join and Shadow Join: Two Parallel Spatial Join Algorithms. In Proceedings of the Eighth ACM International Symposium on Advances in Geographic Information Systems, 54–61. New York: Association for Computing Machinery.

Dhillon, I.; and Modha, D. 1999. A Data-Clustering Algorithm on Distributed Memory Multiprocessors. Paper presented at the Workshop on Large-Scale Parallel KDD Systems, ACM SIGKDD International Conference on Knowledge Discovery and Data Mining, San Diego, Calif., 15 August.

Dietterich, T. G. 1998. Machine-Learning Research: Four Current Directions. *AI Magazine* 18(4): 97–136.

Dietterich, T. G. 2000. An Experimental Comparison of Three Methods for Constructing Ensembles of Decision Trees: Bagging, Boosting, and Randomization. *Machine Learning* 40(2): 139–158.

Dobra, A.; Garofalakis, M. N.; Gehrke, J.; and Rastogi, R. 2002. Processing Complex Aggregate Queries Over Data Streams. In Proceedings of the ACM SIGMOD International Conference on Management of Data, 61–72. New York: Association for Computing Machinery, Special Interest Group on Management of Data.

Dokas, P.; Ertoz, L.; Kumar, V.; Lazarevic, A.; Srivastava, J.; and Tan, P.-N. 2002. Data Mining for Network Intrusion Detection. Paper presented at the 2002 National Science Foundation Workshop on Next Generation Data Mining, Baltimore, Md., 1–3 November.

Domingos P.; and Hulten, G. 2000. Mining High-Speed Data Streams. In Proceedings of the Sixth ACM SIGKDD International Conference on Knowledge Discovery and Data Mining, 71–80. New York: Association for Computing Machinery, Special Interest Group on Knowledge Discovery and Data Mining.

Domingos, P.; Hulten, G.; and Spencer, L. 2001. Mining Time-Changing Data Streams. In Proceedings of the Seventh ACM SIGKDD International Conference Knowledge Discovery in Databases, 97–106. New York: Association for Computing Machinery, Special Interest Group on Knowledge Discovery and Data Mining.

Domingos, P.; Hulten, G.; and Spencer, L. 2001. Mining TIme-Changing Data Streams. In Proceedings of the Seventh ACM-SIGKDD International Conference on Knowledge Discovery and Data Mining, 97–106. New York: Association for Computing Machinery, Special Interest Group on Knowledge Discovery and Data Mining.

Dong, G.; Han, J.; Lakshmanan, L.; Pei, J.; Wang, H.; and Yu, P. 2003. Online Mining of Changes from Data Streams: Research Problems and Preliminary Results. Paper presented at the 2003 ACM SIGMOD Workshop on Management and Processing of Data Streams, San Diego, Calif., June 8.

Dong, G.; Han, J.; Pei, J.; and Wang, K. 2001. Efficient Computation of Iceberg Cubes with Complex Measures. In Proceedings of the ACM SIGMOD International Conference on Management of Data, 1–12. New York: Association for Computing Machinery, Special Interest Group on Management of Data.

Dongarra, J.; Huss-Lederman,S.; Snir M.; Otto, S.; and Walker, D. 1995. *MPI: The Complete Reference.* Cambridge, Mass.: The MIT Press.

Drashansky, T. T.; Houstis, E. N.; Ramakrishnan, N.; Rice, J. R. 1999. Networked Agents for Scientific Computing. *Communications of the ACM* 42(3): 48–54.

Drossu, R.; and Obradovic, Z. 2000. Data Mining Techniques for Designing Efficient Neural Network Time Series Predictors. In *Knowledge-Based Neurocomputing,* eds. I. Cloete, and J. Zurada, 325–368. Cambridge, Mass.: The MIT Press.

Drury, S. A. 1998. *Images of the Earth: A Guide to Remote Sensing.* Oxford: Oxford Science Publications.

National Cancer Institute. Dtp Aids Antiviral Screen Dataset. Bethesda, Md.: National Institutes of Health

Du, W., Using General Grid Tools and Compiler Technology for Distributed Data Mining: Preliminary Report. In Proceedings of the High Performance Data Mining SIAM Conference. Philadelphia, Penn.: Society for Industrial and Applied Mathematics.

Dubes, R. C.; and Jain, A. K. 1988. *Algorithms for Clustering Data.* Upper Saddle River, N.J.: Prentice Hall.

Dunkel, B.; and Soparkar, N. 1999. Data Organization and Access for Efficient Data Mining. In Proceedings of the Fifteenth International Conference on Data Engineering, 522. Los Alamitos, Calif: IEEE Computer Society.

Durham, S. K.; and Pearl, G. M. 2001. Computational Methods to Predict Drug Safety Liabilities. *Current Opinion in Drug Discovery and Development* 4(1): 110–115.

Dzeroski, S. 2001. Relational Data Mining Applications: An Overview. In *Relational Data Mining,* eds. S. Dzeroski, and N. Lavrač, 339–364. Berlin: Springer-Verlag.

Dzeroski, S.; and Lavrac, N. 1994. *Inductive Logic Programming: Techniques and Applications.* Chichester, UK: Ellis Horwood.

Dzeroski, S.; and Lavrac, N. 2001a. An Introduction to Inductive Logic Programming. In *Relational Data Mining,* eds. S. Dzeroski, and N. Lavrač, 48–73. Berlin: Springer-Verlag.

Dzeroski, S.; and Lavrac, N., eds. 2001b. *Relational Data Mining.* Berlin: Springer-Verlag.

Ederer, F.; Mantel, N. N.; and Myers, M. H. 1964. A Statistical Problem in Space and Time: Do Leukemia Cases Come in Clusters? *Biometrika* 20: 626–638.

Efron B.; and Tibshirani, R. J. 1993. *An Introduction to the Bootstrap.* New York: Chapman and Hall.

Egenhofer, M. J.; Herring, J.; and Mark, D. M. 1994. The 9-Intersection: Formalism and Its Use for Natural-Language Spatial Predicates, Tech. Rep., 94–1, National Center for Geographic Information and Analysis, Santa Barbara, Calif.

Eisenberg D.; Marcotte E. M.; and Xenarios I. 2001. Mining Literature for Protein-Protein Interactions. *Bioinformatics* 17(4): 359–363.

Eisenberg, A. 2002. With False Numbers, Data Crunchers Try to Mine the Truth. *New York Times* July 22.

Ellison, H. 1999. *Handbook of Chemical and Biological Warfare Agents.* Boca Raton, Fla.: CRC Press.

Ertoz, L.; Kumar, V.; Lazarevic, A.; Ozgur, A.; and Srivastava, J. 2003. A Comparative Study of Anomaly Detection Schemes in Network Intrusion Detection. In Proceedings of the Third SIAM International Conference on Data Mining. Philadelphia, Penn.: Society for Industrial and Applied Mathematics.

Espino, J. U.; and Wagner, M. M. 2001. Accuracy of ICD-9-Coded Chief Complaints and Diagnoses for the Detection of Acute Respiratory Illness. In *Journal of the American Medical Informatics Association,* Supplement issue on the Proceedings of the Annual Fall Symposium of the American Medical Informatics Association: 164–168.

Esposito, F.; Lisi, F. A.; and Malerba, D. 2001. Mining Spatial Association Rules in Census Data. Paper presented at the Workshop on New Techniques and Technologies for Statistics and Exchange of Technology and Know-How, Crete, 18–22 June.

Estan, C.; and Verghese, G. 2001. New Directions in Traffic Measurement and Accounting. In Proceedings of the First ACM SIGCOMM Workshop on Internet Measurement, 75–80. New York: Association for Computing Machinery.

Ester, M.; Frommelt, A.; Kriegel, H.-P.; and Sander, J. 1998. Algorithms for Characterization and Trend Detection in Spatial Databases. In *Proceedings of the Fourth International Conference on Knowledge Discovery and Data Mining,* 44–50. Menlo Park, Calif.: AAAI Press.

Ester, M.; Kriegel, H.-P.; Sander, J.; and Xu, X. 1997. Density-Connected Sets and Their Application for Trend Detection In Spatial Databases. In *Proceedings of the Third International Conference on Knowledge Discovery and Data Mining,* 10–15. Menlo Park, Calif.: AAAI Press.

Estivill-Castro, V.; and Lee, I. 2000. Autoclust: Automatic Clustering Via Boundary Extraction for Mining Massive Point-Data Sets, Tech. Rep. 2000-03, Dept. of Computer Science and Software Engineering, Univ. of Newcastle, Tyne, United Kingdom.

Etzioni, O. 1996. The World-Wide Web: Quagmire or Gold Mine? *Communications of the ACM* 39(11): 65–68.

Etzioni, O.; and Perkowitz, M. 1999. Adaptive Web Sites: Conceptual Cluster Mining. In *Proceedings of the Sixteenth International Joint Conference on Artificial Intelligence,* 264–269. San Francisco: Morgan Kaufmann Publishers.

Evfimievski, S. 2002. Randomization Techniques for Privacy Preserving Association Rule Mining. *SIGKDD Explorations* 4(2): 43–48.

Fabret, F.; Jacobsen, H.-A.; Llirbat, F.; Pereira, J.; Ross, K. A.; and Shasha, D. 2001. Filtering Algorithms and Implementation for Very Fast Publish / Subscribe Systems. In Proceedings of the ACM SIGMOD International Conference on Management of Data, 115–126. New York: Association for Computing Machinery, Special Interest Group on Management of Data.

Fan, W.; Stolfo, S.; and Zhang, J. 1999. The Application of AdaBoost for Distributed, Scalable and On-Line Learning. In Proceedings of the Fifth ACM SIGKDD International Conference on Knowledge Discovery and Data Mining, 362–366. New York: Association for Computing Machinery, Special Interest Group on Knowledge Discovery and Data Mining.

Fang, M.; Garcia-Molina, H.; Motwani, R.; Shivakumar, N.; and Ullman, J. 1998. Computing Iceberg Queries Efficiently. In *Proceedings of the Twenty-Fourth International Conference on Very Large Databases* 299–310. San Francisco: Morgan Kaufmann Publishers.

Fayyad, U.; Haussler, D.; and Stolorz, P. 1996. Mining Scientific Data. *Communications of the ACM* 39(11): 51–57.

Feit, S.; Kohane, I. S.; Mandl, K. D.; and Pena, B. M. G. 2000. Growth and Determinants of Access in Patient E-Mail and Internet Use. *Archives of Pediatric and Adolescent Medicine* 154(5): 508–511.

Fellegi, I. T.; and Sunter, A. B. 1969. A Theory for Record Linkage. *Journal of the American Statistical Association* 64: 1183–1210.

Ferman, A. M.; and Tekalp, A. M. 1999. Probabilistic Analysis and Extraction of Video Content. In Proceedings of the IEEE International Conference on Image Processing 2, 91–95. Los Alamitos, Calif.: IEEE Computer Society.

Ferman, A. M.; Huang, T. S.; Mehrotra, R.; Naphade, M.; Tekalp, A. M.; and Warnick, J. 1998. A High Performance Shot Boundary Detection Algorithm Using Multiple Cues. In Proceedings of IEEE International Conference on Image Processing, 2, 884–887. Los Alamitos, Calif.: IEEE Computer Society.

Fernandez, F. 1999. Statement Before the Subcommittee on Emerging Threats and Capabilities, Committee on Armed Services United States Senate (DARPA). Washington, D.C.: Government Printing Office.

Fersht, A.; Golbik, R.; Neira, J.; Nolting, B.; Schreiber, G.; and Soler-Gonzalez, A. 1997. The Folding Pathway of a Protein at High Resolution from Microseconds to Seconds. *Proceedings of the National Academy of Sciences of the United States of America* 94(3): 826–830.

Fidelis, K.; Judson, R.; Moult, J.; and Pedersen, J. 1995. A Large-Scale Experiment to Assess Protein Structure Prediction Methods. *Proteins* 23(3): II-V.

Fine, A.; Greenko, J.; Mostashari, F.; and Layton, M. 2003. Clinical Evaluation of the Emergency Medical Services (EMS) Ambulance Dispatch-Based Syndromic Surveillance System, New York City. *Journal of Urban Health* 80(2, suppl 1): i50–i56.

Finin, T.; Joshi, A.; Kagal, L.; and Undercoffer, J. 2002. Vigil: Enforcing Security in Ubiquitous Environments. Paper presented at the Grace Hooper Celebration of Women in Computing 2002 Conference, Vancouver, Canada, 9–12 October.

Finin, T.; Labrou, Y.; and Mayfield, J. 1997. KQML as an Agent Communication Language. In *Software Agents,* ed. J. Bradshaw. Menlo Park, Calif.: The AAAI Press / The MIT Press.

Fisher, D. 1996. Iterative Optimization and Simplification of Hierarchical Clusterings. *Journal of Artificial Intelligence Research* 4: 147–180.

Flach, P.; Kramer, S.; and Lavrač, N. 2001. Propositionalization Approaches to Relational Data Mining. In *Relational Data Mining,* eds. S. Džeroski, and N. Lavrač, 262–291. Berlin: Springer-Verlag.

Flake, G.; Giles, C. L.; and Lawrence, S. 2000. Efficient Identification of Web Communities. In Proceedings of the Sixth ACM SIGKDD International Conference on Knowledge Discovery and Data Mining, 150–160. New York: Association for Computing Machinery, Special Interest Group on Knowledge Discovery and Data Mining.

Floyd, S. 2002. Highspeed TCP for Large Congestion Windows. Berkeley, Calif.: ICSI Center for Internet Research.

Floyd, S.; Handley, M.; Kohler, E.; and Padhye J. 2003. Datagram Congestion Control Protocol (Dccp). Berkeley, Calif.: ICSI Center for Internet Research.

Ford Jr., L. R.; and Fulkerson, D. R. 1956. Maximal Flow Through a Network. *Canadian Journal of Mathematics* 8: 399–404.

Forman G.; and Zhang, B. 2000. Distributed Data Clustering Can Be Efficient and Exact. *SIGKDD Explorations* 2(2): 34–38.

Forman-Kay, J.; Kay, C.; Kay, L.; and Mok, Y. 1999. NOE Data Demonstrating a Compact Unfolded State for an SH3 Domain Under Non-Denaturing Conditions. *Journal of Molecular Biology* 289(3): 619–638.

Fortin, S. 1996. The Graph Isomorphism Problem, Tech. Rep. TR96-20, Dept. of Computing Science, Univ. of Alberta, Edmonton, Canada.

Foster, I.; and Kesselman, C. 1997. Globus: A Metacomputing Infrastructure Toolkit. *International Journal of Supercomputer Applications* 11(2): 115–128.

Foster, I.; and Kesselman, C. 1999. *The Grid: Blueprint for a New Computing Infrastructure.* San Francisco: Morgan Kaufmann Publishers.

Foster, I.; Kesselman, C.; and Tuecke, S. 2001. The Anatomy of the Grid: Enabling Scalable Virtual Organizations. *International Journal of Supercomputer Applications* 15(3).

Foti, D.; Lipari, D.; Pizzuti, C.; and Talia, D. 2000. Scalable Parallel Clustering for Data Mining on Multicomputers. In *Proceedings of the Third International Workshop on High Performance Data Mining HPDM00-IPDPS,* Lecture Notes in Computer Science 1800, 390–398, ed. J. Rolim. Berlin: Springer-Verlag.

Fowler, J.; Machiraju, R.; Soni, B.; Schroeder, W.; and Thompson, D. 2001. EVITA—Efficient Visualization and Interrogation of Terascale Datasets. In *Data Mining for Scientific and Engineering Applications,* eds. R. L. Grossman; C. Kamath; P. Kegelmeyer; V. Kumar; and R. R. Namburu, 257–279. Dortrecht, The Netherlands: Kluwer Academic Publishers.

Frank, I.; and Friedman, J. H. 1993. A Statistical View of Some Chemometrics Regression Tools. *Technometrics* 35(2): 109–148.

Fred, A. L. N.; and Jain, A. K. 2002. Data Clustering Using Evidence Accumulation. In Proceedings of the Sixteenth International Conference on Pattern Recognition IV, 276–280. Los Alamitos, Calif.: IEEE Computer Society.

Freitag, D. 1998. Information Extraction from HTML: Application of a General Learning Approach. In *Proceedings of the Sixteenth National Conference on Artificial Intelligence,* 517–523. Menlo Park, Calif.: AAAI Press / The MIT Press.

Freitag, D.; Joachims, T.; and Mitchell, T. 1997. Webwatcher: A Tour Guide for the World Wide Web. In *Proceedings of the Fourteenth International Joint Conference on Artificial Intelligence,* 770–777. San Francisco: Morgan Kaufmann Publishers.

Freitas, A. A.; and Lavington, S. H. 1998. *Mining Very Large Databases with Parallel Processing.* Dortrecht, The Netherlands: Kluwer Academic Publishers.

Freund, Y.; and Schapire, R. E. 1996. Experiments with a New Boosting Algorithm. In *Proceedings of the Thirteenth International Conference on Machine Learning,* 148–156. San Francisco: Morgan Kaufmann Publishers.

Friedman, N. 1998. The Bayesian Structural EM Algorithm. In *Proceedings of the Fourteenth Conference on Uncertainty in Artificial Intelligence,* 129–138. San Francisco: Morgan Kaufmann Publishers.

Friedman, N.; and Goldszmidt, M. 1997. Sequential Update of Bayesian Network Structure. In *Proceedings of the Thirteenth Conference on Uncertainty in Artificial Intelligence,* 165–174. San Francisco: Morgan Kaufmann Publishers.

Friedman, N.; Getoor, L.; Koller, D.; and Pfeffer, A. 1999. Learning Probabilistic Relational Models. Paper presented at the Sixteenth International Joint Conference on Artificial Intelligence, Stockholm, Sweden, Jul. 31–Aug. 6.

Friedman-Hill, E. J. 1997. Jess, the Java Expert System Shell. Distributed Computing Systems, Sandia National Laboratories, Livermore, Calif.

Fujita, T.; Geiger, F.; Hansch, C.; Muir, R. M.; Maloney, C. F.; and Streich, M. 1963. The Correlation of Biological Activity of Plant Growth-Regulators and Chloromycetin Derivatives with Hammett Constants and Partition Coefficients. *Journal of American Chemical Society* 85: 2817–1824.

Fujita, T.; Hansch, C.; Maolney, P. P.; and Muir, R. M. 1962. Correlation of Biological Activity of Phenoxyacetic Acids with Hammett Substituent Constants and Partition Coefficients. *Nature* 194: 178–180.

Gallopoulos, S.; Houstis, E. N.; and Rice, J. 1994. Computer as Thinker / Doer: Problem-Solving Environments for Computational Science. In *IEEE Computational Science and Engineering,* 11–23. Los Alamitos, Calif.: IEEE Computer Society.

Ganti, V.; Gehrke, J.; and Ramakrishnan, R. 2001. Demon: Mining and Monitoring Evolving Data. *IEEE Transactions on Knowledge and Data Engineering (TKDE)* 13(1): 50–63.

Ganti, V.; Gehrke, J.; and Ramakrishnan, R. 2002. Mining Data Streams Under Block Evolution. *SIGKDD Explorations* 3(2): 1–10.

Ganti, V.; Gehrke, J.; Loh, W.-Y.; and Ramakrishnan, R. 2002. A Framework for Measuring Differences in Data Characteristics. *Journal of Computer and System Sciences (JCSS)* 64(3): 542–578.

Garey, M. R.; and Johnson, D. S. 1979. *Computers and Intractability: A Guide to the Theory of NP-Completeness.* San Francisco: W. H. Freeman and Company.

Garofalakis, M. N.; Gehrke, J.; and Rastogi, R. 2002. Querying and Mining Data Streams: You Only Get One Look. In Proceedings of the ACM SIGMOD International Conference on Management of Data, 635. New York: Association for Computing Machinery, Special Interest Group on Management of Data.

Gehrke, J. 2002. Data Mining for Security and Privacy: Introduction to Special Issues on Privacy and Security. *SIGKDD Explorations* 4(2): i.

Gehrke, J. 2002. Research Problems in Data Stream Processing and Privacy-Preserving Data Mining. Paper presented at the Next Generation Data Mining Workshop, Baltimore, Md., November.

Gehrke, J. 2003. Letter from the Special Issue Editor. *IEEE Data Engineering Bulletin* 26(1): 2.

Gehrke, J.; Korn, F.; and Srivastava, D. 2001. On Computing Correlated Aggregates Over Continual Data Streams. In Proceedings of the ACM SIGMOD International Conference on Management of Data, 13–24. New York: Association for Computing Machinery, Special Interest Group on Management of Data.

Geist A.; Melechko, A.; Ostrouchov, G.; and Samatova, N. F. 2002. Rachet: An Efficient Cover-Based Merging of Clustering Hierarchies from Distributed Datasets. *An International Journal of Distributed and Parallel Databases* 11(2): 157–180.

Ghosh A. 1998. *E-Commerce Security, Weak Links and Strong Defenses.* New York: John Wiley and Sons.

Ghosh, A. K.; and Schwartzbard, A. 1999. A Study in Using Neural Networks for Anomaly and Misuse Detection. In Proceedings of the Eighth USENIX Security Symposium, 141–151. Berkeley, Calif.: USENIX—The Advanced Computing Systems Association.

Ghosh, J. 2002. Multiclassifier Systems: Back to the Future (Invited Paper). In *Multiple Classifier Systems.* Lecture Notes in Computer Science 2364, 1–15, eds. F. Roli; and J. Kittler. Berlin: Springer-Verlag.

Ghosh, J. 2003. Scalable Clustering. In *The Handbook of Data Mining,* ed. N. Ye, 247–277, Mahwah, N.J.: Lawrence Erlbaum Assoc.

Ghosh, J.; and Srivastava, J., eds. 2001. Papers presented at the Workshop on Web Mining, Siam Conference on Data Mining, Chicago Il., April.

Ghosh, S.; Kargupta, H.; and Sivakumar, K. 2002. Dependency Detection in Mobimine and Random Matrices. In *Proceedings of the Sixth European Conference on Principles and Practice of Knowledge Discovery in Databases,* 250–262. Berlin: Springer-Verlag.

Giarratano, J.; and Riley, G. 1998. *Expert Systems Principles and Programming.* Third Edition. Boston, Mass.: PWS Publishing Company.

Gibbons, P. B.; and Matias, Y. 1999. Synopsis Data Structures for Massive Data Sets. In *External Memory Algorithms, DIMACS Series in Discrete Mathematics and Theoretical Computer Science,* 50, 39–70. Providence, Rh. Is.: American Mathematical Society.

Gibson, D.; Kleinberg, J. M.; and Raghavan, P. 1998. Inferring Web Communities from Link Topology. In Proceedings of the Ninth ACM Conference on Hypertext and Hypermedia: Links, Objects, Time and Space—Structure in Hypermedia Systems, 225–234. New York: Association for Computing Machinery.

Gieger, D.; and Heckerman, D. 1995. Learning Bayesian Networks: A Unification for Discrete and Gaussian Domains. In Proceedings of the Eleventh Conference on Uncertainty in Artificial Intelligence, 274–284. San Francisco: Morgan Kaufmann Publishers.

Gilbert, A. C.; Kotidis, Y.; Muthukrishnan, S.; and Strauss, M. 2001. Surfing Wavelets on Streams: One-Pass Summaries for Approximate Aggregate Queries. In Proceedings of the Twenty-Seventh International Conference on Very Large Databases, 79–88. San Francisco: Morgan Kaufmann Publishers.

Gilks, W.; S. Richardson; and D. Spiegelhalter. 1996. Markov Chain Monte Carlo in Practice. Boca Raton, Fla.: Chapman and Hall.

Girosi, F.; Niyogi, P.; and Poggio, T. 1998. Incorporating Prior Information in Machine Learning by Creating Virtual Examples. Proceedings of the IEEE 86(11): 2196–2209.

Glass. Robert L.; and Vessey, Iris 1995. Contemporary Application-Domain Taxonomies. IEEE Software 12(4): 63–76.

Gleb, Frank; Jenkins, Jessica; and Fikes, Richard. JTP: An Object Oriented Modular Reasoning System. Knowledge Systems Laboratory, Stanford Univ., Stanford, Calif.

Gobel, U.; Sander, C.; Schneider, R.; and Valencia, A. 1994. Correlated Mutations and Residue Contacts in Proteins. Proteins 18: 309–317.

Goldberg, H.; and Jensen, D. eds. 1998. In Artificial Intelligence and Link Analysis: Papers from the 1998 AAAI Fall Symposium, ed. David Jensen and Henry Goldberg. Tech. Rep. FS-98-01, American Association for Artificial Intelligence, Menlo Park, Calif.

Goldman, C. V.; Mor, Y.; and Rosenschein, J. S. 1995. Using Reciprocity to Adapt to Others. In Adaption and Learning in Multi-Agent Systems, Lecture Notes in Artificial Intelligence 1042, 164–176, eds. G. Weiss; and S. Sen. New York: Springer-Verlag.

Goldreich, O.; Micali, S.; and Wigderson, A. 1987. How to Play Any Mental Game—A Completeness Theorem for Protocols with Honest Majority. In Proceedings of the Nineteenth Annual ACM Symposium on the Theory of Computing, 218–229. New York: Association for Computing Machinery.

Golombek, D. A.; Heyes, J. J. E.; McLean, B. J.; and Payne, H. E. 1998. New Horizons from Multi-Wavelength Sky Surveys: Proceedings of the 179th Symposium of the International Astronomical Union, International Astronomical Union Symposia 179, Dortrecht, The Netherlands: Kluwer Academic Publishers.

Gorodetski, V.; Karsaev, O.; Popyack, L.; and Skormin, V. 2000. Distributed Learning in a Data Fusion Systems. Paper presented at the Conference of the World Computer Congress (WCC-2000) Intelligent Information Processing (IIP 2000), Beijing, China.

Gouda, K.; and Zaki, M. J. 2001. Fast Vertical Mining Using Diffsets, Tech. Rep. 01-1, 2001 11, Rensselaer Polytechnic Institute, Troy, N.J.

Granger, C. W. J. 1989. Combining Forecasts–Twenty Years Later. Journal of Forecasting 8(3): 167–173.

Green, P. J.; and Richardson, S. 2002. Hidden Markov Models for Disease Mapping. Journal of the American Statistical Association 97(460): 1055–1070.

Grossman, R. L. 2002. Finding Bad Guys in Distributed Streaming Data Sets. Panel Presentation on Resource and Location Aware Data Mining, Second SIAM International Workshop on High Performance Data Mining, Arlington, Va., April 13.

Grossman, R. L.; Bailey, S.; Ramu, A.; Malhi, B.; Sivakumar, H.; and Turinsky, A. 1999. Papyrus: A System for Data Mining Oover Local and Wide Area Clusters and Super-Clusters. Paper presented at the ACM International Conference on Supercomputing, Rhodes, Greece, June 20–25.

Grossman, R. L.; Gu, Y.; Hanley, D.; Hong, X.; Lillethun, D.; Levera, J.; Mambretti, J.; Mazzucco, M.; and Weinberger, J. 2002. Experimental Studes Using Photonic Data Services at Igrid 2002. *Journal of Future Computer Systems* 19(6): 945–955.

Grossman, R. L.; Levera, J.; and Mazzucco, M. 2002. Aggregate Queries on Streams of Data Using a Small Buffer. UIC Laboratory for Advanced Computing Tech. Rep. 2002, Univ. of Illinois, Chicago, Ill.

Grossman, R. L.; Mazzucco, M.; Sivakumar, H.; and Pan, Y. Forthcoming. Simple Available Bandwidth Utilization Library for Highspeed Wide Area Networks. *Journal of Supercomputing.*

Grossman, R. L.; Sivakumar, H.; and Bailey, S. 2000. Psockets: The Case for Application-Level Network Striping for Data Intensive Applications Using High Speed Wide Area Networks. Paper presented at the ACM IEEE International Conference on Supercomputing (SC2000), Dallas, Tx., Nov. 4–10.

Grossman, R. L.; and Moore, R. 1996. Workshop on Scientific Data Management, Mining, Analysis, and Assimilation, San Diego Supercomputer Center.

Grossman, R. L.; Kamath, C.; Kumar, V.; and Namburu, R. 2000. Workshop on Mining Scientific Datasets, Univ. of Minnesota, Minneapolis, Minn.

Grossman, R.; and Mazzucco, M. 2002. Dataspace—A Web Infrastructure for the Exploratory Analysis and Mining of Data. *IEEE Computing in Science and Engineering* 4(4): 44–51.

Grossman, R.; Hornick, M.; and Meyer, G. 2002. Data Mining Standards Initiatives. *Communications of the ACM* 45(8): 59-61. Gruber, T. R. 1992. A Translation Approach to Portable Ontology Specification. *Knowledge Representation* 5(2): 199–220.

Gruber, T. R. 1993. Towards Principles for the Design of Ontologies Used for Knowledge Sharing. In *Formal Ontology in Conceptual Analysis and Knowledge Representation,* eds. N. Guarino and R. Poli. Dortrecht, The Netherlands: Kluwer Academic Publishers.

Guha, B.; and Mukherjee, B. 1997. Network Security via Reverse Engineering of TCP Code: Vulnerability Analysis and Proposed Solutions. *IEEE Network Magazine* 11(4): 40–48.

Guha, S.; Meyerson, A.; Mishra, N.; Motwani, R.; and O'Callaghan, L. 2002. High-Performance Clustering of Streams and Large Data Sets. In Proceedings of the Eighteenth International Conference on Data Engineering (ICDE), 685–694. Los Alamitos, Calif.: IEEE Computer Society.

Guha, S.; Mishra, N.; Motwani, R.; and O'Callaghan, L. 2000. Clustering Data Streams. Paper presented at the Forty-first Annual Symposium on Foundations of Computer Science (FOCS'00), Redondo Beach, Calif., Nov. 12–14.

Guo, Y.; and Sutiwaraphun, J. 2000. Distributed Learning with Knowledge Probing: A New Framework for Distributed Data Mining. In *Advances in Distributed and Parallel Knowledge Discovery,* eds. H. Kargupa, and P. Chan, 113–131. Menlo Park, Calif.: AAAI Press.

Haarslev, V.; and Möller, R. 2001. RACER: Renamed ABox and Concept Expression Reasoner. Inference Engine. Hamburg, Germany: Technische Universität Hamburg-Harburg.

Haas, P. J.; and Hellerstein, J. M. 2001. Online Query Processing. In Proceedings of the ACM SIGMOD International Conference on Management of Data, 623. New York: Association for Computing Machinery, Special Interest Group on Management of Data.

Hall, B. H.; Jaffe, A.; and Trajtenberg, M. 2000. Market Value and Patent Citations: A First Look. NBER Working Paper (W7741), June. National Bureau of Economic Research, Cambridge, Mass.

Hall, D.; and Llinas, J. 2001. *Handbook of Multisensor Data Fusion.* Boca Raton, Fla.: CRC Press.

Hamblen, M. 2002. Privacy Algorithms: Technology-Based Protections Could Make Personal Data Impersonal. *Computerworld* (Oct. 14).

Hamilton, J. 1990. Analysis of Time Series Subject to Changes in Regime. *Journal of Econometrics* 45(1–2): 39–70.

Hamilton, J. 1994. *Time Series Analysis.* Princeton, N.J.: Princeton Univ. Press.

Hamzaoglu, I.; Kargupta, H.; and Stafford, B. 1997. Scalable, Distributed Data Mining Using an Agent Based Architecture. In *Proceedings of the Third International Conference on Knowledge Discovery and Data Mining,* 211–214. Menlo Park, Calif.: AAAI Press.

Han, B.; Obradovic, Z.; and Vucetic, S. 2003. Re-Ranking Medline Citations by Relevance to a Difficult Biological Query. Paper presented at the IAESTED International Conference Neural Networks and Computational Intelligence, Cancun, Mexico, 19–21 May.

Han, E.-H.; Karypis, G.; and Kumar, V. 1999. Chameleon: Hierarchical Clustering Using Dynamic Modeling. *IEEE Computer* 32(8): 68–75.

Han, E.-H.; Karypis, G.; and Kumar, V. 2001. Data Mining for Turbulent Flows. In *Data Mining for Scientific and Engineering Applications,* eds. C. Kamath; P. Kegelmeyer; V. Kumar; and R. Namburu, 239–256. Dortrecht, The Netherlands: Kluwer Academic Publishers.

Han, E.; Joshi, M.; Karypis, G.; and Kumar, V. 2000. Parallel Algorithms for Data Mining. In *CRPC Parallel Computing Handbook,* eds. J. Dongarra; I. Foster; G. Fox; K. Kennedy; L. Torczon; and A. White. San Francisco: Morgan Kaufmann.

Han, J.; and Kamber, M. 2001. *Data Mining: Concepts and Techniques.* San Francisco: Morgan Kauffmann Publishers.

Han, J.; and Koperski, K. 1995. Discovery of Spatial Association Rules in Geographic Information Databases. In *Proceedings of the Fourth International Symposium on Large Spatial Databases,* Lecture Notes in Computer Science 951, 47–66, eds. M. J. Egenhofer, and J. R. Herring. New York: Springer-Verlag.

Han, J.; and Miller, H. J., eds. 2001. *Geographic Data Mining and Knowledge Discovery.* London: Taylor and Francis.

Han, J.; Kamber, M.; and Tung, A. 2001. Spatial Clustering Methods in Data Mining: A Survey. In *Geographic Data Mining and Knowledge Discovery.* eds. J. Han and H. Miller, 188–217. London: Taylor and Francis.

Han, J.; Pei, J.; and Yin, Y. 2000. Mining Frequent Patterns Without Candidate Generation. In Proceedings of the ACM SIGMOD International Conference on Management of Data, 1–12. New York: Association for Computing Machinery, Special Interest Group on Management of Data.

Han, J.; Xin, M.; and Zaiane, O. R. 1998. Discovering Web Access Patterns and Trends by Applying Olap and Data Mining Technology on Web Logs. In Proceedings of Advances in Digital Libraries Conference, 19. Los Alamitos, Calif.: IEEE Computer Society.

Hand, D. J.; Mannila, H.; and Smyth, P. 2001. *Principles of Data Mining.* Cambridge, Mass.: The MIT Press.

Hand, D.; Keim, D.; and Ng, R. eds. 2002. Proceedings of the Eighth ACM SIGKDD International Conference on Knowledge Discovery and Data Mining. New York: Association for Computing Machinery, Special Interest Group on Knowledge Discovery and Data Mining.

Handley, M.; Katabi, D.; and Rohrs, C. 2002. Congestion Control for High Bandwidth-Delay Product Networks. In Proceedings of the 2002 Conference on Applications, Technologies, Architectures, and Protocols for Computer Communications, 89–102. New York: Association for Computing Machinery.

Hardin, C.; Luthey-Schulten, Z.; and Pogorelov, T. 2002. Ab Initio Protein Structure Prediction. *Current Opinion in Structural Biology* 12(2): 176–181.

Harman, D.; and Voorhees, E. M. 1996. Overview of the Fifth Text Retrieval Conference. In The Fifth Text Retrieval Conference (TREC-5), NIST Special Publication 500-238. Gaithersburg, Md.: National Institute of Standards and Technology.

Harmelen, F.; Hendler, J.; Horrocks, I.; McGuinness, D.; Patel-Schneider, P.; and Stein, L. 2003. Web Ontology Language (OWL) Reference Version 1. Cambridge, Mass.: W3C World Wide Web Consortium.

Haveliwala, T. 2002. Topic-Sensitive Page Rank. Paper presented at the Eleventh International World Wide Web Conference, Honolulu, Hawaii, 7–11 May.

Hawkins, D. 1980. *Identification of Outliers.* New York: Chapman and Hall.

Heckman, J. 1979. Sample Selection Bias as a Specification Error. *Econometrica* 47(1): 153–161.

Henderson, D. A. 1999. The Looming Threat of Bioterrorism. *Science* 283(5406): 1279–1282.

Hendler, J. 2000. DARPA Agent Markup Language. Arlington, Va.: BBN, Inc. (www.daml.org).

Hendler, J. A.; and Horrocks, I., eds. 2002. *The Semantic Web—ISWC 2002: First International Semantic Web Conference, Sardinia, Italy, June 2002, Proceedings,* Lecture Notes in Computer Science 2342, New York: Springer-Verlag.

Hershberger, D. E.; and Kargupta, H. 2001. Distributed Multivariate Regression Using Wavelet-Based Collective Data Mining. *Journal of Parallel and Distributed Computing* 61(3): 372–400.

Hershberger, D.; Johnson, E.; Kargupta, H.; and Park, B. 2000. Collective Data Mining: A New Perspective Towards Distributed Data Mining. In *Advances in Distributed and Parallel Knowledge Discovery,* eds. P. Chan, and H. Kargupta, 133–184. Menlo Park, Calif.: AAAI Press / The MIT Press.

Hinton G. E.; Jacobs R. A.; Jordan M. I.; and Nowlan S. J. 1991. Adaptive Mixtures of Local Experts. *Neural Computation* 3(1): 79–87.

Hoballah, I; and Varshney, P. 1989. Distributed Bayesian Signal Detection. *IEEE Transactions on Information Theory* 35(5): 995–1000.

Hobbs, M. H. 1996. Spatial Clustering Using a Genetic Algorithm. In *Innovations in GIS 3,* ed. D. Parker, 85–95. London: Taylor and Francis.

Hobohm, U.; and Sander, C. 1994. Enlarged Representative Set of Protein Structures. *Protein Science* 3(3): 522–524.

Hoch, R.; Lee, J.; Podlaseck, M.; and Schonberg, E. 2001. Visualization and Analysis of Click-stream Data of Online Stores for Understanding Web Merchandising. *Data Mining and Knowledge Discovery* 5(1/2): 59–84.

Hoche, S.; and Wrobel, S. 2001. Relational Learning Using Constrained Confidence-Rated Boosting. In *Proceedings of the Eleventh International Conference on Inductive Logic Programming,* Lecture Notes in Artificial Intelligence 2157, 51–64, eds. C. Rouveirol, and M. Sebag. Berlin: Springer-Verlag.

Hogan, J. W.; Krieger, N.; Lemieux, K.; Waterman, P.; and Zierler, S. 2001. On the Wrong Side of the Tracts? Evaluating the Accuracy of Geocoding In Public Health Research. *American Journal of Public Health* 91(7): 1114–1116.

Holland, J. H. 1975. *Adaptation in Natural Artificial Systems.* Ann Arbor, Mich.: Univ. of Michigan Press.

Honig, B. 1999. Protein Folding: From the Levinthal Paradox to Structure Prediction. *Journal of Molecular Biology* 293(2): 283–293.

Hopcroft, J.; and Ullman, J. 1979. *Introduction to Automata Theory, Languages and Computation.* Reading, Mass.: Addison-Wesley Publishing Co.

Horling, B.; Klassner, F.; Lesser, V. R.; Raja, A.; Wagner, T.; and Zhang, S. X. Q. 1998. Big: A Resource Bound Information Gathering Agent. In *Proceedings of the Fifteenth National Conference on Artificial Intelligence,* 539–546. Menlo Park, Calif.: AAAI Press / The MIT Press.

Hotho, A.; Maedche, A.; Staab, S.; and Studer, R. 2001. SEAL-II—The Soft Spot Between Richly Structured and Unstructured Knowledge. *Journal of Universal Computer Science* 7(7): 566–590.

Hovig, E.; Jenssen, T. K.; Komorowski, J.; and Laegreid, A. 2001. A Literature Network of Human Genes for High-Throughput Analysis of Gene Expression. *Nature Genetics* 28(1): 21–28.

Hsu, W.; Liu, B.; and Ma, Y. 1998. Integrating Classification and Association Rule Mining. In *Proceedings of the Fourth International Conference on Knowledge Discovery and Data Mining,* 8–86. Menlo Park, Calif.: AAAI Press.

Huang, J.; Liu, Z.; and Wang, Y. 1998. Classification of TV Programs Based on Audio Information Using Hidden Markov Model. In Proceedings of the 1998 IEEE Second Workshop on Multimedia Signal Processing, 27–32. Piscataway, N.J.: The Institute of Electrical and Electronics Engineers, Inc.

Huang, T. S.; Naphade, M. R.; and Wang, R. 2001. Supporting Audiovisual Query Using Dynamic Programming. In Proceedings of the Ninth ACM International Conference on Multimedia, 411–420. New York: Association for Computing Machinery.

Huang, W.; Johnson, E.; Kargupta, H.; and Krishnamoorthy S. 2001. Distributed Clustering Using Collective Principal Component Analysis. *Knowledge and Information Systems Journal* (Special Issue on Distributed and Parallel Knowledge Discovery) 3(4): 422–448.

Huang, W.; Kargupta, H.; Krishnamrthy, S.; Park, B.; and Wang, S. 2000. Collective Principal Component Analysis from Distributed, Heterogeneous Data. In *Proceedings of the Fourth European Conference on the Principals of Data Mining and Knowledge Discovery,* Lecture Notes in Computer Science 1910, 452–457, eds. J. Komorowski; D.A. Zighed; and J. Zytkow. Berlin: Springer-Verlag.

Huffman D. 1952. A Method for the Construction of Minimum Redundancy Codes. *Proceedings of the Institute of Radio Engineers* 40: 1098–1101.

Hugh-Jones, M.; Guillemin, J.; Langmuir, A.; Meselson, M.; Popova, I.; Shelokov, A.; and Yampolskaya, O. 1994. The Sverdlovsk Anthrax Outbreak of 1979. *Science* 266(18 November): 1202–1208.

Hussain, F.; and Jeong, J. 1995. On the Identification of a Vortex. *Journal of Fluid Mechanics* 285: 69–94.

Imafuji, N.; and Kitsuregawa, M. 2002. Effects of Maximum Flow Algorithm on Identifying Web Community. In Proceedings of the Fourth International Workshop on Web Information and Data Management, 43–48. New York: Association for Computing Machinery.

Inokuchi, A.; Motoda, H.; and Washio, T. 2000. An Apriori-Based Algorithm for Mining Frequent Substructures from Graph Data. In *Proceedings of the Fourth European Conference on Principles and Practice of Knowledge Discovery in Databases,* 13–23. Berlin: Springer-Verlag.

Inokuchi, A.; Motoda, H.; Nishimura, K.; and Washio, T. 2002. A Fast Algorithm for Mining Frequent Connected Subgraphs, Tech. Rep. RT0448, IBM Research, Tokyo Research Laboratory, Tokyo.

Jacobson, V.; R. Braden, and D. Borman. TCP Extensions for High Performance. IETF RFC 1323, May, 1992.

Jacquez, G. M. 1996. AK Nearest Neighbour Test for Space-Time Interaction. *Statistics in Medicine* 15(17–18): 1935–1949.

Javitz, H. S.; and Valdes, A. 1993. The Nides Statistical Component: Description and Justification, Tech. Rep., Computer Science Laboratory, SRI International, Menlo Park, Calif.

Jennings, N.; and Woolridge, M. 1995. *Intelligent Agents: ECAI-94 Workshop on Agent Theories, Architectures, and Languages.* New York: Springer-Verlag.

Jensen, D.; and Neville, J. 2000. Iterative Classification in Relational Data. In Learning Statistical Models from Relational Data: Papers from the AAAI Workshop, 13–20. Tech. Rep. WS-00-006, American Association for Artificial Intelligence, Menlo Park, Calif.

Jensen, F. 1996. *An Introduction to Bayesian Networks.* New York: Springer-Verlag.

Jensen, V. C.; and Soparkar, N. 2000. Frequent Itemset Counting Across Multiple Tables. Paper presented at the Fourth Pacific-Asia Conference on Knowledge Discovery and Data Mining, Kyoto, Japan, 18–20 April.

Jhung, Y.; and Swain, P. H. 1996. Bayesian Contextual Classification Based on Modified M-Estimates and Markov Random Fields. *IEEE Transaction on Pattern Analysis and Machine Intelligence* 34(1): 67–75.

Jiang, M.; Machiraju, R.; and Thompson, D. 2002a. A Novel Approach to Vortex Core Region Detection. Paper presented at the Joint Eurographics-IEEE TCVG Symposium on Visualization, Barcelona, Spain, May.

Jiang, M.; Machiraju, R.; and Thompson, D. 2002b. Geometric Verification of Swirling Features in Flow Fields. In Proceedings of the 2002 IEEE Conference on Visualization, 307–314. Los Alamitos, Calif.: IEEE Computer Society.

Jin, C.; Wei, D.; Low, S. H.; Buhrmaster, G.; Bunn, J.; Choe, D. H.; Cottrell, R. L. A.; Doyle, J. C.; Feng, W.; Martin, O.; Newman, H.; Paganini, F.; Ravot, S.; and Singh, S. 2003. Fast TCP: From Theory to Experiments. Unpublished paper, California Institute of Technology, Pasadena, Calif.

Joachims, T. 2002. Optimizing Search Engines Using Clickthrough Data. In Proceedings of the Eighth ACM SIGKDD International Conference on Knowledge Discovery and Data Mining, 133–142. New York: Association for Computing Machinery, Special Interest Group on Knowledge Discovery and Data Mining.

Johnson E.; and Kargupta, H. 1999. Collective, Hierarchical Clustering from Distributed, Heterogeneous Data. In *Revised Papers from Large-Scale Parallel Data Mining, Workshop on Large-Scale Parallel KDD Systems, SIGKDD,* Lecture Notes in Computer Science 1759, 221–244. Berlin: Springer-Verlag.

Johnson, E.; and Kargupta, H. 1999. Collective, Hierarchical Clustering from Distributed, Heterogeneous Data. In *Large-Scale Parallel KDD Systems,* Lecture Notes in Computer Science 1759, 221–244, eds. C. Ho, and M. Zaki. New York: Springer-Verlag.

Jolliffe, I. T. 1986. *Principal Component Analysis.* Berlin: Springer-Verlag.

Jones, D. T. 1999. Protein Secondary Structure Prediction Based on Position-Specific Scoring Matrices. *Journal of Molecular Biology* 292: 195–202.

Jonsson, E.; and Lindqvist, U. 1997. How to Systematically Classify Computer Security Intrusions. In Proceedings of the 1997 IEEE Symposium on Security and Privacy, 154–163. Los Alamitos, Calif.: IEEE Computer Society.

Joshi, A. 1995. To Learn or Not to Learn. In *Adaption and Learning in Multi-Agent Systems,* Lecture Notes in Artificial Intelligence 1042, 127–139, eds. G. Weiss and S. Sen. New York: Springer-Verlag.

Joshi, M.; and Kumar, V. 2003. Credos: Classification Using Ripple Down Structure (A Case for Rare Classes). In Proceedings of the Nineteenth International Conference on Data Engineering (ICDE). Los Alamitos, Calif.: IEEE Computer Society.

Kamath, C. 2001. On Mining Scientific Datasets. In *Data Mining for Scientific and Engineering Applications,* eds. R. L. Grossman; C. Kamath; P. Kegelmeyer; V. Kumar; and R. R. Namburu, 1–21. Dortrecht, The Netherlands: Kluwer Academic Publishers.

Kamath, C. 2002. Introduction to Scientific Data Mining. Paper presented at the Mathematical Challenges in Scientific Data Mining, Short Program at the Institute for Pure and Applied Mathematics, Los Angeles, Calif., 14–18 January.

Kamath, K.; and Musick, R. 2000. Scalable Data Mining Through Fine-Grained Parallelism: The Present and the Future. In *Advances in Distributed and Parallel Knowledge Discovery,* eds. P. Chan, and H. Kargupta, 29–77. Cambridge, Mass.: The MIT Press.

Kanade, T.; and Nakamura, Y. 1997. Semantic Analysis for Video Contents Extraction—Spotting By Association in News Video. In Proceedings of the Fifth ACM International Conference on Multimedia, 393–401. New York: Association for Computing Machinery.

Kantarcioglu, M.; and Vaidya, J. 2002. An Architecture for Privacy-Preserving Mining of Client Information. In Proceedings of the IEEE International Conference on Data Mining Workshop on Privacy, Security, and Data Mining 14, 37–42. Sydney, Australia: Australian Computer Society.

Kargupta, H. 2000. Distributed Data Mining: Towards the Next Generation of Knowledge Discovery Systems. Paper presented at the Second Workshop on Mining Scientific Datasets, Minneapolis, Minn., 20–21 July.

Kargupta, H.; and Joshi, A. eds. 2002. Papers from the National Science Foundation Workshop on Next Generation Data Mining, Baltimore, Md., Univ. of Maryland.

Kargupta, H.; Kushraj, D.; Liu, L.; Park, B. H.; Pittie, S.; and Sarkar, K. 2002. MobiMine: Monitoring the Stock Market from a PDA. *SIGKDD Explorations* 3(2): 37–46.

Kargupta, H.; Liu, K.; and Ryan, J. 2003. Random Projection and Privacy Preserving Correlation Computation from Distributed Data, Tech. Rep. TR-CS-03-24, Dept. of Computer Science and Electrical Engineering, Univ. of Maryland, Baltimore County, Baltimore, Md.

Karypis, G.; and Kumar, V. 1998. A Fast and High Quality Multilevel Scheme for Partitioning Irregular Graphs. *SIAM Journal on Scientific Computing* 20(1): 359–392.

Karypis, G.; and Kuramochi, M. 2001. Frequent Subgraph Discovery. In Proceedings of the 2001 IEEE International Conference on Data Mining, 313–320. Los Alamitos, Calif.: IEEE Computer Society.

Karypis, G.; and Kuramochi, M. 2002a. Discovering Geometric Frequent Subgraphs. In Proceedings of the 2002 IEEE International Conference on Data Mining, 258–265. Los Alamitos, Calif.: IEEE Computer Society.

Karypis, G.; and Kuramochi, M. 2002b. An Efficient Algorithm for Discovering Frequent Subgraphs, Tech. Rep. 02-026, Dept. of Computer Science, Univ. of Minnesota, Minneapolis, Minn.

Karypis, G.; and Kuramochi, M. 2002c. Efficient Candidate Generation by Joining for Frequent Subgraph Discovery, Tech. Rep. 02-36, Dept. of Computer Science, Univ. of Minnesota, Minneapolis, Minn.

Kato, H.; Nakayama, T.; and Yamane, Y. 2000. Navigation Analysis Tool Based on the Correlation Between Contents Distribution and Access Patterns. Paper presented at the Workshop on Web Mining for E-Commerce—Challenges and Opportunities (WebKDD 2000) at KDD 2000, Boston, Mass., 20 August.

Katz, R. H. 2002. Pervasive Computing: It's All About Network Services. Invited Talk presented at the International Conference on Pervasive Computing, Zurich, Switzerland, Aug. 26–28.

Kelly, T. 2002. Scalable TCP: Improving Performance in Highspeed Wide Area Networks. Paper presented at the First International Workshop on Protocols for Fast Long-Distance Networks, Geneva, Switzerland, 3–4 February.

Kemmerer, R. A.; and Vigna, G. 2002. Intrusion Detection: A Brief History and Overview. *Security and Privacy, A Supplement to IEEE Computer Magazine* 35(4): 27–30.

Kemp, C.; and Ramamohanarao, K. 2002. Long-Term Learning for Web Search Engines. In *Proceedings of the Sixth European Conference on Principles of Data Mining and Knowledge Discovery,* 263–274, Berlin: Springer-Verlag.

Kender, J. R.; and Liu, T. 2000. A Hidden Markov Model Approach to the Structure of Documentaries. Paper presented at the Workshop on Content Based Access to Image and Video Libraries Held in Conjunction with CVPR, Hilton Head Island, South Carolina, 13–15 June.

Kender, J. R.; and Yeo, B. L. 1998. Video Scene Segmentation Via Continuous Video Coherence. In Proceedings of the 1998 IEEE Conference on Computer Vision and Pattern Recognition, 367–373. Los Alamitos, Calif.: IEEE Computer Society.

Kenji, Y. 1997. Distributed Cooperative Bayesian Learning Strategies. In Proceedings of the Tenth Annual Conference on Computational Learning Theory, 250–262. New York: Association for Computing Machinery.

Keong, W.; and Ong, K. L. 2002. Mining Relationship Graphs for Effective Business Objectives. Paper presented at the Pacific-Asia Conference on Knowledge Discovery and Data Mining, Taiwan, May.

Kernighan, B.; and Lin, S. 1970. An Efficient Heuristic Procedure for Partitioning Graphs. *Bell Systems Technical Journal* 49(2): 291–307.

Khan, F.; Kim, J.; Kirchhoff, F.; and Wilkins, J. 2000. Stability of Si-Interstitial Defects: from Point to Extended Defects. *Physical Review Letters* 84(3): 503.

Kifer, M.; Lausen, G.; and Wu, J. 1995. Logical Foundations of Object-Oriented and Frame-Based Languages. *Journal of the ACM* 42(4): 741–843.

Kimball, R.; and Merx, R. 2000. *The Data Webhouse Toolkit—Building Web-Enabled Data Warehouse.* New York: Wiley Computer Publishing.

King, R. D.; Lewis, R. A.; Muggleton, S.; and Sternberg, J. E. 1992. Drug Design by Machine Learning: The Use of Inductive Logic Programming to Model the Structure-Activity Relationships of Trimethoprim Analogues Binding to Dihydrofolate Reductase. *Proceedings of the National Academy of Sciences of the United States of America* 89(24): 11322–11326.

King, R. D.; Muggleton, S. H.; Srinivasan, A.; and Sternberg, M. J. E. 1996. Structure-Activity Relationships Derived by Machine Learning: The Use of Atoms and Their Bond Connectivities to Predict Mutagenicity by Inductive Logic Programming. *Proceedings of the National Academy of Sciences of the United States of America* 93(1): 438–442.

Kitamoto, A. 2002. Spatio-Temporal Data Mining for Typhoon Image Collection. *Journal of Intelligent Information Systems* 19(1): 25–41.

Kitsuregawa, M.; and Reddy, P. K. 2002. An Approach to Build a Cyber-Community Hierarchy. Paper Presented at the Workshop on Web Analytics, Held in Conjunction with the Second SIAM International Conference on Data Mining, Arlington, Va., 11–13 April.

Kittler, J.; and Roli, F., eds. 2001. *Multiple Classifier Systems,* Lecture Notes in Computer Science 1857. New York: Springer-Verlag.

Kleinberg, J. M. 1999. Authoritative Sources in a Hyperlinked Environment. *Journal of the ACM* 46(5): 604–632.

Knorr, E. M.; and Ng, R. T. 1998. Algorithms for Mining Distance-Based Outliers in Large Datasets. In *Proceedings of the Twenty-Fourth International Conference on Very Large Data Bases,* 392–403. San Francisco: Morgan Kaufmann Publishers.

Knox, E. G. 1964. The Detection of Space-Time Interactions. *Applied Statistics* 13: 25–30.

Kohane, I. S. 2002. The Contributions of Biomedical Informatics to the Fight Against Bioterrorism. *Journal of the American Medical Informatics Association* 9(2): 116–119.

Kohavi. R. 2001. Mining E-Commerce Data: The Good, the Bad, and the Ugly. In Proceedings of the Seventh ACM SIGKDD International Conference on Knowledge Discovery and Data Mining, 8–13. New York: Association for Computing Machinery, Special Interest Group on Knowledge Discovery and Data Mining.

Kohavi, R.; Masand, B. M.; Spiliopoulou, M.; and Srivastava, J. eds. 2002. *WEBKDD 2001— Mining Web Log Data Across All Customers Touch Points,* Lecture Notes in Artificial Intelligence 2356. Berlin: Springer-Verlag.

Kohavi, R.; Spiliopoulou, M.; and Srivastava, J., 2001. Collection of Unpublished Papers presented at the WebKDD2000: Web Mining for E-Commerce—Challenges and Opportunities Workshop. Boston, Mass., Aug. 20.

Kohavi, R.; Masand, B. M.; Spiliopoulou, M.; and Srivastava, J. 2001. Mining Log Data Across All Customer Touchpoints. In *WEBKDD 2001—Mining Web Log Data Across All Customers Touch Points,* ed. R. Kohavi, B. M. Masand, M. Spiliopoulou, and J. Srivastava. Lecture Notes in Computer Science 2356. Berlin: Springer-Verlag.

Koller, D.; and Pfeffer, A. 1998. Probabilistic Frame-Based Systems. In *Proceedings of the Fifteenth National Conference on Artifical Intelligence,* 580–587. Menlo Park, Calif.: AAAI Press.

Kopena, Joe. 2002. DAMLJessKB. Geometric and Intelligent Computing Laboratory, Drexel Univ., Philadelpha, Penn.

Koplan, J. 2001. CDC's Strategic Plan for Bioterrorism Preparedness and Response. *Public Health Reports* 116(Supplement 2): 9–16.

Krishnapuram, R.; Joshi, A.; Nasaoui, O.; and Yi, L. 2001. Low-Complexity Relational Clustering Algorithms for Web Mining. *IEEE Transactions on Fuzzy Systems,* 9(4): 506–607.

Krusl, I. 1998. Software Vulnerability Analysis. Ph.D. diss., Dept. of Computer Science, Purdue Univ.

Kulldorf, M. 2001. Prospective Time Periodic Geographical Disease Surveillance Using Scan Statistics. *Journal of the Royal Statistical Society, Series A* 164(1): 61–72.

Kumar, R.; Raghavan, P.; Rajagopalan, S.; and Tomkins, A. 1999. Trawling the Web for Emerging Cyber-Communities. *Computer Networks* 31(11–16): 1481–1493.

Kumar, V.; and Tan, P. 2002. Discovery of Web Robot Sessions Based on Their Navigational Patterns. *Data Mining and Knowledge Discovery* 6(1): 9–35.

Kuramochi, M.; and Karypis, G. 2001. Frequent Subgraph Discovery. In Proceedings of the IEEE International Conference on Data Mining. Los Alamitos, Calif.: IEEE Computer Society.

Lam, W.; and Segre, A. M. 1997. Distributed Data Mining of Probabilistic Knowledge. In Proceedings of the Seventh International Conference on Distributed Computing Systems, 178–185, Los Alamitos, Calif.: IEEE Computer Society.

Lander, S.; and Lesser, V. R. 1992. Customizing Distributed Search Among Agents with Heterogeneous Knowledge. In Proceedings of the First International Conference on Information and Knowledge Management. New York: Association for Computing Machinery.

Lauritzen, S. L. 1995. The EM Algorithm for Graphical Association Models with Missing Data. *Computational Statistics and Data Analysis* 19: 191–201.

Lawrence, S. 2001. Online or Invisible? *Nature* 411(6837): 521.

Lawrence, S.; Giles, C. L.; and Bollacker, K. 1999. Digital Libraries and Autonomous Citation Indexing. *IEEE Computer* 32(6): 67–71.

Lazarevic, A.; and Obradovic, Z. 2002. Knowledge Discovery in Multiple Spatial Databases. *Neural Computing and Applications* 10(4): 339–350.

Lee, W. S.; Li, X.; Liu, B.; and Yu, P. S. 2002. Partially Supervised Classification of Text Documents. In *Proceedings of the Ninth International Conference on Machine Learning,* 387–394. San Francisco: Morgan Kaufmann Publishers.

Lee, W.; and Stolfo, S. 1998. Data Mining Approaches for Intrusion Detection. In Proceedings of the Seventh USENIX Security Symposium, 79–94. Berkeley, Calif.: USENIX, the Advanced Computing Systems Association.

Lee, W.; and Xiang, D. 2001. Information-Theoretic Measures for Anomaly Detection. In Proceedings of the 2001 IEEE Symposium on Security and Privacy, 130. Los Alamitos, Calif.: IEEE Computer Society.

Lee, W.; Mok, K.; and Stolfo, S. 2000. Adaptive Intrusion Detection: A Data Mining Approach. *Artificial Intelligence Review* 14(6): 533–567.

Lehnert, W.; and Sundheim, B. 1991. A Performance Evaluation of Text-Analysis Technologies. *AI Magazine* 12(3): 81–94.

Lempel, R.; and Moran,S. 2000. The Stochastic Approach for Link-Structure Analysis (SALSA) and the TKC Effect. *Computer Networks* 33(1–6): 387–401.

Levinson, S. E.; Liberman, M. Y.; Ljolje, A.; and Miller, L. G.. 1989. Speaker Independent Phonetic Transcription of Speech for Large Vocabulary Speech Recognition. Paper presented at the DARPA Speech and Natural Language Workshop, Philadelphia, Penn.

Levinthal, C. 1968. Are There Pathways for Protein Folding? *Journal de Chimie Physique* 65(1): 44–45.

Li, H.; and Parthasarathy, S. 2001. Automatically Deriving Multilevel Protein Structures Through Data Mining. Paper presented at the High Performance Computing Workshop on Bioinformatics and Computational Biology, Hyderabad, India, 17–20 December.

Li, S. 1995. *Markov Random Field Modeling in Computer Vision.* Berlin: Springer-Verlag.

Li, W.; Ogihara, M.; Parthasarathy, S.; and Zaki, M. J. 1996. Parallel Data Mining for Association Rules on Shared Memory Multi-Processors. In Proceedings of the 1996 ACM / IEEE Conference on Supercomputing (CDROM). New York: Association for Computing Machinery.

Li, W.; Parthasarathy, S.; and Zaki, M. J. 1997. A Localized Algorithm for Parallel Association Mining. In Proceedings of the Ninth Annual ACM Symposium on Parallel Algorithms and Architectures, 321–330. New York: Association for Computing Machinery.

Lillethun, D.; Mambretti, J.; and Weinberger, J. 2003. Odin: Path Services for Optical Networks. Demonstration of Advanced Optical Networking at Telecom 2003, Geneva, Switzerland, Oct. 12–18.

Lim, E. P.; Moh C. H.; and Ng, W. K. 2000. DTD-Miner: A Tool for Mining DTD from XML Documents. In Proceedings of the Second International Workshop on Advance Issues of E-Commerce and Web-Based Information Systems, 144–151. Los Alamitos, Calif.: IEEE Computer Society.

Lin, M.-J.; Miikkulainen, R.; and Ryan, J. 1997. Intrusion Detection with Neural Networks. In AI Approaches to Fraud Detection and Risk Management: Papers from the AAAI Workshop, 72–77. Tech. Rep. WS-97-07, American Association for Artificial Intelligence, Menlo Park, Calif.

Lindell, Y.; and Pinkas, B. 2000. Privacy Preserving Data Mining. In *Advances in Cryptology—CRYPTO 2000,* Lecture Notes in Computer Science 1880, 36–54, ed. M. Bellare. New York: Springer-Verlag.

Lindell, Y.; and Pinkas, B. 2002. Privacy Preserving Data Mining. *Journal of Cryptology* 15(3): 177–206.

Lippmann, R. P.; and Cunningham, R. K. 2000. Improving Intrusion Detection Performance Using Keyword Selection and Neural Networks. *Computer Networks* 34: 597–603.

Lisi, F. A.; and Malerba, D. 2001. An ILP Method for Spatial Association Rule Mining. Paper presented at the First Workshop on Multi-Relational Data Mining, Freiburg, Germany, 6 September.

Luo, J. 1999. Integrating Fuzzy Logic with Data Mining Methods for Intrusion Detection. Master's thesis, Dept. of Computer Science, Mississippi State Univ., Mississippi State, MS.

Maclin, R.; and Opitz, D. 1999. Popular Ensemble Methods: An Empirical Study. *Journal of Artificial Intelligence Research* 11: 169—198.

Madria, S. K.; Bhowmick, S. S.; Ng, W. K.; and Lim, E. P. 1999. Research Issues in Web Data Mining. In *Proceedings of the First International Conference on Data Warehousing and Knowledge Discovery (DAWAK99),* Lecture Notes in Computer Science 1676, 303–312. Berlin: Springer-Verlag.

Maedche, A.; and Staab, S. 2000. Discovering Conceptual Relations from Text. In *Proceedings of the Thirteenth European Conference on Artificial Intelligence,* 321–325. Amsterdam: IOS Press.

Magliveras, S. S.; Memon, N. D.; and Sayood, K. 1994. Lossless Compression of Multispectral Image Data. IEEE Transactions on Geoscience and Remote Sensing 32(2): 282–289.

Mambretti, J. Omninet. 2002. Northwestern Univ. International Center for Advanced Internet Research (iCAIR). Optical Metro Network Initiative, Evanston, Ill.

Mamoulis, N.; and Papdias, D. 2001. Multiway Spatial Joins. *ACM Transaction on Database Systems (TODS)* 26(4): 424–475.

Mandl, K. D.; and Olson, K. 2002. Use of Geographical Information from Hospital Databases for Real Time Surveillance (Abstract). *Pediatric Research* 51(4): 94.

Manganaris, S.; Christensen, M.; Zerkle, D.; and Hermiz, K. 1999. A Data Mining Analysis of Rtid Alarms. Paper presented at the Second International Workshop on Recent Advances in Intrusion Detection (RAID), West Lafayette, Ind., Sept. 7–9.

Manku, G. S.; and Motwani, R. 2002. Approximate Frequency Counts Over Data Streams. In *Proceedings of the Twenty-Eighth International Conference on Very Large Databases* 346–357. San Francisco: Morgan Kaufmann Publishers.

Mannila, H.; Toivonen, H.; and Verkamo, A. I. 1996. Discovering Generalized Episodes Using Minimal Occurrences. In *Proceedings of the Second International Conference on Knowledge Discovery and Data Mining,* 146–151. Menlo Park, Calif.: AAAI Press.

Mannila, H.; Toivonen, H.; and Verkamo, A. I. 1997. Discovery of Frequent Episodes in Event Sequences. *Data Mining and Knowledge Discovery* 1(3): 259–289.

Manning C. D.; and Schüze, H. 2000. *Foundations of Statistical Natural Language Processing.* Cambridge, Mass.: The MIT Press.

Martin, R. D.; and Yohai, V. 2001. Data Mining for Unusual Movements in Temporal Data. Paper presented at the KDD-01 Workshop on Temporal Data Mining, San Francisco, Calif., 26–29 August.

Masand, B. M.; and Spiliopoulou, M., eds. 2000. *Advances in Web Usage Analysis and User Profiling,* Lecture Notes in Artificial Intelligence 1836, Berlin: Springer-Verlag.

Masand, B.; and Spiliopoulou, M. 1999. Web Usage Analysis and User Profiling, 1999. In *Web Usage Analysis and User Profiling: International WEBKDD'99 Workshop,* Lecture Notes in Computer Science 1836, eds. M. M. Brij and M. Spiliopoulou. New York: Springer-Verlag.

Masand, B.; Spiliopoulou, M.; Srivastava, J.; and Zaiane, O. R., eds. 2002. *WEBKDD 2002— Mining Web Data for Discovery Usage Patterns and Profiles,* Lecture Notes in Computer Science 2703. Berlin: Springer-Verlag

Matthew V. Mahoney and Philip K. Chan. 2001. PHAD: Packet Header Anomaly Detection for Identifying Hostile Network Traffic, Tech. Rep. CS-2001-04, Dept. of Computer Sciences, Florida Institute of Technology, Melbourne, Fla.

Matzner, S.; Pierce, L.; and Sinclair, C. 1999. An Application of Machine Learning to Network Intrusion Detection. Paper presented at the Fifteenth Annual Computer Security Applications Conference, Phoenix, Ariz., 6–10 December.

McCallum, A.; Mitchell, T.; Nigam, K.; and Thrun, S. 2000. Text Classification from Labeled and Unlabeled Documents Using EM. *Machine Learning* 39(2–3): 103–134.

McClean, S.; Scotney, B.; and Greer, K. 2000. Conceptual Clustering Heterogeneous Distributed Databases. Paper presented at the Workshop on Distributed and Parallel Knowledge Discovery, Boston, Mass., Aug. 20.

McClelland, J.; and Rumelhart, D. 1986. *Parallel Distributed Processing: Explorations in The Microstructure of Cognition.* Cambridge, Mass.: The MIT Press.

McGuinnes, D. L.; and Noy, N. F. 2001. Ontology Development 101: A Guide to Creating Your First Ontology, Tech. Rep., Stanford Knowledge Systems Laboratory KSL-01-05 and Stanford Medical Informatics SMI-2001-0880, Stanford Univ., Stanford, Calif.

McHugh, J. 2000. Testing Intrusion Detection Systems: A Critique of the 1998 and 1999 DARPA Intrusion Detection System Evaluations as Performed by Lincoln Laboratory, 262–294. New York: Association for Computing Machinery.

McKay, B. D. 1990. Nauty Users Guide (Version 1. 5), Tech. Rep. TR-CS-90-02, Dept. of Computer Science, Australian National Univ., Canberra, Australia.

McKay, S. J.; Roule, T. J.; and Woessner, P. N. 2001. Evidence Extraction and Link Discovery (EELD) Seedling Project, Database Schema Description, Version 1. 0., Tech. Rep. 2862, Veridian Systems Division, Arlington, Va.

Melville, P.; Mooney, R. J.; and Nagarajan, R. 2001. Content-Boosted Collaborative Filtering. Paper presented at the ACM SIGIR Workshop on Recommender Systems, New Orleans, La., September.

Mendelzon, A. O.; and Rafiei, D. 2000. What Do the Neighbours Think? Computing Web Page Reputations. *IEEE Data Engineering Bulletin* 23(3): 9–16.

Merz, C. J.; and Pazzani, M. J. 1999. A Principal Components Approach to Combining Regression Estimates. *Machine Learning* 36(1–2): 9–32.

Miller, J. 2003. U. S. Is Deploying a Monitor System for Germ Attacks. *New York Times* January 22, 2003.

Mironova, S. Y. 2003. Integrating Network Storage into Information Retrieval Applications. Master's thesis, Dept. of Computer Science, Univ. of Tennessee, Nashville, Tenn.

Minsky, M. 1985. *The Society of Mind.* New York: Simon and Schuster.

Mish, F. C., ed. 1993. *Merriam-Webster's Collegiate Dictionary* Tenth Edition. Springfield, Mass.: Merriam-Webster, Inc.

Mitchell, T. 1999 The Role of Unlabeled Data in Supervised Learning. Paper presented at the Sixth International Colloquium on Cognitive Science, San Sebastian, Spain, 12–15 May.

Mo, K.; Nogues-Paegle J.; and Paegle, J. 1998. Predictability of the NCEP-NCAR Reanalysis Model During Austral Summer. *Monthly Weather Review* 126(12): 3135–3152.

Moe, W. 2002. Buying, Searching, or Browsing: Differentiating Between Online Shoppers Using In-Store Navigational Clickstream. *Journal of Consumer Psychology* 13(1–2) 29–40.

Montalenti, F.; Sørensen, M.; and Voter, A. 2001. Closing the Gap Between Experiment and Theory: Crystal Growth by Temperature Accelerated Dynamics. *Physical Review Letters* 87: 126101.

Moore, R. W.; Baru, C.; Marciano, R.; Rajasekar, A.; and Wan, M. 1999. Data-Intensive Computing. In *The Grid: Blueprint for a New Computing Infrastructure,* 105–129, ed. I. Foster and C. Kesselman. San Francisco: Morgan kaufmann, Publishers.

Morimoto, Y. 2001. Mining Frequent Neighboring Class Sets in Spatial Databases. In Proceedings of the Seventh ACM SIGKDD International Conference on Knowledge Discovery and Data Mining, 353–358. New York: Association for Computing Machinery, Special Interest Group on Knowledge Discovery and Data Mining.

Morphy, E. 2001. Amazon Pushes "Personalized Store for Every Customer." *E-Commerce Times* 28 September.

Moukas, A. 1996. Amalthaea: Information Discovery and Filtering Using a Multiagent Evolving Ecosystem. Paper presented at the First International Conference on Practical Applications of Intelligent Agents and Multi-Agent Technology, London, April.

Moult, J. 1999. Predicting Protein Three-Dimensional Structure. *Current Opinion in Biotechnology* 10(6): 583–588.

Muggleton, S. 1999. Scientific Knowledge Discovery Using Inductive Logic Programming. *Communications of the ACM* 42(11): 42–46.

Muggleton, S. 2003. Stochastic Logic Programs. *Journal of Logic Programming.*

Muggleton, S. H., ed. 1992. *Inductive Logic Programming.* New York: Academic Press.

Muralidhar, K.; Parsa, R. A.; and Sarathy, R. 2001. An Improved Security Requirement for Data Perturbation with Implications for E-Commerce. *Decision Science* 32(4): 683–698.

Muth, P.; O'Neil, P.; Pick, A.; and Weikum, G. 2000. The LHAM Log-Structured History Data Access Method. *The Very Large Data Bases Journal* 8(3–4): 199–221.

Naor, M.; and Pinkas, B. 2001. Efficient Oblivious Transfer Protocols. In Proceedings of the Twelfth Annual ACM-SIAM Symposium on Discrete Algorithms, 448–457. Philadelphia, Penn.: Society for Industrial and Applied Mathematics.

National Aeronautics and Space Administration (NASA). 1999. EOS Reference Handbook: A Guide to NASA's Earth Science Enterprise and the Earth Observing System.

National Aeronautics and Space Administration (NASA). 1999. Workshop on Issues in the Application of Data Mining to Scientific Data, Univ. of Alabama, Huntsville, AL.

National Aeronautics and Space Administration (NASA). 2002. Science Data Users Handbook. Landsat Project Science Office. Goddard Space Flight Center.

Nascimento, M. A.; and Silva, J. R. O. 1998. Towards Historical R-Trees. In Proceedings of the 1998 ACM Symposium on Applied Computing, 235–240. New York: Association for Computing Machinery.

Naus, J. I. 1965. The Distribution of the Size of the Maximum Cluster of Points on a Line. *Journal of the American Statistical Association* 60: 532–538.

Newell, A.; and Simon, H. 1963. GPS, A Program that Simulates Human Thought. In *Computers and Thought,* eds. E. Feigenbaum, and J. Feldman, 279–293. New York: McGraw-Hill.

Ng, R. 2001. Detecting Outliers from Large Datasets. In *Geographic Data Mining and Knowledge Discovery,* eds. J. Han, and H. J. Miller, 218–235. London: Taylor and Francis.

Ng, R.; and Han, J. 1994. Efficient and Effective Clustering Methods for Spatial Data Mining. In *Proceedings of the Twentieth International Conference on Very Large Databases,* 144–155. San Francisco: Morgan Kaufmann Publishers.

Nii, H. P. 1986. Blackboard Systems: The Blackboard Model of Problem Solving and The Evolution of Blackboard Architectures. *AI Magazine* 7(2): 38–53.

Ning, P., Jajodia, S., and Wang, X. S. 2001. Abstraction-Based Intrusion in Distributed Environments. *ACM Transactions on Information and Systems Security,* 4(4): 407–452.

Nolan, J. J.; Simon, R.; and Sood, A. K. 2001. An Atomic Approach to Agent-Based Imagery and Geospatial Problem Solving. Paper presented at the Second Asia Pacific Conference on Intelligent Agent Technology, Maebashi City, Japan, 23–26 October.

Nolan, J. J.; Simon, R.; and Sood, A. K. 2001. Developing an Ontology and ACL in an Agent-Based GIS. Paper presented at the Workshop on Ontologies in Agent Systems (OAS 2001), Montreal, Canada, 29 May.

Nolan, J. J.; Simon, R.; and Sood, A. K. 2002. Sadisco: A Scalable Agent Discovery and Composition Mechanism. In *Proceedings of the Second International Conference on Hybrid Intelligent Systems,* 519–528. Amsterdam: IOS Press.

Olmea, O.; and Valencia, A. 1997. Improving Contact Predictions by the Combination of Correlated Mutations and Other Sources of Sequence Information. *Folding and Design* 2: S25–S32.

O'Toole, T. 2001. The Problem of Biological Weapons: Next Steps for the Nation. *Public Health Reports* 116(Suppl.): 108–111.

Open GIS Consortium 1998. Open GIS Simple Features Specification for SQL, Revision 1. 0, Tech. Rep., Open GIS Consortium, Wayland, Mass.

Osmar R. Zaiane. 1998. From Resource Discovery to Knowledge Discovery on the Internet, Tech. Rep. TR 1998-13, Simon Fraser Univ., Burnaby, British Columbia, Canada.

Ozden, B.; Ramaswamy, S.; and Silberschatz, A. 1998. Cyclic Association Rules. In Proceedings of the Fourteenth International Conference on Data Engineering, 412–421. Los Alamitos, Calif.: IEEE Computer Society.

Padmanabhan, B.; and Tuzhilin, A. 1998. A Belief-Driven Method for Discovering Unexpected Patterns. In *Proceedings of the Fourth International Conference on Knowledge Discovery and Data Mining,* 4–100. Menlo Park, Calif.: AAAI Press.

Page, D. 2000. ILP: Just Do It! In *Proceedings of Computational Logic 2000,* 25-40, eds. J. Lloyd, V. Dahl, U. Furbach, M. Kerber, K. Lau, K. C, Palamidessi, L. Pereira, LY. Sagiv, and P. Stuckey, eds. Berlin: Springer-Verlag.

Page, L.; Brin, S.; Motwani, R.; and Winograd, T. 1998. The Pagerank Citation Ranking: Bringing Order to the Web. Tech. Rep., Stanford Digital Library Technologies Project, Stanford, Calif.

Pandey, A.; Srivastava, J.; and Shekhar, S. 2001. A Web Intelligent Prefetcher for Dynamic Pages Using Association Rules—A Summary of Results. Paper presented at the Workshop on Web Mining, Chicago, Ill., April 7.

Papadias, D.; Tao, Y.; Kalnis, P.; and Zhang, J. 2001. Efficient Olap Operations in Spatial Data Warehouses. In *Proceedings of the Seventh International Sympsium on Spatial and Temporal Databases,* 443–459. Berlin: Springer-Verlag.

Papadias, D.; Tao, Y.; Kalnis, P.; and Zhang, J. 2002. Indexing Spatio-Temporal Data Warehouses. In Proceedings of the Eighteenth International Conference on Data Engineering (ICDE), 166–175. Los Alamitos, Calif.: IEEE Computer Society.

Parent, S.; Mobasher, B.; and Lytinen, S. 2001. An Adaptive Agent for Web Exploration Based of Concept Hierarchies. Paper presented at the Ninth International Conference on Human Computer Interaction, New Orleans, La., Aug. 5–10.

Park, B.; and Kargupta, H. 2003. Distributed Data Mining: Algorithms, Systems, and Applications. In *The Handbook of Data Mining,* 241–258, ed. N. Ye. Mahweh, N.J.: Lawrence Erlbaum Associates.

Park, B.; Ayyagari, R.; and Kargupta, H. 2001. A Fourier Analysis-Based Approach to Learn Classifier from Distributed Heterogeneous Data. In Proceedings of the First SIAM Internation Conference on Data Mining, Chicago, Ill., 2001. Philadelphia, Penn.: Society for Industrial and Applied Mathematics.

Park, B.; Kargupta, H.; Johnson, E.; Sanseverino, E.; Hershberger, D.; and Silvestre, L. 2002. Distributed, Collaborative Data Analysis from Heterogeneous Sites Using a Scalable Evolutionary Technique. *Applied Intelligence* 16(1).

Park, B.-Y.; and Kargupta, H. 2003. Distributed Data Mining. In Ye, N., Ed., In *The Handbook of Data Mining,* 341–364, ed. N. Ye. Mahweh, N.J.: Lawrence Erlbaum Associates.

Parthasarathy, S., and Coatney, M. 2002. Efficient Discovery of Common Substructures in Macromolecules. In Proceedings of the IEEE International Conference on Data Mining, 362–369. Los Alamitos, Calif.: IEEE Computer Society.

Parthasarathy, S.; and Ogihara, M. 2000. Clustering Distributed Homogeneous Datasets. In *Proceedings of the Fourth European Conference on Principles of Data Mining and Knowledge Discovery,* Lecture Notes in Computer Science 1910, 566–574. Berlin: Springer-Verlag .

Parthasarathy, S.; and Subramonian, R. 2000. Facilitating Data Mining on a Network of Workstations. In *Advances in Distributed and Parallel Knowledge Discovery,* ed. H. Kargupta and P. Chan. Menlo Park, Calif.: AAAI Press.

Parthasarathy, S.; Kargupta, H.; Kumar, V.; Killicorn, D. S.; and Zaki, M., eds. 2002. Proceedings of the SIAM High Performance Data Mining Conference, Philadelphia, Pennsylvania. Philadelphia, Penn.: Society for Industrial and Applied Mathematics.

Parthasarathy, S.; Zaki, M.; Ogihara, M.; and Dwarkadas, S. 1999. Incremental and Interactive Sequence Mining. Paper presented at the Eighth International ACM Conference on Information and Knowledge Management (CIKM), Kansas City, Mo., Nov. 2–6.

Parthasarathy, S.; Zaki, M.; Ogihara, M.; and Li, W. 2001. Parallel Data Mining for Association Rules on Shared-Memory Systems. *Knowledge and Information Systems,* 3(1): 1–29.

Patrick, Y. G, 2002. The Design of a Platform for Distributed KDD Components. Paper presented at the Second SIAM International Conference on Data Mining, Philadelpha, Penn., April 11–13.

Pawelzik, K.; Kohlmorgen, J.; and Muller, K. R. 1996. Annealed Competition of Experts for a Segmentation and Classification of Switching Dynamics. *Neural Computation* 8(2): 340–356.

Pearl, J. 1988. *Probabilistic Reasoning in Intelligent Systems.* San Francisco: Morgan Kaufmann Publishers.

Pei, J.; Han, J.; and Mao, R. 2000. CLOSET: An Efficient Algorithm for Mining Frequent Closed Itemsets. In Proceedings of the ACM SIGMOD International Workshop on Data Mining and Knowledge Discovery (DMKD'00), Dallas, Tex., May 11.

Peng, K.; Vucetic, S.; Han, B.; Xie H.; and Obradovic, Z. 2003. Exploiting Unlabeled Data for Improving Accuracy of Predictive Data Mining. Paper presented at the Third IEEE International Conference on Data Mining, Melbourne Fla., Nov. 19–22.

Piatetsky-Shapiro, G. 1991. Discovery, Analysis, and Presentation of Strong Rules. In *Knowledge Discovery and Databases,* 229–248, ed. G. Piatetsky-Shapiro and W. Frawley. Menlo Park, Calif.: AAAI Press / The MIT Press.

Plank, J. S.; Atchley, S.; Ding, Y.; and Beck, M. 2002. Algorithms for High Performance, Wide-Area, Distributed File Downloads. Tech. Rep. UT-CS-02-485, Dept. of Computer Science, Univ. of Tennessee, October 2002.

Plank, J.; Bassi, A.; Beck, M.; Moore, T.; Swany, M.; and Wolski. R. 2001. Managing Data Storage in the Network. *IEEE Internet Computing* 5(5): 50–58.

Pohle, C.; and Spiliopoulou, M. 2001. Data Mining for Measuring and Improving the Success of Web Sites. *Data Mining and Knowledge Discovery* 5(1–2): 85–114.

Pohle, C.; Spiliopoulou, M.; and Teltzrow, M. 2002. Modeling and Mining Web Site Usage Strategies. Paper presented at the Multi-Konferenz Wirtschaftsinformatik, Nuernberg, Germany, 9–11 September.

Pokrajac, D.; Hoskinson, R. L.; and Obradovic, Z. In Press. Modeling Spatial-Temporal Data with a Short Observation History. *Knowledge and Information Systems* 5(3): 368–386.

Pollastri, G.; and Baldi, P. 2002. Prediction of Contact Maps by Recurrent Neural Network Architectures and Hidden Context Propagation from all Four Cardinal Corners. *Bioinformatics* 18(1): S62–70.

Pollock, D.; and Lowery, D. 2001. Emergency Medicine and Public Health: New Steps in Old Directions. *Annals of Emergency Medicine* 38(6): 675-683.

Poritz, A. B. 1982. Linear Predictive Hidden Markov Models and the Speech Signal. In Proceedings of the International Conference on Acoustics, Speech, and Signal Processing (ICASSP), 1291–1294. Piscataway, N.J.: The Institute of Electrical and Electronics Engineers, Inc.

Portela, L. M. 1997. On the Identification and Classification of Vortices. Ph.D. diss., Dept. of Computer Science, Stanford Univ., Stanford, Calif.

Prasetyo, B.; Pramudiono, I.; Takahashi, K.; Toyoda, M.; and Kitsuregawa, M. 2002. Naviz: User Behavior Visualization of Dynamic Page. Paper presented at the Pacific-Asia Conference on Knowledge Discovery and Data Mining, Taipei, Taiwan, May 6–8.

Primmerman, C. A. 2000. Detection of Biological Agents. *Lincoln Laboratory Journal* 12: 3-31.

Prodromidis, A.; Chan, P.; and Stolfo, S. 2000. Meta-Learning in Distributed Data Mining Systems: Issues and Approaches. In *Advances in Distributed and Parallel Knowledge Discovery,* ed. H. Kargupta and P. Chan. Menlo Park, Calif.: AAAI / The MIT Press.

Provost F., Jensen D., and Oates T. 1999. Efficient Progressive Sampling. In Proceedings of the Fifth ACM SIGKDD International Conference on Knowledge Discovery and Data Mining. New York: Association for Computing Machinery Special Interest Group on Knowledge Discovery and Data Mining.

Provost, F. J.; and Buchanan, B. 1995. Inductive Policy: The Pragmatics of Bias Selection. *Machine Learning* 20(1–2): 35–61.

Provost, F.; and Fawcett, T. 2001. Robust Classification for Imprecise Environments. *Machine Learning* 42(3): 203–231.

Quinlan, J. 1993. *C4. 5: Programs for Machine Learning.* San Francisco: Morgan Kaufmann Publishers.

Quinlan, J. R. 1990. Learning Logical Definitions from Relations. *Machine Learning* 5(3): 239-266.

Quinlan, J. R. 1996. Boosting First-Order Learning. In *Algorithmic Learning Theory, Seventh International Workshop,* Lecture Notes in Computer Science 1160, 143–155. Berlin: Springer-Verlag.

Quinlan, J. R. 1996. Induction of Decision Trees. *Machine Learning* 5(1): 71–100.

Quinlan, J. Ross. 1986. Induction of Decision Trees. *Machine Learning* 1(1): 81–106.

Rabiner, L. 1989. A Tutorial on Hidden Markov Models and Selected Applications in Speech Recognition. *Proceedings of the IEEE* 77(2): 257–286.

Ramamohanarao, K.; and Harland, J. 1994. An Introduction to Deductive Database Languages and Systems. *Very Large Data Bases Journal* 3: 2.

Raman, V.; and Hellerstein, J. M. 2002. Partial Results for Online Query Processing. In Proceedings of the ACM SIGMOD International Conference on Management of Data, 275–286. New York: Association for Computing Machinery Special Interest Group on Management of Data.

Ramaswamy, S.; Rastogi, R.; and Shim, K. 2000. Efficient Algorithms for Mining Outliers from Large Data Sets. In Proceedings of the ACM SIGMOD International Conference on Management of Data, 427–438. New York: Association for Computing Machinery Special Interest Group on Management of Data.

Rath, T.; Carreras, M.; and Sebastiani, P. 2003. Automated Detection of Influenza Epidemics with Hidden Markov Models. In *Proceedings of the Fifth International Symposium on Intelligent Data Analysis.* New York: Springer-Verlag.

Read, R. C.; and Corneil, D. G. 1977. The Graph Isomorphic Disease. *Journal of Graph Theory* 1(1): 339–363.

Reinders, F.; Jacobson, M. E. D.; and Post, F. H. 2000. Skeleton Graph Generation for Feature Shape Description. Paper presented at the Joint Eurographics-IEEE TCVG Symposium on Visualization, Amsterdam, The Netherlands.

Reinders, F.; Post, F. H.; and Spoelder, H. J. W. 1999. Attribute-Based Feature Tracking. Paper presented at the Joint Eurographics-IEEE TCVG Symposium on Visualization, Vienna, Austria, May 26–28.

Reis, B. Y.; and Mandl, K. D. 2003. Time Series Modeling for Syndromic Surveillance. *BMC Medical Informatics and Decision Making* 3(2).

Reis, B. Y.; Pagano, M.; and Mandl, K. D. 2003. Using Temporal Context to Improve Biosurveillance. *Proceedings of the National Academy of Sciences of the United States of America* 100(4): 1961-1965.

Richards, B. L.; and Mooney, R. J. 1995. Automated Refinement of First-Order Horn-Clause Domain Theories. *Machine Learning* 19(2): 95–131.

Richards, G. W. 2002. Virtual Screening Using Grid Computing: The Screensaver Project. *Nature Reviews: Drug Discovery* 1: 551–554.

Richie, D.; Kim, J.; and Wilkins, J. 2001. Applications of Real-Time Multiresolution Analysis for Molecular Dynamics Simulations of Infrequent Events. In Materials Research Symposium Proceedings 677, AA5. 1. Warrendale, Penn.: Material Research Society.

Richie, D.; Kim, J.; Hazzard, R.; Hazzard, K.; Barr, S.; and Wilkins, J. 2002. Large-Scale Molecular Dynamics Simulations of Interstitial Defect Diffusion in Silcon. In Materials Research Symposium Proceedings 731, W9.10–5. Warrendale, Penn.: Material Research Society.

Rijsbergen, V. 1979. *Information Retrieval.* London: Butterworths.

Rizvi, S. J.; and Haritsa, J. R. 2002. Maintaining Data Privacy in Association Rule Mining. In *Proceedings of Twenty-Eighth International Conference on Very Large Data Bases,* 682–693. San Francisco: Morgan Kaufmann Publishers.

Roddick, J. F.; and Spiliopoulou, M., 2002. A Survey of Temporal Knowledge Discovery Paradigms and Methods. *IEEE Transactions on Knowledge and Data Engineering* 14(4): 750–767.

Roddick, J. F.; Hornsby, K.; and Spiliopoulou, M. 2001. An Updated Bibilography of Temporal, Spatial, and Spato-Temporal Data Mining Research. In *Proceedings of International Workshop on Temporal, Spatial, and Spatio-Temporal Data Mining,* 147–163. Berlin: Springer-Verlag.

Roddick, J.-F.; and Spiliopoulou, M. 1999. A Bibliography of Temporal, Spatial, and Spatio-Temporal Data Mining Research. *SIGKDD Explorations* 1(1): 34–38.

Rogerson, P. A. 1997. Surveillance Systems for Monitoring the Development of Spatial Patterns. *Statistics in Medicine* 16: 2081.

Rosenblum, M.; and Ousterhout, J. K. 1992. The Design and Implementation of a Log-Structured File System. *ACM Transactions on Computer Systems (TOCS)* 10(1): 26-52.

Rosenschein, J. 1994. Designing Conventions for Automated Negotiation. *AI Magazine* 15(3): 29–46.

Rost, B. 2001. Review: Protein Secondary Structure Prediction Continues to Rise. *Journal of Structural Biology* 134(2–3): 204–218.

Rumelhart, D.; Hinton, G.; and Williams, R. 1986. Learning Representations by Back-Propagating Errors. *Nature* 323: 533–536.

Ryan M. J.; and Arnold, J. F. 1997. Lossy Compression of Hyperspectral Data Using Vector Quantization. *Remote Sensing of Environment* 61(3): 419–436.

Samarati, P.; and Sweeney, L. 1998. Protecting Privacy When Disclosing Information: K-Anonymity and Its Enforcement Through Generalization and Suppression. Paper presented at the IEEE Symposium on Research in Security and Privacy, Oakland, Calif., May 3–6.

Samtaney, R.; Silver, D.; Zabusky, N.; and Cao, J. 1994. Visualizing Features and Tracking Their Evolution. *IEEE Computer* 27(7): 20–27.

Sander, C.; and Schneider, R. 1991. Database of Homology Derived Protein Structures and the Structural Meaning of Sequence Alignment. *Proteins* 9(1): 56–68.

Sander, J.; Ester, M.; Kriegel, H.-P.; and Xu, X. 1998. Density-Based Clustering in Spatial Databases: The Algorithm GDBScan and Its Applications. *Data Mining and Knowledge Discovery* 2(2): 169–194.

Sandholm, T. W.; and Crites, R. H. 1995. On Multiagent Q-Learning in a Semi-Competitive Domain. In *Adaptation and Learning in Multi-Agent Systems,* Lecture Notes in Computer Science 1042, ed. G. Weiss and S. Sen, 191–205. New York: Springer-Verlag.

Santos-Costa, V. 1999. Optimising Bytecode Emulation for Prolog. In *Proceedings of the International Conference on Principles and Practice of Declarative Programming,* Lecture Notes in Computer Science 1702, 261–267. Berlin: Springer-Verlag.

Santos-Costa, V.; Srinivasan, A.; and Camacho, R. 2000. A Note on Two Simple Transformations for Improving the Efficiency of an ILP System. In Proceedings of the Tenth International Conference on Inductive Logic Programming, Lecture Notes in Artificial Intelligence 1866, 225–242, ed. J. Cussens and A. Frisch. Berlin: Springer-Verlag.

Sarawagi, Sunita; and Nagaralu, Sree Hari 2000. Data Mining Models as Services on the Internet. *SIGKDD Explorations* 2(1): 24–28.

Sayal, M.; and Scheuermann, P. 2000. A Distributed Clustering Algorithm for Web-Based Access Patterns. Paper presented at the Second ACM-SIGKDD Workshop on Distributed and Parallel Knowledge Discovery, Boston, Mass., August.

Saygin, Y.; Verykios, V. S.; and Clifton, C. 2001. Using Unknowns to Prevent Discovery of Association Rules. *SIGMOD Record* 30(4): 45–54.

Scarponi, D. 2000. Blackmailer Reveals Stolen Internet Credit Card Data. *Credit Cards Magazine* January 10.

Schneier, B. 1995 *Applied Cryptography.* New York: John Wiley and Sons.

Schoenberg, F. P.; Peng, R.; Huang, Z.; and Rundel, P. 2003. Detection of Nonlinearities in the Dependence of Burn Area on Fuel Age and Climatic Variables. *International Journal of Wildland Fire* 12(1) : 1–6.

Schonbrun, J.; Wedemeyer, W. J.; and Baker, D. 2002. Protein Structure Prediction in 2002. *Current Opinion in Structural Biology* 12(3): 348–354.

Schum, D. A. 1999. Marshalling Thoughts and Evidence During Fact Investigation. *South Texas Law Review* 40(2): 183–209.

Schum, D. A. 2001. Alternative Views of Argument Construction from a Mass of Evidence. *Cardozo Law Review* 22(5–6): 1461–1502.

Schum, D. A. 2001. Species of Abductive Reasoning in Fact Investigation in Law. *Cardozo Law Review* 22(5–6): 1645–1681.

Schuster, A.; and Wolff, R. 2001. Communication Efficient Distributed Mining of Association Rules. In Proceedings of the ACM SIGMOD International Conference on Management of Data, 473–484. New York: Association for Computing Machinery Special Interest Group on Management of Data.

Sebastiani, F. 2002. Machine Learning in Automated Text Categorization. *ACM Computing Surveys* 34(1)(March): 1–47.

Seeger, M. 2001. Learning with Labeled and Unlabeled Data. Tech. Report, Institute for Adaptive and Neural Computation, Univ. of Edinburgh, Edinburgh, Scotland.

Sekar, R.; Gupta, A.; Frullo, J.; Shanbhag, T.; Tiwari, A.; Yang, H.; and Zhou, S. 2002. Specification Based Anomaly Detection: A New Approach for Detecting Network Intrusions. Paper presented at the Ninth ACM Conference on Computer and Communications Security, Washington, D.C., Nov. 18–22.

Sellis, T. K. 1988. Multiple-Query Optimization. *ACM Transactions on Database Systems* 13(1): 23–52.

Sen, S.; and Sekaran, M. 1995. Multiagent Coordination with Learning Classifier Systems. In *Adaption and Learning in Multi-Agent Systems,* Lecture Notes in Computer Science, 1042, ed. Gerhard Weiss and Sundip Sen. New York: Springer-Verlag.

Sen, S. 1997. Developing an Automated Distributed Meeting Scheduler. *IEEE Expert* 12(4): 41–45.

Serfling, R. E. 1963. Methods for Current Statistical Analysis of Excess Pneumonia-Influenza Deaths. *Public Health Reports* 78(6): 494–506.

Shahshahani, B.; and Landgrebe, D. 1994. The Effect of Unlabeled Samples in Reducing the Small Sample Size Problem and Mitigating the Hughes Phenomenon. *IEEE Transactions Geoscience and Remote Sensing* 32(5): 1087–1095.

Sharkey, A. 1999. *Combining Artificial Neural Nets.* Berlin: Springer-Verlag.

Shatkay, H.; Edwards, S.; Wilbur, W. J.; and Boguski, M. 2000. Genes, Themes and Microarrays: Using Information Retrieval for Large- Scale Gene Analysis. In *Proceedings of the Eighth International Conference on Intelligent Systems for Molcular Biology,* 317–28. Menlo Park, Calif.: AAAI Press.

Shekhar, S., and Chawla, S. 2003. *Spatial Databases: A Tour.* Upper Saddle River, N.J.: Prentice Hall.

Shekhar, S.; and Huang, Y. 2001a. Discovering Spatial Co-Location Patterns: A Summary of Results. In *Proceedings of the Seventh International Symposium on Spatial and Temporal Databases,* 236–256. Berlin: Springer-Verlag.

Shekhar, S.; and Huang, Y. 2001b. Co-Location Rules Mining: A Summary of Results. In *Proceedings of the Seventh International Symposium on Spatial and Temporal Databases.* Berlin: Springer-Verlag.

Shekhar, S.; Chawla, S.; Ravada, S.; Fetterer, A.; Liu, X.; and Tien Lu, C. 1999. Spatial Databases —Accomplishments and Research Needs. *IEEE Transactions on Knowledge and Data Engineering* 11(1): 45–55.

Shekhar, S.; Lu, C.-T.; and Zhang, P. 2001. Detecting Graph-Based Spatial Outliers: Algorithms and Applications: A Summary of Results. In Proceedings of the Seventh ACM SIGKDD International Conference on Knowledge Discovery and Data Mining, 371–376. New York: Association for Computing Machinery Special Interest Group on Knowledge Discovery and Data Mining.

Shekhar, S.; Lu, C.-T.; and Zhang, P. 2003. A Unified Approach to Detecting Spatial Outliers. *GeoInformatica* 7(2).

Shekhar, S.; Schrater, P. R.; Vatsavai, R. R.; Wu, W.; and Chawla, S. 2002. Spatial Contextual Classification and Prediction Models for Mining Geospatial Data. *IEEE Transactions on Multimedia* (Special Issue on Multimedia Dataabses) 4(4): 174–188.

Shen, H.-W.; Chiang, L.; and Ma, K.-L. 1999. Time-Varying Volume Rendering Using a Time-Space Partitioning Tree. In Proceedings of the 1999 IEEE Visualization Conference, 371–378. Los Alamitos, Calif.: IEEE Computer Society.

Shenoy, P.; Haritsa, J. R.; Sundarshan, S.; Bhalotia, G.; Bawa, M.; and Shah, D. 2000. Turbo-Charging Vertical Mining of Large Databases. In Proceedings of the ACM SIGMOD International Conference on Management of Data, 22–33. New York: Association for Computing Machinery, Special Interest Group on Management of Data.

Shindyalov, I.; Kolchanov, N.; and Sander, C. 1994. Can Three-Dimensional Contacts in Protein Structures Be Predicted by Analysis of Correlated Mutations? *Protein Engineering* 7(3): 349–358.

Shumway, R. H.; and Stoffer, D. S. 2000. *Time Series Analysis and Its Applications.* New York: Springer-Verlag.

Silver, D., and Wang, X. 1997. Tracking and Visualizing Turbulent 3D Features. *IEEE Transactions on Visualization and Computer Graphics* 3(2): 129–141.

Simenson, L.; Fukuda, K.; Schonberg, L. B.; and Cox, N. J. 2000. The Impact of Influenza Epidemics on Hospitalizations. *The Journal of Infectious Diseases* 181(3): 831–837.

Simon, R.; Nolan, J. J.; and Sood, A. K. 2002. A Light-Weight Agent Approach for Collaborative Multimedia Systems. *Information Sciences: An International Journal* 16(1)(January): 53–84.

Simons, K.; Kooperberg, C.; Huang, E.; and Baker, D. 1997. Assembly of Protein Tertiary Structures from Fragments with Similar Local Sequences Using Simulated Annealing and Bayesian Scoring Functions. *Journal of Molecular Biology* 268(1): 209–25.

Singer, M.; Vriend, G.; and Bywater, R. 2002. Prediction of Protein Residue Contacts with a PDB-Derived Likelihood Matrix. *Protein Engineering* 15(9): 721–725.

Sippl, M. 1996. Helmholtz Free Energy of Peptide Hydrogen Bonds in Proteins. *Journal of Molecular Biology* 260(5): 644–648.

Skolnick, J.; Kolinski, A.; and Ortiz, A. 2000. Derivation of Protein-Specific Pair Potentials Based on Weak Sequence Fragment Similarity. *Proteins* 38(1): 3–16.

Smith, R. 1980. The Contract Net Protocol: High-Level Communication and Control in a Distributed Problem Solver. *IEEE Transactions on Computers* C-12(12): 1104–1113.

Soderland, S. 1999. Information Extraction Rules for Semi-Structured and Free Text. *Machine Learning* 34(1–3): 233–272.

Solberg, A. H.; Taxt, T.; and Jain, A. K. 1996. A Markov Random Field Model for Classification of Multisource Satellite Imagery. *IEEE Transaction on Geoscience and Remote Sensing* 34(1): 100–113.

Sonnhammer E. L.; Eddy S. R.; Birney E.; Bateman A.; and Durbin R. 1998. PFAM: Multiple Sequence Alignments and HMM-Profiles of Protein Domains. *Nucleic Acids Research* 26(1): 320–322.

Sørensen, M., and Voter, A. 2000. Temperature-Accelerated Dynamics for Simulation of Infrequent Events. *Journal of Chemical Physics* 112(21): 9599.

Sparrow, M. K. 1991. The Application of Network Analysis to Criminal Intelligence: An Assessment of the Prospects. *Social Networks* 13(3): 251–274.

Spiekermann, S.; Grossklags, J.; and Berendt, B. 2001. Privacy in Second Generation E-Commerce: Privacy Preferences Versus Actual Behavior. In Proceedings of the ACM Conference on Electronic Commerce, 14–17. New York: Association for Computing Machinery.

Spiliopoulou, M. 1999. Data Mining for the Web. In *Proceedings of the Third European Conference on Principles and Practice of Knowledge Discovery in Databases,* 588–589. Berlin: Springer-Verlag.

Spiliopoulou, M. 1999. The Laborious Way from Data Mining to Web Mining. *International Journal of Computer Systems, Science, and Engineering,* 14(1): 113–126.

Springer, T. 2002. Google Launches News Service. *PC World* 23 September.

Srikant, R.; and Agrawal, R. 1995. Mining Generalized Association Rules. In *Proceedings of the Twenty-First International Conference on Very Large Databases,* 407–419. San Francisco: Morgan Kaufmann Publishers.

Srinivasan, A. 1999. A Study of Two Sampling Methods for Analysing Large Datasets with ILP. *Data Mining and Knowledge Discovery* 3(1): 95–123.

Srinivasan, A. 2001. The Aleph Manual. Computing Laboratory, Mathematical and Physical Sciences Division, Oxford Univ., Oxford, England.

Srinivasan, A.; King, R. D.; Muggleton, S.; and Sternberg, M. J. E. 1997a. Carcinogenesis Predictions Using ILP. In *Proceedings of the Seventh International Workshop on Inductive Logic*

Programming, Lecture Notes in Computer Science 1297, 273–287, ed. S. Dzeroski, S., and N. Lavrac. Berlin: Springer-Verlag.

Srinivasan, A.; King, R. D.; Muggleton, S. H.; and Sternberg, M. 1997b. The Predictive Toxicology Evaluation Challenge. In *Proceedings of the Fifteenth International Joint Conference on Artificial Intelligence* 1–6. San Francisco: Morgan Kaufmann Publishers.

Srinivasan, A.; Muggleton, S. H.; Sternberg, M. J.; and King, R. D. 1996. Theories for Mutagenicity: A Study in First-Order and Feature-Based Induction. *Artificial Intelligence Journal* 84(1): 277–300.

Srinivasan, S.; Ponceleon, D.; Amir, A.; and Petkovic, D. 2000. What Is That Video Anyway? In Search of Better Browsing. In Proceedings of the IEEE International Conference on Multimedia and Expo, 388–392. Piscataway, N.J.: The Institute of Electrical and Electronics Engineers, Inc.

Sriniviasan, A.; and King, R. 1999. Feature Construction with Inductive Logic Programming: A Study of Quantitative Predictions of Biological Activity Aided by Structural Attributes. *Knowledge Discovery and Data Mining Journal* 3: 37–57.

Srivastava, J.; and Mobasher, B. 1997. Web Mining: Hype or Reality? In Proceedings of the Ninth IEEE International Conference on Tools with Artificial Intelligence. Piscataway, N.J.: The Institute of Electrical and Electronics Engineers, Inc.

Srivastava, J.; Cooley, R.; Deshpande, M.; and Tan, P.-N. 2000. Web Usage Mining: Discovery and Application of Usage Patterns from Web Data. *SIGKDD Explorations* 1(2): 12–23.

Staniford, Stuart; Hoagland, James A.; and McAlerney, Joseph M. 2002. Practical Automated Detection of Stealthy Portscans. *Journal of Computer Security,* 10: 105–136, 2002.

Stern, L.; and Lightfoot, D. 1999. Automated Outbreak Detection: A Quantitative Retrospective Analysis. Epidemiology and Infection 122: 103–110.

Stolfo, S.; Prodromidis, A. L.; and Chan, P. K. 1997. Jam: Java Agents for Meta-Learning Over Distributed Databases. In *Proceedings Third International Conference on Knowledge Discovery and Data Mining,* 74–81, Menlo Park, Calif.: AAAI Press.

Stolorz, P.; and Dean, C. 1996. Quakefinder: A Scalable Data Mining System for Detecting Earthquakes from Space. In *Proceedings of the Second International Conference on Knowledge Discovery and Data Mining.* Menlo Park, Calif.: AAAI Press.

Strehl, A.; and Ghosh, J. 2000. A Scalable Approach to Balanced, High-Dimensional Clustering of Market-Baskets. In *High Performance Computing 2000—HiPC 2000—The Seventh International Conference,* Lecture Notes in Computer Science 1970, 525–536. Berlin: Springer-Verlag.

Strehl, A.; and Ghosh, J. 2002a. Cluster Ensembles—A Knowledge Reuse Framework for Combining Multiple Partitions. *Journal of Machine Learning Research* 3 (Dec.): 583–617.

Strehl, A.; and Ghosh, J. 2002b. Cluster Ensembles—A Knowledge Reuse Framework for Combining Partitionings. In *Proceedings of the Eighteenth National Conference on Artificial Intelligence,* 93–98. Menlo Park, Calif.: AAAI Press / The MIT Press.

Strehl, A.; Ghosh, J.; and Mooney, R. 2000. Impact of Similarity Measures on Web-Page Clustering. In Artificial Intelligence for Web Search: Papers from the AAAI Workshop. 58–64. Tech. Rep. WS-00-01, American Association for Artificial Intelligence, Menlo Park, Calif.

Strehl, Alexander; and Ghosh, Joydeep 2002. Cluster Ensembles—A Knowledge Reuse Framework for Combining Partitionings. In *Proceedings of the Nineteenth National Conference on Artificial Intelligence.* Menlo Park, Calif.: AAAI Press / The MIT Press.

Studer, R.; Benjamins, V. R.; and Fensel, D. 1998. Knowledge Engineering: Principles and Methods. *Data Knowledge Engineering,* 25(1–2): 161–197, 1998.

Stumme, G. 2002a. Conceptual On-Line Analytical Processing. In *Information Organization and Databases,* 191–203, ed. K. Tanaka, S. Ghandeharizadeh, and Y. Kambayashi. Dortrecht, The Netherlands: Kluwer Academic Publishers.

Stumme, G. 2002b. Using Ontologies and Formal Concept Analysis for Organizing Business Knowledge. In *Wissensmanagement Mit Referenzmodellen—Konzepte FR Die Anwendungssystem-Und Organisationsgestaltung,* 163–174, ed. J. Becker and R. Knackstedt. Heidelberg: Physica-Verlag.

Sujudi, D.; and Haimes, R. 1995. Identification of Swirling Flow in 3D Vector Fields. In Proceedings of the Twelfth Computational Fluid Dynamics Conference, Paper 95-1715. Arlington, Va.: American Institute of Aeronautics and Astronautics (AIAA).

Sumpson, G. G. 1961. *Principals of Animal Taxonomy.* New York: Columbia Univ. Press.

Sundaram, H.; and Chang, S. F. 2000. Video Scene Segmentation Using Audio and Visual Features. In Proceedings of the IEEE International Conference on Multimedia and Expo 1. Piscataway, N.J.: The Institute of Electrical and Electronics Engineers, Inc.

Sure, Y.; Staab, S.; and Angele, J. 2002. Ontoedit: Guiding Ontology Development by Methodology and Inferencing. Paper presented at the International Conference on Ontologies, Databases and Applications of Semantics (ODBASE 2002), Univ. of California, Irvine, Calif, 29–31 October.

Sure, York; Erdmann, Michael; Angele, Jurgen; Staab, Steffen; Studer, Rudi; and Wenke, Dirk. 2002. Ontoedit: Collaborative Ontology Development for the Semantic Web. In *Proceedings of the First International Semantic Web Conference,* Lecture Notes in Computer Science, 221–235. Berlin: Springer-Verlag.

Sweeney, L. 2001. Computational Disclosure Control: A Primer on Data Privacy Protection. Ph.D. Dis.,, Computer Science Dept., Massachusetts Institute of Technology, Cambridge, Mass.

Szalay, A. S.; Gray, J.; and Vandenberg, J. 2002. Petabyte Scale Data Mining: Dream or Reality? In Proceedings of the SPIE Conference on Advanced Telescope Technologies. Bellingham, Wash.: Society of Photo-Optical Instrumentation Engineers.

Talia, D. 2002. The Open Grid Services Architecture—Where the Grid Meets the Web. *IEEE Internet Computing,* 6(6): 67–71.

Tang, L. R.; Mooney, R. J.; and Melville, P. 2003. Scaling Up ILP to Large Examples: Results on Link Discovery for Counter-Terrorism. Paper presented at the KDD-2003 Workshop on Multi-Relational Data Mining, Washington D.C., August.

Teich, J. M.; Wagner, M. M.; Mackenzie, C. F.; and Schafer, K. O. 2002. The Informatics Response in Disaster, Terrorism, and War. *Journal of the American Medical Informatics Association* 9(2): 97–104.

Teltzrow, M.; and O. Günther. 2003. Web Metrics for Retailers. In *E-Commerce and Web Technologies: Fourth International Conference(EC-Web Prague),* Lecture Notes in Computer Science 2738, 328–338, eds. K. Bauknecht; G. Quirchmayr; A. M. Tjoa. Berlin: Springer-Verlag.

Thampy, S. 2003. Feature Tracking in Two-Dimensional, Time- Varying Data Sets. Master's thesis, Dept. of Computational Engineering Mississippi State Univ., Mississippi State, Mississippi.

Thaper, N.; Guha, S.; Indyk, P.; and Koudas, N. 2002. Dynamic Multidimensional Histograms. In Proceedings of the ACM SIGMOD International Conference on Management of Data. New York: Association for Computing Machinery Special Interest Group on Management of Data.

Thomas, D.; Casari, G.; and Sander, C. 1996. The Prediction of Protein Contacts from Multiple Sequence Aligments. *Protein Engineering* 9(11): 941–48.

Thompson, D.; Machiraju, R.; Jiang, M.; Nair, J.; Craciun, G.; and Venkata, S. 2002. Physics-Based Feature Mining for Large Data Exploration. *IEEE Computing in Science and Engineering* 4(4): 22–30.

Thrun, S. 1996. Is Learning the n-th Thing any Easier than Learning the First? In *Advances In Neural Information Processing Systems-8,* 640–646., ed. D. S. Touretzky, M. Mozer, and M. E. Hasselmo. Cambridge, Mass.: The MIT Press.

Thrun, S.; and Pratt, L. 1997. *Learning to Learn*. Dortrecht, The Netherlands: Kluwer Academic Publishers.

Thuraisingham, B. 2003a. *Web Data Mining Technologies and Their Applications in Business Intelligence and Counter-Terrorism*. Boca Raton, Fla.: CRC Press.

Thuraisingham, B. 2003b. Data Mining, National Security, Privacy, and Civil Liberties. *SIGKDD Explorations* 4(2): 1–5.

Thuraisingham, B.; and Ford, W. 1995. Security Constraint Processing in a Multilevel Distributed Database Management System. *IEEE Transactions on Knowledge and Data Engineering* 7(2) (April): 274–293.

Ting, K. M.; and Low, B. T. 1997. Model Combination in the Multiple-Data-Base Scenario. In *The Ninth European Conference on Machine Learning*, Lecture Notes in Computer Science 1224, 250–265. New York: Springer-Verlag.

Tjaden, Brett; and Wasson, Glenn. 2002. The Oracle of Bacon at Virginia. (www.cs.virginia.edu/oracle/). Charlottesville, Va.: Dept. of Computer Science, School of Engineering, The Univ. of Virginia.

Tobler, W. 1979. Cellular Geography. In *Philosophy in Geography*, 379–386, ed. S. Gale and G. Olsson. Dordrecht, Holland: Reidel.

Toivonen, H. 1996. Sampling Large Databases for Association Rules. In *Proceedings of the Twenty-Second International Conference on Very Large Databases*. San Francisco: Morgan Kaufmann Publishers.

Traub, J. F.; Yemini, Y.; and Wozniakowski, H. 1984. The Statistical Security of a Statistical Database. *ACM Transactions on Database Systems (TODS)*, 9(4): 672–679.

Tsui, F. C.; Espino, J. U.; Dato, V. M.; Gesteland, P. H.; Hutman, J.; and Wagner, M. M. 2003. Technical Description of RODS: A Real-Time Public Health Surveillance System. *Journal of the American Medical Informatics Association* 10(5): 399–408.

Tsui, Fu-Chiang; Espino, Jeremy U.; Wagner, Michael M.; Gesteland, Per; Ivanov, Oleg; Olszewski, Robert T.; Liu, Zhen; Zeng, Xizoming; Chapman, Wendy; Wong, Weng K.; and Moore, Andrew. 2002. Data, Network, and Application: Technical Description of the Utah RODS Winter Olympic Biosurveillance System. In Proceedings of the Annual American Medical Informatics Association Fall Symposium, 815–819. Bethesda, Md.: American Medical Informatics Association.

Tucker, P., and Maier, D. 2002. Exploiting Punctuation Semantics in Data Streams. In Proceedings of the Eighteenth International Conference on Data Engineering (ICDE), 279. Los Alamitos, Calif.: IEEE Computer Society.

Tumer, K.; and Ghosh, J. 2000. Robust Order Statistics Based Ensemble for Distributed Data Mining. In *Advances in Distributed and Parallel Knowledge Discovery*, ed. H. Kargupta and P. Chan. Menlo Park, Calif.: AAAI Press / The MIT Press.

U.S. Army Medical Research Institute of Infectious Diseases. 2001. *Medical Management of Biological Casualties Handbook*. Fort Detrick, Md.: U.S. Army Medical Research Institute of Infectious Diseases.

U.S. Dept. of Health and Human Services. Centers for Disease Control and Prevention. 2000. Biological and Chemical Terrorism: Strategic Plan for Preparedness and Response. Recommendations of the CDC Strategic Planning Workgroup. *MMWR Morbidity and Mortality Weekly Reports* 49(RR04)(April 21): 1–14.

U.S. Dept. of Health and Human Services. Centers for Disease Control and Prevention. 2001. Updated Guidelines for Evaluating Public Health Surveillance Systems. *MMWR Morbidity and Mortality Weekly Reports* 50(RR13)(July 27): 1–35.

U.S. Dept. of Health and Human Services. Centers for Disease Control and Prevention. 2002a. Morbidity and Mortality Tables. Atlanta, Ga.: Centers for Disease Control and Prevention.

U.S. Dept. of Health and Human Services. Centers for Disease Control. 2002b. Syndromic Surveillance for Bioterrorism Following the Attacks on the World Trade Center-New York City, 2001. *MMWR Morbidity and Mortality Weekly Reports* (Special Issue) 51(September 11): 13–15.

U.S. National Institute of Standards and Technology, U.S. Dept. of Commerce. 2003. ACE—Automatic Content Extraction. Washington, D.C.: U.S. Dept. of Commerce.

Undercoffer, Jeffrey; and Pinkston, John 2002. An Empirical Analysis of Computer Attacks and Intrusions. Tech. Rep. TR-CS-03-11, Univ. of Maryland Baltimore County, Dept. of Computer Science and Electrical Engineering, Baltimore, Md.

Undercoffer, Jeffrey; Perich, Filip; and Nicholas, Charles 2002. Shomar: An Open Architecture for Distributed Intrusion Detection Services. Tech. Rep., 12 September. Univ. of Maryland Baltimore County, Dept. of Computer Science and Electrical Engineering, Baltimore, Md.

Undercoffer, Jeffrey; Perich, Filip; Cedilnik, Andrej; Kagal, Lalana; and Joshi, Anupam 2003. Centarusu2: A Secure Infrastructure for Service Discovery and Delivery in Pervasive Computing. *Mobile Networks and Applications (MONET)* 8(2): 114–125.

Underhill, P. 2000. *Why We Buy: The Science of Shopping*. Carmichael, Calif.: Touchstone Books.

Vaidya, J., and Clifton, C. 2002. Privacy Preserving Association Rule Mining in Vertically Partitioned Data. In Proceedings of the Eighth ACM SIGKDD International Conference on Knowledge Discovery and Data Mining, 639–644. New York: Association for Computing Machinery Special Interest Group on Knowledge Discovery and Data Mining.

Vaidya, J.; and Clifton, C. 2003. Privacy-Preserving K-Means Clustering Over Vertically Partitioned Data. In Proceedings of the Ninth ACM SIGKDD International Conference on Knowledge Discovery and Data Mining. New York: Association for Computing Machinery Special Interest Group on Knowledge Discovery and Data Mining.

Valentin, G.; Zuliani, M.; Zilio, D. C.; Lohman, G. M.; and Skelley, A. 2000. DB2 Advisor: An Optimizer Smart Enough to Recommend Its Own Indexes. In Proceedings of the Sixteenth International Conference on Data Engineering (ICDE), 101–110. Los Alamitos, Calif.: IEEE Computer Society.

Vapnik, V. 1998. *Statistical Learning Theory*. New York: John Wiley.

Vendruscolo, M.; Kussell, E.; and Domany, E. 1997. Recovery of Protein Structure from Contact Maps. *Folding and Design* 2(5): 295–306.

Viswanathan R.; and Varshney, P. 1997. Distributed Detection with Multiple Sensors. *Proceedings of IEEE* 85(1): 54–63.

Vlachos, M.; Kollios, G.; and Gunopulos, D. 2002. Discovering Similar Multidimensional Trajectories. In Discovering Similar Multidimensional Trajectories: Proceedings of the Eighteenth International Conference on Data Engineering (ICDE). Los Alamitos, Calif.: IEEE Computer Society.

Voter, A. 1997. Hyperdynamics: Accelerated Molecular Dynamics of Infrequent Events. *Physical Review Letters* 78: 3908.

Voter, A. 1998. Parallel Replica Method for Dynamics of Infrequent Events. *Physical Review B* 57(22): 13385.

Vucetic, S.; Brown C.; Dunker A. K.; and Obradovic, Z. 2004. Supervised Partitioning of Disordered Proteins. *Proteins: Structure, Function and Genetics.* 56(3)

Vucetic, S.; Fiez, T.; and Obradovic, Z. 1999. A Data Partitioning Scheme for Spatial Regression. In Proceedings of the IEEE / INNS International Joint Conference on Neural Networks. Los Alamitos, Calif.: IEEE Computer Society.

Vucetic, S.; and Obradovic, Z. 2000. A Constructive Competitive Regression Method for Analysis and Modeling of Non-Stationary Time Series. In Proceedings of the First International Workshop on Computational Intelligence in Economics and Finance at the Fifth International Conference on Information Science 2, 978–981. Durham, No. Car.: Association for Intelligent Machinery.

Vucetic, S.; and Obradovic, Z. 2000. Discovering Homogeneous Regions In Spatial Data Through Competition. In *Proceedings of the Seventh International. Conference on Machine Learning,* 1095–1102. San Francisco: Morgan Kaufmann Publishers.

Vucetic, S.; and Obradovic, Z. 2000. Performance Controlled Data Reduction for Knowledge Discovery in Distributed Databases. In *Proceedings of the Pacific-Asia Conference on Knowledge Discovery and Data Mining, Kyoto, Japan.* Computer Science Editorial 3, 29–39. Berlin: Springer-Verlag.

Vucetic, S.; and Obradovic, Z. 2001. Classification on Data with Biased Class Distribution. In *Proceedings of the Twelfth European Conference on Machine Learning,* 527–538. San Francisco: Morgan Kaufmann Publishers.

Vucetic, S.; Fiez, T.; and Obradovic, Z. 2000. Analyzing the Influence of Data Aggregation and Sampling Density on Spatial Estimation. *Water Resources Research* 36(12): 3721–3731.

Vucetic, S.; Obradovic, Z.; and Tomsovic, K. 2001. Price-Load Relationships in California's Electricity Market. *IEEE Transactions on Power Systems* 16: (2): 280–286.

Vucetic, S.; Pokrajac, D.; Xie, H.; and Obradovic, Z. 2003. Detection of Underrepresented Biological Sequences Using Class-Conditional Distribution Models. In Proceedings of the Third SIAM International Conference on Data Mining, 279–283. Philadelphia, Penn.: Society for Industrial and Applied Mathematics.

Wagner, M. M.; Tsui, F. C.; Espino, J. U.; Dato, V. M.; Sittig, D. F.; Caruana, R. A.; McGinnis, L. F.; Deerfield, D. W.; Druzdzel, M. J.; and Fridsma, D. B. 2001. The Emerging Science of Very Early Detection of Disease Outbreaks. *Journal of Public Health Management and Practice* 7(6): 51–59.

Waller, L. A. 2000. A Civil Action and Statistical Assessments of the Spatial Pattern of Disease: Do We Have a Cluster? *Regulatory Toxicology and Pharmacology* 32(2): 174–183.

Wang, H.; Yang, J.; Wang, W.; and Yu, P. S. 2002. Clustering by Pattern Similarity in Large Data Sets. In Proceedings of the ACM SIGMOD International Conference on Management of Data, 418–427. New York: Association for Computing Machinery Special Interest Group on Management of Data.

Wang, J. T. L.; Ma, Q.; Shasha, D.; and Wu, C. H. 2001. New Techniques for Extracting Features from Protein Sequences. *IBM Systems Journal* 40(2): 426–441.

Wang, K.; and Liu, H. 1998. Discovering Typical Structures of Documents: A Road Map Approach. In Proceedings of the Twenty-First Annual International ACM SIGIR Conference on Research and Development in Information Retrieval, 46–154. New York: Association for Computing Machinery Special Interest Group on Information Retrieval.

Wang, W.; Yang, J.; and Muntz, R. 1997. Sting: A Statastical Information Grid Approach to Spatial Data Mining. In *Proceedings of the Twenty-Third International Conference on Very Large Data Bases,* 186–195. San Francisco: Morgan Kaufmann Publishers.

Wang, W.; Yang, J.; and Muntz, R. 2000. An Approach to Active Spatial Data Mining Based on Statistical Information. *Journal of Knowledge and Data Engineering* 12(5): 715–728.

Wang, X.; and Wang, J. T. L. 2000. Fast Similarity Search in Three-Dimensional Structure Databases. *Journal of Chemical Information and Computer Sciences* 40(2): 442–452.

Wang, X.; Wang, J. T. L.; Shasha, D.; Shapiro, B. A.; Rigoutsos, I.; and Zhang, K. 2002. Finding Patterns in Three Dimensional Graphs: Algorithms and Applications to Scientific Data Mining. *IEEE Transactions on Knowledge and Data Engineering* 14(4): 731–749.

Wang, X.; Wang, J. T. L.; Shasha, D.; Shapiro, B.; Dikshitulu, S.; Rigoutsos, I.; and Zhang, K. 1997. Automated Discovery of Active Motifs in Three Dimensional Molecules. In *Proceedings of the Third International Conference on Knowledge Discovery and Data Mining,* 89–95. Menlo Park, Calif.: AAAI Press.

Warrender, C. E.; and Augusteijn, M. F. 1999. Fusion of Image Classifications Using Bayesian Techniques with Markov Rand Fields. *International Journal of Remote Sensing* 20(10): 1987–2002.

Wasserman, S.; and Faust, K. 1994. *Social Network Analysis: Methods and Applications.* Cambridge: Cambridge Univ. Press.

Watts, D. J. 1999. *Small Worlds: The Dynamics of Networks Between Order and Randomness.* Princeton, N.J.: Princeton Univ. Press.

Weigend, A. S.; Mangeas, M.; and Srivastava, A. N. 1995. Nonlinear Gated Experts for Time Series: Discovering Regimes and Avoiding Overfitting. *International Journal of Neural Systems* 6(4): 373–399.

Weininger, D. 1988. Smiles, A Chemical Language and Information System: Introduction to Methodologiy and Encoding Rules. *Journal of Chemical Information and Computer Sciences* 28(1): 31–36.

Weir, N.; Fayyad, U.; and Djorgovski, S. 1995. Automated Star / Galaxy Classification for Digitized POSS-II. *Astronomical Journal* 109(6): 2401–2412.

Weislow, O.; Kiser, R.; Fine, D. L.; Bader, J. P.; Shoemaker, R. H.; and Boyd, M. R. 1989. New Soluble Fomazan Assay for HIV-1 Cytopathic Effects: Application to High Flux Screening of Synthetic and Natural Products for Aids Antiviral Activity. *Journal of the National Cancer Institute* 81(8): 577–586

Weiss, G. 1995. Adaption and Learning in Multi-Agent Systems: Some Remarks and a Bibliography. In *Adaption and Learning in Multi-Agent Systems,* Lecture Notes in Artificial Intelligence 1042, 1–21, eds. G. Weiss; and S. Sen. New York: Springer-Verlag.

Welty, Chris. 2000. Towards a Semantics for the Web. Paper presented at the Dagstuhl Symposium on Semantics for the Web, Dagstuhl, Germany, May.

Widom, J.; and Ceri, S., eds. 1996. *Active Database Systems: Triggers and Rules for Advanced Database Processing.* San Francisco: Morgan Kaufmann Publishers.

Williams, P. 2002. Patterns, Indicators, and Warnings in Link Analysis: The Contract Killings Dataset. Tech. Rep. 2878, General Dynamics Information Systems and Technology Group, Veridian Systems Division, Arlington, Va.

Williams, P.; and Woessner, P. N. 1995a. Nuclear Material Trafficking: An Interim Assessment. Transnational Organized Crime 1(2): 206–238.

Williams, P.; and Woessner, P. N. 1995b. Nuclear Material Trafficking: An Interim Assessment, Ridgway Viewpoints. Tech. Rep. 3, Ridgway Center, Univ. of Pittsburgh, Pittsburgh, Penn.

Winter, R.; and Auerbach, K. 1998. The Big Time: 1998 Winter Very Large Data Bases Survey. *Database Programming Design* 11(8).

Wirth, R.; Borth, M.; and Hipp, J. 2001. When Distribution Is Part of the Semantics: A New Problem Class for Distributed Knowledge Discovery. Paper presented at the PKDD-2001 Workshop on Ubiquitous Data Mining for Mobile and Distributed Environments, Freiburg, Germany, September 3–7.

Witten, I. H.; and Frank, E. 1999. *Data Mining: Practical Machine Learning Tools and Techniques with Java Implementations.* San Francisco: San Francisco: Morgan Kaufmann.

Woessner, P. N. 1995. Chronology of Nuclear Smuggling Incidents: July 1991–May 1995. *Transnational Organized Crime* 1(2): 288–329.

Woessner, P. N. 1997. Chronology of Radioactive and Nuclear Materials Smuggling Incidents: July 1991–June 1997. *Transnational Organized Crime* 3(1): 114–209.

Wolf, W. 1997. Hidden Markov Model Parsing of Video Programs. In Proceedings of International Conference on Acoustics Signal and Speech Processing. Piscataway, N.J.: The Institute of Electrical and Electronics Engineers, Inc.

Wolf, Y. I.; Grishin, N. V.; and Koonin, E. V. 2000. Estimating the Number of Protein Folds and Families from Complete Genome Data. *Journal of Molecular Biology* 299(4): 897–905.

Wolfson, H.; and Rigoutsos, I. 1997. Geometric Hashing: An Overview. *IEEE Computational Science and Engineering* 4(4): 10–21.

Wolpert, D. 1992. Stacked Generalization. *Neural Networks* 5(2): 241–259.

Wolski, R.; Spring, N.; and Hayes, J. 1999. The Network Weather Service: A Distributed Resource Performance Forecasting Service for Metacomputing. *Future Generation Computer Systems* 15(5–6): 757–768.

Wrobel, S. 2001. Inductive Logic Programming for Knowledge Discovery in Databases. In *Relational Data Mining,* 74–101, ed. S. Dzeroski and N. Lavrač. Berlin: Springer-Verlag.

Wu, Y.; Tian, Q.; and Huang, T. S. 2000. Integrating Unlabeled Images for Image Retrieval Based on Relevance Feedback. In Proceedings of the Fifth International Conference on Pattern Recognition 1, 21–24. Piscataway, N.J.: The Institute of Electrical and Electronics Engineers, Inc.

Yamanishi, K.; Takeuchi, J.; Williams, G.; and Milne, P. 2000. On-Line Unsupervised Outlier Detection Using Finite Mixtures with Discounting Learning Algorithms. In Proceedings of the Sixth ACM SIGKDD International Conference on Knowledge Discovery and Data Mining, 320–324. New York: Association for Computing Machinery Special Interest Group on Knowledge Discovery and Data Mining.

Yan, X.; and Han, J. 2002. GSpan: Graph-Based Substructure Pattern Mining. In Proceedings of the IEEE International Conference on Data Mining. Los Alamitos, Calif.: IEEE Computer Society.

Yao, A. C. 1986. How to Generate and Exchange Secrets. In Proceedings of the Twenty-Seventh IEEE Symposium on Foundations of Computer Science, 162–167. Piscataway, N.J.: The Institute of Electrical and Electronics Engineers, Inc.

Yasnoff, W. A.; Overhage, J. M.; Humphreys, B. L.; LaVenture, M.; Goodman, K. W.; Gatewood, L.; Ross, D. A.; Reid, J.; Hammond, W. E.; Dwyer, D.; Huff, S. M.; Gotham, I.; Kukafka, R.; Loonsk, J. W.; and Wagner, M. M. 2001. A National Agenda for Public Health Informatics. *Journal of Public Health Management and Practice* 7(6): 1–21.

Ye, N.; and Chen, Q. 2001. An Anomaly Detection Technique Based on a Chi-Square Statistic for Detecting Intrusions Into Information Systems. *Quality and Reliability Engineering International* 17(2): 105–112.

Yip, K.; and Zhao, F. 1996. Spatial Aggregation: Theory and Applications. *Journal of Artificial Intelligence Research* 5: 1–26.

Yip, R.; and Levitt, K. 1998. The Design and Implementation of a Data Level Database Inference Detection System. In Proceedings of the International Federation for Information Processing TC11 WG 11.3 Twelfth International Working Conference on Database Security XII: Status and Prospects. New York: Association for Computing Machinering

Yona, G.; Linial, N.; and Linial, M. 1999. ProtoMap: Automatic Classification of Protein Sequences: A Hierarchy of Protein Families, and Local Maps of the Protein Space. *Proteins* 37(3): 360–378.

Yoshida, K., and Motoda, H. 1995. CLIP: Concept Learning from Inference Patterns. *Artificial Intelligence* 75(1): 63–92.

Ypma, A.; and Heskes, T. 2002. Categorization of Web Pages and User Clustering with Mixtures of Hidden Markov Models. In *Workshop on Web Knowledge Discovery and Data Mining) Lecture Notes in Computer Science 2703,* 31–43. Berlin: Springer-Verlag

Zaki M. J.; and Hsiao, C. J. 2002. CHARM: An Efficient Algorithm for Closed Itemset Mining. In Proceedings of the Second SIAM International Conference on Data Mining, 457–473. Philadelphia, Penn.: Society for Industrial and Applied Mathematics.

Zaki, M. J. 2000. Scalable Algorithms for Association Mining. *IEEE Transactions on Knowledge and Data Engineering* 12(3): 372–390.

Zaki, M. J. 2002. Efficiently Mining Frequent Trees in a Forest. In Proceedings of the Eighth ACM SIGKDD International Conference on Knowledge Discovery and Data Mining. New York: Association for Computing Machinery Special Interest Group on Knowledge Discovery and Data Mining.

Zaki, M. J., and Gouda, K. 2001. Fast Vertical Mining Using Diffsets. Tech. Rep. 01-1, Dept. of Computer Science, Rensselaer Polytechnic Institute, Troy, N.Y.

Zaki, M. J.; Jin, S.; and Bystroff, C. 2000. Mining Residue Contacts in Proteins Using Local Structure Predictions. In Proceedings of the IEEE International Symposium on Bioinformatics and Biomedical Engineering. Piscataway, N.J.: The Institute of Electrical and Electronics Engineers, Inc.

Zelezny, F.; Srinivasan, A.; and Page, D. 2002. Lattice-Search Runtime Distributions May Be Heavy-Tailed. In *Proceedings of the Twelfth International Conference on Inductive Logic Programming.* Berlin: Springer-Verlag.

Zelle, J. M.; and Mooney, R. J. 1996. Learning to Parse Database Queries Using Inductive Logic Programming. In *Proceedings of the Fourteenth National Conference on Artificial Intelligence,* 1050–1055. Menlo Park, Calif.: AAAI Press.

Zhang, B.; Hsu, M.; and Forman, G. 2000. Accurate Recasting of Parameter Estimation Algorithms Using Sufficient Statistics for Efficient Parallel Speed-Up: Demonstrated for Center-Based Data Clustering Algorithms. In *Proceedings of the Fourth European Conference on Principles and Practice of Knowledge Discovery in Databases.* Berlin: Springer-Verlag.

Zhang, P.; Huang, Y.; Shekhar, S.; and Kumar, V. 2003. Exploiting Spatial Autocorrelation to Efficiently Process Correlation-Based Similarity Queries. In *Proceedings of the Eighth International Symposium on Spatial and Temporal Databases.* Berlin: Springer-Verlag.

Zhang, T.; Ramakrishnan, R.; and Livny, M. 1996. Birch: An Efficient Data Clustering Method for Very Large Databases. In Proceedings of the ACM SIGMOD International Conference on Management of Data, 103–114. New York: Association for Computing Machinery Special Interest Group on Management of Data.

Zhao, C.; and Kim, S. H. 2000. Environment-Dependent Residue Contact Energies for Proteins. In *Proceedings of the National Academy of Sciences of the United States of America* 97(6), 2550–5.

Zhao, Y.; and Karypis, G. 2003. Prediction of Contact Maps Using Support Vector Machines. In Proceedings of the Third IEEE International Symposium on Bioinformatics and Biomedical Engineering. Piscataway, N.J.: The Institute of Electrical and Electronics Engineers, Inc.

Index

534 INDEX

AND gates, secure computing, 257
ANMI (average mutual information)
 direct optimization of, 54
 as measure of mutual information, 53
 supra-consensus function for, 58
anomaly detection
 counterterrorism and, 179
 link analysis and, 180
 in MINDS (Minnesota Intrusion Detection System), 202–206
 network intrusion and, 199–200
anonymity, 268–269
anthrax
 attacks, 185–187
 dataset, 331
antitrust laws
 corporate collaboration and, 264
 price fixing by airlines, 266
AOL (America Online), web community, 417
application events, semantic web mining
 atomic, 470–474
 complex, 474–475
 knowledge acquired from, 475–477
 overview of, 469–470
application level data, web usage mining, 408
application server logs, web usage mining, 408
applications, DDM (distributed data mining), 5–9
 mobile and wireless, 5–7
 multiparty, privacy-sensitive data and, 8–9
 scientific, business and grid mining, 7–8
Apriori algorithm
 data streams and, 107–108
 distributed association rule mining, 16
 frequent itemset identification, 127, 134
 frequent-pattern mining, 105–106
architecture, intelligence data
 global information sphere, 30–31
 local information sphere, 29–30
 overview of, 28–29
architecture, knowledge grids, 68–69
archiving intelligence data, 34–35
ARIMA time series model, 192
artificial intelligence. *see* AI (artificial intelligence)
association analysis module, MINDS

challenges of, 211–214
 illustration of, 214
 overview of, 209–211
association patterns, 210
association rule mining
 counterterrorism, 178–179
 distributed data, 16
 DSR (data stream reduction) and, 137–142
 e-commerce web sites, 464
 environmental data, 351–353
 periodic associations, 36
 protein folding, 297
 spatial data, 351–353, 371
 support and confidence measures, 127
association rule mining, sampling-based, 126–136
 comparing FAST and EA, 133–136
 EA (epsilon approximation) computation, 132–133
 EA (epsilon approximation) halving method, 129–132
 FAST algorithm and, 127–129
 future directions, 140–141
 overview of, 126–127
association rules
 privacy of data and, 259
 used as decision rules, 267
ASTER images, 336
astronomical datasets, mining techniques for, 287
atomic application events, semantic web mining, 470–474
attack class, in target centric intrusion ontology, 445
attacks, cyber
 buffer overflow, 446, 456–457
 content-based, 208
 DDoS (distributed denial of service attacks), 13
 DoS (denial of service) attacks, 445, 448–452
 internal/external attacks, 164–165
 logic exploit, 446
 Mitnick, 451–456
 Syn Flood, 450–451, 453
attacks, physical
 anthrax, 185–187
 chemical, 167–168, 172–173
 infrastructure, 169, 173
 nuclear, 167–168, 173
attributes, MINDS continuous, 211–212
attributes, spatial objects, 358